Europe: A Cultural Hi

D0084412

The successor to Peter Rietbergen's highly acclaimed *Europe: A Cultural History*, which has been a major and original contribution to the study of Europe, this excellent second edition brings the reader up-to-date with Europe's current cultural trends.

From ancient Babylonian law codes to Pope Urban II's call to crusade in 1095, and from Michelangelo on Italian art in 1538 to Sting's lyrics in the late twentieth century, the cultural history of Europe is a diverse and wide-ranging subject. This exceptional text expertly condenses it, explains it and introduces it to the reader in a thorough and highly readable style.

Presented chronologically, *Europe: A Cultural History* examines the many varied cultural building blocks of Europe, their importance in the continent's cultural identity and how the perception of Europe has changed over the centuries.

Starting with the beginnings of agricultural society and ending with the mass culture of the early twenty-first century, the book uses literature, art, science, technology and music to examine Europe's cultural history in terms of continuity and change. Rietbergen looks at how societies developed new ways of surviving, believing, consuming and communicating throughout the period. His book is distinctive in paying particular attention to the impact of other cultures on Europe, from its Celtic and German origins, to the influence of the Greeks and the Romans, the role of Christianity and the modern-day contact with Islam.

The text has been thoroughly revised for the late twentieth and early twenty-first centuries, and with a wide selection of excerpts to support the arguments, lyrics from contemporary songs and many illustrations, this book is an excellent student resource for both historical and cultural studies.

Europe

A Cultural History

Second Edition

Peter Rietbergen

Routledge
Taylor & Francis Group

LONDON AND NEW YORK

First published in 1998
by Routledge
2 Park Square, Milton Park, Abingdon, Oxon OX14 4RN

Simultaneously published in the USA and Canada
by Routledge
270 Madison Ave, New York, NY 10016

Reprinted in 1999, 2003, 2004

Second edition published 2006

Routledge is an imprint of the Taylor & Francis Group

© 1998, 2006 Peter Rietbergen

Typeset in Bembo by
Keystroke, Jacaranda Lodge, Wolverhampton
Printed and bound in Great Britain by
Antony Rowe Ltd, Chippenham, Wiltshire

British Library Cataloguing in Publication Data
A catalogue record for this book is available from the British Library

Library of Congress Cataloging in Publication Data
Rietbergen, P. J. A. N.
    Europe: a cultural history / Peter Rietbergen.—2nd ed.
        p. cm.
    Includes bibliographical references and index.
    ISBN 0–415–32358–4 (hardback) — ISBN 0–415–32359–2 (pbk.)
1. Europe—History. 2. Europe—Civilization. I. Title.
    D20.R42 2006
    940—dc22   2005012198

ISBN10: 0–415–32358–4 (hbk)
ISBN10: 0–415–32359–2 (pbk)

ISBN13: 9–78–0–415–32358–1 (hbk)
ISBN13: 9–78–0–415–32359–8 (pbk)

Contents

List of plates   xiii
List of maps   xv

Prologue   **xvii**
Europe – a present with a past   **xvii**
Europe: old Europe, new Europe, old borders, new borders   xvii
Europe: ideas   xx
Europe: realities   xxiii
Europe: on the problems of writing its (cultural) history   xxvi
On choices: the scope and structure of this book   xxix
On the use of this book   xxxv
Acknowledgements   xxxvi

PART I
Continuity and change: new ways of surviving   **1**

1 **Before 'Europe': towards an agricultural and
   sedentary society**   **3**
Beginnings in Africa and the eastern Mediterranean, or
the non-European origins of European culture   3
The advent of agriculture, temple and state   7
Invasion, conquest and change: the first wave   13
BABYLON, THE SEVENTEENTH CENTURY BC: THE LAW
  CODE OF HAMMURÁPI   16
Beginnings in Europe: after the last Ice Age   17
Invasion, conquest and change: the second wave   20
A 'marginal' culture? Religion and state formation in Israel   22
A 'marginal' culture? Trade and communication in Phoenicia   23
A 'marginal' culture? Democracy and its limitations in Greece   24
A 'marginal' culture? Tribal society in Celtic Europe   33

The 'birth of Europe' and the Greek 'world-view', or how
   to define one's own culture 35
The world of Alexander the Great 37

2 **Rome and its empire: the effects and limits of cultural
   integration**   41
Between the Alps and the Mediterranean, between the Etruscan
   and the Greek worlds: the expansion of the early Romans 41
From an informal to a formal empire 45
ROME, THE SECOND CENTURY AD: A LEGAL SYSTEM, A
   LEGAL SOCIETY – THE ROMAN CONTRIBUTION 50
Roman culture 53
The Roman Empire and the worlds beyond 55

3 **An empire lost – an empire won? Christianity and the
   Roman Empire**   61
Developments within the Jewish world: the genesis of
   Christianity 61
From Jews – and Gentiles – to Christians: the role of Jesus
   of Nazareth and his followers 62
Religions in the Roman Empire 67
A sect of 'hopeless outlaws' 68
CARTHAGE, AD 180: ARGUMENTS AGAINST AND FOR THE
   RELIGION OF THE CHRISTIANS 71
Towards an empire Roman as well as Christian 72
Rome and its neighbours in the fourth and fifth centuries AD:
   'decline and fall'? The division and loss of the political
   empire – the survival of the cultural empire 77
Empire and language 82

PART II
Continuity and change: new forms of belief   85

4 **Towards one religion for all**   87
The Christian world-view: the survival of classical culture
   within the context of Christianity and Europe 87
MOUNT SINAI, AD 547: KOSMAS EXPLAINS THE CHRISTIAN
   COSMOGRAPHY 89
One religion for all: the fusion of Christianity and Europe 95
The rise of a new empire: Frankish statecraft and Christian
   arguments 97

Culture and cohesion: the role of ideology and education in
the shaping of Carolingian Europe, or the 'First Renaissance'? 101
The impact of monasteries 105

**5 Three worlds around the Inner Sea: western
Christendom, eastern Christendom and Islam**   **108**
Confrontation and contact from the sixth century onwards 108
The world of the Prophet: Islam 108
God's kingdom among men: orthodox Christendom 114
A far corner of the earth: Roman, Catholic Christendom 118
The Crusades: western Christendom versus Islam and
eastern Christendom 120
CLERMONT, 26 NOVEMBER 1095: POPE URBAN II CALLS
FOR A CRUSADE 122

**6 One world, many traditions. Elite culture and popular
cultures: cosmopolitan norms and regional variations**   **127**
Europe's 'feudal' polities 127
The Church and the early states 130
Economic and technological change and the early states 133
Stronger states – stronger rulers? 137
The towns and the early states 139
A Christian world or a world of Christian nations? 145
Elite culture and popular cultures: cosmopolitan norms and
regional variations 151
LONDON, AD 1378: GEOFFREY CHAUCER DESCRIBES HIS
WORLD 154
The importance of the universities 159

Interlude. The worlds of Europe, *c.*1400–1800   **166**
A world of villages 167
A world of towns 175
Two worlds? 180

PART III
**Continuity and change: new ways of looking at man and
the world**   **185**

7 A new society. Europe's changing views of man   **187**
The survival of classical culture and the beginnings of
Humanism 187

The loss of Byzantium – the gain of Europe: the further
development of Humanism in Italy 189
From Humanism to the Renaissance in Italy 194
ROME, AD 1538: MICHELANGELO TALKS ABOUT ITALIAN
ART 197
Humanism and the Renaissance: Italy and beyond 201

8 **A new society: Europe as a wider world**   205
Economic and technological change and the definitive formation
of the 'modern' state 205
From manuscript to typescript 208
Gunpowder and compass 212
THE HAGUE, AD 1625: HUGO GROTIUS EXPOUNDS 'THE
LAW OF NATIONS' 215
Church and State: the break-up of religious unity 216
Printing, reading and the schools: education for the masses? 221
Unity and diversity: printing as a cultural revolution 227
Europe and its frontiers: nation-feeling and cultural
self-definition 236

9 **A new society: Europe and the wider world since the
fifteenth century**   239
The 'old' world and the 'older' world 239
The 'old' world and the 'new' 245
The 'Columbian exchange' 249
EUROPE, THE EARLY SIXTEENTH CENTURY: OPINIONS
ON THE CONQUEST OF AMERICA AND ITS
CONSEQUENCES 255
Images of America and mirrors of Europe 256
Further cultural consequences of European expansion 264

10 **A new society: migration, travel and the diffusion
and integration of culture in Europe**   272
Migration, travel and culture 272
Non-voluntary travel: the cultural significance of migrations 273
Three types of cultural travel 276
ROME, WINTER 1644–5: JOHN EVELYN VISITS THE
ETERNAL CITY 288
The practice of travel 290
To travel or not to travel? 293
Travel as an element in growing cosmopolitanism and cultural
integration 295

11 A new society: the 'Republic of Letters' as a virtual and virtuous world against a divided world   **297**

The Republic of Letters: a quest for harmony 297

The Republic of Letters and the ideal of tolerance: theory and practice 298

CHATEAU MONTAIGNE, NEAR BORDEAUX, AD 1580: MICHEL DE MONTAIGNE ON EUROPE AND 'THE OTHER' 299

The Republic of Letters and its enemies: national cultural policies, or the political uses of culture 304

The Republic of Letters, or how to communicate in an invisible institution 307

The Republic of Letters and the 'intertraffic of the mind': three examples 310

12 A new society: from Humanism to the Enlightenment   **314**

Humanism and empiricism between 'ratio' and 'revelatio' 314

From – scientific – empiricism to new visions of man and society 318

EUROPE, THE EARLY SEVENTEENTH CENTURY: VIEWS ON THE SCIENTIFIC METHOD OF FRANCIS BACON AND RENÉ DESCARTES 320

From Humanism to Enlightenment: a long dawn 325

Enlightenment and Romanticism: poles apart? 330

PART IV
Continuity and change: new forms of consumption and communication   **337**

13 Europe's revolutions: freedom and consumption for all?   **339**

Material culture and conspicuous consumption: Europe's process of consumer change until the end of the eighteenth century 339

Production and reproduction: a process of economic and demographic change until the end of the eighteenth century 343

A process of social and cultural change: the convergence of elites until the end of the eighteenth century 346

Two 'revolutions': one political, one economic, both cultural 350

PARIS, 27 AUGUST 1789: THE CULTURAL IMPORTANCE OF
THE 'DÉCLARATION DES DROITS DE L'HOMME ET DU
CITOYEN' 353
Urban, industrial culture: the regulation and consumption
of time 361

**14 Progress and its discontents: nationalism, economic
growth and the question of cultural certainties**   **366**
The revolutions and their aftermath 366
Elements of nationalism: the political culture of the nineteenth
century 370
New elites, new mechanisms of cultural diffusion, new
manifestations of culture 373
BASLE, THE MIDDLE OF THE NINETEENTH CENTURY:
JACOB BURCKHARDT (1818–97) CRITICIZES
CONTEMPORARY CULTURE 380
Money and time, goods and leisure: towards a consumer culture 389

15 Europe and the other worlds   **392**
Europe and its expanding world 392
Europe and Latin America: a severed relationship? 393
The 'old' world and the 'new': North America as a vision of
freedom 395
Capitalism and consumerism: freedom or slavery, progress or
decadence? 398
NEW YORK, 1909: HERBERT CROLY (1869–1930) INTERPRETS
'THE PROMISE OF AMERICAN LIFE' 400
Europe and 'America': a cultural symbiosis, or the growth of the
'western world' 401
To the 'heart of darkness': Europe and Africa 403
The 'old' world and the 'older' world 405

**16 The 'Decline of the Occident' – the loss of a dream?
From the nineteenth to the twentieth century**   **414**
The sciences: positivism and increasing relativism 414
BERLIN, 1877: HEINRICH STEPHAN REJOICES IN THE FIRST
GERMAN TELEPHONE SERVICE 415
Europe in hiding, Europe surviving 422
A growing sense of *fin de siècle* between pessimism and
optimism 427
A world between wars 432

17 Towards a new Europe? **441**

Science, culture and society 441

After the Second World War: deconstruction and reconstruction 448

A culture of time versus money 454

From 'familyman' to 'salaryman' – from group identity to
individual identity? 460

Dimensions of identity – culture as communication: towards an
'anonymous mass culture'? 464

EUROPE SINCE THE 1960s: POPULAR MUSIC – HIGH
CULTURE? 472

Epilogue **478**
Europe – a present with a future

Notes 494
Index 529

Plates

1 View of the 'Museum Island' in Berlin's Spree River xxi
2 Limestone statue of the scribe Heti with a papyrus scroll,
  *c.*2–3000 BC 11
3 Cave painting at Niaux, France, dated c.20,000–10,000 BC 15
4 Bronze chariot from a seventh-century BC grave at Strettweg,
  Styria 21
5 Scene from a funerary monument found at Neumagen, Germany,
  dated *c.*AD 190 48
6 Mosaic of Empress Theodora, wife of Justinian, dated sixth
  century, from the church of San Vitale, Ravenna, Italy 48
7 Shrine dedicated to the service of Mithras, located under the
  Christian church of San Clemente, Rome 69
8 Fresco depicting 'a meal of fraternal love', found in one of the
  Roman catacombs 69
9 Germanic limestone tombstone, from the eighth century, from
  Alskog Tjangvide on the island of Gotland, Sweden 88
10 Fifteenth-century fresco cycle in the church at Briançon, France 121
11 The teaching of theology at the Sorbonne, from a fifteenth-century
  French manuscript 157
12 Water-driven flour-mill on the bank of the River Vltava at
  Prague, in a colour-wash, pen drawing by the Dutch artist
  Roelant Savery, *c.*1610 158
13 Anonymous engraving showing various aspects of agricultural
  labour, 1502 168
14 An illustration from the *De re metallica* of Georg Agricola, 1556 169
15 A Roman mosaic allegedly depicting Plato's academy, at the
  National Museum of Naples 196
16 Eighteenth-century engraving showing the observatory for
  astronomical research of the Jesuit mission in Peking 254
17 Jacob Fugger, the Augsburg banker, and his chief accountant,
  Matthäus Schwarz, depicted in the Fuggers' headquarters in 1516 278

18   Engraving showing people watching heretics and witches being
     burned in a straw hut, depicted in a text on criminal law and
     procedure, the *Cautio Criminalis* of 1632   299
19   Water-driven organ/automata devised by the learned Jesuit
     Athanasius Kircher (1602–80)   319
20   Eighteenth-century print making fun of science, in a vision of
     an air-borne world   319
21   The first German railway between Nuremberg and Fürth, in a
     contemporary engraving, 1835   354
22   A view of the Krupp firm's factories at Essen, Germany, in an
     engraving of *c.*1860   364
23   Lithograph showing the Parisian 'Au Bon Marché', the great
     department store, *c.*1870   381
24   Late nineteenth-century (coloured) lithograph of a Parisian
     telephone exchange   415
25   Engraved representation of the 'Hall of the French Machines'
     at the 'Exposition Universelle' held at Paris in 1878   418
26   Engraving showing how machines in the family home could
     free women of heavy household chores   418

Maps

1 Migrations in Western Eurasia, third to first millennium BC   14
2 Extent of Greek influence in the ancient Mediterranean world, *c.*400–300 BC   39
3 Roman Empire in AD 211   49
4 Linguistic boundaries, *c.*AD 1200 (with eleventh- and twelfth-century pilgrimage routes)   156
5 European expansion at the end of the Middle Ages to *c.*1540   243
6 Agencies and commercial interests of the Fugger trading and banking house, *c.*1500   277
7 Major spheres of European cultural influence, *c.*1800   408

Prologue
Europe – a present with a past

Es irrt der Mensch, so lang er strebt.

Man shall err as long as he strives.

God, in the 'Prologue' to Goethe's *Faust I*[1]

Europe: old Europe, new Europe, old borders, new borders

Few people thinking about the part of the Eurasian land mass commonly called Europe will realize that, according to the geographers at least, its geographical centre is located some dozen kilometres north of the Lithuanian capital Vilnius, a city itself situated near the border of Russia. Given this fact, we should accept that, geographically speaking, Europe is a world that extends from what is the westernmost part recognized as such – the Irish Atlantic coast – to the Urals.

Yet many Europeans have difficulty in accepting that the inhabitants of the Baltic countries of which Lithuania is one, which became members of the European Union in 2004, really belong to 'their' continent – let alone that they would consider Russia a 'natural' part of it. Nevertheless, travelling in those Baltic countries, one becomes very much aware of what Europe is. One experiences the urban culture of cities like Tallinn – formerly Reval – and Riga, the capitals of, respectively, Estonia and Latvia. This is a sea-oriented culture that became European because these cities were founded as port-towns in the thirteenth and fourteenth centuries by merchants of the German Hanse: they were part of the great shipping route that connected Flanders and the other Netherlands, on the North Sea, all the way around Denmark and the cities of northern Germany via the Baltic Sea to the upper reaches of the Finnish Gulf.[2] As the Hanse was a sociocultural as well as a commercial-financial network, Hanse cities show all kinds of similarities. Thus, the churches of Tallinn and Riga have the typical, purely ornamental brick bands of the ecclesiastical architecture one also finds in Stralsund, Rostock and Lubeck, to name but a few finely restored cities of the Hanseatic heartland, but also in small Dutch Hanse towns like Doesburg. Other traces of an old common culture have recently been discovered and uncovered: the frescoed medieval saints who were plastered over during the iconoclast furies of the sixteenth century that happened here as elsewhere in Europe. In these towns, church schools were established where knowledge European-style – which, from the sixteenth century onwards, also meant through the printed book – was dispensed.

Though the – German-speaking! – elites of these Baltic towns turned Lutheran after the Reformation, they used the Italian baroque style – notwithstanding its 'popish' connotations – for their pulpits and baptismal fonts and richly carved pews and, indeed, for their funerary monuments as well. Besides grand churches, the burghers of these Baltic towns – traders and descendants of traders – also built grand town houses for their own use and even grander town halls and guild halls to express their collective identity, with gothic façades of glazed bricks; in later centuries they added baroque staircases and classicist assembly rooms.

Yet these Baltic cities survived within a rather different culture: the culture of the heirs of the Crusader German knights, who had first occupied these territories – for themselves and for the Church – in the thirteenth century, like the Spanish Christian knights had conquered the Muslim parts of Iberia from the tenth century onwards.

The German Balts, like their Spanish contemporaries, appropriated the land, dividing it into huge estates, and reduced the indigenous population – whom they converted from their own so-called 'heathen' religions to Christianity, as had happened to the Muslim population of central and southern Spain – to the harsh conditions of serfdom.

In the seventeenth century, this imported, but by now local aristocracy had to accommodate another imported elite: the Swedish rulers who came to create an empire encompassing the entire Baltic Sea. Although they became land-owners as well, they tried to introduce some freedom for the populace, as had become the policy in Sweden itself. The Swedish kings also founded a university, at Dorpat, which soon became a centre of regional learning.

A century later, the tsarist empire occupied these lands. Now the local nobility, itself the product of different earlier cultures, became part of the cosmo-politan, Enlightenment culture that was first introduced from western Europe at the imperial court at St Petersburg in the early eighteenth century and, from there, spread to the seats of the regional aristocracy all over Russia. Tsar Peter I built his wife a baroque summer palace in Tallinn, while some decades later the favourite of one of his successors constructed a Versailles-like chateau in the depths of Latvia.

Thus, in the Baltic region, both an urban-bourgeois European culture and an aristocratic-feudal but equally European culture existed side by side, model-ling itself, during the nineteenth century, on St Petersburg but also on Berlin and Paris. Yet, this was also a border region, with a 'different' culture: for unlike in western Europe, most of what was European in the towns and in the country houses never really touched the majority of the population. And whereas in Europe the lot of the masses slowly improved, certainly from the late eighteenth century onwards, the conditions of the peasantry in the Baltic region deteriorated until, in the early twentieth century, the serfs were finally freed.

Then, for the first time, they started to participate in the culture of their own region, to become its bearers, also because they became part of the larger, town-based economies that were now growing. At the same time, these regions, to stress their independence from the imperialist aspirations of Russia – meanwhile turned communist – showed a tendency towards cultural nationalism, as had so many other regions in north-western, southern and central Europe. Trying to find proof of their historic roots as a cultural community, they stressed the uniqueness of their language – Estonian, Livonian, Latvian – and of their art and customs to create their own national identity as the basis for a newly won statehood.

But the Baltic states became border countries again when, after the Second World War, communist Russia occupied them. The Russian occupants created a culture of dependence, of fear, instilling anti-European, anti-Western feelings in these states now turned satellites.[3]

The same happened in Lithuania, though it shows a different culture: visiting Vilnius in the early twenty-first century, one is very much struck by its almost southern European character, with its churches – baroque, Roman Catholic – dominating a hill-top town. For hundreds of years, this too was a border region conquered and contested, mostly by Poland and Russia. Out of this struggle arose another national culture – one, moreover, which showed an aspect that, though largely absent in Estonia and Latvia, was very much part of the European experience as well: the Jewish aspect. For Vilnius was the 'Jerusalem of Lithuania' from the seventeenth century onwards: a town where almost one-third of the population was Jewish until, between 1940 and 1945, first some of the Roman Catholic inhabitants themselves – restrained all too little by the Lithuanian Church – then German Wehrmacht and SS soldiers and, finally, Soviet occupants slaughtered tens of thousands of Jews – as also happened in Latvia.

Not only did the Jewish Lithuanians create the better part of the country's industrial economy and, therefore, its prosperity, they also created a magnificent Yiddish culture – around their synagogues (one built, incidentally, in the same baroque style and by the same architect who designed some of the city's grandest eighteenth-century churches), their schools and their charitable institutions. In the early twentieth century, this essentially religious culture, like the other religious cultures all over Europe, produced not only a secular variant, in the so-called 'Yiddische Wissenschaftliche Institut' (the Jewish Scientific Institute), but also such outstanding men as Jascha Heifetz, the violinist, Itzak Lipschitz, the sculptor and Chaim Soutine, the painter.

In short, the experience of these regions – often seen as peripheral from a western European perspective, while the regions themselves considered their culture pure European, and rather thought of Russia as a border region – in many ways mirrored what has happened and is still happening elsewhere in the world we call Europe. Out of a continuous process of amalgamation that resulted from and, at the same time, existed alongside forms of multiculturalism, identities have grown – and are still growing – on a local, regional and even national level.

At the same time, at least some people felt there was yet another identity overarching these, which they called European. Indeed, identities can and often do exist alongside each other, fulfiling different needs. Thus the Estonians, having won statehood and a national identity, as well as membership of the European Union, look for other forms of cohesion too. Together with the Finns and the Livonian-speaking minority in Latvia who, like their compatriots, have also opted for Europe, they want to stress their Finnish-Ugric identity, which linguistically they share with the Magyar-speaking part of Hungary. On the other hand, the many Russians living in the Baltic states, feeling their role has diminished with the demise of Soviet power, would like to create a Russian axis along what is now the eastern border of the European Union – a border that, even by that very fact, may well be extended further eastward during the forthcoming decades.

By the twenty-first century, all over geographical Europe, 'nations', mostly imagined communities created, like the Baltic ones, out of older, regional cultures, have to come to terms with institutional Europe: the Europe of the Union, of Brussels and its seemingly endless stream of rules and laws. But they also face another Europe, which terms itself the actual foundation for that very Union: a cultural Europe that, according to many, makes the political, social and economic Europe both logical and viable. Yet, over the centuries, but especially since the nineteenth century, many people, including historians, have questioned this cultural Europe: they have questioned its component parts, its divisions, its boundaries, even its very existence, arguing that it is no more than a convenient prop for politicians who dream of unity for the sake of increased power or to maintain their own state's independence, or that it is a romantic but unrealistic notion cherished by artists, men of letters and, yes, some politicians as well, who all dream of unity because they cannot deal with diversity. Admittedly, I do not share the criticism implicit in these views, though the arguments are often useful tools for further analysis. Obviously, many questions remain to be answered.

Europe: ideas

In 1999, UNESCO put the so-called 'Museuminsel' of Berlin on the world cultural heritage list. Yet, in thus rightly honouring one of Europe's most impressive museum complexes, situated on an island in the Spree River, the UNESCO managers probably did not realize they were actually endorsing a complex vision of history, closely related to the genesis of European culture and the European self-image.

When, in 1830, the first museum on the island opened its doors, on a severely classicist building built from 1824 onwards to the designs of Prussia's leading architect, Karl Friedrich Schinkel, the visitors read the following inscription on the façade: 'Studio antiquitatis omnigenae et artium liberalium' – for the study of the origins of all people and of the free arts. The 'Altes Museum' was built to house the antiquities collected by Prussian princes and private persons in,

Plate 1 View of the 'Museum Island' in Berlin's Spree River, with the Greek temple-like structure built from designs by Friedrich August Stuler between 1862 and 1876 to house the new German National Gallery. It stands amidst a number of other magnificent museum buildings, such as the 'Altes Museum', the Pergamon Museum, the Bode Museum etc. The entire complex was obviously meant to convey the idea that the German capital was, in a sense, Athens reborn, with this 'Acropolis of the Arts' enabling Europeans to study their civilization from its beginnings to their own times.

Source: CKD RU Nijmegen

mostly, ancient Greece and the ancient Near East. Obviously, these regions, both culturally and geographically, were only marginally related to nineteenth-century Europe, if at all. Yet, most Europeans, pondering and wondering about their origins, felt that, at least partly, they lay in these very regions – indeed, they had to lie in these regions. Thinking their own time was, in a sense, the epitome of human achievement, they felt the need to explain its genesis and therefore appropriated those earlier, neighbouring cultures which contained elements that had seemingly prefigured Europe's contemporary culture. Europeans wanted to somehow show that their world had built its great civilization on a millennial tradition, that Europe was, in a sense, the rightful heir to these traditions. Consequently, in the vestibule of the 'Altes Museum' a cycle of paintings followed the history of mankind, beginning with man's dispersion after the destruction of the Tower of Babel. Moreover, looking at the objects in the 'Altes Museum' that – as in so many other museums created in Europe during that period – were presented in a very persuasive (chrono)logical sequence, people began to think of themselves as the final product of the traditions embodied therein. In reconstructing history into a process of cultural continuity, nineteenth-century Europeans were actively creating a past that suited their present. This continuity, though empirically largely false, by the very fact of its creation became, in another sense, true. As the American poet Ezra Pound once remarked: 'Not what happened, but what is remembered is significant'.

In 1841, King Friedrich Wilhelm IV of Prussia decided the entire Spree River island should be dedicated to the arts and humanities. Expeditions to Egypt[4] and Mesopotamia enlarged the kingdom's collections of ancient Near Eastern art and artefacts. The king himself left an inscription on the great pyramid of Giza to record Prussia's and, therefore, Europe's cultural appropriation of Egypt. Moreover, in Berlin a 'Neues Museum' was built to exhibit the shiploads of artefacts. Again, the message of continuity was preached to the visitors the very moment they entered the museum: in the frescoed decoration of the so-called 'Fatherland Hall', the history of Egypt was, in a complicated way, connected to ancient Norse epics such as the *Edda*, which told the history of the early German people – or so they thought.

In the early twentieth century, the Pergamon Museum was constructed to house the huge monumental remains of the former Graeco-Roman world as well as of Assyria and Babylonia, excavated by state-sponsored archaeological expeditions. It was large-scale robbery, some people now say. Others argue that it was the timely preservation of works of art and other testimonies of the past that, would have disappeared if Europe had not rescued them.

From 1865 onwards, yet another museum was built on the Spree island, for the Prussian state's growing picture collection. The building itself, however, once more illustrates the underlying idea of Europe's cultural continuity. The (Alte) 'Nationalgalerie' is obviously modelled on the Parthenon, the temple of the goddess Pallas Athena that crowns the Athens Acropolis. Continuing a long tradition among the European intellectual elite, by the nineteenth century many believed that ancient Greece, and more specifically Periclean Athens, the

Athens of the fifth century BC – with its perfectly proportioned figures sculpted in pure, white marble, with its democracy and its man-oriented philosophy – was the cradle of all that was beautiful and noble in European civilization.[5] Inside, continuity is the message, too, on a huge frieze depicting the 'great men' of German culture that runs around the stair well.[6] Of course, the German tribes who, according to the accepted view of history, created the states that, by the 1870s – when the museum was opened – merged into the German Empire, had no direct links to the Graeco-Roman world. Yet, in this building dedicated 'To German Art' according to the huge inscription on its façade, the inventors of this tradition stretched the line of civilization from the Romans – who were seen as the heirs of Greece and of Greece's cultural example, Egypt – and from the Christian heirs of Roman culture to their own times.

Although the Berlin museum complex is of a rare and fascinating sophistication, all over nineteenth-century Europe people were similarly occupied with inventing their history, their past – in museums, in history textbooks, in history painting and, soon, also in motion pictures set in the past[7] – to show that it was precisely and, indeed, only Europe that had inherited everything mankind ever had created by way of things humane. Only Europe was truly civilized.

Europe: realities

There is a Europe beyond the idea and the ideal of it, a Europe forever between old and new borders; a Europe of people who have a shared history, a shared culture that identifies them, and makes them what they are – for, as the French philosopher Jean Paul Sartre wrote: 'je suis mon passé' – I am what my past has made me.

Despite all varieties of time and place, retrospectively Europeans have tackled the problems posed by nature – including the problems posed by their own bodies – to somehow solve the problems of living together in a society, and, finally, to have invented means of representing their natural surroundings, themselves and their society in such a way that the accumulated knowledge of these fields allowed them to survive through successive generations. Taken together, these three aspects of human action constitute human culture.

Or should one rather use the term civilization? Actually, the distinction is not an easy one. Culture is, easily, the older term, having been used by Roman authors to denote the entirety of man's actions, especially in relation to nature. Civilization is of far more recent vintage. It is actually an eighteenth-century French noun, formed from the older adjective 'civilise', civilized, which was used as an alternative for 'poli', polite, polished – hence, for example, in Dutch 'beschaafd', shaven, smooth, polished, as against 'ruw', rough. Referring to such older concepts as 'civility', or the Italian 'civiltà' – the culture of a 'civitas', a town, where people knew how to behave, because they were not rustics or, even worse, barbarians – the new noun, too, soon came to signify a certain aspect of culture, perhaps more its superficial aspect than its essence. However, though it was incorporated into many European languages, 'culture' continued to be used as well. But while some used the two words indiscriminately, in German, for example, 'Kultur' – together with the concept of 'Bildung' – was considered to identify something of a more complex and indeed higher-ordered nature than 'Zivilisation', the latter sometimes seen as no more than a veneer, a polish. However, in France, it was civilization that prevailed, to indicate 'high' or elite culture; as French elite culture was, indeed, cosmopolitan, the notion spread to other countries. When, in 1879, the English anthropologist E.B. Tylor published his famous *Primitive Culture*, about the life of the North American Indians, he specifically chose this title to challenge the distinction between civilization and culture; he felt that civilization had become rather too hierarchical and, indeed, exclusive and that culture was the more inclusive term. Since then the two terms have come to be used interchangeably, as I do.

Culture can be lived and, indeed, be experienced as an identity on various levels: of the individual, the family, the clan, the tribe, of the street or the neighbourhood, of the peer group, of the village, the town, the region, the nation or the state. And, perhaps uniquely so, it can be lived and experienced on the level of that very Europe. For while, during the past millennia, Africans, Native Americans and Asians have not identified themselves as such, Europeans have done so increasingly over the past centuries.

Now, despite all of the above, nothing about the genesis of the actual culture of Europe is 'natural', logical, pre-conditioned. What continuities there are, are balanced by as many changes that, in the end, make it impossible to describe European cultural history in terms of an evolutionary process. Moreover, at the beginning of what most people term European history, little that was achieved in this geographical region was 'typically European'. Yet, especially over the past five centuries, a culture has grown in what we call Europe that has not only become different from most other parts of the world but has also changed many other parts of that world. To start with, in a world of agrarian civilizations – the Amerindian and African-sub-Saharan, Islamic, Indian, Chinese, Japanese and Polynesian – Europe existed, but was no more distinctly recognizable than these others. Then, in a situation that was entirely contingent, many of its otherwise unremarkable features came together remarkably to create a transformation that was at that time unique: the transformation of an agrarian into an industrial culture and society that, for better or for worse – according to one's perspective – came to dominate large parts of the world, economically, politically and culturally. This transformation started slowly in the fifteenth century, accelerated in the late eighteenth century and came to an end in the twentieth century. By that time, however – and through the cultural appropriation described above – Europe had gained characteristics as well as a cohesion most of the other worlds (still) lack.

But what, then, is Europe if we may question calling it a continent and attributing to it the specious security of a distinct geographical entity, as so often happens, and if its culture is not a 'natural fact' either? If anything, Europe is a political and cultural concept, invented and experienced by an intellectual elite more specifically whenever there was cause to give a more precise definition of the western edge of Eurasia, the earth's largest land mass. When was there cause to give such a definition? Often in a moment or period of crisis, of confrontation. After all, it is only when self-definition is necessary that people become self-reflective and describe their own identity.

Thus, the question why the term and, even more so, the concept of 'Europe' was coined at all leads to another question: namely, when was it first used, and by whom? Of course it is equally important to know what was its content at different times in history, and for whom and in what way it was a living reality. Since the seventh century BC, when the word was first heard in the Mediterranean region called Hellas, much has been thought, written and said about Europe, right up to the present day. Europe has been described first, as an Asian princess of that name, subsequently, as a Greek demigoddess, and finally as the queen of the world. Europe has been expressed metaphorically in images and words that encode emotions. In short, Europe has been the result of ways of thinking, of ideologies that actively contributed to the creation of realities. Europe has even become an objective geographical concept. Because of all that, Europe now is a more or less strongly felt bond between those living in it. Europe is situated in that area of tension which links dream to deed, thinking to doing. But it has always been and still is an excluding criterion for those who want to distinguish themselves from an outside world as well.

To find answers to the above questions, one needs to go back far into the past before returning to the situation that developed from the fifteenth century onwards and, more specifically, to the years following the Second World War. For it really was only then that politicians, who were mainly economists and lawyers, attempted to bring to fruition what they, interpretively and sometimes manipulatively, presented as the 'idea of Europe', attributing it, sometimes rather idealistically, to a long historical tradition.[8] They felt the strong need to forever suppress the chances of the European states once more destroying themselves with their own arms — for the two so-called 'world wars' of the twentieth century were, rather, European wars inflicted by Europe upon itself and the world. Therefore, they began to present Europe as a 'culture' or a 'civilization', as a unity with features distinctly its own that, ideally, would do away with interstate rivalry. To further the acceptance of what they felt to be a political, military and economic necessity, to help achieve the 'integration' of the European states, they tried to give it an ideological foundation. Admittedly, this idea had been raised in earlier ages too, but in circles rather more restricted. By now, through mass communication and education, 'Europe' was held up as an ideal to the majority of its peoples, urging them to give up some of their proudly felt but potentially always dangerous dreams of independence to realize, instead, a dream of cohesion, peace and prosperity. In short, insofar as a European consciousness exists among the majority of the peoples living in Europe, it is a consciousness that is of very recent vintage.

Yet, the fact that the 'idea of Europe' was often voiced explicitly either as an ideal community, a utopia, and/or as the instrument of a political elite — as, for example, the elite of Prussia, who wanted to create a basis for their own national identity and, consequently, power – in no way means that it has not become a reality of sorts in the course of time, first for that elite and, during the last century, for far larger groups of people. As Friedrich Nietzsche wrote: 'Ein Traum, ewig wiederholt [kann] durchaus als Wirklichkeit empfunden und beurteilt werden' ('The continuous repetition of a dream may well turn it into a reality felt and judged').[9]

Yet, in attempting to accelerate the process of European unification – of realizing the dream? – the twentieth-century politicians who started building the European Community, which has now become the European Union, have embarked upon a course whose consequences have reached – and still are reaching – much further than in any previous period, pitting a still much-debated belief in the power of a collective, European ideal against the tenacity of older local, regional and national allegiances.

Europe: on the problems of writing its (cultural) history

In view of the above, we need a historical analysis of the phenomena that have contributed to Europe's cultural cohesion, to its past and present reality.

Writing history is always a cultural and political, perhaps even a moral dilemma. Indeed, historians of necessity involve their own culture and self in their writing. If they do not create a contemporary picture of the past, few will want to read them. But, if the images they conjure up are too period-bound, they will quickly fade. My search for Europe is unavoidably a wilful journey along a number of paths, some of which are not yet taken, others obviously well trodden. Whether my stroll leads anywhere is for the reader to decide. I hope this book will provide a time- and place-bound journey through selected fields of Europe's cultural history, guiding readers past various points of recognition and yet stimulating their thought.

Obviously, this book cannot even begin to describe all the features of the European landscape, past and present. Nor does it intend to definitely define what cannot be defined, namely, what Europe really is, for Europe will continue to change, to be itself in new ways. Regardless of the extent to which one's perspective is determined by the views of earlier travellers, what we see is always new. Just as a landscape and our perspective of it change during a journey, similarly, when we think about Europe its contours shift and its characteristics rearrange themselves. For Europe is a series of world-views, of peoples' perspectives on their reality, sometimes only dreamt or desired, sometimes experienced and realized as well.

This was never clearer to me than when I had finished the first draft of the book. Obviously, a text like this is not written or published without being scrutinized by a number of readers, both critical friends and professional reviewers, who remain anonymous for the very reason that the publisher asks them to comment on the text in view of its scholarly acceptability and its commercial viability. By and large, their comments had prepared me for the criticism that a book on European culture was bound to receive and, that, now that I am writing its revised edition, I know it has received.

A basic problem is, of course, how to give body to the concept, the definition of culture outlined above. Many authors writing about the 'culture' of Europe – or, indeed, about 'the' culture of Europe – only vaguely indicate the actual design and extent of their research. Do they plan to study the 'concept of Europe' only, as argued in texts that claim for Europe a cultural and spiritual unity, voicing ideas and ideals that frequently betray an unspoken yet only barely concealed moral basis and bias? Or should one approach the problem of Europe by searching for and then analysing behavioural patterns and institutions, ways of looking at man and society, the things man makes – 'manifestations of meaning' – all of which collectively constitute a given 'culture' and, consequently, can help answer the question of what elements, and when, did they (begin to) distinguish the region identified by them from other parts of the world.

Inevitably, these alternatives touch upon the much-discussed problem of the difference between cultural history conceived as, on the one hand, a history of ideas and ideologies and, on the other hand, as a far wider-ranging history of the great variety of cultural forms, namely the manifestations of man's handling of nature, of himself and of the society he lives in and of his representations thereof, that both give and constitute meaning.

Obviously, both are respectable approaches. As views of what has characterized, and continues to characterize Europe are so charged with norms, values and political aspirations, it seems sensible to try to combine both perspectives. After all, if one would study articulate ideas about Europe without considering them in the context of the time, the circumstances and the social framework in which they were formulated, and on the basis of the very diverse cultural forms in which they became manifest, there would be a real danger of seeing such ideas as timeless and universal and to attach too much value to them. If the past has anything to teach us, it is that ideas claiming absolute validity are always dangerous.

Some critics have argued that an undertaking of this magnitude – describing the infinitely complex cultural history of Europe – is doomed to fail if the author does not harness his data in an economic or sociological 'grand design' such as, for example, the ones chosen by the French historian Fernand Braudel[10] or the German sociologist Norbert Elias,[11] or judges them against some all-embracing and explaining concept or even 'theory' of culture. I cannot but say that though I have found many of the ideas put forward by cultural historians *largo sensu* during the past decades immensely fruitful, I have nevertheless found none that will satisfactorily allow me to use any of them as an overall, structural concept, let alone theory.[12]

Some critics vehemently accused me of being too irreverent regarding the biblical sources of Christian tradition. I persist in saying that no sources should ever be beyond critical analysis. Others, however, felt that the text should not give such prominence to the influence of Christianity on European culture as it does. I happen to think that in every culture of this world, the role of religion(s), and of institutionalized churches cannot be overestimated. Yet other critics argued that a cultural history of Europe should at least chastise the churches for the iniquities perpetrated by them or in their name, showing that Europe's Christian record is far from unblemished, indeed, that there is a definite black side to European culture – which, of course, there is and which I do acknowledge. In short, I should have written extensively on the various inquisitions, on witch-hunts and, in another context, on the genocide perpetrated by so-called Christian Europeans against their Jewish co-Europeans. Of course, I also should have used the gender perspective to analyse how a patriarchal society not only suppressed the female part of its population but also succeeded in silencing its voice in the story that is history or, as some would rather have it, her-story. Yet, though I actually did and do write about all these issues – but, apparently, not enough to satisfy the tastes of these critics – I admittedly do not think that writing history is about apportioning praise or blame to the actions of those who have lived before us, who thought and acted under different circumstances and from different moral precepts. Rather, writing history is about trying to understand them, in their own time and place. Indeed, we can actually try to do so, for contrary to the views of some of the more extremist postmodernist theorists, the texts, the stories historians produce are not only fictions or interpretations, they are solidly and scholarly, scientifically based on facts.[13]

In a comparable vein, some took me to task for not writing about 'the masses', the 'common people', if only because, according to these critics, they suffered most in the making of Europe. However, there seems little sense in expatiating on the human costs of the cultural process, both in Europe and elsewhere. Though it is important to know, for example, how many people worked on the construction of the colonnades in St Peter's Square in Rome and, also, how many died in the process, yet to give such an indication for each and every one of Europe's great buildings or, in another context, to try and work out how many died at the hands of each of Europe's institutions – for example, the Spanish inquisition, or the Soviet Russian army – is both tedious and often fraught with problems of methodology and statistics. Others, however, wondered why this cultural history contained so many details about the economic and political background in the first place. So, yes, while I do think cultural history is, in a way, all-encompassing and, consequently, should pay attention to those human actions we term economic or political, I do not think it should be burdened by graphs and tables.

Some wondered whether the text did not prove what they had always thought and said, namely that cultural history is nothing but a paean to great men and great ideas. Others noted the dozens, nay hundreds of eminent culture makers that I failed to mention, arguing that its art, its literature and its music constitute Europe's most precious heritage and, indeed, its very identity. Not surprisingly, perhaps, the past culture makers I failed to include in my pantheon often proved to be the compatriots of the present reviewers; the latter were not convinced by the argument that any attempt at strengthening the old canon of 'great men (and women)' – or, for that matter, creating a new one – would invite only a host of hostile reactions.[14] Yet, I do feel that culture is made by people; that, consequently, a cultural history should name the men and women who, somehow, have contributed to its making. However, I also feel that, rather than describe people with whom almost everyone is familiar from the age of primary school onwards, it is far more revealing to quote those men and women who, though lesser known, are equally representative of their place and time.

Finally, a few readers were convinced I was in the pay of the European Union, writing an apologia for the ideologies of its power brokers. Others, however, blamed me for being a Euro-pessimist, for presenting altogether too bleak a view of the reality of the values that during the past fifty years have been presented as uniquely European, and of the blessings of the unification that is, according to the Euro-optimists, logically based upon them.

If writing this book – and reading the reviews it has elicited – has taught me anything it is that in talking and writing about Europe the biggest problem is actually the reality of present passions aroused by Europe's past, whether these be religious, moral, nationalist or political. Indeed, even before the present book's first edition was published, I was confronted with some reviewers who, after its first publication, were nothing less than vituperative in their criticism, revealing a bias that, I felt, was both extreme and definitely uncalled for in the scholarly debate that a review always is. While others showed genuine passion, I yet realized that Europe continues to change in time, its idea differing from individual to individual, from group to group. As in the early 1990s, when I had wondered whether I should not renounce my project altogether, when asked to write a revised edition, I felt I should perhaps decline the offer. However, in re-reading my own position, I felt I did need to reconsider some issues as there was some truth in many – though certainly not all – of the critical remarks made over the past ten years. Thus, the challenge and the pleasure involved in presenting a revised text have prevailed.

On choices: the scope and structure of this book

Writing history means making choices. These choices are made against a background of complex factors, including the questions a writer poses himself, his assumptions about his reader's interests and the mass of disorganized details from different and often discordant sources about the past at his disposal. Ultimately, all these factors contribute to the story. But in the last instance, of course, the author's interpretation is the result of an effort to ask meaningful, which means present-minded, questions while trying to avoid meaningless, that is to say present-minded, answers.

In view of all this, writing a 'cultural history of Europe' is not an easy task. One not only must determine the chronological scope of such a tale, more importantly one must decide where, both geographically and culturally, Europe begins and ends. Having dealt with my definition of culture in the previous section, a definition is now called for of the other constituent element of this book: Europe in its spatial and temporal dimensions.

Must everything be described which has happened from the North Cape to Gibraltar, from the west coast of Ireland to the Urals – the accepted geographical definition of Europe as a continent? Or should only those developments be emphasized that can help us understand Europe's culture as it is seen today? Rather than engage in a futile attempt at writing an all-inclusive, encyclopedic and, consequently, unreadable book – and aware of the risk of taking too teleological a view – I have decided to follow the latter approach. However, in doing so choices have been made that limit both the geographical scope of the Europe described and the elements of culture discussed, knowing that to some these restrictions will be disappointing, not to say painful.

As a result of many geoeconomic, geopolitical and cultural-religious developments, some of which can be traced far back into past millennia, while others are of more recent origin, many internal divisions have come into existence creating a multiplicity and diversity of culture(s) in the Europe geographically defined above. Perceptibly the most obvious is the 'dividing line' separating western Europe from what, geographically at least, is called eastern Europe. This 'line', actually a wide transitional zone sometimes referred to as central or even central-eastern Europe, stretches from the Baltic to the Balkans and roughly coincides with the Baltic states, Poland, the Czech and Slovak Republics and Hungary.

This book mainly, though not exclusively, records events that occurred in the western zone, dwelling somewhat less upon the central European countries and their cultures, and giving but scant attention to Russia and the Balkans. Although there are sound scholarly reasons, besides considerations of a politically correct nature, to induce an author to fully include the cultures of eastern Europe, I have chosen not to do so. First of all, I lack the language skills necessary to delve into the relevant literature. More important, however, I believe that this non-inclusion can be defended on the basis of past developments themselves. With its many 'accidents', history has forged links between a number of regional cultures in western and central Europe which increasingly have shown a comparable historical development, resulting in a more widely experienced culture that, however diverse in many of its elements, has yet grown towards an overall unity.[15]

One factor often named as determining the relative unity of this area is the way of life and of thinking which was paired with and is still coloured by the development of western Christianity after the break-up of the Carolingian Empire in the tenth century and the schism between the churches of Rome and Byzantium in the eleventh century. However, another, far more important element is the fact that a number of countries in western and central Europe, while being ruled by 'absolute' monarchs up until the end of the eighteenth century, have yet developed towards consensual and finally even constitutional government. Moreover, these parts of Europe first experienced a slow transition from a mainly agrarian to an industrial economy and culture. Over a long period, a tradition of civic societies has evolved there, characterized by increasing economic and political freedom for the individual and, from the late nineteenth century onwards, also by some sort of collective care for that individual – a mixture of consumerism, liberalism and social democracy. If judged by those criteria, the Europe that now projects itself with such a pretence of historical inevitability is, indeed, only a recent creation;[16] some would even say that it is really a creation of the late nineteenth century.[17]

Due to a number of historical accidents as well as to the absence of certain preconditions, in eastern Europe such structures and traditions have not developed, or only marginally so. Obviously, even as I write and, certainly, in the near future, economic and political changes will result in a growing integration not only of already superficially comparable lifestyles but also of the views of the people and societies of, respectively, western(-central) and eastern Europe. In this process, people in the west increasingly will be forced to reconsider their notions of what Europe is.

However, my conscious choice to make this cultural-geographical restriction does not solve the problem of other choices. Looking backwards, one has to establish which of the traditions one feels Europe is characterized by – each one of them perhaps not specifically, let alone uniquely 'European' – which, taken together, do constitute a coherent culture, a heritage that is worth exploring from a historical point of view.

This first involves choosing the amount of detail to give on developments and cultures that, while geographically speaking are manifestly not European, yet are traditionally included in most histories of Europe. Thus, the so-called 'neolithical' revolution, which introduced agriculture and the forging of iron to the world, did not occur in Europe first – though it soon spread there and influenced the environment there and elsewhere as, since then, only the Industrial Revolution has done.

Precisely because of the search for continuity outlined above, most European histories nowadays begin with an extensive analysis of all that occurred in Egypt, the Near East and Greece from *c.*5000 BC, acting on the assumption that the world of the eastern Mediterranean was the 'cradle of European civilization'. As this is indeed where Graeco-Roman culture and Christianity began, and became probably the two most important ideological cornerstones of the concept of 'European' civilization, developments in this region will be described, albeit only sketchily, in Part I, chapters 1, 2 and 3. However, limiting the story to these 'roots' of Europe would do no justice to what was occurring at the same time in, from a modern perspective, Europe proper and, more specifically, in its western and central regions. Therefore, this aspect is included in the story as well, also in the first chapters.

In trying to isolate the relevant traditions, or sources of inspiration, of these cultures in their chronological appearance, we should first, but cautiously, name the nascent democracy of ancient Greece, specifically Athens – cautiously because it was a democracy that left out the majority of the town's population. We should then go on to the legal structures devised in classical Rome, which protected both life and property, and to the moral values of Christianity that tried to teach that protecting only oneself would not result in a humane society.

Specifically, the fusing of the classical tradition with the beliefs of Christianity, and the characteristics of the society that brought about this fusion – and was formed by it – are described in Part II, chapters 4, 5 and 6.

Following these two extended introductory parts, an Interlude looks at Europe from another point of view, namely as a world that, for many centuries, consisted largely of local, enclosed, rural cultures and of more open, urban cultures. Through their more dynamic culture, the latter were, many historians have argued, the motors that brought about the change that altered Europe from the fifteenth century onwards.

Following the idea that Europe slowly underwent its most important trans- formation since that period, Parts III and IV take up two-thirds of the book, covering Europe's history since then. According to the German sociologist Max Weber (1864–1920), Europe during these centuries acquired some of its prevailing characteristics: nationalism, as well as rationalism and scepticism; while the first phenomenon embedded Europeans in an often 'invented' tradition that tried to give them security, the other two represented a process in which Europeans became, in a sense, 'disenchanted'. This development, Weber felt, was exemplified in the bipolarity of the Enlightenment, with its glorification of the 'logos', and Romanticism, with its continued search for the inspiration of the 'mythos'. The tension seems to characterize European culture to the present day.

Also, in Parts III and IV I have chosen to highlight the relationship between Europe and the other worlds as, to me, this seems as important as the question of Europe's pre-European roots discussed in Part I.

Europe and Europeans – as everything and everyone – exist only by virtue of their contrasts, their opposites. Moreover, they have an 'un-known side', i.e. some characteristics of fears and desires which define them. Man, and therefore also European man as he sees himself, has made and known himself through a confrontation with the 'other', and will always do so. Therefore it is crucially important not to forget that from the earliest times onwards a diversity of peoples living in 'Europe' as well as, more visibly and to Europe more profitably – especially between the fifteenth and the twentieth centuries – peoples from other worlds have played an important, not to say an essential part in shaping Europe's culture. Conversely, Europeans themselves have always had a perspective on those other worlds, the more so as they came to dominate large parts of them – culminating, of course, in the inclusion of North America in its own culture, which resulted in the concept of the 'Western World'. Though for those parts of Asia and Africa that came into its orbit, European dominance effectively lasted only two centuries, covering the short period of *c.*1750 to *c.*1950, its consequences for the culture of the present world, and for the process of globalization, have been enormous. Indeed, if Europe is to be called 'unique', as some do, one of the reasons given surely should be that no other culture has ever influenced the globe as completely, for better or for worse.

Also, it is precisely in these two centuries that Europe really came to acquire the characteristics it now prides itself on. It seems to me that in this period the economic importance of Europe's Eurasian, Atlantic and African empires, and the complex interaction of these empires with the building of a consumer-oriented, literate, democratic society in Europe itself, really constitute the 'miracle of the West'. Without at least indicating the role that various non-European worlds and their peoples and cultures played in its creation, my story of the European world would be both partial and incomprehensible. Consequently, justice must be done to the global aspects of Europe's past, too, to avoid mis-representing history.

In Part III, I have stressed the various ways in which, since the sixteenth century, forms of tolerance have been slowly developing both through inter-regional and interconfessional contacts within the narrow confines of Europe and through intercultural relations between Europe and the 'other worlds'. At the same time, we should stress the intolerance that often characterized the daily practice of the majority as against what was preached by only a minority.

I have also chosen to stress the invention of the art of printing as the first communications revolution since the introduction of scripture: an essential stimulus not only to the wider distribution of knowledge and to the diffusion of a spirit of criticism and debate but, perhaps more important, a road to better education and consequently to more widely spread opportunities for cultural diversity and personal development, although this only became a mass phe-nomenon since the nineteenth century. By then, Europe had become the first 'knowledge society' of the world. But as the information density increased from the nineteenth century onwards – not as a result of any political will but, basically, as a consequence of technological developments – the context of identity in which European people lived was much enlarged as well. In this ongoing process, inevitably people increasingly search for distinction – when 'others' become too near, people retire to their 'self', and its trusted social and cultural parameters that are often local and regional rather than national, European or global. Consequently, tolerance, multiculturalism even, and the perceived need to retain one's own identity are certainly not easily reconciled.

Meanwhile, forms of representative government emerged in intricate inter-action with economic changes that, between the fifteenth and the nineteenth centuries, turned Europe from a mainly agrarian society in which, through a complex set of social and legal rules, equality of chances was largely absent, into an industrial society with opportunities that were, at least in principle, open to all. The process in which people articulated ideas of social equality and social justice eventually resulted in the concept of human rights, a concept not unequivocal but certainly inspiring.

Of course, we should be well aware that much of the above represents ideas and ideals that neither were nor yet are fully realized in practice. On the contrary, Europeans have often been untrue to their vision of themselves and of the heritage they claim. One of the historian's tasks, I think, is to evaluate – though, again, not to judge – past practices precisely to allow people to determine what they feel to be important enough to preserve as an inheritance for the future.

Throughout the book, I will try to establish how Europeans, often but certainly not exclusively intellectuals and scholars, shaped their lives, created culture, in increasingly complex manifestations. Many if not all of these manifestations were formed within the fundamental cultural context Europe acquired when, from the first century AD onward, a fusion started between Graeco-Roman traditions and Christianity, a creed in itself the product of several Near Eastern, 'Asiatic' religions. This fusion resulted in a frequently difficult partnership of resolute rationalism on the one hand and beliefs based on revelation on the other hand. For the past 2,000 years, this has stimulated a creative tension that has become one of the motors of European culture, influencing both the thoughts and actions of those Europeans who remained religious and of those who, precisely because of that tension, sought new ways.

This book also hopes to show how, as a result of this process, many ideas were absorbed as normative values in the self-image of Europe, which was mainly articulated by the intellectual elite. Though elites, certainly intellectual elites, are groups whose cohesion is determined by various socio-economic and cultural factors, they share a way of thinking which determines their spoken and – much more powerful – written words as well as, at least partly, their deeds. In this way, and as long as they dominate society's communication and, thus, information processes, they have a strong influence on the cultural expressions of society at large, certainly on those expressions that one encounters on the surface: political and social ideas, the public manifestations of power, customs and manners, and so on.

All this does not mean that this book deals with 'elite culture' only and omits any reference to 'popular culture'. These concepts, also referred to as the 'great' and 'small' traditions, are too simple and, hence, distorting to be tenable. Rather, I prefer to stress that precisely the question of what people thought and, more important, how and in which circumstances they acted gives direction to every study of cultural history.

Having made all of the above choices, including the one not to search for an all-encompassing framework to present the data that follow from these choices, I still felt that I needed to avoid a simple chronology – though, of course, there is no denying the influence of time evolving, of new generations choosing from the inheritance of their forebears, changing it, adding to it. Yet, having said that, I need to stress that cultural histories never follow the strict chronology used by the more traditional political histories. Moreover, for various reasons categories like 'the Middle Ages', the 'Early Modern Period' and 'Contemporary History', long in use, are more or less inadequate, if not actually misleading. The patterns shown by different domains of culture and, also, in different sectors of society can sometimes remain static for centuries, and sometimes change in quick succession within relatively short periods. Therefore, searching for useful beginnings and endings, for synchronicity, would mean distorting the past only to suit the format of a textbook.

To give some structure to a story that stretches over thousands of years, this book charts Europe's past along the lines of what I have termed four grand phases of continuity and change. These phases can be summed up in the following phrases.

The *effort at survival*, characterizing the history of all of mankind from the beginning, produced a great change in European culture with the transition, from the fifth millennium BC onwards, to an agricultural society, and a rather more secure livelihood. The move towards *one dominant religion* in Europe, which really started in the fourth century AD, had enormous consequences for life and thought. With some rhetorical exaggeration, one might say that from the sixteenth century onwards the genesis of *a broader view of the world* brought Europeans slowly out of the confines of the village into the orbit of the state, of Europe, and finally even of other worlds. Last but not least, the development towards *mass consumption and communication* in the nineteenth and twentieth centuries gave European culture its present characteristics; also, more than anything that came before, it robbed Europe of many of its traditional cultural forms.

Obviously, this is not to say that the phases outlined above were peculiar only to European history, for at least the first and second definitely occurred in other regions of the world as well. But it may be maintained that, taken together and seen in their historical interaction, they represent both the result of and a framework for choices that have contributed to Europe's singularity, to its cultural identity as it stands today.

On the use of this book

In view of all the above arguments of definition and limitation, any cultural history of Europe is a selection. It is influenced not only by an author's field(s) of interest, the scope of his reading and the choices he makes – which I have dealt with in the preceding pages – but also by the format of the book to be published, the latter the outcome of a confrontation between the author, a publisher's policy and the presumed audience.

Now, although it is hoped that the interested lay reader will find this book a stimulating point of entry into European cultural history, it is primarily intended as an introduction for students in their early years of academic study. Some caveats are therefore appropriate.

As this book presumes to be a cultural history in the broad sense, it has to consider economic, social and political structures and processes as well. Yet as any cultural history is, inevitably, an attempt at a synthesis, trying to recreate and analyse the lifestyle of a number of more or less cohesive groups in a specific region, it cannot give a lengthy, in-depth treatment of these aspects of the past. Readers who want to be thoroughly informed of these will have to turn either to more specialized works in these fields or to works which pretend to cover European history in all its aspects.

Moreover, the nature of a cultural history of Europe that tries to explain present structures and manifestations through an analysis of past developments, almost automatically leads to a selection and discussion of precisely those aspects and episodes that clarify the process of continuity and change that transformed the past into the present. Writing history that way is, therefore, the (teleological) chronicling of the behaviour and achievements of the 'victors', whether they were individuals or groups, whose actions or concepts contributed to today's cultural fabric. Some historians argue that the 'losers', those who have been sidetracked by history, are just as important. They feel we can learn just as much from the possibilities that once existed but which were never realized, as a result of circumstance – coincidence, the exercise of power, choice. The questions implicit in this view are intriguing but unanswerable. Some would feel that, in fact, none of the energy that once existed really has been lost; that all thoughts and trends, even if they have at particular moments been condemned or cast off as too alternative or irrelevant, as heretical even, have only temporarily sunk into oblivion: they may well play a role at any time in the fruitful interaction between 'past' and 'present' which always creates a 'future'. For as William Shakespeare wrote in *The Tempest*: 'Whatever is Past, is Prologue'.

Finally, I envisaged a book that would be of use to a large audience, implying that, if anything, it should not be so voluminous as to be daunting instead of inviting. Therefore, I have tried to write a short book. To increase its readability, a large number of quotations have been used, hoping that the reader, for whom the past is, by definition, a foreign country where people do things differently, will still feel that he can travel there. For the same reason, longish extracts from original sources have been used to provide opportunities for discussion, reflection and further investigation. The annotation of the text is meant to serve both as a bibliography and as an incentive to further reading. Therefore, a separate bibliography has not been included.

Acknowledgements

First of all, I would like to thank my colleague, Professor Dr Anton Hagen, who, though no historian, through his enthusiasm for the project stands at the beginning of this book.

The way I learnt to experience Europe during my journey has been made decidedly less one-sided by the comments of a number of people who, unlike the anonymous ones referred to above, can and should be mentioned with gratitude. Among them, I would like to give special thanks to my colleague from Louvain-la-Neuve, Professor Rudolph Reszohaszy, as well as to Professor Paschalis Kitromilides of the University of Athens, Professor Inge Jonsson of Stockholm University and Dr Jan van der Harst, University of Groningen. Both they and M. Jacques Walch, former director of IBM Europe, took pains in going through parts of my text, censuring it wherever necessary. The book as it now appears has gained considerably from their candid criticism as it has, too, from remarks made and suggestions offered by those reviewers of the first edition who did not obviously have an agenda all of their own, and from the observations of those readers who prefer to remain nameless but may yet recognize where their contributions have made a difference.

Yet the book owes just as much to the questions raised by my Nijmegen students, in the lectures and seminars in Mediterranean History, in Intellectual History and in the History of Cultures and Mentalities. With this book I hope to repay a debt of gratitude every teacher owes to his pupils. The fact that in these programmes Dr Meindert Evers has for long been my closest colleague has added as much to the pleasure of teaching as it did to the necessity of continuing to ask new questions. Last but not least I thank Dr Catherine Brölmann, who put up with the first version of this book for a long time and whose meticulous reading saved my text from many inconsistencies. Of course, any defects that remain in this revised edition are solely my own.

All illustrations have been provided by the Centre for the Documentation of Art History of the Radboud University, Nijmegen, the Netherlands, which has taken care that all copyrights that were ascertainable have been honoured. Those who think that their right to any of the illustrations has not been honoured should contact the Centre.

'Cruise Missiles' and 'Berlin': Lyrics by John Watts, reproduced by kind permission of Complete Music Ltd. 'Public Enema Number One': Composed by Bruce Dickinson/David Murray, published by Zomba Music Publishers Ltd, used by permission, all rights reserved. 'History Will Teach Us Nothing': Words and Music by Sting © 1987, reproduced by permission of G.M. Sumner/EMI Music Publishing Ltd, London WC2H 0QY.

Peter Rietbergen
The Dutch Institute, Rome, Italy

The Radboud University, Nijmegen, the Netherlands

The Netherlands Institute for Advanced Studies (NIAS), Wassenaar, the Netherlands

Christ Church, Oxford, England
July 1994–November 1997; July 2000–December 2004

Part I

Continuity and change

New ways of surviving

1   Before 'Europe'

Towards an agricultural and sedentary society

Beginnings in Africa and the eastern Mediterranean, or the non-European origins of European culture

Already in the seventeenth and eighteenth centuries, European scholars were searching for the origins of man in a past far remote from and in developments more complex than the simple picture painted – and accepted by most of their contemporaries in – the Christian Bible. To most Europeans, the Holy Book was still the only touchstone of truth, teaching that the earth and man came into existence when God created the universe on the morning of a momentous day in the year 4004 BC.

In 1698, an English medical doctor, Edward Tyson, visited the docks in London – famous as a place where other worlds entered Europe – having heard that a chimpanzee was being displayed there. When the animal died, he asked permission to dissect it. He studied all its aspects and functions and compared these with those of humans. Observing many differences, he yet considered the number of similarities to be greater and more significant. His conclusion, in a book called *Orang-Outang, sive Homo Sylvestris*, 'Orang-Outang, or the Wild Wood Man' (London 1699), was that a fundamental distinction between humans and certain simian types was scientifically untenable.[1] Tyson scrupulously refrained from elaborating on the implications of his observations for the traditional view of man's history as the final, most perfect stage of God's creation. However, these cannot have escaped his more perspicacious readers.

In 1819, a young Dane, Christian Jurgensen Thomsen (1788–1865), was entrusted by the king with the task of classifying archaeological finds made in Denmark which by royal order were from now on to be sent to Copenhagen. Wondering how to comply with his instructions, Thomsen finally decided on a course of action that nowadays would be considered simple logic but at that time was not part of a European's mental framework: archaeological objects were mainly judged on their aesthetic merits. Thomsen, however, divided his objects according to their material and functional aspects. On the basis of this classification he concluded that the three earliest stages of man's history should be termed the Stone Age, the Bronze Age and the Iron Age, reflecting both growing technological skills and cultural progress. He presented this development as historically significant in itself, thus establishing the study of material culture and of man's past before the invention of writing as an object of scientific study rather than of aesthetics.[2] Some scholars were enthusiastic but the general public could not yet share Thomsen's grand vision of man's past, deeming the objects he had found too primitive to be considered proof of anything that could be termed European culture.

In 1847, the Frenchman Jean Boucher de Perthes published a book called *Antiquités celtiques et antediluviennes* (Paris 1847), in which he described the findings of his excavations at Abbeville, on the Somme river. Although some acclaimed him as an original scientist, the larger public derided his ideas: how could one possibly accept that remnants of 'antediluvial man' remained and, moreover, remained in Europe?

Indeed, until well into the nineteenth century such views and their implications were unacceptable, not to say repugnant, to most Europeans, even to the well educated. 'Civilization', 'culture' – these words and concepts referred to the temples and philosophy of the ancient Greeks, to the powerful, legal structures of the Romans, to the universal norms and values propagated by the Christians. Cave dwellers, whose features were more ape-like than human and who worked with 'primitive' stone tools, simply did not fit into the European self-image. Yet, the progress of archaeological research in the nineteenth and twentieth centuries eventually forced Europe to drastically adjust its self-image, finally accepting even that man had come from Africa, the continent viewed so long as a world of darkness, a world without culture.

Obviously, the question of what distinguishes man from the chimpanzee, its nearest relative in the common ancestry, or pan-lineage, is much discussed, centring around such questions as what intelligence actually is, in relation to self-reflection, the ability to learn and to use that learning to improve one's existence, etc.[3] According to the latest findings and the interpretations that have been given to them, hominids, among them *homo habilis*, who may have been the first to craft stone tools and later may have been the first to master the art of making fire (and probably was also the first to engage in big game hunting), originated in Africa sometime between *c.*3,000,000 and 2,000,000 years ago, inhabiting large parts of the continent. Sometime around 1,700,000 years ago, *homo ergaster* moved out of the area in north-east Africa where, perhaps, his migrations in search of food and a better clime had brought him, and into Eurasia, where recent finds have shown traces of him in Georgia but also in northern China. At a much later date, perhaps some 800,000 years ago, a species of *homo ergaster* settled in present-day France and Italy. Yet, we know this only because of the worked stones they left behind: there is not a trace of these people themselves, not even genetically.[4]

Between 700,000 and 400,000 BC, some groups or perhaps only one group of *homo ergaster* evolved into *homo heidelbergensis* – where and when exactly is still under debate – who, in turn, moved to Europe too, as his name indicates. As late as *c.*250,000 BC, another type of *homo ergaster/heidelbergensis* called *Neanderthal* man entered the scene, named after the region near Düsseldorf, in

Germany, where his remains were first found; he actually inhabited the wide stretch of Eurasia from France and Spain to Uzbekistan. Fossils give us an idea of his appearance: very robust and stocky, on average between 1.55 and 1.65 metres tall, with short legs and a long torso enabling him to cope with the dearth of food resources in winter, when he survived on fat reserves accumulated by gathering in seasons of relative plenty. Neanderthal man's brain volume was, moreover, bigger than that of any other creature. He used these greater cranial capacities to develop a stone-based technology, consisting largely of prepared-core flaking, which indicates that he consciously planned his basic survival strategies.[5]

Influenced by the seasons, these earliest inhabitants of Europe travelled around their regions seeking semi-permanent shelter in caves. Gradually, 'conscious' habitation grew, especially with the coming of fire. But scholars are divided over the question of whether these Europeans already had a language; if not, they would have lacked the communicative capacity that can, for instance, organize a hunter society.

None of the genetic material of these more recent representatives of *homo ergaster* survives in the present population of the world; whether they became extinct through natural causes or because they could not compete with newer types of hominids is still discussed. For example, due to climate changes and the further development of the brain, *homo sapiens* had come into being *c*.200,000 years ago. Where and when did he originate?[6] Also in (sub-)tropical Africa, from where groups of his species, too, started migrating in search of the kind of food that held the protein they now needed to become the ancestors of the modern world's population. DNA research seems to show that small bands of them moved from present-day Eritrea to the Yemen – crossing the Red Sea, which at that time was partly dry land. From the Arab peninsula, men and women moved – gathering and now hunting too – into Asia, reaching southern Asia some 70,000 years ago. Adapting to the different climes they encountered, their skin colour might have taken on a lighter or, conversely, a darker hue and some of them might have grown taller or even become smaller; indeed, as recent as 2004 the remains of hominids of about 1 metre tall were discovered in Indonesia. Thus, man's physical variety was the result of multiple mutations. Only some 40,000 years ago, the species called *homo sapiens* migrated into Europe as well. In Europe, he is often called *Cro Magnon*, named after the French site where he was first discovered. Anatomically and behaviourally, he basically resembled modern European man.

In retrospect, this was a turning point. Periodically, the climate on earth enters an 'Ice Age'. Some 40,000 years ago, northern and western Europe as well as the regions around the Alps and the Pyrenees once again were in the grip of a harsher climate, with glaciers rapidly expanding from the principal mountain ranges. During the following millennia, this Ice Age came to a slow end, and the world gradually started to get warmer again; at this time the most recent variety of *homo sapiens* started to spread throughout Europe, via the Mediterranean and the Danube. Though there is an ongoing dispute about what occurred between the older inhabitants and the new ones, most scholars, taking into account genetic research, hold that the Neanderthals, by then the most numerous type of archaic man in Europe, turned out to be far less capable of surviving; they were displaced and, whether through natural causes or as a consequence of large-scale genocide at the hands of the newcomers, finally became extinct. However, when this occurred exactly and for how long the two species did, perhaps, live alongside one another and even interacted together is still being debated.

As proof of the changes that occurred in these millennia, archaeologists have found signs of a far more complex economy, society and culture. Hunting was clearly one of the principal strategies for survival, but long-distance trade, too, now seems to have become common; tools, both of stone and bone, and weaponry became more sophisticated: a more refined technology had developed. Also, these people looked for dwelling places other than caves: open-air encampments with substantial houses made of wood and bone have been discovered on the plains of Czechoslovakia and southern Russia as well as in France.

Even more fascinating is that people started to create symbolic representations both of themselves and of the world around them.[7] Paintings made with natural pigments − another technological innovation − have been found on the walls of caves, concentrated mainly in southern France and northern Spain. Until 1995, the most revealing were considered to be those discovered at Lascaux by a group of adventurous boys in the summer of 1940; others of the same kind are situated in the Pyrenees and at Spanish Altamira. In 1995, a new and even more spectacular find was made in the Ardèche: there, cave paintings depict all kinds of animals hitherto unknown about in early Europe; they seem to date as far back as 30,000 years. However, the discussion over the interpretation of these artefacts is not yet settled. Was it art for art's sake, or a means to instruct the young men and women of the tribe in the seasonal stages of a hunting economy, with references to the male and female elements in man and society? Then again, the caves may have been used as religious centres, where shamanistic rituals were enacted and where the paintings reflected trance-like voyages into the world of the animals that were essential to the survival of man.[8] The concentration of cave paintings in what, at that time, were apparently the most crowded areas of Europe may point to the need for ceremonial activities intended to integrate and coordinate the growing population. Besides paintings, representations of humans and animals were made in bone and ivory, splendid examples of which, created in *c*.35,000 BC, were found in caves in southern Germany. The many so-called 'Venus' figures are especially fascinating. These female figurines, both stylized and naturalistic, have been found all over central Europe. They may well point to the matrifocal character of these societies.

Did language already exist? As indicated above, the scholarly debate on the origins of language is fraught with vehemently expressed and often contradictory opinions.[9] Theories diverge widely, placing this evolutionary development anywhere between 400,000 and 100,000 BC. As speech preceded writing, there will probably never be any evidence for the exact period of its genesis. Yet both the organization needed for hunting in a profitable way and the very complexity of the many artefacts or 'art' forms, pointing to a culture that used symbolic representation, intriguingly suggests the possibility of other, perhaps older, forms of communication beyond mere sounds and gestures.

It is also noteworthy that these cultures, precisely in the articulation of domestic structures and the various 'art' forms, already show their own regional identities, which may have resulted in the formation of separate, self-conscious 'ethnic' groups. For we should not forget that western and central Europe's distinctive physical-geographical features must have favoured the genesis not only of culture in general – that, of course, came about everywhere – but also of incipiently diverse cultures. Unlike the vast steppes stretching from Russia to central Asia, these parts of Europe, a relatively small corner of the earth, showed an incredibly varied landscape: surrounded by seas on three of the four sides, criss-crossed by navigable rivers connecting the inland areas with those seas; it was a region with contrasting but congenial ecologies, with demanding and challenging climates, and with natural barriers that stimulated development through both seclusion and communication.

The advent of agriculture, temple and state

For hundreds of thousands of years, all humans were gatherers and, later, hunter-gatherers. So were the inhabitants of North Africa and the Near East until approximately 10,000 BC. In the Sahara, then not a desert but a humid and fertile region, living conditions were favourable and people continued to go on as they always had done, even developing the art of pottery. However, the Near East, the 'land bridge' that, when the Red Sea had become a sea again, still allowed African man to move into Europe and Asia, was climatically and geographically somewhat less favoured, as it had been left relatively arid after the last Ice Age. People there had to start collecting wild grasses and grind them to get edible seeds; the skeletons of women found there show the spinal distortion this created. When the seeds were sown, first by chance and soon deliberately, agriculture had been 'invented'.[10]

The introduction of a cereal diet from *c.*9,000 BC onwards allowed for population growth and, in turn, for the intensification of agriculture. This occurred in the Levantine region (Israel, Palestine, the Lebanon and Syria), in south-eastern Turkey, in southern Russia and in present-day Iraq. Whether similar developments took place in other parts of the world or whether agriculture spread from this one region is another of early history's great debates: many scholars hold that the 'invention' of agriculture occurred simultaneously in, for example, China though, on the other hand, it may have come to India from the Near East. Demonstrably, farming reached the western end of Eurasia from that region, first spreading to the coasts of the Black Sea, then still a fresh water lake. During the following millennia, it was taken up in the innumerable small coastal valleys of the eastern Mediterranean and by the Aegean islands, in fact in almost all places where streams, running down from the mountains, deposited their sediment and could be used to irrigate the fields. From the eastern Mediterranean and the Danube basin, agriculture spread into parts of Italy, Spain and France, and into central Europe.[11]

We have only archaeological evidence to document the slow transition to an agrarian economy and the changing lifestyles and new social and cultural forms that accompanied it. Still, the process can be reconstructed. It seems that soon after the introduction of agriculture in the Near East, both natural or artificial irrigation as a means to ensure higher yields and animal husbandry were developed there, with the domestication of a limited number of crops and animals,[12] such as olives and vines, and woolly sheep. Certain nomadic or semi-nomadic groups now became sedentary, settling more or less permanently in villages, which they often surrounded by earthen or stone walls, if only to protect themselves against the hunter-gatherers, whose competitors they were for the use of the land. Sometimes, these villages were quite large. Thus, for example, the ruins of Catalhöyük, in Anatolia, give evidence of what almost can be termed a town, built *c.*7000 BC by a people of neolithic cattle breeders; it housed a population of some 10,000 in small dwellings that were entered from the roof. Sculpture and gaily coloured frescoes indicate that these people had thoughts that went far beyond mere physical survival. For reasons as yet unknown, the settlement was deserted some 2,000 years later. Another famous example of an early town is the walled city of Jericho, in Palestine, which probably also dates as far back; as people continue to live there even now, it is sometimes referred to as the 'oldest inhabited town in the world'.

This settling process was often accompanied by a transition to institutionalized private ownership. Although this certainly did not lead to just and humane structures as we view them, from a purely economic perspective this form of production has proven the most successful throughout human history: only for his own gain man seems to be driven to produce a surplus that then becomes the basis for intricate social and cultural structures.

Indeed, where conditions for agriculture were particularly favourable, complex societies and specialized forms of organization did develop. The great river valleys led the way: Egypt, where the annual flooding of the Nile left a narrow strip of fertile mud in the desert from which farmers could reap a rich harvest; and Mesopotamia, the 'Land between the two Rivers', namely the Euphrates and the Tigris. The latter not only provided plenty of water for irrigation – artificial irrigation[13] – but, perhaps even more important, allowed for transport between the two emerging food-producing areas of the Near East, northern Syria and the lower reaches of these two rivers. Soon, communities evolved which based their prosperity both on agriculture and on the manufacture of products not necessary for mere survival, such as beautifully worked tools and weapons, made of stone and later bronze, or finely crafted pottery for cooking and to store grain in. They also made added-value products that were ideologically important, to be bought and displayed by those who could afford to do so on the basis of their agriculturally produced surplus wealth:

things such as costly textiles, artful metalwork and jewellery set with precious stones. Thus, trade networks developed in which rivers played a significant role, but also overland routes, along which the newly found forms of traction by camel and donkey could be used.

In these as yet mainly agricultural civilizations, which were extremely dependent on water and other natural resources, people were intensely interested in the heavenly bodies; determining night and day but, more importantly, governing the change of the seasons and the coming of the rains – and the floods; they held power over the land's fertility. Indeed, natural forces could change the existing cultures and systems entirely. When, some 4,200 years ago, one of the recurring 'small ice ages' occurred, the level of the Nile sank and large parts of agricultural Egypt became deserts again; harvests failed year after year, people died and the so-called Old Dynasty that had ruled the country for many centuries lost its power, to be replaced by new rulers only when the situation improved after some hundred years of poverty and chaos. The forces behind such changes could not yet be interpreted in any scientific way, at least not according to science as it is now defined.[14]

In this situation, where the power of nature was felt to be a mystery both fascinating and tremendous, religions developed that worshipped the forces of nature and the heavenly bodies as magical, as divine. Soon, those who maintained they could make valid predictions of their movement or even claimed influence or power over them were especially honoured. Dedicating themselves to studying and explaining these phenomena, they became magi, mediating between the divine and the human world. Farmers gladly gave them some of their surplus products hoping they would gain the gods' favour.[15] Frequently, these mediators developed into a closed caste of priests, basing their power on hereditary claims, administering the religion in which people expressed their relationship to the incomprehensible or ineffable by creating gods. While the divine might keep its natural form – a river, a spring – it also came to be represented in man-made forms. While at first the gods were imagined as animals, reflecting the view of the world of a pastoralist-nomadic society, in the urban agricultural communities anthropomorphic images were made as well. These were worshipped in ever more elaborately built cult sites, often centred around mountains or mountain-like artificial structures to represent the idea that the gods lived on high, ruling both the skies and all that lived under them. To these sanctuaries, the faithful went with their gifts of grain or cattle. From these temples, the priests exercised a growing power over society.

In the most advanced agricultural civilizations the first divisions of time, calendars, were created, based on a thorough scrutiny of the heavens. In the Nile delta the year was invented, consisting of 365 days divided into twelve months, each made up of thirty days with leap days to even out the differences. Thousands of years later, the Romans took over this system. In 46 BC, Julius Caesar introduced an improved version of the Egyptian calendar that, with several adjustments in later centuries, is still used in Europe and the entire western world.

As some agricultural societies grew more complex, a more regulated form of administration became necessary, especially when non-working priests, no longer satisfied with periodical gifts, started asking farmers for regular contributions in kind or in money to finance the cost of religious services, of increasingly sumptuous temples and, of course, of the clergy themselves.[16] Probably because of the bureaucratic needs of this kind of 'taxation' arising in these temple societies, the invention of some non-oral communication system to store or transmit data became a necessity. The Inca civilization of Peru developed its system of knotted strings. At a far earlier stage, the river civilizations of India as well as, perhaps, the cultures of early China developed writing, as did the societies of the Near East.

In the centuries between 3400 and 3200 BC complicated writing systems evolved both in Egypt and Mesopotamia, comprised partly of simplified pictures (pictograms), partly of symbols (ideograms), partly of signs for syllables, and partly of one-letter signs. Egyptian 'hieroglyphics' – the Greek for 'holy incisions' – were written on papyrus or incised in stone or clay tablets; this, and Sumerian 'cuneiform', named after the wedge-like signs used in its scripture, became the means of communication in the eastern Mediterranean. Soon, it ceased to be only a 'holy' script; it was adapted to the serve the needs of the trade that now came to connect the different agricultural civilizations of Egypt, Mesopotamia and, quite probably, north-western India. As surplus production enabled people to specialize in all kinds of manufacture, trade networks that used rivers, the sea as well as overland routes brought agricultural products and other man-made wares to those who specifically lacked or desired them. At this time shipbuilding became one of the Mediterranean world's great industries. But while ships were a means of transport, of commerce, they were also a major means of communicating other forms of culture. One of the earliest examples proving this is a vessel constructed some 3,300 years ago, recently discovered on the Turkish south coast: it was found to carry wares from Italy, but also ivory and rhinoceros teeth from Africa, copper and tin (to make bronze) from Cyprus and spices from Asia. Yet, in making the trip to all the ports supplying or selling these products, the people aboard must have carried tales as well, telling about the peoples and cultures they encountered.

Besides needing temples and priests to regulate relations between the natural and the supra-natural world, and some sort of scripture to record the obligations between mortals and gods and, soon, between men themselves, these societies also sought means to defend themselves against internal unrest or external attack. As the priests had done, those who took up military duties now also claimed part of the harvest and often appropriated land which tenant farmers – or more often slaves – had to work to ensure the livelihood and the military provisions of this new class. A new social group who did not work with their hands was now born; they developed into a class of 'aristocrats' or 'nobles'. Soon, they competed with the priests over the exercise of power. Their leaders, sometimes turning into absolute monarchs, often drew their authority from the interface between religious and military power. Divine powers were often

Plate 2 Limestone statue of the scribe Heti with a papyrus scroll, showing traces of the original painting. It can be dated to Egypt's 15th dynasty, i.e. *c.*3–2000 BC. Such statues proclaim the importance of a class of literate men for the functioning of the religious and secular bureaucracy of early temple-states of which pharaonic society was one.

Source: CKD RU Nijmegen

attributed to them as they, too, claimed to be able to comprehend and even predict the course of nature, more specifically of the agricultural cycle and the prosperity it brought.

On the fertile borders of the Nile this priestly monarch was the pharaoh, worshipped as 'son of the Sun', who ruled over Upper and Lower Egypt, which had been united about 5,000 years ago. The authority of this god-king, who fused religious with military might, was such that – contrary to what was believed until recently – the peasantry built the enormous pyramids and temples erected in their name of their free will: as paid labourers, well taken care of by the enormous organization and bureaucracy responsible for the operations on the Giza plateau.

In the many city-states that between them possessed the fertile lands of Mesopotamia, between the two rivers, the priest caste initially ruled all. On their initiative the gigantic, terraced temple-mountains were built of brick tiles, the local material: the traces of these adobe structures still dot the erstwhile rich countryside, much of it now returned to a desert state. In later centuries these priest-kings had to share their power with – or even completely relinquish it to – leaders emerging from the military caste who, however, nearly always induced or forced the priests to divinely legitimize their authority.

On the islands of the Aegean and all around its shores, royal civilizations also flourished: in the fertile valleys of Mycenae and Tiryns on the Peloponnese as well as on Crete where, besides agriculture, sea trade became an important source not only of income[17] but also of contact with other cultures, as witnessed by the Cretan-style frescoes with the characteristic bull-fighting scenes found in some of Egypt's palaces. Since the 1970s, Cretan civilization has become a hot topic again. When Arthur Evans discovered and 'restored' the ruins of the palace of Knossos in the 1930s, he reconstructed this city's culture as one of peace and sun, of youthful, elegant men and women – perhaps unconsciously recasting them in the image he had of an ideal English society? Yet, there now seems to be evidence of another, rather different side to this culture: one wherein children were sacrificed and the followers of the various goddesses violently fought one another.

The further development of the structure we now know as 'the state' was made possible by two interconnected phenomena occurring within the partly agricultural, partly commercial temple-societies described above: the invention of writing – for example, the Cretans, too, developed their own script, known as 'linear A', which has not yet been deciphered – and the gradual extension of large-scale trade, together with the introduction of coinage. The former enabled the elaboration and, more important, the codification of law regulating disputes over property and inheritance. The latter soon demanded the creation of accounting and credit facilities. Together, these formed the basis for a fiscal system that could support large armies which, aided by good communication systems and proper logistics, helped the state to increase its power, both internally and externally, and thus to expand. But these states, whether pharaonic Egypt or the city-states of Mesopotamia and the Aegean, by their growing power and wealth increasingly attracted the unwelcome attention of outsiders, be they driven by hunger or greed.

Invasion, conquest and change: the first wave

Around 5000 BC, the region now comprising southern Ukraine and southern Russia, bounded by the Caspian Sea, was inhabited by tribal peoples; after the burial tumuli they built, they are named 'Kurgan' in Russian. Their language is lost now, but scholars have named it proto-Indo-European, as it was the origin of a number of languages spoken at later times both in Europe and in parts of the Near and Middle East – in present-day Turkey as well as in Iran (formerly Persia) – and in India. Linguists have discovered striking parallels between these languages, in the words used for such diverse fields of culture as kinship relations and agricultural practice, for pottery and for numerals. This may indicate that, over a very long period of time, successive groups from among the Kurgan peoples migrated west, east and southwards.[18] Other scholars claim that people much like them in culture, but perhaps inhabiting a region slightly further south, in eastern Turkey and northern Iraq and Iran, were the ones to start these big migrations and the spread of the languages which resulted in the tongues now spoken in Europe and parts of Asia.[19]

These nomadic-pastoralist tribes were ruled by military elites who maintained their power by, among other things, the use of a new invention: their horse-drawn chariots, which altered the art of warfare. Although their economy included some agriculture and various forms of barter trade, it consisted mainly of cattle-grazing; consequently, they led a frugal life of near-subsistence on their vast tundra or steppe-like plains. Worshipping the sun and the sky gods, they were well aware how precarious their circumstances were though, of course, they did not know its precise cause, i.e. that a drop in long-term temperature, however minute, greatly affected their economic basis because the amount of pasture available for their herds was then reduced. As such climatic changes occurred regularly, these peoples were often forced to leave their homelands and move west, south or east in search of more equable climes. With their horses and wheeled vehicles, they were able easily to move their families and herds whenever natural conditions or their own inclinations drove them to do so.

Obviously, belligerence or hunger made the wealthy agricultural civilizations around the eastern Mediterranean and in Mesopotamia the favourite target of these nomads. These societies were not only threatened from the north – the horsemen from the Eurasian plains and the Bedouins from the Syrian and Arabian deserts were equally jealous of their neighbours. Egypt was relatively safe, as the deserts that bordered the Nile were inhospitable to man. However, the 'fertile crescent' – the area of the Euphrates, the Tigris and the coast of the Levant – as well as the river valleys of mainland Greece were frequently the target of successful attacks or outright invasions.

Indeed, in the decades after *c.*2200 BC, such tribes from central Eurasia, while moving into northern India and central Europe, also settled on the mainland

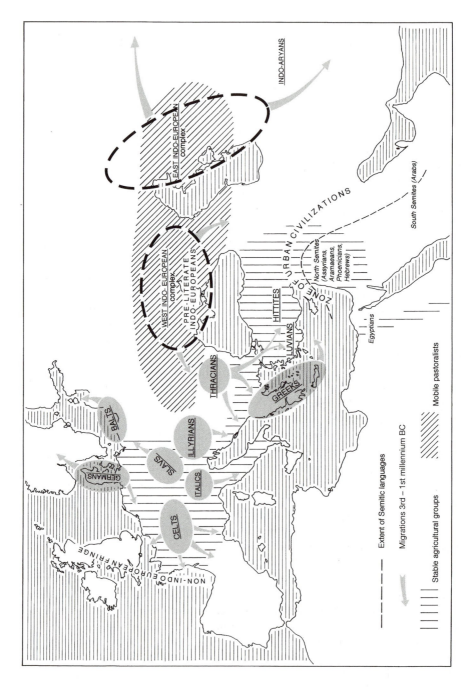

Map 1 Migrations in western Eurasia, third to first millennium BC

around the Aegean, where 'Kurgan'-like structures have been found dating from that time. Perhaps they also introduced the horse there. They spoke an Indo-European language from which Greek later developed. But the invasion by these 'Greeks' is only one manifestation of a process that was occurring continuously on the Eurasian landmass, resulting in intermittent crises in all the neighbouring worlds: there, indigenous societies would be uprooted by migrants turned invaders and conquerors; often, however, they merged with the cultures they encountered.

It is believed, therefore, that in the two centuries after 2200 BC as well as, again, in the period between *c.*1500 and 1100 BC, nomad leaders gained control not only over the Peloponnese but also over the 'Land between the two Rivers'. Many of them founded new states that, from a cultural perspective, always incorporated a mixture of existing 'native' and new 'foreign' elements. Indeed, it was not long before the foreign became native – showing that thinking in such terms can be dangerous.

Hammurápi (1792–1750 BC), the ruler of the city and state of Babylon, in Mesopotamia, descended from such nomads. He founded a vast empire and became famous as one of the first lawmakers of the western part of the world.[20] A diorite stele, or column, more than 2 metres high shows him standing before the sun god Shamash, from whom he accepts the task of writing his 'law code'. In this way he showed that his legal prescriptions were divinely sanctioned.

Plate 3 A deer's head in yellow, red, brown and black, from a cave painting at Niaux, France, dated *c.*20,000–10,000 BC. The artist has captured the animal with its head thrown back, its antlers thrust forward, preparing for attack – a scene which must have been part of prehistoric man's daily life.

Source: Centre for Art Historical Documentation, Nijmegen, the Netherlands

———————◆———————

BABYLON, THE SEVENTEENTH CENTURY BC: THE LAW CODE OF
HAMMURÁPI

The pillar on which Hammurápi's 'law code' is inscribed was discovered by
French archaeologists in Susa, Iran, in 1901–2, and is now in the Louvre
Museum in Paris. Its public function – indeed, one that, despite its differences
from our own system, still appeals to us, as it did to its discoverers – was obviously
to allow anyone who could read or be read to to invoke 'the law', ensuring that
arbitrariness was to a certain extent abolished.

The text, divided into 282 articles, reveals the existence of a complex,
definitely patriarchal society, characterized by a combination of agriculture and
commerce. Intricate regulations establish the rights and duties of the upper class,
the nobility, towards the state, the temple and the rest of the citizens who were
not part of the nobility, mostly farmers and traders. The prescriptions primarily
deal with land development and use but also address the problems of an already
quite advanced trade system, heavily emphasizing the safeguarding of the rights
of property. In a number of cases the punishment for offences committed by
the nobility against commoners is noticeably less severe than for offences
committed by people against others from their own class: equality before the
law had not been realized, but some forms of public safety had, through the
state's monopoly on public violence.

Many of Hammurápi's laws recur in the oldest laws of the Jews that, though
written much later, especially in the Old Testament books of Exodus and
Deuteronomy, show the influence of Mesopotamia on the societies of the
Mediterranean coast.

1   If a seignior accused another seignior and brought a charge of murder
     against him, but has not proved it, his accuser shall be put to death.
2   If a seignior brought a charge of sorcery against another seignior, but has
     not proved it, the one against whom the charge of sorcery was brought,
     on going to the river [the Euphrates, regarded as god], shall throw himself
     into the river, and if the river has then overpowered him, his accuser shall
     take over his estate; if the river has shown that seignior to be innocent and
     he has accordingly come forth safe, the one who brought the charge of
     sorcery against him shall be put to death, while the one who threw himself
     into the river shall take over the estate of his accuser.
6   If a seignior stole the property of church or state, that seignior shall be put
     to death; also the one who received the stolen goods from his hand shall
     be put to death.
15   If a seignior has helped either a male slave of the state or a female slave of
     the state, or a male slave of a private citizen or a female slave of a private
     citizen to escape through the city-gate, he shall be put to death.

38   In no case may a soldier, a commissary, or a feudatory deed any of his field, orchard, or house belonging to his fief to his wife or daughter, and in no case may he assign them for an obligation of his.

39   He may deed to his wife or daughter any of the field, orchard, or house which he purchases and accordingly owns, and he may assign them for an obligation of his.

104   If a merchant lent grain, wool, oil, or any goods at all to a trader to retail, the trader shall write down the value and pay (it) back to the merchant, with the trader obtaining a sealed receipt for the money that he pays to the merchant.

106   If a trader borrowed money from a merchant and has then disputed (the fact) with his merchant, that merchant in the presence of god and witnesses shall prove that the trader borrowed the money and the trader shall pay to the merchant threefold the full amount of money that he borrowed.

142   If a woman so hated her husband that she has declared, 'You may not have me', her record shall be investigated at her city council, and if she was careful and not at fault, even though her husband has been going out and disparaging her greatly, that woman without incurring any blame at all, may take her dowry and return to her father's house.

153   If a seignior's wife has brought about the death of her husband because of another man, they shall impale that woman on stakes.

195   If a son has struck his father, they shall cut off his hand.

196   If a seignior has destroyed the eye of a member of the aristocracy, they shall destroy his eye.

198   If he has destroyed the eye of a commoner or broken the bone of a commoner, he shall pay one mina of silver.

264   If a shepherd, to whom cattle or sheep were given to pasture, being in receipt of his wages in full, to his satisfaction, has then let the cattle decrease, has let the sheep decrease, thus lessening the birthrate, he shall give increase and profit in accordance with the terms of his contract.

268   If a seignior hired an ox to thresh, twenty *qu* of grain shall be its hire.

269   If he hired an ass to thresh, ten *qu* of grain shall be its hire.

282   If a male slave has said to his master, 'You are not my master', his master shall prove him to be his slave and cut off his ear.[21]

Beginnings in Europe: after the last Ice Age

As the climate in Europe started to get warmer again, and the ice cap covering it started melting, the continent assumed much of its present shape. The sea level rose, creating a Baltic Sea considerably larger than the present one, as well as the Zuiderzee – which the Dutch began reclaiming since the early years of our era until they finally converted the last part of it into farmland in the late nineteenth and early twentieth centuries.

With the glaciers receding, north-western Europe also acquired its present contours of high ridges bordering low-lying plains. At the same time, however, the tremendous forces inside the earth continued to work, as they still do, for example in causing northern Scandinavia to rise by 1 metre per century. This can be seen from the fact that many early settlements which, according to archaeological data, were situated on the coast a thousand or more years ago have been unearthed in places now high and dry, inaccessible to any shipping. Meanwhile, south-western and southern Europe continued slowly to sink, as it still does. Over the last millennia, this has caused the flooding of large coastal plains and the continuous battle of man against water all along these coasts. Sometimes, the process has created huge coastal lakes, like the Marismas in southern Spain, or the Pontine Marshes south of Rome, which then became uninhabitable because of malaria. Yet again, in other areas the alluvial deposits brought to the sea by Europe's rivers resulted in coastlines prograding steadily: the ancient port of imperial Rome, Ostia, once on the Tyrrhenian Sea, is now situated some 3 kilometres inland.[22] Obviously, these processes, however slow, did deeply affect man's life for many centuries; indeed, until well into the nineteenth century when some, though certainly not all, of them could be halted or even reversed by technological means.

Of more immediate impact to man was the ecological change brought about by the end of the last Ice Age: all over Europe, the tundra and steppe-like landscape turned into dense forests. This process was completed by about 10,000 BC. Consequently, the animal population decreased, forcing humans to adapt their behaviour to a sharply reduced food supply. This seems to have resulted in a different, generally less sophisticated pattern of economic and social organization, evinced by the decreasing production of symbolic forms. Hunting, the exploitation of aquatic resources and the gathering of plant foods, mostly hazelnuts, became the basis of subsistence.[23]

But by the seventh or sixth millennium BC, a new element slowly began entering this European environment from the Near East, dramatically changing people's lives: agriculture and animal husbandry were adopted in Europe; staples not native to this region, such as wheat and barley, as well as sheep and goats, were now introduced. Farming and cattle breeding were slowly adopted by the inhabitants of the great plains of the central-western part of the continent. The process, a gradual revolution, beginning in the countries bordering the eastern Mediterranean, first affected Greece and the Balkans and then spread, by sea, to the islands of the Mediterranean and to Europe's southern shores. By *c.*5000 BC, possibly via the Danube valley that enters deep into the heartland of Europe, it reached the central regions and began its voyage to the north-west. By this time, both the physical and the cultural landscape of Europe had changed forever.[24]

The limits set on food supply and, consequently, on demographic development, first by a hunter-gatherer and later by a nomadic-pastoralist way of life, were broken. In Europe's new agricultural economy, a new way of life, a new culture evolved as well, based on the security and prosperity provided by agriculture, always in combination with hunting. As in the great river civilizations of the Near East, in Europe, too, agriculture and the surpluses of food and, hence, of wealth that came with it resulted not only in population increase but also in the development of more complex institutions both in the sociopolitical field and in the realm of religion.

Hamlets and villages, mostly palisaded, now covered the temperate woodlands. Houses were built – of stone and clay in the south-east, of timber in central and western Europe. Pottery was introduced, painted in red and white in the Aegean and in the Balkans, decorated in linear patterns in central Europe. People, though still donning leather clothing and grass capes, began to wear jewellery as well, made not only of shells but of the precious, very hard to work, obsidian.

Extensive burial sites have been discovered, with graves that were both formal and individual. Shamanistic rituals, including the smoking of narcotic weeds and human sacrifice, characterized religion. Fired clay figurines, mostly female – perhaps referring to woman's prime role in creation and reproduction – have been found in and near many settlements.[25] Culture in Europe, quite possibly a culture which continued to centre around a mother-goddess, became ever more recognizable.[26]

Thus, from the fifth millennium BC onwards, various developments slowly altered the area designated as Europe by researchers of prehistoric culture, that is, from Ireland to the Danube and the great rivers of Russia. The increasing abundance of archaeological findings allows us to chart better the changes, resulting in an ever more complex picture. Roughly three cultural regions can be distinguished: the north, the middle and the south of Europe.

For a very long time, in the cold, relatively unattractive and sparsely populated north the economic, social and political situation did not change much. The agricultural economy remained the principal means of existence; stone remained the primary raw material for tools and weapons, and the village remained the main form of settlement. Nevertheless, this culture was able to erect, first, huge wooden temples, like the one discovered in 1997 near Stanton Drew, in southwest England, dating from *c.*3000 BC – consisting of nine concentric circles made up of some 500 10-metre high, ornamented wooden poles. Hundreds of years later, this and comparable structures were built over with large stones, to form so-called megalithic monuments, also in circular form, like the great sanctuary at Stonehenge. Other examples of a new creativity are the Danish, Dutch and Breton oblong barrow graves. All in all though, society here was less affected by the great changes occurring in the middle and southern regions of Europe.

By *c.*5000 BC, agriculture had fully developed in the more temperate parts of Europe, with the introduction of the olive and the grape, as well as the woolly sheep and, perhaps a millennium later, the plough. From the south, viticulture eventually reached the frontiers of the temperate zone, in mid-England, the Netherlands, Germany, southern Poland and southern Russia. From a smoking culture, Europe became a drinking culture. Woolly sheep, bred in runs by the women, allowed for the manufacture of textiles; this in turn revolutionized clothing, which soon became a social sign as well. Moreover, the wheel and the horse revolutionized both military and economic life: the chariot and the cart, as well as long-distance overland trade, now became part of European culture.[27]

Quite probably, the chariot was introduced by the peoples who continued to ride in from the great Eurasian steppe. Not surprisingly, temperate Europe's fertile fields held great attraction for these Indo-European migrants. As they did in the Near East and India, these people, trekking westward, also invaded the worlds of Europe's older cultures, changing them, probably, from more matriarchal to more patriarchal societies, while, of course, being changed themselves by the contact – sometimes the conquest – as well.

Increased commerce may have been due to the proximity of these parts of Europe to the more complex economic and cultural centres of the eastern Mediterranean. There, the kingdoms and cities of the Aegean and the Near East developed a growing need for the mineral riches Europe could provide. For the chariot-driving peoples had also brought new techniques to the regions they entered. Around *c.*2500 BC, they had developed bronze casting in southern Russia and the northern Near East. This method required enclosed clay-lined furnaces driven by bellows. However, the basic metals of bronze – copper and tin – were not widely available around the Mediterranean and in Mesopotamia. This must have been one of the prime factors behind the development of long-distance trade within and soon also outside these regions. This trade, in turn, decisively changed the long-static economies and societies of western and central Europe.[28]

Complex trade routes began to connect the mineral resources of the Carpathians, Austria and southern Germany with the Aegean. This brought great wealth, resulting in a changing material culture that has left many traces. The previous existence or the genesis of substantial elites in these regions can now be proven. They 'emerge' from the rich grave-offerings that have been discovered: chieftains and their families were buried with their horses and bronze chariots, with carefully crafted drinking vessels and beautifully tooled and decorated weapons, all of which indicate prestige but also, of course, surplus wealth. Even in more northerly regions, where copper and tin were not available for exchange, skilfully worked bronze was sought; there, amber and fur were used as barter. By 1300–1100 BC, most of south and central Europe had entered in their 'Bronze Age'.

Invasion, conquest and change: the second wave

The second great wave of invasions – others would say migrations – into the eastern Mediterranean occurred during the fifteenth and fourteenth century BC. It was particularly destructive. While scholarly opinion on this period is characterized by many conflicting interpretations, it seems likely that tribes probably coming from or through the Balkans and Italy penetrated into the eastern part of the Mediterranean. Wearing horned helmets and bearing large

Plate 4 Bronze chariot showing a procession of warriors and other people, some of them leading a (sacrificial?) deer, surrounding a figure (of a mother goddess?) carrying a shallow bowl in which offerings could be placed. From a grave from the seventh century BC found at Strettweg, Styria.

Source: Steiermärkisches Landesmuseum, Johanneum, Graz, Austria

round shields and spears, these invaders seized power in many places.[29] Called 'sea raiders' by the Egyptians, they even conquered the pharaonic kingdom, as is shown by the commemorative engravings depicting their attacks that cover the walls of the great temple of Medinet Habu, built by Pharaoh Rameses II a century later.

Though many splendid monuments, like the royal palaces of Knossos, on Crete, were lost during these invasions, all sorts of culture, such as language, writing and religion, were retained by the new societies that now evolved, for the original inhabitants of the Aegean world soon mixed with the newcomers.[30]

In consequence of these changes, new developments took place all over the eastern Mediterranean. From a modern European point of view, the most interesting ones occurred mainly on the margins of the great civilizations of Egypt and Mesopotamia.

A 'marginal' culture? Religion and state formation in Israel

In about 1000 BC, trading cities – some of them merchant republics, others monarchical city-states – dominated the coastal area occupied by present-day Syria, Lebanon and Israel. Culturally, they fulfiled an ancient and important role as intermediaries between the civilizations of the Aegean, Asia Minor, Mesopotamia and Egypt.[31]

This region's interior was mainly inhabited by semi-nomadic tribes. Some of these, the tribes of Israel, had created a religious system veering towards monotheism, with Yahweh as the only invisible God. Although forms of 'henotheism' did exist, in which one particular god was seen as the supreme creator – 'Lord of Heaven and Earth, The Earth did not exist, You have created it', says a text of one of the non-Israelite cultures – 'pure' monotheism as in Israel was an exception in the Near East. Rather, varieties of polytheism were the rule: every tribe usually worshipped several gods, represented in human or animal form.

The history of the Israelites, inextricably bound up with their religion, was recorded by a multitude of authors over hundreds of years, until it came to form the Old Testament part of the *Bible*, from the Greek word for 'book'. Showing the long struggle of some Jewish groups to keep their faith with their chosen God – recent research has shown that other Jews frequently reverted to henotheism or even polytheism – it also shows the slow formation of a Judaic state out of a tribal community where physical survival in semi-arid areas was a constant concern, as affirmed by the Bible's manifold food references: God rewarded those who served him well with plenteousness.

In an early period, war erupted between the interior and coastal societies and, according to tradition, a number of Jewish tribes united under kings anointed by priests in Yahweh's name. A new kingdom thus came into being, which was given a governmental, ceremonial and religious centre when King David took the city of Jerusalem from a neighbouring tribe in about 990 BC. There, the Arc of the Covenant was now placed and Yahweh worshipped in a splendid temple built – or so the story goes – by David's son and successor, Solomon.

However, tensions quickly surfaced. On the one hand, the 'modern' kings, aided by the priestly elite, strove for a kind of theocratic centralization though, at other times, they sought support from gods other than the unseen Yahweh. On the other hand, so-called prophets regularly strove to see the old, holy traditions maintained; acting as self-appointed protectors of the ordinary people, they created their own power base.[32]

When it came to ethics, precisely these prophets pressed the need to live righteously in Yahweh's name. An essential part of this was showing mercy to the less fortunate. The powerful and rich had a duty to protect the poor, since they had virtually no rights shielding them from all sorts of exploitation and oppression. Thus, in the society of ancient Israel, justice was proclaimed to be a religious and moral duty, though certainly not a socially and politically enforceable right.

A 'marginal' culture? Trade and communication in Phoenicia

By several thousand years BC, trading cities had already flourished both along the coast of northern Syria and in Phoenicia, the name later given by the Greeks to, specifically, the narrow strip between the foothills of the Lebanese and Syrian mountains and the sea. The cities originated in the little pockets of arable land beside the streams running down from the mountains. Lack of further agricultural potential turned the people living there to the sea. Soon, they began to trade along the almost natural routes that, from east to west and north to south, crossed this land: for here, the Syrian and Palestinian coast and its flat, relatively fertile hinterland connected to the Mediterranean, and to Anatolia, present-day Iraq – and to the civilizations along the Indus River in north-western India – but also to Egypt. Although the Phoenician region never became politically united, these cities shared similar governmental structures. Moreover, their peoples spoke the same language and often worshipped the same gods.[33]

Prosperity increased in this region when, in somewhat later times, the Phoenicians discovered that many of their trading partners lacked raw materials like copper and tin, essential for manufacturing bronze weapons and tools, and wood. Thus, at an early stage, old cities like Jericho, in the Jordan valley, as well as new ones such as Byblos, Sidon, Tyrus and Ugarit, on the coast of present-day Lebanon and Syria, began to flourish. In 1975, a team of Italian archaeologists searching the plains of north-western Syria discovered the ruins of the once-great town of Ebla. In it, they found the remains of a huge archive containing tens of thousands of clay tablets covered in cuneiform script.[34] Thanks to these, we now know a lot more about the economic, political and cultural aspects of these societies: their customs, their rituals, their food, and the way all aspects of life in this region developed through interaction with and between the other three main areas of civilization now existing in the Near East: Asia Minor including, soon, the Greek world around the Aegean, Mesopotamia and Egypt.

During the turbulent years between 1500 and 1100 BC, many of the great kingdoms and the city-states in the Near East were either weakened or even destroyed by the wave of invaders and migrants. When peace returned, some of the Phoenician cities took the opportunity to expand. They (re-)established contacts with the fertile and wealthy valleys around the Aegean but also with northern Africa – where slaves, ivory and gold were to be had, as well as all kinds of agricultural products – Italy, southern France and eastern Spain, the latter important for its silver deposits. Whenever possible, they even established settlements and colonies in these places, to allow part of their own population to emigrate. Thus, they exported many elements of eastern Mediterranean culture to regions that were not yet as technologically advanced yet.

Somewhere in the middle of the second millennium BC, in the Syrian city of Ugarit, the many hundreds of signs used for writing in Mesopotamia had been reduced to some thirty. In around 1000 BC, the Phoenicians further developed this system, whereby each sign ('letter') came to stand for only one sound, usually the first sound of the object which the sign had originally been associated with: *alef*, from the first sound for 'cow', became the letter or sound 'a', and so on. This revolutionary discovery can, perhaps, be explained by the commercial milieu in which it was made. Whereas in the temple-states of Egypt and Mesopotamia, reading and writing the complicated sign system was deliberately restricted to a small group of highly educated and hence powerful people – though simplified systems did develop there later, for everyday use – such trading societies as Ugarit and the Phoenician cities needed a simple way of writing that would be easy to learn by a large group who could not afford to spend long years at school.

A 'marginal' culture? Democracy and its limitations in Greece

As indicated in the introduction, many Europeans look upon ancient Greece as one of the roots of their civilization. Yet, nowadays, their image of it is largely shaped by film and other forms of popular culture.[35] If anything, these tend to romanticize the world of the Greeks and, also, make it less alien, more like a society that twenty-first century people can 'relate' to. It is, therefore, necessary to understand not only to what extent Greek culture was a precursor of the modern world, but also which aspects of it were indeed very different.

By the twelfth century BC, the Mycenaean and Cretan civilizations had disappeared from Greece. New Indo-European, so-called Dorian, tribes settled there between 1200 and 800 BC. While they did adopt some elements from the civilizations they conquered or merged with, they by and large maintained their own lifestyles.[36] This new society was concentrated around military leaders, local 'rulers' who were, however, more like rustic gentleman farmers than the splendid kings of old who had lived a refined palace culture in great cities. Writing largely disappeared and bards became the bearers and transmitters of a mostly oral culture, singing the praises of their heroic ancestors in epic poems.

Two collections survive: the *Iliad*, which tells of the battle between a number of rulers from the Greek mainland and the king of Troy, a city which is now in north-western Turkey; and the *Odyssey*, which describes the subsequent fate of one of the heroes of the Trojan War, who manages to return home only after a long and perilous journey that takes him across the Mediterranean. While the existence of Troy has been debated among historians for more than a century after its discovery by the German archaeologist Heinrich Schliemann – who, incidentally, set out to do so precisely to refute beliefs that the *Iliad* was romance rather than history – nowadays we do accept that it did exist. Situated in north-western Turkey, in a commercially and militarily strategic place, it was named *Ilios*, or *Wilusa* and it is quite likely that a war was fought over it between the *Achai(w)oi*, the Mycenean Greeks, and the city's inhabitants.[37] Both epics were and still are attributed to the poet Homer, who lived *c.*750 BC. While some scholars doubt his authorship altogether, others maintain that even if he was the writer, he was certainly not the only one. While he evidently composed his part of the text by codifying much older, anonymous, orally transferred traditions, it was in turn added to by later contributors, also anonymous.

From these poems a 'romantic' or rather chivalrous culture emerges, with valorous men who treated women both as objects of desire and as the spoils of war: in the *Iliad*, war breaks out when Helen, a princess, is captured and must be won back – it was a theme that resulted from the Indo-European stock of stories and would become one of the great topics of European literature. It was also an intensely competitive culture, which considered physical prowess to be a sign of power and might. Yet it was a culture which also displayed fascinating elements dating from the period before 1500–1100 BC and the following centuries.

Precisely the oldest elements in these tales have much to teach us about the situation at the end of the previous, second millennium: comparison of Homer's text with the oldest stories from ancient Israel recorded in the first books of the Bible and with the epic poems from Egypt and Mesopotamia shows the fundamental unity shared by the cultures around the eastern Mediterranean, certainly until the invasions and migrations of 1500–1100 BC. They shared such spectacular stories as the tale of the Flood, which is found in the Noah episode of the Biblical book of Genesis and in the much older Babylonian epic of the hero Gilgamesh. It probably had its historical basis in the huge inundations caused by the breaking of the salt barrier between the Aegean and the great lake that became the Black Sea, in the fifth millennium BC. These cultures also shared more profound views on the creation of man and his relations with the divine.

Whereas some scholars think that in Greece this 'oriental' influence had effectively ended with the Dorian invasions, others hold that right down to the eighth century BC the military and economic expansion of the Near Eastern states was such that the eastern Mediterranean remained a cultural continuum – a continuum, however, that during the seventh and sixth centuries BC was slowly taken over by the Greeks.[38]

However that may be, even as Homer was recording stories from the Greeks' distant and not so distant past, the society which he was part of was already changing. The populations of the Greek communities around the Aegean were growing; this necessitated not only agricultural expansion, but also a turn to trade, to provide an additional means of existence. In the process, the gap between rich and poor seems to have widened. Also, farming villages began to cooperate, creating a new structure called the *polis* – hence 'politics' as the all-inclusive word for the management of a community's socio-administrative processes, including its legal and military aspects.

In most Greek *poleis*, the tribal monarchy gradually disappeared, to be replaced by government by nobles from the most powerful families who had also, in the past, been military leaders: those who called themselves the community's best men, the *aristoi*. The rivalry between these families frequently led to chaos; sometimes a single person seized power and ruled as a tyrant; at other times efforts to achieve peace resulted in power sharing between several socio-economic groups.

This is what happened in Athens during the so-called classical age.[39] When, at the beginning of the fifth century BC, Solon introduced reforms trying to establish the rule of law, factional strife was not eradicated. In the year 508 BC, after nearly 100 years of war between successive tyrants and aristocratic cliques, Kleisthenes, a nobleman, decided to broaden his power by incorporating the people, the *demos*, into his support base – hence, 'democracy'. Men from more than one hundred *deme*, or neighbourhoods, which comprised Athens were elected by lot to various administrative bodies, the most important of which was the Council of Five Hundred, or *boule*. However, the People's Council had the last word – each adult male citizen, some 30,000 persons, having the right to vote.

We should be wary of idealizing this situation or comparing it to present-day representative democracy – if only because Athens was, by and large, a society based on a huge number of slaves who had no political rights whatsoever. Moreover, besides being a politically male-only system, attendance at the democratic meetings, which took place almost every week, meant the loss of a day's work, especially for those men who did not come from the city centre. In practice this probably meant the wealthy citizens who lived in the centre were the ones who exercised their democratic rights. In addition, only the rich could be elected to the most senior positions, since they had the time and the education necessary to execute complex daily administrative tasks, as well as the prestige and financial means to ensure public support for their election. To put an end to the resulting corruption, it was decided that state subsidies would be made available to the poor to enable them to attend the People's Council and various jury courts. This improved the situation though it still did not prevent the wealthy from frequently winning votes by a show of power, carefully selected charity and some plain bribery, allowing them to gain the offices and positions from which they could continue to exercise the same power. Also, the kind of communication that ensures well-informed decision-making among voters was mostly lacking. To start with, most Athenians knew how to read only rudimentarily, if at all.[40] Moreover, while people may have discussed politics often, at decisive meetings the political leaders delivering their speeches simply could not be heard by everyone present during these large open-air meetings. Demagogy, or the capacity to somehow influence the *deme* and its voters by winning over, first, a small group – e.g. those sitting in the front rows – and through them collect the votes of the larger community, was widely used by various power seekers.

Since Athenian society knew no equality of property or income, the rich could afford to accept the theory and to a certain extent even some of the practice of political democracy. Thus, the freeborn poor were given legal equality and seem not to have suffered institutionalized tyranny and exploitation; also, they could at least partly benefit from the practice of consultation and control in the exercise of power. Yet it is not without significance that two of classical Greece's most influential political thinkers, Plato (428/27–348/47 BC) and Aristotle (384–322 BC), held rather negative views of the democratic system. Plato, in his *Politeia*, sketches democracy as the regiment of unlimited freedom in which all desires exist together. The ensuing anarchy cannot but result in a subsequent phase of tyranny. According to Aristotle, in his *Politika* – part III, 1278–9 – democracy, far from being the *ariste polis*, the 'best form of government for a city-state', is the rule of the poor. Describing the state and its political-constitutional structure, he presupposed a *polis* of manageable proportions, necessary because in the Greek view democracy was immediate rather than representative. However, he also presupposed a system in which the citizens proper were relatively free from day-to-day toil because immigrant workers, the *metoikoi* – Aristotle himself came from this group – and even outright slaves, perform the heavy manual tasks.

Thus, while Greek thinkers have proposed fascinating theories about the various forms of political organization, we should not uncritically proclaim them the progenitors of western parliamentary democracy.[41] Indeed, both theoretically and practically, their ideas diverged considerably from the ideas and practices that developed in Europe during a far later period. But the discussion their ideas engendered has definitely been fruitful.

Herodotus (*c.*485–425 BC), a merchant and traveller who has often been called the 'father of history' because of his *Historiai*, was born in Helikarnassos in Asia Minor but spent most of his life in Athens. In the third book of his 'Histories', he describes a discussion between three men about the best, or at least the most preferable, form of government. He uses three fictitious high-ranking Persians as his mouthpiece, yet it is clear that he presents a debate that had already been going on in Greece for decades. In its condemnation of monarchical govern-ment, his text was directed both against the Persians, the Greeks' most dreaded enemy, and against those Greeks who showed monarchic tendencies themselves. Yet, Herodotus' analysis is far from being an ode to democracy; rather, it is an outstanding description of the phases that government in many Greek *poleis* actually went through. It summarizes the arguments for and against democracy, oligarchy and monarchy, pointing out, for instance, the ease with which uneducated public opinion can be manipulated, the greed and self-interest of cliques and factions and the tyranny of a king. These arguments continue to be of vital interest in our own age and, as such, have lost none of their relevance:

> The first speaker was Otanes, and his theme was to recommend the establishment in Persia of democratic government. 'I think,' he said, 'that the time has passed for any man among us to have absolute power. Monarchy is neither pleasant nor good. . . . How can one fit monarchy into any sound system of ethics, when it allows a man to do whatever he likes without any responsibility or control? Even the best of men raised to such a position would be bound to change for the worse – he could not possibly see things as he used to do. The typical vices of a monarch are envy and pride; envy, because it is a natural human weakness, and pride because excessive wealth and power lead to the delusion that he is something more than a man. These two vices are the root cause of all wickedness: both lead to acts of savage and unnatural violence. . . .
>
> A king again, is the most inconsistent of men; show him reasonable respect, and he is angry because you do not abase yourself before his majesty; abase yourself,

and he hates you for being a toady. But the worst of all remains to be said – he breaks up the structure of ancient tradition and law, forces women to serve his pleasure, and puts men to death without trial.

Contrast this with the rule of the people: first, it has the finest of all names to describe it – equality under law; and, secondly, the people in power do none of the things that monarchs do. Under a government of the people, a magistrate is appointed by lot and is held responsible for his conduct in office, and all questions are put up for open debate . . . the state and the people are synonymous terms.'

Megabyzus . . . recommended the principle of oligarchy in the following words: 'In so far as Otanes spoke in favour of abolishing monarchy, I agree with him; but he is wrong in asking us to transfer political power to the people. The masses are a feckless lot – nowhere will you find more ignorance or irresponsibility or violence. It would be an intolerable thing to escape the murderous caprice of a king, only to be caught by the equally wanton brutality of the rabble. A king does at least act consciously and deliberately; but the mob does not. Indeed, how should it, when it has never been taught what is right and proper, and has no knowledge of its own about such things? The masses have not a thought in their head; all they can do is rush blindly into politics like a river in flood . . . let us ourselves choose a certain number of the best men in the country, and give them political power . . . it is only natural to suppose that the best men will produce the best policy.'

Darius was the third to speak. 'I support,' he said, 'all Megabyzus said about the masses but I do not agree with what he said of oligarchy. Take the three forms of government we are considering – democracy, oligarchy, and monarchy – and suppose each of them to be the best of its kind; I maintain the third is greatly preferable to the other two. One ruler: it is impossible to improve upon that – provided he is the best. His judgment will be in keeping with his character; his control of the people will be beyond reproach; his measures against enemies and traitors will be kept secret more easily than under other forms of government. In an oligarchy, the fact that a number of men are competing for distinction in the public service cannot but lead to violent personal feuds; each of them wants to get to the top, and to see his own proposals carried; so they quarrel . . . and from that state of affairs the only way out is a return to monarchy – a clear proof that monarchy is best.

Again, in a democracy, malpractices are bound to occur; in this case, however, corrupt dealings in government services lead not to private feuds, but to close personal associations, the men responsible for them putting their heads together and mutually supporting one another. And so it goes on, until somebody or other comes forward as the people's champion and breaks up the cliques which are out for their own interests. This wins him the admiration of the mob, and as a result he soon finds himself entrusted with absolute power, all of which is another proof that the best form of government is monarchy.'[42]

As noted above, although a number of Greek cities had created a democratic government, one should realize that in Athens, the city we know most about, not only the slaves but also half of the freeborn adults, namely all women, were excluded from politics as, indeed, they were from many other aspects of public life.[43] For legally, too, women were considered unfit to speak or even act for themselves, and had to accept male guardianship all through their life, first of a father or a brother, later of a husband or a son. Their first duty was to bear children, preferably many, as only four in ten would survive infancy. While parents were required to educate their sons in preparation of at least a minimal participation in city affairs, they kept their daughters in close confinement at home. Even there, females were restricted to the women's quarters. Of formal, literary education for girls, little evidence survives. Women took care of the household chores, preparing the meals that, with population growth and the conversion of precious soil from pasture into arable land, came to consist more and more of fish than of meat; incidentally, they were not supposed to eat with the male members of the family.

Lower-class women may have gone out to work, although in a slave society most menial jobs were taken already. Middle- and upper-class girls who went out into the streets never did so unaccompanied; they may even have worn a veil. It is doubtful whether women were allowed to visit the theatre, where the plays enacted, articulated and shaped much of the views and attitudes of the Athenians. Still, women did participate in the processions honouring some of the gods. In the so-called mystery cults, presided over by priestesses, they even found a domain partly outside immediate male control.

Yet, all in all, Athens and other Greek cities were largely male-dominated societies.[44] Even Greek vase-painting seems to confirm this. Whenever women are depicted, both the freeborn and the slaves, they are shown serving the men, in the house, in the tavern or in the brothel. Men went out to the gymnasium, participating in the many sports that Greek culture set such store by precisely because they enhanced the virtues of manly valour. Men went out to the regular meetings of the fraternities that took care of funerals, organizing collections to allow the member-families to have a proper feast on the day of the burial. Men went out to dinner, drinking from cups painted with scenes representing sexuality in all possible forms, mostly objectifying the female role.

Outside marriage, free Athenian women were simply unavailable as sexual partners; slaves or foreign-born prostitutes took that role. Also, sexuality was not gender-structured, divided into heterosexuality and homosexuality. Rather, it was conceived as an act between an active and a passive participant, the active one mostly being male, older and of higher status, as opposed to the passive one, who could be either male or female. This resulted in a situation wherein it was quite common for men to practise what is now called homosexuality, a word the ancient Greeks themselves did not use. It was certainly not frowned upon or stigmatized, and practised only in an age-structured form, i.e. a younger man, eager for education in all fields of life, was sexually subservient to an older one. He himself would assume the role of mentor when he too came of age.[45] Some scholars have argued that, at least among the elite, emotional and sexual relationships between adult and slightly younger men prevailed. But while it is true that marriage was more of a social and procreative norm than a sexual and emotive force excluding other attachments, the idea that bisexuality was actually practised widely throughout Greek society may very well reflect present-day wishful thinking in search for past legitimation.

Indeed, there is ample material indicating that male–female sexuality was the norm. Even though marriages were always arranged, and the man, marrying at around age 30, was usually twice as old as the woman, partners often seem to have come to love each other. Yet it is also true that for a man, divorce was very easy indeed, a simple declaration before witnesses being sufficient. Women, on the contrary, could separate for only a few very grave causes and had to go through complex legal procedures.

Thus, the position of women in classical Greece much resembled that in traditional Islamic cultures. The *Iliad* and the *Odyssey* had summarized the female situation: Helen's infidelity created chaos, while Penelope's housebound faithfulness to her husband, presumed dead, restored order. However, the playwright Euripides showed that he was aware of the problems prevailing attitudes provoked among the female part of the population when he gave Medea, the heroine of his eponymous tragedy, the words: 'Of all living, thinking beings, we women are the most unlucky'. Nor was the philosopher Plato unaware of the imbalance. He is supposed to have given thanks to nature, first because he was human rather than animal and, second, because he was a man rather than a woman – continuing the enumeration of his good fortunes by adding how lucky he was to be a Greek rather than a foreigner and, lastly, an Athenian citizen living at the same time as Socrates. In the later decades of the fifth century BC, however, Plato, among others, voiced ideas about female emancipation, but they were not implemented. Only in the third and second centuries BC did women acquire greater freedom, expressed, amongst other things, in and through the education that now became available to elite girls as well as to boys.

However, in dealing with all these questions, we should be aware that the evidence we have is overwhelmingly urban and, indeed, Athenian, as well as upper class. It is hard to judge if the situation was different in other cities and in the countryside. Even the ideas of female beauty may reflect this complex bias: we know that women who could afford to do so liked to wear a thick layer of white facial make-up, obviously to show they were not forced to go out to work for a living or, worse, labour in the fields as farmers and slaves did. Whether the lips, painted a bright red, and the hair, dyed a golden blond, also indicated a subconscious desire to emphasize a racial difference is difficult to say.

Political, social and cultural life in the city was mostly concentrated around a holy place, a shrine – generally located on the highest point of the *polis*, the *akro-polis*, easiest to defend and nearest to heaven – and a meeting place, *agora*, where the adult men from the *polis* gathered for communal affairs. Young men from the elite were educated not only in reading and writing and in the classical tales about gods and heroes, but also in rhetoric, a way of speaking and thinking specifically geared to public action and politics. Precisely this education both reflected and contributed to the further development of a standard Greek language and a specifically Greek cultural pattern.

Both in Greek and in other Mediterranean cultures, the gods were represented as humans, admittedly with more power than ordinary mortals but still with the same urges and desires, virtues and vices.[46] This meant that, from the point of view of ethics, the norms people used to guide themselves in their lives, in society, were determined by social rather than religious or moral considerations. Honour and shame with respect to one's own group were the dominant values, not guilt and atonement resulting from subjection and surrender to a morally superior or even perfect god. Indeed, it seems that in the classical era many Athenians spent a considerable amount of their time fighting those whom they thought to have blemished their honour – in court, however, rather than through blood feuds as in the archaic age.[47]

Yet there was little agreement with regard to the foundations of human actions in norms and values. In the fifth century BC, when the so-called Sophists dominated higher education, they argued that the application of a logical, rational way of thinking which enabled man to discover the rules which seemed to govern the structure of language and nature should also lead him to conclude there were no such things as absolute laws, regardless of whether these were given by the gods; rather, life and human action were based on conventions which men had agreed upon among themselves. A thinker like Socrates (469– 399 BC) opposed such views, maintaining that laws were solidly anchored in absolute moral norms which existed independent of man, time and place. It is an opposition that still fuels discussion about the validity of values in present-day society.

However, most people did relate their everyday experience to a larger order, as Greek thinking about life and society was embodied in a corpus of myths, in stories about the world of the gods and their relationship to the world of man. Myths were collective representations of man's subconscious visions of the world of landscapes, of nature, but also of family structure and the community. Thus, myths came to be sources of great authoritative meaning in Greek society, up to the third and second centuries BC.[48]

Related to norm-describing myths, on the interface between the worlds of the gods and of man was the theatre. Attic drama, in its two forms of tragedy and comedy, developed from the festive celebrations for the fertility god Dionysus. Vying for the honour to be invited to write plays for such an event and thus instruct and please the public who attended it led to creative competition between, for example, the dramatists Sophocles and Euripides. Consequently, they and many others produced inspiring texts that still fascinate a twenty-first century audience. For despite their time-bound context, they often articulate problems modern Europeans also wrestle with.[49]

In tragedy, the relations between man and the gods was the central theme, while comedy developed as a form of political cabaret. Both were staged for the edification and enjoyment of the people but also were used to legitimize political ideas, and ideologically manipulate the electorate.[50]

Political, social and cultural structures comparable, in varying degrees, with those in Athens evolved in many Greek *poleis*. Yet, through its sociopolitical constellation as well as on its great wealth, Athens became one of the most powerful city-states in the fifth and fourth centuries BC. But although they repeatedly tried to do so, the Athenian leaders did not succeed in gaining control over the other Greek cities.[51] Nevertheless, their town became an exemplary centre, attracting talent in diverse fields from all over the Greek world. Relative freedom, an educated people and an economy which had been functioning well for some time led to a vibrant intellectual climate in which many forms of culture developed and were then copied elsewhere in the Greek world.[52] In this way, Athenian Greek culture gained a glory which far exceeded its relative political importance.

Even though the Greek cities had a common identity, not only in their language and in the organization of their polytheistic pantheon but also in the political and philosophical discussions that were central to the cultural life of the elite, the *poleis* jealously guarded their independence, as did the Phoenician city-states. Partly because policies of aggression and expansion within the Greek world itself were either briefly successful, or failed altogether, most cities had to find other ways of solving their internal problems, mostly economic and demographic. Colonization was one such option.

As a result of trade, the Greek and Phoenician cultures had already intersected in the tenth and ninth centuries BC. Perhaps the Phoenicians, expanding their power in the western part of the Mediterranean, were an example for the Greeks: from the seventh century BC, many *poleis* began settlements there, first as trading posts, but soon as colonies, too. Thus, the culture of these Greek cities spread to southern Italy, southern France and eastern Spain.[53] One element deserves specific mention.

In the time of Homer, the Greeks had adopted Phoenician 'alphabetic' writing. Adding to it signs representing the vowels the Phoenician system lacked, they greatly facilitated scripture, making it more compact and less equivocal. Now, in southern Italy, dominated by the Greek colonies, first the Etruscans and later the Romans took over the new system. Thus the 'alpha-bet', this 'Asian' discovery, provided the origins for the system of writing that came to be used first in Europe and then throughout the whole of the western world.

Besides the alphabet, the Greeks have contributed one undisputedly advantageous element to the culture of Europe and, over time, of the west: their way of reasoning, of describing everything that exists and, then, of analysing and interpreting it by means of scientific conceptions. Obviously, the Greeks did not differ from a number of other cultures either in their basic cognitive capacities or in developing a logic to deal rationally with the questions raised by their observations of nature and culture. Indeed, the Chinese, for example, did reason by way of a logic perhaps as systematic and critical as that of, say, Aristotle. Yet, the Greeks showed a special interest in radical questioning and arguing perhaps because of their political experience, of violent debate both within and between the many city-states.[54] The resulting rationality, soon adopted by the Romans and introduced by them into the education of their empire that subsequently became Christian and European, has deeply influenced western thinking over the past 2,000 years. Admittedly, however, it has not resulted in a single concept of science that can satisfactorily describe the many-dimensional nature of reality. Indeed, even some of the Greek 'philosophers' themselves already admitted that there might be more than one way to capture the truth, because each way is likely only to be able to describe part of the truth.

A 'marginal' culture? Tribal society in Celtic Europe

Meanwhile, in the first millennium BC, life in Europe, beyond the regions the Greeks knew about, had changed again precisely because, as in the eastern Mediterranean, new groups moving south and west from their homelands in Russia and central Asia made their influence felt. As always, archaeological finds provide evidence of the ensuing developments.

People continued to live in clans and tribes, dominated by aristocratic families who owed their power to their military leadership and the wealth produced by dependent farmers. Druids and sages, shamanistic medicine men, continued to control the contacts with the 'other' world through magic and various forms of ritual. Lentils were introduced, as well as broad beans and millet, which now became a staple, being strong and growing quickly. But villages made way for hill forts, large walled-in spaces, probably erected to protect against external attack,[55] and burying the dead in graves was replaced by cremation and the preservation of ashes in funerary urns – hence the name 'Urnfield culture' given to this period. The new practice seems to reflect a deeper, spiritual change: rather than stressing the need to preserve the wholeness of the body for the afterlife, the corpse was now allowed to decay because it was valueless. In the visual arts, scenes depicted men – warriors – performing heroic deeds: action and glory are what remains for posterity, while the soul lives on, borne to another world by birds and boats, symbols that start to occur frequently, also in the boat-shaped stone settings for the buried urns.

This culture and society, which came to dominate the greater part of Europe for the next 1,000 years, has been named Celtic, simply because the Greek traveller and writer Herodotus had named the peoples living in these regions *Keltoi*.[56] The Celts or Gauls truly were the builders of a 'Europe before Europe', the bearers – since *c*.1300–1100 BC – of the first civilization which encompassed the whole continent, from Brittany to the Balkans and the Baltic.[57] However, it is a civilization which has left only material remains – enormous stone structures, magnificent gold jewellery and many other objects which are evidence of transcontinental trade.

The centres of Celtic culture were, roughly, eastern France, southern Germany and western Czechoslovakia, with a definite core in the Hallstatt region, near the Salzkammergut, and the La Tène areas near Lake Neuchâtel. There, a number of chiefdoms ruled by military aristocracies controlled rich reserves of copper, silver and tin. They also controlled some of Europe's main waterways – the Seine, Saône and Rhône, the Rhine and the Danube – stretching into the farthest corners of the continent. Their position was greatly strengthened when, once more in the eastern Mediterranean, men took metallurgical techniques one step further, going beyond the making of bronze to the melting of iron, for iron ore was abundantly available in these Celtic lands.[58] This resulted in increasingly intricate trade networks, that soon came to include Spain as well: the great reserves of silver found there allowed the silver coins to be minted which were the motor of the growing economy of the eastern Mediterranean cultures.[59]

Indeed, iron and silver were among the main reasons why, by the ninth century BC, both the Greeks and the Phoenicians decided to settle in the western Mediterranean. The Greeks founded Massalia – Marseilles – which controlled the trade routes to the north, via the Rhône; they also settled in Ampurias, near present-day Barcelona, and traded with the Guadalquivir region, where the so-called 'Tartessos kingdoms' had become wealthy; these, however, were Phoenician foundations, as were the trading posts on Ibiza.

Actually, the whole of Europe now became a series of interlocking systems of trade, connecting Cadiz with the Shetland Islands: we know about this from documents like the Massaliote *periplous*, a sixth-century sailor's manual about trade routes from Spain to Ireland. But the same systems also were linked to the Black Sea and the Danube, as well as to the shores of the Baltic Sea.

The fact that the climate in Europe deteriorated in these centuries may have influenced these changes as well. Northern Europe became far more humid, and huge tracts of arable land slowly turned into peat bogs in the seventh and sixth centuries BC. People had to find new ways to survive. From the sixth century BC, the Celts, driven by overpopulation in an agricultural society that had reached the limits of its productivity, began to expand to the south and south-east, over the Alps to the rich Italian peninsula and through the Balkans to the world of the Greeks and the empires in Asia Minor.

But if anything, these migratory movements strengthened the already complex trade area; cultural exchanges increased as shown, for example, by the magnificent *krater* found in a chieftain's grave in Vix, France: it is a bronze drinking vessel, 1.68 metres high, clearly of Near Eastern, Greek-influenced workmanship. It is only one of many finds that tell us that Mediterranean influences slowly began to pervade Celtic culture, just as Celtic motifs turn up in Greek and, later, Roman art.[60]

Regrettably, we know little about the Celts. For although Celtic myths and legends such as, perhaps, the story of King Arthur and the romance of Tristan and Isolde have come down to us, transmitted orally for centuries and written down only at a far later stage, the Celts themselves did not write. Therefore, one can only speculate about the precise details of their life and culture, which was rediscovered only in the eighteenth century. In the nineteenth century, viewed by Europeans who by that time had begun to look for their earliest roots – and were not always happy to have to do so in the Mediterranean and the 'Asian' Near East – Celtic civilization was increasingly romanticized as the 'dawn of Europe'.[61]

The 'birth of Europe' and the Greek 'world-view', or how to define one's own culture

Actually, one has to return to the early Greeks to see when the name of Europe originated and what those who conceived it meant by it.[62] Europe first and foremost was a geographical term which came into use in Greece from the seventh century BC. The Greeks had but a very limited idea of the earth's situation: they considered the Mediterranean to be, literally, the centre of all lands, or, as the sixth-century prose writer Hekataios of Miletos told in his 'history', the sea that divided the two known worlds: Asia, 'the world of the rising sun' – after an Assyrian word – which at first also included North Africa; and Europe, a name the Greeks had coined themselves.[63] They held certain ideas about their own culture which reflected a mental mechanism found all over the world: most cultures define civilization – normality and identity – by describing certain peripheral areas and their inhabitants as not conforming to their own norms, branding them as foreign and even uncivilized; this enables people to define what is their 'own' and what is 'another's'.

The ancient Greeks felt that Africa, which was given its independent geographical status several centuries later in the writings of the widely travelled Herodotus, was black and uncivilized, with the exception of Egypt, whence came many of the arts prized by the Greeks.[64] Asia they deemed more civilized but politically and militarily unsound; this, in fact, was wishful thinking rather than the truth, reflecting, actually, Greek fear of their most powerful neighbours. Europe, or rather the Greek sphere of influence – the first mention of Europe, in the seventh century, speaks of 'the Peloponnese, Europe and the islands whose shores are lapped by the sea'[65] – was the most civilized and consequently, it was thought, the strongest region. It was strong because civilization was concentrated in free, independent and – at least according to Greek political and cultural propaganda – democratic city-states which between them maintained a balance of power. These states, sharing the same language, Greek, and the same religious and cultural traditions, constituted *Hellas*, not a political structure nor, indeed, a specific geographical entity but a cultural community, a civilization. It celebrated its cohesion in such manifestations as the games held every fourth year near the great temple of Zeus at Olympia, in the Peloponnese, or in the pilgrimages made to the famous Pythia, the oracle at the sanctuary of Delphi, with its processional way climbing a mountain overlooking the Gulf of Corinth and lined with sumptuous monuments and statues presented by cities and private citizens alike. As a cultural community of independent states, the Greek cities differed greatly – though perhaps not as completely as the Greeks would have it – from the 'other' world, from Asia, where there were large political systems encompassing numerous communities and luxury-indulging despots who ruled these vast territorial unities with brutal force.

And yet, the name 'Europe' was coined in a mythical story about the rape of the maiden Europa, a Phoenician princess, who was abducted by the father of the gods, Zeus, and taken to Crete. Did the Greeks thus recognize and even honour their many cultural debts to the Near East, to Asia? Herodotus did not fail to mention that the alphabet had been a Phoenician invention. And, of course, Plato, who may have travelled south to see the other worlds, wrote admiringly about the religious and philosophical ideas of Egypt. Indeed, scholars during recent decades have found increasing evidence of Greek indebtedness to 'Asian' cultures, typically saying that even the Acropolis, considered by many the exemplary manifestation of Greek culture, would not have been built but for Greek knowledge of the great Persian palaces.

On a deeper level, the Greeks felt they could explain how their civilization had been shaped and why it was different. The prime cause was climate, which was so varied in Europe that four seasons followed each other in one year: the annual change of temperature, between cold and warmth, made people flexible and active, both physically and mentally. In Africa and Asia the situation was different: there, temperature was more even, and warmer, too, causing body and spirit to be less flexible and more sluggish; consequently, people in these parts were indolent and inactive, easily led by tyrannical kings and emperors. In short, they were different, foreign. This was expressed in their language, too: they spoke no Greek! They were 'babblers', 'barbarians'. Whether this rather exclusive stance, implying a fairly negative view of most Africans and Asians, also entailed discriminatory practices based on race or skin colour, is a topic still debated by historians.[66]

Obviously, this geographical-cum-climatological approach and the characteristics attributed to various cultures on the basis of it were only a cover for a fascinating but certainly also biased political and cultural argument, one which not least was intended to support continued Greek independence against the constant threat posed to them by their neighbours, especially to the east.[67] It is one of the first examples of the power which a geographical representation, a 'mental' map, can have over man and his ideas.[68] However, despite their intriguing arguments and also despite their conceit, the small Greek city-states in the long run proved to be not strong enough to effectively resist the expansionist politics of adjoining states.

For while the Greek *poleis* acquired their character as independent powers, a number of empires came into existence in Asia Minor which threatened that very independence. In particular, the Medes and the Persians who, in the sixth century BC, had their power base in present-day Iran, expanded their territory at the expense of the Greek cities that ruled the coast of Asia Minor. Their armies even marched to within a short distance of Athens. It is true that Greek coalitions knew how to halt the Persians – in 490 BC at Marathon and in 480/479 at Salamis and Plataiai – but this did not prevent Persian pressure being noticeably felt, especially in Greek Anatolia. Precisely in this context, the linguistic distinction between Greek and non-Greek gradually acquired political content, emphasizing the difference between 'Greek freedom' and 'oriental despotism', as made plain with dramatic power in Aeschylus' famous political play *The Persians*. Thus, the cultural stereotypes developed in the Greek world as a result of the necessity to militarily confront the Persians greatly helped to create a 'national' Greek identity.

Still, in the end even the great alliances between the Greek city-states set up on Athens' initiative were unable to withstand the force of events, the more so because time and time again the *poleis*' mutual jealousy opened the way for foreign influences.

The world of Alexander the Great

In the fourth century BC, a young man ascended the throne of Macedonia, a somewhat rustic principality on the northern periphery of the Greek cultural world. Bringing the city-states under Macedonian control, he finally dealt the deathblow to Greek freedom. Yet at the same time, his actions were instrumental in diffusing Greek culture to an extent until then not realized.

Alexander the Great (356–323 BC) had been raised in the best traditions of 'classical' Athens by his teacher Aristotle. After succeeding to the throne, he followed in his father's expansionist footsteps, conquering not only the whole of 'Greece' proper but also the Greek world of Asia Minor, the trading cities of the Levant, Egypt and large parts of the Persian empire. Much has been made of Alexander's vision. He has even been presented as a proto-global ecumenicalist. However that may be, his dream – of heroic power, basically, and, perhaps, of a post-bellum utopia – came at a price: the carnage, unnecessary probably even considering the mores of his own times, of hundreds of thousands of soldiers and civilians.[69]

Transversing Persia, Alexander reached the Indus River and thus the confines of the great civilizations of south Asia. When Plutarch, some 500 years later, wrote about Alexander's campaigns, he took care to emphasize that Alexander had founded many cities there and, indeed, had brought the essence of civilization to these regions, giving them the Greek language and the values cherished by the Greeks, such as love for one's parents. While thus defining Greece's own culture by juxtaposing it with neighbouring ones, he and other Greek writers could not suppress their admiration for the Zoroastrian culture of Persia, with its vision of the world as a battlefield between good and evil, and man's need to bring justice to all, especially the poor, as well as for the Hindu culture of India, with its accomplishments not only in the fields of religion, philosophy and cosmology, but also in the applied arts and in technology.

Alexander's empire did not last. After his untimely death, his generals divided the spoils. Yet, in the various kingdoms into which the Alexandrian Near East was subsequently split, an intriguing mixture emerged of elements from Greek culture and the pre-existing traditions of those regions. This resulted in a civilization which has been called 'Hellenistic'.[70]

Certainly, Hellenism was a veneer, laid over millions of unassimilated Mediterraneans and Asians who were now confronted with a new kind of kingship, theocratic, totalitarian – an inheritance that would affect Europe by way of the Romans. And yet, thousands of artists, intellectuals and scientists had followed Alexander on his travels to the east, eagerly absorbing new ideas. Through the stability he created, future generations would continue to travel. Thus, from the fourth century BC onwards, the life of the urban elites in the world around the eastern Mediterranean was altered. Many adopted both the Greek language and the Greek literary tradition as well as Greek art; combining these with their own Babylonian, Egyptian, Persian or Syrian heritage they produced a fascinating mosaic; sometimes, the result was a harmonious fusion, at other times one still sees the different parts existing side by side in art, religion, literature and the sciences. The world of the *polis* was past. The time of the 'cosmo-politan', the 'citizen of the world', had come. A new culture emerged.[71]

This culture became most strikingly manifest in one of the many cities founded by and named after Alexander. From its birth in 331 BC, Alexandria, in the Nile delta, became an international port, the most prosperous city in the Mediterranean, in western Eurasia even, where the sea routes from east to west and from south to north linked up with the land routes to and through East Africa, the Arabian peninsula and the rich world of east Asia.

Indeed, Alexandria probably owed much of its cultural standing to its economic function as the gateway through which the Mediterranean, and Europe, could reach the civilizations of Africa and even more of the Orient, of Asia. From the third century BC, trade from the Persian Gulf across the deserts of the Near East, but even more through the Indian Ocean and up the Red Sea, brought the wealth of Asia to Alexandria: not only diamonds and pearls, pepper and sugar, ebony and sandalwood, ivory and silk, but also cotton and wool. From the Mediterranean world came slaves, and sesame seed, flax and wine, copper, lead and tin.[72] But this trade also served as an exchange mechanism for all sorts of ideas perhaps even more than for actual objects, greatly facilitating a diffusion of knowledge and its applications in all fields of culture, in which the question of original invention is hardly ever to be answered, if not actually meaningless. Such high-tech gadgets as milometers, altimeters, earthquake detectors and armillaries, which explained the movements of the planets within our system, that could be found in Alexandria were to be found in India and China as well, showing the varied interests, especially, of the maritime and mercantile communities of the Near East and of Asia.

But in Alexandria, this 'interface' between cultures, in this cosmopolis, where great riches were stored, the phenomena known as libraries and museums first came into existence: cultural institutions that, much later, would become focal points of European civilization as well as centres of tradition and renewal. It was precisely the great 'Museion', museum, library and university at the same time, which became a fulcrum of science and learning. This was the milieu where the Homeric tradition was first researched and where Euclid (*c*.300 BC) wrote his textbook on mathematics, the *Elementai*. It was the place where Eratosthenes (280–200 BC), having put two sticks in the sand and observing the different length of the shadow they cast, decided the earth was not flat and went on to calculate the earth's circumference at 40,000 kilometres – his fault margin later

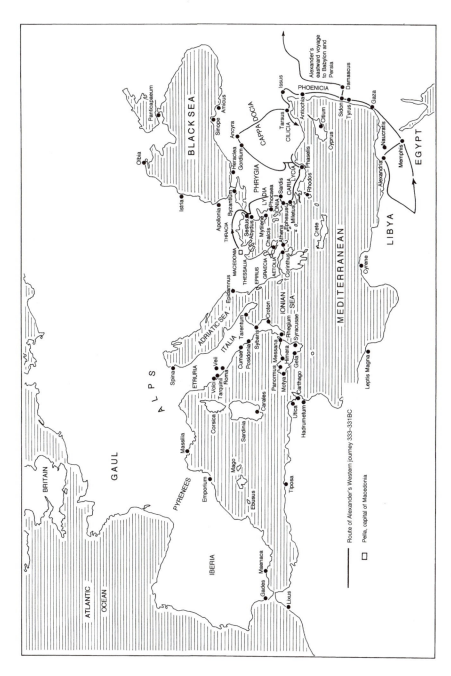

Map 2 Extent of Greek influence in the ancient Mediterranean world, *c.*400–300 BC

proved to be less than 100 kilometres. It was also the place where, later, Ptolemy (*c*.100–*c*.170 AD) developed the geocentric model of the cosmos as well as naming the continents of the earth and their various parts. It was the town where Archimedes, who hailed from Syracuse, on Greek Sicily, studied applied physics and engineering. It was also the town whose school of medicine was famous all over the Hellenistic world. At an earlier time, the Greeks, borrowing perhaps from Indian insights, had evolved a rational system of diagnosis and treatment; consequently such practitioners as Galen, who was a student at Alexandria in the second century AD, could become the first doctor to describe the circulation of the blood.

Politically, this 'Hellenistic world' was soon threatened by the armies of the nascent Roman Empire which, starting in the second century BC, crossed the borders of the Italian peninsula and within two centuries conquered all lands surrounding the Mediterranean Sea.[73]

Yet despite the decline and fall of the independent Greek cities and the rise of hegemonic political structures, the concept of fostering individual spiritual development, of a citizen's (i.e. a free man's) civil rights as opposed to a powerful state, remained a powerful background thought. Admittedly, during the following 2,000 years of European and world history most peoples were not exactly granted much political freedom, at least not until the revolutions of the late eighteenth century AD drastically changed European society. However, the core of a theory about the political rights of citizens – whether or not within the context of the immediate but yet limited form of democracy that had been the practice of many Greek cities – was formulated by a number of Greek philosophers. Several centuries later this fundamental idea would be given additional strength in the legal systems devised by a number of Roman philosophers and jurists and embodied in the 'legal state' of Rome. If only for this reason, the role played by Rome in the history of Europe deserves closer attention.

2 Rome and its empire

The effects and limits of cultural integration

Between the Alps and the Mediterranean, between the Etruscan and the Greek worlds: the expansion of the early Romans

While Edward Gibbon's study *Decline and Fall of the Roman Empire* dominated the European popular image of Rome during the nineteenth century, together with an astonishing amount of novels inspired by it, for most of the first half of the twentieth century dozens of epic movies of the toga-and-sandal variety have helped conflate the history of Rome with the history of its emperors and its gladiators. In the 1970s, the hugely popular television series *I, Claudius*, based on a famous novel by Robert Graves, represented Rome through the intrigues and in-fighting within the family of the Emperor Augustus. In 2000, Rome returned to the cinema with a vengeance, as *Gladiator* became both a huge commercial success and something of a cult film.[1] However, few of these images even begin to convey the complexity of Roman society and culture, while, of course, they not only deserve study for their own sake but are also of major importance to a better understanding of the development of Europe.

In the twenty-second century BC, when the first Greeks settled on the Peloponnese, tribes speaking an Indo-European language and probably coming in from the Near East or central Asia had entered Italy, settling in the centre of the peninsula. They are now called Latins.

More than 1,000 years later there was a new invasion, by a people known as the Etruscans.[2] Their language has been only partly deciphered; therefore, little can be said for certain about their origins. We know them, largely, through the lavish grave gifts with which they buried their dead; these are important cultural phenomena, providing an excellent guide to the study of the development of their society; they indicate the lifestyles of the various sociocultural groups as well as the power of the ruling elite. Their societies developed in the fertile region between present-day Florence and Rome; they organized themselves in independent city-states in which a warrior aristocracy ruled the older, indigenous population. In the eighth and seventh centuries BC, they succeeded in expanding both northwards and southwards. Their power was a result of their wealth, which was based on trade in metalwork and pottery; the quality of their craftsmanship was such that their products were in great demand all over the Mediterranean.

The Etruscan elite, eager for the products of Greek culture in southern Italy, soon adopted alphabetic writing as well; indeed, the oldest known example of Greek writing has been discovered in an Etruscan woman's grave in Osteria dell'Osa. Yet their influence also reached beyond the Alps, penetrating deep into the Celtic world. This was certainly one reason why, in the sixth and fifth centuries BC, Celtic tribes, driven by overpopulation and the hope of riches, entered Italy.[3]

One of the cities the Etruscans had conquered in the seventh century was Rome, a mixed Latin-Samnite community situated in the fertile plain along the banks of the Tiber river, where trade routes linked the sea, and its precious salt, with the interior and the mountains, with their valuable grain and cattle. The legendary 'seven hills' probably served as places where the population of the valley sought protection when they were attacked.

Etruscan kings ruled Rome for more than a century in an often tense partnership with a local aristocracy which was united in an advisory board, the Senate.[4] By the sixth century BC, the Etrusco-Roman community became fully urban, adopting the characteristics of the southern Italian Greek *poleis*. The aristocrats, known as patricians, based their power on property ownership; as 'patrons' they relied on the backing of their 'clients', a group of dependent farmers. The remaining population of free citizens, mostly traders and artisans, were known as plebeians.

In about 500 BC – the official date given is the year 509 – the patricians forcibly expelled their Etruscan overlords. Rome became an oligarchic republic, ruled by two magistrates, or consuls, chosen annually from the ranks of the patricians who, assembled in the Senate, now formed the republic's governing body. Rome was certainly not a democracy of equal citizens. Indeed, the Roman Republic mainly guaranteed the rights – *libertates* – and the property of the aristocracy; their retainers enjoyed only limited rights.[5]

In the following centuries the city of Rome cast a greedy eye over the fertile land of its neighbours. Since the Etruscans were busy trying to ward off continued Celtic attacks from the north, Rome was more or less able to do as it pleased, especially to the south.[6] Increasing numbers of Latin cities were forced to recognize its suzerainty even if they retained some measure of internal self-government, provided the ruling elites cooperated, that is, submitted to Rome's demands. This basically meant supplying troops and other aid for the wars Rome now continuously waged. Rome began to establish colonies in strategic positions in conquered areas, partly to relieve the pressure of a growing population in the city itself.

Thus, in the fifth, fourth and third centuries BC, a process of Romanization began, which imposed both the language and other cultural elements of the 'Urbs', 'The Town', as it proudly called itself, on the entire region, although there was, of course, also interaction with indigenous cultures; in particular, local deities from subjected cities were incorporated in the Roman pantheon.

Contact with, and the gradual subjugation of, Greek colonies in southern Italy had especially far-reaching consequences: soon, the Roman elite came to admire and absorb Greek culture – especially in its artistic and literary forms.

Meanwhile, in Rome itself political and social tension grew with expansion. Not only did wealthy plebeians demand access to power, the whole non-governing population now insisted on written laws to protect them against magisterial arbitrariness. Legal codification was first realized in 451 BC. Moreover, both rich patricians and rich plebeians tended to gradually merge into a single group of *nobiles*, which in 367 BC led to the requirement that one of the consuls must be a plebeian. In 287 BC, the so-called *concilium plebis*, the gathering of all free male Roman citizens, was given legal status.[7] As in Athens, this did not create a democracy in Rome in the present-day sense. By the second century BC, the body of electors already consisted of approximately 250,000 men and therefore could not possibly assemble. In fact, power lay in the hands of the *de facto* administrators, the nobles, who continued their oligarchic government through their experience in and monopolization of bureaucracy, manipulating the electorate with all available means.

The waging of war became a Roman characteristic in the fourth and third centuries. War certainly was a social 'release'. As so often in history, expansionist politics and the 'creation' of foreign enemies were instruments used to avert internal tensions by providing the population with an external challenge. Indeed, many of Rome's wars were not defensive but, under the pretext of preventive action, blatantly aggressive. War was also a way for the Roman elite and sometimes for ordinary men, too, to achieve fame, wealth, status and thus power.

Inevitably, Rome's southward expansion resulted in a conflict with the rich and powerful trading city of Carthage, one of the colonies founded by the Phoenicians on the coast of North Africa, since by now it controlled parts of southern Italy, Sicily and a large part of the western Mediterranean.[8] When the elder Cato (234–149 BC), one of Rome's most influential statesmen, decided to throw a handful of ripe figs at the feet of his fellow senators, he did so to underscore the message he had been proclaiming for some time: 'Carthage must be destroyed', both for its wealth as the centre of North African agriculture and for its commercial and political hold over the western sea. From 264 BC onwards, the two cities had been at war. The prize was supremacy over the Mediterranean, over trade and the riches that consolidation and further expansion would bring. In 202 BC, a decisive, though by no means final battle was fought: the Carthaginian general Hannibal was defeated and the road now lay open for Rome's rule over the western Mediterranean.

This only provided a challenge for further expansion. In the years following 197 BC, Roman legions marched against the Celts in the Po valley and even into southern France and Ibero-Celtic Spain. In the same years they marched on Greece, conquering such independent city-states as remained, and on Asia Minor, where the kingdoms of Alexander's successors had to yield to them. The Greek cities retained a measure of internal autonomy, partly as a result of the esteem in which the Roman elite held Greek culture. In the west where, certainly in the transalpine regions, no strong state-systems existed, the fortified cities on which Celtic tribal connections centred were placed under Roman government, often after bloody battles and sometimes with the deportation of all the inhabitants, as happened during Caesar's wars. As in Greece, the local elites were usually allowed to keep their power, provided they met Rome's military, fiscal and cultural requirements.

The empire now taking shape was partly informal, still based, as it were, on the patron–client relations of early Rome, and partly formal. Its expansion brought about the growing power and wealth of the city that was its centre and its symbol. But the population of Rome was mushrooming at a spectacular rate. On the one hand, this was caused by the increasing number of slaves, the prisoners of war who bred and thus also multiplied slaves.[9] On the other hand, more and more people migrated to the *Urbs* in search of fame and fortune, including many impoverished Italian farmers; they had lost their property to rich Romans who bought more and more land which they then exploited as large-scale slave-worked enterprises. Thus, the majority of the town's population was poor, the more so as the Roman economy remained largely artisanal, not branching out into large-scale industries. This led to new tensions, especially manifest in food supply.[10]

The proletariat that now developed increasingly turned into an instrument in the power politics of the elite. Indeed, some have characterized Roman society as a system wherein the rich used their money to manipulate and discipline the people's freedom, mostly through the organization of elaborate festivals that were supposed to show that the rulers served the ruled, thus serving as symbolic proof of the rulers' right to rule.[11] As it was quite easy to bribe those who, though poor, were free and had the right to vote with promises of 'bread and games', many Roman politicians, who were usually aristocrats, took advantage of this situation. Some were principled in their use of such 'bought' votes, sincerely wanting to bring about political and social change; others only seemed intent on increasing their own power. In 122 BC, it was decided that the state was to subsidize food supplies for the population and in 58 BC free distribution of food was instituted. All this put an enormous financial burden upon the state, which prompted more wars to increase the number of people who could be forced to make financial contributions to the empire, to Rome and to a system that became ever more cruel and exploitative.

However, by now, Roman society itself became dangerously divided.[12] From 91 BC, civil wars raged almost uninterruptedly, coming to an end only when the aristocratic general Gaius Julius Caesar took power. He had first risen to political eminence by flaunting his class traditions, courting the common people by going about the streets, giving them magnificent mock battles in the amphitheatre and expending largesse on a grand scale. Charming and, perhaps, even sexually seducing both men and their wives, acting like a truly populist politician, he strengthened his power base before taking on the governorship of Rome's northernmost province, Gaul. Operating from there, he rebuilt his wealth and, being both a brilliant albeit ruthless general and a very clever propagandist, acquired fame as a successful commander. Finally, he decided to return to Rome. Marching on the city with his troops – a mortal sin in Roman eyes – he soon showed he was not going to content himself with another temporal office, to be shared with another ambitious leader. Having appointed himself dictator, however, he was murdered in 44 BC by a group of aristocrats who, as was to be expected, wanted to regain their class's previous position.

Chaos ruled until power was seized by Gaius Octavius, who had the support of the army, which honoured him as Caesar's cousin and adoptive son, and of a sizeable proportion of the old aristocracy, who were not only willing to trade their former independence for law and order but also hoped to retain some of their power under an aristocratic leader.[13] By a deft manipulation of the various factions in Rome and in the empire, Octavius finally succeeded in rallying the support of the whole realm. Avoiding the trap so many of his predecessors had fallen into, he liked to uphold the fiction that he ruled as *princeps*, the first of citizens, instead of as the imperial autocrat he obviously was. Another of the images he liked to project of himself was that of 'Father of the Fatherland'. Yet, in 27 BC, he let himself be 'forced' by the Senate to accept the title of *Augustus*, the 'Exalted One'. His successors are simply known as the Roman emperors.

From an informal to a formal empire

In the first and second centuries AD, the Roman Empire reached its final, enormous extension, spreading its influence over large parts of Europe, the Near East and North Africa, and continuously proving its great strength. Simultaneously, however, and indeed partly as a result of this expansion, the empire's weaknesses slowly began to appear.[14]

Admittedly, in the north-west, England was successfully invaded. The wall built in the border region with present-day Scotland by the Emperor Hadrian came to form a frontier to ward off the 'uncouth' and warring Picts. Prosperous cities with temples and public baths, such as *Verulamium* (St Albans) and *Aquae Sulis* (Bath), arose south of this border. The countryside was covered by army camps and fortified *villae*, manor houses that were also centres of a, by now, Romanized Celtic culture.[15]

However, the wars that intended to extend the empire eastwards to the Elbe river were unsuccessful. After many bloody battles with the tribes living in central Europe, Rome finally accepted the Rhine as the *limes*, the frontier of its empire in the north and east. Depending, of course, upon the length of the communication lines with Rome, the areas within its borders underwent intensive Romanization, especially in regions around the imperial administrative centres, the cities that sprang up along the line, often around the forts where the Roman legions were garrisoned.[16]

Thus, in Roman Gaul as well as in present-day Belgium and the Netherlands, a provincial but nonetheless often splendid variant of Rome's culture became manifest, of which the material remains can still be found today, for the outer regions of the empire tried in everything to emulate the glorious centre, Rome.

Temples were built where the supranatural was honoured – both the Roman gods and the older, local ones, Romanized but still recognizable to the indigenous people. Aqueducts were constructed, bringing water to the inhabitants, baths were built where they used to relax, amphitheatres were erected where games were organized, as well as, in the larger centres, theatres where plays were staged. And the people, not only locals but often Roman colonists or retired legionnaires and their offspring lived there, in dwellings small and great; the more luxurious, many-roomed ones were adorned with mosaics and frescos, as in the cities of Italy itself.

To the north-east of the *limes*, the Dacians and Thracians, unruly tribes inhabiting the Balkans as far as the Danube, were slowly incorporated into the empire and also underwent Romanization, expressed in, among other things, their language and material culture.

Sending their legions further eastwards, the Romans had also reached the Euphrates and the Tigris. There, however, they were halted by the Parthians, who ruled over an enormous empire in present-day Iraq and Iran, but of whom we know relatively little as yet. Though the Emperor Trajan once reached the Persian Gulf, reminiscing about his great predecessor, Alexander, and the eastward journeys he had undertaken, the Parthians did not allow the Romans to use this route to the riches of Asia.

By and large it was Egypt, and more specifically Alexandria, that, via the Arabian peninsula and the Red Sea, played the most important role in the empire's communication with the Orient. The Romans thought a great deal about Asia, writing not only about its geographical but also its philosophical characteristics and fantasizing about its fabulous wealth. Indeed, so great was the demand for Asian products in the Roman world that according to the writer Pliny the Younger, authorities started to worry about the serious silver drain from the Mediterranean to the world of 'India'.[17] Undoubtedly, the ships that carried gems and gold, silk and spices also carried ideas and beliefs, which were then incorporated into the syncretic religions and philosophies of the Graeco-Roman world of the eastern Mediterranean.

In the southern provinces of the empire, on the Mediterranean coast of grain-rich Africa, splendid cities were built, with magnificent colonnaded market squares, temples and amphitheatres. Yet here the deserts and the semi-nomadic Bedouins who lived there created a real boundary beyond which the Romans could not expand: apparently these opponents, knowing the harsh terrain as no others did, were too formidable.[18] Still, this does not mean that the indigenous peoples living there, trading across the sand sea, did not form another interface of culture, through which notions of the world of Africa beyond the Sahara crept into the Roman-Mediterranean world as well.

How did this empire hold together? Obviously, an intricate legal-administrative apparatus was needed; yet, however efficient, this by itself would not have been sufficient to rule effectively such an enormous region. Infrastructurally, the famous 'Roman roads', with the bridges that allowed them to traverse low-lying valleys or unfordable rivers, were of prime importance, and great energy as well as huge sums were spent on them, so much so that after 2,000 years many European roads still follow their course. Constructed by the legions as they advanced further and further from the central milestone that marked the empire's heart in Rome, they allowed the armies to move swiftly from one part of the empire to another, from one camp to another.[19] Both the roads as well as the camps, which often became the nuclei of larger, civilian settlements, provided a network with nodal points that gave cohesion and security; they also helped to spread all kinds of technical skills and even literacy to the frontier regions of the empire. But for all its military might and efficiency, the empire would not have survived for several centuries if its institutional structure had not been strong.

Beginning with the rule of Augustus, the capstone of the system was the emperor, the lawgiver, the master of life and death.[20] No wonder, then, that his person gradually acquired superhuman traits. The emperors used these as propaganda to further increase the legitimacy of their power. The tradition of divine rulers, which had existed for a long time in such kingdoms of the eastern Mediterranean as Egypt and Persia, and had been adopted by Alexander partly to facilitate his own rule in these regions, was broadened into an 'emperor cult' enforced throughout the empire.[21] The artistic elite at court glorified the emperor with all the means at their disposal, and his images were worshipped in temples. Certainly, in the eyes of the masses the emperor became a sacrosanct figure.

But while everyone had to honour and obey the emperor, it was, perhaps, far more important that everyone also had to respect the basic principles of the empire as codified in its legal system. This ensured that all free persons were treated equally under uniform laws, whether they lived in *Londinium* (London) on the Thames, in *Augusta Treverorum* (Trier) on the Rhine, in *Carnuntum*, near Vienna, on the Danube, or in *Doura Europos* on the Euphrates, in *Hadrumetum* (Hammamet) on the Tunisian coast, or in *Tingis* (present-day Tangier) commanding the Maghrebine coast opposite the rock of Gibraltar – that, of course, did not yet bear its eighth-century name, but was known as one of the Pillars of Hercules.

From the first century AD onwards, the empire underwent important changes.[22] Augustus and his successors increasingly controlled the entire system of government. Financially they were able to do so because of the gigantic domains granted to them by the Senate and the estates they inherited from wealthy citizens who wanted to court their favour; also, people were frequently compelled, with varying degrees of force, to bequeath their property to the emperor. Moreover, the emperors gained direct control over a large number of precisely those provinces which were the most prosperous in the empire: Gaul, with its trade, Spain, with its mineral deposits, Syria, where the wealth of Asia was brought to Europe, and grain-rich Egypt. This position enabled them to employ the financial resources of government to consolidate and increase their own power, as well as manipulate the food supply, thus placating the people of Rome. The army, certainly in a formal sense, was also under the emperor's

Plate 5 A Roman teacher, with the beard of manhood and authority, and his class, reading their parchment scrolls; as schools for the general public were usually crowded, and pupils would use only wax tablets, this probably represents a private and privileged class. To embark on a career in such an intensely 'legal' society as that of the Roman Empire, it was necessary to study the three Rs. From a funerary monument found at Neumagen, Germany, dated *c.*AD 190.

Source: Landesmuseum, Trier, Germany

Plate 6 The wife of the great Roman 'law-giver', Justinian: Empress Theodora, with her ladies-in-waiting, from the sixth-century mosaics in the church of San Vitale, Ravenna, Italy.

Source: P.J.A.N. Rietbergen

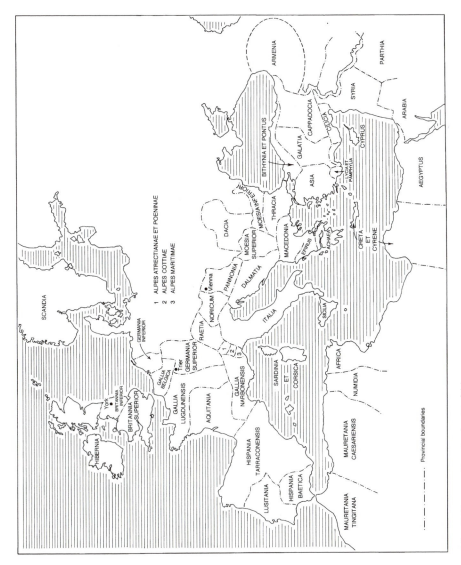

Map 3 Roman Empire in AD 211

SCANDIA

HIBERNIA

BRITANNIA
INFERIOR
York
BRITANNIA
SUPERIOR

GERMANIA
INFERIOR

GALLIA
BELGICA
Trier
GERMANIA
SUPERIOR
RAETIA

GALLIA
LUGDUNENSIS

AQUITANIA

NORICUM · Vienna

PANNONIA

1 ALPES ATRECTIANAE ET POENINAE
2 ALPES COTTIAE
3 ALPES MARITIMAE

2
3

GALLIA
NARBONENSIS

ITALIA

DALMATIA

MOESIA
SUPERIOR

DACIA

MOESIA INFERIOR

THRACIA

BITHYNIA ET PONTUS

ARMENIA

GALATIA

CAPPADOCIA

ASIA

CILICIA

SYRIA

PARTHIA

ARABIA

LYCIA ET
PAMPHYLIA

CYPRUS

MACEDONIA

EPIRUS

ACHAEA

SICILIA

SARDINIA
ET
CORSICA

HISPANIA
TARRACONENSIS

LUSITANIA

HISPANIA
BAETICA

AFRICA

NUMIDIA

CRETA
ET
CYRENE

AEGYPTUS

MAURETANIA
TINGITANA

MAURETANIA
CAESARIENSIS

-·-·-·- Provincial boundaries

control. To win the support of the soldiers, who were an important but unreliable power source, the emperors provided them with pensions and promises of farms after they retired from the army – Spain was Romanized not least because of the many veterans who settled there, managing agricultural estates and breeding the horses which the army needed.[23]

As the empire grew, so did its bureaucracy. Many of the new offices were held by the emperor's own candidates, directly appointed by him. The Senate and the consuls gradually had to yield most of their power. Meanwhile, the legal system, which principally aimed at guaranteeing the individual's rights, specifically the material ones, was extended. This provided the foundation for a juridical-institutional pyramid with the emperor at its peak: in the administration of justice, he was the final court of appeal. Surely, it was this very system, and the rules that it helped to uphold, that must be considered one of the central elements in the longevity of the Roman Empire.

ROME, THE SECOND CENTURY AD: A LEGAL SYSTEM, A LEGAL
SOCIETY – THE ROMAN CONTRIBUTION

In the course of several centuries, Roman jurists – legal scholars and lawyers – elaborated a system which, as the following extracts clearly show, in many ways still provides the basis of the law in large parts of Europe and, indeed, in consequence of European imperialism from the sixteenth century onwards, in considerable parts of the non-European world. This process began and developed in parallel with the expansion of the Roman Empire, when more and more subjected nations and states adopted the basic principles of Roman law, which had originally been the law of the city of Rome.

These principles were expounded in the second century AD, in Gaius's *Institutiones*, a fundamental legal text in which one can recognize such basic notions as, for example, that the spirit of the law prevails over its letter, as well as the increasing emphasis on the claims of equity and the principle of the benefit of the doubt. Gaius's reference to the law of nations, which, according to him, has universal application, is equally important; it reflects and embodies an acceptance of the human condition in that it presupposes war and the organization of states, as well as the right to property and the necessity of legal commerce. As Roman law was considered to be in conformity with this 'natural' law, it could and did claim to be universal as well.

> Every people that is governed by statutes and customs observes partly its own peculiar law and partly the common law of all mankind. That law which a people establishes for itself is peculiar to it, and is called civil law [*ius civile*] . . . while the law which natural reason establishes throughout all mankind is followed by all peoples alike and is called the law of nations [*ius gentium*], as being the law observed by all peoples [*gentes*]. Thus the Roman people observe partly their own peculiar law and partly the common law of mankind. . . .

The laws of the Roman people consist of statutes, plebiscites, decrees of the Senate, imperial constitutions, edicts of those possessing the right to issue them, and responses of the learned. . . . An imperial constitution is what the emperor by decree, edict, or letter ordains; it has never been doubted that this has the force of statute, seeing that the emperor himself receives his *imperium* through a statute.

The right of issuing edicts is possessed by the magistrates of the Roman people. . . . The responses of the learned are the decisions and opinions of those who are authorized to lay down the law. If the decisions of all them agree, what they so hold has the force of statute, but if they disagree the judge is at liberty to follow whichever decision he pleases. . . .

The principal distinction in the law of persons is that all men are either free or slaves. Next, free men are either freeborn or freedmen. Freeborn are those born free, freedmen those manumitted from lawful slavery.[24]

This last point is explained in more detail in the most famous codification of Roman law, the *Corpus iuris civilis*, which consists of a textbook (Gaius's *Institutiones* mentioned earlier), a series of imperial decrees, the so-called *Codex*, and the *Digesta*, a collection of notions mainly about private law. These were all brought together in AD 533, during the reign and on the explicit order of Emperor Justinian. In the *Digests* it is posed that:

Manumissions are also comprised in the law of nations. Manumission is the dismissal from hand, that is, the giving of freedom. For as long as anyone is in a state of slavery, he is subject to hand and control; when manumitted, he is freed from control. This has its origin in the law of nations, seeing that by natural law all were born free and manumission was not known since slavery was unknown; but after slavery made its appearance . . ., the benefaction of manumission followed. . . .

Under this same law of nations, wars were begun, peoples distinguished, kingdoms founded, ownerships marked off, boundary stones placed for fields, buildings erected, commercial relations, sale, hire, and obligations instituted.

Among the general tenets formulated in the *Digests* we read:

That which is faulty in the beginning cannot become valid with the passage of time.

. . . No one who has the power to condemn lacks the power to acquit.

. . . Anything not permitted to the defendant ought not to be allowed to the plaintiff.

. . . In cases of doubt, the more liberal interpretation should always be preferred.

. . . In all matters certainly, but especially in the case of law, equity should be given due regard.

. . . It is right under natural law that no one should increase his wealth through harm or injury to another.

. . . No one suffers a penalty for what he thinks.

. . . Every individual is subjected to treatment in accordance with his own action and no one is made the inheritor of the guilt of another.[25]

In such an intensely legal culture, the position of free women, too, seems to have been rather more closely safeguarded and, from a modern point of view, rather more humane than in Greece. Although Roman society was deeply patriarchic, with the *pater familias* having extensive authority over all members of his household, marriage contracts gave women the right to retain their own property and, indeed, the management of it.[26] They presided over the household, as symbolized also in their presence at dinner. Nor was a Roman woman as confined to her own domain as her Athenian counterpart. Moreover, women were held in far greater public respect than in Greece, occasionally even participating in literary and political life.

Yet there seems to have been a growing aversion to marriage, at least in Rome itself, as early as the second century BC. As this caused the birthrate to fall, government measures had to be taken – Augustus's rule that a woman was to be free of male guardianship after she had borne three children must be also interpreted with this objective in mind. One famous censor, Cecilius Metellus, is reported to have delivered a speech in which he said: 'If we could get on without a wife, Romans, we would all avoid the annoyance, but since nature has ordained that we can neither live very comfortably with them nor at all without them, we must take thought for our lasting well-being rather than for the pleasure of the moment'.[27]

Whether he was being ironic or referred to homosexuality as the preferred alternative is a matter for debate. Yet, as in Greece, and for the same reasons, the practice was widespread and not morally condemned either. The famous eighteenth-century historian of the Roman Empire, Edward Gibbon, rather scandalized, had to admit that all but one of the first 14 emperors of Rome were either bisexual or exclusively homosexual.

Despite their greater legal freedom, most females led a restricted existence. Normally marrying at around the age of 12, Roman girls were first and foremost supposed to bear children and educate them to become proper Roman citizens. Tacitus admonished them to breast-feed their offspring themselves, as the Germanic women did, rather than follow the old custom of employing a wet-nurse. Sex outside the marriage, while considered normal and even status-enhancing for men, was deemed totally unacceptable for women, the more so as their sexual appetite was seen as insatiable, as noted by the poet Horace in one of his odes; he, of course, was only following Aristotle, who had argued as much in his 'History of Animals'.[28] Reading the many literary descriptions of women engaging in sexual adventures with as much gusto as men, therefore, should not blind us to the fact that Roman poets and prose writers portrayed only the lifestyle of the elite.

As in Greece, Roman women sought refuge in religion, especially in the many mystery cults that centred round female deities. Particularly popular, all over the empire, was the cult of the ancient Egyptian goddess Isis, supposedly able to give women the same power as men. The poet Juvenal, writing at the beginning of the second century AD, felt forced to comment in some very satirical, even bitter verses upon this phenomenon, which may indicate the still essentially patriarchal character of Roman society.

Children, often born to mothers we would consider children themselves, were not treated like small adults, although male children especially were encouraged to live up to the virtues society expected from them. Indeed, contrary to former belief, Roman families did not sigh under the yoke of harsh paternal authority. Perhaps the image of Augustus as 'Father of the Fatherland', and his consistent use of the imperial family as the model for all families and, indeed, for the empire as a whole, did contribute to this situation.[29]

Roman culture

From the second century BC onwards, the Greek–Hellenistic civilization that had come to dominate most of the eastern Mediterranean during the later years of Alexander's conquests now became embedded in a new world: the expanding Roman Empire. The Mediterranean empire of the Romans spanned three continents, many different peoples and even more religions. It was relatively tolerant. Whether, as is often argued, this confluence of cultures was free from racist attitudes or, on the other hand, the inevitable cultural and ethnic distinctions did produce some sort of racism, is highly debated.[30] Certainly, status and power were mainly determined by wealth and the prestige a person acquired by adapting to the culture of the elite via the *paideia* (see below). Indeed, perhaps one of the most important factors contributing to the cohesion of the Roman Empire and its culture was that, regardless of all differences in race, language and religion, the steep way to the top, to a career in the centres of provincial power, or even in the imperial capital, was, in principle, open to all free people living within the *limes*, if they had the ambition to embark on such a road.

The condition, of course, was that one was a Roman citizen. Admittedly, citizenship and the rights that went with it were not given to everybody, but during the first and second centuries AD, it was gradually granted to one town after another until, in the second decade of the third century, all free inhabitants of the empire were made citizens – if only to secure their fiscal contribution to the state.

If one was a Roman citizen, one could become a member of the elite, maybe not within one but certainly within two generations, provided one had absorbed the *paideia* ideal which had been the basis of Greek cultural and especially moral-philosophical texts and had been adopted by the Roman upper class. It actually meant that one had learned to read, write and, in particular, speak Latin well, within the rhetorical tradition that had developed under Greek influence.[31]

In his *Institutio Oratoria*, 'The Elements of Oratory', the Roman writer Quintilian (*c.*AD 35–96) clearly outlined the elements deemed essential to the education of a proper citizen of the Roman Empire. From a pedagogical perspective, his views are still surprisingly modern.

> Above all, make sure that the infant's nurse speaks correctly. . . . Of course, she should without doubt be chosen on the basis of good moral character, but still make sure that she speaks correctly as well. The child will hear his nurse first, and will

learn to speak by imitating her words. And by nature we remember best those things which we learned when our minds were youngest.

[I, 1, 4–5]

I am not so foolishly unaware of a child's stages of development as to think that young children should be harshly forced to begin with the three Rs or should have real work pressed upon them. Above all else we must take care that a child who is not yet old enough to love learning should not come to hate it and dread, even when he is older, an experience which was once bitter. Let his lessons be fun, let him volunteer answers, let him be praised, and let him learn the pleasure of doing well. If, on occasion, he refuses instruction, bring in someone to serve as a rival, someone with whom he can compete; but let him think that he is doing well more often than not. Encourage him with the rewards or prizes in which his age group delights.

[I,1, 20]

As soon as a boy has learned to read and write, it is time for him to study with a *grammaticus*. I won't distinguish between Greek and Latin teachers, although I would prefer that priority be given to a Greek teacher. But both offer the same curriculum. And this curriculum can be divided very briefly into two main subjects: the art of speaking correctly and the interpretation of poetry. However, the curriculum offers much more in the details of the programme than is at first apparent on the surface. For example, the art of speaking and the art of writing are connected. And flawless reading precedes interpretation. And critical judgment is required in all the cases. . . .

It is not sufficient to have read only poetry. Every kind of writer must be thoroughly investigated, and not simply for his topic or theme, but for his vocabulary, because words often acquire authority according to the writer using them. And your studies with the *grammaticus* cannot be complete without the study of music because this education should include a discussion of meter and rhythm. You cannot understand the poets if you know nothing about astronomy since the poets so often use the rise and setting of the constellations (to give one example) in indicating time. Nor should this level of education overlook the study of philosophy, not only because many passages in almost every poem require our understanding of an intricate or minute detail of natural science but also because some poets, such as Empedocles among the Greeks, and Varro and Lucretius among the Romans, actually wrote down doctrines of philosophy in verse.

[I, 4, 1–5][32]

All the texts Quintilian referred to were available to those who could afford them; until the first century AD, everything was written on rolls, *volumina*, of papyrus, and then in books, *codices*, consisting of sheets of parchment folded a number of times into pages.

Not surprisingly, to succeed in Rome, a good knowledge of Greek itself was to be recommended. Often extremely phil-Hellenist, the majority of the Roman elite frequently looked up to Greek philosophy, literature and the visual arts. Roman youths from the better families, the future leaders of this upstart empire, completed their education with a tour of the Hellenic cultural centres, and filled their villas and city palaces with Greek 'classical' art treasures or, more often, copies of them. Those who considered themselves the real heirs to classical Greece, the inhabitants of Athens and of other Greek cities, also in Asia Minor, often looked down on 'barbaric' Rome. 'The Town' itself was deeply offended by this contempt – after all, had not the *Pax Romana* saved Greek civilization from destruction by Asian barbarism?

Despite often slavishly following Greek examples, so much so that, for example, in sculpture Roman copies could hardly be distinguished from Greek originals – indeed, we know what Greek sculpture looked like mainly through the numerous copies made for a Roman clientele – the Romans did create a culture of their own. Cicero, the famous orator, spoke and wrote in such a way that he became the norm for Roman rhetoric, for a way of speaking and, thus, thinking that every civilized person was supposed to practise. In poetry, Horace's lyric odes became classics. Meanwhile, Virgil continued the story of Homer's *Odyssey* with his impressive epic about the tribulations of Aeneas, son of the royal house of Troy who, after his escape from the ruins of his city, was supposed to have fled westward and begot the first Romans: thus, Rome symbolically made itself the heir to the culture of the eastern Mediterranean, but also claimed to have created a new civilization.

Instead of indulging in such mythmaking but propagandistically effective poetry, Tacitus set new standards of prose writing and of a rigorous, 'objective' analysis of history, in his often blood-curdling tales about the vicissitudes of the empire under the rule of the first imperial family.

A certain ease in citing all these classical, normative texts would help an ambitious man to hold his own amongst his rivals and to prove himself as a 'cultured' person. Yet money was certainly helpful too, if only because it provided ambitious and well-to-do parents from the 'province', who had not been reared in the Roman tradition themselves, with the means to give their children the education and, thus, the opportunities which they themselves had not had.

Thus, the Roman Empire, with its advanced communications network, its *lingua franca* and its relatively open cultural ideal, created an educated elite who, though numerically limited, may still have been the single largest such group in the world before the global changes of the late nineteenth and twentieth centuries. It is doubtful whether, without these foundations and this group, the Europe we know today would have come into existence.

The Roman Empire and the worlds beyond

As a result of its expansionist policy, Rome soon ruled a large part of the area already known as Europe. Its knowledge of the wider Europe steadily increased as its legions continued to conquer new regions, extending the empire towards the north and east.

By the second century AD, the imperial frontier, the *limes*, had reached its furthest extension. Yet, even the peoples living beyond it, for example, the so-called Germanic tribes, were known to the Romans and influenced by them.[33]

Only the north of Scotland, parts of Scandinavia and northern Russia were still uncharted on the Roman 'maps'. Actually, the Romans did not have maps, nor did they have any accurate notion of the real extent of their territories, beyond the concept that the empire was made up of all those places that had, or as with India, for example, were believed to have acknowledged the authority of the emperor. To Rome, the world was an extension of linear itineraries, stretching out from the capital, the Urbs, the centre of the world. Any pictorial representations of the world that existed were distorted, giving the viewer an idealized, Romanocentric view, in which the emperor could sit on the globe.[34]

While the inhabitants of these areas beyond Rome's northern and eastern borders, usually semi-nomads living in tribes, remained largely unknown, they posed a constant threat to the empire, which attracted them because of its fabulous wealth. As they frequently gave in to that lure and tried to cross the *limes*, with violence if necessary, they were seen as enemies and stigmatized by the Romans as foreign, as a 'babbling', 'barbaric', uncivilized rabble just as the Greeks had described the Romans in earlier times.[35]

Satyrs and titans – these were the terms of abuse, mingled with admiration, used by the Romans to describe the Celts or Gauls when they first came to know them. The Roman writer Ammianus Marcellinus (*c.*AD 330–95) describes their appearance and behaviour as follows: 'Almost all of the Gauls are of tall stature, fair and ruddy, terrible for the fierceness of their eyes, fond of quarrelling and of overbearing insolence'.[36] The geographer Strabo (*c.*64 BC–AD 19) had already told his readers that: 'On whatever pretext you stir them up, you will have them ready to face danger, even if they have nothing on their side but their own strength and courage'. He adds:

> To the frankness and high-spiritedness of their temperament must be added the traits of childish boastfulness and love of decoration. They wear ornaments of gold, torques on their necks and bracelets on their arms and wrists, while people of high rank wear dyed garments besprinkled with gold. It is this variety that makes them unbearable in victory and so completely downcast in defeat.

Another writer added some information about their customs:

> When several dine together, they sit in a circle; but the mightiest among them, distinguished above the others for skill in war or family connections, or wealth, sits in the middle like a chorus-leader. Beside him is the host and next on either side the others according to their respective ranks. Men-at-arms, carrying oblong shields stand close behind them while their bodyguards, seated in a circle directly opposite, share in the feast like their master.

In short, the Celts were considered irritable, ambitious and belligerent characters, as the Romans had discovered at first hand. The famous *De Bello Gallico*, 'On the Gaulic War', in which the Roman general and later autocrat Gaius Julius Caesar had described his campaigns north of the Alps (58–51 BC), concurs with the handful of earlier and later accounts we have of them.

While Celtic civilization flourished in south and central Europe, partly as a result of the interaction with Rome and the Mediterranean world, society and culture in northern Europe remained largely unchanged for a long time. This area, too, was inhabited by Indo-Germanic peoples who had congregated mainly in Scandinavia, present-day Germany and Poland. In about 90 BC, the Greek writer Poseidonios had named them 'Germans', a concept later taken over by the Roman general Caesar. Following Caesar's conquests in present-day France and the various attempts by the first Roman emperors to expand the borders of their empire towards the north and east, Roman contact with the 'Germans' steadily grew. In AD 98, the historian Tacitus even devoted a separate study to them, 'On the origins and region of the Germans'.[37]

As the Germans had not yet begun to write their own history, Tacitus's account is an important supplement to archaeological research. Relying on data procured by Roman officers and other eyewitnesses, he described the peoples who lived beyond the Rhine, the empire's border, but frequently crossed from there into areas occupied by the Romans. As to the name 'Germans', Tacitus had ideas of his own. He writes:

> The name Germany . . . is modern and newly introduced, from the fact that the tribes which first crossed the Rhine and drove out the Gauls, and are now called Tungrians, were then called Germans. Thus what was the name of a tribe, and not of a race, gradually prevailed, until all called themselves by this self-invented name of Germans, which the conqueror had first employed to inspire terror.[38]

He continues:

> For my own, I agree with those who think that the tribes of Germany are free from all taint of intermarriages with foreign nations, and that they appear as a distinct, unmixed race, like none but themselves. Hence, too, the same physical peculiarities throughout so vast a population. All have fierce blue eyes, red hair, huge frames, fit only for a sudden exertion. They are less able to bear laborious work. Heat and thirst they cannot in the least endure; to cold and hunger their climate and their soil inure them.

This verbal portrait is very similar to Ammianus Marcellinus' description of the Celts, indicating that, at least to these Mediterranean observers, all northerners looked very much alike.

In fact the term 'Germans' referred to dozens of tribes who between c.800 BC and the beginning of the Christian era occupied the entire region between the Rhine, the Danube and the Weichsel: Burgundians, Franks, Frisians, Goths, Longobards, Saxons, Vandals and so forth.[39] They inhabited that enormous part of Europe which had not fallen into Roman hands, even though some tribes settled within the empire's borders, especially in present-day Belgium and the Netherlands. We know most about the situation in Scandinavia, northern Germany and the Netherlands; however, as systematic excavations in central and eastern Europe are slowly beginning, our picture may well alter during the coming years.

The Roman writer Pliny the Elder, who died in AD 79 in Pompeii, of an attack of asthma shortly after the fateful eruption of Mount Vesuvius, wrote a 'Natural History', which, in fact, was an encyclopedia of sorts, including the data he had collected about the peoples Romans had heard of but did not yet know much about. He told his readers that the Frisians, in those northern regions, lived on their terps, 'looking like seafaring folk when their lands are inundated, but like shipwrecks when the water recedes'.

Germanic tribes usually consisted of a number of clans, each comprising several families who recognized a common, sometimes mythical, ancestor and who lived together in one village – this was not a society that needed cities.[40] Animal husbandry was the dominant economic feature, while barley was the most important staple, used for both food and drink, when made into beer; it was supplemented with various wheats and cultivated vegetables. Culturally, religion was of the greatest importance. The heavens were ruled by such fertility goddesses as Freya and Njörd, and by the war gods Odin/Wotan and Donar/ Thor; priest-kings celebrated sacrifices for them, both in holy groves and in wooden temples.[41]

Political and military power was in the hands of a warrior aristocracy, consisting of families who traced their ancestry back to the gods. For the rest, society was made up of free farmers, who were included in political and military decision-making, and of families whose members were wholly or partly unfree and hence had fewer or no rights. These included, for instance, members of other tribes who had been forced into submission and prisoners of war who had been enslaved.[42]

Many of the Germanic tribes fought fiercely among themselves, driven by a lack of fertile farmland, overpopulation and the hope of the spoils of war. Besides, from the beginning of the first century AD the proximity of the prospering border areas of the Roman Empire provided a constant challenge. These wars were sometimes led by anointed, 'sacred' kings and sometimes by dukes, chosen for the occasion. Thus, in the Cherusci tribe the noble warrior Hermann, or Arminius, was appointed duke to lead his people against the Roman aggressor in AD 9 in the famous and, to Rome, disastrous battle of the Teutoburger Forest, where three legions are supposed to have been slaughtered. Obviously, nineteenth-century Germans, celebrating their past, decided to honour their heroic ancestor with a huge monument.

Besides astonishment at the completely different political and social structure of the Germans, Tacitus' text expresses a certain admiration as well: it almost seems as if he thought these Germans still lived in a happy state of primitiveness.[43] Describing their way of life, he analyses the fascinating differences that existed, and to a certain extent still exist, between Mediterranean village life and the north European practice of settlement. He writes:

> They obtain their kings on the basis of birth, their generals on the basis of courage. The authority of their kings is not unlimited or arbitrary. Their generals control them by example rather than command, and by means of the admiration which

attends upon energy and a conspicuous place in the front line. . . . The strongest incentive to courage lies in this, that neither chance nor casual grouping makes the squadron or wedge, but family and kinship.

On small matters, the chiefs consult, on larger questions the community, but with this limitation, that even the matters whose decision rests with the people are first handled by the chiefs. They meet . . . on specified days. . . . It is a failing of their freedom that they do not meet at once, when commanded, but waste a second and third day by dilatoriness in assembling. When the throng is pleased to begin, they take their seats carrying arms. Silence is called for by the priests, who thenceforward have power also to coerce. Then kings or chiefs are listened to, in order of age, birth, glory in war, or eloquence, with the prestige that belongs to their counsel rather than with any prescriptive right to command. If the advice tendered is displeasing, they reject it by shouting; if it pleases them, they clash their spears. . . .

Conspicuously high birth or signal services on the part of ancestors confer the rank of chief, even in the case of very young men; they mingle with others of maturer strength and long-tested valour, who are not ashamed to be seen among their retinue. In the retinue itself, degrees are observed, depending upon the judgment of whom they follow. There is great rivalry among the retainers to decide who shall have the first place with his chief, and among the chieftains as to who shall have the largest and most spirited retinue. To be surrounded always by a large band of chosen youths means rank, strength, glory in peace, protection in war. . . .

It is well known that none of the German tribes lives in cities and that they do not even allow houses to touch one another. They live separately and scattered, according as spring, meadow or grove appeals to each man. They lay out their villages not, after our fashion, with buildings contiguous and connected; everyone keeps a clear space round his house.

A 'myth' had been born, for during the next 2,000 years this picture, in a way highly flattering to 'the Germans', was influential in shaping the self-image of the inhabitants of the region between, roughly, the Rhine, the Baltic, the Oder and the Alps, who have often been proud to call themselves the heirs of Tacitus' heroes.

According to archaeological research, around *c.*2500 BC the world further east, the huge area between the Baltic Sea, the Dnieper River, the Carpathian Mountains and the Oder was inhabited by the so-called proto-Slavic tribes. Their economy and society seem to have been based both on agriculture and pastoralism. As they left no written records, and did not come within the sphere of influ-ence of the Roman Empire, little is known of them up until the fourth and fifth centuries AD.[44] By then, the combined influence of Rome and of Christianity had imbued the population of western Europe with a vision of culture that viewed the continent's Slavic region as being, at most, on the margin of the 'civilized' world, i.e. of Europe; to many, it did not belong to it at all. This vision was certainly reinforced by another wave of invasions of war-like tribes from the Eurasian plains, who after conquering these regions mingled with the indigenous population, and then went on to attack the Roman Empire's frontiers.

The work of Ammianus Marcellinus shows how a culture such as the Roman one, based on agriculture, a sedentary population and a rigid, institutionalized structure regulated by laws, viewed these nomadic pastoralists, who were attracted by the riches of Rome and who, in the course of the fourth century, began to cause the Roman legions more and more trouble:

> The people of the Huns . . . all have compact, strong limbs and thick necks, and are so monstrously ugly and misshapen that one might take them for two-legged beasts. . . . They are so hardy in mode of life that they have no need of fire nor of savoury food, but eat the roots of wild plants and the half-raw flesh of any kind of animal whatever, which they put between their thighs and the backs of their horses and thus warm a little.
>
> They are never protected by any buildings . . . roaming at large amid the mountains and woods, they learn from the cradle to endure cold, hunger and thirst. . . . They are subject to no royal restraint, but they are content with the disorderly government of their important men, and led by them they force their way through every obstacle. . . . They are all without fixed abode, without hearth, or law, or settled mode of life, and they keep roaming from place to place, like fugitives, accompanied by the wagons in which they live.[45]

On the south-eastern frontiers lived

> the Saracens whom we never found desirable either as friends or as enemies [and who], ranging up and down the country . . . laid waste whatever they could find, like rapacious hawks which, whenever they have caught sight of any prey from on high, seize it with swift swoop. . . .
>
> I will now briefly relate a few more particulars about them. Among those tribes whose original abode extends from the Assyrians to the cataracts of the Nile and the frontiers of the Blemmyae [perhaps the Pygmies of Central Africa], all alike are warriors of equal rank, half-nude, clad in dyed cloaks as far as the waist, ranging widely with the help of swift horses and slender camels in times of peace or of disorder. No man ever grasps a plough-handle or cultivates a tree, none seeks a living by tilling the soil, but they continually rove over wide and extensive tracts without a home, without fixed abodes or laws.[46]

Ammianus' descriptions clearly define the elements which he thought were the foundation of Roman civilization, and which were lacking in the lives of these barbarians. Yet such tribes as the ones he wrote about were not the least important among the factors that, in the end, brought about the 'decline and fall' of the Roman Empire.

3 An empire lost – an empire won?

Christianity and the Roman Empire

Developments within the Jewish world: the genesis of Christianity

In order to determine the role of Christianity in the Roman Empire it is first necessary to give a general outline of the course of Jewish history preceding the birth of Christ. As a result of internal tensions, the temple-state of Israel had at an early stage split into two parts, Israel and Judaea. It lost its independence when both kingdoms collapsed under the expansion of, first, the Late Assyrian Empire (722 BC) and, thereafter, the Babylonians (597 BC). Part of the Jewish population was even driven into exile in present-day Iraq.

It was precisely in their milieu that cultural traditionalism could flourish, yet now with a new religious element: the oppression of life in exile was seen as Yahweh's punishment for the Jews' deviation from strict monotheism and the loose life lived by many believers. Therefore, the need for repentance and for strict compliance with the religious laws as articulated in the first part of the Old Testament, the so-called 'five books of Moses' or *Pentateuch*, was stressed. Indeed, perhaps these texts were codified only now. Such men as Isaiah, Jeremiah and Ezekiel vehemently attacked degenerated Judaism and pointed the way to its regeneration, sometimes prophesying that a 'Messiah' or 'anointed one' would arise, a king who would renew the bond between the people of Israel and their God and make them mighty once again.

Having lost their own sovereign state, many Jews who had not been deported left for more challenging places in the region and thus spread all over the Near East. Often gaining a leading role in the big commercial towns of the region, they were envied by the local populations. Their prosperity and their obviously different religion made them easy scapegoats when a community, feeling the need to relieve internal tensions, took their anger out on 'foreigners'.

Meanwhile, the Persians conquered Babylon and allowed the departed Jews to return to their homeland. The orthodox believers, having suffered for the good cause during their 'Babylonian Exile', naturally wanted to be the leaders of the newly restored kingdom. They soon found they were not the only ones with definite ideas; others made clear that they, too, were dedicated to Judaism, though perhaps not as devotedly and strictly as the former exiles. Moreover, other religions were now practised in the Jewish state as well, for in the fourth and third centuries BC the entire Near East came under the influence of Greek culture.[1] In the course of the second century, the greater part of the Jewish elite was Hellenized. To counter this process, all sorts of orthodox groupings in Jewish society tried to gain greater power: the 'Hassidics', the 'pious ones', and later the Pharisees, and especially the zealot sect of the 'Essenes' cherished strongly ritualistic beliefs paired with an intense hatred of foreigners.

External threats in the second and first centuries BC, first from the Hellenist rulers who picked up the fragments of the imperial dream of Alexander the Great, and later from the Romans, reinforced the need felt by faithful Jews for a charismatic leader, a 'Messiah', who would bring salvation and make Israel independent again. All kinds of visions of an approaching 'end of time' and a glorious new beginning now connected with the need to be cleansed of sin, as has become clear from the discovery of the so-called Dead Sea Scrolls in 1947 and the following decades. This fascinating corpus of texts has proved the existence of a group of Jews living at Qumran, on the edge of the Dead Sea, in the century preceding the birth of Christ. According to their texts, they held ideas which were later to be presented as typically Christian as well.

From Jews – and Gentiles – to Christians: the role of Jesus of Nazareth and his followers

Some 2,000 years ago, in that Jewish world, a world of bickering prophets and rival sects, a man stood up and preached and, soon, was hailed as a prophet, though in all probability he was the illiterate son of a simple country artisan in a small farming village. His followers, a tiny band at first, but soon a growing group, were probably dissatisfied men, who felt their world was changing in unacceptable ways, as their very own leaders, the Jerusalem elite, gave in to the attractions of the new, Greek culture that had reached even their lands.[2] They felt this Hellenized world impinged on their cultural and religious independence and, therefore, denounced it as decadent, depraved even. They eagerly looked for someone who would restore the original purity of their religion: a 'Messiah', a 'man anointed by God'. They found him in Jesus of Nazareth.[3]

Jesus's followers not only saw him as a 'Messiah', they also hailed him as the new 'King of the Jews'. They were prepared to die for his – for God's – cause: martyrdom for these Jews was a sign of election, a challenge to the foreign aggressors and a step on the way to realizing Yahweh's kingdom. Those who grouped themselves around Jesus of Nazareth included not only a small number of faithful disciples, later known as 'apostles', but also an increasing crowd of people both from the Jewish faith and from other Near Eastern religions, called heathens, or 'gentiles' by the Jews. After Jesus's death, they became known as Christians, the people who followed the man who was now referred to as 'Chreistos', the Greek word for the Hebrew 'Anointed One' – Greek being, of course, the language of culture in the larger part of the Near East, including Israel.

As Jesus could not write, we do not have his own words to tell us what he thought and taught. We only know what some of his disciples, probably writing long after his death, felt that they should tell about him – not recording his life's history, but edifyingly presenting his teachings as they percieved them and wanted to present them to those who never had heard him in person. Thus, his disciples interpreted his message: as a call for charity, especially towards the poorest, as a plea for belief in the one true, invisible God, as a warning against the futile attractions of earthly life, and as a view of a better world to come.

Only the few testimonies written by his closest followers tell us what attracted people to the new Messiah. In the record of Jesus's teachings written by Matthew, we read the following:

> When he [i.e. Jesus] saw the crowds he went up a mountain. There he sat down, and when his disciples had gathered around him he began to address them. And this is the teaching he gave:

> Blessed are the poor in spirit: the kingdom of Heaven is theirs.
> Blessed are the sorrowful; they shall find consolation.
> Blessed are the gentle; they shall have the earth for their possession.
> Blessed are those who hunger and thirst to see right prevail; they shall be satisfied.
> Blessed are those who show mercy; mercy shall be shown to them.
> Blessed are those whose hearts are pure; they shall see God.
> Blessed are the peacemakers; they shall be called God's children.
> Blessed are those who are persecuted in the cause of right; the kingdom of Heaven
>   is theirs.

Another disciple, Luke, gave his own version of what happened on that occasion. He presents Jesus as saying:

> to you who are listening I say: love your enemies; do good to those who hate you; bless those who curse you; pray for those who treat you spitefully. If anyone hits you on the cheek, offer the other also; if anyone takes your coat, let him have your shirt as well. Give to everyone who asks you; if anyone takes what is yours, do not demand it back.

> Treat others as you would like them to treat you . . . you must love your enemies and do good, and lend without expecting any return; and you will have a rich reward: you will be sons of the Most High, because he himself is kind to the ungrateful and the wicked. Be compassionate as your Father is compassionate.

> Do not judge, and you will not be judged; do not condemn, and you will not be condemned; pardon, and you will be pardoned; give, and gifts will be given you.[4]

But whatever the spiritual quality of these words, there is no corroborating evidence that they represent historical fact. Even the 'Gospel of St Thomas', the one text that is quite likely to represent Jesus's original words more trustworthily than the three so-called synoptic gospels recognized by the Christian churches, is not a history at all. Indeed, not only do we not really know what Jesus said, our knowledge of him as a historical person is scant, too.[5] The oldest text accepted as 'gospel' by the Christians, that of Mark, does not even have his birth story,[6] nor indeed do we have his exact year of birth. We do know, however, that, during his lifetime, the Romans conquered most of the Near East and soon held sway over Israel as well. They saw Jesus as a bothersome rebel, one of the many prophets whose agitation made the Jews such an unruly people. A number of factions among the Jews themselves also viewed Jesus and his disciples as a threat: some were afraid he would overturn the power of Jerusalem's priestly elite, others felt they did not need a new king at all, and feared that his actions, enraging the Romans, would only increase Roman pressure on their society. Therefore, the Nazarene was accused of being an enemy of the state. A trial ensued and once he was found guilty it was decided that he should be put to death. According to tradition, he was crucified in AD 33.

Everything else that is told about Jesus largely stems from the descriptions of his life that were recorded after his death. For example, what eventually became 'the tradition', the three synoptic gospels of Matthew, Mark and Luke recognized by the Christian churches, were all written at least 50 years later. As testimonies to their writers' faith, they are fascinating and to Christians entirely convincing. As historically trustworthy sources on which, moreover, the Christian churches have long based their claims to power, they are to be read with the greatest caution.

Yet, to Jesus's followers, these texts, together with the Jewish Old Testament, came to constitute the second, but more important part of the Bible. The majority of Jews, of course, who did not acknowledge Jesus as the Messiah, do not accept this 'New Testament' either. Meanwhile, in the decades and centuries that followed, a number of texts providing information and interpretations that, for one reason or another, displeased those of Christ's followers who now became leaders of the Christian communities were destroyed. As a result, some of the oldest writings documenting Jesus's teaching virtually disappeared, though some of them, like that of Thomas and, also, of Barnabas, have been discovered in the twentieth century, providing new and sometimes startlingly different perspectives on early Christianity.

In short, the life and thoughts of Jesus of Nazareth are trapped in stories that try to make sense of and give sense to the ideas of a man his followers wanted to hold up to the world as the 'anointed one', the Christ, who had purified religion, offering a sure path to god. The situation famously mirrors the one that had occurred some 500 years earlier, when the disciples of Siddharta Gautama, the Buddha, the 'enlightened one', had created the tales that now tell us what his followers wanted posterity to remember; rather than writing records of what he actually did say, these stories inevitably conceal the historical person. Some 600 years later, the very same thing happened when the followers of Muhammad started recording his sayings, and the stories of his life that seemed to support them. He, of course, was that other great religious reformer, purifier, who called himself, significantly, the 'seal of the prophets', thus firmly establishing himself in the Judaeo-Christian tradition.

Despite the grave scientific problems surrounding our historical knowledge of Jesus – problems that need and indeed do not upset those who truly believe – the Christian Near East, for the past 1,900 years, and Europe, for more than 1,500 years, have created their culture around this man and founded their society upon the ideas that his followers have codified. It is, therefore, necessary to know what we can, with some certainty, say about Christianity.

First of all, one has to accept that the words of Jesus, insofar as they can be reconstructed at all,[7] will have referred to a Jewish world and to Judaism which, in itself, is a religion steeped in traditions it shared with the major religious systems of the Near East.[8]

We also know that the teachings of the Christian churches as they evolved in the three centuries following Jesus's death, little resemble the words he may have spoken. The changing exigencies of time and place resulted in a traditional body of knowledge, a christology and, indeed, a theology, that served the needs of a creed fast becoming an institutional religion, a power structure moreover.

Finally, we should acknowledge that Christianity, especially Roman Christianity and the reformed varieties thereof, for all their association with Europe – indeed, for all their cultural Europeanization that came about between the fourth and tenth centuries – has remained a very non-European religion.

Not only did some of the second-generation 'Christians' – the name was only used after Jesus's death – try to liberate their belief from Judaism, many soon felt the need to engage in competition on the religious market of the region, a need born from the necessity to survive through strength of numbers or the proselytizing urge. They had to systematize their own religion, and, consequently, fill in the gaps it showed, with so few facts to go by; these had to be filled if they wanted to win over those still seeking a religion to satisfy their needs. In doing so, they could not help being influenced by the very religions that seemed both successful and attractive and subconsciously or in good conscience introduced elements from them.

Thus, Jesus came to be born from a virgin, an image spread widely in the major religions of the Near East.[9] That he first saw the light in a grotto – the manger is a later version – and, being both man and god, went on to spend his life helping mankind combat the evil it carried, was probably borrowed from the highly popular cult of the Persian god Mithras. Mithraism, adopted by Roman soldiers in the eastern parts of the empire, had travelled westward with the army to conquer the entire Roman world: Mithraic temples have even been found along the imperial frontier on the Rhine and also in Britain.[10] Indeed, Mithraism was, many scholars argue, one of Christianity's greatest competitors. Meanwhile, the very notion of a man who dies only to be resurrected again, originated in the ancient cult of the Babylonian deity Marduk, whose liturgy, annually celebrated in the month of Nissan, enacted that scene.[11]

While Judaism was strictly patriarchic and, therefore, at least officially, did not allow the concept of a female god – though, again, in various periods of their history, the Jews did adore goddesses – the Christians knew very well that alienating half of their potential following was not in their best interest. While stressing Jesus's unique position as man–god precluded introducing any female counterpart, they did introduce the cult of his mother, the Virgin Mary. Among other things, Mary took on all the attributes created by a far more ancient cult, that of the Egyptian goddess Isis, which had gained enormous popularity in the Roman Empire – particularly amongst women.[12] Divine Isis, mother of the god Horus, is always shown with her child on her lap, giving him her breast to suck. Often, she was depicted standing upon the moon, surrounded by stars. Not only did these images become Christian icons, the ancient Egyptian litanies prayed or sung to the goddess were also translated to be used to invoke the Virgin.[13]

Thus, the mythobiography of Christ – and his mother – slowly evolved, largely to appeal to the mass of potential Christians and, indeed, to those who needed such stories and images to be able to believe in the first place. Yet, the leaders of the early Church fully realized that they had to create a rather more refined discourse to win over the Roman elite – another necessity for the Church's survival and growth. In debates with Roman intellectuals throughout the second and third centuries, they developed a Christian cosmology that, by and large, based itself on the favourite philosophy of the Romans, neo-Platonism. The abstract notions about man and the cosmos of neo-Platonism were, in a sense, personalized to fit in with the Christian idea of a personal god, of his creative act and of his divine–human son.

At the same time though, Christianity was unavoidably engaged in a debate with another, potentially far more disruptive set of ideas, nowadays collectively referred to as 'gnostic'. All over the Near East, people in search of salvation were influenced by preachers, writers who offered them 'gnosis', wisdom, as the path thereunto; the path, however, was beset with many difficulties because creation itself was both good and evil and, therefore, man had to choose wisely indeed in order to reach his goal, to overcome the evil within him. In presenting Christ as the one road to salvation, the Christians were, in a very real way, involved in this search and, thus inevitably, in debates with all those who offered rival interpretations and opportunities – including, quite probably, Buddhist monks who travelled westward to preach their own way.

In short, Christianity, originating in the Near East, that commercial and cultural crossroads between the Mediterranean and Asia, inevitably developed in a complex interaction with all the other religions of the Near East and, also, those further east. It could not have been otherwise as is, perhaps, tellingly shown by the parallel development of a later creed, that of the prophet Mani. Born in third-century Syria, of Jewish-Christian parents, in a short time he gained followers from Persia across to Spain. Manichaeism, too, shows the complexity of religious interaction in, precisely, the Near East. Though Mani was heavily indebted to Christianity, he freely took ideas from Persian Zoroastrianism – that, itself, at earlier times had influenced Mithraism and, thus, Christianity – but also adopted Buddhist notions.[14] No wonder then, that many who looked for faith found his teachings attractive, as did the young Augustine, in north African Hippo. When, in later life, he converted to Christianity, to become one of its leading lights up to the present day, he did so precisely in an intricate dialogue with the Manichaeism he rejected, meanwhile incorporating some of it into his own version of his new-found faith.[15]

Religions in the Roman Empire

The writer Minucius Felix, who lived in the second half of the second century AD, told how the Roman Empire, which incorporated more and more different cultures because of its expansionist politics, also embraced a multitude of religions. In his dialogue *Octavius* he analysed the way the Romans themselves accepted everything which appeared salutary to them.[16] However, he also criticized a number of what were, according to him, the more banal and untrustworthy cults: for instance, the mystery cults proliferating in the oriental parts of the Roman Empire.[17] Showing the acuity of a twentieth-century religious anthropologist, he particularly targeted the extremely popular cult of Isis, which had come to the imperial capital from Egypt:

> Hence it is that . . . we see each people having its own individual rites and worshipping the local Gods – the Eleusinains Ceres, the Phrygians the Great Mother, the Epidaurians Aesculapius, the Chaldaeans Baal, the Syrians Astarte, the Taurians Diana, the Gauls Mercury – the Romans one and all. . . . In captured fortresses, even in the first flush of victory, they reverence the conquered deities. Everywhere they entertain the gods and adopt them as their own; they raise altars even to the unknown deities, and to the spirits of the dead. Thus it is that they adopt the sacred rites of all nations, and withal have earned dominion. . . .
>
> Consider the sacred rites of the mysteries. You find tragic deaths, dooms, funerals, mourning and lamentations of woebegone gods. Isis, with her Dog-head and shaven priests, mourning, bewailing, and searching for her lost son; her miserable votaries beating their breasts and mimicking the sorrows of the unhappy mother. Then, when the stripling is found, Isis rejoices, her priests jump for joy, the Dog-head glories in his discovery. . . . Is it not absurd either to mourn your object of worship, or to worship your object of mourning? Yet these old Egyptian rites have now found their way to Rome, so that you may play the fool to the swallow and sistrum of Isis, the scattered limbs and the empty tomb of your Serapis and Osiris.[18]

The Roman authorities could accept these creeds as long as they had posed no grave political threat. Thus, the cult of the Indian-Persian god Mithras, whose birth in a cave, last supper before death and ascension to heaven were depicted on the walls of countless underground temples all over the empire, was hugely popular among the soldiers of Rome from the first century AD onwards – they had encountered it from the Near East and were instrumental in its subsequent spreading – and, if only for that reason, it was even favoured by the emperors themselves, whose power almost totally depended on the army. However, some cults were deemed positively threatening such as, for instance, the one founded by the Jewish-Christian prophet Mani, whose teaching, stressing the battle between good and evil, became very popular in the third century AD, spreading from the Near East all the way to Spain. Many of these new religions showed a drift towards monotheism. Like Judaism, which had been gaining influence outside Israel, these cults, too, tended towards the belief in one God. It was this particular tendency that the emperors vigorously opposed, as stated in Diocletian's edict of AD 296:

> Excessive idleness . . . sometimes drives people to join with others in devising certain superstitious doctrines of the most worthless and depraved kind. In so doing, they overstep the bounds imposed on humans. . . . Wherefore it is our vigorous determination to punish the stubborn depraved minds of these most worthless people.
>
> We take note that . . . those Manichaeans have set up new and unheard-of sects in opposition to the older creeds, with the intent of driving out to the benefit of their depraved doctrine what was formerly granted to us by divine favour. We have heard that these men have but recently sprung up and advanced, like strange and unexpected portents, from the Persian people, our enemy, to this part of the world, where they are perpetuating many outrages, disturbing the tranquility of the peoples and also introducing the gravest harm to the communities.
>
> And it is to be feared that . . . they may try, with the accursed customs and perverse laws of the Persians to infect men of a more innocent nature, namely the temperate and tranquil Roman people as well as our entire empire with what one might call their malevolent poisons. . . .
>
> Therefore, we instruct that their followers, and particularly the fanatics, shall suffer a capital penalty, and we ordain that their property be confiscated for our fisc.

A sect of 'hopeless outlaws'

Amidst all these competing sects, the Christians, too, developed into a prominent religious movement all over the Near East, on the Asian periphery of the Roman Empire. Perhaps precisely because they creatively incorporated a great number of the characteristics of their competitors, they succeeded in becoming one of the region's major religions within the time span of only one century, between *c.*AD 40 and 140, i.e. 'after Christ's birth', or *Anno Domini*, the Christian chronology, which, however, was introduced in western Europe only in the eighth century.

Christianity soon spread all over the Roman Empire.[19] Of major importance was the preaching of the apostle Paul who, in the fifth and sixth decades of the first century AD, told his audiences, first in Asia Minor and then in imperial Rome itself that Christianity was not a religion for former Jews only, but indeed was open to every person. He and a number of his fellow apostles used the safe and easy communications provided by the empire to travel over vast distances, divulging the word of their teacher and bring the 'good news' to all who wanted to listen. When, in AD 70, Jerusalem was taken by the Romans again, the temple destroyed and the Jewish state effectively dismantled, Christianity – and, for that matter, Judaism itself – were freed of the constraints of ancient Israel; certainly

Plate 7 A shrine dedicated to the service of Mithras, one of the great competitors of Jesus, the Christ. In the centre is the altar table, showing the winged god riding his bull; around the walls are seats for the believers who gathered here to share their sacramental meal. The shrine is located under the Christian church of San Clemente, Rome.

Photo: Alinari

Plate 8 A fresco depicting a 'meal of fraternal love' or 'Agape', the cultic meal of the early Christians, found in one of the Roman catacombs.

Photo: Marc de Kleine, Nijmegen

for Christianity this meant it could present itself as a religion that, though it might have originated in Judaism, offered salvation to the gentiles as well.

At first, many Romans looked upon Christianity with contempt, as a sect that succeeded in winning over mainly slaves and women, and was mostly practised underground; an obscure religion to which people surrendered in perhaps good but always foolish faith. And yet, such was the power of the Christian message that from the second century AD the entire Roman Empire, i.e. all the world around the Mediterranean, gradually took on a Christian character.[20]

At least three elements of Christianity were attractive to a wider strata of society: revelation, which allowed even the uneducated to grasp vital truths;[21] conversion, which gave the Christians the kind of moral excellence formerly attainable only by those who could afford the costly Graeco-Roman education that was supposed to be the model road towards perfection; and lastly, of course, the highly appealing idea of salvation, of a life after death, given to each and every believer, however sinful, because of the redeeming offer made by Christ of his own life, symbolized in the wine and bread of the Eucharist – another food ritual. It gave the Christians a sense of a personal relationship with a personal God, and a perspective from which to judge and, in many cases, endure the vicissitudes of life on earth, so painful to many. No wonder many were won over by this fundamental vision of man's equality before an impartial God who would justly judge each according to his merits, as well as by the feeling of belonging, the sense of community created by this non-local, indeed 'universal' sect.

Minucius Felix listed the objections raised against the Christians: their origins in the lowest social strata, their secrecy, their refusal to worship Roman deities and, politically even more unacceptable, the deified emperors, as well as their contempt for this life and their belief in a resurrection of soul and body alike. The propaganda against the Christians was determined, at least in part, by a lack of familiarity with their symbols and rites, which had largely developed underground. However, much of it was the result of pure malice:

> Is it not deplorable that a faction . . . of abandoned, hopeless outlaws makes attacks against the gods? They gather together ignorant persons from the lowest dregs, and credulous women, easily deceived as their sex is, and organize a rabble of unholy conspirators, leagued together in nocturnal associations and by ritual fasts and barbarous foods, not for the purpose of some sacred rite but for the sake of sacrilege – a secret tribe that shuns the light, silent in public but talkative in secret places. They despise the temples . . . they spit upon the gods, they ridicule our sacred rites . . . they pity our priests; half-naked themselves, they despise offices and official robes. What amazing folly! What incredible arrogance! They despise present tortures yet dread uncertain future ones; while they fear to die after death, they have no fear of it in the meantime; deceptive hope soothes away their terror with the solace of a life to come. . . . This plot must be completely rooted out and execrated. They recognize one another by secret signs and tokens; they love one another almost before they are acquainted. Everywhere a kind of religion of lust is also associated with them, and they call themselves promiscuously brothers and

sisters, so that ordinary fornication, through the medium of a sacred name, becomes incest. . . .

[They] say that a man put to death for a crime and the lethal wooden cross are objects of their veneration. . . .

What is told of the initiation of neophytes is as detestable as it is notorious. An infant covered with spelt to deceive the unsuspecting is set before the one to be initiated in the rites. The neophyte is induced to strike what seems to be harmless blows on the surface of the spelt, and this infant is killed . . . its blood – oh, shocking – they greedily lap up. . . .

Furthermore, they threaten the whole world and the universe itself and its stars with fire, and work for its destruction . . .; they say that they are reborn after death from the cinders and ashes.[22]

At first, the Roman authorities were not overly worried, regarding the Christians as yet another crazy sect. Soon, however, they were irked by some of the tenets of the Christians' faith, especially its abhorrence of emperor worship, and began to persecute them. Until AD 250, only individual Christians were prosecuted as enemies of the state. Later, their religion as such was made illegal, and bloody, large-scale prosecutions started, which also affected related sects like the Manichaeans.

CARTHAGE, AD 180: ARGUMENTS AGAINST AND FOR THE RELIGION
OF THE CHRISTIANS

The governor of Roman North Africa, proconsul Vigellius Saturninus, whose seat was in the ancient Phoenician town of Carthage, interrogates six Christians brought before him – three men and three women. The act of interrogation reads as follows:

The proconsul Saturninus said: 'You can secure the indulgence of our lord the emperor if you return to your senses.'

Speratus said: 'We have never done any wrong; we have lent ourselves to no injustice; we have never spoken ill of anyone. . . .'

The proconsul Saturninus said: 'We, also, are religious, and our religion is simple; and we swear by the genius of our lord the emperor and pray for his welfare, as you ought to do. . . .'

Speratus said: 'The empire of this world I do not recognize; but rather I serve that God whom no man has seen nor can see with human eyes. I have not committed theft; if I buy anything, I pay the tax. . . .'

The proconsul Saturninus said to the others: 'Cease to be of this persuasion. . . . Do not participate in this madness.'

Cittinus said: 'We have none other to fear except only our Lord God who is in heaven.'

Donata said: 'Honour to Caesar as to Caesar, but fear to God.'

Vestia said: 'I am a Christian.'

Secunda said: 'What I am, that I wish to be.'

The proconsul Saturninus said to Speratus: 'Do you persist in being a Christian?'

Speratus said: 'I am a Christian.' And they all concurred with him.

The proconsul Saturninus said: 'Do you desire some time to reconsider?'

Speratus said: 'In a matter so just, there is no reconsidering.'

The proconsul Saturninus said: 'What are the things in your box?'

Speratus said: 'The Books, and the letters of Paul, a just man.'

The proconsul Saturninus said: 'Take a postponement of thirty days and reconsider.'

Speratus said again: 'I am a Christian.' And they all concurred with him.

The proconsul Saturninus read out the decree from the tablet: '. . . it is my decision that they be punished with the sword.'

Speratus said: 'We give thanks to God.'

Nartzalus said: 'Today we are martyrs in heaven: thanks be to God.'[23]

In AD 197, the Roman scholar Tertullian wrote his Apologeticum, an extensive apologia for the Christians. He analysed their actions, practices and way of life, dismissed all false accusations, and stated, finally, that the principal objection to them was not their religion but their refusal to recognize the emperor's authority as divine. In passing, he actually reversed the accusation, saying the Romans themselves feared their rulers more than their gods:

'You do not,' say you, 'worship the gods; you do not offer sacrifice for the emperors.' It follows by parity of reasoning that we do not sacrifice for others because we do not for ourselves: it follows from our not worshipping the gods. So we are accused of sacrilege and treason at once. That is the chief of the case against us, the whole of it, in fact. . . .

So now we have come to the second charge, the charge of treason against a majesty more august. For it is with greater fear and shrewder timidity that you watch Caesar than the Olympian Jove himself. . . . So that in this too you show more fear for the rule of a man. In fact, among you perjury by all the gods together comes quicker than by the *genius* of a simple Caesar. . . . So that is why the Christians are public enemies: because they will not give the emperors vain, false, and rash honours. . . .

We invoke the eternal God, the true God, the living God, for the safety of the emperors. . . . Nothing is more foreign to us than the state. One state we recognize for all: the universe.[24]

Thus, Christianity had already defined itself as a universal religion, recognizing no political boundaries: it meant its empire to be of the whole world.

Towards an empire Roman as well as Christian

In the course of the fourth century AD, all official connections between the Roman state and the old religions slowly came to an end. In AD 313, Emperor Constantine (*c.*AD 280–337) and his associate in the eastern part of the empire promulgated what later became known as the 'Decree of Milan'. This was actually a series of orders addressed to the most important civil servants, commanding them to end the prosecution of the Christians and to grant them freedom to practise their religion on a par with the worshippers of the other creeds that flourished in the Roman Empire.

Reading the 'Decree of Milan', the preference that most of Constantine's successors would finally give to the new religion can already be noticed, despite the text's attempt to treat all religions impartially:

> When I, Constantine Augustus, as well as I, Licinius Augustus . . . were considering everything that pertained to the public welfare and security, we thought that, among other things which we saw would be for the good of many, those regulations pertaining to the reverence of the Divinity ought certainly to be made first, so that we might grant to the Christians and to all others full authority to observe that religion which each preferred; whence any Divinity whatsoever in the seat of the heavens may be propitious and kindly disposed to us and all who are placed under our rule . . . so that the supreme Deity, to whose worship we freely yield our hearts, may show in all things His usual favour and benevolence.
>
> Therefore, your Worship should know that it has pleased us to remove all conditions whatsoever, which were in the rescripts formerly given to you officially, concerning the Christians, and now any one of these who wishes to observe the Christian religion may do so freely and openly, without any disturbance or molestation. . . . your Worship will know that we have also conceded to other religions the right of open and free observance of their worship for the sake of the peace of our times, that each one may have the free opportunity to worship as he pleases; this regulation is made that we may not seem to detract aught from any dignity or any religion.[25]

As a result of the decree, all property previously confiscated from the Christians was returned to them, with the state indemnifying those who had acquired such property. Thus, not only was the religion of the Christians given equality with other religions, it gained an economic base which the new Church used to extend its institutional power. The role of the old religions was gradually eroded and, at the same time, the flourishing Christian community and its leadership were given the chance to strengthen their own position. On the one hand, measures were taken that definitely limited the appeal of the traditional creeds:

> No person at all, of any class or order whatsoever of men or officials . . . whether he is powerful by the accident of birth or is humble in descent, legal status and fortune, shall sacrifice an innocent victim to senseless statues in any place at all or in any city. He shall not, through more secret wickedness, venerate his household god with fire, his *genius* with wine, his *Penates* with fragrant essences . . . But if anyone should dare . . . he shall be reported in accordance with the example of a person guilty of high treason.[26]

On the other hand, many privileges were accorded to the new religion. In AD 313, Constantine decreed that:

Since it appears from many things that the setting at naught of divine worship, through which the highest reverence for the most holy power of heaven is preserved, has brought great dangers to the state, and that the lawful restoration and maintenance of this have bestowed good fortune on the Roman name and extraordinary prosperity on all the affairs of mankind – for it is divine Providence which bestows these blessings – it is our decision that those men who, with due holiness and devotion . . . offer their services in the performance of divine worship, should receive rewards for their labours . . . Wherefore it is my will that those persons in the Catholic Church . . . who devote their service to this holy worship – those who are customarily named clerics – shall once and for all be kept completely exempt from all compulsory public services . . . nor be disturbed in any way from devoting themselves completely to serving their own law. For when they render supreme service to the deity, it seems that they confer the greatest possible benefits upon the state.[27]

Eventually – or so the story goes – Constantine himself became a Christian: on his deathbed, in AD 337, he was baptized.[28] Historians disagree as to whether this was the result of political opportunism or of religious conviction, although it seems likely that political necessity and a sense of the sociocultural irreversibility of the Christianization process heightened the emperor's own sensibility.[29]

Meanwhile, in the process of its rise to cultural and political pre-eminence, the Christian Church inevitably lost some of its pristine qualities. Initially, the idea of 'gnosis', referred to above, of an inner enlightenment attainable by everyone who strove after it in a life that was, of necessity, torn between matter and spirit, between evil and good, had greatly influenced early Christianity. As it stressed individual responsibility rather than living life according to the rules of a stifling authority, the authoritarian structures now developing within the Church did not look kindly upon it. Indeed, gnostic ideas were declared heterodox, or even heretic. Many historians have also argued that, in this period, the largely egalitarian relationship between men and women that had characterized the early Church also disappeared.[30]

Inevitably, Christianity was soon rocked by fierce factional strife. Specifically, the doctrine of the divinity of the human Christ and the concept of Holy Trinity, of God the Father, his Son and the Holy Spirit, were hotly debated, if only because many felt unconvinced by the theological and philosophical basis of these notions. Obviously, either for personal or political reasons, the emperors could and would not tolerate such heated discussions, which led to open fights and even outright schisms. Therefore, they frequently attended the councils during which the Christians tried, usually in vain, to reconcile their differences. They also supported those Church leaders who persecuted dissenting Christians, trying to root out heterodox ideas. Hence, Constantine himself was present at the famous Council of Nicea in AD 325. Eusebius, the emperor's contemporary and biographer, describes the drama in his *Vita Constantini*, III, vi–x, *passim*:

Constantine summoned a general synod, inviting the bishops in all parts with honorary letters to be present . . . at that time there were to be seen congregated in one place persons widely differing from one another not only in spirit but also in physical appearance, and in the regions, places, and provinces from which they came . . . from all the churches which had filled all Europe, Africa and Asia. . . . Present among the body were more than 250 bishops . . . for the council which was to put an end to the controversies.

The Council ended with the promulgation of the famous Nicene Creed, a text meant to reconcile the participants and, thus, to restore unity. Increasingly, the Church, aided by the state, tried to formalize and control public discourse in religious matters, in order to establish an orthodox doctrine. Indeed, Church councils' decisions were always presented as consensual.[31] It all helped to develop a society with an overtly pyramidal, authoritarian pattern of relationships.

However, precisely because the ecclesiastical leadership increasingly ruled out discussion, arguments continued unabated. Later, in AD 380 and 381, Emperor Theodosius determined that:

It is our will that all peoples ruled by our Clemency shall practise that religion which the divine Peter the Apostle transmitted to the Romans; that is, according to the apostolic discipline and the evangelical doctrine, we shall believe in the single deity of the Father, the Son, and the Holy Spirit, under the concept of equal majesty and of the Holy Trinity. We order that those persons who follow this rule shall embrace the name of Catholic Christians. The rest, however, whom we judge demented and insane, shall have the infamy of heretical dogmas, their meeting places shall not receive the name of churches, and they shall be smitten first by divine vengeance and secondly by retribution of our hostility. . . .

The contamination of the Photian pestilence, the poison of the Arian sacrilege, the crime of the Dunomian perfidy, and the sectarian monstrosities . . . shall be abolished even from the hearing of men.[32]

Meanwhile, as a result of Constantine's politically inspired decisions, Christianity became the religion of the Roman state. Inevitably, ever more people now felt called on to embrace the new faith. Even members of the elite now converted, out of conviction or from a wish to hold on to their positions.[33] Consequently, Christianity became thoroughly saturated with those elements from the old 'heathen' culture that did not openly conflict with it, such as classical rhetoric, aspects of philosophy, mainly of a neo-Platonist bent, and many themes and forms from architecture and the visual arts: the Christian church was modelled on the Roman basilica, and Christ himself was often depicted as 'the good shepherd', like the hugely popular Greek god Dionysios, to give but two examples. In the end, even the Christian calendar and the veneration of saints and relics showed many aspects of the older, pagan cults.

Thus, all around the Mediterranean – including, therefore, a large part of Europe – a situation developed in which only one religion governed the society and came to pervade the wider culture of this world empire; it was, indeed, a new phenomenon in world history. Moreover, this religion was not polytheistic but monotheistic, requiring everyone to submit completely to an unseen yet personal God. Faith, not reason, was its central principle. Anything humans had invented but that Church leaders considered to conflict with professed religion was now condemned as heresy, unless it could somehow be fitted into the new theological system.

Indeed, the new religious elite wanted to extirpate completely the power that all sorts of cults and religions, usually older than Christianity, still held over the population. In this aim, they knew the emperors, who had increasingly chosen to attach themselves to Christianity, would be on their side. For the rulers of the Romans strove to maximize the unity of thought and action among their subjects; therefore, they gladly supported policies of cultural homogenization. In a decree of AD 357, the Emperor Constantius Augustus told his people:

> No one shall consult a soothsayer or astrologer or diviner. The evil teaching of augurs and practitioners of magic shall become silent. The Chaldeans and magicians and all the rest . . . shall not attempt anything of this sort. The curiosity of all men for divination shall forever cease.[34]

Of course, this did not mean such practices really disappeared. On the contrary, many Christian priests consciously or unconsciously took over the functions of the old magicians and sorcerers, precisely because the population needed a priesthood who could communicate with and if necessary placate the incomprehensible forces of nature.

Gradually, everyday life became structured according to the Church's rules. All sorts of advantages were accorded to the new religion and its followers. Also, many elements of the older cultures were integrated into Christian practice in the interest of cultural and, thus, social homogenization. This can be seen from imperial decrees of AD 386 and 392:

> On the day of the Sun, which our ancestors rightly called the Lord's Day [Constantine had ordered this in AD 321], the prosecution of all litigation, court business and suits, shall be entirely suspended. No person shall demand the payment of a public or private debt, nor shall there be any cognizance of controversies before arbitrators. . . . Contests in the circuses shall be prohibited on the festal days of the Sun . . . in order that no concourse of people to the spectacles may divert men from the reverend mysteries of the Christian law.[35]

The emperors, most of whom by now had been educated within a Christian culture themselves, were increasingly severe with the adherents of the older cults, not primarily because they opposed them from a religious point of view but because such cults posed a threat to public stability, offering opposition groups an alternative ideology. In AD 395, and again in later years, they ordered that:

> If any images still stand in the temples and shrines, and if they received or do now receive the worship of pagans anywhere, they shall be torn from their foundations. . . . The buildings themselves of the temples which are located in cities or towns or outside the towns shall be confiscated to public use. Altars shall be destroyed in all places.[36]

In AD 425, an imperial edict was promulgated that clearly showed how much had changed in less than a century after Constantine's decision: it was patently obvious that Christianity had become victorious. All ideas diverging from accepted doctrine were now forcefully suppressed. Moreover, the emperor had given the pope – the bishop of Rome who, as the successor of the apostle Peter, claimed supremacy in the Church's hierarchy – his unambiguous support as the only spiritual leader of all Christendom:

> We command that the Manichaeans, heretics, schismatics, astrologers, and every sect inimical to the Catholics shall be banished from the very sight of the City of Rome, in order that it may not be contaminated by the contagious presence of the criminals. An admonition, moreover, must he especially issued concerning those persons who by perverse persuasion withdraw from the communion of the venerable Pope, and by whose schism the rest of the common people also are corrupted.[37]

However, this edict also shows that, whatever power the Church had acquired, it still had not managed to force everyone in the Roman Empire into the straitjacket of Christianity.

Rome and its neighbours in the fourth and fifth centuries AD: 'decline and fall'? The division and loss of the political empire – the survival of the cultural empire

Certainly from the first century AD onwards, the Roman Empire, parallel with its territorial growth had become increasingly economically dependent on natural resources and manpower that had to be imported from outside its borders. In particular, slaves, who were needed to keep the system going, could be obtained only by wars of conquest – indeed, such wars had always been and still were the 'motor' of Roman imperialism; when, by the end of the second century AD, the empire had reached its greatest size because further expansion proved militarily and financially unfeasible, slaves had to be purchased from barbarian middlemen beyond the frontiers. An indication of the 'problem' is that by the end of the first century AD, in Italy alone 2 million of its 6 million inhabitants were slaves; this meant that a fresh supply of 150,000 new slaves was needed annually.

Strangely, perhaps, as a result of this situation, the Roman economy became a powerful stimulus to the economies of neighbouring regions. In northern and central Europe, for example, the provisions needed by the empire's enormous armies led to increased cattle-rearing among the German tribes beyond the Rhine, who provided leather for tents, boots, saddles and other horse gear. Archaeological finds also testify to a growing demand for luxury goods in the areas that provided the empire with raw materials and slaves. Such finds also evidence technological improvements in the various border regions, which were perhaps influenced by intensified contacts with the Roman world, as shown by the beautiful filigree, gem-encrusted jewellery discovered in a chieftain's grave at Sutton Hoo, in England.

As indicated above, for as long as we know, central Eurasia was the home of a great many nomadic-pastoralist communities. Especially when climate conditions worsened, they started moving, in tribes but also in more loosely constructed bands, gathered around an inspiring and successful leader who promised them booty. From the middle of the first millennium BC, another period of almost continuous movement set in, that lasted until the end of the first millennium AD. It can be called appropriately 'The Age of Migration'. To Rome, these migrating groups, fighting, regrouping, sometimes settling for a protracted period, then moving again, were uncivilized, barbarians even. Obviously, this is one perspective only. Actually, they were societies of whose culture we know little because, mostly, they did not write. Often, in the process of moving and settling and moving again, they did come to form what one might call ethnic identities, acquiring a common language, constructing a common history, praying to common gods. However, when new groups came out of central Eurasia, these identities might be destroyed or, rather, reformed. It was, in a sense, a Domino-process that constantly repeated itself, changing both the worlds of Europe beyond the imperial frontier and Roman culture and society itself.

By the second century AD, Romans became particularly aware that peoples in northern and central Europe had begun moving again, partly due to population increases, and partly due to climate changes – which affected their incipient agrarian economies – and social instability on the eastern periphery of Europe: the region of present-day Poland and western Russia. This led to the Longobards crossing the Danube in the latter part of the century, and the Franks, Frisians and Saxons emerging at the Rhine border, and sometimes crossing it during the first half of the third century. Often, these were war bands of uncertain ethnogenesis; they confederated because they saw possibilities in the weakening of Roman authority in the frontier regions.

Further east, a heterogeneous congeries of Germanic tribes as well as even more loosely organized, roving groups made up of a wide range of ethnic elements, probably originating from the Vistula basin, now entered written history as 'the Goths', the name given them by the terrified people of south-east Europe,[38] who were first confronted with their attacks in the late second and early third centuries.[39] They settled near the Roman border on the Danube and soon even converted to Christianity. There, Bishop Wulfila or Ulfilas (*c*.AD 310–82/3) decided to give his people the Bible in Gothic. Its earliest known manuscript copy, probably produced in the sixth century, was written in beautiful silver letters on purple vellum; this *Codex Argenteus* is now kept in the University Library at Uppsala. Wulfila had to invent an alphabet to achieve his aim, for his people's culture was as yet without writing.[40]

Actually, there never was an original, distinct Goth culture. During two centuries of raids, invasions, settlements, removals and resettlements, the mixture of nomadic elements, Germanic influences and the Graeco-Roman culture of the Balkans and the Black Sea coast came to constitute something that could be called a Goth civilization which was then introduced into western Europe.

When the Huns advanced over the Eurasian steppe by the end of the fourth century, the Goths were forced to penetrate further into the relative safety of the Roman Empire. They eventually conquered the wealthiest regions of its western part. Some of their bands set up a kingdom in northern Italy, based at Ravenna, where the monumental remains of a marvellous mixture of Roman and Germanic cultural elements can still be seen. Others founded a kingdom in southern France, based at Toulouse; they adapted easily to the local Gallo-Roman culture.

In Iberia, present-day Spain, too, the existing Roman elements mixed with the German heritage of the Goths, resulted, among other things, in a thriving intellectual life that lasted until the coming of new conquerors in the seventh century. It produced such great spirits as Isidore, archbishop of Seville (*c.*560–636), a major scholar in various fields. He wrote a 'History of the Goths' that, significantly, starts with a *Laus Spaniae* (a 'praise of Spain'), indicating that the Goth conquerors wished to merge with the existing, Romanized population; it was a first expression of Spanish 'national' feeling. He also compiled a history of the world, a treatise on astronomy and cosmography and, most important perhaps, a fascinating work called *Etymologiae*, one of Europe's first encyclopedias and a foundation of philosophy and scholarship for centuries to come.

The coming of the Huns also led to the migration of peoples in western Europe. One year, at the beginning of the fifth century, the Burgundians crossed the frozen Rhine, settling around Worms, Speyer and Strasbourg. Later, their army was destroyed by the hordes from Asia. This disaster, told and retold countless times in heroic songs by Burgundian bards who embellished and added to it, finally resulted in the famous *Nibelungenlied*, providing Europe with a fecund legend that was set to music by Richard Wagner in the nineteenth century – although he incorporated a lot of material from Norse and Icelandic sagas as well – and, in the early twentieth century, filmed in silent but evocative images by the Austrian film-maker Fritz Lang.

Meanwhile, the keepers of the empire, the Christian emperors of the fourth and fifth centuries, had to accept that not even the new religion would provide the divine protection they had so dearly hoped for. The pressure on the borders from outside increased. Soon, the tribes and peoples who were driven from central and eastern Europe and central Asia by the changes that affected their agriculture and cattle-raising became a threat more than ever before.[41]

We know now that internal developments also caused 'the Fall of Rome'.[42] The empire's structural flaws were becoming glaringly manifest. Its very size was, perhaps, one of the main reasons for its demise; also, the bureaucracy and economy were unable to adequately mobilize the forces needed to police the state and to defend its frontiers; moreover, communications between the capital and the provinces took too long; finally, on the peripheries there was increasing distrust of the parasitic, wasteful centre, Rome, with its continuous demands for money and goods. As central power and, thus, authority waned, regional differences turned out to be centripetal after all. Consequently, the regions that once had been incorporated in the empire, now gradually went their own way; in the process, the cultural varieties that had continued to exist underneath the Roman veneer became visible again. In the east, Greek had remained the common language, while in the west Latin had gradually gained the upper hand.

Other factors were at work, too. Thus, in the decades after AD 160 and, again, in the years following AD 541, a wave of epidemics swept over the empire. It was both the result of economic problems that debilitated general health and, thus, the power to resist, while, of course, in its turn it caused further, long-term agricultural recession; the ensuing poverty affected the population and led to continuing demographic and economic decline, though the effects were different in various parts of the empire. By and large, the new situation was most noticeable in the centres of Roman power and culture, the cities.[43] As the rule of the emperors gradually became weaker, many members of the urban elites who implemented state power on the regional and local level acquired greater political independence; however, they also began to look upon the Church as the one institution that could guarantee the old values, a process that can be witnessed, for example, among the urban elites of Roman Gaul.[44] In many towns, the Christian bishops, by now expert in governing large communities, even took over as secular rulers.

By the end of the third century AD, under attack from all sides, and with its inner structure weakening, the empire could no longer be ruled with economic, military and organizational unity, precisely when it needed this unity most. Unity was indeed lost when central government was no longer able to effectively defend the borders. Therefore, considerations of a logistic-military nature led to the decision to formally divide the empire into an eastern and a western half, to be ruled in concord by two emperors. Though, in retrospect, this decision may seem foolish and though it did prove fateful, at the time it was the logical thing to do.

From the fourth century onwards, a Greek or Byzantine Empire developed in what formerly had been Greece and Asia Minor. It considered itself the true heir to ancient Rome, creating a vision of its capital, Byzantium, as the 'new Rome' even though it was renamed Constantinople in AD 330.[45] The western Roman Empire, the *imperium occidentalis*, the empire of the Occident, became known as the Latin Empire because of the dominant cultural language. Though Rome remained its capital, for long periods such northern cities as Milan and Ravenna fulfilled that function, too.

During the last centuries of its existence, the Roman Empire, by now permanently divided, was increasingly forced to adopt a policy of accommodation; gradually, not only were foreign peoples allowed to enter the empire, they were also assimilated into Roman culture. Often, the foreign war bands were positively hailed, providing the soldiers that the great senatorial, landowning families of the empire needed to fulfil the role they increasingly took upon themselves, i.e. defending and policing the region they dominated, now that imperial authority was weakening. This, of course, contributed to the Romanization of the immigrants.

Consequently, by the late fourth and early fifth centuries, certainly in the northern and western parts of the empire, imperial power was mostly controlled by non-Roman generals and finally passed outright into the hands of new-comers. One such, Theodosius, though a descendant of the Visigoths, a people who only shortly before had been described as a 'barbaric' tribe, could yet become ruler of the western empire in AD 381. Showing that a loss of memory can be politically expedient, the orator Themistius praised this upstart as the saviour of the old culture, saying: 'The Barbarians have still not defeated the Romans for after all, form triumphed over formlessness, order over chaos, courage over fear, obedience over disobedience'.[46] However, the ideas of this intellectual, who swam with the tide and yet managed to nicely articulate the essence of Roman culture in the face of this powerful new leader, were not shared by all 'real' Romans. In AD 399, the somewhat more conservative orator Synesius addressed Emperor Arcadius as follows: 'That these fair-haired people, who arrange their hair in Euboian styles, are our slaves in private but our rulers in public is outrageous, a shocking spectacle'.[47] These words betray an attitude that people in Europe would frequently display when they wanted to brand others, migrants, as a 'danger' to their own position and culture.

Meanwhile, a certain defeatism came to characterize the empire's inhabitants. The Christian scholar St Jerome (331/47–419/20) wrote:

> I come now to the frail fortunes of human life, and my soul shudders to recount the downfall of our age. For twenty years now and more the blood of Romans has every day been shed between Constantinople and the Julian Alps. Scythia, Thrace, Macedonia, Thessaly, Dardania, Dacia, Epirus, Dalmatia, and all the provinces of Pannonia, have been sacked, pillaged and plundered by Goths and Sarmatians, Quadians and Alans, Huns and Vandals and Marcomanni. How many matrons, and how many of God's virgins, ladies of gentle birth and high position, have been made the sport of these beasts! Bishops have been taken prisoners, presbyters and other clergymen of different orders murdered. Churches have been overthrown, horses stabled at Christ's altar, the relics of martyrs dug up. . . . The Roman world is failing, and yet we hold our heads erect instead of bowing our necks.[48]

This attitude of proud resignation did not prevent the end of the empire. In August of the year AD 410, the Goth leader Alaric laid siege to Rome, conquering and sacking it. The 'eternal' symbol of the unity and power of the Roman Empire was, for the time being, destroyed. But St Jerome's words indicate the chance of survival which he ascribed to a world no longer Roman but still Christian.

Nor was he mistaken. At the end of the fifth century, some of the war bands who had settled within the empire in the region of the Rhine, Moselle, Somme and Loire were united under one Chlodwig, who shook off the yoke of the Romanized rulers of that region and established a kingdom, utilizing the traditional instrument of German politics, the creation of a partly fictive tribal structure with its basis in equally fictive family relationships, sometimes stretching back to the times of heroes and gods, to create a 'people' now called the Franks.

But as so many Germanic war leaders and their followers had done before him, Chlodwig converted to Christianity; according to tradition, he was baptized in Rheims on Christmas night in AD 497. He may have been persuaded to do so because Christian missionaries assured him such a move would bring him the power and wealth associated with the old empire. Certainly, his descendants used this argument to style themselves the successors of the Roman emperors – and Rheims remained the place where, if possible, French kings were crowned until the French Revolution, 1,500 years later. But whatever Chlodwig's motives, he linked himself and his people with the culture of the Romans, as did a great number of the Germanic tribes who continued to enter the empire that was now definitely lost.

Empire and language

By the fifth century AD, the linguistic map of Europe had become very complicated. During many centuries of migration, numerous tribes and 'nations' had brought their languages to this part of the world. By and large, most languages originally stemmed from the so-called 'proto-Indo-European', spoken by the semi-nomadic peoples inhabiting the southern Russian steppes, northern Turkey and northern Iran sometime during the millennia between 7,000 and 5,000 BC.[49] Although this 'original' language does not exist any more and, moreover, its nature and its 'originality' are still hotly debated, efforts at reconstruction have revealed some of its cultural characteristics, which show that the society which used it was a patriarchic one, subsisting both on agriculture and pasturing.

A number of tribes or more loosely formed bands from this linguistic-cultural 'pool' had begun to migrate to the Danube area between 5,000 and 3,500 BC and reached the Adriatic region somewhere before 2,000 BC. Meanwhile, they had also moved into Iran and India, where their language developed into the Indo-Iranian tongues, among which are old Persian and Sanskrit, the language of India's oldest and holiest books, the *Vedas* – though, admittedly, unlike most Europeans, Indians even now have great problems in accepting the idea that the most venerated elements of their culture, its ancient, sacred language and its religious ideas and customs, were quite probably imported or at least heavily influenced by peoples from central Eurasia; indeed, many Indians claim a more national, indigenous origin.[50]

In Europe, the spread and development of the Indo-European languages closely followed the pattern of two millennia of migration and conquest before the beginning of the Christian era. In Greece, the Greek language has been attested from the fifteenth century BC onwards. In the end, it became the *lingua franca*, the language commonly used in the eastern Mediterranean from the third century BC until the seventh century AD, when it was superseded there by Arabic.

The first Indo-European people to spread their language over central and western Europe were the Celts, during the last millennium BC. As the German tribes came in from western Russia, partly by way of Scandinavia, Celtic was largely marginalized; it remained the language of the western periphery of Europe: Ireland, Wales, Cornwall and Brittany.

But while the Germanic languages were formed – Gothic, now lost, and the Anglo-Saxon, Scandinavian and German varieties – they also encountered a powerful competitor. Around the Adriatic basin, the Italic languages had evolved, among which Latin soon became the tongue of conquerors. For as the Roman Empire consolidated its hold over ever greater parts of south-west Europe, the spoken or 'vulgar' version of Latin became predominant because it was the language of the political and cultural elite and, soon, also of the new, Christian Church. Indeed, the spreading of the Christian message was obviously favoured greatly by the communication possibilities provided by that highly unified cultural and linguistic structure which was the Roman Empire with its Graeco-Latin civilization. In its turn, the spreading of Christianity resulted in the spreading of a Latinized language as well.

Eventually, this complex situation gave birth to the so-called 'Romance' languages, the regional, vernacularized varieties of Latin: Italian, Sardinian, French, Occitan, Spanish, Catalan, Portuguese and, of course, Romanian. These gradually supplanted the languages previously spoken in these regions, whether of yet older Indo-European origin or, as in the case of the only survivor, Basque, even dating back to pre-Indo-European times.

Looking at the map of the Roman Empire in the fourth and fifth centuries AD, one must conclude that the military *limes* had become, to a large extent, a cultural, linguistic frontier, too. South-west of it, the Romance tongues continued to predominate and while in the north-western corner the Germanic languages – English, Frisian, Dutch and German – consolidated themselves, in later centuries there has been considerable interaction with, especially, Latin and later French. North and east of the frontier, the other Germanic languages flourished largely uninfluenced, though further east a last wave of invasions in the sixth and seventh centuries AD brought the Baltic and Slavonic branch of Indo-European to central Europe and the Balkans; it first branched out into a number of dialects from which, eventually, separate languages stemmed, among them Polish, Czech, Slovak, Serbian, Croat, Bulgarian and, of course, Russian.

Thus, it seems that the secret success of any language is muscle, first, and perhaps, mission and money, second. Greek marched with the armies of Alexander, Latin spread with the legions of the Romans and the missionaries of the Christians and, in later times, Arabic would conquer three continents in the wake of Islamic traders and troops, while, of course, Spanish began its victory in the sixteenth century in the wake of a global conquest both material and spiritual. To a far lesser extent, from the seventeenth century onwards, the Dutch and the French established their language overseas as well. Last, but not least, English first started on its road around the world when the British built their empire.

Part II

Continuity and change
New forms of belief

4 Towards one religion for all

The Christian world-view: the survival of classical culture within the context of Christianity and Europe

It is important to note that, within the time span of three centuries, the small sect of the Christians, originating in a very localized, tribal, religious tradition, Judaism, developed into a fully fledged church. Moreover, it came to encompass the entire Roman Empire and was deemed so influential that the emperors not only adopted it but also sought to dominate it, showering it with land grants and exempting its priests from public service. Yet this very church, while accepting these privileges, for a long time shied away from the State, arguing that a true believer could not well serve two masters. On the other hand, the Christian Church soon adopted the organizational structure of the State, the Roman State, creating its own hierarchy of authorities culminating in the bishops, the patriarchs and the pope, as well as adopting the structure of the Roman public meeting place, the 'basilica', as the model for its churches. Indeed, as the institutions that sustained the empire grew weaker, the leaders of the Church often felt forced to step in where civic authorities failed to cope, offering protection and security to the people and, thus, assuming secular power as well.

It is interesting to wonder what happened, meanwhile, to that pseudo-geographical concept, Europe, a concept that, in fact, entailed a world-view, a cultural representation of the Graeco-Roman world?[1] For an inhabitant of the Roman Empire such as Augustine (AD 354–430), a patrician's son from Thagaste in North Africa who converted to Christianity and later became a saint of the new Church, the world actually consisted of two parts: an eastern part, which coincided with the continent of Asia, which to him was the Near East, and a western part, which consisted of Europe and Africa, separated but not divided by the Mediterranean: 'The reason why Europe and Africa have been made into two continents lies in this, that all the water from the ocean comes between the two, flowing between their lands and forming the great sea for us.'[2] Obviously, Augustine had no great use for the concept of Europe. Even though he knew that another world existed beyond its frontiers, what counted for him was the Roman Empire, the huge, culturally unified world that encircled what was known as *Mare Nostrum*, 'our sea'.

Plate 9 A Germanic limestone tombstone, from the eighth century, from Alskog Tjangvide on the island of Gotland, Sweden, showing another cosmology. Its runic inscription dedicates it to the memory of one Jurulv, murdered by relatives. The stone shows the 'Ship of the Dead', below, and in the upper part the deceased's arrival, on Odin's eight-legged horse, at Valhalla, the home of the Gods – a great hall as the ones actually built in north-western Europe at that time.

Source: Centre for Art Historical Documentation, Nijmegen, The Netherlands

Not only Augustine converted to the new religion. So, increasingly, did many of the empire's citizens. In the process, Christianity inevitably developed in the crucible of existing cultures, consciously and unconsciously feeding on many of its elements. Consequently, the new religion soon provided an attractive and, for many, convincing mix of characteristics of other popular religions and systems of thinking. Among these were the teachings connected with the Indian-Persian god Mithras, and also the cult of the Invincible Sun God, who for many years had been the Emperor Constantine's tutelary deity: the rites celebrating the birth of Mithras and the feast of the Sun both helped to shape the Christian feast of 'Christmas', as the birth of the Saviour and the return of Light. Equally influential was the worship of the Egyptian goddess Isis who, often painted and sculpted as a mother-goddess with the child Osiris in her lap, clearly became a model for the representation of the Virgin Mary. And, of course, there were the ideas of a number of Greek philosophers, including Aristotle and Plato, popular among the Graeco-Roman elites precisely in the period during which the Christian Church tried to convince and convert them as well.

In the cultural synthesis that ensued, the view people had of the world changed, both in a physical and in a metaphysical sense.

MOUNT SINAI, AD 547: KOSMAS EXPLAINS THE CHRISTIAN
COSMOGRAPHY

In about AD 547, the Greek Kosmas, who had become a monk after a life of travelling and trading as far as India, wrote his *Kristianike Topographia* (Christian Topography). A ninth-century copy of the text is in the Vatican Library in Rome. It is illustrated with the earliest Christian maps.

In this work, Kosmas tried to reconcile pagan geography and the information about the physical world known to him with the notions that Christian Holy Scripture seemed to dictate. Kosmas's view of the world seems to run counter to the global world-view that had been central to Ptolemaic cosmology. From now on, for more than a thousand years, all Europeans bar a small, scholarly elite thought of the earth as a flat world, as a vast expanse of land in an even vaster expanse of water, contained under the vault of heaven. Indeed, like Kosmas himself, the majority of the clergy, too, was convinced that this was the way God had created the world. Obviously, this view entailed specific explanations of the nature of the relations between land and sea, earth and heaven, and the movements of the heavenly bodies.

> We have said that the figure of the earth is lengthwise from east to west and breadthwise from north to south, and that it is divided into two parts: this part which we, the men of the present day, inhabit, and which is all round encircled by the intermedial sea, called the ocean by the Pagans, and that part which encircles the ocean, and has its extremities bound together with those of the heaven, and which men at one time inhabited to eastward, before the flood in the days of Noah occurred, and in which also Paradise is situated. . . .
>
> The northern and western parts of the earth which we inhabit are of very great elevation, while the southern parts are proportionally depressed. For to what extent of its breadth the earth is imperceptibly depressed, it is found to have an elevation of like area in the northern and western parts, while the ocean beyond is of unusual depth. But in the southern and eastern parts the ocean beyond is not of unusual but of the medium depth. When these facts are considered, one can see why those who sail to the north and west are called lingerers. It is because they are mounting up and in mounting up they sail more slowly, while in returning they descend from high places to low, and thus sail fast, and in a few days bring their voyage to an end . . .
>
> The eastern and southern parts again, as low-lying and over-heated by the sun, are extremely hot, while the northern and western, from their great elevation and distance from the sun, are extremely cold, and in consequence the inhabitants have very pale complexions, and must keep themselves warm against the cold . . .
>
> Since then the heaven and the earth comprise the universe, we assert that the earth has been founded on its own stability by the Creator, according once more to the divine scripture, and that it does not rest on any body. . . .
>
> We therefore first depict along with the earth the heaven, which is vaulted and which has its extremities bound together with the extremities of the earth. To the best of our ability we have endeavoured to delineate it on its western side and its eastern; for these two sides are walls, extending from below to the vaults above.

There is also the firmament which, in the middle, is bound together with the first heaven, and which, on its upper side, has the waters according to divine scripture itself . . .

To the extremities on the four sides of the earth the heaven is fastened at its own four extremities, making the figure of a cube, that is to say, a quadrangular figure, while up above it curves round in the form of an oblong vault and becomes as it were a vast canopy. And in the middle the firmament is made fast to it, and thus two places are formed.

From the earth to the firmament is the first place, this world, namely, in which are the angels and men and all the present state of existence. From the firmament again to the vault above is the second place – the Kingdom of Heaven, into which Christ, first of all, entered, after his ascension, having prepared for us a new and living way.

Since the heavenly bodies then, according to divine scripture, are moved in their orbits by invisible powers, and run their course through the north, and pass below the elevated part of the earth, it is possible, with such a configuration, for eclipses of the moon and the sun to be produced. For the angelic powers, by moving the figures on rational principles and in regular order, and with greater speed than lies in us to apprehend, produce these phenomena, plying their labours by night and by day without ever pausing.[3]

On Kosmas's map, the nether world is, by and large, the same as the world of the Christians: Europe and the Holy Land, or rather the Christian Near East, symbolically centred around Jerusalem and Rome, with Asia and Africa only sketchily represented, not least, obviously, because so little of it was actually known.[4]

Obviously, a confrontation between the cosmos as seen through the eyes of the holy book of the Christians and the knowledge and world-view of the 'Ancients', long held by the elite of the Roman Empire and their intellectual successors, was inevitable, the more so as views did not differ only as to physical nature, but also as to the nature of creation itself – was it the work of a personal God, or of an impersonal, natural force? Over the centuries, the resulting tension became a structural element in European culture and, right up to the twentieth century, continued to elicit debate and, indeed, feed doubts among those who were raised within the world of Christendom. Consequently, Europe's intellectual history has comprised alternating periods of time when men harked back to classical civilization, and when they emphasized an original Christian purity, which gradually became more and more idealized. Always, when tension became too great, a synthesis that would reconcile both ideas was sought. However, a system that pleased and convinced everyone was not found.

Three forms of tension, voiced most clearly in the (always overlapping) fields of philosophy, religion and science seem to have been perennial: between the immortal soul and the mortal body, between good and evil and, intertwined with the first two, between faith, in the unreasoned authority of a higher power, and reason, as the essential capacity of the free-willed human being to finally understand every problem with which the cosmos presented him.

Long before the genesis of Christianity, one of the central questions that had been asked repeatedly was: is everything in the universe, including man, who considers himself a thinking and free agent, actually material? The Greek philosopher Demokritos (*c*.470–360 BC) had already answered in the affirmative. In his atom theory, he proposed that everything that existed consisted of a more or less complex series of smaller parts. More importantly, he also argued that the human 'spirit', or soul, was no more than that and would, therefore, die with the rest of the material body.

Such concepts, of course, were diametrically opposed to the notion of bodily resurrection which was precisely the idea the Church needed to neutralize the second fundamental tension. Christ and his followers had actually fought the presence of misery and injustice on earth, of 'evil', evident to so many, with the promise of a life of eternal goodness and happiness in the hereafter to which both body and soul would be resurrected if man had made his peace with God. Although this notion appealed to many, there were those who still asked themselves why a God who was presented as all-good as well as all-powerful and who, moreover, had promised man resurrection had permitted evil to enter the world in the first place.

In the first four centuries of the Christian era, the discussions between Christians and other intellectuals in the Roman world resulted in all sorts of ideas and even theories that hoped to solve this dilemma. As outlined above, some of these, collectively known as *gnosis*, or knowledge, argued that good and evil, spirit and matter, were essential characteristics of man and, therefore, of God, who had created man. According to these Gnostics, salvation could be achieved only through understanding these characteristics and accepting their consequences. However, this rather personalized way of thinking, popular among a number of Christians ever since, was anathema to the religious establishment.

Within Christianity, what in the end became accepted tradition was largely based on the ideas of the patrician from Thagaste in his major theological-philosophical works, the *Confessiones* and the *De Civitate Dei* ('On the City of God'). Augustine, despite being attracted to gnosticism in his youth, finally concluded that man exists because he thinks, considers and doubts. Next, Augustine asked himself how man came into existence and then argued that this resulted from the creation by an eternal God who stands outside and above the cosmos, having created both space, that is, motion, and time, as well as matter. Augustine's ideas show the influences of the Graeco-Roman culture in which he was raised and in which Christianity had developed as a new system of thought, seeking to synthesize what, according to many, cannot be synthesized – religion, or belief, especially as the unconditional surrender to a revealed God, and science, as a series of concepts trying, through reasoned argument, to explain the physical reality of the world and of man. To Augustine, the world, and in it both the Church – which he saw as the only road to salvation – as well as its members, were all imperfect though still indicated the perfection they would realize when they turned to God.

The teaching of Augustine owed quite a lot to the philosophy of Plato (428–348 BC), principally as it had been assimilated and reformulated by Plotinus (*c.*AD 204–70). As a result of studying Plato's philosophy, Christian intellectuals constructed a way of thinking and living that appealed to the cultural elite as well as to the masses. Several of Plato's concepts were interpreted in such a way that the more intellectual opponents of Christianity let themselves be convinced. After all, in his *Symposium*, the Athenian philosopher had stipulated that there are two worlds: the world of the imperfect body in which people operate with their impressions and senses, and which they can therefore know, and the world of 'Ideas', the higher principles which, although man is partly unaware of them, exist in every human being. In his *Timaios*, Plato had articulated his views on creation: 'Ideas' are the thoughts of the *Nous* (the Intellect or the Divine Soul), in which the *Hen* (the One) has become conscious. These 'Ideas' manifest themselves in the *Psyche* (the Soul) of the world but also in the souls of individual people, who thus become animate matter.

Inevitably, however, Christian intellectuals also had to come to terms with Aristotle, Plato's most distinguished student. As often happens with students, he had in many ways defied his teacher. Arguing that the 'Ideas' were only 'names', not 'real things', Aristotle did talk of 'forms' in which undefined matter, 'substance', was given shape, resulting in physical nature. The 'pure form', which sets everything in motion, is the 'prime mover', pure thought – God, who thinks himself and therefore creates himself. Combining what they felt was useful and convincing in the two schools, the Christian thinkers-theologians of the first three centuries AD reworked the essence of this Platonic-Aristotelian body of ideas in a Christian sense.

Although the founding fathers of Christianity relied heavily on the philosophical speculations of the ancient Greeks, they were not at all happy with the notions the Greek philosophers had deduced from their study of physical nature. Man would not reach his destination, the Heavenly City as envisaged by St Augustine, by futilely delving into the secrets of microcosm or macrocosm. Indeed, these were not his to know. Nor were they of any use in man's efforts to ameliorate a life on earth that only served as preparation for a better life in the hereafter; indeed, the suffering inherent in that life was a necessary component of that preparation.

Meanwhile, the Christian intellectuals, in creating their synthesis, were opposed by such forceful critics as the scholar Porphyry (AD 234–301/6), Plotinus' student. He denounced the new movement as completely irrational and unphilosophical in his *Contra Christianos*, an attack against which Augustine, for instance, could defend himself only with some difficulty. However, as the Christian emperors intervened in theological debate, regarding discussions on cosmology and philosophy, they decided not to tolerate any destabilization of the religion of their choice: the works of men like Porphyry were publicly burnt on Constantine's orders.[5]

Of course, the ins and outs of these learned discussions eluded the majority of Christians. However, they were readily convinced by the notion of the existence of good and evil, and by the idea that man could escape his own inclination towards evil and, hence, injustice and misery only by submitting to God, whom one must love as one did one's neighbour. Moreover, they soon accepted it was only possible to obtain God's mercy and, thus, salvation by obeying the teachings and rules of the Church which God's son, Christ, had established on earth. These, then, were the foundations of the views of man and the world held by most 'Europeans' for almost the following nearly 2,000 years.

Meanwhile, in the prolonged 'crisis' that marked the end of the political unity of the Roman world in the fourth and fifth centuries, both in the eastern and the western empire intellectuals felt the need to articulate their own identity, to define a common fate. Whether poets, chroniclers or Church authorities, they all were part of the political elite and wrote their works in the service of State or Church.[6]

In the western empire – the region on which this book will mainly concentrate – this common fate gradually became linked to Christianity, now increasingly seen as the one basic characteristic and indeed the redeeming characteristic of a geographically well-defined world, which by and large coincided with (western) Europe.

Soon, the bishops of Rome, or 'the popes', saw their newly gained power over the Christian world threatened by their main competitors within the Church, the Christian patriarchs of Constantinople. Fundamentally, their claim to supremacy was founded on a passage in the gospel of Matthew – chapter 16, verses 18–19 – wherein the disciple Simon acknowledges Jesus as God's son. Jesus then tells Simon that as Peter, 'the Rock', he will be the foundation stone of Christ's Church, with the power 'to bind and loose both in heaven and earth'. Hence, a tradition arose in which Peter was proclaimed to have been Christ's first Vicar on Earth and the first bishop of Rome. From the fourth century onwards, St Peter's grave, reputedly situated in a Roman cemetery below the seventeenth-century marble altar under a huge baroque bronze canopy that now fills the enormous space beneath the cupola of St Peter's in Rome, became a centre of pilgrimage for many believers. However, their religious supremacy was by no means absolute, not even in the western empire, although they tried to turn it into an independent religious and cultural region over which, as by divine right, they now claimed political dominion as well. As there was no gospel text to base this claim on, the popes invented the so-called 'Donation of Constantine', which had purportedly given them secular rule over the western half of the Roman Empire when the emperor himself had left for the eastern part.

Despite these power struggles, the bishops of Rome – the historical continuity of their line is much disputed – often came out victorious in the many doctrinal disputes with other Christian groups in the Mediterranean-Christian world. However, though they now claimed both spiritual and temporal control over the entire Church, their power, such as it was, was effectively limited to the Roman parts of western Europe. Increasingly, though, from the fifth century onwards they sent out missionaries to Christianize the worlds beyond the old Roman frontier, thus soon extending their power to northern and central Europe as well, bringing to those regions a new culture. I will try to indicate what that culture was, and how it was spread to become, in the end, the foundation of European culture as we know it.

As the old Greek notion of Europe – a world, a society defined by its geography and climate – was incorporated into Christian thought during the early centuries of the Christian era, the conversion of the old Graeco-Roman elite, schooled in the ideals of *paideia*, ensured that the concepts of man and civilization, which had been attached to this world, now became part of Christian culture as well. Soon, the educated Christians interpreted the central text of the Christians, the Bible, and especially the Old Testament, with the Greek geographical names and the concepts implicit therein at the back of their mind.

After all, this readership, the elite of the Christian faithful, had to try and understand why the world as they knew it, the world around 'our sea', was so varied, especially in its different races and cultures. More specifically, the political and cultural leaders needed to show why their civilization was the most important and therefore worth defending and, even, expanding.

This resulted in a fascinating religious-cultural construction. It was based on a story told in Genesis, the first book of the Old Testament: the story of Noah who, with his family and a specimen of each of the animal species, was the only one to survive the great flood that destroyed mankind. In Christian thinking, his three sons now were identified with the inhabitants of the three known worlds. Thus, Shem became the patriarch of the Semites, the inhabitants of Asia. Ham, who, having mocked his father for his drunkenness, had been cursed for it, became the patriarch of the Hamites, the inhabitants of Africa; at a much later date Europeans used the story to argue the inherent cursedness of the Africans and, thus, their natural slavery. Finally, Japheth became the patriarch of the Japhites, the inhabitants of Europe.[7] In most European texts describing the earth – for example, the seventh-century *Historia Brittonum* – these are the three groups who populate the three continents, i.e. the entire world. At the same time, in his seventh-century encyclopedia, Isidore of Seville, the leading intellectual light of the Visigoth kingdom of Spain, argued that the people living in his specific part of the world were especially blessed by God. For their world, unlike the worlds of Africa and Asia, was the 'Christian world'.[8] Inevitably, it was also the world of civilization, because it had first been the Roman world. Moreover, not only the Romans but all those who had come into contact with the Roman Empire, such as the Franks – and, of course, the Visigoths to whom Isidore himself belonged – were the progeny of one of Japheth's descendants, Alanus.[9]

One religion for all: the fusion of Christianity and Europe

Indeed, many of the 'barbaric' tribes who had been migrating into western Europe had absorbed the conquered region's culture, religious as well as linguistic, for example in adopting Latin or one of its regional variants. The process can best be witnessed in the elites of these peoples who, even if they may not always have accepted Roman-Christian religion and culture out of conviction, quickly realized that it was an effective means of retaining or even increasing their power.

By AD 403, the Christian intellectual Prudentius had already internalized a fascinating teleological vision of history in which, even before the birth of Christ, the Roman Empire had developed as an ideal political and cultural unity precisely because, at a later stage and according to God's plan, it had to provide the basis for the spreading of the Christian message that would ultimately save mankind. For Prudentius, the Roman Empire's borders inevitably coincided with those of the Christian world: there, faith and reason would now merge. This, of course, is a significant pronouncement on the two elements which, according to Prudentius, had been introduced into European life by the Christian and Roman cultures, respectively. However, observing that 'Life, but not merit, is given to everyone', he also asserted that 'an abyss separates the Roman forms of life from the barbaric, just as man is separated from the animals, the mute from those who speak'.[10]

Indeed, the tribes and peoples from northern and eastern Europe who continued to advance on the prosperous south-west between the fourth and tenth centuries, settling within the Roman-Christian world, often were viewed with disdain by those who had already been Romanized at an earlier stage. One of these tribes were the Longobards, who conquered northern and central Italy and were soon felt to threaten the Pope's position. Consequently, in AD 739, Pope Gregory III sought the help of the Frankish leader, Charles Martel who, formally speaking, usurped the throne that had been held by the Merovingian kings, the descendants of Chlodwig,[11] and therefore needed the Pope's help to legitimize and even sanctify his rule. A papal chronicler wrote:

> The province subject to Roman government was smitten by the wicked Longobards and their King, Liutprand. Coming to Rome, he pitched his tents in the field of Nero, ravaged the Campagna, and forced many Roman nobles to shave and dress in the Lombard fashion. Therefore the man of God [i.e. Pope Gregory III], oppressed with grief on every side, took the holy keys from the grave of the blessed Apostle Peter and sent them by sea to the land Francia, to the most wise Charles [i.e. Charles Martel], who then ruled the Frankish kingdom, by his ambassadors, the most holy Bishop Anastasius and the priest Sergius, to ask the most excellent Charles to free them from this great oppression by the Longobards.[12]

After one or two generations, the erstwhile foes had mostly been assimilated into Roman-Christian culture. Soon, they internalized its merits and virtues to such an extent that one of their chroniclers could clearly, albeit idealistically, describe his situation as follows:

> The Longobards . . . have abandoned their barbaric savagery, perhaps because they married natives and begot children who derived something of the mildness and wisdom of the Romans from the blood of their mothers and from the properties of the country and climate. Even now they retain the elegant Latin speech and polished manners. In the government of their cities and the service of their commonwealth they still copy the skilful methods of the ancient Romans. They are so eager for freedom that they recoil from excess of power and are ruled by the will of consuls rather than of dictators [*imperantes*]. And as it is known that there are three estates among them, consisting of captains, vavasours and people, consuls are chosen, in order that arrogance may be suppressed, not from one estate alone, but from every estate; and lest they be seized with a lust for power, they are changed nearly every year. Hence it happens that almost all the land is divided between the cities . . . and it is almost impossible to find any noble or magnate, even in so wide an area, who does not obey the orders of his city. The cities . . . do not scorn to promote to knighthood and to offices of various ranks young men of inferior condition, and workers engaged in low, even manual trades, whom other peoples thrust out like the plague from the freer and more honourable pursuits. Hence it happens that they far surpass all other cities in the world in wealth and power.[13]

Meanwhile, Christianity itself had become as expansionist as the Roman Empire had ever been. In about AD 550, St Prosper of Aquitaine argued that 'Christ's mercy was not satisfied only to reach the borders of Rome: it has already brought many peoples who were never compelled by Rome's arms to submit to the lordship of the Church of Christ'.[14] This argument highlights an important development. With the demise of the Roman Empire, the Christian Church felt it had become its heir in many respects. Having adopted its bureaucratic structure, it had gained great organizational strength. Now, it also took on the civilizing ideology of the Romans, proclaiming that to a world of 'barbarians', a world of tribal chiefs and their loosely organized kingdoms, it would bring such important, albeit mundane services as literacy and legislation, which helped create centralized power besides, of course, promising them eternal salvation.

It was precisely the Roman popes who felt they could use the fading memory of a once powerful empire to build a new one. For example, in AD 597, Pope Gregory the Great sent the monk Augustine to England, not because, as the story went, he was struck by the angelic beauty of the blond boys sold in the Roman slave market but because he remembered that 'Anglia' had once been a thriving part of the Roman Empire. Relying on the structures, cultural and political, that still remained, might not Roman missionaries induce the local rulers to submit to the Church's growing dominion?[15] Gregory was not disappointed. Within fewer than twenty years, the monks sent by the Pope had helped the Anglo-Saxon kings to codify more than ninety laws,[16] not forgetting to ensure the position of the new religion.

Indeed, in the process of Christian expansion that took place between the fourth and tenth centuries and went far beyond the former Roman frontier, a new 'cultural space' came into existence, hesitantly at first but gradually more noticeably. In the eighth century, Christianity, and with it Graeco-Roman culture, reached present-day central Germany. Here, among the 'wild tribes of Germania', Boniface (*c.*674–754), coming from England, preached a new religion. He had first travelled to Thuringen via 'Bavaria and the border areas of Germania's unknown areas' to convert the heathen tribes there. Later, while in Rome, the Pope honoured him with 'a book in which were written the holy laws of the Church, laid down by the synods of bishops, and an order . . . that he teach the people entrusted to him according to these examples'. And so he tried. Finishing Boniface's biography, the monk Willibald was able to record the saint's successes: 'and so it happened that the message of his sermons became known everywhere, to such an extent that his name resounded almost all over Europe'.[17] Christianity and Europe slowly but surely became 'one'. The process was not an easy one. Boniface, for one, paid for it with his death – but gained his martyrdom and sainthood.

The rise of a new empire: Frankish statecraft and Christian arguments

The various tribes who had settled in central and western Europe during the last centuries of Roman rule soon developed some sort of state-structure. However, at least until the twelfth century, power in these early states was actually exercised by regional or even local lords and their soldiers, rather than by central authorities, if only because to be effective in an illiterate society any order had to be given by mouth, and its effects checked personally. And illiterate the new, post-Roman culture certainly was.

Often, the conquerors or war leaders gave land grants to those members of their family or followers who had aided them, thus creating a lineage-system society. They also confirmed the possessions of those families of the indigenous, older, senatorial aristocracy who had not opposed them; the latter, however, enjoyed their income, derived from the farming population, not so much by right of kinship with the new ruler, but under an older tributary tradition that had developed in the Roman Empire. Soon, these two systems merged. For even though the power relationships in these proto-states were, at the beginning, highly personalized, over the following centuries the situation was slowly stabilized and formalized. Increasingly, the new landowners, too, rather than invoking an ever more distant connection with the original conqueror and his successors, ruled their subjects by right of birth, and by right of the political-administrative functions they had acquired within the state, which often became hereditary. By and large, the farming population of Europe retained its freedom, though, of course, the new rulers eagerly adapted the pre-existing systems of taxation and 'corvées' – or forced labour – to their own use.

Inevitably, sometimes, the new ruling families gradually lost part of their power to the magnates of their state, precisely because, in trying to defend the independence of their new states, they often needed to buy military support by again granting the magnates lands from the princely domain.

However, within those regions of Europe that had formerly been part of the Roman Empire, the new central rulers seem to have retained some of their authority, because it was now based on the residual Roman notion of a state governed by a lawful sovereign who dispensed justice to the state's subjects.[18] Often, though, this was enforced by some kind of divine right, invoked through a supposed relationship with ancient heroes, or demigods, even though this pagan notion was Christianized as well, with the kings now being anointed by the senior priest of their state. Indeed, it was by virtue of this fiction that until the end of the seventeenth century, both the English and the French kings, after their coronation-cum-anointing, would lay their supposedly healing hands on hundreds or even thousands of people suffering from such illnesses as scrofula.

Inevitably, both the ruling princes as well as the magnates sought to increase their power by means of dynastic alliances or simple conquest. As indicated above, on the territory of Roman Gaul, the leaders of the Franks successfully did so. However, despite the successes of the Merovingian dynasty, the ensuing process of unification by which the remains of the western empire which largely came to coincide with the world of Roman Christendom is always identified with Charles (*c.*742–814) – whose epithet 'the Great' was added later. He was the energetic and apparently charismatic member of the Carolingian family who, having deposed the Merovingian kings, used the tradition of their authority and skilfully manipulated the Frankish nobles to greatly expand their royal authority.[19] This was, however, achieved, perhaps, at the cost of granting them more royal land and even certain sovereign rights in the field of local jurisdiction.

Charlemagne himself, succeeding to power in a kingdom that encompassed large parts of present-day France, Belgium, Switzerland and the south of the Netherlands, soon succeeded in also gaining power over western and central Germany, northern Italy and northern Spain, in the process establishing Christianity among all the tribes that he subdued.

Realizing that a strong kingdom could exist only on the basis of a strong economy, Charlemagne continued an economic policy adopted by his predecessors.[20] He knew, as they had known, that a strong economy could not rely on agriculture only, certainly not if it were to produce the surplus and hence the fiscal revenue the Frankish kings needed for their expansionist policy. Trade had to be revived and to stimulate it, a common, stable, reliable currency had to be introduced if he were to reach his aim. Therefore, he encouraged Frankish trade through the network of major trading towns that stretched from the northern Netherlands to northern Germany and Scandinavia and, from there, to the eastern coasts of the Baltic Sea, whence trade routes led through Russia, along the Volga basin, to the Black Sea. In this seemingly improbable way, Frankish trade reached the markets of the Near East and central Asia and, thus, the silver the Frankish rulers needed to reform the coinage was obtained.

Of course, Charlemagne also tried to revitalize trade between the Mediterranean coasts of Europe and the trading centres of northern Africa and the Levant. In this, too, he was successful. During his reign, both the wealth and the power of the Frankish kingdom grew.

Without anyone being aware of it, Frankish policy was considerably helped by the fact that in the fourth and fifth centuries, another climate change had occurred. Europe now became drier, and water seems to have been in short supply – folklore and legends talk about this problem. However, with the seas less stormy, and the Alpine passes open for longer periods of the year, both sea trade and overland trade could only profit from the new situation.

To further enhance his authority and thus his power, in the year 800, Charlemagne went to Rome, the holy city of Christianity, there to be rewarded by the Pope with the imperial crown. Thus, he became the first in a long line of 'Holy Roman Emperors' which ended only when, in 1806, Napoleon I of France decided to dismantle the Holy Roman Empire. To contribute to a growing sense of European identity, what happened in Rome more than 1,200 years before was soon interpreted as follows:

> After handing over the empire to Christ's vicar, Constantine went to Thrace, where Europe ends, and established a city there named after him. That was where the seat of the empire was until the time of Charles, in whose person Pope Adrian transferred the empire from the Greeks to the Germans.[21]

Thus, in historiography the Roman popes were accorded the power to bestow the imperial crown and title on whomever they wished, in this case transferring the heritage of Rome from the east, from Constantinople, to the west, to Charles's seat at Aachen, where the new emperor built a chapel deliberately echoing Roman ecclesiastical architecture – specifically and significantly harking back to the great octagonal church built by Constantine over the grave of Christ in Jerusalem.

To many – or at least to the intellectual elite of the west – it seemed as if the glory of the former Roman Empire had been resurrected, as if a true *renovatio imperii* had been realized. The two founts of ideal power, the terrestrial, realized in the 'universal' State, and the celestial, realized in the 'universal' Church, were again in communion. The Church, embodied in the Pope, Christ's Vicar on Earth and established in Rome, and the State, embodied in the emperor who sought his legitimacy at least partly in that state *par excellence*, the Roman Empire, were now locked in a holy alliance. Of course, the spiritual support of the Church of Rome and the military power of the empire were of mutual benefit to Pope and emperor – as long as they did not compete for actual supremacy both in religious and secular matters. Yet, however profitable it might seem in the short run, the collaboration between two such power institutions could not but be problematic in the long run.

Those who articulated imperial propaganda were the men of the Church. It was they who now controlled the imperial court – as the ruler's trusted collaborators – rather than the regional magnates, who were his competitors. Thus, the intellectuals of Charlemagne's time, mainly monks and priests,[22] proclaimed that God supported this young king from a young people and blessed his victories, the obvious reward for the emperor's piety and his policy of the Christianization of civilization. What could be more meaningful now than to define the area over which he claimed dominion as 'Europe' and thus present it once again as a logical, complete unity?[23] Soon, Charlemagne's principal confidant, Alcuin (*c*.735–804), and the emperor's biographer, Einhard (*c*.770–840), presented him as the man who did indeed wield the *regnum Europae*.[24]

However, Charlemagne not only embarked on a policy of Christianization, thus broadening the power of this ecclesiastical court elite, but he also attempted to preserve what little was left in the west of Graeco-Roman civilization. Indeed, though he could not have done so without the help of his clerical advisors, it was he himself who had the vision to make this culture into a way of life for his court as well as for the warrior elite who administered his realm. The obvious reason was, of course, that Charlemagne and his supporters needed an ideology that would give cohesion and unity to the constantly expanding Frankish Empire.[25]

Thus, the Frankish kings situated themselves in the tradition of the ancient Roman emperors and proclaimed themselves the rightful heirs to their empire, as is shown from a letter which, in 871 AD, one of Charlemagne's successors, Emperor Louis II, sent to his colleague and 'competitor', the Byzantine *basileus* Basil I. The latter, as well as his ancestors, in trying to uphold the fiction of the one, undivided Roman Empire, were willing to recognize the rulers of the barbarians in the west only when they acceded to be the 'representatives' of the only true Christian emperors, who, as Constantine's successors, ruled in Byzantium. Now, the arguments used by the Franks were mostly derived from the Bible and the merit the Carolingian kings had earned by their own conversion to Christianity and their policies of converting other peoples. However, historical and cultural arguments were also used in another way. The policy of the Jews towards Christ is interpreted negatively, and the bond between the Franks on the one hand, and Rome and Latin on the other – the city and the language of civilization – are emphasized. Note, too, how the Byzantines' use of Greek and their 'abandonment' of Rome are held against them. In fact, the text presents all the elements that would determine the self-image of the Europeans in the west for centuries to come:

> the Frankish race has borne the Lord much very fertile fruit, not only by being quick to believe, but also by converting others to the way of salvation. Hence the Lord rightly warned you: 'The Kingdom of God shall be taken from you and given to a nation which bears him fruit' [Matthew 21.43] God was able, out of stones, to raise up children for Abraham [Matthew 3.9], and so he could also, out of the hardness of the Franks, raise up heirs to the Roman Empire. If we belong to Christ, we are, according to the Apostle, the seed of Abraham [Paul to the Galatians 3.29]; and if we belong to Christ, we can, by his grace, do everything which those who belong to Christ can do. As we, through our faith in Christ, are

the seed of Abraham, and as the Jews for their treachery have ceased to be the sons of Abraham, we have received the government of the Roman Empire for our right thinking or orthodoxy. The Greeks for their cacodoxy, that is, wrong thinking, have ceased to be Emperors of the Romans – not only have they deserted the city and capital of the Empire, but they have also abandoned Roman nationality and even the Latin language. They have migrated to another capital city [i.e. Byzantium] and taken up a completely different nationality and language.[26]

Culture and cohesion: the role of ideology and education in the shaping of Carolingian Europe, or the 'First Renaissance'?

The influence of scholars like Alcuin strongly persuaded Charlemagne to advance the cause of education all over his empire. Senior clergymen were urged to take the lead but the court nobles, who ruled the various parts of the realm, were asked to provide their establishments with schools – for the children of servants as well as for the sons of the free men who wanted an education.

The new educational ideal was clearly founded in a Christian way of life, since a better understanding of Holy Scripture would result in morally better and hence more civilized behaviour. Probably in AD 794 or 796, Charlemagne wrote to the well-known *Epistola de litteris colendis* ('Memorandum on the cultivation of learning') Abbot Baugulf of Fulda, admonishing this prelate and all the others who received similar orders as follows:

> Be it known to You, whose devotion is pleasing to God, that we and our loyal servants have considered it profitable that the bishoprics and monasteries committed by Christ's favour to our guidance should in addition to following the monastic way of life and living together under a holy rule, offer earnest instruction in the study of literature to those who, by the gift of God, are capable of learning, according to the capacity of each of them. Observing a rule imparts order and grace to honourable conduct, and perseverance in teaching and learning does the same for correct speech: so that those who are eager to please God by rightly living may not neglect to please Him by speaking correctly. . . .
>
> For although correct conduct may be better than knowledge, nevertheless knowledge precedes conduct. . . . Because of failure to learn, the uninstructed tongue could only faultily express what devout piety was faithfully dictating to the mind. Hence we began to fear that, there being too little skill in writing, there might also be far too little wisdom in understanding the Holy Scriptures. . . . Therefore we exhort you . . . not to neglect the study of letters. . . . Let men be chosen for this work who have the will and ability to learn and the desire to instruct others. And let this be done with a zeal as great as the earnestness with which we command it. We wish you, as befits soldiers of the Church, to be devout in thought and erudite in speech, chaste in your strict conduct and learned in your eloquence, so that if anyone seeks to see you out of reverence for the Lord or because of your noble and holy life, he may both be edified by your appearance and enlightened by the wisdom he perceives in your reading and singing, and may go home joyfully rendering thanks to Almighty God.[27]

Arguing, as some critics have done, that this educational policy only benefited the Church and the clergy seems to be a misreading the emperor's own political intentions to create a truly educated elite that would contribute both to cultural and religious unity and, hence, to the better governability and welfare of the empire. The emperor's ideas can be observed from a number of statements. Thus, addressing the clergy of his realm, he wrote:

> Therefore, because we take care constantly to improve the condition of our churches, we have striven with watchful zeal to advance the cause of learning, which has been almost forgotten by our ancestors; and, by our example, also we invite those whom we can to master the study of the liberal arts. Accordingly, God aiding us in all things, we have already corrected carefully all the books of the Old and New Testaments, corrupted by the ignorance of the copyists.

In AD 789, he admonished a number of his senior officials to 'join and associate to themselves not only children of servile condition, but also sons of free men. And let schools be established in which boys may learn to read'.[28] Of course, the ability to read, the teaching of reading even, presupposes texts that can be read. We know that Charlemagne ordered books from all parts of his realm to be collected in the imperial library at Aachen.[29] His biographer also tells us in the twenty-ninth chapter of the *Vita Karoli*, that the Emperor ordered the codification of German tribal laws as well as of the German heroic songs, both of which until then had only been transmitted orally.

Through the efforts of Charlemagne and his ecclesiastical advisers, the culture of the elite of the Christian Church slowly, and in a modified form, became the culture of the secular upper class as well. In the process, the Frankish state, which now covered a considerable part of western Europe, gradually acquired a character that was Germanic as well as Christian and, in fact, also Roman, with the remnants of Greek civilization being received mainly through the filter of Rome and through Latin. However, in a sense, this old, revived culture was now shared by a greater population than it had reached during Roman times since, under Charlemagne, a policy of expansion and colonization was initiated which pushed the borders of the Frankish Empire increasingly northwards and eastwards. Moreover, even though the Picts and the Frisians, the Goths and the Wends, the Balts and the Slavs were not subjected, they too came under the cultural influence of the Frankish Empire.

Admittedly, the political unity that such a large part of present-day western Europe had achieved under Charlemagne was lost again soon after his death. Yet western Europe's expansionist policies into central Europe continued. Often undertaken with the Church's wholehearted cooperation, these policies were pursued by the emperor's successors from the late ninth century onwards, specifically by the rulers of the German states that emerged from the break-up of Charlemagne's empire, until, in the fourteenth century, the limit of this expansion was reached: in the Baltic area, in Poland and in the Balkans. There, western European expansion encountered a formidable contestant for the possession of these regions: Greek Christianity, backed by the Byzantine emperors. Soon, the elites surrounding the Pope and emperor in the west decided that Graeco-Byzantine culture was decidedly 'different' and, even, a hostile and threatening force, despite its Christian character. Therefore, this region became an uncertain border area, disputed and, consequently, divided culturally, religiously and politically. Here, for centuries peoples have been confronted with choices that still tear them apart today.[30]

With the spread of Roman Christianity through missionaries who were supported equally by the popes, the Holy Roman Emperors and the various European princes, the Roman Church took on the organization of religious life in the entire area to the west of the invisible line stretching from the Baltic to the Balkans.[31] A truly transcontinental Church was now created. It became visible in the persons and the power of bishops and priests, in the monasteries and cathedral schools that educated the elites who now came to share and cherish the same norms and values all over this vast region. Consequently, in northern and central Europe, too, the Church and, with it, the cultured elite, began to refer to Rome as the one and only centre, as the south and west had done for some centuries already. These regions, though they had never submitted to the Roman Empire, now adopted a common, Christian ideology, and became part of its discourse. Gradually, this ideology was presented ever more outspokenly as a universal ideology, as, unquestionably, even the very essence of civilization.

To foster this communal ideology, the Church of Rome needed to give the hugely diverse peoples and tribes of Europe a common history. In this new history, in which all sorts of older legends about people's origins were adjusted or rewritten, the roots of the secular world – of power and culture – were traced back to the ancient Romans. The Romans, in their turn, were linked by their ancestor, Aeneas, to his forefathers, the Trojans, who were, *en passant*, identified with Greek culture, that could thus be made part of Europe's cultural ancestry. On the other hand, the roots of the religious world, the world where God's plan of salvation was played out, were inevitably traced to the Bible, to the Old and the New Testaments. However, in both spheres – secular and religious – the process that history was presented as having reached its fulfilment in Europe, in the West – or, as the historian Otto von Freising (d. 1158) wrote: 'As I said earlier, all human powers and possibilities, in this case, wisdom, come from the East, from Babylon, in order to be completed in the West'.[32]

In this one, simple sentence, the specific elements which were now seen as constituting Christian – 'European' – culture were clearly identified: power, to be understood as the result of human knowledge, wisdom, which in its turn was to be understood as the product of learning – and both, of course, the gift of God. Significantly, for Otto, the origin of this wisdom lay in Asia. Not, as one might have expected, in the Holy Land, but even further east in Mesopotamia where, it was assumed, God had first created man, had given him the powers of knowledge and had placed him in the garden of Eden.

To implement this ideology, which consisted of a history as well as a vision of the future, a specific curriculum – taught in Latin – had been devised, in which the seven *artes liberales* were divided into the *trivium*, the three fundamental subjects of grammatica, rhetorica and dialectica, and the *quadrivium*, the four more complex subjects of arithmetica, geometrica, astronomia and musica. In the centuries following the reign of Charlemagne, the teaching programme of the school attached to the imperial palace at Aachen became the prototype for numerous schools founded by the clergy all over Europe. These establishments now became the real centres of European culture.[33] As a result, Latin rapidly gained the character of a 'universal' language, facilitating communication between scholars in this nascent 'western world'; thus, language too contributed in no small degree to the genesis of a common culture in this region.

Still, to term the complex policy sketched above a 'first Renaissance', as has been done, is perhaps to misjudge it. It may seem like an attempt at a cultural *renovatio* of the old Roman Empire, but the actual aim was, mostly, pragmatic, i.e. to create the foundations of a Christian, Frankish Empire. Given the fact that this policy was instigated and executed by the Church, it did not aim at an 'objective', independent appreciation of ancient, Graeco-Roman culture in its own right – if only because many of its manifestations were condemned as pagan. Yet, in the process, many individual scholars, though all clerics, did preserve the better part of that pagan, classical culture for posterity.

Meanwhile, Roman Christianity ceased to be the religion and culture of an elite only. Indeed, it was practised by most people in the western part of Europe, although almost always in combination with numerous pre-Christian customs and all sorts of beliefs which the Church termed 'superstition' or, again, pagan. These included ways of thinking which for one reason or another were anathema to the ecclesiastical authorities, ranging from what was seen as sorcery and witchcraft – though a distinction was made between white and black magic – to soothsaying and alchemy, as well as various forms of astrology and kabala. Still, it is quite clear that well into the seventeenth century, i.e. for nearly 1,000 years, it was the clergy who continued to act both as the official, Church-appointed mediators between man and the divine as well as assuming the roles formerly played by the druids of the Celts or the priests of the German gods, often performing age-old rites which had been condemned by their own Church.

Indeed, as by now the majority of people in the Carolingian Empire were of Germanic origin, a 'Germanization' of Christianity was inevitable. The Church accepted this situation in a rational as well as emotional and psychological way, Christianizing many Germanic cultural phenomena: such festivals as the ones celebrating mid-winter and the subsequent return of light were fused with the holy day of the nativity of Christ to become an ever more complex Christmas feast. Such customs as, for instance, the festive annual markets were linked to the holy day commemorating the consecration of the local church, to sacralize and Christianize a secular occasion, and give the Church power over it. Even certain people, such as local seers, miracle workers or heroic rulers were often canonized, their cults being turned into the feasts of Christian saints.[34] In this way the various regional cultures were effectively merged into the one Christian culture.[35] Precisely because those cultural elements that most strongly influenced people's emotions – though they might be considered pagan and profane by the elite – were now brought under ecclesiastical influence, the diffusion of the basic ideas of Christianity was much facilitated.

Yet, religious and cultural uniformity were never completely realized. Indeed, deviant ideas, branded as heresies, were constantly formulated, showing that the Church was not able to provide all the answers to people's spiritual and material needs. Whether because of religious or intellectual scruples, or for economic, political and social reasons, individuals and groups would formulate and advocate alternative views of man, society and salvation, calling into doubt the certainties, the order and the security provided, at a cost, by the Church. Often, these people would try to reach the masses, using the vernacular instead of Latin, the language of the Church, which remained incomprehensible to most people in Europe. Thus, criticism, dissent and heterodoxy contributed to the growth of regional cultures, undermining the pretended unity of the Christian world.[36]

The impact of monasteries

The basic institutional structure of the Church as it had developed in the last centuries of the Roman Empire – fundamentally the system of bishoprics and, increasingly, the supremacy of the Roman papacy – continued to exist in most countries of western Europe that developed on territory formerly under Roman rule. Moreover, it was exported beyond that territory as Christianity itself spread to the north and east through the missionary efforts of its clergy and, often, the zeal of regional magnates and princes. Yet Christianity would not have become a major religious and cultural factor without the contribution of another of the Church's institutions, the monastery.

The monastic tradition – which, of course, is not unique to Christianity but also characterizes Hinduism and Buddhism – had its origins in the very regions where Christianity was born, i.e. in Palestine, Syria and Egypt. Retreating from the worries of the world into a private sphere of prayer and introspection, men and women used to go into the desert to live the solitary life of a hermit, or congregated into small communities devoted to pious contemplation. The 'first' Christian monastery proper – with separate establishments for males and females – was founded by St Pachomius in the Nile valley in the fourth century AD. Soon, many of these communities decided to adopt a common rule, to give cohesion to their congregation.

It was not long before the monastic tradition moved to the north, to the Byzantine Empire – even nowadays, Mount Athos in northern Greece is a veritable cluster of monasteries – and to the west, to northern Africa and to Europe. Mostly, these communities were looked upon with awe and reverence by common people and rulers alike, even when times were violent and devastation reigned. They were seen as places that belonged to God, where men and women communicated with heaven, setting an example to a world that would not or could not live a life of continuous piety.[37]

The mainstream tradition of western monasticism originated with Benedict of Nursia (*c.*480–543/7) – a Roman of noble ancestry who had entered the Church and, disappointed with its growing power and wealth, ended up founding a monastery on Monte Cassino – who decided to adapt an earlier, anonymous set of guidelines to structure his community. In the following centuries, this rule, later known as the 'Benedictine Rule', was adopted by hundreds of monasteries all over Europe, finding wide though not exclusive acceptance.

Benedict's ideas resulted in a variety of monastic manifestations. As to the monastery's formal organization, mature men wishing to enter, or boys influenced and inspired by their elders to do so, were usually obliged to spend some time in the 'novitiate' before being allowed to take the vows of chastity, obedience and poverty that constituted the essence of monkhood. Collectively, the community of monks in a given monastery elected an abbot, who ruled the establishment until he died, consulting the community when necessary. In female monasteries, the same rules prevailed.

The fundamentals of Benedictine life can be summed up in the two actions of praying and working. Prayer, seven times a day during the span of twenty-four hours, was combined with contemplation, through the study of theology and the reading of devotional literature and, soon, with a life of learning in general. To this end, the monastic *scriptoria*, where monks painstakingly copied the texts the Church needed, began to manufacture bibles and other texts for daily devotional use.[38] But monasteries also began to collect or transcribe texts of general literary and scientific interest, and to produce original scholarship. Codifying and commenting on the Gospels and on the wisdom of the fathers of the Church but also on the ideas of all those who had somehow contributed to humanity's welfare. Now, as indicated above, the European intellectual elite soon felt that somehow this had to include the works of those scholars and writers who had lived before the advance of Christianity. Indeed, there were even monks who stressed the need to preserve pre-Christian poetry as important and valuable for the development of a Christian culture,[39] although the often explicit sexual contents of, for example, Roman literature led to the expurgation or even elimination of a good many texts. Although it is unlikely that a number of texts that scrutinized the secrets of nature, of God's creation, all too closely were destroyed, over the centuries the Christian monks have been the major force in helping to preserve the manuscripts that contained the cultural heritage of antiquity.[40] In the twelfth century, the abbey of Cluny, in France, one of the grandest and wealthiest in Christendom, owned some 570 volumes – or *codices* – of manuscripts, while the cathedral of Durham, in England, had a library of 546 books, and the cathedral of Bamberg, in Germany, preserved 365 texts.[41]

Inevitably, being centres of learning, with important libraries, many monasteries became centres of education as well, producing scholars who, for centuries, have been influential in almost all fields of European culture. Thus, the magnificent monastery of St Gallen, in Switzerland, and later the abbey of Cluny, to name but two, attracted students from all over Europe, as did the schools attached to the cathedrals (these were the churches where a bishop resided, enthroned in his 'cathedra' or bishop's throne).

By pursuing a monastic career, some European women, whose opportunities in a secular, male-dominated society were severely restricted, were able to contribute to culture in a major way. The lady Hroswitha, abbess of the monastery of Gandersheim (*c*.930–70), left an important oeuvre of Latin poems on religious themes, an epic devoted to the Emperor Otto I and a series of plays which make her the first playwright of the post-classical European world.[42] The lady Hildegard (1098–1179), abbess of the Benedictine monastery of Bingen, also rightly gained fame in a number of fields: as a seer and a visionary, whose literary works are of great beauty and show her to have been thoroughly conversant with classical literature and philosophy; as an exorcist, who left fascinating texts with medical-magical ideas and conjurations; and also as a musical theorist.[43]

Besides daily prayer and, for those who were capable of it, scholarly endeavour, work in these monasteries was understood to be daily, manual labour in the fields, providing sustenance for each monk or nun and, thus, making the monastery as independent as possible of the world and its numerous distracting influences. Consequently, though individual poverty was part of 'the Rule', institutional wealth was soon in evidence all over monastic Europe. The majority of monasteries became very rich indeed, both through their own industry and through the often considerable bequests and donations, in money and landed property, from the faithful who wanted the monastic clergy to pray for their souls or to engage the support of these increasingly powerful institutions in all kinds of political machinations. Many monasteries became grand agricultural enterprises that were often worked by numerous tenant farmers who further increased the abbey's wealth with their rents. The more vigorous male monastic orders often chose to settle in agriculturally unpromising regions where, through the reclamation of vast stretches of waste land – for example, in parts of France and England, in the northern Netherlands, and in Pomerania and Silesia – they changed the countryside, thus altering Europe's visual aspect as well as its ecology.[44] While contributing to a 'Christianization' of the landscape, through their cultural influence they altered the European mind as well.

5 Three worlds around the Inner Sea

Western Christendom, eastern Christendom and Islam

Confrontation and contact from the sixth century onwards

With the gradual decline of an empire that had spanned the entire Mediterranean, the 'Inner Sea' became both a bridge and a battleground between the three religious traditions that were the heirs of the Roman Empire's Graeco-Hellenistic and Latin cultures. Between them, they divided this world, both politically and culturally.

In the south-east, the Arabs, driven by the inspiration of Islam, gained mastery over a large part of the Mediterranean's Asian and African shores. Islamic civilization – which, as will be argued below, is not Arab civilization – was one of the three successors to the Roman Empire[1] in that it was both stimulated by and resulted from opposition to the older Judaeo-Christian tradition and to Greek culture in the Near East. The power of Islam soon confronted the Byzantine Empire that had grown around the Aegean Sea in the north-east; it was a state that was also a Church and for 1,000 years desperately tried to hold on to the former eastern territories of Rome. And, finally, Islam collided with a Europe narrowly defined; it was a Europe that, in the north-west of Eurasia, mainly through the drive of the Roman Church had preserved the culture of ancient Rome to become the civilization of the Frankish world of the Occident. It has been argued that the strength and the longevity of these three empires derived from the vital alliance between state power and monotheistic religion and that, indeed, as long as heresies were somehow contained, their political structures remained intact as well.

The world of the Prophet: Islam

In the sixth century AD, a prophet appeared on the Arabian peninsula who preached a new religion. As with most prophets, for a long time his people did not heed him. Basically, when Muhammad (c.AD 570–632) began to teach his ideas about God and the world, the culture of the Arabs was the culture a deeply divided, tribal, nomadic economy and society, which interacted fruitfully with a series of prosperous ports, on the perimeter of the largely poor peninsula.

These formed a network in which commerce between the coasts of the Mediterranean and the Indian Ocean, and hence East Asia, was conducted via the Red Sea and the Persian Gulf.[2] The desert Arabs worshipped the forces of nature. The city dwellers adhered to a variety of religions, among which Judaism and Christianity figured prominently, alongside a number of other cults such as the one surrounding sacred objects like the famous Black Stone even now revered in Mecca's holy precinct, or *haram*. In Mecca, one of the rich trading towns on the edge of the vast desert, Muhammad was born around 570 of the Christian era, into the Hashemite clan of the wealthy tribe of the Kuraysh.

From AD 610 onwards, Muhammad, who had been a merchant all his life and, hence, had travelled widely, encountering many of the peninsula's cultures and religions, began receiving messages from Allah, which he soon started to communicate to his relatives. Slowly, his prophecies became more complex. Memorized and transmitted orally by a small but growing band of disciples, Muhammad's new religion and its precepts were only clearly revealed when, after the his death in AD 632, his teachings were codified in a manuscript text, the *Koran*, i.e. the 'Reading'. By then, the Prophet's followers knew that Allah was the only, invisible and yet omnipotent God, to whom all believers striving to attain the joys of paradise should profess their faith. In testimony of this, they should lead a life of honesty and piety. They should pray five times a day, they should fast during the month of Ramadan and, if at all possible, at least once in their lives make the pilgrimage, or *haj*, to Mecca and Medina, the cities where, respectively, Muhammad was born and died. By then, too, it was clear that Muhammad considered himself the last of a long line of prophets, which he himself traced back to Jesus of Nazareth, first, and from him to his earlier Jewish predecessors.

Indeed, Muhammad's new religion obviously owed much to this Christian-Judaeo-tradition.[3] Thus, in the second chapter of the *Koran*, Abraham is mentioned as the progenitor both of the Arabs, via his son Ishmael, and of the Jews, via his son Isaac. Abraham is also represented as the builder of the *Ka'ba*, the 'House of Worship' at Mecca, where the Black Stone was kept and which now became the central sanctuary of Islam. Indeed, Muhammad acknowledged that Islam, with both the Jewish and the Christian faiths, formed a unique triad, the *Ahl al-Kitab* (the 'People of the Book'), the three monotheistic religions that had shared origins in the world described in the Jewish Old Testament.

Studying the *Koran*, as well as the tales about the Prophet's life and sayings – the 'tradition' or *Sunna* – one is struck by the similarities both between the teaching and the life of Muhammad as it is now presented and the stories that, some 500 years earlier, had been woven around Jesus. As in Jesus' case, all discordant versions of Muhammad's sayings were soon suppressed and, finally, destroyed after his death to ensure that his successors controlled his tradition as it was embodied in the holy book, the believer's guide *par excellence*. Reading the first *sura* or chapter of the *Koran*, the *Sura al-Fatiha* ('Opening Chapter'), also called the *Umm al-Kitab* ('Mother of the Book'), it says:

In the Name of Allah, the Compassionate, the Merciful

1 Praise be to Allah, the Lord of the Worlds;
2 The Compassionate, the Merciful;
3 Master of the day of Judgment;
4 You alone do we worship, and to You alone we pray for help;
5 Guide us to the straight Way;
6 The Way of those whom You have favoured;
7 Not of those who have incurred your wrath. Nor of those who go astray.[4]

At first, Muhammad's views were not looked upon kindly by the majority of the Meccan people, if only because the religious elite of this multi-religious town feared competition from yet another creed. Hence, in AD 622, the Prophet had to flee, taking refuge in the city of Jathrib, later renamed *Madinat al-Nabi* ('The City of the Prophet') or Medina. This flight, known as the *hegira*, or *hijra* was later taken as the beginning of the Muslim calendar. In Medina, Muhammad's charismatic personality soon made him into a religious as well as a political and military leader. With his followers, who swore to wage a holy war or *jihad* in defence of their new faith and its prophet, he succeeded in capturing Mecca in AD 630. By his death, *Islam* – literally, the 'surrender to Allah's will' – had spread over the greater part of Arabia.

As the Prophet had not fathered any male children, the position as his successor or *caliph*, both in the religious and in the political leadership of the Islamic world, was disputed between, on the one hand, an elected heir and, on the other, his son-in-law Ali, the husband of his favourite daughter Fat(i)ma.[5] The bloody struggles that ensued shook the community of believers. Indeed, with the murder of Ali's son Husayn, in AD 680, the *umma* (the Islamic world) finally split into two. One part, believing in the resurrection of Ali's descendants, formed the Shi'ite community, most of whom inhabit present-day Iraq and Iran. The other, by far the larger group (70 to 80 per cent), are known as the Sunnites, who claim to be the true keepers of the Prophet's tradition. Both groups soon developed doctrinal differences, although they are easily recognizable as stemming from the same root.

Despite and, indeed, sometimes in consequence of the wars of succession, the armies of Islam succeeded in conquering Syria, in AD 639, and Egypt, in AD 642 – the major Near Eastern possessions of the Byzantine Empire. From there they entered the west, capturing Byzantine North Africa.[6] In the East, too, Islam was successful. In AD 651, the caliphs even occupied faraway Persia. Meanwhile, merchants and traders, converted to the new faith, who tradition-ally sailed the Indian Ocean along the 'Spice Road', spread Islam to India and even to the Far East, especially present-day Indonesia, as did those who dared follow the desert trail – the Silk Road – into central Asia and the western provinces of China.

Ruling first from Damascus and, as the centre of Islamic economic and political power moved eastwards, from Baghdad, the caliphs' first concern was to pacify and unite their vast territories in North Africa and the Near East. On the whole, wherever possible they respected local religion and custom – in other words, the Christian culture established there. Yet, to ensure their military and political control over their growing realm and its enormous fiscal possibilities, they pursued a policy of colonization, settling persons of unquestionable Islamic rectitude all over their dominions. Still, in the end, the erstwhile political unity of Islam was lost, precisely because the empire had, after all, grown too big and, hence, had become ungovernable.

From AD 711 onwards, Islamic forces crossed the Straits of Gibraltar – *Gibr al-Tarik*, the 'Rock of Tarik' – and began to conquer the Iberian peninsula, completing their conquest in AD 718 but for a small group of Christian principalities in the unhospitable north-west. However, these conquerors were not Arabs at all, but Islamicized Berbers from the Maghreb who, moreover, soon disclaimed their obedience to the Islamic caliph in the east. In 'Spain', they set up a number of states of their own, of which the caliphate of Cordoba was by far the most powerful. Exploiting the fertile fields of *al-Andalus* (the south), as well as the rich trade with their native North Africa and, from there, with sub-Saharan Africa and the Levant, Islamic Iberia grew wealthy indeed. Soon, the city of Cordoba was also a major cultural centre, with a huge mosque, founded in AD 786 to rival the main Islamic sanctuaries of Mecca and Jerusalem – where the 'Dome of the Rock' now marked the place from where Muhammad had been allowed to enter heaven. Attached to the Cordoba mosque an important university and a great library catered for the needs of students and scholars from all over the Islamic world who gathered there to study, to teach and to do research.

Besides Islamic Spain, the Maghreb and Egypt soon claimed independence of the Baghdad caliphate, too. Consequently, from the ninth century onwards, the Islamic empire was divided up into many independent dynasties. Still, Islamic culture retained its unity, precisely because of the strength of its two major unifying factors: the religion preached by Muhammad and the Arabic language, which was now considered the unique, the holy language because it was the language in which Allah had revealed the *Koran*.

Significantly, since the Prophet had declared himself the last of God's messengers, Islam could not accept the authority of a priesthood that would presume to further develop its theological and other religious ideas. Indeed, after many disputes, the *Koran* itself, as God's revelation of his eternal truths – in the second *sura*, the *Sura al-Baqara*, it reads: 'This is the Book in which there is no doubt, in it is guidance for those who fear God' – was widely held to be eternal with God and, hence, unchangeable. In consequence, it could not even be translated. This, obviously, was an unworkable situation, for if a religion does not live and change, even slightly, then it will inevitably disappear. It was not long before a number of learned men claimed they were well suited to explain all that was unclear in the *Koran*'s 144 *suras* and, even more so, in the vast corpus of sayings attributed to Muhammad. Consequently, by the ninth century, the six books of the *Sunna* supplemented the holy book as a source from which rules for Islam could be dictated. Together, the holy book and the tradition of the Prophet now provided the basis for daily life in its religious as well as in all its secular forms, welding together the disparate cultures of the many worlds conquered by Islam, which soon stretched from Morocco to Malaysia.

The second factor in this process of unification was the common language: Arabic. It was the language of the holy book, of Muhammad and his first followers and hence also the language of the first generation of Islamic conquerors, the new elite. Soon, in the many states of the Islamic world, everyone aspiring to a position of influence under the new regime realized not only that conversion to Islam was mandatory but also that Arabic was the language of religion and, therefore, of power. However, it has to be admitted that, up to the present day, to the vast majority of the inhabitants of the Islamic world, Arabic, the Arabic of the *Koran*, is an entirely artificial language – as was, of course, the case with Latin in the Christian world. Basically, Koranic Arabic was and is memorized – if not always comprehended – through assiduous recitation of the holy book. Consequently, though fully mastered by only, a small, and marginally understood by, only a wider readership, outside the Arabian peninsula it never became a vehicle for the everyday culture. For daily usage, the newly converted peoples continued to speak their own language. In some regions, though, new languages originated from a mixture of the old, regional tongues and the recently imported Arabic one – here, again, mirroring linguistic-cultural developments in Europe in the wake of the growing religious–intellectual pre-eminence of Latin.

As to the civilization of Islam, it has to be understood that in many of its manifestations it was, indeed, a splendidly creative continuation the conquerors had encountered when confronted with the Greek-Byzantine culture of the Near East and North Africa. However, with the advance of Islam, this Islamicized Greek-Byzantine culture spread far beyond that world to large parts of Africa and Asia, where it continues to flourish to the present day. Some would even argue that the Muslim victory was the final fulfilment of antique civilization, since the God-given power claimed by the early caliphs was nothing less than the continuation and perhaps even realization of the political and religious universalist dream of Constantine – a dream that lives on in some of the pan-Islamic tendencies of today.

Yet, in many ways the new Islamic or Islamicized intellectual and artistic elites went far beyond this Greek-Byzantine culture. For example, in AD 830, the Caliph al-Ma'mun founded the famous 'House of Wisdom' in Baghdad – a library and an academy for the translation of texts deemed important for a culture that truly honoured Allah's creation, as well as for original research.[7] Again, one might argue that this development had its parallel in the Christian world of Charlemagne, though at this stage the intellectual breath and vigour of Islamic culture undeniably far surpassed what went on in the west.[8] In Baghdad, such scholars as the Nestorian Christian Husayn ibn-Ishaq, a physician by training, produced translations of the medical treatises of classical authors such as Dioskurides, Galen and Hippokrates. At the same time, Islamic doctors engaged in such practical research as, for example, the anatomy of corpses – not allowed in the Christian world – and the analysis of brain functions and of blood circulation. Together, these two approaches resulted in both a medical theory and a medical practice that were far superior to the dismal state of medical science and health care in the west. In Baghdad, too, Plato's *Republic* and several of Aristotle's texts were translated. However, they also were commented upon. For while diligently translating Greek scientific literature – and thus preserving it for posterity as the Christian monks did – Islamic scholars soon contributed their own ideas as well. Often, an originally Greek text, whether scientific, philosophical or medical would evolve into a different one, offering critical perspectives and new views. Thus, in the field of mathematics, while using Greek as well as Hindu concepts – Islamic scholars developed the much more sophisticated 'algebra'. Moreover, Al-Khwarizmi (AD 790–840) wrote in 830 AD, a treatise in which he dealt with the proper use of the Arabic (but actually Indian) numerals – the original one to nine to which he added the zero – which helped make arithmetic a simple system, greatly facilitating its use both for scientific and practical purposes, in education and, of course, commerce. Indeed, when, at a much later stage, counting in Arabic rather than in the cumbersome old Roman way was introduced into European commerce, it revolutionized European practices as well. Continuing a long Greek-Near Eastern tradition of empirical observation of the heavens and earth, Islamic scholars also made great headway both in astronomy and the earth sciences, including geography, and in the related fields of technology, producing star charts, maps and nautical instruments.

In the decorative arts as well as in architecture, Islamic architects created beauty beyond the prototypes they found in the Hellenistic-Byzantine world, as shown by the great mud mosques of Djenne and Timbuktu, in sub-Saharan Mali, and the stone- and brick-built ones of Cordoba, in Spain, with its huge minaret – now the bell-tower of the cathedral that was built within the mosque after the Christian conquest of the town –, of Cairo in Egypt, where the Ibn Tulun mosque stands out, and of Isfahan, in Iran or of Samarkand, in Uzbekistan. Of course, there are also the palaces of Granada, the famous Alhambra, and of Delhi, the equally famous Red Fort. Given the fact that, basically, Islam did not allow the representation of religion – hence, no religious art comparable to the Christian tradition developed – people found an outlet for their artistic desire in decorating buildings, tapestries and, indeed, texts in geometric designs and in calligraphy; consequently, illuminated Koranic manuscripts are still among the best splendours of Islamic artistic culture.

In literature, too, Islamic writers produced major works. Thus, the fecund storytelling tradition of the nomadic Arabs soon combined with motives and themes from the older folklore of the regions they now conquered – the Egyptian, Greek and Hebrew tales. This resulted in the great collection of the *Thousand and One Nights*. Fascinatingly, long before its final codification in the fourteenth century, numerous stories told by the ill-used Scheherazade – the female teller who, to prevent death for herself and her friends, has to entertain her cruel master with an endless succession of amusing and exciting tales – had found their way to the Christian west, due to one of the most untraceable but also most persistent ways of cultural transfer, oral communication. Consequently, a considerable part of the stories Europeans have deemed to be part of their own tradition from time immemorial – and indeed they were handed down from generation to generation by the storytellers who toured the countryside and the towns in England, France and Germany – first came to Europe from the Islamic world. Admittedly, they originated even beyond the Near East, coming from as far as Persia and India. In lyric poetry, too, the Arab world achieved marvellous results which, again, influenced Europe, specifically via Islamic Spain.

In short, it has been said, not without some truth, that 'while al-Rashid and al-Ma'mun [two of the early caliphs] were delving into Greek and Persian philosophy, their contemporaries in the West, Charlemagne and his lords, were reportedly dabbling in the art of writing their name'.[9] An exaggeration though this may be – the story that Charlemagne could not really write is a fable – by the eighth and ninth centuries AD, the cultural achievements of the Islamic east far outshone those of the Christian west and continued to do so for several hundred years to come. Indeed, for 1,000 years, the economic and cultural capitals of the (Eurasian) world were not London, Paris or even Rome. They were Baghdad, Cordoba and Damascus or, for that matter, Constantinople and, one might add, Hangzhou, Heyan-kyo and, in the Americas, Tenochtitlán.

God's kingdom among men: orthodox Christendom

Since the fifth century, the Roman emperors of the east, accepting the impossibility of keeping the entire empire under their control, decided to concentrate on the domains of Asia Minor, Syria, Egypt and North Africa, leaving the west, reluctantly, to the Franks, who were, to them, the barbarian usurpers of Italy and Roman Gaul. Byzantium, their capital on the Bosporus, had now become Constantinople, a magnificent city, with marvellous marble palaces sprawling over the hilltops, and crowned by the Hagia Sophia, the huge church of 'Holy Wisdom', adorned with golden mosaics and surmounted by an enormous cupola – a feat not only of architecture and engineering but also of Christian faith.

Indeed, in the Byzantine Empire, Church and State, faith and politics were closely associated, not to say intrinsically linked: they constituted one organic structure, a mimesis, or imitation on earth of the kingdom of heaven. This theocracy was ruled by the *basileus*, the emperor, a semi-sacerdotal figure, God's immediate representative among men.

If anything, Byzantine civilization was the most direct heir of the Graeco-Hellenistic culture that for hundreds of years had dominated the eastern part of the Mediterranean. Yet it was fundamentally influenced by the introduction of Christianity. The Orthodox Church, so called because it claimed to be true to the original Christian faith – unlike the Church of Rome – became the prime creative element in Byzantine culture, shaping every single aspect of life there.

Indeed, political dispute and strife were always connected with, if not directly caused by, theological issues, if only through the great degree of informed lay participation in Church affairs.

On the one hand, the Byzantine elite consisted of the patricians of 'The Town' – after all, they thought of Constantinople as the true successor to that first of towns, Rome, styling themselves the inhabitants of the second or rather 'new' Rome – with their huge estates spread all over the empire. However, the realm was also ruled by the leading oligarchies of the provincial capitals. Together, they held to the ideal of the Christianized *paideia*. The higher ideal, however, was union with God – through asceticism, which explains the great regard for, and even greater power of, the many monasteries in the empire; indeed, in the Byzantine world, monastic might surpassed the influence of the great abbeys in the world of Roman Christendom.

On the whole, Byzantine society was an educated one. Primary education, widely available, sometimes even at the village level and, what is more, for both sexes – a thing unheard of in the Christian west until some 1,000 years later – ensured a high level of literacy. Female participation in culture, generally, was extensive, with many aristocratic women studying, engaging in research and writing. Scholarship was held in high esteem, fostered both in the great university of Constantinople, founded in AD 425, and in the important institutions of learning in such major provincial cities as Antioch and, of course, Alexandria.

The empire experienced its first flowering in the sixth century, specifically during the reign of Emperor Justinian, an able administrator who ordered the codification of ancient Roman Law as it then functioned, thus contributing greatly to its survival. The seventh and eighth centuries, however, saw both internal dissension and external assault.

A great conflict broke out when the worship of icons, the images of Christ and the saints, which by many educated believers was considered idolatry, was forbidden. However, the majority of the population and, even more, the monasteries, the main repositories of the icons and the recipients of the vast wealth their veneration brought, were furious. Peace was restored only when the images were restored. If anything, it gave even more power to the monasteries, such as the great complex on Mount Athos. Soon, they became a major factor in economic life, not only in agriculture but also in trade.[10]

Meanwhile, with the advance of Islam in the Near East and North Africa during the seventh century, the Byzantine Empire, relinquishing so many of its provinces lost not only a considerable part of its fiscal capacity and hence of its military power – taxes were raised in the remaining parts of the empire, resulting in growing popular unrest – but also the line of defence that shielded its capital. From then on, the empire was more or less continuously at war against the forces of Islam. It was a war it would finally lose, with the famous fall of Constantinople in 1453. There was little consolation in the fact that, in the mean time, its civilization had greatly contributed to the formation of Islamic culture.

From the sixth century onwards, cultural contacts with the 'Franks', as the people of the west were often called, slowly increased.[11] The great commercial centres of Italy, such as Venice and Genoa, which tried to re-establish trade in the Mediterranean after the chaos of the fifth and sixth centuries, were especially influenced by Byzantium. The decoration of the great churches at Ravenna – a sometime outpost of the Byzantines – as well as the mosaics and stained glass that still adorn St Mark's basilica in Venice evince their Byzantine origins. Indeed, all over Italy, religious art and, moreover, the liturgy of the Church itself were for a long time influenced by Byzantine examples. And although one may question the claim that western painting originated in the Orthodox east, for several centuries religious painting all over the Christian world of Europe was undeniably influenced by Byzantine examples, as witnessed by the art production at the court of Charlemagne, which shows some Byzantine traces,[12] and the 'iconic' style of the frescos that adorned the walls of the great abbey church at Cluny.

In one field at least, a truly complex and fascinating amalgam seems to have been created. Recent musicological research suggests that what the western Church calls Gregorian chant, the liturgical music of Rome that originated in the fifth century AD, cannot have sounded as we have heard it over the past 150 years. Rather, it must have resembled its actual origins: early Byzantine and perhaps even Jewish music and, moreover, at least in those parts of Roman Christendom that were influenced by Islam, such as southern Italy and southern Spain, the music that can still be heard in North Africa and the Near East, where continuous oral transmission has caused traditions to remain much stronger than in Europe.

Yet interaction between 'Rome' and the 'new Rome', the two 'sibling cultures', the two halves of the greater, Christian Europe, was far less intensive than might have been expected,[13] despite the cultural influence of such dynastic ties as the one which in AD 972 brought a Byzantine princess, Theophano, to the west to become the wife of Emperor Otto II.[14] Basically, the growing doctrinal differences between the Church of Rome and the Church of Constantinople, and the obvious wish, on both sides, to increase their own sphere of influence, prevented a more intensive and fruitful exchange.

This became clear when, with the gradual loss to Islam of its southern and eastern territories, from the eighth century onwards, Byzantium sought compensation to the north. Its expansion in the Balkans, where the Christian powers from western Europe were advancing as well, was greatly facilitated by the close links between Church and State. Just as, a century before, Charlemagne's conquests in central Germany had profited from Rome's missionary efforts, so now the Byzantine rulers extended their power to Bulgaria, Transylvania and Wallachia in the wake of Orthodox missionaries. The fact that, unlike their Roman counterparts, the Greek Christians did not insist that their language be retained as the language of the holy book certainly contributed to the success of their conversion policies among the Slav peoples in the face of Rome's efforts to introduce Latin Christendom in these debated lands. Realizing that the liturgy and the religious texts would be more effectively introduced if translated into the vernacular, such ninth-century Byzantine missionaries as the brothers

Methodius and Cyrillus, unconsciously following the example of Bishop Ulfilas among the Goths, are even reputed to have devised an alphabet for the then illiterate Slavs. The so-called 'Cyrillic writing' spread over the Balkans and even further, and still retains its use there, mostly in religious culture.

In the region we now call Russia, Viking rulers from Scandinavia had established their regime around the two trading cities of Novgorod and Kiev in the ninth and tenth centuries. However, they soon engaged in diplomatic relations with their Byzantine neighbours.[15] Slowly, Orthodox Christianity – and the Cyrillic script[16] – was introduced among the 'Russians', too, showing its cultural creativity in the monasteries, with their rich music and their churches painted with icon-like frescos, and culminating a few centuries later in the works of the great Andrej Rublev (*c.*1360 to *c.*1430), who decorated the cathedral at Vladimir and the monastery of Zagorsk.

While the Byzantine Empire was successful in expanding its political and cultural dominance to the north, it was less fortunate in keeping its Mediterranean possessions, losing, in particular, Sicily, which went, first, to Islamic conquerors and then to the Norsemen. Nevertheless, its cultural influence there remained strong, judging, for example, by the famous medical 'School of Salerno' where Greek-Byzantine, Jewish and Islamic scholars gathered under the enlightened tutelage of the Norman kings in southern Italy.

Meanwhile, relations between the two Christian Churches were also marred by the fact that the Byzantine emperors wanted total control over their Church, both institutionally and doctrinally. To effect this, they nominated and deposed the patriarchs of Constantinople who were its nominal leaders. The popes in Rome, on the other hand, claiming supremacy over the entire Christian world, could not accept such control, nor were they willing to tolerate the patriarchs as their equals. This resulted, in 1054, in a schism between Rome and Constantinople, which aggravated the already inimical feelings between these two Christian Churches, as both sides now increased their efforts to make propagandist use of the incipient cultural-religious self-consciousness in their respective regions.[17]

What with their disappointments in the Balkans, and the Byzantine refusal to acknowledge their supremacy, the popes in Rome did their best to incite the Christian princes of western Europe against their eastern European competitors. As economic competition in the Mediterranean grew fiercer as well, concentrating on Byzantium's hold over some of the most profitable trade routes to the Near and Far East, the clash of both religious and other interests only deepened the chasm between the two Christian worlds, hindering contact between intellectuals too – the more so as by now few western scholars still read any Greek.

Indeed, by and large, Byzantine cultural contacts with the west were scant. In so far as they existed at all, they mostly developed via the 'intercultures' created by the presence of, in particular, Genoa and Venice in Byzantium, where, across the Golden Horn, the 'Frankish' commercial communities of Galata and Pera provided a gate between east and west. Moreover, the European merchants who settled in the scales, i.e. the ports towns of the Levant, from Antioch to Alexandria, were cultural intermediaries as well. Significantly, a Venetian scholar who was raised in the Byzantine Empire and settled in present-day Hungary engaged upon the translation from Greek into Latin of one of the most important philosophical works of late antiquity: John of Damascus' *Fountain of Wisdom*. Thus, he provided one of the basic elements for Thomas Aquinas' famous *Summa Theologica*, which would influence western (religious) culture for centuries to come. Yet, the most important contributions of ancient Greek culture to Europe were not made through the medium of Byzantium, but through the texts produced by the other heir of the Graeco-Roman world, Islam.

A far corner of the earth: Roman, Catholic Christendom

Certainly from the seventh century onwards, educated people in western Europe wanted their world, their Christian community, the source of their norms, values and ideas, to coincide as much as possible with the geographical concept of Europe. Undeniably, the break-up of relations between the Roman Church, which now called itself the 'Catholic', that is to say 'Universal' one, and the eastern or Orthodox Church, contributed to a growing Euro-centredness. Indeed, the division increased the feeling of unity among the literate people in the west. To them, *Christianitas*, the world of (Roman) Christendom, and Europe – basically western and central Europe – now became synonymous, even though the latter term was still not used frequently. Incidentally, in the same way, the Islamic world did not describe itself geographically but rather culturally and religiously, as *Dar ul-Islam*, the 'House of Islam'.

It was precisely Islam that was another factor in the nascent cultural unity of Europe. Under Muhammad's successors, a conflict over power between the Islamic caliphate, the Frankish kingdom and the Byzantine Empire – incidentally all engaged in Mediterranean trade – was inevitable, for economic, political and, perhaps, religious reasons.

In the Christian countries on the north-west coast of the Mediterranean, men like Alcuin, mentioned above, gradually became aware that Christianity as they professed it was now actually contained within this part of the world – it no longer held any power over the Balkans, North Africa or the Near East, whence it had once come. Charlemagne, praised as the defender of this world of 'Christendom', was one of the first rulers who had to decide how to react to the two rivals in the Mediterranean region: Islam, threateningly present on the southern, Iberian border of his empire, and the Greeks on its eastern flanks.

Indeed, many Christians felt that the new religion, Islam, was getting dangerously close. Monotheistic like Christianity, by force of arms it had quickly spread not only through the Near East but also into North Africa. There, Christianity had flourished for centuries, indeed both longer and more intensely than in Europe. Now, in the eighth and ninth centuries, most Christians in the Levant and North Africa gradually converted to the teachings of Muhammad. Sometimes they were forced to do so, but actually conversion mostly occurred as a natural process of social and cultural adaptation to the norms of a new class of rulers that only few could resist.

Soon, the threat of Islamic expansion was felt on European soil as well. From the newly conquered Islamic states on the Iberian peninsula, Islamic raiders and even small armies crossed the Pyrenees to strike at the Carolingian heartland. The rise to power of Charles Martel, Charlemagne's grandfather, had been partly due to his success in raising an army among the Frankish nobles and defeating the 'Saracens' near Poitiers, in AD 732. However, from North Africa, Islamic troops also reached southern Italy, via the islands of Malta and Sicily. Moreover, via Anatolia and the Bosporus, they increasingly threatened Constantinople, which the west – some might say politically and religiously narrow-mindedly – considered to be not altogether a bad thing. However, there was always the danger that Islam would enter the Balkans, the much-disputed backyard of the Byzantine Empire and, potentially, the west's soft underbelly.

Yet, it is important to acknowledge that Europeans have long held a distorted their view of the past, precisely by introducing into it an image that represents Islam only as an aggressive force. However, to understand what happened in Europe at that time, it is important to know what, only in recent decades, historians have come to understand themselves.

In the ninth and tenth centuries, with the population in the western and central parts of Europe slowly growing, tensions within the agricultural economy with its strictly limited food production forced the powers in this region to embark on a policy not only of the peaceful reclamation of waste lands but also of aggressive expansion into territories inhabited by people that, if only for that reason, had to be stigmatized as enemies and barbarians. Undoubtedly, Europeans began to put increasing military pressure on the eastern and southern frontiers of their world. However, the contemporaneous extension of the Byzantine and Islamic spheres of influence meant that there were only a few opportunities for expansion. In north-western Spain, a number of small-sized, poor Christian principalities sought to extend their domain southward, leading to a process of direct conflict with the Islamic states of Iberia which was to last for several centuries. In the east and south-east of Europe – largely the Balkanic region – the advance forces of western Christendom met the frontier garrisons of the Orthodox world, aggravating the rivalry between these two Christian 'Europes'. If anything, this contributed to the militarization and marginalization of south-east Europe, with results which can still be noticed today. The forces of western expansion also met the 'heathen' hordes of the Slavs in present-day Hungary, the Czech and Slovak Republics, Poland and in the coastal regions of the eastern Baltic. In the process, some of the peoples living in central-eastern Europe were Christianized by Rome. However, from the German heartland land-hungry migrants also swept into these parts, and were to colonize and rule them for a very long time indeed. This, of course, resulted in tensions in every field of economic, political and cultural life. Obviously, the expansion of Byzantine influence among the Balkanic peoples described above certainly was partly caused by these demographic-economic factors as well. Indeed, in the Islamic world, too, the same developments stimulated both migration and military expansion, both in the Mediterranean world – which inevitably then became the battle ground between the three cultures that surrounded it – and in the East, in the world of Asia.

The Crusades: western Christendom versus Islam and eastern Christendom

When the power of Islam started to spread along the northern coasts of the Mediterranean, it began to co-determine the history of Europe, and has done so ever since.[18] One might have thought that a coalition between the Greek and Latin Christians against Islam was the obvious reaction to what both saw as a definite threat. Yet the political and cultural pretensions of Byzantium, and the dreams of political and cultural domination of Charlemagne and his successors could not be combined. One must also question whether in each of these two worlds, the Graeco-Roman civilization that both felt to be an essential characteristic of their culture, had not changed. In both, differing outside influences had become manifest in the previous four centuries and had gradually merged with the remains of the Roman heritage: in western Europe the Germanic cultures that originated in central Europe and the further regions of Asia, in south-eastern Europe the imports from Asia Minor and Egypt.

Be that as it may, it was very clear that, because of divergent political interests, a common, anti-Islamic ideology was out of the question. Though the threat of Islam was felt in the Christian east for 700 years and in the Christian west for 900 years – from the eighth to the fifteenth and seventeenth centuries respectively – the two Christian rivals failed to create a common policy, either to defend themselves or to mount a combined attack. However, from the start the threat posed by Islam led to greater internal cohesion in both parts of Europe. Yet, only in the western part did it result in the further articulation of a notion of 'Europe', as witnessed already in the words of the seventh-century chronicler Isidore of Seville, who described as 'Europeënses' the troops who, under King Charles Martel's leadership, had stymied the 'Saracens', thus preventing further Islamic penetration into Europe beyond the Pyrenees.

For 900 years, the Church of Rome successfully tried to convince these 'Europeënses' that there was great danger outside their own, safe Christian world. From the pulpit, priests proclaimed that everything that they held dear – the Christian faith, the Church, their own norms and ways of life – would be destroyed unless everyone could forget old feuds, form a united front and prepare for battle.

For, alas, world history teaches us that nothing more effectively contributes to a sense of solidarity than the creation of a common enemy. In the specific interaction between the Islamic and Christian worlds, such an enemy was finally

Plate 10 European, Christian pilgrims, both laymen and priests, arriving at their holy city, Jerusalem, from a fifteenth-century fresco cycle in the church at Briançon, France.

Source: Centre for Art Historical Documentation, Nijmegen, the Netherlands

born during the Crusades, which were presented as 'holy wars' against the Muslims, just as Islam presented its raids against the Christian world as *jihad*. During the Crusades, Islam became Europe's most 'significant other', which means it became a world characterized by everything Europeans disliked – also in themselves – and therefore projected onto their neighbouring culture. Since Islam has been forced to continue to play this role up until the present, it is no wonder that in its turn it has cast Christianity in a similar role.

At the same time, the Crusades were effectively European armed invasions of the Holy Land and the wider Islamic Near East, as well as, sometimes, Christian Byzantium. For two centuries, beginning in 1095, Crusades were undertaken with great regularity.[19] Christian propagandists convinced people – and were, quite likely, themselves convinced – that there existed a dire need to safeguard the access of Christian pilgrims to the holy sites of Christendom in Palestine, the land where Jesus had lived and died, and the land that had been occupied by the Muslims. However, one should, of course, realize that power politics and economic motives played a considerable and, according to some, pre-eminent role as well: the western world sought to expand into the eastern Mediterranean both at the expense of the Byzantine Empire and of the emerging Islamic states. While the majority of Crusaders felt a deep need to preserve the Christian sanctuaries, the religious elite also hoped to gain renewed control over the Orthodox Church in the Near East. The secular powers – Europe's princes, but also

Europe's trading towns – may also have been sincere in their Crusading zeal, but they certainly had an ulterior motive too: they craved control over the trade routes that led from the Near East to central Asia, Europe's source of indispensable silver and thus of economic and political power, and which linked the Mediterranean to the Indian Ocean, from where the import of silk and spices satisfied Europe's increasing demand for luxury goods.

CLERMONT, 26 NOVEMBER 1095: POPE URBAN II CALLS FOR
A CRUSADE

In the autumn of 1095, Pope Urban II, attending a Church council at Clermont in France, used this gathering to express his concern about the situation in the Holy Land. The reports of his words show that at least one thought guiding his public announcements was his hope that a common assault on Islam would put an end to the many disputes and wars between rival princes and nobles that ravaged European society, and to the social unrest which was caused, for instance, by itinerant robber barons and plundering gangs of dispossessed farmers.

Although the papal words have not been recorded verbatim, various people present have given their version of them. The following, obviously idealized interpretation was recorded by Fulcher of Chartres, who, however, only wrote his account after the dream of the conquest of Jerusalem had become a fact. Though this text should be judged against the background of both ignorance and increasing suspicion between the two religions, it will not fail to remind any reader of the danger of religious fundamentalism.

> O children of God, he [i.e. the Pope] said, since you have promised God, more earnestly than usual, to keep the peace among yourselves and faithfully maintain the rights of the Church . . . it is vital that you should make a rapid expedition to help your brothers who live in the east, who need your assistance and have now many times appealed for it. For, as most of you have already been told, they have been invaded as far as the Mediterranean sea . . . by the Turks, a Persian people, who have overrun an increasing amount of Christian territory on the frontiers of Romania [i.e. the Byzantine world] . . . killing or capturing many of them, ruining churches and ravaging the Kingdom of God. . . .
>
> It is not I but the Lord himself who begs and exhorts you, as the heralds of Christ, to persuade all men, be they knights or common soldiers, be they rich or be they poor . . . to devote themselves to helping their fellow Christians like a hurricane, to sweep away this evil race out of our people's country. . . .
>
> Let those who are brigands become soldiers of Christ; let those who have been fighting against their own brothers and kinfolk now fight lawfully against the barbarian; let those who are hired for a few sous now find eternal rewards. . . .
>
> Those who are going must not delay their journey, but lease their property and gather the money they need, and when winter ends and the spring follows, let them set forth eagerly upon the way, with the Lord going before them.[20]

However, other versions of the papal words, like the account of the monk Robert, were considerably more bloodthirsty:

> A race from the kingdom of Persia, an accursed race, a race utterly alienated from God . . . has invaded the lands of those Christians and has depopulated them by the sword, pillage and fire. . . . They destroy the altars, after having defiled them with their uncleanness. They circumcise the Christians, and the blood of the circumcision they either spread upon the altars or pour into the vases of the baptismal font. When they wish to torture people . . . they perforate their navels, and dragging forth the extremity of the intestines, bind it to a stake. . . .
>
> Let the deeds of your ancestors move you and incite your minds to manly achievements; the glory and greatness of king Charles the Great, and of his son Louis . . . who have destroyed the kingdoms of the pagans, and have extended in these lands the territories of the Holy Church. Let the holy sepulchre of the Lord our saviour, which is possessed by unclean nations, especially incite you. . . .
>
> When Pope Urban had said these and very many similar things . . . he so influenced to one purpose the desires of all who were present, that they cried out: 'It is the will of God!'.[21]

Rallied by this strong language, many Christians in western Europe felt compelled to 'take the Cross'. Leaving their hearths and their families, they banded together and made their way eastward, to reconquer the holy cities of Christianity. In 1098, the first army succeeded in taking Jerusalem and the other places where Christ had lived and preached.

Though Christian tales of the Crusades mostly stress the glorious deeds of the European knights and their soldiers, inevitably there was another side to the story. The Islamic historian 'Izz ad-Din ibn al-Athir (1160–1233) thus describes the conquest of Jerusalem by the 'Franks':

> Jerusalem was taken from the north on the morning of Friday 22 Sha'ban 492 [15 July, 1099]. The population was put to the sword by the Franks, who pillaged the area for a week. A band of Muslims barricaded themselves into the oratory of David and fought for several days. They were granted their lives in return for surrendering. The Franks honoured their word, and the group left by night for Ascalon. In the Masjid al-Aqsa [i.e. the great mosque on the Temple Mountain] the Franks slaughtered more than 70,000 people, among them a large number of Imams and Muslim scholars, devout and ascetic men who had left their homelands to live lives of pious seclusion in the Holy Place. The Franks stripped the Dome of the Rock of more than forty silver candelabra, each of them weighing 3,600 drams, and a great silver lamp weighing forty-four Syrian pounds, as well as a hundred and fifty smaller silver candelabra and more than twenty gold ones, and a great deal more booty. Refugees from Syria reached Baghdad in Ramadan, among them the qadi Abu Sa'id al-Hárawi. They told the Caliph's ministers a story that wrung their hearts and brought tears to their eyes.

One of the most lively and illuminating Islamic accounts of the Christians who now created the so-called 'Crusader kingdoms' and settled there in increasing numbers, is given in the autobiography of Usama ibn Munqidh, lord of Shaizar (1095–1188), a witty, cultured nobleman whose life spanned almost the entire first century of the Crusaders' presence in the Near East. The following are some of his stories, showing both the opportunities and the limitations of cultural *rapprochement*, not least because of Christian arrogance as is most clearly revealed in the last fragment:

> This is an example of Frankish barbarism, God damn them! When I was in Jerusalem I used to go to the Masjid al-Aqsa, beside which is a small oratory which the Franks have made into a church. Whenever I went into the mosque, which was in the hands of the Templars who were friends of mine, they would put the little oratory at my disposal, so that I could say my prayers there. One day I had gone in . . . when a Frank threw himself on me from behind, lifted me up and turned me so that I was facing east. 'That is the way to pray!', he said. Some Templars at once intervened . . . and took him out of my way, while I resumed my prayer. But the moment they stopped watching me he seized me again and forced me to face east. . . . The Templars intervened and . . . apologized to me. . . .
>
> I paid a visit to the tomb of John the son of Zechariah – God's blessing on both of them! [These two Christian saints are venerated as prophets by Islam.] . . . After saying my prayers, I came out. . . . I found a half-closed gate, opened it and entered a church. Inside were about ten old men, their bare heads as white as combed cotton. They were facing east, and wore . . . on their breasts staves ending in crossbars. . . . took their oath on this sign, and gave hospitality to those who needed it. The sight of their piety touched my heart, but at the same time it displeased and saddened me, for I had never seen such zeal and devotion among the Muslims.
>
> [Later, a friend takes him to a Muslim monastery, where:] I saw about a hundred prayer-mats, and on each a sufi, his face expressing a peaceful serenity, and his body humble devotion. This was a reassuring sight, and I gave thanks to Almighty God that there were among the Muslims men of even more zealous devotion than those Christian priests.
>
> A very important Frankish knight was staying in the camp of King Fulk. . . . We got to know one another, and became firm friends. He called me 'brother' and an affectionate friendship grew up between us.
>
> When he was due to embark for the return journey he said to me: 'My brother, as I am about to return home, I should be happy if you would send your son with me . . . so that he could meet the noblemen of the realm and learn the arts of politics and chivalry. On his return home he would be a truly cultivated man.'
>
> A truly cultivated man would never be guilty of such a suggestion; my son might as well be taken prisoner as go off into the land of the Franks.[22]

For two centuries, from 1096 until 1291, the Crusading movement greatly intensified contact between the Christian west, the Byzantine Empire and the Islamic Near East, as a result of the constant travelling between Europe and 'Outre Mer' (beyond the sea), as the Christian principalities established in the Levant were now called. For the first time in their history, many people from the western part of Europe were confronted with the differences and similarities between cultures. But while the Crusading ideal continued to be a stimulus to Christian unity even after the Christian soldiers and settlers had to withdraw from the Holy Land following the fall of their last bulwark, Acre, in 1291, actual contact decreased again in the thirteenth century. Moreover, as people in Europe realized that the popes in Rome mainly continued to propagate the holy war in order to increase their own power in Italy and elsewhere, interest declined even further.[23]

Yet during these two centuries, the Crusades had a great impact on European culture indeed. In waging war on a common enemy, the inhabitants of western Europe increasingly felt they were one community, 'Christendom' – an emotion felt again after the Second World War when 'the West' – of Europe, combined with the United States and Canada – opposed 'the East' – of Europe, the Communist world – and, asked, 'Who are we, what is Europe?', and knew they were a free and democratic society.

The monk William of Malmesbury, in his version of the address given by Pope Urban II in 1095 at Clermont, had another answer. It is a fascinating one, because it clearly shows in what ways Christians then thought they were both distinct – from others – and distinguished themselves. Malmesbury argues that Christians are no barbarians but display *virtus*, i.e. they lead civilized lives; also, they cherish a common cultural language and are, at the same time, detached from culture and the world (this is a monk writing!). Moreover, Europe produces people 'whose inspired texts will make them immortal as long as anyone cherishes Latin literature'. But Europeans also respond to calls to defend their high ideals. After all, 'Love of one's own hearth must not prevent you, because for the Christian the world is, in a sense, a place of exile, but, on the other hand, the whole world is his country'.[24] Steeped in the learned, Christian culture of his day, William here provides the arguments that helped him and the other members of Europe's intellectual elite to propagate a number of ideals they define as specific to their world. However, he also admonishes his readers to look beyond Europe, to realize the ideals of Europe elsewhere. Thus, the seed of European expansion is sown here.

While the Crusades that William wrote about certainly created some sense of European unity, they also gave the many people involved some insight into what made their culture different from Islam. Yet, significantly, the image of Islam as the great enemy was mainly a creation of those who never left home. Those who actually journeyed to the Holy Land and lived there for an extended period often experienced not only the differences but also the similarities between the two cultures.

However, the importance of the Crusades for Europe lies elsewhere too. For the first time in European history, large groups of people from diverse regions came into contact with each other. While all were defending the same high ideals, many soon noted that very different motives played a role as well, if only because rulers and 'nations' had their own agendas. Moreover, they also became aware of the many ways in which they differed from each other: they were 'arrogant' French, 'gluttonous' Germans or 'dishonest' Italians. Indeed, the chronicles of the Crusades are full of stereotypes in the making. Although, arguably, the Crusades were a supreme moment of Christian universalism, with Christian culture proving its power and might, they also awakened many Europeans to the existing and increasing differences within their own culture.

6 One world, many traditions

Elite culture and popular cultures: cosmopolitan norms and regional variations

Europe's 'feudal' polities

In the course of the ninth century, the Carolingian Empire collapsed, mainly for the same reasons that many past empires have not survived: it was too big, and due to its reliance on personal power that, again, was based on personal relationships between central rulers and local magnates, it lacked the kind of formal bureaucracy that could hold it together in a situation wherein, after the death of a strong leader, weak successors were faced with bids for independence by their subordinates. After several divisions between successive generations of Charlemagne's heirs, the former unity was lost and Carolingian Europe was fragmented into a number of warring principalities.[1]

Wherever large states did emerge, mostly based on an agricultural economy, authority nominally rested in the hands of a single ruler. Sometimes, the origins of such power still lay in tribal leadership, based on a mixture of military prowess and divine sanction, as in those parts of Europe where the Germanic tradition was strong. Such power might grow by the gradual assumption of ever more functions by the ruler, whether or not with the willing assent of others in his peer group of landowning nobles. Often, however, rulers rose to power, or acquired yet greater power simply through conquest, defeating those who could or would not try to hold on to their own territory. Initially, therefore, most European states were anything but static and changes occurred incessantly. For though power mostly was or became hereditary in the family of the man who had first 'founded' the state, a ruler might not only lose it through force of conquest, he could also increase it through inheritance. Hence dynastic alliances were important, and great value was placed on princely marriages.

This rather unstable situation at the end of the first millennium of the Christian era was aggravated by the southward migrations of the Norsemen or Vikings, the still largely pagan, i.e. non-Christian Germanic inhabitants of Scandinavia. Long pictured as cruel marauders, we now know that their background and motives were rather more complex. Admittedly, they had been pirating the Carolingian frontiers since the end of the eighth century and now, seeing their chance and using their marvellous longboats, they invaded and plundered all of north-western Europe. But overpopulation, changing climatic conditions and the ensuing agricultural problems, as well as the quest for easy booty and new trade routes all contributed to their large-scale migration to England, the Netherlands, the German lands and France, where they settled as farmers, craftsmen and merchants. Soon, the Viking trading towns became important centres of cross-European commerce.[2] As indicated in Chapter 5, both in present-day Sicily and in Russia, the Vikings created principalities, as they did, of course, in the state that bore their name, Normandy. Meanwhile, the south-eastern flank of Europe was attacked by the Magyars who crossed the Danube in the ninth century, wreaking havoc both in the former Carolingian Empire and in the Byzantine territories.

In this situation of declining central authority and hence security, of migration and economic upheaval, people looked for new ways to safeguard their survival. Finding the emperors and kings who nominally ruled from the ninth and tenth centuries onwards increasingly unable to effectively protect them from internal injustice and external aggression, they now turned to regional military leaders, warrior-aristocrats. The latter, whose power was based on their own estates, saw a chance to increase both that power and holdings by offering safety to the weaker – who might be other aristocrats, or clergy or peasants – in exchange for personal, mostly military services, or goods. Soon, the most successful local magnates not only increased their economic and political-military power, but also arrogated powers of jurisdiction over their dependants, thus effectively eliminating the reality and, to many ordinary people, even the concept of a central state, or ruler, as the dispenser of justice.

In a famous letter to William, Duke of Aquitaine, Fulbert, bishop of Chartres from 1006 until 1028, gave a clear exposé of the way economic, military and political structures were ever more strongly perceived in terms of personal relationships of protection and service, or obedience. Analysing the mutual duties of a lord and his bondsman, his vassal, Fulbert stressed the strong personal ties of trust and obedience that were considered essential to a well-structured sociopolitical life:

> To William, the most glorious Duke of the Acquitanians, Bishop Fulbert offers the aid of his prayers.
>
> Having been told to write something about the nature of fealty, I have briefly noted the following points for you on the authority of the books. A man who swears fealty to his lord ought always to remember these six words: unharmed, safe, honourable, profitable, easy, possible. Unharmed, because he must not do to his lord any physical injury. Safe, because he must not betray his secrets or damage the defences by which his lord can be safe. Honourable, because he must not detract from the lord's jurisdiction or from anything else which pertains to his rank. Profitable, because he must not cause the loss of any of his property. Easy and possible, lest he make it difficult to do the good deed which his lord could otherwise easily perform, or make impossible what would otherwise have been possible. It is right that the vassal [*fidelis*] should beware of doing harm in this way. But he does not earn his fief merely by so restraining himself . . . He must still loyally aid and advise his lord on the above six points. . . The lord ought in all these things to do

the same for his vassal. And if he does not do so, he will deserve to be considered a man of bad faith. . . . I would have written to you at greater length had I not been occupied with many other matters, even with the restoration of our city and our church, all of which was burnt down recently in a terrible fire. Although we cannot fail to be somewhat affected by this loss, nevertheless we breathe again in the hope of consolation from God and from you.[3]

The question is, of course, whether and how this ideal worked out in practice. The answer seems affirmative, to judge by the so-called 'formulae of Tours', a set of models for all sorts of legal documents dating from the seventh century. One of the forms was meant for use by a person feeling too weak to survive on his own and wanting to offer his services to a stronger man. In doing so, he would become that man's vassal, but would receive protection, clothing and food in return:

> I, A, to the magnificent lord B.
> As it is well known to everybody that I have no means of feeding and clothing myself, I have asked you, in your pity, permission to hand over and commend myself to your protection and your goodwill has granted me it. And I have therefore done so, on the understanding that you must aid and comfort me with food and clothing, according as I am able to serve you and deserve well of you; and that, so long as I live, I must extend to you service and obedience of the kind expected of a free man; and throughout my life I shall have no power of withdrawing from your power and protection, but must remain all the days of my life under your power and protection.[4]

This was the basis of the so-called 'feudal system', which, however, was no system at all. The term 'feudalism' was coined by legal historians only in the seventeenth century, in an effort to describe and comprehend the complex economic, military and political relationships that had given structure and cohesion to European society in the centuries following the decline of Roman authority. Nor did these relationships concern only great noblemen who strove for an alliance with a still mightier ruler. They could equally well involve a simple peasant who sought the protection of a local landowner.

What, effectively, evolved in these centuries was a hierarchy of loyalties, within which one vassal received his sustenance – whether or not in the form of property, *feudum* – from or was guaranteed it by a lord who, in his turn, might be the vassal of someone more powerful, as can be seen from the agreement reached in 1076 between the Count of Hainault and the bishop of Liège who was, himself, a vassal of the Holy Roman Emperor:

> In assigning all these allods and fiefs to the church of Liège, and in the liege homage of this great man the Count of Hainault, it was laid down that the Count of Hainault owed his lord the Bishop of Liège service and aid for all purposes and against all men with all the forces of his vassals [*homines*], both infantry and cavalry, and that once the Count was outside the County of Hainault these forces should be maintained at the Bishop's expense. . . . If the lord Bishop summoned the Count

of Hainault to his court or to any conference, he had likewise to pay him his expenses. If the lord Emperor of the Romans summoned the Count of Hainault to his court for any reason, the Bishop of Liège ought at his own expense to bring him safely to and from the court and appear on his behalf and answer for him in the court. . . . Should the Count of Hainault lay siege to any fortress which belonged to his own honour . . . the Bishop must at his own expense assist the Count with five hundred soldiers, whilst the Count must provide the Bishop with means to buy victuals at a fair price. If there were grass or other fodder necessary to horses in the fields, the Bishop and his men might take this at the Bishop's choice.[5]

In his turn, the Count of Hainault had vassals who did not always fulfil their obligations, as demonstrated in 1176:

> That same year, disputes arose between the Count of Hainault and his vassal and kinsman Jacques d'Avesnes over certain wrongs which said Jacques was doing to the lord Count. Hence the lord Count summoned Jacques to his court and required him to restore the castle of Condé. Jacques . . . eventually refused outright to restore the castle. The lord Count called upon his [other] vassals . . . to decide what was to be done about this. Hence it was judged that Jacques had no further rights in his castle. . . . The Count of Hainault mobilized his army and at Easter 1176 launched a fierce attack. . . . Since Jacques could not withstand the forces of his lord the Count, he begged for mercy, prostrated himself at the foot of the armed Count and restored the castle of Condé to his authority.[6]

Yet despite these multiple dependencies, there were many parts of Europe where rulers remained relatively strong and where most men, noblemen and commoners, while retaining their possessions as so-called 'allods' (i.e. as free, unalienated property), gave military service to the lord of the land not because they were his vassals, but because they were his subjects, and he was the ruler. However, the bureaucracies that now took on an increasing share of government – at least in the stronger states – while devising a new legal system in which to define the ruler–subject relationship, sometimes rewrote existing obligations in such terms that they closely resembled not only those of the 'feudal ideal' but, at the same time, of the real vassalage that existed elsewhere.[7]

The Church and the early states

By the end of the tenth century Europe slowly began to recover from the political and economic crisis that had begun at the end of the ninth century. First, the relative cold that had prevailed for more than a century came to an end; this, of course, provided a boost to agriculture and thus to population growth and consequently, trade and industry were stimulated too. Also, the Norsemen and other invaders were either driven back by force or, more often, permanently established themselves in their newly won principalities, marrying into the indigenous population. Indeed, in present-day France, the Viking-descended dukes of Normandy were soon among Europe's strongest rulers. In the German lands, King Otto I stopped the advance of the Magyars, who then settled in present-day Hungary.

Even in those regions that lacked powerful princes, the concept of a society ruled by law – one of ancient Rome's great cultural achievements – had been preserved and, in its way, implemented by the Church, the only great institution to survive both the Roman and the Carolingian Empires. It had kept alive the idea and the ideal of a legal society, if only because the popes, trying to preserve and increase their power, adapted Roman Law for their own use, thus creating the corpus of Canon Law.

Arguably, this ability of the Christian Church to manage those strong states that otherwise might have created a civil society which did not evolve, has been hugely important for Europe's further development. Basically, the Church succeeded in integrating the local and regional communities of Europe through legislation that combined secular aims with religiously legitimized rules. It first tried to contribute to a more peaceful climate through the imposition of Sunday as the Lord's Day, on which no one was to attack his enemy. Soon, the increasing number of saints' days – to which the same rule applied – coupled with so-called 'truces of God', helped also to create a more peaceful society; so did a ban on fighting on market-days – no mean stimulus to economic growth. Also, the Church successfully kept the more bloody forms of warfare within bounds, though it did apply different rules of warfare between Christians and between Christians and infidels. Even more successfully, it managed if not to eradicate, at least to curb the ubiquitous blood feuds. Undeniably, in the beginning, the rules laid down by the Church were but poorly observed, though in some regions the clergy could build on and expand pre-existing 'peace associations' wherein groups collectively took oaths to assume responsibility for law and order in their community. Soon, new legal systems turned the exercise of blood vengeance into a prerogative, first, of the Church and its courts, and then of the secular authorities. The process was, one might say, a colonization from within.[8] Very slowly, Europeans began to implement this vision of a legal, civil society, wherein the members of any given community might expect to be treated equally, although this was often only theory.[9]

No less important was the Church's policy towards marriage and family matters. It seems that, from the beginning, Christianity has stressed matrimony as something sacred, not only attaching to it great social importance, as, in their way, the people of classical Rome and Greece had done, but also investing it with a unique moral, religious value, to the exclusion of other forms of relationship.

Undoubtedly, strengthening the ideal and practice of a priest-sanctioned marriage gave the Church greater control over its flock than otherwise would have been the case. As secular authorities, too, were quick to see the advantages of a regulated, single-system society, this policy met with considerable success. Of course, for the majority of Europeans – the peasants, the poor – procreation was a dire necessity, whatever their inclination. Without children to help work the land, the life of a farmer, especially an ageing one, would have been practically unlivable. Also, in an (agricultural) society that valued the transfer of patrimony and privilege along proven bloodlines, the sacredness of a union that by and large guaranteed the legitimacy of children was very important.

On the other hand, in both the peasant world and in other socio-economic groups, same-sex contacts were certainly not uncommon, partly because women were not available, partly because they evaded the problems of unmarried mothers, with all the concomitant problems for the offspring in an acutely ancestor-and-kinship-conscious society. This may have been one of the reasons why, for a long time, homosexuality continued to be widely practised without strong opposition by the Church. It is, however, debatable whether, as some historians have argued, this also meant that homosexuality existed as an 'identity', a way of living together that was even officially sanctified by the Church in same-sex unions.[10]

On the whole, there is abundant evidence that European culture increasingly tended towards heterosexual relations and, moreover, towards the expression of sexuality as 'legitimate', as acceptable in the eyes of God only within the sacred marriage bond, with the sole aim of procreation. Indeed, while the Church stressed the fact that man's salvation was best served by celibacy, it could not deny the obvious necessity of the reproduction of the species. Thus, men and women who did not aspire to a monastic life were told that marriage and parent-hood was their only viable option.[11] Inevitably, the Church itself, although it had tolerated married priests for a long time, in the end became the victim of the sacred social order it successfully sought to impose on society at large: priests who did not live up to the ideals which, though only partly, were now internalized by the common people, became the object of violent persecution.[12]

Undeniably, Europe was a culture that afforded men far more opportunities than it did women. Of course there were a few, mostly noble-born female artists – writers of courtly and mystic poetry, mostly – as well as noble ladies who patronized the arts. There was even a small number of women scholars.[13] However, they were the exceptions, rather than the rule. Most women were told and were, indeed, convinced that their life had to run the course from being a 'clean maid' to being a 'true wife': chaste motherhood was their real vocation, following the example of that mother *par excellence*, the Virgin Mary, whose cult was increasingly stimulated.[14] If a woman's husband died, she might, of course, marry again, but preferably she should spend the rest of her life as a steadfast rather than a merry widow.[15]

Increasingly, from the eleventh century onwards, the growth of a society made up of small nuclei embedded in a family system legitimized both by sacred and secular law loosened whatever might have remained of strong extended kinship networks in the older, tribal societies. However, Church family and marriage policy was also influenced by the fact that, for several centuries, large parts of Europe lacked strong states. Almost inevitably, such states would have been predatory organizations, which would have resulted in the insecurity of the tenure of landed property. Now the Church, which neither could nor would adopt such a predatory attitude itself, tried to ensure the legal possession of property instead. Whether this was for motives of easier cultural and religious control or for economic reasons after all – detaching property, land, from large kinship systems to facilitate transfer to the Church – is not altogether clear. Certainly, self-interest played a role, for the Church received many grants of land in return for the prayers said by priests and monks that enabled the donors to comfortably live their lives on earth, and yet be assured of a place in heaven. Still, the security of property was a powerful incentive to invest in land, both on the part of the big landowners and of the smaller, free-holding peasants. All this contributed to a growing individualism which, in itself, strengthened the market orientation of European economic life and, in its turn, the growth of a well-ordered, legally structured society – Church-dominated, of course, but only for the time being.[16]

Economic and technological change and the early states

Despite increasing trade, both regional and, largely via the Mediterranean and the Baltic, interregional, this economy and this society were still agricultural at heart. Europe was a world of manors and estates with, at the centre of a hamlet or village, the homes of the landowners: castles or fortified houses. These ranged from simple wattle-and-daub structures, scarcely more comfortable than the dwellings of the peasants, to magnificent, stone-built fortresses that might be more spacious but, mostly, were equally uncomfortable. Whereas the castle or manor house was one pole of economic, social and political life, the parish church was its spiritual and cultural counterpart. In this world, the peasants lived and worked: as free men who usually fitted into this system of lordship one way or another, and as unfree, the villeins and the serfs, who were largely bound to the soil and its owner, a nobleman or knight.

Food supply was dependent both on a mixture of climatic and soil conditions and on human technology. This, of course, was the same all over the world. In Europe, however, certain conditions as well as inventions allowed for a slowly different development.[17] For the greater part, Europe was a rainfall agriculture, allowing each farmer to work a considerable number of square metres, instead of the rather small plots that had to be worked in more arid regions which depended heavily on irrigation. Moreover, an ingenious method of crop rotation was used within the so-called 'open field' system, wherein at any one time half the land was cultivated while the other half lay fallow. Soon, an even more ingenious system was adopted, the three-field or three-course system, which allowed for summer and winter sowing while the last third of any property was left to recuperate. Such sources of energy as the watermill – known to the Romans but not widely used by them because they had a dependent (indeed a slave) peasantry to do the work and were loath to invest in this rather costly piece of engineering – were used all over Europe from the sixth century onwards, and from the twelfth century windmills were introduced as well, greatly facilitating such activities as fulling and sawing.

Of course, the topic of technology forms an integral part of cultural history. As, in this context, we have to view the relationship between Europe and Asia, we touch upon the problematic question of the diffusion of knowledge and technology between civilizations as opposed to the parallel development of indigenous inventions.

Non-European inventions would not, of course, have been adopted in Europe if Europeans had not already possessed the skills necessary to modify, adapt and develop them to suit their own use. Also, the early indigenous invention or adaptation of non-human energy, mostly in the form of water and, later, wind, in a certain way made Europe equal to the civilizations of China and Islam. The fact that windmills were used in Europe only from the middle of the twelfth century onwards, and that according to some scholars they were introduced from Persia or even the Far East, does not detract from that statement, for even if they were not a local invention, it seems that at least the change from a vertically shafted mill to a horizontally shafted one was definitely a European improvement.[18]

Indeed, the improvements in European technology from as early as the fifth century onwards were such that many historians have argued that, largely because of the use of water-driven machines,[19] by the twelfth century not only the utilization of energy had been drastically changed but also the use of man-power, as waterpower had helped to do away with the need for a slave-worked economy. First introduced in the world of the monastic economies – not, however, for economic motives, but to enable these communities to retain their isolation from the wicked world by assuring a great degree of autarky – water-power was soon adopted by lay entrepreneurs as well; they saw its possibilities for material profit, and inevitably made it the object of extensive investment, and of continuous improvement. Consequently, a veritable 'medieval' industrial revolution took place.[20] By the twelfth century, corn, olives, grapes, wood, iron, leather and paper could all be, and often were, processed by water-driven machines with a remarkable range of applications, although for the majority of small-scale operators such machinery was too expensive, and manual production continued to be the norm. Therefore, some historians maintain that though the aptitude to improve technologies was there, the incentive to actually do so was largely lacking. Also, it is undeniable that technological development was predominantly incremental, based on experience, rather than on application of abstract conceptual knowledge. Moreover, as land continued to be the major source of all raw organic material and, thus, energy, those who held power over it controlled the economy.[21] Indeed, though peat and soon coal were used for fuel and a considerable mining industry developed, water-power continued to remain Europe's main source of energy well into the eighteenth century. Hence, the beginnings of the so-called Industrial Revolution were arguably based as much on the waterwheel as on the steam engine.

As early as the Middle Ages, however, new methods of producing energy were combined with an increase in the production of iron in wind-driven mills, which resulted in the manufacture of more effective wheel-driven ploughs, with mould-boards and better shares, and the increased use of horses in agriculture – horses, especially second-hand ones, being cheaper than oxen which could be used for meat. All this helps to explain how the average agricultural yield in Europe rose considerably between the ninth and the thirteenth centuries. Walter of Henley, who in the thirteenth century wrote a widely copied and therefore supposedly also widely read treatise on land husbandry, stated that for mere survival, a ratio between seed and yield of one to three was necessary. By his time, an average manor seems to have realized a yield of one to five.[22] This situation, and the resulting improvement in the European diet, which was probably superior to most other parts of the world, goes a long way to explaining the almost continuous population rise, the further development of the European economy and the changes in European culture in this period.

Still, by the twelfth century, the technologies of the worlds of Asia were far broader in scope than those of Europe. In almost every field this had resulted in machinery more sophisticated than anything so far invented in the west. Consequently, Europe continued to learn from Asia.

While in geopolitical terms, the world of Islam both separated and linked the worlds of east Asia and Europe, these worlds were united in one very specific way. What has been called the 'microbial unification of the world' became manifest in the great bubonic plagues that spread from central Asia both to China and to Europe, first ravaging the Islamic Near East and the Byzantine Empire from the sixth century onwards, and then creating havoc all over Eurasia from the twelfth to the fifteenth centuries.

Due to its geographical situation, the Mediterranean was the road *par excellence* connecting the two worlds, economically and culturally. In Europe, therefore, Italy and, via the passes of the Alps, southern Germany became the centre of economic productivity and of cultural, and also technological, exchange, change and progress. Of course, Islamic Spain, though slightly less important economically, greatly influenced the diffusion of an immensely wide variety of ideas: originating both from ancient Greek science and philosophy, and from ancient and contemporary Islamic-Asiatic science and technology, they were taught at the universities of the Islamic cities of Iberia where, soon, some daring Christian students from Europe arrived to gain new knowledge. Thus, through the filter both of Islamic scholarship and of Mediterranean commercial, largely maritime practice, science and technology from the east travelled to the west.

The process was accelerated when, from the tenth century onwards, the Christian princes of northern Spain succeeded in advancing on the Islamic world that bordered their territories to the south. When Toledo, one of the great Islamic cities, fell to the Christians in 1085, and European scholars were introduced to the enormous stock of knowledge stored there by generations of scientists, they eagerly adopted Indian medicine and, even more important, Hindu numerals, including the symbol for zero. As indicated above, these numerals and the resulting decimal system, so much easier to use than the laborious Roman system, helped simplify mathematics to such an extent that they became fit for use in everyday European economic life which, in a certain sense, was as big a revolution as the introduction of the simplified Phoenician script had been to Mediterranean trade three millennia earlier.

The Christian scholars and students flocking to Toledo were also fascinated by the manuscript books that discussed mechanical devices of all sorts. Thus, the idea of the weight-driven clock, probably originating in India, entered Europe as well. Among the really important technical devices that came to Europe along the Islamic-African-Spanish road were pedal-operated looms, which left the weaver's hands free to pass the shuttle backwards and forwards. These were probably introduced into Europe during the twelfth century.

However, by far the most revolutionary were the paper-making techniques that employed vegetable fibres pounded in water until a pulp was formed that could be made into paper sheets. The technique had first been invented in China and according to some sources had entered the Islamic world as early as the eighth century, via central Asia.[23] It was perfected in Baghdad, both through the addition of starch which created a paper suitable for the use of quills or pens, instead of brushes – which influenced the art and clarity of writing – and through the introduction of a water-driven machine that operated hammers for pounding the fibres into pulp. These inventions stimulated the production of (manuscript) books and thus advanced the dissemination of knowledge in a remarkable way. The subsequent westward spread of manuscript books in the ninth and tenth centuries in turn led to the westward spread of the new papermaking techniques as well; consequently, the first paper mill was established in Spain in 1151.

Whereas Islamic Spain seems to have been the main channel through which important scientific notions and technological devices reached Europe, actually there were three more roads connecting the worlds and technologies of further Asia with the Christian west. Islamic Sicily was the first. The use of sophisticated labour-saving reeling machines for the processing of silk thread from the cocoons, which had been in use in China for ages, travelled to Byzantium and the Near East at some time in the eleventh century. One hundred years later, silk manufacture is mentioned in northern Italy. Significantly, however, by then the machine had been modified and, indeed, improved into the throwing machine with a circular frame.

At approximately the same time, the Crusades created a second link between Europe and the Near East. For two hundred years, it brought such diverse techniques to Europe as food processing for the production of pasta and the making of certain incendiary weapons. The use of the latter was, of course, not only to revolutionize European civilization but, eventually, would also give it one of its greatest holds over the rest of the world.

The first real intimation of the possibilities of high-nitrate powder became evident when the Mongols began their expansionist campaigns in the thirteenth century, thus creating the third road that connected east Asia with Europe. Thus, for example, well into the fourteenth and fifteenth centuries, captives from Mongol armies were brought as slaves to Italy, quite likely introducing various skills first developed within the Chinese-Mongol cultural sphere.[24]

Europeans, of necessity, soon became very interested in the new superpower of central Asia, and decided to get to know it better. Soon, the popes sent their ambassadors to the great khans, hoping to find them allies in their battle against Islam. On his return from Mongolia in 1257, the Franciscan friar, William of Roebroeck, told of the military use of explosive powder, which the Mongols had learnt from the Chinese – the often-told tale that the Chinese used what we call gunpowder only for innocently artistic fireworks is a fable. A year later, experiments with gunpowder and rockets were made in Cologne, and Roebroeck's friend, the learned monk Roger Bacon, wrote a tract explaining the new invention to the scientific world of Europe. At the same time, the new weaponry had become known to Europeans in the Near East as well. There it had been improved as part of the creative interaction between the worlds of Islam and China. Soon, yet more advanced ideas about the military use of gunpowder also reached Europe.

Although gunpowder is normally associated with handguns, the earliest really useful gunpowder weapon, the bronze-barrelled cannon, seems to have been developed in Manchuria only in the last decades of the thirteenth century, as was the smaller Chinese-Manchurian handgun. By the beginning of the fourteenth century, these new devices appear in European drawings and are soon in material evidence as well. The invention had probably reached Europe by way of the Mongol-dominated regions of Russia and, perhaps, by the trade routes connecting these regions with the Baltic: some of the earliest cannons have been unearthed in Sweden.

The case of gunpowder and guns is especially significant because it shows that object diffusion and idea diffusion have coincided here, while at the same time it is obvious that to simply characterize the process as an example of the transfer of technology would be wrong. Rather, one should explain what happened in terms of a dialectic, a technological dialogue, or an inventive exchange.

Stronger states – stronger rulers?

The above technological developments, whether indigenous or imported, as well as the sociolegal and ideological structures created or favoured by the Church, gradually resulted in the formation of stronger states, both by contributing to their cohesion and military power and through the growth of the economy and, hence, their fiscal capacity.

For a long time, such princes as there were shared their sovereign authority with numerous other lords. A centralized state, with a non-lineage-based structure and a bureaucracy that ensured some sort of rational government as well as a revenue for public purposes and that held power over all subjects within its territory, had yet to evolve. Yet this was precisely what many monarchs strove for and, indeed, actively set out to create. Of course, this resulted in continuous strife with their neighbouring princes as well as with the magnates of their own state who were unwilling to give up their independence and their income from a growing economy which, besides profiting from improved agriculture, now began to have its base in trade as well. Slowly, however, at least some European rulers were successful in acquiring a more than equal share of sovereign power.

In England, during the invasions of the Norsemen, the local chieftains had gradually come to accept the authority of one king who eventually came to rule over the seven former Anglo-Saxon overlords. It was King Alfred of Wessex, surnamed 'the Great' (849–99) – whose life was written by the bishop of Winchester, Asser – who was credited with this feat.[25] Indeed, he gained a status in English history close to the mythical Arthur, who was supposed to have united the country in the period when Roman authority disappeared. Soon, Anglo-Saxons and Vikings intermarried, even producing a new dynasty, and a slow process of administrative and fiscal unification started. This formed the basis on which William 'the Conqueror' – the Viking-descended Duke of Normandy who crossed the English Channel in 1066, bringing not only an army but also an already proven system of central government – could start enlarging royal power in England.

The territory of present-day France was divided between many independent rulers although a number of them nominally recognized the sovereignty of the king who, in fact, held real power only over his own domain, the region of Paris. Yet through war, marriage, inheritance and diplomacy, these successive 'kings of France' succeeded in acquiring ever more territories. Though they left regional customs well alone, they employed a complex bureaucracy to secure a fiscal efficiency that significantly enlarged their financial and military possibilities. From the thirteenth century onwards, an important new development occurred. As large parts of western France were controlled by the kings of England – basically by right of marriage – the rulers of France began to exploit anti-English sentiments among the population to create an embryonic 'national feeling', asking the feudal lords of France as well as the common people to unite and fight under their banner.[26] Of course, this was the context for the famous episode of Joan of Arc (*c*.1412–31), the peasant girl who led a French army and took Orleans from the English, but was later captured by them and burnt at the stake.

In the German-speaking part of Europe, a system had evolved wherein numerous ecclesiastical and lay lords, while ruling their own principalities, elected one of their group to the kingship – a man who then usually received the imperial title, as the heir of Charlemagne's tradition and hence of Rome and all it implied. However, the actual power of this Holy Roman Emperor was small, depending mainly on the extent and wealth of his own domains. In the fifteenth century, the imperial title became all but hereditary in the Habsburg family, who had their real power-base in Austria.

Elsewhere in Europe, too, states emerged from the eleventh and twelfth centuries onwards, in Sweden as well as in Denmark, in Poland as well as in Hungary and, of course, in the Iberian peninsula, where a wealthy kingdom developed in Aragon, around Barcelona, largely based on profitable trading across the Mediterranean. Still, by and large the sovereigns had but little power because their functions were limited and hence their subjects' inclination to pay taxes was also limited. Indeed, with the Church performing most services now considered within the public sphere – education, the care of the sick, the orphaned and the ageing – the kings, except in times of real danger to the state, were not very successful in extracting money from their subjects, whether noble or common. The common people realized that any revenue was mostly used to finance wars that brought them only misery, whereas the aristocracy knew the kings probably would use their armies to curb their power to compete.

However, most people did see the advantages of a peaceful, structured society wherein the use of arms was not each and everybody's privilege and wherein legal transactions of any kind were binding under a superior authority. This is what gave most aspiring monarchs a real chance to increase their power. Setting themselves up as the state's supreme judicial authority, to guarantee property and security if not yet equality before the law was a service that made them increasingly popular. In this, they could expect to find support among the many communities – parishes, villages, municipal governments, guilds – that had been enacting collective legislation from the tenth century onwards, although, of course, frictions inevitably arose over the question of who, in the end, would hold legislative and judicial power.[27] Working towards their own aims, these princes could also rely on the basic equality of all men stipulated by Christianity. This equality, however theoretical in most cases, allowed for the slow growth of a sociopolitical climate characterized by agreement and consensus, competition and contractual relationships, both in the field of economics and of politics.[28] This was to prove highly important to the further development of European society. Developing a uniform system of rules, mostly derived from the basic tenets of Roman Law, often via papal Canon Law, all over Europe princes furthered the acceptance of their dominion by projecting themselves as the keepers of the 'community', and demanding, in return, payment of taxes and submission to their 'absolute' authority.[29] In so doing, they were beginning truly to build a state.

Even though, as a result of this process, the regional magnates gradually lost out in their competition for power, they continued to defend their independence vis-à-vis growing state authority. In trying to retain some of their influence, they often felt forced to compromise with the monarch. Accepting the latter's ultimate sovereignty, they would demand that the ruler acknowledged their right to be his first advisers which would allow them a major voice in the business of government. This became manifest in England in 1215, when the great barons forced the reigning king to accept the *Magna Carta*, the 'Great Document'. Listing a number of fundamental rights of the English people, it basically proclaimed that everyone, including the monarch, had to obey the law. Comparable developments took place all over Europe.

The towns and the early states

Into this society now came a new player, or rather an old one that acquired a new importance. However, the genesis and development of the towns that were to play such an essential part in the economic, political and cultural life of Europe has not been a uniform process. Actually, the nuclei around which urban structures evolved were quite varied.[30]

In those parts of Europe where the Romans had created their administrative and military centres – often building, too, upon pre-existing settlements – urban traditions continued even during times when the European economy was, by and large, an agricultural one. Thus, we find a continuity of city life all over Italy, where the battles between popes and emperors had actually resulted in a power vacuum,[31] as well as in southern France and parts of Spain, but also in such former Roman frontier colonies as Cologne, Trier and Vienna. But life in these *civitates* which, after the gradual disappearance of Roman or Romanized civic rule in the fourth and fifth centuries, were often ruled by a Christian bishop – for example, Winchester in England – did not really differ from life in the surrounding countryside. Mostly, these towns had a distributive, rather than an industrial function for agricultural products and farm-produced manufactures.

Other pre-urban nuclei developed as a *portus* (a port town) – like the important and extensive eighth-century settlement of Dorestad on the lower reaches of the Rhine – or a *vicus* or *wike*, a street of houses outside but under the immediate protection of a castle or a monastery. However, many of these towns did not survive the period of crisis in the ninth and tenth centuries.

Yet, when peace and stability returned in the eleventh century, and the economy revived, a number of these old cities, like the great episcopal towns along the Rhine, re-established themselves. Some communities developed on commercially suitable spots, whether a ford where people crossed a river or the intersection of two or more trade routes. The Anglo-Saxon kings founded new centres on a large scale. Also, once more, towns evolved around the religious cores of Christendom – the monasteries which commanded huge estates and needed a central market – as well as around the more important strongholds of regional magnates trying to dominate a greater area. Thus abbeys and castles became regional centres, to which peasants flocked to sell their products, and where merchants settled to ply their trade. Artisans might then join the community, and the typical traits of a town – a variety of economic activities – would begin to emerge.

From the eleventh century, when the population of Europe began to grow again, in the urban centres in particular a surplus of labour became available that could turn to large-scale manufacture for an expanding regional market. Merchants and moneylenders gained importance, gladly fostering such efforts. Banking was soon dominated by the Jews; the reasons for this were manifold. First money-lending, if it involved usury, was a forbidden practice among Christians. Also, the Jews themselves were a literate community in the midst of a largely illiterate society and as, under Christian law, they were forbidden to own land, they applied themselves successfully to this complicated but lucrative business although it made them even more vulnerable to the periodic outbursts of anti-Semitic virulence of which they were the victim.

Besides trade, the mainstay of most urban economies became some kind of proto-industry, with textiles easily being the major sector. Indeed, many towns started producing first linen and later fine woollen cloth, as did Ghent, in Flanders. The need to provide the looms with supplies of high-quality wool stimulated trade between such industrial centres and the regions producing wool, as is shown by the trade links that were established between north-eastern England with its economy based on sheep, and the continent, especially the north of France, Flanders and Holland. In northern Italy, especially around Milan and in Lombardy, silk manufacture stimulated trade with the Levant and the production of ironware led to transalpine trade. Both generated great prosperity.

As factory-organized production did not yet really exist, the household itself was the basic economic as well as social unit. For most townspeople, the house was both a dwelling and a workplace, often open to the street during day time.[32] The owners, whether they were artisans-and-shopkeepers, or bankers, merchants and tradesmen, usually employed not only members of their own family, including their wives, but also unmarried apprentices and salaried workers. As the latter mostly lived in, we should not think of these groups in terms of a 'nuclear' family. The concept of 'household' would more accurately describe the situation. This, of course, influenced the lives of all involved in a variety of activities. Urban lower- and middle-class women, rather than being restricted only to the house, participated in economic and hence public life to a considerable extent. Children were often brought up by elderly relatives. With many people sharing a restricted space – mostly, separate bedrooms did not exist, nor, of course, were there any bathrooms – modern ideas of privacy simply did not apply.

Whatever their origin or specific characteristics, whenever a town became sufficiently important it would try to gain some sort of (political) independence. As trade, from the eleventh century onwards, became the backbone of Europe's economic and financial development, the leaders of the towns, who often based their wealth on financial or mercantile transactions, would try to exploit their political importance vis-à-vis the rulers whose day-to-day exercise of power mainly depended on the money made available to them by urban financiers. Often acting as tax-farmers, these financiers would advance lump sums to the state, thus growing rich in the fiscal business as well. By necessity, this mutual dependency had to result in a political *modus vivendi*. However, in the highly personalized power structures that existed during these centuries, the position of a collective entity such as a town was not an unproblematic one. New kinds of relationships had to be devised. Soon, these were codified in the so-called town charters, documents pledging the liberties or privileges granted to city dwellers by the rulers.

The right to hold a market and certain guarantees of undisturbed trade were, of course, considered basic. Often, regional potentates would gladly grant market charters, realizing their importance for the economy and thus for their own power. So did the German kings who wanted to revitalize trade with the Balkans and the Middle East via their border regions in central Europe. To further develop these market functions, towns were also given a lord's special protection.[33]

Another important privilege was that by living in a city for 'a year and a day' a serf would be liberated from his obligations towards the lord of the land to which he had been tied, giving him the status of a free man instead. This obviously attracted many people and besides contributing to the growth of towns, it also changed the structure of society. In 1188 King Philip Augustus of France granted such rights to the community of Pontoise:

> In the name of the holy and indivisible Trinity, Amen.
>
> Philip, by the grace of God King of the French. All men, present and future, shall know that we have established a commune at Pontoise, reserving fealty to us and our successors and saving all customs, in this wise:
>
> That all who dwell in the parishes of Pontoise and St Martin shall by perpetual right be free and immune from every unjust tallage, from unjustified arrest, from unfair use of the right to purchase their goods, and from all unreasonable exactions. . . . If anyone brings within the walls somebody who has unwittingly done wrong to a member of this community, and if that person can prove upon oath that he did this in ignorance, he shall . . . be allowed to go free and in peace. . . .
>
> Anyone who comes to market within the walls shall be allowed to come and go in peace. . . .
>
> Traders who are in transit or who dwell in Pontoise shall at all times be left in peace. . . .
>
> If anyone living outside the walls has committed any offence against the community, and has refused to make amends on being summoned to do so, the community may punish him for it in whatever way it can. . . .
>
> All the men shall as a community provide for common needs, such as the watch, the prisons and the moats and all things pertaining to the defence and security.[34]

In those towns that were not ruled by a merchant elite, but by a local or regional, secular or religious prince, forms of co-government often developed. The inhabitants organized themselves to negotiate with their lord a number of other rights. Mostly, the townspeople would first try to gain jurisdiction in commercial matters, but gradually in every other aspect of town life and government. Thus, many towns managed to ensure a certain degree of self-government, either with or without the supervision of a lord's representative. In this way, political structures developed whereby the community was able to operate as an independent entity, instead of individuals having to confront other individuals.[35]

Indeed, the urge to gain greater independence increased by the high degree of united action that characterized town life, as can be witnessed in the phenomenon of the guilds. These organizations of artisans and merchants specializing in a specific branch of industry or trade fostered a definite sense of self-sufficiency. Women, operating independently, played an important role, especially in the crafts' guilds, making up a large minority of their members in many towns.

Soon, the guilds developed a sense of social and cultural solidarity as well as a sense of power. This became obvious in such manifestations as the care they took of their sick and ageing members, sometimes creating hospitals and retirement homes for them. It also showed in their willingness to help save the souls of their deceased brethren by spending freely on masses to be said for the dead in the local church, and in the construction of special guild chapels, adorned with specifically commissioned altar pieces honouring the guild's patron saint. In many towns, too, they had magnificent guildhalls erected, where they would convene for special meetings or celebrations.

As indicated above, most European towns were actually governed by small elites, consisting either of men from the landowning nobility who had interests in the towns as well – as was often the case in Spain and Germany, and especially in Italy – or of wealthy merchants, as, for example, in most towns of the southern and northern Netherlands and in England. Depending upon the town's major economic function, both groups might have a stake in its rule. However, eventually the two groups tended to merge into one single ruling class, a veritable oligarchy. Mostly, the members of the ruling elite held the major administrative positions and dominated the city council even when this was composed through some sort of election by a larger group of the inhabitants.

From the eleventh century onwards, towns became a major influence in western and central Europe, both in economic and in political life. Aware of their unique position, and of the advantages it gave them, they sometimes tried to organize even across state borders. In the twelfth century, the Hanseatic League emerged, a network of trading cities that covered a large part of northwestern Europe, facilitating the movement not only of goods but also of ideas, commercial, technical and artistic.[36]

By the fifteenth century, cities and their ruling elites were a power factor that could no longer be disregarded, and they knew it. In 1458, an anonymous merchant in Naples recorded his thoughts on his profession. His words evince a highly developed self-awareness, based on an ideal-type vision of the importance of the merchant class to the economy, society and culture. Strikingly, to him, trade was not only the essential motor for the economy, ensuring prosperity along with the agricultural sector, but also the essential factor in the proper functioning of the state, since bureaucracy and taxation depended on it. Moreover, he presented the merchant as the 'ideal' citizen. He reasoned as follows:

> The dignity and office of merchants is great and exalted in many respects, and most particularly in four. First, with respect to the common weal. For the advancement of public welfare is a very honourable purpose, as Cicero states. . . . The advancement, the comfort, and the health of republics to a large extent proceed from merchants. . . . Through trade . . . sterile countries are provided with food and supplies and also enjoy many strange things which are imported from places where other commodities are lacking. Merchants also bring about an abundance of money, jewels, gold, silver, and all kinds of various crafts. Hence, cities and countries are driven to cultivate the land, to enlarge the herds, and to exploit the incomes and rents. And merchants through their activity enable the poor to live; through their initiative in tax farming they promote the activity of administrators; through their exports and imports of merchandise they cause the customs and excises of the lords and republics to expand and consequently they enlarge the public and common treasury.

> [A merchant is] sparing, temperate, solid, and upright . . . ; no professional man understands or has ever understood the monarchies of this world and the states in regard to management of money upon which all human states depend as does a good and learned merchant.[37]

In the centuries following the decline of the Roman Empire, though states usually assumed a monarchic form of government, political organization in Europe sometimes developed along republican lines as well, with final sovereignty over a town and a larger territory being exercised by a small urban elite, as, for example, in the great merchant republics of Venice and Genoa, or the powerful towns of Hamburg, Bremen, Lübeck and Danzig in northern Germany. For a long time, these town-states managed to resist incorporation into the usually bigger territorial monarchies. Yet, these became the European norm: all over the west, the tendency was towards princely rule.

Inevitably, with the growing power of the towns – both the independent ones and those functioning within the princely states – their roles multiplied. Economically speaking they have been essential to Europe's growing prosperity. Also, the specific way of life that developed in urban conditions contributed to a slow but gradual change from an agricultural society and culture to an artisanal and proto-industrial one, which at least partly created different values. Finally, urban political structures became of major importance to the further development of the European states. In the traditional struggle between monarchs trying to increase their power and nobles trying to retain as much of it as possible, the towns, if only because of the revenue they generated, became potential political allies for either party. It was the princes who, conferring ever more privileges on the urban communities, succeeded most in tying them to their interest. However, precisely in doing so, they introduced an element in state politics that would finally alter the concept of absolute princely power.

For as the towns, or rather the urban elites, acquired their own stake in the preservation of central power, they increased their demands to participate in state government. Most princes were fully aware that they could not but admit the urban representatives to the consultative assemblies that came into existence all over Europe as a result of the complicated play for power between the various power groups – namely, central government, the Church, the nobility and the towns. In England, a 'parliament' including the representatives of towns was first convened in 1295. A decade later, in France, King Philip IV called for the assembly of the 'États-généraux' when he needed his realm's support in his struggle against the power of the Pope.

Thus, in most states, a balance was eventually struck between kings, the nobles – who usually cooperated with the Church since most positions of ecclesiastical power were held by nobles – and the towns.[38] While each group tried to realize its own particular goals, however, they knew it was in their own interest to preserve the power of the state that was increasingly seen as a common responsibility, a guarantee against chaos, war and poverty. Depending upon the quality of the balance, a state could be strong or weak. Still, it simply could not survive without the active or at least passive participation of the cities and their elites.

A Christian world or a world of Christian nations?

The dream of a new empire coinciding with the territory of (western) Europe, which seemed to materialize during the realm of Charlemagne, had evaporated after the emperor's death. The political fragmentation that characterized the west after the collapse of the Carolingian Empire in the ninth century had, by the tenth century, already led to the creation of states which frequently embodied specific ethnolinguistic unities. Soon, the division between those parts of Europe where the Romance languages were spoken, and the part where 'Thios', 'Diutsch', 'Deutsch' (i.e. German) was the basis of the languages was widely felt.[39] By degrees, the various states acquired their own 'proto-national' character despite the unity of religion and, at least in the upper classes, of culture that still seemed to bind them to the larger concept of Christendom, or Europe. Indeed, there were some who did not want to accept this new situation of a Europe divided into national states and argued for a continued universal hegemony, either papal or imperial.

Three men whose stories present a view of their world can help us to better understand the history of this period. In the last decades of the twelfth century, a learned and witty cleric named Walter Map wrote his *De Nugis Curialium* ('On Courtiers' Trifles'), a fascinating series of, mostly satirical, stories about his own times. This Welshman, grown rich in the service of king and Church, had studied in Paris and had been one of the English representatives at the third Lateran Council in Rome. About France, which he knew well – after all, a large part of it still belonged to the English Crown – he was brief: it was 'the mother of all mischief'. The Greeks were dealt with at somewhat greater length. They were 'soft and womanly', 'voluble and deceitful' and 'of no constancy or valour against an enemy'. Rome, by mouth of one of his storytellers, was curtly characterized indeed: ROMA stands for '*radix omnium malorum avaricia*', or 'the root of all evil is avarice'. But with a definite note of self-confident self-mockery, Map described his compatriots, the Welsh, as wholly unfaithful to everybody – to each other as well as to strangers'.[40]

In about 1200, a well-travelled, anonymous clergyman from Saxony wrote what is considered to be the oldest chronicle of the world in German. Starting with God's creation, the story quite quickly proceeds to the early Christian era. Constantine's reign is, of course, an essential marker:

> Do he do cristen wart, do wart gehoget over all de werelt de cristenlike name . . . di hilege ecclesia gewan grote sekerheit unde grote vrede.[41]

> As he became a Christian, the name of Christ was exalted all over the world . . . and Holy Church created safety and peace.

A little further on in, the author tells us that 'de Engelsaxen gewonnen Brittanniam unde besaten dat lant wante an disen dach, dat is nu Engelant' ('the

English conquered Brittany and possess it up until the present day; it is now England'). Other states are mentioned as well. Yet, the framework within which they function is 'de Cristenheit' (Christendom).

Of course, he talks of the rise of Muhammad, presented as a false prophet who misled the witless masses with a promise of a heaven full of eating, drinking and fornication. Contrast this then with Charlemagne:

> Der keiser Karl . . . mit deme quam dat rike an de Vranken, unde darna an de Dudischen herren . . . was an godes dieneste vlitich, wande he was wol geleret; he san oc selven mit sinen kapellanen. . . . He merede de Dudische sprake mit der Walschen . . . de keiser Karl let sine kindere alle leren.

> The Emperor Charles, with whom the empire fell to the Franks, and afterwards to the German lords, served the Lord with great fervour, for he was well educated; he also sang [during mass] with his chaplains. He added Latin to the German tongue. The Emperor Charles caused all his children to study.

Obviously, this is an intellectual speaking, someone who attaches importance to showing how literate this exemplary emperor was. In Anglo-Saxon England, the king who had introduced unity and Christianity, Alfred the Great, was put forward as an example for the people in a similar way. It is an intellectual speaking, a man who, significantly, indicates that the vernacular can be enriched by additions from the standard cultural languages, the 'Walsch' ones, i.e. the languages derived from Latin, mostly Italian and French. It is an intellectual speaking, a man who identifies the distinguishing criteria of contemporary culture and society: reading and preferably writing. In short, this is an intellectual who, like his clerical colleagues all over Europe, is consciously creating a socio-cultural and thus psychological dividing line between *literatus* and *illiteratus*, a dividing line which increasingly separated the powerful from the powerless.[42]

The world-view presented by a Viennese burgher is different but quite as intriguing. In about 1276, one Jansen Enikel composed a gigantic rhymed chronicle of world history, 27,000 stanzas long. It is in the vernacular as well, but much juicier than the lines of the anonymous author of the Saxon world history.[43] Enikel's story, too, begins with the creation and then quickly moves on to Noah and his sons:

> der ein was Sem genant/des tugent zieret wol ein lant/der ander hiez Japhet zwar/der was an tugent gezieret gar/des dritter sones nam was genant Cham/und war der tumbist under in.

> the one was named Sem, whose virtue adorned a land; the other was called Japhet, who possessed great virtue; the third son was called Cham, and he was the most stupid of them all.

A prejudice with long-lasting and far-reaching results had been born: the Chamites, the people of black Africa, were dismissed as 'dumb'.

Jansen attaches great importance to the foundation of Rome, and to the history of the ancient emperors and of the popes which he integrates into one seamless narrative, thus suggesting a pre-given continuity. Not once does he use the word Europe, however. To him, Orient and Occident were the two constituent parts of the known world, until Constantine the Great appeared on the scene, after which, in his story, the word 'Kristenheit' is always used, to denote a complex geographical-cultural-religious entity. However, Jansen's 'Kristenheit' is divided into independent countries: 'Frankenlant, Engellant, Yspaniënlant, Italië, Oesterreich', or peoples: the 'Beier, Laniparten, Sahsen, Ungern'.

Notably, he later specifies the division of Europe in an overview of the twelve languages – the number is symbolic – which are spoken in his world; obviously, German is given pride of place. These languages now identify people – nations? – as well. Somewhat surprisingly, the Greeks are the fifth group, and the Armenians the ninth – perhaps because both still belonged to the 'Kristenheit'? What is definitely surprising is to see the Moors in Spain form the tenth group. Does this indicate that, though their religion would not speak for their inclusion, they still form part of Enikel's world because, beyond Christendom, he already thinks in terms of a geographically defined Europe?

Significantly, Jansen adds a special characteristic to each language group, often reflecting an apparently long-standing prejudice about the national character of those concerned but also something about their diet – we must not forget that in these centuries food was central to most people's thinking precisely because it was such a scarce commodity:

> Beiern is ein diutsch lant/daz ist mir wol bekant/daz sint gûtig liute . . . [And] ze Tyrol in dem lande/da lebt man an schande/und ze Görz ist ir vil . . . Die Kernder auch diutsch kunnen/der ern muoz man in gunnen . . . hirsbrin ist ir spis.[44]

> Bavaria is a German land – that I know well; the people who live there are good people. In the land of Tyrolia, people live without honour . . . and they have a lot of corn. The Carinthians also know German, I have to admit; they eat wheat porridge.

Yet, during these centuries the way people thought about Europe was changing. At the beginning of the fourteenth century, Alexander von Roes, a senior civil servant, wrote:

> It is now appropriate for me to describe the borders of Europe, and the different habits of the diverse peoples and groups. After all, Europe has four important empires, namely, the Greek in the east, the Spanish in the west, the Roman in the south and the Frankish in the north, while there are still more small kingdoms on the borders.[45]

The text contains two striking elements. Like Jansen Enikel, von Roes does include the Greek Christians in the world he now calls Europe. Unlike Jansen, however, he does not once describe European unity in terms of the *Christianitas* idea. Europe, now, is simply made up of different political entities, each with its own culture.

Indeed, by now most states were trying to create some kind of collective identity, in order to create greater cohesion and, thus, power. In a Christian culture, what better way than to make the national heroes into saints, or the saints into national heroes? Thus, for example, in France, the religious and popular cults of St Clovis, St Denis, St Louis and St Michel provided the subjects of the French king with a rallying point, specifically useful when wars had to be fought against encroaching neighbours.[46]

The new idea – of Europe rather than Christendom, and of states making up this Europe – certainly reflects the fact that by now the Church and the states, which both considered themselves universal, were actually no longer able to cooperate. This had become manifestly clear when they started fighting each other continuously during the tenth, eleventh and twelfth centuries. Struggling for sole or at least supreme power, pope and emperor each called on what was, in terms of content, a very different 'renovation' of the old Roman hegemony. Their fighting greatly damaged what there was of cultural and political unity in 'Europe',[47] eroding the *Christianitas* concept, the very base of their power claims. While the popes had great moral authority – as well as a very efficient bureaucracy, also in fiscal affairs – they had no army to help them wield real power. The emperors on the other hand lacked a proper bureaucracy and, indeed, beyond their own domains, a manageable territory to draw power from – the 'German Empire' stretched from the Baltic to Brindisi and from The Hague to the lands beyond Vienna, and was already divided into a multitude of small states that only nominally accepted imperial suzerainty.

No wonder, then, that various thinkers were intent on finding ways to heal the rift they felt threatened Europe. In 1310, the Florentine poet Dante Alighieri proposed in his tract *De Monarchia* that the spheres of State and Church should finally be separated: the emperor, using the law, was to give secular society its ideal form on earth, while the Pope, with the help of God's revelation, was to lead mankind to its ultimate destination, heaven.[48]

At almost the same time, the French writer Pierre Dubois formulated a statement about papal power, designating it the 'universal' authority while establishing that the emperor could not have a similar hegemony. However, despite the Pope's spiritual power, Dubois felt that it was the duty of the various sovereign princes to guarantee the law in the independent states of which the Christian world was in fact now comprised. Instead of an imperial hegemony in secular matters, Dubois envisaged an assembly of states or a 'council', in which the Christian world, which he does not call Europe, would be united.[49]

Meanwhile, there were stormy discussions between the popes in Rome and the various secular princes of Christian Europe, with the emperor in the lead, mainly about the question of whether Roman authority was supreme both in spiritual as well as in secular matters. Innumerable arguments for and against were put forward, often referring to the texts of such classical writers on politics as Aristotle and Plato that, though not yet available in their entirety, were avidly read and commented upon.

The Italian scholar Marsiglio of Padua (*c*.1275–*c*.1342), doctor, philosopher and rector of the Sorbonne in Paris, took a very daring stand in his work *Defensor Pacis* (1324), demanding absolute autonomy for every political unity – city-state, principality, kingdom and empire. He also advocated the establishment of a 'Christian council' to deal with general problems concerning all believers and, thus, states. Inevitably, papal censorship tried to prevent this potentially danger-ous text being read or spread. Yet Marsiglio's words, certainly in retrospect, were a great moment in the development of ideas about the position of man as a citizen, and of the body of citizens as the basis of all authority. Thus, they greatly influenced political and, also, ecclesiastical thought in Europe:

> [I, 15.2] Let us say, in accordance with the truth and the doctrine of Aristotle . . . that the efficient power to establish or elect the ruler belongs to the legislator or the whole body of citizens, just as does the power to make laws. . . . And to the legislator similarly belongs the power to make any correction of the ruler and even to depose him, if this be expedient for the common benefit. For this is one of the more important matters in the polity; and such matters pertain to the entire multitude of the citizens. . . .
>
> The method of coming together to effect the aforesaid establishment or election of the ruler may perhaps vary according to the variety of provinces. But in whatever way it may differ, this must be observed in each case, that such election or estab-lishment is always to be made by the authority of the legislator who, as we have very frequently said, is the whole body of the citizens, or the weightier part thereof. . . .
>
> [II, 20.2] And now I am going to show that the principal authority, direct or indirect, for such determination of doubtful questions belongs only to a general council composed of all Christians or of the weightier part of them, or to those persons who have been granted such authority by the whole body of Christian believers. . . . Let all the notable provinces or communities of the world, in accordance with the determination of their human legislators whether one or many, and according to their proportion in quantity or quality of persons, elect faithful men, first priests and then non-priests, suitable persons of the most blameless lives and the greatest experience in divine law.[50]

Still, anyone travelling through Europe in these ages would still have seen many signs that marked its continuing cultural unity under the tutelage of the Church, however disputed its political power might be.

Each city of importance would position itself in the landscape with the spires of its many churches. Entering the gates, one would often find, dominating the central square, a cathedral, whether in the Romanesque style, with heavy walls and small windows with rounded arches, or in the newer fashion which only later was called 'Gothic' – characterized by soaring vaults, pointed arches and huge windows, as in the famous cathedrals of France, like Chartres and Lyon, or Germany, like Bamberg or Cologne. Indeed, the daring inventiveness of the architects of these ages seemed to know no bounds, as is shown by the breathtaking perpendicular fan-vaults and the almost completely stained-glass window-walls of Henry VI's chapel at King's College, Cambridge. Cathedrals, far from being separate, self-sufficient entities, were the living heart of an episcopal town, structures where many people found employment, and where both individual religion and civic pride found its expression in daily devotion, magnificent feasts and great works of art.[51]

The portals of these churches, the great as well as the lesser, that now arose in every city were decked with sculpted visions of hell and heaven, of the devils that lived in the realm of eternal damnation, where no true Christian ever hoped to end, and of the saints floating in paradise. Inside these churches, which were not sterilely white as we often see them nowadays, but very brightly painted with biblical and hagiographic scenes, people made the round of the many side-chapels and chantries with their altars and altar-pieces, painted or sculpted in stone or wood, while, in the apse, the high altar always presented a mighty vision of life on earth and in heaven.

Indeed, though, at this time, most art in Europe – in any of its manifest expressions – was still religious art, both in function and in content, yet, in the papal capital and in the wealthy towns of Tuscany, specifically religious painting – commissioned not only by cardinals and prelates, religious orders and nobles, but also by rich burghers and civic fraternities – now began to show traces of a new 'realism'. Around 1300, Pietro Cavallini, in his fresco cycles for the great papal basilicas in Rome and, slightly later, Giotto di Bondone in the churches and chapels of Assisi, Florence and Padua depicted men and women as real people, rather than idealized types. Such religious art flowered all over Europe. In the grand retable made by Veit Stoss for one of Cracow's main churches, sculpture and painting are united in one stupendous vision of what still was a deeply religious world.

Dotting the countryside, there were the monasteries, both big and small, many of them already centuries old, others the manifestation of the constantly new inspiration and vigour in the Christian monastic movement. Everywhere, one found the offspring of the great abbey at Cluny. First built in 909, through its 'reformation' it had set an example to many others who strove for a more strict observance of monastic rules. The ensuing vast network of daughter foundations now contributed to Cluny's great wealth.

At the end of the eleventh and the beginning of the twelfth century, a new call for monastic austerity and purity was heard, this time from the monks at Citeaux, led by St Bernard. The Cistercian movement, too, found followers everywhere. They established several hundred monasteries all over Christendom, mostly engaging in agricultural and industrial business,[52] but all the while functioning and acting as the centres of an all-pervading religious culture.

Elite culture and popular cultures: cosmopolitan norms and regional variations

After the decline of the old Romanized elites in the fourth, fifth and sixth centuries, almost without exception those who held power in the Church, the monks and the priests, were the only ones who could still read and write. As writing (or rather literacy) is an essential means of exercising power in every complex society, with the rise of the Frankish Empire and other kingdoms in Europe from the eighth century onwards, the clergy came to hold great power in the secular world as well, as already indicated above.

Besides, at princely courts, the Christianization of civilization occurred mainly in the '*scriptoria*', the writing rooms of the monasteries, and in the classrooms of cathedral schools.[53] There, the clergy raised its pupils, who were either the sons of the nobility, often trained for military and administrative functions in the State or for senior positions in the Church, or the sons of commoners, who were almost always educated for an ecclesiastical career. In this milieu, the clergy preserved and commented on a tradition of knowledge based on those elements of classical culture which the Church was prepared to endorse, to the extent, that is, that they did not conflict with the biblical and other arguments used by Rome.[54]

From the sixth century onwards, in a process of sifting and selecting, the clergy expanded the corpus of knowledge which the Church allowed educated people to digest and to use to exercise power.[55] Although the artistic, philosophical and scientific way of thinking in which Christian theology and the classical tradition slowly merged was basically the culture of an ecclesiastical and secular elite,[56] inevitably it filtered down into the wider society, gradually evolving into what we now recognize and define as 'European culture', even though no one would have used that term.

Yet, in this Europe, the outlines of a common cultural ideal became increasingly visible. As a result of the political discord following Charlemagne's death, to many literate Europeans, the 'guardians of tradition', his empire, the revived Roman Empire, became a vision of past glory. Indeed, his reign was increasingly idealized as a 'golden era', as a world, moreover, that should be retrieved. Such a dream occurs, for example, in the works of influential historians like Notker Balbulus and Nithard,[57] contributing to the 'myth' of a perfect world that, effectively, coincided with Europe, with Christendom. Obviously, they often, consciously or subconsciously, elaborated on Rome's wish for the borders of the religious and political worlds to overlap, to form one unified culture over which the Church did claim power.

Although the Church did not actually succeed in realizing this vision, it did create a unity that was the more substantial because it survived many political changes, devastating wars and grave economic crises. The Christian world was one, in belief, liturgy and institutions. The laws of the Church, or Canon Law, evolved out of and were now preserving the concepts of Roman Law, and contributed to people thinking of the relations between the individual and state government in legal terms that were soon proclaimed universal, overruling all local customary law. Meanwhile, the Christian calendar that structured the

European year around the major feasts of the Church as well as the many saints' or holy days – and the ritual that went with it – now came to regulate European daily life from dawn until dusk: church bells would wake the peoples of Europe in the morning, tell them when it was noon, try to bring them to mass on Sundays, at least, announce birth, marriage and death, the coming of enemy armies, or the great events of the State, in short they would circumscribe every single detail of daily life, all the year round, making European culture a Christian culture in every respect.

Precisely this culture has been termed the 'small tradition'. It provided a framework for the whole of western and central Europe within which everyone arranged their lives.[58] Yet this common basis did not result in a common feeling, at least not for the vast majority of people, most of them somehow tied to the soil, almost all of them illiterate. Their horizon was, in fact, limited to their own locality. Their habits and lifestyles mostly took form within the confines of their self-enclosed farming communities, frequently attached to a nobleman's manor, with a castle and perhaps a village as its secular centre.

Churches and chapels were the religious centres, where most people's ideas of the world were shaped. It was there that the clergy proclaimed the message central to the lives of many Europeans as Christians: life on earth is temporary. Hence, do not attach too much importance to it. Also, accept suffering as a result of man's imperfection, of his fundamental state of sinfulness: man will regain his perfection in the hereafter. It is, in the end, God's mercy that will help him to reach this goal.[59]

Thus, although the mindset of Europeans was, basically, the same, they did not experience it as a common culture. On the contrary, anyone who arrived in the local community from beyond the horizon was seen as foreign and differ-ent. Yet this local awareness was not absolute. From all layers of society people travelled beyond the horizon at least once in their lives: they were the pilgrims who, like their fellow believers in the Islamic world, considered that a 'sacred journey', a journey to the holy cities was essential for their salvation. As Dante Alighieri (1265–1321) indicates in the introduction to the fortieth sonnet, '*O pilgrims*', of his *Vita Nuova*:

> Those who travel over seas are called palmers,
> as they often bring back palms;
> Those who go to St James' shrine in Galicia are called pilgrims,
> because the burial place of St James was further away from his country than
>   that of any other apostle;
> And Romeos are those who go to Rome,
> which is where those whom I call pilgrims were going.[60]

By sea or over land, often following the highways which had been constructed centuries ago by the Roman legions, pilgrims journeyed from the west, north or eastern parts of Europe to the south, to the cradle of Christianity – Rome and Jerusalem.[61] Along the way they met other people, whose languages and ways of life were different. Yet all shared the same faith, all were heading for the same sanctuaries, all held the same expectations of the hereafter, all eagerly anticipated paradise in heaven. And though, in the phenomenon of pilgrimage, devotion and trade often went hand in hand, this only strengthened its influence on the development of Christianity as a pan-European culture.

The major pilgrim route led to Jerusalem, either by ship from Venice or another Mediterranean port, or overland through the foreign and very dangerous Balkans. After the end of the Crusades, however, people were less inclined to travel to the world of Islam. Indeed, the popes, while still fostering the Crusading ideal, used the actual situation to draw attention to their own city as the holiest place of Europe, where St Peter and St Paul had lived and died, together with hundreds of other saints and martyrs. The *Pieterpad* or 'St Peter's Way' led from Scandinavia through the Netherlands to Rome, to the graves of the apostles and the sanctuaries of all those other holy men and women. A third major route developed from the ninth century onwards: from all over Europe, the *Camino de Santiago* directed the faithful to the shrine of St James at Santiago, in Galicia, the most northwesterly province of present-day Spain.[62] All these routes were 'roads of civilization', along which all sorts of major and minor forms of culture spread over the entire Christian world: the sculpted shell pattern associated with Compostela, the expressive forms of early Romanesque architecture and sculpture a vision of the remnants of ancient Rome whose ruins rose around the Christian shrines, the elements from dialects and languages, European as well as Semitic, which crept into the pilgrims' parlance, the food habits people picked up on their journey.

Of course, people went on interregional pilgrimage as well. Thus, from the whole of north-west Europe people travelled to Canterbury, in England, where St Augustine was buried and where, later, Thomas à Becket was venerated, or they made a somewhat more modest but still considerable journey within their own region as, for instance, in the Netherlands to the shrine of St Servaas in Maastricht.

Pilgrimage was not restricted to members of the elite only. Indeed, its cultural importance precisely stems from the sheer number of people from the un-educated classes who, through their travel, often gained a new vision of the world. Still, it has to be doubted whether they contributed much to a further articulation of fundamental European unity. For besides being illiterate and, thus, unable to communicate beyond their own communities, through pilgrimage people also became aware of each other's peculiarities, of the 'strange' habits and 'weird' morals which, inevitably, had developed in local or regional isolation and which frequently led to mutual irritation or, even worse, derision. Judgement soon became prejudice – and condemnation. The twelfth-century *Liber Sancti Jacobi*, part of which for hundreds of years has served as the travel guide for all pilgrims going to Santiago, named the Gascons 'braggarts and lecherous drunkards', and the Spaniards 'uncivilized'. Similar texts warned the traveller against the dirty tricks played on one with double-bottomed beakers containing far less beer than bargained for, or against people who saw no problem in sexually assaulting man and animal alike. On the other hand, Dante significantly noted that most pilgrims were barely interested in what they saw and experienced during their journeys:

> Ye pilgrim-folk, advancing pensively
> As if in thought of distant things, I pray
> Is your own land indeed so far away –
> As by your aspect it would seem to be –
> That nothing of our grief comes over ye
> Though passing through the mournful town midway;
> Like unto men that understand to-day
> Nothing at all of her great Misery?[63]

Meanwhile, however, though monks and priests, warriors and courtiers and, increasingly, the wealthier townspeople shared many of the same cultural premises of the peasants, they were nevertheless far more influenced by a wider world, a world of education in the literate or even scholarly tradition; in that world, they were confronted with ways of thinking, with problems and questions – philosophical, theological, scientific and literary – which, from the perspective of the 'ordinary people', must have seemed a different world altogether. This world, this culture has been called the 'great tradition'.

LONDON, AD 1378: GEOFFREY CHAUCER DESCRIBES HIS WORLD

In his *Canterbury Tales*, written between 1378 and 1400, Geoffrey Chaucer (1342–1400), an English civil servant who travelled widely on the continent, has left us a vivid picture of life and culture during these years, presented through the stories told by a number of persons from all walks of life while on their pilgrimage to the shrine of St Thomas à Becket, in Canterbury. Characteristically, the first person we meet is a knight, whom Chaucer portrays in a highly stylized and idealized way, stressing the true knightly values: he is a gentle, noble man, not arrogant but modest – he does not offend others. Of course, he defends the frontiers of Christendom and, crossing the Mediterranean and the plains of central Europe, even seeks out the Infidel in his own world:

> There was a Knight, a most distinguished man,
> Who from the day on which he first began
> To ride abroad had followed chivalry,
> Truth, honour, generousness and courtesy,
> He had done nobly in his sovereign's war
> And ridden into battle, no man more,
> As well in Christian as in heathen places,
> And ever honoured for his noble graces.
> When we took Alexandria, he was there,
> He often sat at table in the chair

Of honour, above all nations, when in Prussia.
In Lithuania he had ridden, and Russia,
No Christian man so often, of his rank.
When, in Granada, Algeciras sank
Under assault, he had been there, and in
North Africa, raiding Benamarin;
In Anatolia he had been as well
And fought when Ayas and Attalia fell,
For all along the Mediterranean coast
He had embarked with many a noble host.
In fifteen mortal battles he had been
And jousted for our faith at Tramissene:
Thrice in the lists, and always killed his man. . . .
He was of sovereign value in all eyes.
And though so much distinguished, he was wise
And in his bearing modest as a maid.
He never yet a boorish thing had said
In all his life to any, come what might;
He was a true, a perfect gentle-knight.[64]

———————————+———————————

This part of Chaucer's *Canterbury Tales* is a late reminder of Europe's 'age of chivalry' and the role of the knight in it, who shows his indefatigable valour and courageous deeds, and also his modesty and good manners which distinguish him from the boors, the peasants. Obviously, this image goes back to such earlier knightly tales as the eleventh-century *Chanson de Roland* that extolled the '*gestes*', the chivalrous actions of the paladins, the companions of Charlemagne in their battle against the Saracens, who were probably Basque warriors living in the Pyrenees;[65] with its vivid details, it was the most influential example of the much-loved genre of the '*chansons de geste*', the heroic poems, originally composed in old French – actually, it was one of the first literary texts in the French vernacular – but translated into English, German and Dutch as well.

These tales in their turn probably relied on a very old, orally transmitted tradition. They continued to be sung or chanted, perhaps accompanied by one or more instruments, to a noble audience. A mixture of fact and fantasy, they illustrate the values held by and the struggles within the European warrior class,[66] telling of noble heroes who live for their loyalty to their prince and for the dignity of war, especially war for their lord and against the Infidel. Often, these poems were first composed to rally the world of Christendom against those whom it felt to be its enemies. Unlike 'Roland's Song', whose protagonists are difficult to identify among a number of historical heroes, the twelfth-century '*Poem of my Cid*' – typically, 'Cid' was taken from the Arab word *Sidi* (lord) – was based on the life of Rodrigo Díaz de Vivar (*c.*1043–99), who had led Castilian troops against Muslim Valencia. The poem enjoyed great popularity.[67] In later times, its theme was reworked by the French seventeenth-century

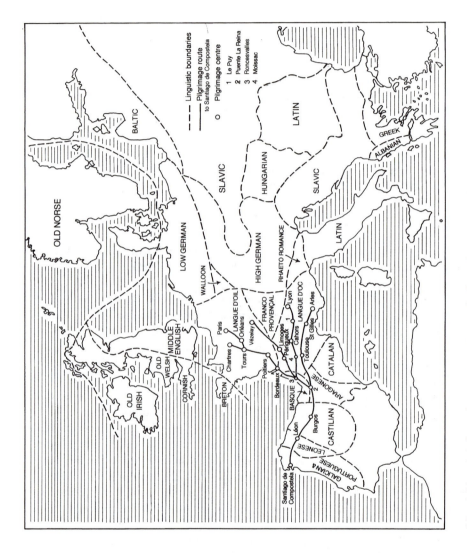

Map 4 Linguistic boundaries, c.1200 AD (with eleventh- and twelfth-century pilgrimage routes)

Plate 11 The teaching of theology at the Sorbonne, from a fifteenth-century French manuscript.

Source: Centre for Art Historical Documentation, Nijmegen, the Netherlands

playwright Pierre Corneille (1606–84), and set to music by numerous eighteenth- and nineteenth-century composers.

Besides the *chansons de geste*, these centuries saw the rise and development of the poetry of courtly love, possibly influenced by comparable genres in the Islamic world of Spain. Beginning with simple, lyric statements, it culminated in the *Romance of the Rose*, which explores the psychological depths of a situation wherein a lover, a knight, completely abases himself for his beloved. In a certain sense this is adulterous poetry, for the beloved is always a married woman, unreachable, the wife of the knight's lord, who will decide on his advancement, and whose favour, in a way, he seeks by paying court to his lady. Often, this lyricism of illicit love, with its barely veiled sensuousness, was frowned upon by the Church, which sought to redirect the nobles' amorous fervour towards a more spiritual goal, the Virgin Mary. In both forms, this poetry and its themes continue to inspire writers up until the present day. However, as the *chansons de geste*, courtly poetry, described an idealized, past world, the world of 'the knight', it was, in a sense, escapist poetry, for when it was recorded, the world that enjoyed it had already become a more complex social and cultural reality.[68]

It is precisely Chaucer's stories that give us a glimpse of this more complex society, in which the old power structure, the idealized rather than factual three-tiered order of Church, aristocracy and peasantry,[69] was rapidly changing under the influence of urban culture. As well as describing priests and knights, and even a liberated woman *avant la lettre*, the garrulous but strong-willed 'wife of Bath', Chaucer gave his readers the tales of merchants and lawyers, the representatives of a commercial, urban society. This 'new' world, first manifest in

Plate 12 A water-driven flour mill on the bank of the River Vltava at Prague, in a colour-wash, pen-drawing by the Dutch artist Roelant Savery, *c.*1610.

Source: Centre for Art Historical Documentation, Nijmegen, the Netherlands

the thriving urban culture of northern and central Italy, was vividly depicted in the hundred tales–within–a–tale written, under the title *Decameron* (1353), by the Florentine writer Giovanni Boccaccio (1313–75). Boccaccio's Florence is peopled by well-to-do burghers and wealthy patricians. It is a world of close-knit families, living within close-knit neighbourhoods. While theirs is not a carefree society, what with their city being under threat from the Great Plague, yet fear and the concomitant turning to religion are remarkably absent; rather, the stories the protagonists tell one another to while away the time in the seclusion of a hillside villa are about man and his foibles, seemingly taken from contemporary daily life. While the intrigues sometimes revolve around the use of a well-turned phrase or clever repartee in this new urban society, most dwell on sex. They portray, often wittily, a world of henpecked husbands and cuckolding wives, of fornicating priests, even.

Undeniably, the 'great' tradition of which men like Chaucer and Boccaccio were part was firmly embedded in the all-encompassing Christian culture of Europe, the 'small tradition'. Yet, the people depicted by Chaucer and Boccaccio surmounted the limitations of that very 'localized' culture precisely through texts, that gave them information from and about a wider world; and through travel – for their economic and social position allowed them to move around – they met other people and exchanged ideas.

Warriors and courtiers travelled, as Chaucer's knight amply illustrates, if only to join a band of mercenary knights or to participate in a big tournament, to attend a dynastic marriage with a great show of power and might, or to finish some business at an important administrative conference. Thus, the career of the Burgundian nobleman Guillebert de Lannoy (1386–1462) almost exactly mirrors the one described by Chaucer in his 'Knight's Tale'. He journeyed to eastern Europe several times where the Brandenburg or Teutonic knights warred against the Slav tribes, who lived along the Baltic coast and in western Russia; as these peoples were largely 'heathen' still, they were felt to live beyond the world of civilization and were therefore 'barbaric'; consequently, this region was seen as a 'field of honour', where Chaucer's literary knight went as well. Lannoy also attended jousts in Castile and, with what could be called a mixture of duty and pleasure, fought the Moors twice on the Christian–Islamic border in central Spain, another region where fame could be earned. Some time later he visited the Nasrid sultan's palace in Granada, almost as a tourist. But he also travelled on a diplomatic-military mission (i.e. as a spy) to the nascent Turkish Empire in Anatolia. Finally, he made his pilgrimage to the Holy Land.[70]

Likewise, merchants travelled, although, at this time, real transcontinental business trips were not yet customary. But they did often journey beyond the rivers and mountains that bounded their own region. Establishing their own permanent communities in far-away cities, as Italian traders used to do in Flanders, while creating a home away from home, they could not but experience the otherness of a strange environment: it was Christian, but still different. And, of course, monks and priests travelled, leaving their monastery or village parish to go to the nearest episcopal court or even to Rome, to the papal Curia. Increasingly, however, they took to the road to study at some famous cathedral school in another part of Europe.

Indeed, during the course of the eleventh century, the first universities were founded – the Latin word '*universitas*' was first adopted in Paris, in 1221, to indicate not a place or building, but the 'body of masters and students', the community of scholars. This new development was basically an urban phenomenon. In Europe's major towns, cathedral schools had paved the way for the expansion of higher education that was now in increasing demand due to the need for well-trained men for the service of both Church and State.[71] Soon, some of these urban academies achieved a supra-regional renown and function, such as the one at Bologna, famous all over Europe for the excellence of its teaching of Roman Law.

The importance of the universities

From the eleventh century, students and teachers began to pour into the universities. Soon, the new phenomenon was one of the major causes of the further development of Europe's Christian elite culture into an integrated, truly European culture.[72] The meeting of minds from different backgrounds and regions resulted in the development of critical thinking, a creative mentality, which, despite the stultifying atmosphere that soon came to characterize these institutes of learning, proved of great importance to the development of new ideas in every field.

In order to improve the conditions under which the scholarly community could develop, in November 1158, the Holy Roman Emperor Frederic I issued a decree to all his dominions. Among other things, he ordered that safe conduct was to be given to all students and teachers who travelled for the sake of learning:

> Bishops, abbots, dukes and all the judges and most eminent men of our sacred palace having diligently considered the matter, we grant this favour of our dutiful love to all scholars who are travelling for the sake of their studies, and especially to teachers of the divine and sacred laws: that they and their representatives may safely come to the places in which letters are studied and live safely in them.
>
> For we consider it fitting . . . that we should with a certain particular love defend from all harm all those by whose knowledge the world is enlightened and the lives of subjects are moulded into obedience to God and to us, his servants. They all excite compassion, for they have made themselves exiles for love of knowledge.[73]

At university, students might follow the method devised by the famous 'scholastic' Petrus Abelardus or Peter Abelard (1079–1142). Shortly after 1120, he had prepared a syllabus in which he juxtaposed conflicting passages taken from the works of the Church fathers. In the foreword to this text, known as *Sic et Non*, Abelard explains how a real, that is critical, scholar ought to work:

> We should . . . take great care that we are not being deceived by a false attribution or by corruption of the text itself. For a great many apocryphal writings were headed with the names of saints, that they might carry authority; and some even of the texts of the Holy Testaments were corrupted through the fault of the copyists. . . . Let us simply say that it is written in Matthew and John that the lord was sacrificed at the sixth hour, but Mark says the third hour. This was an error of the copyists, and 'the sixth hour' was originally written in Mark, but many thought the Greek letter was a gamma. . . . So if perchance there appears to be something in the writings of the saints which is not in harmony with truth . . . either we should suppose that that portion of the text is not faithfully translated or is corrupt, or we should confess that we do not understand it. . . .
>
> When different things are said about the same matter, it is necessary to discuss thoroughly what is intended as a binding precept and what as a dispensation relaxing the law or an exhortation to perfection, so that we may seek to resolve the conflict by taking into account the difference of intentions. . . . We can easily resolve a great many disputes if we can maintain that the same words have been used with different meanings by different authors. . . . If it happens that there is such an obvious conflict that it cannot be resolved by any argument, then the authorities must be compared, and the one whose testimony is more robust and more fully confirmed should be preferred. . . .
>
> The outstanding canonical authority of the Old and New Testaments is in a different category from the books of later writers. If anything in the Bible strikes you as absurd, it is not permissible to say 'The author of this book did not uphold the truth', but that either the manuscript is false, or the translator made a mistake, or that you do not understand it. But if the little works of later men which are contained in innumerable books are thought to diverge from the truth (perhaps because they are not understood in the original sense), then the reader or listener is free to judge, and to approve what he likes and condemn what he dislikes and

anything of that kind, unless the argument or account in the book is supported by sure reasons.[74]

This rationalistic, logical, almost experimental way of observing the world and everything in it, may well have been stimulated by the contacts between Christian scholars and the Islamic universities of the Iberian peninsula. Indeed, it has been argued that the European universities themselves, as well as the structure of their curricula, originated in or were heavily influenced by the Islamic colleges or *madrassas* and their teaching methods.[75] Though this may be overstating the case, the importance of Europe's cultural contacts with the Islamic world in this field, too, should not be underestimated.

For since the eleventh century, the process of cultural fusion between the Christian and the Islamic world, long in the making, intensified, mainly on the island of Sicily, which was 'reconquered' from the Islamic Berber rulers by Norman rulers who cleverly played the Christian against the Islamic world. There, the University of Salerno came to serve as a window through which Europe could catch a glimpse of a culture, especially a scientific culture, far in advance of developments in peninsular Italy and elsewhere. Through Salerno, medical research, elaborated by Islamic scholars from the ideas of the Greek physicist Galen, came to Europe. Soon, such notions as blood circulation or the advanced treatment of women's diseases based on empirical research, though received with deep distrust by traditional practitioners, could not fail to influence the vision of man and his body.

Meanwhile, as indicated above, Islamic kingdoms had flourished on the Iberian peninsula since the eighth century, ruling most of what is now Spain. There, too, a thriving learned culture developed, again to an extent not yet achieved in Christian Europe. When the eleventh-century jurist Said al-Andalusi, of Toledo, described the world, he maintained that the Christians, whom, *nota bene*, he placed in the lowest of the three classes of human beings, were a stupid people, if only because they did not study physics and the other exact sciences.[76] He was, of course, not entirely wrong. During these centuries, the *Koran*'s admonition that the faithful should study Allah's creation in all its manifold aspects, had created an empirical, scholarly strain in Islamic thinking that was as yet absent in Christian thought.

The cultural situation had become more complicated when Christian princelings from the mountains of northern Spain started to 'reconquer' the peninsula.[77] Soon, several Christian kingdoms occupied the entire northern half of Spain. In 1492, the last Islamic kingdom, Granada in Andalusia, was taken by Ferdinand of Aragon and Isabella of Castile, the heirs of two long lines of Christian-Iberian princes, whose earlier marriage had laid the basis for the future Spanish state. With the fall of Granada, 'Europe' as a geographical entity was a Christian world once again. Yet, in the process of the *Reconquista*, Europe had not only absorbed large parts of the classical inheritance that had been preserved in the 'heathenish world' of Islam, it also had, mostly unconsciously, adopted part of Islamic culture itself. In short, the Islamic-Greek influence had so fundamentally confronted Christian civilization with its classical origins that at least the educated culture of Europe, the intellectual or 'great tradition', had changed completely.[78]

The process had, however, been a long one. With the gradual establishment of Christian rule over the Islamic states of Spain, the great centres of Islamic learning became the capitals of Christian princes and, of course, of the Christian clergy. Often, bigotry led to the destruction of irreplaceable cultural treasures. Luckily, however, some conquerors were aware of the unique opportunity that now presented itself to broaden their horizons.

The most cosmopolitan among them was, of course, King Alfonso X of Castile (1221–84), rightly called '*el Sabio*' (the Learned). A gifted poet himself, who left a great collection of song texts, written in Galician, the poetical language of the time, he also protected and propagated the work of the so-called 'Toledo School of Translators'. This was a group of men who spent their lives studying the Arabic and Hebrew texts they had found in the conquered cities. Incidentally, the Jews, often oppressed in the Christian world, had been made welcome in the Islamic world, where they were esteemed both for their commercial cleverness and for their intellectual qualities. Now, the Christian scholars who had arrived with the new regime, in close cooperation with their Islamic and Jewish colleagues, produced a great number of translations, both in Latin and in Spanish, the latter of which King Alfonso made the state language. Soon, all kinds of new knowledge were revealed to Christian Europe for the first time.

The process was accelerated when the fame of the libraries of the renowned Islamic universities started attracting students from all over the Christian world. For about 300 years, from the twelfth to the fifteenth centuries, while the Christian Spaniards pushed their political dominion to the south, these men – clerics and laymen alike – flocked to Toledo, Cordoba and, finally, Granada to study the Latin translations of the Arabic versions of ancient Greek works on law, philosophy and the sciences, texts which had disappeared from Europe or which the Church had deliberately 'forgotten' because they conflicted with Christian doctrine. Of course, they also came to know the texts that Islamic scholars themselves had written, commenting on the Greek tradition and, in doing so, elaborating it.

Returning to Europe, to their monasteries and universities, these scholars soon argued, for example, for the wider acceptation of the Ptolemaic world-view, which presented the world as a globe. Gradually, the notion of a flat earth, until then held by most, albeit not all Europeans, was replaced with a new vision. They also spread new ideas in the fields of astronomy and mathematics. Most important, perhaps, was the diminishing importance of the idea that man's earthly existence only served to prepare him for life after death, in heaven, the traditional basis of Church doctrine. With new notions about the cosmos, the world and about man himself came the conviction that what really mattered was, indeed, man's duty to further investigate the whole of God's creation.

Inevitably, traditional scholastic Christian culture and the new ideas about man and nature now conflicted, intensifying the traditional tension between classical heritage and Christian theology. Inevitably, this shift of paradigms – the differing sets of values that structured the old and the new world-view – called for a new synthesis. It was produced by Thomas Aquinas (1225–74). As with all Christian scholars, his learning was deeply steeped in Augustine's writings – the writings of a man who, in the fourth century, had confronted the opposition between faith and reason. Now, Aquinas, acknowledging the vast amount of new information he could draw on, searched for ways to reconcile the two worlds. On the one hand, he wanted to retain the Church's interpretation of the Bible and, on the other hand, he wanted to incorporate in it Aristotle's ideas about man and nature, society and learning, which could now be better understood through the translated texts of such Islamic scholars as Ibn Sinna (980–1037) and Ibn Rushd (1126–98), known in Europe as Avicenna and Averroës, respectively.[79]

Ibn Sinna had written important works on medicine, which, combining Greek and Indian learning with many practical insights, greatly influenced Jewish doctors, almost the only scholarly practitioners in this field in all of Europe. He was also a philosopher, who argued that the 'forms' – souls – flowing from God became manifest in matter, which exists eternally with God, who is the 'unmoved mover'. Ibn Rushd elaborated on this idea. For him, religion was the 'visible' presentation of that which can be reasoned about philosophically, aiming primarily at all those who could not simply follow this reasoning, namely the majority of people.

Thomas Aquinas proposed that man is endowed with an insubstantial, immortal soul. One of the most important aspects of the soul is reason, so that even 'the humanity of man flows from his participation in reason'. Reason enables man to achieve knowledge. Thus, man can know all that has been created: nature. That which apparently cannot be reasoned about, God, will nevertheless be accepted by man as true, from the deepest part of his being. Thomas therefore wrote, among other things, that 'Because it transcends understanding, our belief cannot be proven by intellectual reasoning. However, because it is true and thus does not conflict with reason, it also cannot in any way be toppled by oppressively rational arguments'.[80] However, the tensions Thomas hoped to resolve have remained inherent in Christian culture, if only because the process of assimilating classical elements into it was pursued with unabated vigour, creating both greater knowledge and greater doubt.

Meanwhile, European universities, where increasingly the old and the new were taught, where Thomas's thoughts flourished while heterodox sounds could be heard as well, were certainly no quiet havens of learning and research. What academic life was like in practice can be inferred from the writings of Jacques de Vitry (*c.*1180–*c.*1240), a prominent clergyman. The picture he paints of Paris, where the Sorbonne counted as one of the foremost universities in Christendom, is decidedly less than elevating. De Vitry not only shows that teaching standards were not very high but also that many students were attending university for the wrong reasons. Moreover, he is keenly aware of the important role played even then by national rivalry and prejudice and the harm such emotions do to the ideal of the university. Quite obviously, there were all sorts of cultural stereotypes, some very old already, such as remarks on the uncouth behaviour of Germans during feasts – we have seen these in Tacitus and other Roman authors who wrote about the Celts and Germans. Notably, de Vitry indicates that in the lands we now call France and Italy, people saw themselves as part of very different 'nationalities': these corresponded with regions then conceived as separate political unities, such as the county of Poitou, the duchy of Burgundy, the Lombardy region, and so on:

> Almost all the students at Paris, foreigners and natives, did absolutely nothing except learn or hear something new. Some studied merely to acquire knowledge, which is curiosity. Others to acquire fame, which is vanity. Others still for the sake of gain, which is cupidity and the vice of simony. Very few studied for their own edification, or that of others. They wrangled and disputed not merely about the various sects or about some discussions; but the differences between the countries also caused dissensions, hatreds and virulent animosities among them, and they impudently uttered all kinds of affronts and insults against one another.
>
> They affirmed that the English were drunkards and had tails. The sons of France proud, effeminate and carefully adorned like women. They said that the Germans were furious and obscene at their feasts. The Normans, vain and boastful. The Poitevins, traitors and always adventurers. The Burgundians they considered vulgar and stupid. The Bretons were reputed to be fickle and changeable. . . . The Longobards were called avaricious, vicious and cowardly. The Romans, seditious, turbulent and slanderous. . . . After such insults from words, they often came to blows.
>
> I will not speak of those logicians before whose eyes flitted constantly 'the lice of Egypt', that is to say, all the sophistic subtleties, so that no one could comprehend their eloquent discourses in which, as says Isaiah, 'there is no wisdom'. As to the doctors of theology, 'seated in Moses' seat', they were swollen with learning, but their charity was not edifying. Teaching and not practising, they have become 'as sounding brass or a tinkling cymbal', or like a canal of stone, always dry, which ought to carry water to 'the bed of spices'. They not only hated one another, but by their flatteries they enticed away the students of others; each one seeking his own glory, but caring not a whit about the welfare of souls.[81]

No wonder Pope Gregory IX felt it was necessary to interfere. On 13 April 1231, he issued a bull about education and the management of university institutions; he also gave specific rules about what should constitute science and scholarship:

> Bishop Gregory, servant of the servants of God, to his beloved sons, all the masters and scholars of Paris, greeting and the apostolic blessing.
>
> May Paris, the mother of sciences, be famous in her riches. . . . Since untidiness can easily creep in where there is no order, we grant you the power to make prudent statutes and ordinances concerning the time and the manner of lecturing and disputing; on the regulation dress; on the burial of the dead; and on who of the bachelors must lecture, and when and on what subject they must do so. . . .

We further ordain that masters of art shall always give one lecture on Priscian and shall lecture on one book after another in an orderly fashion. They shall not use at Paris those books of natural philosophy which have on sure grounds been prohibited at a provincial council until they have been examined and cleansed of every suspicion of error. Masters and students of theology shall strive to employ themselves in the faculty which they profess, and shall not parade as philosophers. . . .

They shall not speak in the language of the people, nor confound the sacred language with the profane, but shall discuss in the schools only those questions which can be determined by means of theological books and the treatises of the Holy Fathers.[82]

Language, of course, has always been and always will remain an important cultural factor, not only in communication but also in defining different groups within society. Often, it is divisive: for example, the Latin used by the Church and by scholars was not understood by the majority of Christians, or Norman French, the language of the conquerors that had been imposed upon Anglo-Saxon-speaking England.[83] Yet, by using the same Latin as 'lingua franca', or through personal multilingualism, often in some of the many forms of German or French then extant, or even talking some pidgin language made up from all of these elements, people such as the bureaucrat Chaucer and the nobleman De Lannoy, as well as the students travelling all over Europe to seek out the best universities, were able to communicate. Such multilingualism existed not only in the great European capitals and centres of learning but also on the periphery, for instance at the count of Holland's court in The Hague, where both Latin and forms of Dutch as well as French were in use.[84] Thus, language was both a divisive and a unifying factor in contemporary European culture.

A certain community feeling gradually emerged, most markedly among the people who were part of the 'great tradition', which ever more clearly became the basis for an 'idea of Europe'. However, the greater 'cultural competence' of the people involved did not always prevent them from being judgmental, prejudiced and condemnatory.

Intitally, any new development in European culture still spread along the roads worn into the landscape of Europe by the two largest groups of travellers, the anonymous armies using the highways constructed by the Roman legions, and the pilgrims who trod the routes linking northern and central Europe to the south-east and the south-west from the time Christianity had been introduced. Soon, however, this communications network was strengthened by new routes or, even, proper roads, connecting monasteries, towns and universities and allowing new forms of culture to be transferred.[85]

Interlude
The worlds of Europe, *c*.1400–1800

As this book attempts to find out when and how the geographical Europe became the cultural Europe, the central problem is obviously whether and, if so, when and to what extent there existed a 'European awareness' among the people living in Europe? Rather than addressing this problem repeatedly throughout the text, I have concentrated some of the issues involved in this 'interlude'. To answer the question, one must first determine how those who inhabited the continent in the past actually lived. The next question would be whether, within their cultural condition, they could actually know about the various and differing regions surrounding them and, on the basis of this knowledge, understand and value each other's ideas and lifestyles? Only then will it be possible to decide whether there was a common culture that bound together regions and countries, states and nationalities across the many natural and artificial borders that divided the European part of the world.

In the previous chapters, the many and radical changes which economy, society and culture went through in the course of the thirteenth, fourteenth and fifteenth centuries have been outlined. However, it is vitally important to establish that for the great majority of the population many of these changes and, indeed, the subsequent technological innovations were hardly, if at all, noticeable. Indeed, one must be aware that up until *c*.1800, Europe actually consisted of 'two nations'. On the one hand, there was the agricultural population who lived their lives according to a rhythm fixed largely by nature and which remained fairly constant until the end of the eighteenth century.[1] On the other hand, since the eleventh and twelfth centuries, there were the inhabitants of the cities, places that in many respects remained distinct from their rural hinterlands; there, trade, banking and incipient industry flourished; there, political life was played out;[2] there, new ideas were formulated and discussed in schools and universities.

Of course, there was a measure of interaction between these two worlds: economically they were increasingly dependent upon one another, and culturally they shared a number of characteristics. The relationship was stronger in Europe's more urbanized regions, such as northern and central Italy, parts of France, southern and Rhineland Germany, Flanders, Holland and southern England. There, new notions and inventions were developed and introduced into the countryside from the towns where they were first formulated or practised – increasingly from the sixteenth century onwards.[3] However, the larger part of rural Europe experienced little or no such influences up until the late eighteenth and even early nineteenth centuries.

Consequently, it has to be maintained that in the majority of cases, towns and countryside largely had their own cultures: whereas western Europe may have had some 20,000 towns, it had some 160,000 villages, where the majority of Europeans lived.[4]

A world of villages

From the beginnings of agriculture in Europe, in the centuries between 10,000 and 5,000 BC, until the eighteenth century AD, between 70 and 80 per cent of Europe's population were farmers or, to be more precise, survived on the basis of agricultural labour. People worked their own farms or tenanted other people's property, always employing their next of kin, both females and children, for the farming economy was very much a family economy. If one were born without property, one would seek employment as a farmhand on a large rural estate. But whatever their condition, people in the countryside spent their lives tied to the soil, sometimes legally but always materially. In large parts of Europe, especially the central and eastern regions, it was not even possible for them to leave the land they tilled because they were, to a greater or lesser extent, bound to their landlord in some form of serfhood.

Fundamentally, a farmer's life was determined by the need to cultivate the soil in order to provide that most basic commodity, food. Not surprisingly, the one and only material supplication in the most important prayer of the Christian world, the 'Our Father', was: 'give us this day our daily bread'. But the Old Testament told believers they had to earn this bread with their own sweat. Their success determined whether they could keep going on the right side of the line which separated survival from death by starvation, the very thin line which in our time is still so horribly obvious in the so-called 'Third World'.[5]

Farming life was governed by a simple, iron regularity. Getting up with the sun to plough, to sow or to harvest, and to tend the cattle, and going to bed when dusk fell. Usually, there was no money for lighting the house during the dark evening hours. Thus, people had no opportunity to indulge in what nowadays we think of as normal forms of after-work relaxation. Moreover, a farmer's job was a tough one; one needed all one's strength and therefore all the sleep one could get, which was preciously little between sunset and sunrise. Moreover, the majority of the farming population was physically not very strong. The composition of the daily diet was limited and, by our standards, unhealthy. Consequently, an endemic illness caused by certain worms could account for a general weakness among hundreds of thousands of farming people.[6] Healthcare was mostly unavailable to country people, since most qualified doctors lived and worked only in towns. Generally speaking, the general public's physical condition was bad indeed. In short, most people lacked the time, the money and also the energy to spend on sports or play. As to other forms of culture, such as reading and studying, these were almost totally absent in peasant societies.

This brings us to the question of what means of communication would have enabled Europeans to become acquainted with each other's ways of life? Before the range and quality of communication was enlarged – first with the gradual penetration of print culture in the sixteenth century, but, effectively, only with the advance of mass communication in the late nineteenth century – there were really only two channels through which information was transmitted: oral and handwritten communication and, to a lesser extent, the visual messages of paintings and frescos and, again, from the sixteenth century onwards, printed images. However, a more detailed consideration immediately shows the limitations even of these media.

Until the nineteenth century, Europe's farming population was largely illiterate.[7] Apart from the expense involved in education, for most people a formal training was totally irrelevant. Reading, writing and arithmetic were of no conceivable use when handling a plough or a hayfork. And, moreover, how could farmers' children have found time to learn? As soon as they knew how to walk they were expected to give a helping hand on the farm. There simply was no time or money allowing them to go to school. Admittedly, in wintertime farming partly came to a standstill. Children could have attended school then.

Plate 13 This anonymous engraving from 1502 shows various aspects of agricultural labour, such as ploughing and keeping the birds from eating the newly sown seed. Until the coming of the Industrial Revolution, agriculture and the heavy manual labour associated with it – country life was no idyll – was the occupation of by far the majority of Europeans, men, women and, often, children.

Source: CKD RU Nijmegen.

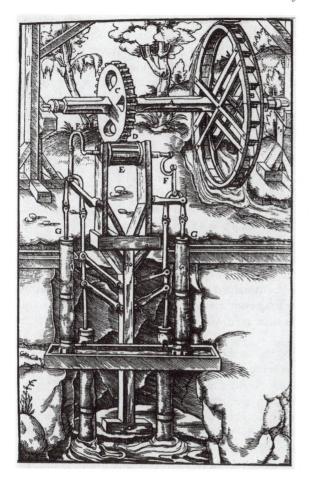

Plate 14 Most Europeans, being engaged in agriculture, would only use very simple implements, such as the ones shown in plate 19. However, in the early modern period, water was used for a variety of sometimes complex mechanical devices. The *De re metallica*, of Georg Agricola, whose name actually means 'farmer', was published in 1556. One of its many illustrations shows falling water being used to drive a wheel which then motors a pump that removes water from a shaft, thus enabling people to mine copper or iron ore, and other minerals.

Source: CKD RU Nijmegen

But for most the question of how to get there would have presented a huge problem. Only rich farmers possessed a donkey or horse, but such traction animals were too valuable to agricultural work to be spared to carry children to school every day. Of course, children could have walked, but not every village had its own school – actually, these were located only in the larger rural centres or in cities of some size. Thus, a walk to school would have meant a journey of some ten or more kilometres every day. Therefore, school attendance and, consequently, learning to read and write were largely precluded, except for those who overcame all these problems and, at least in winter when their help was not needed, sought some basic education. Even those who were sent to school after all, went there not really to learn how to read and write, but to be taught a certain discipline and some notions of how to behave.[8] In short, their way of life was such that for most people the transfer of culture through the written word was barred.

Other forms of large-scale communication were also lacking in the agrarian communities that comprised the larger part of Europe. For one thing, most commodities moved only short distances and in low-density flows; this provided little economic incentive for investment in road building, which obviously limited communication. Also, to people engaged in agriculture, travel, certainly travel for pleasure, was an unknown concept. Every trip cost time and money, precisely the two things farmers did not have to spare. For the majority, a visit to the weekly market was the only moment that their life on the farm and in the village community connected to the larger, outside world – a world that began in the city.

For the countryside in Europe, the city was friend and foe, nearby and yet far away, a separation, a cultural division that in many regions lasted until the nineteenth century. Entering the city gates, country folk were confronted with different habits and morals, with people who often looked down on farmers as rustics. Indeed, to city dwellers, 'peasant culture' was a contradiction, for the agrarian way of life was considered less sophisticated, uncivilized even: peasants could not read or write, they lived in and with nature, and many of their favourite traditions reflected the untamed, dangerous elements of that nature. A mixture of disdain and fear frequently characterized the attitude of town folk towards country folk who, in their turn, were inclined to distrust city dwellers as stuck-up cheats.[9]

Yet to country folk, going to the weekly market, while an economic necessity, also meant having an outing, seeing other people, hearing the stories of travelling pedlars and listening to actors and singers, who opened a window on the world, on life outside their own small village communities. But primarily the market was serious business: farmers had to sell their produce there, and to buy the necessities not available in the village. There was little time left to relax in the tavern or just stroll along the street to listen to the latest news. At most, they might hear some strange tales, told in bits and pieces, without being able to grasp the details.

People from the countryside had to leave the city before dusk, primarily because at nightfall the gates were shut, and those who did not live within the walls were expected to remove themselves. Moreover, it was not advisable to travel the Lord's roads after night had fallen. Until the late eighteenth century, large parts of the European countryside were perilous indeed. Few people left the safety of their own surroundings for pleasure, simply because travelling was not free of danger. One should not forget that huge parts of Europe were not cultivated but consisted of vast moors and dark forests. Highwaymen could rob you of the profits of a week's hard work, not to mention worse. Besides roving bands of professional robbers one might encounter plundering soldiers, 'living off the land' to improve their meagre pay, or farmers who had become penniless, landless and rebellious through failed harvests or other economic disasters; they all made the countryside a very unsafe place indeed, the more so as a regular police force was simply non-existent there. Also, the roads were mostly unpaved, unlit and not signposted. Hence, manifold dangers persisted in the rural areas of the Netherlands and England certainly until the eighteenth century, and in the remote and sparsely populated parts of Scandinavia, France, Germany, Italy and Spain, as well as in central and eastern Europe well into the nineteenth century.

It was not only people, however, who made life difficult for the traveller. One might encounter imagined ghosts and spirits, who had all sorts of nasty plans up their sleeves, and even devils, like the wicked Moenen, who meets a girl Mariken, in the play *Mariken van Nieumeghen*, written around the year 1500 in the eastern Netherlands. This is a gripping, even fascinating tale and, moreover, a historical source which has much to tell us about the culture and mentality of 'ordinary' people during these centuries of transition.

On market day, Mariken, who keeps house for her uncle, a priest, walks to Nijmegen to do her shopping. She has to cover a considerable distance and in the evening, after an exhausting day and an unsettling experience with a distant relative, she has to go home again. Returning, as darkness falls, she realizes that she will not be able to reach home in time and starts looking for shelter in the roadside woods. There, the devil Moenen confronts her. With promises of plentiful and delicious food, of wealth and also of knowledge, he seduces her. She decides to accompany him to the big city, Antwerp, at that time the trading metropolis not only of the Netherlands but also of north-western Europe. The life they embark on there is filled with all the sins known to Christian man in the late fifteenth century: excessive food and wine, whoring and, moreover, too much seeking after knowledge of heaven and earth – a privilege not of man but of God. In presenting these pleasures, the play actually spells out a series of morals and warnings, which the spectators would have understood from their own experiences. One of the messages was: do not travel, certainly not by night – it will lead only to misery.

Consequently, people did not travel unless they absolutely had to. As they could not read either, they lacked the two most obvious and influential means of communication and information: contact with other people and ideas through meeting them in the flesh, and contact with other people and ideas through the written word. In short, the culture and mentality of the majority of Europeans, i.e. those who lived in Europe's agricultural communities, were severely limited. These limitations were three-fold: material – a lack of money; spatial – distances too great to cover on foot; and mental – the lack of communication.

As a result, the factual and mental horizon of most Europeans only reached as far as they could see: to the end of the field, to the edge of the village. Every community was largely closed in on itself, had its own local culture which, despite its wealth of orally transmitted ideas, of social organization and custom, was only slightly and slowly influenced by external factors of change. Life revolved around work, was interrupted only by such moments of relaxation as the annual harvest festival – the origin of the village fair – and the many days the Catholic Church had marked as special, such as Christmas, Easter, the feast of the patron saint of the local church and a number of other 'holy' days – hence 'holidays'. On those days, if no famine reigned, villagers would feast on beer and meat, there would be dance and music, as well as games, and itinerant musicians and players would perform.

Let us pause for a moment to reflect on the role of the Catholic Church, the Church of Rome. It called itself universal as, indeed, it was until about the year 1500 when all the people of western and central Europe were still Catholic. The Church tried to govern the very essence of the lives and actions of these people, as well as, precisely to guide those actions, their deepest thoughts and emotions. Each community had a church as its visual anchor, its social and cultural centre. The local priest, besides being a shepherd of souls, frequently doubled as a doctor, a village arbiter and, if possible, a schoolmaster, although most of the supposedly literate clergy often bordered on illiteracy themselves. The Church taught people to love their neighbours and to obey the ecclesiastical and secular authorities as well as telling them about the existence of heaven, hell and purgatory, where they would go after they died. Above all loomed the constant presence of a severe yet good God. Indeed, that was what the Church taught, and what, in this largely illiterate society, it showed to the people, mostly in devotional pictures. Thus, in Orvieto cathedral's San Brizio chapel, between 1499 and 1504, the artist Luca Signorelli depicted heaven as a place where the elect lived their blissful lives: their bodies perfect, their heads crowned with garlands, surrounded by the saints and angels, all lauding God[10] – for Christian heaven partly derived from the Jewish concept of it, which, simply, described it as man's union with God. Yet, most people in rural Europe may well have preferred another vision, that of a peasants' heaven as painted by Pieter Breughel, the Elder, in whose 1567 painting of the 'Land of Cockayne' there was plenty of food, sex and other merry-making – precisely the things most people lacked in their daily lives.[11] Significantly, however, there were, in this world, far more paintings of hell than of heaven – reflecting, obviously, the fears that beset people every day of their lives: of violence and torture, of illness and physical corruption.

The role of the Church presents us with an apparent contradiction. For centuries, the Roman Catholic clergy were the pre-eminent guardians of a long tradition of knowledge that was passed on from generation to generation, by means of manuscript texts. Yet their flock, the faithful, unable to read, could participate only with eye and ear in the culture that these priests controlled. Nor did the Church really want to provide extensive instruction to the masses. As an institution, it actually considered knowledge of and insight into the great problems of theology and cosmology superfluous and even dangerous for ordinary man. It would only keep him from his daily work or, worse, tempt him to a life of sin, as Mariken had experienced.

Because the clergy, at least in part, were the 'information caste', they wanted to preserve their exclusiveness. In fact, they derived their position from an almost magical power. Ideally, they could read and write, which already resembled magic in the eyes of many; they knew and understood more of the world than most other people did; they could explain or even predict some of the natural phenomena that so terrified most men. Not surprisingly, they wanted to retain this position of power. Knowledge was, therefore, not shared with as many people as possible. On the contrary, it was monopolized by monks and nuns in their monasteries, and by the 'secular' representatives of the Church, the village priests, who often were the only educated men in Europe's rural world.

Whatever the Church chose to teach to the masses was mainly taught through the spoken word, from the pulpit, and through images, visual representations: statues and paintings. On the façades and portals of churches and chapels, on their walls and ceilings, stories from the Bible and edifying scenes from the saints' lives were depicted for all those believers who could not read. After the advent of printing, simple and cheaply printed images were used as well.

In this world of villages and of villagers, were the inhabitants Europeans? Word and image had ensured that in the period beginning with the time that Christianity first became established, i.e. the fifth and sixth centuries, and ending *c.*1500, all Europeans up to the invisible dividing line running from the Baltic to the Balkans still recognized the Pope in Rome as the head of their Church. When Mariken, by Divine Providence, was brought to repent of her sins, she travelled to Rome to ask forgiveness. Everyone felt Christian in the Catholic sense. Yet what this meant in the daily routine of those who dwelt on the other side of mountains and rivers was something most people never asked. Christianity had created a common culture, but its solidarity seldom was or had to be tested in practice.

Thus the mental world of Europeans, of farming communities in particular, differed greatly from what we can imagine today. What occupied Europe's rural population? Certainly few or none of the things we fill our lives with. There was no television, no films, no radio, even. There were no newspapers and, for most people, no books. Sport did not exist either as an organized leisure activity, or as passive entertainment. Indeed, outside the circles of the aristocracy and the well-to-do urban middle classes, leisure was not a known concept.[12] Politics hardly played a role, at least, not in the sense of national or world politics, if only because there was virtually no information that would have elicited public debate. Moreover, political parties, party programmes, all the things that nowadays stimulate political awareness or discussion did not exist either. Only in the big cities did any sort of political consciousness actually exist.

Of course, people knew about wars, but mainly as events which periodically occurred in their own world: until the end of the seventeenth century, small or great wars were waged somewhere in Europe every year. Yet ordinary people hardly understood the larger issues behind them as there were no news analyses and commentaries. War was simply a part of daily life, incomprehensible, as was so much else; it was certainly not an intellectual or moral problem.

What did actually occupy people, historians have tried to infer from the stories they told each other, the songs they sang and the poems they recited. In the evenings, especially in winter, the villagers gathered together to listen to story-tellers and singers – local men or travelling ones – who were the preservers of the complex collective memory of the village community, circumscribing a world at once local and cosmic, through tradition and myth. Stories, songs and poems were passed on orally, from generation to generation. It was not until the eighteenth and nineteenth centuries that assiduous scholars began to collect and record them: the German J.G. Herder in the late eighteenth century and, later, Charles Perrault, in France, and the brothers Grimm, again in Germany, carried out pioneering work in this field. They, and a host of other scholars who studied popular culture, or folklore, gave us a chance to look back into the past through those stories, to uncover the lives and probe the minds of those who did not normally record their actions, ideas and feelings. Although these tales are heavily filtered by time, by centuries of oral transmission and, of course, by the writing of their final recorders, the other sources which document the life of ordinary people certainly are as biased, if not more so. For though secular and ecclesiastical records yield fascinating insights, too, they nearly always represent popular culture through the eyes of educated middlemen – clerks and chroniclers, for whom the world of written words was the dominant narrative, into which the world of 'others' had to be fitted.[13] Combining all available sources, and using visual and material evidence as well, historians nowadays venture to present an image of what went on in that largely oral culture.[14]

People were mainly occupied by what conditioned their daily lives. Food and eating, therefore, dominate many stories: the misery caused by the lack of it and the joy when there was plenty for a change can be sensed in almost all texts. Sexuality was also important, without, however, being unrestrained.[15] Especially in the countryside, people enjoyed sex rather freely and talked about it openly until the nineteenth century, when a large-scale civilizing campaign staged by the Churches and the urban middle class declared many things sexual to be taboo; this situation was only reversed in the 1960s and 1970s. Moreover, from a psychological perspective entirely different from ours, sexuality was probably much more essential than we can imagine now. Not only was it necessary that many children be born in order to guarantee the reproduction of the species and ensure that adults had someone to take care of them in old age, since society made no provisions for this, also, according to psychologists, sexuality, letting go of oneself, was actually the only way to escape the fear of the transitory nature of life and of inevitable death.

Death, for the average European, was always uncomfortably close. Infant mortality was appallingly high and most of those who survived still died between the ages of 30 and 40. And then, of course, there were wars. Whether great or small, they seemed to be waged continuously. With everyone having some experience of war in their own life, it was spoken and sung of a great deal, if only to defy the threat and the misery they caused.

Finally, natural phenomena, such as lightning and thunder, comets and solar or lunar eclipses, played a very important role in tales, poems and songs; they, too, threatened everyday life, the more so as they were not yet understood. Hence, ghosts and spirits and also witches and wizards constantly appear in all sorts of stories. The former were the manifestations of the incomprehensible, of all those things for which no simple remedy could be found; the latter, if properly managed, were potential helpers in the ongoing struggle with this other world that seemed the continuation of daily life. Indeed, fear in the face of a world that, rather than orderly, presented itself as chaotic and unruly, was perhaps a central emotion in this Europe. To master this fear, people devised all sorts of strategies that were entirely rational within their mental paradigm. Not surprisingly, the supreme vision of an ordered world, where there was no fear, no want, no suffering, was paradise, a garden as unlike actual nature as possible: an 'enclosed garden' where every valley had been made plain, everything crooked straight.[16]

The one organization that helped people create order was, of course, the Church, the keeper of a faith that may be interpreted as the collective attempt of the people living in Europe to bring man and nature into a balance, to make comprehensible, acceptable and livable what was incomprehensible, unacceptable and unlivable without the help of God and the promise of heaven: the misery of every new day, the pain of life with its many illnesses, its unavoidable death, and the question of what the purpose of it all was. Yet precisely because much of what the Church tried to teach was relatively complicated, people needed concrete help, and sought refuge with those same wizards and witches, as well as with sayings and charms. Most of these forms of culture, albeit denounced as superstition by the Church, were in fact the very forms of a vast, ancient repertoire that the Church had not absorbed into its own arsenal of ritualistic action devised to make life controllable.[17] Indeed, the priests themselves often acted within and made use of a complex scenario of primeval ways and means which were definitely not accepted by the small group who defined right speaking and acting within the Church. This situation has caused historians to ask to what extent this culture really was Christian at all, in its ideal sense, rather than a complex mix, under different names, of more ancient beliefs branded as 'paganism' by the Church.[18]

A world of towns

The majority of city dwellers consisted of salaried labourers and free artisans, with a 'middle class' made up of entrepreneurs in various fields of trade and industry, as well as professional people who served the needs of these groups in so far as they necessitated the creation of written records: lawyers, public notaries and town officials. This, in turn, presupposed another group of people: teachers, at various levels, who were capable of instructing all these men in the arts of literacy and numeracy. For besides reading and writing, arithmetic had become increasingly essential, especially to urban society. What with bookkeeping, handling an abacus, trying to account for constantly shifting exchange rates between the hundreds of different monetary systems, measuring the contents of ships and carts, of tuns and bales, Europe, urban Europe, was becoming a rational, measurable, quantifiable society.[19]

Whereas these teachers might be priests or monks, i.e. part of the clergy who constituted a considerable proportion of the population in almost every European city up until the sixteenth century – indeed, even the fabric of the city was itself often dominated by the sometimes huge, walled properties of churches and monasteries – this situation changed when the influence of the Church decreased; in the course of the sixteenth century, secular, professional teachers began to set up schools as well.

The ruling elite, the urban patriciate might consist either of the wealthiest entrepreneurs or of a mixture – sometimes through intermarriage – of this group and of nobles from the surrounding countryside. The latter, however, might themselves be descended from traders or bankers who, in earlier generations, had acquired landed estates and sometimes even titles of nobility. For the distinctions between classes, especially in those regions where trade and industry became important, were certainly not as rigid as is often assumed.[20] Nobles would invest or even actively participate in banking and trading, and wealthy tradespeople would retire to the country to enjoy a more 'noble' life, building luxurious houses, collecting books and paintings, if only portraits of faked ancestors and, invoking that most aristocratic of privileges, going out to hunt.

Economic life, in the city, was of a different nature to that in the countryside. Artisanal production could be family-centred, as of old, with both women and children being integral parts of a 'family economy', but it often developed into big enterprises, employing dozens or even hundreds of workers, sometimes assembled under one roof in a system of proto-industrial manufacture.

Trade, too, could be small-scale, specialized and local, or cover many products and regions, and conducted by firms who set up networks of 'counting' houses all over Europe, such as the firm of Francesco Datini, the 'merchant of Prato', one of the richest men in fifteenth-century Europe. Normally, entrepreneurs liked to staff these offices with family members, being the most trustworthy, for the ties of kinship, even outside the conjugal family, were felt strongly, as is still common business practice in Asia. However, when more capital was invested, the need to expand, to specialize and to attract the most capable men soon resulted in the employment of non-relatives as well; for a long time, however, it was customary that a newcomer marry one of his boss's daughters.

Meanwhile, increasing competition in the urban economy, especially in times of crisis, such as those in the late sixteenth and early seventeenth centuries, resulted in a growing tendency to prevent women from taking an active role in the production process. All over Europe, the corporations or guilds wherein production in any field was mostly organized, adopted rules which forced women, who had set up business for themselves, or had inherited it from their deceased husband, to either remarry, choosing a male member of their guild, or to sell out to such a person. This is not to say that women did not work. The poorer ones most certainly did, especially in the big cities, where they would be likely to make up most of the marketing population, or else serve in the more affluent households.[21]

With changing labour relations, a shift in gender roles came about as well, especially among the prosperous trading classes. Men who tried to emulate the elite would prefer their womenfolk not to work. Those families who could afford to exempt their females from participation in the labour process often did so, aping the wealthier groups in society, especially the (titled) aristocracy who still functioned as the cultural role model. As in the aristocracy, the main role of a prosperous bourgeois woman now became one of providing her husband, and his family, with preferably male children to continue the line and to inherit the property, but she should not interfere in business or encroach on other male domains.[22] For aristocratic women did not normally work. In the upper reaches of the nobility, they would lead a life of luxury, participating in court society, showing off the status of their husband's family. At most, such noble ladies would supervise a large household. Still, this might entail very practical work as well, as is evident from that fascinating cache of documents called the 'Paston Papers', which reveal the life of a well-to-do English landowning family at the end of the fifteenth century.[23] Indeed, Margaret Paston often acted as her husband John's steward during his absence, mostly on military duty; she managed his estates, advised him on his business and legal affairs and even took decisions on her own. But though the Pastons owned manor houses and castles, Margaret's lifestyle would seem to have been more bourgeois than aristocratic. Among the high nobility, women would mostly not demean themselves with such tasks.

Running a large household was increasingly the task that fell to women from the affluent middle class. This, however, led to new ideals about femininity as well. A 'good' woman was, first, a good mother and, second, a good housewife. Yet it has to be said that while women in this group generally retreated from active participation in public life, their hold over their families increased, and with it their power to shape the conduct of all involved.[24]

This became more evident as economic specialization, greater wealth and the desire to demonstrate that wealth and the way of life that went with it, all resulted in a situation wherein such traditional practices as using the house as an office, a shop and a warehouse at the same time were discontinued. With the separation between work and home amongst the more prosperous urban groups came an awareness of the home as a private place where, within the intimacy of the family, presided over by the mother, people lived a life different from the one they presented to the public.[25]

What life was like in these bourgeois households, where there was both leisure time and money to spend on a comfortable, hospitable interior, on good food, on lighting in the evening, and so on, is shown in contemporary painting, especially from such a quintessentially urban, bourgeois society as that of the Dutch province of Holland – even though these pictures may have had some moralistic purpose, depicting desired instead of actual behaviour. They show mothers keeping an eye on their children while preparing dinner, as well as, in the evening, people sitting around the table, playing cards or singing together, or reading by themselves – such as the old man with his glasses, who has fallen asleep over his book.

With growing wealth and, consequently, bigger houses, notions of privacy not only separated the house from the office or the shop, but also came to extend to the spheres of parents on the one hand, and children on the other. This seems specifically to have affected the experience of sexuality as something that belonged to the adult domain of married life. Nevertheless, the various bodily functions and, indeed, the body itself were not yet surrounded with the notions of intimacy, shame or taboo that they were to acquire in the nineteenth century: in sixteenth- and seventeenth-century paintings, while women publicly breast-fed their children, one sees men urinating in public as well, although the latter was already associated with rustic boors rather than with refined urbanites.

All this, in turn, also contributed to the genesis of the concept of childhood amongst the more well-to-do people. After infancy, the period during which they were being cared for by their mother, young boys and girls, though they might be physically able to participate in work as, indeed, their counterparts in the working classes both in the countryside and in towns were forced to do, now entered into a stage of childhood; people became aware that the young needed time to grow up, and had to be further educated, in relative freedom.[26] Still, we should realize that the moment these children were considered to have reached adulthood occurred in their early teens rather than, as nowadays, in their early twenties.

Although during the period *c.*1400 to *c.*1800 most educated people theoretically defended the position that man and woman were created equal, at the same time women were increasingly seen as docile, subservient even. In many countries, women's legal rights were limited. In parts of Germany, a woman could not even stand trial because, *de jure*, she was considered to be like a child, who could not be held responsible for a crime. Indeed, if women failed to comply with the new ideals, they might be branded as 'different', as bad women. Some scholars have seen this development as the birth of the concept of the evil witch, who was to become a disciplining warning to European women until the end of the eighteenth century, when the last witches were burnt at the stake. Of course, the phenomenon of the witch was far more complex, involving the psychology of close-knit communities, with their need to define insiders and outsiders and, equally, the need to project tensions onto specific persons, as scape-goats.[27]

In their turn, men were impressed with the notion that they were chosen to take on a double responsibility: as the '*pater familias*', they were both the provider for their household and their family, as well as its public face.

The institution of marriage was the ideal basis for such ideas. However, in the thirteenth, fourteenth and fifteenth centuries, a great variety of forms of concubinage had come into use, were condoned and indeed often sanctioned by the Church. Thus, it was quite common for a couple to enter upon an engagement to be married at the church door and then to return home and live together as man and wife until the wife became pregnant; when this proof of the viability of the relationship had been obtained, the couple would return to church for the final marriage vows at the chancel steps and then proceed to the altar for Eucharist. This explains why, in contemporary paintings of French weddings, the bride radiantly shows her pregnancy. However, numerous constructions undesirable to the Church had been devised, as witnessed by Chaucer's 'Wife of Bath', who married five times at the church door without finalizing her vows. All kinds of secular relationship rituals existed as well; for example, when prospective partners sealed their intention to live together by jumping over a broom in front of witnesses.

While the Church was losing control over marriage and sexuality, the State became increasingly concerned about an ordered society, preferably one in which working males, the majority of tax-paying subjects, could be held responsible for the rest of the population, their families. Hence, in the late fifteenth and early sixteenth centuries, the two powers joined forces, trying once more to legalize and sacralize marriage as the only institution in which sexuality could be expressed, and out of which legitimate offspring could be borne, and the family or household as the fiscal basis of society, its legal microcosm. It was understood that in both, the father would rule supreme.[28]

Much like the countryside, towns, too, whether great or small, were not quaint, idyllic communities, as nineteenth-century romantic writers or twentieth-century conservationists would sometimes have it. Admittedly, some research indicates that neighbourhoods were seemingly comfortable, close-knit groups, where the quarrels that occurred were solved through the intercession of the community's representative, where people attended each other's funerals, even paying a penalty if they failed to turn up, and where annual gatherings were organized in the form of huge drinking and eating parties to physically and symbolically stress group harmony.[29] Other case studies, however, tell of poisoned letters, of abuse and defamation, of violent quarrels ending in murder and of people trying to kill their neighbours using black magic.[30]

Increasingly, the wealthy tended to congregate in a safe, comparatively spacious and clean part of town, usually its centre, while the poor would live on the periphery. However, as urban populations grew and overspilled the area protected by the city walls – most European cities were walled until the middle of the nineteenth century – the poor would go and live in new but often very squalid quarters which, if only for that reason, were looked upon disdainfully by the more affluent burghers. Houses here would be built of wood, and have straw roofs well into the nineteenth century. In most cities, the majority of streets often remained unpaved, and mostly unlit at night. Closed sewage systems were absent and dirt was piled on the streets and in backyards. Consequently, all kinds of illnesses spread easily, creating havoc amongst the population, especially those who lived in cramped surroundings. Also, crime in violent forms was quite normal, even in the bigger cities, where there was already some kind of police system. Prostitution, too, showed itself quite openly; it was not yet morally frowned upon, and heavily punished only when it brought syphilis into the armies.[31]

Both phenomena are amply attested to in such major towns as seventeenth-century papal Rome, where a prominent citizen, Giacinto Gigli, filled his diary with notes of murders, rapes and, indeed, rampant 'superstition', as well as describing the vain efforts of the papal government to increase the moral tone of this capital of Catholic Christendom. He also noted the ways in which the authorities reacted to many kinds of undesirable behaviour, setting the 'stage' for death – for serious crimes, until the end of the eighteenth century, were harshly dealt with: criminals were burned at the stake, hanged or quartered, while noblemen might claim the privilege of being beheaded – such public executions were meant to show what the norms of society were, and impress upon onlookers that order would always be restored.[32] The people would flock to these theatrically presented occasions, sometimes giving in to an almost orgiastic celebration of sin and redemption.[33]

Two worlds?

The above survey is, necessarily, a very general one. It synthesizes innumerable details about the equally innumerable local, self-centred and enclosed communities that comprised rural Europe. It juxtaposes these communities with the often different economic, social and cultural reality of towns. Obviously, such a representation can always be invalidated by citing individual cases wherein the differences between town and countryside appear less extreme. Specifically, in terms of culture, towns, especially smaller ones, greatly resembled villages, in that there, too, one would encounter widespread illiteracy, the predominance of oral traditions, little proof of communication with the wider world and many manifestations of what the Church called superstition.

Yet if one looks at Europe from about the fifteenth to the eighteenth centuries, bearing in mind all the details presented so far, one must conclude that there existed a deep chasm in European society. It was a chasm that was not only economic and social but primarily cultural in nature.

Inevitably, the mass of peasants, living in their communities limited by the walking-distance horizon, with no appreciable means of communication, had a restricted world-view. Consequently, most people lived in great fear of everything that was not familiar and hence different. People or things that were 'different' were easily seen as alien, even dangerous.[34] Thus, all kinds of phenomena in the physical world surrounding them, but also, of course, illnesses, threatening as they were, were often blamed on witches. The belief in witches, while being of all ages and cultures was, in the last decades of the fourteenth century, spreading through Europe. By that time, the Church itself was changing its position, and enlarging the power of the Inquisition to deal with it. Until the end of the seventeenth century, the 'witch craze' raged; consequently, some 40,000–50,000 women and men died, most being burnt at the stake. Geographically, the phenomenon was concentrated in central and northern Europe,[35] and continued in regions where the Reformation took over. Indeed, in the Roman Catholic Mediterranean parts of Europe, there seems to have been little witch-hunting and even less prosecution than in the Protestant world. It is, however, important to accept that it was not an irrational outburst; the lawyers and judges involved were men who tried to make sense of the accusations that led to and, indeed, the confessions that were made during the trials, finding that the people they faced had made a pact with the Devil – which was a sin, because it aimed at the subversion of God's plan for the world – and were engaged in working harm on their 'neighbours', on their society by supernatural means.[36] This also helps us understand why the craze ended: i.e. when the better part of Europeans ceased to believe that such means existed, which was sometime during the late seventeenth and early eighteenth centuries. Still, why the 'witch craze' occurred when and where it did has not yet been satisfactorily explained.

Nor were local cultural forms consciously experienced as part of a communal European tradition. After all, education, if it reached people at all, reached most of them only as an attempt to learn to read and write. Even if they succeeded, a simplified version of the message of the Bible, frequently reduced to allegories and metaphors, was often their only frame of reference. To them, the culture of Greek and Roman antiquity was a closed book. Also, many of the finer points – some historians would even argue the essence – of Christianity eluded them. Travel, unless professionally necessary, was a senseless and useless action. From itinerant preachers and pedlars they might have heard, though vaguely at most, about the Mediterranean, about the worlds of Byzantium and Islam; they would probably have known even less about the worlds beyond the wide seas. The past, history, consisted of stories about the village and the village community in earlier times and of folk tales and legends which put everything strange and incomprehensible in its place in a largely magical context. In short, most people lacked any reference that could give 'Europe' the status of a concept, let alone make it a lived reality; at most, it was a meaningless word.

Crossing a 'border', such as a river or a mountain, one would encounter people living according to different social codes, showing different habits and often speaking different tongues as well, for even within a single-language community, the various dialects would not be understood. Hence, the concept of solidarity was applied only to the limited community of a person's own village or city. Beyond their family, people were attached first and foremost to their *patria*, their *Heimat* or their native soil. Some, but certainly not all, felt themselves part of the regional state that would have absorbed the village or city in days of old: these might be farmers' sons who, as soldiers, had served a regional leader, or village administrators who visited the regional capital with some regularity.

Regional leaders themselves – low- or high-ranking nobles and city administrators – equally held to their particularistic outlooks. This was certainly the case when they had to defend their power against an increasingly mighty central elite: the nobility at a princely court and the senior administrators who were the main instruments of state formation in the emerging capital cities. In view of this complex situation, it was a long time before people finally began to feel part of the new, larger political structures that were slowly being formed.

However, one should also remember that in the new states at least, the 'ordinary man', unable to even understand people from neighbouring villages, could certainly not talk to his 'fellow citizens' from another region. After all, in most countries there was still no single 'national' language, taught to and spoken by everyone.[37] Until the fourteenth century the English elite spoke French and therefore experienced difficulties communicating with the English-speaking population at large, while the Norwegian elite used Danish for much longer.

In Spain, the inhabitants of Catalonia or of the old kingdom around Valencia, vexed by their subjection to the Castilians, considered foreign oppressors from the region around Madrid who did not speak their language, emphatically tried not to use Castilian, if only to express their deep-rooted opposition. In France, the majority of the inhabitants of Provence or Brittany thought of themselves as nations which, unfortunately, had failed to withstand the imperialism of the kings, who hailed from the region around Paris. If only for that reason, Bretons and Provençals did not master the language now called French – originally the Parisian dialect. It also meant that they were usually unable to understand the officials who ruled them in the name of the government in the capital. Thus, communication between, for example, city officials in Gascony and the Parisian bureaucrats was possible only through an interpreter.[38] Indeed, until the nineteenth century, many 'French' people spoke languages or dialects of languages which their fellow countrymen could hardly understand.[39]

All over Europe, central governments attempted to codify one of the languages in their state as the 'national' language and to impose this, by force if necessary, on the entire population of the state; yet it was a policy which, due to prevailing illiteracy, did not yield large-scale success until the introduction of general compulsory education in the nineteenth century. Only then did the farming population in the more isolated parts of France feel themselves to be French citizens.[40] And as for the Northern Netherlands, reading the minutes of the Nijmegen city council in the seventeenth century one could be forgiven for thinking that they were written in one of the varieties of Low German that even nowadays is spoken in the Rhineland and Westphalia; it little resembled the standard Dutch that is now the country's language. Indeed, people did not feel Dutch but rather identified themselves as Frisians, Gueldersmen or Hollanders; yet, to most even that would be a futile form of reflection.[41]

In consequence of all this, the 'great tradition', culture as a system of ideas and ideals articulated in the whole of Europe, was not a part of the thoughts or the lives of the masses. Obviously, an idea of 'Europe' did exist, held by the few who were knowledgeable about the earth's shape and did not think a map an incomprehensible, unreadable document. Yet for most of these people, too, it remained a geographical notion only. Europe as a dream of cultural unity continued to function in and for the very limited group who had invented it: the intellectuals, the scholars and others who had had the benefit of education and who were able to travel, to see other places and meet other people – in a nutshell, the elite. They were 'the people with history', members of an increasingly self-conscious, cosmopolitan and, to a very large extent, urban society.

By the fifteenth and sixteenth centuries, the European elite had slowly changed both in composition and in outlook, growing more complex. Besides the monks and the warriors, the merchants had been acquiring increasing economic power since the twelfth century. In the succeeding centuries, this power was also translated into political terms and forms. Thus, the elite was by no means a closed circle any more. It was composed of the leaders of the First

Estate, the lords spiritual, the clergy with their Christian and thus, according to their own definition, universal culture embracing the whole of Europe and, indeed, the worlds beyond. It was also composed of the leaders of the Second Estate, the lords temporal or the nobility, who, it is true, had participated in that culture since the eighth and ninth centuries but who had begun to think more and more 'nationally' within the framework of the various budding states where their power lay.

However, increasingly in evidence was a Third Estate, made up largely of wealthy entrepreneurs and professionals, the most powerful group in the urban middle class. Their bases were the cities; as these often had become largely independent of government control, the urban elites felt that, unlike the noble-military class and the clergy, they did not fit into such large unities as State and Church, which transcended local borders. Partly as a result, they formed values that were different, at least to a certain extent. Though their banking or trading connections might give them an international outlook, economically, politically and culturally they would more often have a very local orientation. And while they would model their material culture on the example of the older elite, genuinely aristocratic values, especially those associated with knightly culture, remained alien to them. Looking for economic and political power, they sponsored both education and the sciences, if only for utilitarian motives. They were also an important factor in the development of controlled tolerance, but, yet again, would largely profess it for pragmatic reasons. For tolerance or, to frame the idea in a larger context, the idea of a civil society, regulated by rules of law which applied to each and every person indistinctly, proved an essential prerequisite for the expansion and power of this group.

Regardless of their socio-economic complexity, at the same time this elite unequivocally remained a cultural upper class because of its common background. After all, it consisted of people who accepted the ideology of Christianity because they were raised in Christian doctrine from childhood. Its members also shared common norms of civilized behaviour; these came into existence precisely during these centuries as a result of the increasingly literate interaction between classical antiquity and Church teaching, an interaction particularly expressed in formal further education but also in such tracts as written by the Rotterdam scholar Desiderius Erasmus, on child education, the relationship between man and wife, between parents and children, etc.

These three groups of clergy, nobility and urban bourgeoisie – both independently and through increasing interaction – became the main agents of a variety of new developments which, from the fifteenth century onwards, began to alter the world that, in this very period, was called Europe.

Part III

Continuity and change

New ways of looking at man
and the world

7 A new society

Europe's changing views
of man

The survival of classical culture and the beginnings of Humanism

It is worth bearing in mind that a resurgence of interest in the culture of the classical Greek and Roman worlds occurred at the court of Charlemagne, while yet another resurgence is notable from the twelfth century onwards rather than, as is so often stated, only as late as the fifteenth and sixteenth centuries. Indeed, we would probably do best to realize that this fascination with the 'Ancients' had always been present since the decline of the Roman Empire in the third and fourth centuries. Though many classical texts were deliberately destroyed or simply lost in the course of time, the Catholic Church assiduously retained all those elements of classical civilization that in their underlying ideas did not conflict with Christian doctrine, and had passed these on through the manuscript texts which were the primary carriers of information. Thus, the 'great tradition' was born, in which Europe's cultured elite always had access to, and communicated with, the culture of the ancient Mediterranean.

A man like Dante Alighieri provides a prime example of this 'great tradition'.[1] Fully versed in classical and later Latin, as well as in the poetical traditions of Provence – such as the *Romance of the Rose* – and the north of France, looking at the painter Giotto's efforts to bring new life into his pictures but also gazing at the Graeco-Byzantine mosaics of Ravenna which told of an older tradition, this descendant of a crusading knight also lived the life of a Florentine citizen. He lived in, and observed with wonder and, sometimes, horror, the world of popes and emperors, listening to their political and theological arguments about power and salvation, as well as participating in the party strife of his own town. Given this background, one can understand how his masterpiece, *The Divine Comedy*, which he finished in the year of his death, 1321, came to chart the totality of history as it was known to him. It narrates the author's trip through time and space, where he meets with figures historical and mythical. It culminates in his visit to heaven, where he lovingly contemplates the perfection of creation. For in doing so, man can begin to understand the *lieto fautore* (joyful Creator), who gave him his soul and thus the possibility to enjoy this very creation. It is in his insistence on the essential importance of belief for man's total experience of life and death that Dante is a typical representative of a Christian world-view. But in other ways he was the precursor of a group of men, urban middle-class laymen rather than clergy or landed gentlemen, who in the following decades would manifest a new way of looking at things, who created a culture that would later be designated as 'humanist'.

Due to the capital generated by Mediterranean trade and a flourishing manufacturing sector, Italy was certainly Europe's wealthiest region during the thirteenth, fourteenth and fifteenth centuries. The many city-states and principalities, with Florence and Venice, Mantua and Urbino and papal Rome in the lead, were governed, politically and culturally, by enormously wealthy merchants and bankers, counts and dukes, by the Pope and cardinals. Living in the magnificent palaces and villas they built, they enjoyed all the good and beautiful things their money could buy. Their attitude to life gradually became more secular, that is to say, more centred on man and the here and now than on God and the hereafter. In adopting this attitude they felt confirmed by their reading of the classical texts in which the same mentality, centred on a creative concept of life, was abundantly evident.

During these centuries, in many Italian cities, learning and learning-infused art acquired increasing prestige among the wealthy interested in these forms of culture, who were greatly influenced by the artists and scholars with whom they often surrounded themselves for reasons of status. In this milieu, a more individualistic view of man was systematically developed and conceptualized. These men – and, increasingly, women – no longer saw man as an anonymous member of the mass of God's obedient creatures, but as a unique being, supreme in his rational and creative capacities that marked him as an individual. Though men had lived the 'I' in previous centuries, the thinkers of these times made the 'I' the centre of their spiritual credo, arguing that the optimal development of the individual should be the central aim and value of a man's life.[2] People came to think of every person as having his own, special qualities, given to him because God willed it; consequently, man would honour God most by making the best of all his possibilities and his qualities.

To develop these qualities, however, one had to study, and more specifically study the *studium humanitatis;*[3] these were the traditional academic subjects of the so-called 'trivium', namely grammar, rhetoric, and logic, and the 'quadrivium', namely geometry, arithmetic, astronomy and music, the latter being considered a mathematical science rather than an 'art'. These subjects by no means embraced all disciplines then taught at universities, but their study was now seen to defeat the rather narrow aims of scholastic education, with its stress on a sophistical analysis of concepts many found no longer relevant. More important, however, these studies were deemed to help a man to realize his innate human, creative potential, which was summed up in the concept of *virtù*, which cannot be equated to our present concept of virtue. By using his *virtù*, man could live his life as fully as possible, within the community he was supposed to serve, and thus fulfil an essential moral obligation. Only in doing so, would he realize the richness of creation as God had intended it. Therefore, without losing their belief in the basic tenets of Christianity, the outlook of many of these humanist thinkers and writers, artists and musicians, besides becoming more individualistic, also became decidedly more secular.

The study of the humanities called for texts which would help man to better understand these ideals. Not the texts produced by the Church and its musty, restricting scholastic tradition but, preferably, classical texts, giving a glimpse of the pure culture of ancient Rome that, once again, was now seen as the touchstone of civilization. Humanists, therefore, started searching for such texts, and found them in abundance – most often in the manuscript repositories of the very churches and monasteries they despised as centres of old-fashioned lore; many were even found in the transalpine countries that were not held in great cultural respect by the humanists for, despite their claims to universality, they were more than a touch proud of being Italians. Thus, from southern Germany came unknown works by Cicero, Petronius and the *Institutes of Oratory* of Quintilian, which taught a man how to speak in public, an important asset in view of the fact that the humanists wanted their *virtù* to express itself in service to the community, to their town.

In the thirteenth, fourteenth and fifteenth centuries, new information about classical, humanistic culture also came to Europe from regions that had not been controlled by the Catholic Church. During these centuries, Europeans completed a process which, more forcefully than ever, integrated the non-Christian, classical, Graeco-Roman part of its past with its own culture;[4] remarkably, once again this occurred to a large extent by way of, or at least with the help of, Islam. Indeed, following the earlier contacts with the Islamic world on the Iberian peninsula, it was now the Graeco-Byzantine civilization of Europe's orthodox Christian south-east that provided new impulses to the culture of the Christian world in the west.

The loss of Byzantium – the gain of Europe: the further development of Humanism in Italy

Despite the growing power of rulers who tried to maintain their claims to sovereignty by steering a middle course between the Church, the landed aristocracy and the increasingly powerful elites of the cities, the urge for a central ideal that might give them a hold in troubled times developed among many people, especially but not only intellectuals. One of the reasons was, of course, that the budding national states were frequently involved in long-lasting conflicts causing chaos in the lives of each and all. But the need for more unity increased further when outside threats were again felt during the course of the fifteenth century.

Word had spread of the growing might of the Ottoman Turks, a militant tribe originating in central Asia, who, after moving into Anatolia in the twelfth century, had converted to Islam and had quickly developed into a regional superpower. Now the Ottoman sultans' assaults on the last remnants of the Byzantine Empire and, thus, the borders of Catholic Europe, created a fear which again fanned the flames of the centuries-old feud between the Christian and Islamic worlds. In short, Europe trembled. This not only led to frantic attempts to settle mutual hostilities within the world of western Christendom, as had happened so often in European history – the Council of Constance (1414–18) had been a sign of this – but also resulted in a resolve to try for common action.

The advance of the Turks into what Europeans thought of as the homeland of Greek culture reached a dramatic climax when, in 1453, the Ottomans conquered the Byzantine capital of Constantinople. Now, the eastern part of the area defined as Europe seemed to lose not only its Christian fundament – a claim already being disputed by many westerners who despised the orthodox variety of Christianity – but also, in western eyes, its 'European' status precisely because Islam was now established there. It is hardly surprising, when the fall of Byzantium seemed imminent, that Pope Pius II had launched an appeal for a crusade, but with a new slant. For Pius was also Aeneas Silvius Piccolomini (1405–64), a scholar well versed in the classics.

As pope, he was pragmatic and realistic enough to accept the multiplicity of states as an irreversible characteristic of what Europe now was. He admitted as much, deliberately paying attention to the historical and cultural diversity of peoples in Europe.[5] He was well aware that the universal power of the emperor continued to exist only on paper. And perhaps he even told himself that Rome's leadership of the Church was no longer undisputed.[6] All this was precisely why a new ideology was called for that would help to create unity at home as well as stimulate powerful action abroad. Instead of a geographical-religious area, *Christianitas*, ruled by the universal Church with or without the support of an all-powerful emperor in the secular sphere, Pius now talked and wrote of *Europe*, describing it in politically rather vague terms but yet defining it as a general cultural category in which religion, Christianity, would naturally continue to play a central role in everyday life. In the words of this pope, Europe became 'our home', and being a European meant, simply, being a Christian.[7] But Pius also wrote 'Greece is now broken and ravaged – you all know what a cultural loss this is for us after all, you know that the whole civilization of the Latin world stems from Greek sources'.[8] Equally significant, Pius believed that eastern Europe, the world of Greek Christendom, had to be reconquered in order to reintegrate Europe culturally.[9] Even if, like his immediate predecessors, he did have ulterior motives in wanting to heal the rift between Catholic and Orthodox Christians and thus increase his own papal power, his interest in Greek culture was entirely genuine. As the true scholar he was, he had been part of the development of the *studium humanitatis*; and all humanists knew that the Latin culture they were now rediscovering and indeed recreating had its roots in the civilization of ancient Greece.

Meanwhile, this renewed acquaintance with classical culture was intensified hugely when, faced by the Turkish threat, numerous members of the Byzantine Empire's cultural elite fled the Balkans and Greece. The scholars and artists who now took to Europe mostly sought a safe haven on the Italian peninsula. In 1396, the government of Florence had already asked the leading Byzantine scholar Manuel Chrysoleras to come and teach at the university, which he did, creating a generation of Italian humanists who now began to study and translate Greek texts. In the 1430s, the Greek philosopher Pletho had taught a course on the difference between the Aristotelian and Platonic systems. The latter, less tainted by adoption and interpretation by the Church, was deemed by some to offer an attractive alternative to the former. In his wake, a group of scholars, the so-called *Accademia Platonica* – founded in 1475 with the support of the vastly wealthy Florentine patron of the arts and sciences, Cosimo de Medici – tried to reach a new synthesis. In particular, Marsilio Ficino (1433–99) sought to reconcile a renewed Platonism with Christianity.[10] Also, Florence had been the town where, in 1438, a council was organized to bring the Greek and Roman Churches closer to one another.

To this refuge, the Byzantine scholars brought their Christian tradition, coloured, to a far greater extent than in the west, by the influence of classical Greek civilization.[11] In their luggage, the exiles from Byzantium carried dozens of manuscripts which had preserved the thoughts of the great Greek thinkers and other writers hardly known in the west. The *Iliad* and the *Odyssey*, the great poems attributed to Homer, could now be read. Also, better or even entirely new versions of Aristotle's and Plato's reflections on man and society became available, as well as Dioskurides' survey of the plant and animal worlds, to name but a few.

Essentially, the necessity to reconquer the Greek cultural world was now considered vital from a political and religious as well as a cultural point of view by intellectuals like Pius II; it was the almost logical outcome of the virtually continuous interaction mentioned earlier between the two cores of Christian civilization, the religious values of the Bible, and the more secular cultural elements of Mediterranean antiquity. It was an interaction which had first peaked in the third and fourth, and once more in the eighth and ninth centuries, and which had intensified from the twelfth century onwards. Now, even though Greece was liberated from the Ottomans only in the early nineteenth century – for Pius's crusading plans failed – from the fifteenth century onwards Europeans tried to intellectually reconquer the Mediterranean world, as one of the most important elements in its cultural formation. It was a reconquest which certainly contributed to European supremacy in 'science and every branch of learning',[12] as Pope Pius had promised, defining Europe's cultural character in precisely the terms which one might expect from an intellectual.

Understandably, the enthusiasm for the ideas of the ancient Greeks and Romans was paralleled by an interest in the languages in which they had written. Classical Greek and Latin were now seen as far more elegant and lucid than the Latin that had been used in previous centuries by the Church and in Church-dominated scholarship. Admittedly, Latin did, by the fifteenth century, include many corrupted words and, moreover, in order to remain a living language had of necessity absorbed all sorts of new words. However, humanist scholars now thought it had to be purified to become a language that was as precise as possible, preferably resembling the Latin used by the Roman rhetorician Cicero. It was to be the medium for a logical expression of ideas that would allow man to articulate his new questions and insights about himself and the world. Actually, in seeking this purity and precision of language, the humanists, too, created a new Latin.

In the century following the death of Thomas Aquinas, the study of classical texts and the new attitude towards man and the world that emerged inevitably led to questions and doubts that had lingered at the back of many a mind now acquired a new urgency. What exactly was the relationship between man and God? Was the Bible the only source of knowledge about creation, as the Roman Church preferred to present it? Or could man himself, by observing and analysing the world around him, finally fathom nature and his own place in it, as the Greek thinkers had asserted? Could man thus acquire knowledge of the order of the cosmos and God's intentions for it?

At least one man thought along such lines, fully realizing they differed from what most of his contemporaries thought. He was Nicholas Chrypffs, the 'Crayfish', better known as Nicholas Cusanus, bishop of Brixen and cardinal of the Holy Roman Church (1401–64),[13] From his training as a theologian and his interest in mathematics and in astronomy, he went on to speculate about the cosmos and its creator. Some of his ideas have a decidedly modern ring. Not only did he conclude that the geocentric model was untenable, but also that the universe, far from being the Ptolemaic globe encapsulated in a fixed heaven, actually knew no bounds and was filled with many planets probably not unlike the earth. It had been willed by God, who was the absolute and infinite, the centre and the circumference, the beginning and the end, the synthesis of all opposites, the *coincidentia oppositorum.* In writing about God, Cusa used mathematics as well, musing that one might imagine Him by thinking of the radius of a circle as infinite, which then would cause the circumference of the circle to coincide with a straight line. With these and other speculations, he was indeed far ahead of his time. That he was able to voice his thoughts at all shows the relative openness of the Church in matters concerning doctrine and learning – although, of course, the authorities must have realized that there was little danger of ordinary people being corrupted by such abstruse notions, formulated in Latin and written in manuscript texts.

Far less speculative were those who, following men like Abelard, asked themselves whether the Bible and the texts from the first years of the Christian Church had not been corrupted by 1,500 years of use? They wondered whether much of what was actually considered incomprehensible or unreasonable in the ideas of the Church was just the result of texts that had been copied incorrectly. However, they also wondered whether the Bible and other fundamental texts of the Church had been worded rather differently at the moment of their origin. Soon, their questions could, at least partly, be answered. For from the Byzantine world now came the old Greek version of Holy Scripture. When compared with the younger, Latin text traditionally used in the west, exciting and even shocking discoveries were made: over the course of time many errors had indeed entered the standard Latin version.

On the one hand, this allowed scholars to prepare new, better editions of the Bible, especially when Hebrew and Aramaic texts were brought in for comparison as well. Consequently, in the sixteenth and seventeenth centuries a number of so-called 'Polyglot' Bibles were produced, which published the holy texts in six, seven or even eight languages in parallel, making the similarities and differences in language and time very clear indeed.

On the other hand, it was precisely these scientific analyses of Holy Scripture that started to undermine people's belief in its absolute value. The Bible now appeared to be the product of history, a man-made creation. As a result, the authority of the Church, which had, after all, based its claim to absolute power on the absolute, timeless truth of the Bible, was to a certain extent affected. Not surprisingly, even nowadays the unchangeableness of the Koran is being hammered home in the Islamic world. If Islamic clergymen did not do this, their power would decline considerably. A comparable process began in Christian Europe in the late fifteenth century. It quickly led to fierce differences between the traditional religious and cultural establishment, the Roman Catholic Church, and those who pleaded for a new culture. Their position was made abundantly clear in a text by one of their protagonists, the Dutch-born scholar, Desiderius Erasmus (*c.*1465–1536).[14]

Partly due to his critical reading of religious texts, partly because he was a keen observer of contemporary reality, Erasmus began to disapprove of institutions like the Catholic Church that asked people to unquestioningly accept the Bible and other fundamental texts as literally and eternally true. In his later years he showed a growing aversion to the ecclesiastical power structures that, in his opinion, could not always withstand the test of intellectual and, hence, critical analysis. Yet, in the end he did not become a real reformer, though he did cleanse the Old and especially the New Testament of all sorts of incorrect readings and outright mistakes. He also published new, scholarly editions of the works of important theologians from the first centuries of Christianity.

In his *Anti-Barbari*, Erasmus vehemently attacked contemporary culture, especially the way it was served by the Roman Catholic clergy, who dominated most of the primary and secondary schools in Europe. He accused them of hypocrisy and ignorance because of their refusal to base education on a sound study of the secular literature of the ancients, the *bonae litterae*. Instead of striving to raise the level of culture through the advancement of knowledge and learning, they tried, or so Erasmus felt, to keep people ignorant and hence unhappy. Elsewhere, Erasmus observed that at least part of the religious establishment was, indeed, loath to lose its comfortable position as the keeper of tradition; they would not relinquish the power they held through their monopolization of magic, ritual and science, the keys to the world of incomprehensible nature, of God. In a letter, he wrote:

> These people see only too plainly, that their own authority will fall to the ground, if we have the Sacred Books accessible in an amended form, and seek their meaning at the fountain-head. And so high a value do they set upon their own

importance, that they had rather have many things unknown, many things misread and cited amiss from the Divine Books, than appear ignorant themselves of any point.[15]

And yet, in spite of Erasmus's rather over-pessimistic sketch, European civilization was changing rapidly. The fifteenth and sixteenth centuries once again became a period of heightened tension between its two components. Many intellectuals no longer thought that the intellectual tradition, which had developed from the twelfth century onwards in an effort to reconcile the Bible and the Church fathers with the Greek philosophical and scholarly body of thought handed on by Islamic culture, was a convincing framework for thought and action. Obviously, their own increasingly intense acquaintance with classical civilization greatly influenced their critical position. To them, what had been presented as culture in Europe was no longer an adequate representation of classical values, including the Latin language, they were worded in, nor indeed did that culture adequately represent the original Christian principles. A new analysis and synthesis were needed, which had to result in a true 'rebirth' of both traditions in the purest forms of their past.

From Humanism to the Renaissance in Italy

Gradually, during the fifteenth and sixteenth centuries, not only scholars, but also artists, architects, musicians and creative writers were now educated in and shaped by the culture of Humanism. They began to experience a more general sense that their society had entered upon a new age, an age reborn after the 'darkness' of the preceding centuries: the 'Renaissance'. While this interpretation of their own past was exaggerated and although they did overemphasize the actual newness of the ideas they professed and the material culture they produced, a new vision of man was undeniably being created. The 'new man' was considered sovereign in the world and, with his reason and creative powers, was able to penetrate any secret, make anything he invented. Indeed, while Humanism denotes, basically, an intellectual movement, circumscribing the world of intellectuals mostly, the Renaissance nowadays is understood as representing a much wider idea. It stands for creativity in a great variety of fields, especially, but not only, in the visual arts, in literature and in music.

To many, Leonardo da Vinci stands out as the Renaissance man *par excellence*. Undeniably, he realized his *virtú* in an astonishing number of fields, demonstrating in all of them one of the basic characteristics of the Renaissance, which stemmed, basically, from the Humanist attitude towards establishing truth: its empirical attitude towards the world and everything in it. Leonardo, and many others in his time, felt that before proclaiming something true, it should be tested, proven. This, they felt – and Leonardo's famous notebooks do fully attest to it – could only be done by observing, describing, analysing whatever came to occupy one's mind. He was driven by an insatiable curiosity – a habit now seen by many as a prime virtue. This not only shows in often scrupulously detailed and deeply observant paintings – among other things, in depicting gesture, he felt he was representing 'mental events' which is, of course, a very fundamental observation. Leonardo's curiosity also shows in an astonishing variety of inventions, from tanks to aeroplanes, to name but two; often, these predate their re-invention or actual application by many centuries.[16]

Inevitably, the Renaissance artists even presented a new physical image of man. People now went in search of the material remains of classical culture as assiduously as they had searched for ancient texts: consequently, the fifteenth and sixteenth centuries saw the birth of archaeology. Soon, numerous works of art were discovered, especially in the ruins of ancient Rome, and reinforced the new view of man that had been developing in the previous century. More specifically, the idea that a perfect culture, which had produced the great texts, could not but be the product of perfectly shaped people induced many artists to produce works based on such revealing examples of classical art as the Roman copies of Greek originals like the 'spear bearer' and the 'wounded amazon'. A multitude of paintings and sculptures of 'perfectly' proportioned men and women were the result. A new, ideal-type human being was created, which has held western man captive ever since: in the twentieth century, it influenced not only the state-controlled breeding programmes of Nazi Germany but also the Hollywood star cult and the fashion industry.[17]

Besides incorporating the secularist and individualist aspects of Humanism, the reborn age or Renaissance favoured realism as well. Consequently, in painting, attempts were made to represent everything as it appeared to the scrutinizing eye. Though not totally absent in previous ages – as seen in the marvellously minute renderings of beasts and plants and even people in illuminated manuscripts – one can certainly maintain that for many centuries realism had been relatively unimportant, since the religious idea and the intention behind it determined both the message and the form in which art was cast, whether in painting or in sculpture. However, in the fourteenth and fifteenth centuries, during the first phases of Humanist culture, painters and sculptors increasingly tried to reproduce reality rather than represent preconceived ideas of what was morally or religiously acceptable. Increasingly, what the eye could measure or observe – distance, depth, colour and even ugliness – was portrayed. Thus, also, this was the time when perspective made its appearance in European painting.

In sculpture, too, people were individualized, with recognizable faces, whereas the art of the preceding centuries had mainly depicted types. For more than 1,000 years most sculpture had been a component of an architectural background – reliefs more than free-standing figures. Now, sculpted images started presenting man in his newly won vision of himself as an independent, moving, walking, running and if necessary fighting, but always free and recognizable, individual.

At the same time and, in a sense, as the logical outcome both of the glorification of man and of the wish to present him as he was, a pride in the beauty of the body – even or perhaps especially of the naked body – became manifest, showing not only the male but, in view of the conventions of the preceding age rather more surprisingly, the female. Whereas woman had been stereotyped

Plate 15 A new combination of mind and body. An ancient Roman mosaic allegedly depicting Plato's Academy, showing a number of scholars engaged in discussion, at the National Museum of Naples. It was this academy which inspired the humanist, neo-Platonist group who gathered around Marsilio Ficino working at Florence in the fifteenth century. Looking at these well-made men, who had, obviously, been the classical world's leading lights, many humanists realized that the body, too, was God's gift.

Source: Centre for Art Historical Documentation, Nijmegen, the Netherlands

for a long time as either an unapproachable saint or an untouchable whore, due to the restrictions imposed upon her roles by the Church, she now seemed to regain some stature as an individual person, in whose body the perfection of God's creation was made as visible, as in the male.

However, one should remember that new ideas always tend to become fashionable. The same individuals who had themselves depicted 'true to life' – in the so-called 'warts and all'-mode – also wanted to conform to the new aesthetic ideal. The Florentine ruler, Lorenzo de Medici, patron of painters and writers and himself a poet and thinker of some merit, allowed his face to be modelled from life by Michelangelo, who was the sculptor, while his body was cast into the mould of an 'ideally' proportioned Greek god. Therefore, one must be wary in accepting as 'real', or realistic, what was produced in painting and sculpture, as European art historians tended to do in the nineteenth and the first decades of the twentieth century. There certainly is more and also more conscious realism in Renaissance art than in the preceding period. However, both sculpture and painting were subject to normative and even moral rules and ideals, as well as, simply, to changing fashions; these were different from but no less compulsive than the mainly religious conventions of the preceding age. Thus, there was a definite tendency to present the world and everything in it rather more harmoniously than it really was; in particular, geometric proportions were seen as harmonious and, hence, ideal, reflecting the innate ideal-ness of the universe, and, therefore, they had to be strictly adhered to because only in doing so could real art be produced and nature, which art was supposed to imitate, perhaps be improved.

Nor should we forget that by far the majority of paintings and sculptures still served religious purposes, and were composed in such a way as to elicit an appropriate devotional reaction in the viewers, whether these were private owners contemplating a picture of the Madonna and her child, by the Italian painter Raphael, in the solitude of their bedroom, or the flocks of the faithful who attended mass and looked up at the huge frescoes, mosaics and statues that adorned walls, ceilings and cupolas in an angel-crowded vision of heaven.

ROME, AD 1538: MICHELANGELO ANALYSES ABOUT ITALIAN ART

In the year 1538, the Portuguese miniature painter Francesco de Hollanda was present at several conversations in which Michelangelo took part as well. The notes de Hollanda took of the artist's sayings are among our more precious testimonies of the painter's ideas. Though, at first, one might think that Michelangelo is taking a rather narrow, chauvinistic stance, in the end it is clear that he is actually defending a style, in fact the only style, namely that of ancient Greek painting preserved and now even resurrected in Italy.

Elsewhere, de Hollanda specifically records Michelangelo's words about Flemish painting, revealing the master's opinions not only on the 'sublime' rather than realistic characteristics of true, i.e. Italian painting, but also about the relationship between certain aspects of taste and aesthetics and persons of a specific class or sex.

> Only works which are done in Italy can be called true painting, and therefore we call good painting Italian, just as if it were done so well in another country, we should give it the name of that country or province. As for the good painting of this country, there is nothing more noble or devout, for with wise persons nothing

causes devotion to be remembered, or to arise, more than the difficulty of the perfection which unites itself with and joins God; because good painting is nothing else but a copy of the perfections of God and a reminder of His painting. Finally, good painting is a music and a melody which intellect only can appreciate, and with great difficulty. . . .

And I further say . . . that of all climates or countries lighted by the sun and the moon, in no other can one paint well but in the kingdom; and it is a thing which is nearly impossible to do well except here, even though there were more talented men in the other provinces, if there could be such, and this for reasons which we will give you.

Take a great man from another kingdom, and tell him to paint whatever he likes and can do best, and let him do it; and take a bad Italian apprentice and order him to make a drawing. . . . You will find, if you understand it well, that the drawing of that apprentice, as regards art, has more substance than that of the other master. . . . Order a great master, who is not an Italian, even though it be Albrecht [i.e. Dürer], a man delicate in his manner, in order to deceive me . . . and I assure You that it will be immediately recognized that the work was not done in Italy, nor by the hand of an Italian. I likewise affirm that no nation or person (I except one or two Spaniards) can perfectly satisfy or imitate the Italian manner of painting (which is the old Greek manner) without his being immediately recognized as a foreigner. . . . And if by some great miracle such a foreigner should succeed in painting well . . . it will be said that he painted like an Italian. Thus it is that all painting done in Italy is not called Italian painting, but all that is good and direct is, for in this country works of illustrious painting are done in a more masterly and more serious manner than in any other place. We call good painting Italian, which painting, even though it be done in Flanders or in Spain (which approaches us most) if it be good, will be Italian painting, for this noble science does not belong to any country, as it came from heaven; but even from ancient times it remained in our Italy more than in any other kingdom in the world, and I think that it will end in it. . . .

The painting of Flanders will generally satisfy any devout person more than the painting of Italy, which will never cause him to drop a single tear, but that of Flanders will cause him to shed many; this is not owing to the vigour and goodness of that painting, but to the goodness of such devout person; women will like it, especially very old ones, or very young ones. It will likewise please friars and nuns, and also some noble persons who have no ear for true harmony. They paint in Flanders only to deceive the external eye, things that gladden you and of which you cannot speak ill, and saints and prophets. Their painting is of stuffs, bricks and mortar, the grass of the fields, the shadows of trees, and bridges and rivers, which they call landscapes, and little figures here and there; and all this, although it may appear good to some eyes, is in truth done without reasonableness or art, without symmetry or proportion, without care in selecting or rejecting, and finally without any substance or nerve.[18]

Increasingly, the *studium humanitatis* and the general cultural climate of the Renaissance produced texts that showed this deepening interest in the essence of what made man a more civilized, humane being and which were therefore called *litterae humaniores*. Mostly, these were the old texts, written by classical authors in Greek or Latin. However, new texts were now designated 'humane texts' as well, whether they were carefully composed in the purified Latin of the fifteenth and sixteenth centuries or in Europe's new cultural language, the Italian of Tuscany, the language of Petrarch (1304–74), the writer who was considered a real humanist, and was famous for his beautiful sonnets immortalizing his beloved Laura.

The subject matter an author chose was actually less important than his ability to show that he understood what man was and could achieve, both as an individual and as a member of society. This resulted in a broad variety of works. Inevitably, in a day and age that so valued both realistic observation and the expression of the self, the new genre of the autobiography was born in humanist circles. Its most splendid early example is surely the hundreds of pages that the famous goldsmith and sculptor, Benvenuto Cellini (1500–71), began to write in 1558, telling the story of his own life. It is a secular, individual and realistic work *par excellence*. His 'I' takes central stage – indeed, life is often presented as drama in autobiography which, of course, should warn readers not to accept it as objectively true. In Cellini's 'Vita', everything is seen and described from his perspective. His readers are forced to see the world around him through his eyes, not according to all sorts of idealizations which Church or State required of people, but, at least from his own point of view, realistically, with all the deception and filth he found in the world but also the beautiful, mostly made by man himself, that exists in it.

Thus, Cellini writes of the necessity to record one's deeds, analyses his own character, unwittingly lets us know that, being a city man, he had no idea of the geographical layout of the surrounding countryside, tells of the ancient monuments that inspired him, gives an idea of the sense of life and movement in the work of Michelangelo Buonarotti, graphically describes his quarrels with his competitors, and so on:

> No matter what sort he is, everyone who has to his credit what are or really seem great achievements, if he cares for truth and goodness, ought to write the story of his own life in his own hand; but no one should venture on such a splendid undertaking before he is over forty. [. . .]
>
> Like the raw young man I was I answered my poor, distressed father back, and, taking the few wretched clothes and the odd couple of coins that I had left, went out of the house and began walking towards one of the city gates. I had no idea which gate was the one for Rome, and I ended up at Lucca, and from Lucca I went on to Pisa. I went to see the Campo Santo while I was at Pisa, and there I discovered many beautiful antiques, that is, marble sarcophagi. In various other parts of Pisa I came across many other ancient works, and I used to study them assiduously whenever I had time off from work. [. . .]

[Michelangelo] depicted a number of infantrymen who because of the summer heat had gone down to bathe in the river Arno: he caught in his drawing the moment when the alarm is sounded and the naked soldiers rush for their arms. He showed all their actions and gestures so wonderfully that no ancient or modern artist has ever reached such a high standard. [. . .]

I grew so angry that I was utterly determined to make mischief, and anyway I am rather hot-blooded by nature. . . . I left . . . fuming with rage and rushed back to my workshop. There I seized hold of a stiletto and hurried round to where those enemies of mine lived. I found them sitting down at dinner, in their home above the shop, and as soon as I appeared that young Gherardo who had started the quarrel hurled himself on me. I stabbed him in the chest, piercing his doublet and jacket right through to the shirt . . . and I shouted out: 'You traitors, today I'm going to kill the whole bunch of you'.[19]

At the other end of the broad spectrum of humanist writers, one finds, for instance, Niccolò Machiavelli (1469–1527), a Florentine scholar, who, in his famous 1513 tract *Il Principe* (The Prince), analyses man's role in that segment of society which is called politics. Machiavelli, too, is secular and a realist. He shows that, in political life, the will to power is a dominant principle. Though often couched and cloaked in nice words of a religious, ethical or social nature, upon closer reading it reveals itself in all its nakedness as pure self-interest:

Everyone perceives how praiseworthy a king is who keeps to his word and is candid instead of sly in political actions. Yet the experience of our time teaches us that those rulers who gave their word easily have come far, who knew how to deceive people with their sly tricks and, finally, they have gained the upper hand over those who lived honestly. . . .

It is therefore clear that a sensible ruler cannot and may not stick to his word if this is to his disadvantage and if the reasons why he gave his word are no longer valid. . . . A ruler therefore does not necessarily have to have all the good qualities which I outlined earlier; he only has to give the impression that he has them. . . . He must appear sympathetic, trustworthy, without guile, and pious, and actually be like that. But at the same time his character and nature must be such that, if he has to be the opposite, he can also behave that way. . . . He must be flexible, following fate and circumstance. In short, he must not deviate from the way of goodness, as long as that is sensible, but he must know how to be bad when necessary.

Education was among the most important institutions through which the classical cultural tradition was transmitted. In a letter to one of his pupils, the humanist scholar Leonardo Bruni (1370–1444) explained the essence of a good education:

Devote Yourself to two kinds of study. In the first place, acquire a knowledge of letters, not the common run of it, but the more searching and profound kind in which I very much want You to shine. Secondly, acquaint Yourself with what pertains to life and manners – those things that are called humane studies because they perfect and adorn man. In this kind of study Your knowledge should be wide, varied, and taken from every sort of experience, leaving out nothing that might seem to contribute to the conduct of Your life, to honour and to fame. I shall advise You to read authors who can help You not only by their matter but also by the splendour of their style and their skill in writing; that is to say, the works of Cicero and of any who may possibly approach his level. If You will listen to me, You will thoroughly explore the fundamental and systematic treatment of those matters in Aristotle; as for beauty of expression, a rounded style, and all the wealth of words and speech, skill in these things You, if I may so put it, borrow from Cicero . . . for I would wish an outstanding man to be both abundantly learned and capable of giving elegant expression to his learning. . . .

What riches will compare with the rewards of these studies? Perhaps the study of law will more easily get You a job, but it is a long way behind those others in utility and dignity. For they combine to produce a good man than which nothing can be thought more useful; the law does nothing of the sort.[20]

Inevitably, trade and travel, military conquest and diplomatic contacts linked the new culture of the Italian towns and courts with the world beyond. The new culture was admired and imitated all over Europe although, of course, by the better educated and the wealthy only. Both south and north of the Alps, Humanism and the Renaissance were elite phenomena. But few of the new ideas and thoughts filtered down to the ordinary man who, after all, could not read or write the *bonae litterae* and, therefore, continued to be semi-barbaric because, in the eyes of this elite, he lacked the means to fully realize his *virtù*.

Humanism and the Renaissance: Italy and beyond

In spite of what many Italians like to think, the new culture was certainly not limited to their peninsula. From Poland to Portugal, from Sweden to Switzerland, people wrote, painted and built, aiming to bring European, Christian civilization to a new flowering by confronting it with its roots, by a return to its sources. These activities took place within institutional frameworks comparable with those of Italy, namely in the palaces of the rulers, in academies sponsored by princes or nobles, but also in the universities they founded.

In Bohemia, the Emperor Charles IV (r. 1346–78) encouraged both the Latinization of his court, and the purification of German. In 1348, he also gave his realm its first university, at Prague, basing it on the examples of Bologna and Paris. In his great castle, Karlstein, frescos were painted in the style of Giotto. Meanwhile, his friend, the Polish King Casimir III (r. 1353–70), followed the same policy, establishing a university in the capital, Cracow, in 1364. At Vilnius, in Lithuania, and at Visegrád, in Hungary, the kings built huge Renaissance-style palaces that became the centre of a court culture that was also a learned culture.

At the same time, all over Europe learned culture continued to flourish in the oldest centres, the monasteries and their libraries. There, too, the monks explored new ways of thinking about the world, and representing it in words and in images. Importantly, however, humanist learning and Renaissance art were also popular with new milieus, the urban elites, who delighted in the idea that, modelling their own vernacular language on the classics, they could give it a new dignity as, of course, they now aimed to give a new dignity to their towns and their own houses by building and decorating them in the new style.

Meanwhile, while the fifteenth century saw the peak of the Renaissance and Humanism in Italy, during its final decades a complex mix of factors began to make cracks in the material basis of the new culture – for, of course, a material basis it had and, indeed, without it the culture would not have flourished. The lucrative trans-Mediterranean trade, the basis of the prosperity of most Italian cities and states, gradually collapsed as a result of disruptive conflicts between the major powers of the Islamic Near East that affected the caravan trade in the Levant and, inevitably, led to sharply rising prices of the oriental products that were the staple of Italian commerce; as the value of silver, up until then the main currency in the Mediterranean, had been steadily rising for a long time because of problems in central Asia, where most of that precious metal came from, the economic climate deteriorated. Also, many Mediterranean port cities had for a long time looked longingly at the rich trade and the even more promising gold that seemed to be for the taking in the Maghrebine port towns. Now, partly as a result of the discovery of America and of alternative routes to Asia, around the Cape of Good Hope, the economic centre of Europe slowly but definitely shifted from the Mediterranean to the Atlantic Ocean, where, of course, great wealth had been accumulated already by the French, Flemish and Dutch towns through commerce and industry. The latter, moreover, were able to produce the consumer goods Europe sought at more competitive prices than Italian artisans could.

At the same time, the Italian peninsula became the most important pawn in the fight for political hegemony in Europe between the Habsburgs, who ruled in Spain, Austria, the German states and in the seventeen Netherlands as well as in southern Italy, and the kings of France who desperately sought to break Habsburg domination. In 1494, French soldiers invaded northern Italy and caused havoc there. A horde of German mercenaries in the Habsburg service followed in 1527, even destroying Rome, the symbolic centre of Italian and indeed European culture, both as the papal capital and as the 'eternal city'.[21]

Yet, although some historians disagree, Italy, or rather the new forms of culture that had developed there, did survive these blows.[22] In the course of the sixteenth and early seventeenth centuries, Italian artistic culture still manifested itself in notable products, especially in the so-called baroque period, up until *c.*1660. Michelangelo Buonarotti, besides being a great painter and sculptor – and, often forgotten, a notable poet, too – was the architect who, after decades of changing inputs by a range of other people, produced the final design for a new St Peter's, which after 1,000 years was to replace the great basilica first erected in the fourth century by the Emperor Constantine over the reputed sepulchre of the Apostle Peter, the first pope. With its mighty cupola and its new-fangled architecture in the classical vein, it provided Christianity with an effective symbol of ecclesiastical, papal power precisely at a time when criticism of the Church's teaching was ever more openly voiced. Meanwhile, Giovanni Pierluigi da Palestrina composed his beautiful masses for the papal Sistine Chapel, which had also been decorated by Michelangelo with his awesome vision both of creation, in the ceiling fresco, and of the Last Judgement, on the altar wall. The much-applauded writer Torquato Tasso produced such great epic poems as *Gerusalemme Liberata* (Jerusalem Delivered), which took their inspiration from the stories of magic and knightly chivalry generated by the Crusades. In the last years of the sixteenth century, the first opera was composed by a group of humanists in Florence, who wanted to revive the classical Greek ideal of tragedy which, they understood, had always been accompanied by music. Soon, at the ducal court of Mantua, Claudio Monteverdi not only delighted his audiences with his madrigals extolling both earthly and divine love, but brought operatic music to its first apogee in such seminal pieces as *Il ritorno d'Ulisse in Patria* and *L'Incoronazione di Poppea* – the subject matter taken, obviously, from Greek and Roman history respectively. And yet, the Italian cities and states gradually lost the pre-eminently active role they had played in earlier times, even though the whole of Europe continued to look to and admire the peninsula not only as the cradle of European civilization but also as the place where it had been born again after what were now rather disparagingly described as 'ages of darkness' – the 'middle ages', the period between the brilliant culture of the ancients and its newly reconstructed version.

In the sixteenth century, Renaissance and Humanism increasingly became manifest north of the Alps as well. Spain became enormously wealthy through its new American colonies. In the German states, the economy prospered through the distributive trades which connected central Europe with the big trading cities along the North Sea, and in England and the Netherlands the economies were given a new impulse from the textile industry and grain trade which had to feed and clothe Europe's population, now growing again after the great economic and demographic crises of the fourteenth century. Thus, the material conditions for a new flowering of culture were abundantly present there. Its effects were soon felt, the more so because in transalpine European thought, too, ideas about the relations between man, the world and God had changed dramatically.

From the late fourteenth century, Church authorities had impotently watched as some of the more intellectual and spiritual of their flock, both men and women, chose to live an exemplary Christian life in the world rather than enter the closed existence of the monastery that kept them under Church control. Thoughts about man's own individual relationship with God, and his individual religious and therefore also social responsibility in the world, were now less controllable. No longer safely confined within monastic walls, these new ideas began to spread. One movement advocating the new thinking, significantly called the *Devotio Moderna* (Modern Devotion), became quite influential, especially in the Netherlands and the neighbouring German states.[23] One of the most powerful writers in this context was Thomas Haemerken, better known as Thomas à Kempis (*c.*1380–1471), whose text *De Imitatione Christi* (On the imitation of Christ), offered many believers a new, more simple and personally intense view of Christianity – it became Europe's second most popular book, after the Bible, of course. Precisely because this group expressly aimed to raise people's awareness and chose education as the most effective means of communication, it posed an outright threat to established culture. Indeed, the Church considered the members of such groups to be much more dangerous than the scientists who, with their complex arguments, might sow the seeds of doubt but, after all, would only ever reach a handful of colleagues.

In the fifteenth and early sixteenth centuries, the educational institutions of the Modern Devotion produced many humanists. Like their Italian colleagues, learned men, north of the Alps, also began to focus on the classical Greek and Roman texts and on the accuracy of the holy book of the Christians. Desiderius Erasmus, mentioned earlier, was easily the most famous of these northern European humanists.[24] In a series of tracts, he tried to lay down the rules for an educational system that, while remaining devoutly Christian, was yet imbued with the critical spirit of Humanism. Indeed, one should not forget that, contrary to what has often been suggested, most people living the culture of Renaissance and Humanism did not display a 'heathenish', pagan spirit at all but remained firmly tied to a view of man and the world as, essentially, redeemable only by God. Looking at Hieronymus Bosch's painting *The Prodigal Son*, probably finished in 1510, we see man – the prodigal son – depicted as a free agent who, while looking back on scenes of a past life of waste and sin, still turns towards the future, the possibility of salvation through the cross, which is the painting's emphatic centrepiece.

The Church was fully aware that the new spirit of criticism and free will that now pervaded Europe had indeed created a new concept of man and thus was, if slowly, giving birth to 'the new man'. As long as this revolutionary view of man and the world, of man and God, was entertained by and spread among only an elite, via education, via texts, pictures and illustrations, the danger was small. But changing perceptions of man can also affect and change large groups of people if the appropriate means and channels of communication are available. It was precisely in this field that the Church's continued power, its supremacy over the people of Europe, was really threatened.

8 A new society

Europe as a wider world

Economic and technological change and the definitive formation of the 'modern' state

The fifteenth century saw a changing world in Europe, which experienced momentous economic progress, after a period of prolonged depression. In the twelfth and thirteenth centuries, a serious crisis had developed partly because the temperature on earth dropped slightly – the phenomenon of the 'small ice age'. The climate had become cooler and wetter, with a sharp dip in the fourteenth century. The abandonment of settlements and the inundation of coastal plains were but a few of the visible manifestations. Then a succession of very wet years resulted in poor harvests, in cruel famines, in malnutrition and, soon, in widespread disease – typhus and malaria. All this caused long-term chaos in the still largely agricultural economy. In a spiral of undernourishment, growing child mortality and a decreasing birthrate, a demographic decline set in, not least because in this situation the Black Death – first attested in Messina, in 1347 – and other epidemics caused hundreds of thousands of deaths, which many, not knowing any of these causes and effects, simply blamed on divine anger at human depravity.[1]

During the fourteenth century, however, the climate improved, and by the beginning of the fifteenth century, the epidemics had subsided and economic and social disruption had been overcome. People, desperately trying to rebuild their personal lives as well as make up for demographic losses, started marrying earlier and produced more offspring. Though effects differed from region to region and, indeed, between urban communities and the rural countryside, by the beginning of the fifteenth century, western Europe in particular began to experience a period of spectacular economic growth. The agricultural sector expanded, the population increased, and surplus production resulted in an extension of regional and interregional trade; in consequence of all this, the fiscal base of governments was considerably broadened. The complex structures of expanding states needed to be managed. Fiscal systems were organized on the basis of mathematical calculations, armies and navies were built like perfect machines in which soldiers functioned according to rules of combat that were planned mathematically as well. Besides, learning, science and technology were increasingly used to maximize commercial and thus state income.

Many craftsmen and scientists whose qualities enabled them to realize all the state's new needs offered their services to Europe's princes. They were men – for in this group, few women participated – who now thought about quantifiable results first, and about the old, religious-metaphysical questions second, if at all. Slowly, a chasm emerged between those for whom knowledge and wisdom were forms of speculation about the relation of man to nature and the supernatural and those who only sought to 'technically' control man and nature. It was a split that in the seventeenth-century debate on the quality of culture was translated in terms like 'old' and 'new', 'ancient' and 'modern'. Actually, the 'reasonable', rational explanations seemed to hold the future, given that they were so obviously successful in the creation of power and wealth. The branches of knowledge which produced these explanations therefore meant 'cultural capital' for those whose profession it was, providing them with an entrance to the world of power, to a position in society which otherwise could only be attained by those with money or of noble birth.

During the fifteenth and sixteenth centuries, states in Europe, building on the foundations laid from the twelfth century onwards, definitively acquired the structure that still characterizes them now. In a process of alternately violent and bloody interaction or peaceful negotiation between the rulers, the various aristocratic power groups and the patrician elites of the major towns, most states developed into complex, centralized bureaucracies, a cultural phenomenon, a 'work of art' even, created by human hands as were the artistic and literary products of the Renaissance.

If only because the process of state formation was so often painful, many literate Europeans increasingly stressed the necessity for a rational, uniform legal system and for a clear circumscription of state power. They based this conviction not only on their reading of classical texts on political theory but also on their empirical observation of the reality of their world, a world of states eager to extend their power internally and externally. Hence, Roman Law was elaborated as a system guaranteeing state subjects at least some minimal, inviolable rights while at the same time stressing the supreme authority of the monarch, and complex ideologies were devised to legitimize a prince's right to rule while yet safeguarding the liberties of the subjects. Mostly, these referred to the divine origin of princely power but, increasingly, secular contract law was invoked to enhance the legality of the relationship between the State, embodied in the prince, and the subjects.

In the sixteenth century, Niccolò Machiavelli had already opined it was precisely the many relatively small states into which Europe was divided that gave this part of the world its *virtù*.[2] These states proved to be stronger whenever the old ruling elites – clergy and nobility, as well as state bureaucracy – realized that a properly functioning economy was the necessary basis of power, that a relatively strong middle class was the principal bearer of such an economy, and that it must therefore be allowed a certain say in public matters and even in politics. These ideas recurred in political analyses produced during the following centuries. The extent to which the ideas expressed therein – state control over the economy and the empowerment of the middle classes – were actually realized in the various states of Europe would greatly influence not only the development of political institutions but also of culture, in each individual state as well as in Europe at large until, finally, the revolutions of the late eighteenth and early nineteenth century brought about both the victory of the central State as well as of the middle classes as its prime power group.

Meanwhile, in 1752, more than two centuries after Machiavelli, François-Marie Arouet, better known by his pen name Voltaire, looking back upon the history of Europe in the seventeenth century in his *Le Siècle de Louis XIV* (The Age of Louis XIV), noted that:

> all [states] resemble each other. They all have the same religious foundation, even if it is divided into different denominations. They all employ the same principles of public law and policy, which are unknown elsewhere in the world.[3]

Voltaire's contemporaries, such as Charles de Montesquieu and Adam Smith, looking at the past of their world, probed even deeper in trying to explain the ways in which Europe functioned and exercised its power. They, too, noted the fact of these comparatively small states, with their rapidly evolving production systems, which they ascribed to their continuous competition but also to their inevitable, creative communication. They saw Europe as a world unified by Christianity, but with religion not being overly powerful. Nor, for that matter, was this European world dominated by one secular ruler only; indeed, the numerous princes who embodied the various states were not all-powerful either. Moreover, though these authors were critical of the situation in many European states, they especially admired the balance which had been achieved in the Dutch Republic and in England, where liberty, equality and wealth, the main elements of a 'virtuous' state, contributed to their prominent position both in Europe and in the wider world.

By and large, later historians have supported these analyses and have named the phenomenon of the centralized, competitive states and the elaboration of public law as some of the most important formative elements in the establishment of the 'wonder' that was Europe.[4]

All these developments were enhanced if not made possible in the first place by technological inventions that had far-reaching economic, political and cultural effects. Their significance is made clear in a revealing statement by the famous English statesman, philosopher and scientist, Sir Francis Bacon (1561–1626). In 1620, he published his *Novum Organum* (The New Instrument), its very title referring to Aristotle's celebrated work on the nature of science, the 'Organon'. In his introduction, Bacon says:

> We should note the force, effect and consequences of inventions, which are nowhere more conspicuous than in those . . . which were unknown to the Ancients, namely, printing, gunpowder, and the compass. For these . . . have changed the appearance and state of the whole world.[5]

Bacon not only ascertains which inventions or rather instruments Europe had adopted, or discovered, to now see them bring about cultural and social changes, but also establishes that these instruments were unknown in the ancient world and that they are, therefore, the achievements of contemporary Europe. In this, he implicitly distances himself from the widely held belief of the humanists that no further progress would be possible once the level of civilization of the ancient Greeks and Romans had again been reached: against the 'Ancients', he positioned himself as a 'Modern', someone who believed in the power of contemporary society to perfect itself.

From manuscript to typescript

Indisputably, Christian Europe changed radically through the influence of two adjoining cultures, the Islamic and the Byzantine, which intellectually both hailed back to the ancient Graeco-Roman culture whence all three had originated. The classical tradition, the 'great tradition', i.e. not only the norms and values but also the outward forms of the culture of Greece and Rome, certainly became more dominant in the fourteenth and fifteenth centuries, both among the monks and the warriors, the two traditional 'orders' who still formed the backbone of Europe's cultural elite, and among the new urban aristocracy. Yet the cultural forms we now catecorize by the terms Renaissance and Humanism would never have acquired their enduring significance if another development had not taken place.

Culture exists thanks to communication and even is, to a large extent, communication. If people do not share their thoughts with others, these thoughts will not endure. They will never be shaped or become manifest as recognizable utterances, which then mark a group of people as sharing common characteristics, as sharing a culture.

Of course, the spoken word was and still is probably the most important mode of communication, but what is said is transient and does not last. What is written more easily survives the moment it was first thought or spoken. It begins a life of is own, becoming transferable information, and moreover the basis for recognizing common thoughts and behaviour. That which is written may also may turn into knowledge, a corpus of information which, by somehow being deemed important enough to be passed on from generation to generation, thus continues to exist. This was acutely felt by the Graeco-Byzantine scholar, Johannes Bessarion (1403–72) who fled to Italy and became a formative influence on humanist culture. In 1468, he donated his enormous collection of manuscripts to the city of Venice, on condition that they be made available to the public. In the letter presenting his library to the Doge, he writes of his books:

> They live, they converse with us, they teach us, they form us, they comfort us, they point us to that which we have forgotten. . . . So great is the power of books, their value, their glory, yes, even their divine force, that we would all be awkward

and ignorant if books did not exist; there would be no knowledge of the past, no examples, no learning about divine and human things. The tombstone which covers the body of man would also cover up his name. . . . After the fall of Greece and the lamentable captivity of Byzantium, I, with unprecedented intensity, used all my strength, all my care, all my material possibilities to trace Greek texts. . . . And so I have collected all the books of the Greek philosophers, especially the rare ones, which are difficult to find.[6]

Bessarion's letter not only indicates the prime importance of texts as carriers of culture, but also shows that in his time 'books' were rare. Until late in the fifteenth century, handwritten texts were the only vehicle of textual information. Moreover, texts were rare also because they were expensive: written, by hand, on hides turned into the very costly 'vellum', or parchment. Consequently, the group who based its knowledge on texts was necessarily small, an elite. At first, texts were initially produced in the scriptoria of monasteries. From the twelfth century onwards, the universities began to cater for the demand for textbooks for both professors and students: professional scribes would copy what students needed. Subsequently, even more professional workshops were set up to meet the wishes of private collectors, bibliophiles, who ordered luxury manuscripts that were mainly if not solely valued for their beautiful illustrations. Yet, by its very economic and social context as well as by its nature, for centuries both the amount and the communication value of handwritten texts was severely limited.[7]

For example, in the relatively poor region which was the northern Netherlands before *c.*1400, not more than a few texts were produced.[8] In the southern Netherlands and present-day northern France the situation was somewhat better until the economy declined there.[9] In wealthy Sicily, the biggest number of books possessed by any private person in the late fourteenth and early fifteenth centuries amounted to only twenty.[10] Indeed, in about 1450, when Europe had approximately 100 million inhabitants, the number of manuscript books kept in the libraries of cathedrals, monasteries, palaces and castles probably ran to only several tens of thousands. Private citizens, regardless of their wealth and prominence – kings, nobles, senior clergy, the great merchants and bankers – seldom owned more than a few manuscripts. If they bought texts at all, these tended to be illuminated bibles, prayer books and missals or, again, treatises dealing with the art of living as a nobleman or the management of great estates, as well as, perhaps, one or two courtly romances.

Therefore, any technique that made possible the exact reproduction of a particular text in great numbers would be revolutionary from every point of view. It would reduce the time and cost of repeatedly copying a particular text by hand. It would greatly increase the amount of copies of a particular text. And it would remove the many errors that inevitably occurred when a text was copied, which meant that, in the manuscript culture, the essential points of a particular work were often so mutilated over the course of several generations that the original meaning had partly or completely disappeared, as had become painfully obvious when the humanists started scrutinizing the Bible.

In China, this central communication problem had been solved before the beginning of the Christian era by using block printing or xylography. The cutting of texts into wooden blocks had been combined with another invention, paper, on which the ink-covered blocks were impressed. Even before the year 1000 AD, block printing helped to produce and spread not only the 150-odd volume edition of the works of Confucius, the founding father of Chinese social and political philosophy – which in its turn spawned a veritable Chinese Renaissance – but also more than 5,000 volumes in which the Buddhist canon, the *Tripitaka*, was divulged.[11]

In the twelfth century, the Koreans developed and used the technique of individual signs cast in metal, which was also introduced into China. However, the fact that the Koreans do, but the Chinese do not have a phonetic alphabet meant that in China some 30,000 separate characters were needed to print a scholarly text. With manual labour being cheap – usually the main reason for discarding the large-scale application of technological inventions – for the time being, the Korean invention was not adopted in China.

It is certain that Europe knew about Chinese printing methods as early as the late thirteenth century, if only through the tales of the Venetian traveller, Marco Polo. Also, news may have reached Europe about the type-casting developments in twelfth-century Korea and in the realm of the Uigur Turks, bordering on the Islamic world, who started using wooden letters at roughly the same time.[12] Indeed, block printing was in evidence in Europe from the fourteenth century onwards, in the production of playing cards as well as religious prints. It certainly occurred in the Rhineland around the 1370s and had probably been introduced there from the Islamic world. Yet, it is impossible to determine if, in the case of the early fifteenth-century efforts at type-casting in the Netherlands and of the subsequent, more successful efforts of Johann Gutenberg (*c.*1400–67) – again, in the Rhineland – we are dealing with regular technology transfer, with more complex idea diffusion or with independent invention.

Whatever the answer to this question, from the late fifteenth century onwards, the west continued along the path of typography, whereas China held on to its xylographic tradition. For a long time, the two were compatible at least in the sense that the amount of time and expense it took to found and set the type for a western-style book page was the same as the amount of time necessary to produce a carved page for a xylographically reproduced book. Only in the late nineteenth century, when labour in China became far more expensive, and the technique of typographic or 'European' printing was greatly improved with the introduction of the rotation press, could the west begin to successfully introduce its own system in the land of origin, where understandably it had been discarded as less than practical a millennium earlier.

In Europe, the credit for realizing the great leap from a manuscript to a print culture is traditionally given to the German Johann Gutenberg, though the Dutch have long staked the claim of the Haarlem-based printer Laurens Jansz Coster. Gutenberg experimented with individual, raised letters of uniform height and width cast in metal; he fiddled around with ink, manufactured on the basis of oil paint; he developed a press which printed the letters, set in line as words and sentences in wooden frames, onto paper, instead of placing the paper on the woodcut letters, as in China.

Between 1438 and 1452, Gutenberg, besieged by spies – industrial espionage can be said to have begun then – developed his technique, shrouding his experiments in secrecy. However, operating on the basis of borrowed capital, inevitably his backers asked to see their money's worth. In the course of the year 1453, the Fust firm, that had invested in Gutenberg's research, on being told he could not yet deliver, demanded their money. As Gutenberg could not pay, he had to hand over his materials, just when he was ready to test his invention in practice. In the same year, the first printed book appeared, the result of a technique still used today, although, of course, digital methods have begun to take over from traditional printing presses. Significantly, the first printed book was 'The Book', the Bible. It was a monument to what was quickly called the *Ars artficialiter scribendi*, 'the art of artificial writing'. 'The Gutenberg Bible', as it is referred to, was a splendid, clear print in a number of exactly identical copies. Nowadays, a single copy is worth millions of dollars, euros or pounds.

Gutenberg's inventions brought about a veritable revolution in European society: economic, technical and cultural. One might even argue that it was the beginning of the most important cultural revolution that western man had experienced in many thousands of years.[13] Printers, who were simultaneously publishers and booksellers, quickly set up business in all the large European cities. Book production now became an economic factor and an industry. In the world of manuscript culture, a copy was usually made because an individual client had asked for it. Now that books could be printed in larger numbers, and presses, which were of course expensive, should preferably be kept running, a printer-publisher had to investigate and sometimes even create a market. He did this by, among other things, advertising his product, which he offered to customers who did not yet know that they needed it. He advertised a still unknown text by a classical Greek or Latin writer, an even better version of the Bible, yet another hymn book. But publishers also worked to create a market, e.g. for a new cookery book – one of the most magnificently illustrated ones ever produced was the *Opera dell'arte del cucinare*, written in 1570 by Bartolomeo Scappi, court chef to Pope Pius V; for a new treatise on the education of children, such as Erasmus's tract *De Ratione Studii*, of 1516, and his *De pueris statim ac liberaliter instituendo*, of 1529, wherein the 'liberal' refers to what makes man 'humane' or, indeed, free; or for a new series of erotic or even pornographic stories, complete with revealing pictures. For the latter, the famous painter Tiziano and the equally famous writer Pietro Aretino teamed up to produce a highly successful illustrated book of stories-cum-pictures, considered to be not only 'dirty' but outright sinful by the Roman Catholic Church which banned its sale, only to increase its sales, of course. In short, the new medium literally created new texts, which previously had not existed because there was no market for them. Precisely because all sorts of texts could be produced properly and cheaply, they were now written and printed. As a result, life in Europe changed fundamentally.

The price of books dropped dramatically, both because it was now possible to produce and sell a large number of identical copies and because paper was used instead of the much more expensive parchment, or vellum. The technique of manufacturing paper, also developed by the Chinese, had become known in Europe in the thirteenth and fourteenth centuries, again via the Arab-Islamic world of Spain. Consequently, the transcriber's or copyist's profession started to disappear during the sixteenth century though, of course, texts that would serve only a limited readership continued to be copied by hand well into the eighteenth century. Indeed, recent research has revealed that even in the world of scholarship, manuscript texts remained in use for a long time, influencing intellectual debate and, thus, the development of ideas in ways that, by the perishable nature of such handwritten notes, are often now difficult to trace.

The new printing technique, however, was soon perfected. All sorts of type-faces were developed, intended to guarantee greater precision in printing, and for use in small-format books, which now quickly appeared. Gutenberg's Bible had been an enormous, unwieldy tome. In the sixteenth century, the Venetian printer-publisher Aldus Manutius developed more convenient texts, pocket-size books, as an answer to a growing need, which was also a sign of the demand for the product. The Chinese literati, of course, had produced them long before, calling them 'sleeve-books'.

Gunpowder and compass

Undeniably, the instruments named by Bacon have been of central importance in the development of Europe from the fifteenth century up until today. It is therefore necessary to pause and consider their role. The cases of the printing press, the gun and the compass are also illustrative of a situation which contributed to significant developments in the entire field of European technology and, consequently, of the European states but also of Europe's position in the wider world.

While printing may be considered a European invention, devised independently from, although far later than in China, neither gunpowder nor the compass were European discoveries. Yet Europe applied both instruments in ways that had not been thought of or elaborated elsewhere. It is one of the fascinating aspects of human history that certain inventions, while causing little or no change in a given culture, can bring about a revolution in a different setting.

The very fact that Europe was made up of a great number of small, increasingly competitive political entities may well have been one of the main reasons for the progress made in creatively modifying techniques that arrived from Asia. In later periods, this competition continued to stimulate indigenous inventions.

In view of their demographic expansion, Europe's many polities were forced to exploit to the utmost their meagre resources. But this very division into small states may also have helped Europe to overcome the depressing effects of the global agricultural and economic crises of the fourteenth century and its accompanying 'pandemic'. Europe's population, decreasing from *c*.80 million to *c*.60 million between 1300 and 1400, started rising again in the fifteenth century. Indeed, Europe entered upon a phase of great expansion in every field. In China, however, a population that had numbered *c*.115 million in 1200 dropped to 85 million in 1300 and to 75 million in 1400. There, this very crisis seems to have been one of the causes that heralded a prolonged period of relative stagnation, which may be explained by a growing tendency towards conservatism in the upper echelons of the huge, monolithically ruled empire.[14] Thus, for the first time in history, the technological and consequently economic balance between the two civilizations was reversed.

Nevertheless, the combination of a discernible resurgence of conservative, agriculturally orientated ideologies in China and, less so, in Japan and India, from the fifteenth century onwards, and the increased interest in technical innovations in Europe cannot entirely explain the technological gap that grew between the west and the east. For while China surprisingly decided to give up maritime expansion after the great and evidently successful expeditions of Admiral Cheng Ho in the mid-fifteenth century, it still continued to produce inventions, such as, for example, the three-spindle spinning wheel and the calendering roller in the textile industry. Nor is it sufficient to note the fact that food prices and, consequently, wages seem to have been higher in Europe than in Asia, which on the European side of the globe stimulated the introduction and perfection of machines in most fields of production.

Rather, it seems that the main cause for the growing gap between east and west lay in the notion, propagated by such men as Sir Francis Bacon, that science should be studied systematically, through the collection, classification, analysis and interpretation of ever greater amounts of empirical data and, moreover, that such scientific work should be strictly organized. Such positivist ideas certainly had their origins in the earlier method of philological empiricism developed by the humanists from the thirteenth century onwards to deal with biblical and classical texts. Of course, the slow permeation of this view of the world as a mental attitude, contributing to the growth of the habit of abstract thought, was greatly strengthened by the availability of information through printing – the invention of which coincided with the first age of maritime expansion. Printing, besides the numerous other cultural changes it brought about, was certainly immensely important too in facilitating, broadening and speeding up the development of new technology in Europe.

As to scientific developments in sixteenth-century Europe, one may assume that thinking in terms of systematic organization and operation had developed from the large-scale mental absorption of the processes observed in early machinery; among these, the clock was probably the most influential, both in providing a vision of order and in imposing a sense of regulated time, which, when introduced into economic life, also began changing people's attitudes towards work and leisure.[15] In its turn, this way of thinking was transferred to various fields of human endeavour. In the long term, all this resulted in a mental and organizational change in general industrial production, too, from a craft-orientated attitude to an assembly-line mode.[16] In the short term, two sectors of public life were drastically changed.

After its introduction in the fourteenth century, gunpowder in Europe was soon used not only to fire heavy cannon, but also to provide ammunition for light arms to be carried and used by single men operating on foot rather than on horseback. This new application led to a major change in European society, affecting life far beyond the military sphere.

Small, inefficient armies of knights, riding expensive, heavily armoured horses were replaced with increasingly large armies, consisting mainly of cheap mercenaries armed with guns. The phenomenon of the armaments industry was born, but so was the arms race; increasingly large masses of troops were deployed, and military technology as well as investments in it came to play a more essential role. New types of weaponry were developed and new ways of protecting cities against the volleys of far-reaching guns and cannons had to be devised. While wars became bloodier, they also became costlier. Even in times of peace, armies continued to demand their toll as soldiers, when not sent home but retained in garrisons, had to be paid, fed and clothed.

Reforms in military organization in particular, such as the arms drill in marching and the use of weapons practised by Prince Maurice of Nassau in the northern Netherlands and King Gustavus Vasa in Sweden, were highly influential in creating a mentality tuned to the systematic division of labour. This also resulted from the need of early modern armies for the production of food, clothing and weaponry along uniform lines and in great amounts. But attitudes towards the State in general were influenced by a more technical, machine-influenced image. The state could be seen as a clock, as it was a complex mechanism made up of numerous people all doing their part to make it run. The prince was, of course, if not the actual clock-maker, still the person who wound it.

From the sixteenth century onwards, a steadily growing proportion of national revenues went to the military. Therefore, the European states needed to increase their income. To the extent that their fiscal capacity did not suffice, foreign expansion could offer a solution. Since a certain balance of power had been reached in Europe, expansion outside Europe continued out of necessity. This is one of the reasons why Europeans, who for 1,000 years had hardly dared venture beyond the borders of their own world, now began to leave their safe territory in ever-increasing numbers, heading for unknown lands and, increasingly, waters: individually, they may have sought adventure, fame and wealth; collectively, they looked for opportunities for economic expansion that would be the basis for greater power, abroad but more importantly at home.

In this context, the compass acquired its importance. European sailors, having become acquainted with the new instrument in the thirteenth or fourteenth centuries, now used it to venture onto the open seas. With new geographical notions finding wider acceptance following the humanists' rediscovery of such ancient writers as Ptolemy and Strabo, some mariners now even dared to cross the oceans, hoping, and later knowing, that the earth was, indeed, round, and that each journey outward could also be a journey homeward. Thus began the voyages of discovery, and, with them, European colonialism: the compass provided the assurance of direction at sea, and firearms provided certainty and ascendancy in the newly discovered lands. Europe spread its wings and began commercially and territorially to conquer large parts of the world. But the men who did so acted for the European states, beginning with Vasco da Gama and Christopher Columbus, employed by the Portuguese and Spanish crowns respectively.

THE HAGUE, AD 1625: HUGO GROTIUS EXPOUNDS 'THE LAW OF NATIONS'

In 1625, the famous Dutch legal theorist and lawyer Hugo de Groot (1583–1645) published his *De Iure belli ac pacis* (On the Right of War and Peace), a systematic account of all legal thinking relevant to the relationship between individual states which, in their development towards formalized and centralized structures, had become increasingly competitive. The need to regularize this often bloody competition induced Grotius to think thoroughly about the problems involved. In these excerpts, Grotius's concern about the conflict between practice and theory, power politics and the rights of human dignity, becomes clear:

> Many have endeavoured to write explanatory commentaries or concise surveys of the municipal law, for instance, of Rome or of a man's own country. Few, however, have attempted the law which applies to the relations of several nations or of their rulers, whether it be derived from nature itself or instituted by custom or tacit contract, and no one so far has treated it completely and systematically. Yet mankind has a concern that this be done. . . .
>
> True, man is an animal, but of a very superior kind, a great deal more removed from the others than their species differ from another; many activities peculiar to the human race show this. Among the special characteristics of mankind is a desire for society, that is for a life in common lived not anyhow but in tranquility and (to satisfy one's intellect) arranged with men of one's own kind. So the supposition that every animal naturally seeks its own advantage is true of other animals, but of man only before he has achieved the employment of his peculiarly human qualities. . . .
>
> That preference for society . . . of which I have already spoken is the source of *ius* properly so called. It involves abstention from another's property, its restitution to him if we do happen to possess it, reparation of damage done by fault, and an admission that punishment may be applied among men. . . .
>
> It is quite wrong to suppose, as some imagine, that in war all laws cease to apply; indeed, war should never be engaged in except to obtain lawful ends, nor once engaged in should it be waged except within the bounds of law and good faith. Demosthenes was right to argue that war is an action directed against those who cannot be constrained by process of law. . . .

Holding it thus firmly established that there exists among nations a common law with force for and in wars, I had many and weighty reasons for writing a book about it. Throughout Christendom I saw a readiness to make war of which even barbarians might be ashamed. Men take up arms for light causes or none at all, and once at war they discard all respect for the laws of God and men. . . . The sight of such atrocities has induced a good many truly reputable writers to forbid Christian men all recourse to arms since it is their special duty to love all men. . . .

[Concluding that this situation is unrealistic, Grotius continues to ponder about the regulation of war.] Touching those who are truly enemy subjects, that is from a permanent condition, the law of nations permits them to be injured, as to their persons, in any place. When war is declared against anyone it is simultaneously declared against the men of his people. . . . We may therefore lawfully kill them on our own soil, on enemy soil, or on soil belonging to no one, or on the high seas. It is not permitted to kill them on [neutral] territory remaining at peace. . . .

How widely this liberty extends may be seen from the fact that the killing of children and women is held to be lawful and included in this law of war. . . . Not even prisoners are exempt. . . .

The violation of women is variously regarded as permitted or not. Those who allow it consider only the injury done to the person, which they hold it agreeable to the law of arms to inflict on anything belonging to the enemy. The other opinion is better: it takes into account not only the injury but also the act of unbridled lust and concludes that something pertaining to neither safety nor punishment should be no more lawful in war than in peace. This latter view is not the law of all nations, but it is the law of the more respectable ones.[17]

Whether or not they heeded the law of nations, it was these states that, from the fifteenth century onwards, wondered what kind of Europe they wanted. What they definitely did no longer want was a situation in which one hegemonic system limited their sovereignty, the more so because, since the effective demise of the imperial authority one associated with the Holy Roman Empire, the only remaining organization with such pretensions, the Catholic Church, partly derived its authority from its power over the incomprehensible, the magical, through ritual and sacrifice. Most people in Europe continued to be deeply influenced by this kind of power. As the Church's might was still based on it, it made its authority potentially all-embracing. Thus, it was all the more frustrating for rulers and their bureaucrats, who were striving to attain absolute power over the people they now considered primarily to be the subjects of their states.

Church and State: the break-up of religious unity

Until the fifteenth century, the Catholic Church was the only bearer of a religion practised everywhere in Europe. It was an institution which, transcending the borders of manors, counties, duchies and kingdoms, had created a common religion with a number of values derived from it, and a common cultural awareness, at least among the elite. In the tenth, eleventh, and subsequently the fourteenth and fifteenth centuries, under the influence of the repeated revival of the crusading idea, the habit had developed of equating the term *Christianitas*, which defined the world of Christianity as opposed to the world of Islam, with geographical 'Europe', suggesting that the latter represented a certain cultural unity as well.

However, in the fifteenth and early sixteenth centuries, the Church of Rome finally lost its millennial monopoly of power in the Christian west. Though criticism of the Church's doctrinal views and moral practices, as well as of growing papal authority, both within the Church itself and in secular politics, had increased significantly during the fourteenth and fifteenth centuries, the Church's structure, though crumbling somewhat, had largely remained intact. Admittedly, there had been strong dissenting voices, such as, for example, those of the Englishman John Wycliffe and the Czech Jan Hus, who had both clearly expressed their dissatisfaction. Yet their influence had remained regionally limited. After all, they could spread their ideas only by word of mouth or through handwritten texts. Hence, they were unable to mobilize multitudes of followers over large parts of Europe. A true 'reform movement', gathering adherents from all over the Christian world, was simply not possible at this time. However, by the beginning of the sixteenth century, the situation was considerably altered as became obvious when the ideas of the German theologian Martin Luther (1483–1546) proved instrumental in shaking the foundations of the Roman Catholic Church and altering the religious landscape of Europe forever.

Luther, deciding that discussion of the conclusions he had reached on the basis of his study of the Bible and other important texts from early Christianity was necessary, if only because the Catholic Church's practices were found wanting, took the course normal in the scholarly world. He formulated his ideas in a number of propositions and, or so the story goes, advertised them in public – in this case by nailing his handwritten theses to the door of the church at Wittenberg. It was then 31 October 1517.[18]

Raised in the humanist tradition, Luther finally broke with the traditions of the Church of Rome in all those areas wherein, according to him, they were no longer founded on the oldest Christian texts as scientifically established. Central to the many doctrines that Luther derived from his thorough study of the sources of Christianity was the idea that the core of God's revelation is found only in Holy Scripture. He questioned the value of several of the seven sacraments because in his opinion they had not been instituted by Christ and, moreover, had become mere acts without any content. Indeed, Luther observed that many Christians had no notion whatsoever of the norms and values presented in the Bible, simply accepting, uncritically and even super-stitiously, as salutary the magic of all sorts of actions performed by priests. Hence, he wrote:

> Thus it is not baptism that justifies or benefits anyone, but it is faith in that word of promise to which baptism is added. This faith justifies and fulfils that which

baptism signifies. . . . It cannot be true, therefore, that there is contained in the sacraments a power efficacious for justification, or that they are 'effective signs' of grace. . . . For if the sacrament confers grace on me because I receive it, then indeed I receive grace by virtue of my work, and not by faith; and I gain not the promise in the sacrament but only the sign. . . . Therefore let us open our eyes and learn to pay heed more to the word than to the sign, more to faith than to the work or use of the sign.[19]

More fundamentally, Luther disputed the concept of free will: man himself does not determine whether, as a result of his way of life, he will be blessed with salvation. God has already predetermined this. Only a person's faith, given him by the mercy of God at the beginning of creation, will save him from damnation, if that is, he lives according to it. Luther proves himself to be a real humanist here. After all, this doctrine of divine providence is clearly derived from the study of early Christian ideas that, in their turn, had been influenced by Greek Stoicism and Persian Manichaeism.

In a debate with Erasmus, who fiercely defended the doctrine of free will as central to Catholic theology, Luther wrote a rejoinder in his *De servo Arbitrio* (On the Bondage of the Will), published in 1520:

> It is then fundamentally necessary and wholesome for Christians to know that God foreknows nothing contingently, but that He foresees, purposes, and does all things according to His own, immutable, eternal and infallible will.
>
> . . .The will of God is effective and cannot be impeded, since power belongs to God's nature; and His wisdom is such that He cannot be deceived. Since, then, His will is not impeded, what is done cannot but be done where, when, how, as far as, and by whom He foresees and wills. . . .
>
> I frankly confess that, for myself, even if it could be, I should not want 'freewill' to be given me, nor anything to be left in my own hands to enable me to endeavour after salvation; not merely because in the face of so many dangers, and adversities, and assaults of devils, I could not stand my ground. . . . but because . . . I should still be forced to labour with no guarantee of success, and beat my fists at the air. If I lived and worked to all eternity, my conscience would never reach comfortable certainty as to how much it must do to satisfy God.[20]

The introduction of such ideas effected a profound change in the traditional views of man and the world and, as a result, in all sorts of cultural forms. While many derived a pious optimism from Luther's teachings, hoping they might develop a more personal relationship with God, through a life of good works, many others were steeped in sombre thoughts of doom and gloom, in apathetic pessimism.

From the 1520s onwards, a very successful movement for religious reform developed, first in Luther's name, but soon around other divines as well; for example, John Calvin, who taught in Geneva, quickly proclaimed his own dissident views of theology and Church organization. Besides addressing doctrinal issues, Luther and his fellow critics were vociferous in condemning many ecclesiastical practices that had developed over the centuries. They vehemently attacked the phenomenon of Church tithes and of the sale of indulgences that channelled much of the wealth of the faithful into the coffers of Rome. They also denounced the often disappointingly low intellectual and spiritual level of the clergy, who, largely uneducated themselves, kept their flock ignorant of even the most basic tenets of Christian belief. Such criticism was quickly adopted not only in the many states of the German Reich, but also in the Low Countries. There, for example, the plays produced by members of the urban elite of Ghent for the town population increasingly voiced Lutheran ideas until, in 1539, central government, afraid of civic unrest, decided to ban such plays altogether.[21]

As indicated above, long before the voices of Luther and his other reformist contemporaries were heard, critical members of the Roman Catholic clergy had themselves voiced concerns over the state of the Church, mostly at the Church's general councils that had convened during the fifteenth century. The new criticism and the demands that went with it would have been as ineffective as the earlier ones if it had not been for two important factors. Of course, one of them was the influence of the first mass-medium of Europe, printing, which greatly facilitated the spread of new ideas, as will be shown below. Equally important, however, was that the calls for reform now were taken up by a number of European princes. Some of them were genuinely concerned about the many malpractices affecting their people through the Church, but many just felt that the power wielded by Rome and its regional representatives impinged rather too much upon their own authority, politically and economically, which, precisely during this period, they tried to increase. Thus, they eagerly seized upon this opportunity, using the prevailing climate of protest either to force Rome into a number of concessions, mostly of a financial and political nature, that gave them greater independence in the affairs of the Church in their own realm, or to sever altogether the ties that had bound them to the papacy for almost 1,000 years.

The kings of France and Spain, for example, while remaining staunch Roman Catholics, yet greatly reduced Rome's influence in their states, whereas the king of England, followed by the monarchs of Denmark and Sweden and a number of German princes, went over to the Reformation, as the entire movement came to be called. However, due to circumstances that varied from state to state, the movement eventually developed rather differently in north–west and in central Europe.

Basically, the actions of Luther and the other reformers created a fundamental split in what there had been of European unity. They caused the one Church that had given Europe cultural coherence for more than 1,000 years to become divided into many religious denominations, all, true enough, Christian, yet quickly manifesting very different value concepts and, indeed, cultures. The Reformation divided the people of Europe into Catholics, who remained loyal to Rome and, thus, to Latin as the language of worship and culture, and Protestants of all sorts who translated the Bible and the liturgy into the vernacular and in doing so made a considerable contribution to further linguistic and hence cultural nationalism.

During the Council of Trent (1545–63), the Catholic Church showed its resilience, formulating positions intended to buttress anew the power of the institution that still called itself the Universal Church. Probably more radically than ever before, this restored Roman Church did indeed influence virtually all areas of culture through religion. On the central level, the Congregation of the Inquisition, a court judging the (im-)propriety of doctrine, became an instrument to ensure orthodoxy; obviously, it could also be used to stifle any form of critical thinking remotely affecting, or threatening to affect, the teaching and thus the power of the Church. However, one has to realize that it was not very effective outside the Italian states and the Spanish kingdoms. Indeed, despite all its efforts, the papacy did not succeed in making its reformed version of Christianity 'universal' once more.

Due to the political background and backing of the Reformation, in most of the 'reformed' parts of Europe, State-dominated Protestant churches came into existence, controlled by both secular and spiritual authorities cooperating in an often uneasy balance. For though the reformers had the princes and their bureaucracies to thank for their effective support in introducing the new doctrine, they would have preferred to be left free to run their own religious communities. Instead, the states used them to introduce and impose their own views even in the field of doctrine, very much as the Church of Rome had always done and still did in Catholic Europe.

Despite this tendency towards uniformity, the reformers' insistence on the individual's primary obligation and responsibility vis-à-vis his Maker may have contributed to or even resulted in a situation wherein alternative thinking, both in matters religious and in matters social and political, slowly began to take root more easily in the Protestant states of north-west Europe than in the south-eastern regions still dominated by the Roman Church. For a long time, this situation has been used as part of the wider argument that asserts that, on the whole, from the sixteenth century onwards, Protestant societies and states 'did better' than Roman Catholic ones, more specifically in paving the way for modernization and progress. This, of course, is a highly complex matter. It must suffice, here, to say that this supposition is not borne out by recent research.[22]

However, by and large, the influence of religion on society remained undiminished, whether in Protestant or in Catholic Europe. Following the adage 'cuius regio, illius et religio' (who rules the land also decides upon its religion), most princes continued to use religion both as a channel for propaganda and, in many cases, as an instrument to enforce cultural cohesion in their state, with the sole aim of increasing their own power. To the extent that the states of Europe still felt the need to capture their subjects by ritual and sacrament, the kings were increasingly presented as rulers sent and sanctioned by God. They were or became the embodiment of the state or the nation.

Once again it was the intellectual elite who helped to shape this ideology. An elite, as always, of scholars and even, by now, of 'intellectuals', of men who, making the accumulation and transfer of knowledge their profession,[23] set out to influence society through their power over the word and through the ways in which they used and manipulated images and symbols. They were writers of chronicles and histories, political theorists and propagandists. However, they were no longer, as in the time of Charlemagne, recruited exclusively from the ranks of the Church which, at that time, had still supported the State. Instead, they were increasingly laymen, servants of the State, often even hostile to every claim the Churches still dared to make, and certainly enemies of the one Church which did so by calling on its unique function as the protector of Europe's unity.

The rise of the Reformation and the growing opposition to papal authority, even in Catholic circles, meant that the sixteenth century saw neither the formation of a common European front based on a common religious foundation, for instance against Islam, nor the genesis of a parallel sense of identity. 'Rather Turkish than popish' was a slogan often heard. Perhaps precisely because many people rejected the papacy, which underpinned its claims to supremacy by calling on a universal Christianity that was presented as identical with Europe, more and more people also rejected the 1,000-year-old identification of their world with *Europe* with *Christendom*. In short, as a result of a variety of developments, the notion of *Christianitas* was gradually abandoned and the concept of *Europe* became firmly established. But even though most educated people may now have thought in these terms, they still saw Europe exclusively as a composite world, a context of interaction, perhaps, made up of independent sovereign nations, whose task it was to realize peace and prosperity by maintaining a balance.[24]

Printing, reading and the schools: education for the masses?

Until the fifteenth century, education had been restricted largely to the elite. In schools directed by monks or other clergymen and attached to monasteries and cathedrals, the sons of the upper classes received a rudimentary education in which reading and writing were the staple curriculum. Future knights and even government officials did not actually need much more to be able to fulfil their roles in society.

Someone desiring a career in the ranks of the Church was naturally supposed to acquire other skills – in Latin, theology and philosophy. Moreover, a career in the Church was the only chance for a decent education for boys from non-aristocratic backgrounds, since the Church did not make any social distinction when recruiting clergymen, although the highest positions in the hierarchy were increasingly given to those who not only boasted a good education, but also the family background that gave them easy access to patronage and power.

It was precisely because of their education that clergymen were frequently asked to fulfil all sorts of functions in secular politics as well. One regularly sees them as advisers to kings, who often preferred unmarried priests to members of the aristocracy, who, after all, would want to enlarge their own power and that of their offspring, often at the monarch's expense.

In the fifteenth and sixteenth centuries, when princes began to expand their power through, among other things, a policy of administrative centralization, they knew they needed an effective bureaucratic apparatus. For indeed, a powerful state can exist only if it is based on a large, well-organized civil service. To create such a bureaucracy required many well-educated people who were not only able to read and write but were also at home with the principles of taxation and public finance. Besides this, they had to be especially well acquainted with the foundations of Roman Law. Whether or not Roman Law was mixed to varying degrees with the 'Germanic' legal tradition, it was considered by virtually all of Europe as the basis of political-administrative thought and of the legal system, which, of course, was the major factor in ensuring the uniformity and homogeneity necessary to a powerful state. At the same time, the economy also needed improved education: international trade and banking naturally required different skills from running the corner shop.

Thus, the need for more and better education was felt all over Europe. But it could only be realized after the invention of printing. Without the printed word, education on a large scale would have been virtually impossible. Now, textbooks covering all areas of learning were printed at prices affordable for parents from the middle class and not just the social elite. For it was precisely the well-to-do burghers who wanted to give their sons the chance to climb the social ladder through careers in the new sectors: the swelling government bureaucracy, banking, commerce, overseas trade and early industrialization.

Indeed, in the fifteenth, sixteenth and seventeenth centuries, the number of schools increased significantly; thus education indisputably became one of the 'basic structures of culture' in Europe.[25] For instance, in England there was a definite trend towards more schools, offering education for more people as the fifteenth century drew to a close, which became more intense in the following centuries. This was helped by the fact that English slowly replaced French as the spoken language of the elite and as the written language of government, a development stimulated by growing political differences between England and France.[26] As education, apart from 'the three Rs', consisted mainly of religious teaching, the choice by the English Reformation for the vernacular as the language of worship and the emphasis on independent reading of the Bible in the translated, so-called King James version (1611) was an influential one. For the same reasons the use of the Dutch so-called 'State Authorized Version' (*Statenvertaling*) (1637) had an effect on the standardization of Dutch and the reading ability and language use of people in the Dutch Republic, both those who attended school and those who were confronted with it only at home.

Yet the effects of education based on the new print culture differed greatly in Europe, according to region and especially social group, and were not felt as quickly everywhere. Considering the lowest level of education, that is, reading and writing one's own language, it has been established that literacy slowly increased. Admittedly, most research has taken the ability to write one's signature as the only proof of this development. Measured in this way, illiteracy dropped to 80 per cent for men and 95 per cent for women in the England of Queen

Elizabeth I. Still as high as that in about 1600, the figures dropped to 70–90 per cent in about 1650, 55–75 per cent in about 1700 and 40–60 per cent in about 1750. Then stagnation set in, lasting well into the nineteenth century.[27] In France, using the same gauge, 70 per cent of men and 90 per cent of women were still illiterate even by about 1700, a situation which hardly improved in the following 150 years.[28]

While this rate of progress may not be impressive, the low level of literacy is not surprising, if only because in large parts of Catholic Europe badly educated clergymen were the sole teachers. When, in 1671, Grenoble's new bishop, Monseigneur Le Camus, made a tour of inspection in his new diocese – the first such tour for 200 years – he encountered some devoted and cultured parish priests, but the majority were alcoholic, fornicating and almost illiterate, and one of them had never even heard of the New Testament.[29] One may well wonder what the peasants were supposed to learn from such men. Nor was the situation any better in the 'reformed' parts of Europe. Reading the autobiography of the seventeenth-century English theologian Richard Baxter, one still feels his dissatisfaction with a youth not nourished by well-educated, high-principled clergymen:

> We lived in a country that had but little preaching at all. In the village where I was born there were four readers successively in six years time, ignorant men, and two of them immoral in their lives. . . . The clerck could not read well. . . . Within a few miles about us were near a dozen ministers that . . . never preached . . .; poor, ignorant.[30]

However, historians have long argued that the level of literacy in Protestant countries, where, after all, the Bible had been translated into the vernacular and the reading of it was encouraged, was certainly higher than in Catholic states. There, the decrees of the Council of Trent (1545–63) had forbidden translations of Holy Scripture, thus making it impossible for most people to read it, so that the clergy continued to form the only 'information caste'. Yet, this assertion appears to be wrong: in those German states that had embraced the Reformation, people were confronted only with the very simplest of excerpts from the Bible and could hardly understand even these. Historians have also highlighted the Swedish situation, arguing that there, through the efforts of the Lutheran Church, the reading proficiency of large sections of the population was already high by the seventeenth century. Yet here, too, scattered indicators point to the fact that this reading ability, largely limited to Holy Scripture as it was, in no way meant that people actually understood what they were reading. Indeed, all over the world the 'reading' of, specifically, sacred texts seems largely to have been and often still is more a matter of rote learning than an indication of effective literacy.

Meanwhile, in Rome the spiritual authorities did try to use cheap prints to promote different forms of popular piety to enhance the vision of the Church as they saw it, a situation of which, of course, printers eagerly took advantage.[31]

But on the whole, both the Catholic Church and the Protestant Churches seem to have pursued a fairly restrictive policy with regard to the extent to which they wanted their believers to become independent thinkers through the printed word.[32]

Many who were taught to read and write actually learned little else. By far the majority of people in Europe attended 'vernacular schools', where both dictation, the didactic method most popular in the fourteenth and fifteenth centuries, and the few new teaching methods developed in their own times, remained in use for the following centuries.[33] When debate about improving popular education began in the eighteenth century, it appeared that in France, which called itself 'enlightened', most thinkers, for reasons of economic and social expediency, did not consider it wise to burden pupils from the masses with anything more than reading, writing and arithmetic: grand ideas would lead only to political and social criticism and dissatisfaction.[34]

From a 'primary school', one could proceed to a 'Latin School', as it had always been called, because of the language of instruction there. From the fifteenth century onwards, all over Europe the curriculum of these schools was deeply influenced by the *studium humanitatis*, to which the classical texts, now reconstructed as close to the original as possible, were central. Specifically, Cicero became the model for elegant prose. Mostly the same subjects were taught at these Latin Schools as, until the middle of the twentieth century, were taught at the traditional 'gymnasium', 'lyceum' or grammar school: the curriculum greatly stressed the value of the classical tradition, presented in a broader cultural framework which established the norms that Christianity imposed on everyone from early childhood.

Certainly, education both at these Latin Schools and at the academies or universities that a small group of boys would subsequently attend was authoritarian and, moreover, imitative rather than creative.[35] One person only seems to really have tried to improve the system. He was Johann Amos Komensky, or Comenius (1592–1670).[36] Born in Moravia, he became a priest and a poet – in his native Czech – as well as a scholar and a didactic. He advocated ecumenicism, i.e. unity among the religions, and the need for Christian pacifism, emphasizing the necessity to create an international legal order and a universal language. While living in Poland, he composed his *Dialactica*, in which he set out the importance of studying creation and all its *realia* besides the Bible and the *litterae humaniores*; he also suggested that only the inclusion of sports and other forms of play would result in a proper curriculum; finally, he proposed that boys and girls be educated together. In Sweden, he was allowed to introduce some of his ideas into the school system. In Hungary, he was finally able to set up a school entirely along his own lines. While in Comenius's ideals we can recognize many ideas that have contributed to modern educational notions, by and large his ideals proved too much in advance of his age and only very slowly gained recognition. Thus, for a long time girls were excluded from public schools beyond the primary level. If they were given any further education at all, this was done at home or, in the Catholic world, in monastic establishments. In the

Protestant world, schools providing secondary-level education for girls were only established in the seventeenth century, in the form of private boarding schools.

Despite the didactic and intellectual, the economic and social and, indeed, the gender restrictions of most Latin Schools, they must be considered a major pillar of European civilization. For centuries, the forms of classical antiquity combined with the values of Christianity provided a firm intellectual and moral world for Europe's literate classes, i.e. for the people who would create the more articulate manifestations of culture of their own time and who can thus be called, with some rhetorical exaggeration, the 'bearers' of European civilization.

From the Latin School, talented or wealthy male pupils would go on to university. Whereas in earlier centuries most universities had originated in cathedral and monastery schools, in the fifteenth and sixteenth centuries the number of new, secular foundations grew explosively. The new states promoted secondary and higher education from understandable self-interest, especially to create a reservoir of highly educated people from which an administrative elite could be recruited. Also, a university was considered to lend prestige to a city or state. Finally, the Reformation led to the creation of many new academies for the academic training of Protestant theologians; often, these soon evolved into fully fledged universities such as, for example, Strasbourg (1538) and Leiden (1575).

But as always, this was education for an elite and scholarship carried out by an elite, even though these elites did not entirely overlap, socio-economically speaking. Though from the sixteenth century onwards the number of students rose considerably, secondary and higher education were definitely not available to all. Moreover, certainly at university level, the subject one studied was strongly influenced by financial factors; for example, studying medicine was expensive and thus beyond the reach of most.

Yet the great expansion of academic education in the sixteenth century meant that the percentage of the European population who could participate in it rose,[37] significantly changing the cultural character of Europe. However, at the end of the seventeenth century, a new elitism slowly became apparent;[38] the attendance percentage dropped again.[39] Partly as a result, the climate of social and intellectual openness which had come to characterize Europe through, among other things, the universities, seems to have altered during the eighteenth century. Not until the twentieth century did the percentage of those participating in higher education again reach the same levels as in the sixteenth and early seventeenth centuries.

Those educated Europeans, who had gone from primary school to Latin School, and perhaps even on to university, wanted to understand their place in the world in all its facets. The fifteenth and sixteenth centuries were precisely the period in which the world became vastly more complex. The first overseas discoveries, the new medium of printing and the increased possibilities of acquiring an education meant that more information than ever before now reached an audience larger than ever before. In a world that was getting bigger every day, people tried to fit the multitude of new data and ideas into their traditional but inevitably slowly changing frames of reference. As a result, the literate classes had to redefine their position both in relation to their fellow men and to society and in relation to their Creator. A changing culture led to stimulating questions but also frequently to nagging doubts.[40]

In short, the interaction between the norms and values inculcated by the combined forces of classical scholarship and Christianity was reinforced by the challenge that the increasingly complex world presented to Europeans. Together, these forces determined secondary and higher education as well as the world of learning. The two concepts of Renaissance and Humanism embodied these forces, circumscribing a cultural ideal that for a long time has characterized European thought and, in a changed, adapted form, obviously still does.

One might argue that the religious differences which ravaged Europe in the sixteenth century – the rupture in the universal Catholic Church, the split between Rome, Wittenberg and Geneva – preclude a general pronouncement on the 'European character' of education and learning. Yet we should not forget that, despite many differences, to a certain extent the same questions arose in both the Catholic and Protestant worlds. People discussed the same issues and, even if they did not discuss these together, they did share a number of educational ideals and practices. Thus, the pedagogical concepts of the Protestant humanist Jacob Sturm (1507–89), who lived in Strasbourg and all his life strove for unity in the Christian world, greatly influenced the *ratio studiorum*, the curriculum of the Jesuits. All over Roman Catholic Europe, from the sixteenth century onwards until, sometimes, the present day, the followers of Ignatius of Loyola have formed in their boarding schools generations of boys schooled by the Jesuits, who were allowed to enter into the cultural, and also sociopolitical, elite.

Reflecting on the common ground between the two religiously defined cultures of Europe, one should first point to the theological discussion among both Catholics and Protestants about the text and content of the Gospels and, indeed, the entire Bible, as well as about the normative function of the early Christian Church. Both camps also struggled with questions concerning the core concept of grace, as well as the increasing tension between faith and reason, between man's knowledge of nature and the far more complicated question of his place therein in relation to God. Nor should one forget that there were innumerable areas where religious differences were less pressing, where people of opposing religious views still could and did actively debate with each other, the more so as communication was still relatively easy since, for the time being, Latin remained the common language of traditional learned culture, and mathematics, a universal symbolic language, became the vehicle for the new sciences.

In short, all over a Europe religiously divided, sites of education and learning, which had been given such an enormous boost by the invention of printing, did indeed share many fundamental characteristics that made them institutions in which a truly 'European' culture was being preserved and spread, as well as being criticized and expanded.

Unity and diversity: printing as a cultural revolution

The most important, but obviously largely unforeseen results of the invention and introduction of the art of printing were cultural in the widest sense. Indeed, there were no areas of European life wherein even those who could not read or write were not somehow influenced by the advent of the printed word. But precisely because we can hardly imagine a society without printed communication it is so difficult to appreciate that a veritable cultural revolution actually took place.

Obviously, the effects of printing first became manifest in scholarship, where the need for communication was probably most acutely felt. In the time of manuscript communication, scholars usually had great problems in simply hearing about other people's ideas in their field. Most scientific texts were available in a few copies only. There was, therefore, hardly any continuous and widespread accumulation of knowledge. New notions might develop around a particular person or in a particular region but did not spread easily and swiftly to contribute to discussion and an increase of knowledge elsewhere.

This changed momentously under the influence of the process of printing. When, in Venice, Aldus Manutius began his systematic edition of classical Greek texts, based partly on the manuscripts introduced by Greek-Byzantine refugee scholars like Bessarion, Europe acquired the *Iliad* and the *Odyssey* and, thus, the subject matter of many a learned debate of a philological and historical nature. When well-researched and complete editions of Aristotle and Plato appeared for the first time, European philosophers could not believe their luck. And (as discussed above) the text of the Greek Bible, showing the incompleteness and inconsistency of the Latin version used by the Catholic Church, set Roman theologians and philologists to work on a new edition which also led to vehement discussions, with repercussions in various domains, including Church politics.[41] Thus, the seemingly simple but essentially scholarly, scientific work of establishing a 'correct' text and making it public through the process of printing contributed greatly to the sense of community among Europe's learned elite – as it had done in other cultures which had developed this process, namely China, Japan and Korea.

One of the most important aspects of the printed word is that it gives those who hold power over it the opportunity to exercise or increase their power through its use. Therefore, the two main components of the European elite, the leaders of both State and Church, were among the first to appropriate the new instrument.

In 1539, King François I of France issued the edict of Villiers-Cotterets, in which he made it known that from then on the dialect of Paris, French, would be the official language of his entire kingdom. Writing and publishing all official documents in this one unequivocal language – the laws and regulations were now printed in Paris and spread as pamphlets or broadsheets all over France – the king might actually expect to reach the majority of his subjects. Of course, the new policy was meant to buttress royal authority and extend its scope, for the many regional languages spoken in France – as in Spain, England, the German states and in fact the whole of Europe[42] – prevented the various peoples of his state from understanding each other. This severely limited the power of central government in Paris. Under these circumstances, a real feeling of 'we, Frenchmen', a 'national awareness', could never develop; conversely, it also meant that the different parts of the state of France retained their own cultural identity and were therefore better able to resist the often unwelcome intrusion in regional and local government by the royal officials sent from Paris. The lack of a 'state' language caused great practical difficulties as well. The collection of taxes and the administration of justice did not function properly because officials and citizens literally did not speak the same language. By making one language compulsory, King François now hoped to eliminate all these problems. Yet he knew the printing press was the principal, indeed the only, instrument to effectuate his new edict. For without educating his entire realm in this one language, it would remain just a dead letter. And, without cheap texts in this one language or, in other words, printed texts, large-scale education would be impossible. With the help of the printed word, however, he might expect to greatly enlarge his royal power.

As in France, all over Europe, printing led to crucial developments in language itself. How should children be taught the one 'national' language, the language, therefore, of the elite? How could the dialect of Paris become French, or the dialect of Holland, Dutch?

First, textbooks establishing the rules of grammar were written and published. And, as mentioned before, in the Protestant countries, the Bible was translated and printed in that specific variety of the vernacular that now became the national language. As the holy book was by far the most important story – indeed, often the only story – children were told, the language in which it was read to them before they were taught to read it themselves was one of the most influential factors in shaping the 'national' language. However, those languages which were not promoted and codified in this way – as happened in France to its many 'regional' languages – became 'mere' dialects, spoken still, but written or printed no longer. These 'second-rate' languages also withdrew from cultural life precisely because they lost their status. People who wanted to be part of the establishment, political or cultural, had to start learning French instead of staying with Breton or Provençal, English instead of Gaelic, Dutch instead of Guelders. In this way, language became a characteristic of national unity. It also became an instrument for central government, for princes and their bureaucracies.

Through incipient mass education, based on printed textbooks, uniform 'national' languages were now formed in France and in other European countries. Central governments began to express and impose regulations and ordinances in these languages, which were now understood in the same way by every educated citizen. In France, in the early seventeenth century, Louis XIII even decided to found an official newspaper to make his government's opinions known to as great a readership as possible.

These developments had their reverse side as well. Those who disagreed with the government also began to use the weapon of print. Thus, the sixteenth century was the first to see large-scale propaganda and anti-propaganda, through an official and a clandestine press. Inevitably, governments soon introduced yet another new weapon, one that until then had hardly been necessary – namely censorship, under which all printed material had first to be officially approved.[43] However, the clandestine press refused to be silenced; increasingly, subversive texts were printed in secret or abroad, and distributed underground.

Through the printing press, propaganda acquired other forms and uses than the printed word. The public display of power by kings, which most people never witnessed because they did not travel and therefore never visited the capital, was now depicted in printed pictures which could be sold cheaply and in large quantities, as, for example, in the royal almanacs which were spread all over France in the seventeenth century, to proclaim the glories of Louis XIV, and of France. Coronations, court celebrations and parades for military victories could all be virtually 'seen'. Thus, the state's power, symbolized by and in the king, was brought to the masses. Even the king himself, who was certainly considered unique by the ordinary people, inhabiting an exalted sphere halfway between heaven and earth, could now be 'seen' by them as he too was made visible. Engraved portraits showed people what their ruler looked like and, understandably, princes ensured that they presented themselves as impressively as possible, with all the pomp of their dignity and power. Their portraits, painted by their court painters, were used as the basis for engravings which were then printed and distributed.

That other government, the Church, also used the printed word to divulge its ideas and to impose and enforce these as uniformly as possible. In the late fifteenth century, the Rome had already realized the potential of the printing press as a means of spreading its dogmas and rules to strengthen its power and to enforce uniform behaviour among as wide a readership as possible and under as closely controlled circumstances as could be contrived. Rome even proclaimed that the invention of printing was proof of the very superiority of Christian civilization. The argument was heard again in the first great political campaign ever directed with the help of the press: the call to mobilize Europe against the Turks in the late fifteenth and early sixteenth centuries, when the sultan's soldiers, having already seized Byzantium, stormed the Balkans and even came to threaten the walls of Vienna.

Yet Rome manifestly did not want the press to spread alternative opinions, to encourage the individualistic interpretations of the man–God–world relation, increasingly voiced by those schooled in the views of Renaissance culture and humanist thinking. Therefore, the Roman Catholic Church tried to introduce censorship in the form of the so-called *Index*, a list of banned, forbidden books, of publications that proper Catholics were forbidden to read – a form of censorship that could be expected of an organization trying to hold on to its power in an increasingly literate culture. However, here too one has to admit that this power was limited, as it relied largely on the reader's moral acceptance of Rome's bans. More effective was the demand made of printers in the Catholic states to obtain permission from the Church authorities before publishing a text, though this prescript, too, was frequently disregarded. Indeed, it seems that the efforts of the secular authorities to create an effective censorship system as a weapon against political criticism were, for the most part, far more successful, as is demonstrated by the example of France, although there, of course, the trade in 'forbidden books' was both widespread and lucrative indeed.

As mentioned above, instead of relying on traditional methods of dissemination only, Luther's friends and followers also saw the opportunity for a much greater debate which the new print culture offered.[44] Not only did they ensure that Luther's propositions were printed, but they also had them distributed. One way of doing this was through the travelling bookseller, a recent cultural phenomenon. He journeyed from city to city and especially from village to village to provide with reading material those who could read but had no regular access to bookshops. It is known that in 1517, 1518 and 1519 many booksellers in the German states were paid by Luther's followers to stock themselves with only one sort of text, Luther's publications, instead of their usual selection. Many customers, either curious or simply for the love of reading, bought and read Luther's works and were frequently affected by his ideas.

Between 1517 and 1520 no fewer than 300,000 copies of Luther's works were sold in this and other ways. Thus, his ideas could become the basis for an effective religious reformation, unlike the equally radical alternatives that had been proclaimed in earlier years. Like the popes of the late fifteenth century, Luther also said, with good reason, that the invention of the art of printing had been 'God's greatest mercy'. Soon, in Germany, illustrated broadsheets and picture books provided visual propaganda for the illiterate and the semi-literate, exploiting popular belief as well as producing it.[45] However, the Reformation also relied on the more traditional methods of mass indoctrination long used by the Roman Catholic Church: despite a certain aversion to religious painting, as part of a systematic evangelism among a half-literate laity still at the picture-book stage, thousands of devotional paintings and tens of thousands of such prints were produced during the sixteenth and seventeenth centuries.[46] In England, too, the new visions about man's relationship with God were widely popularized through broadsides combining catchy music – godly tunes – with religious pictures to instruct those who could barely read, or couldn't read at all.[47]

The Catholic Church's reaction to the actions of Luther and other reformers has been called the Counter-Reformation – a nineteenth-century term – or the Catholic Reformation, as many would prefer.[48] In fact, Rome's approach to the many issues that had presented themselves since the late fifteenth century was mainly formulated during the twenty or so years that the Church's main representatives sat in council, albeit intermittently, in the Italian town of Trent. It fitted into of a millennial tradition of councils which had been convened whenever the Church's local and regional spokesmen rather than the Curia and the popes in Rome itself felt the need to deliberate on internal and external problems and re-establish unity. To a considerable extent, the so-called

Tridentine reforms became a success thanks also to the printing press. From 1530 onwards, Rome increasingly used the printed word to publicize its answer to Luther and the other reformers. Soon, an increased religious uniformity was imposed and enforced through all sorts of books. The *catechism* comprehensively summarized the central points of Catholic doctrine for the general public; the *breviary* and the *missals* made the liturgy the same all over the Catholic world; sermon books instructed priests on the best, psychologically most effective ways to approach the faithful.

Among the many instruments devised by the Church of Rome to effect social control and discipline, the reform and strengthening of the sacrament of confession was, perhaps, the most profoundly successful. The Council of Trent's new stress upon confession as a central sacrament and the subsequent policy of educating priests to actually introduce and enforce it in their parishes, aided by printed confession books, resulted in a moral and indeed cultural conformity at the deepest level, that of people's innermost thinking in terms of what was accepted behaviour and what was not, in the eyes of God, of the Church and of society. Analysing one's sins, confessing the ways in which one had not obeyed the rules of the Church, to a priest who was the representative of that Church, in due time created a complex psychological and social interaction between a set of rules imposed from above and their acceptance both by individuals and groups who increasingly began to live according to these precepts.

The introduction of the tenets reformulated or newly conceived by the Council of Trent was greatly facilitated by the foundation of new religious orders, among which the Society of Jesus was the most conspicuous. The Jesuits and their like especially concentrated on education, trying to create a truly Roman Catholic elite by recruiting pupils from the urban middle and upper classes, who eagerly flocked to their colleges because of their reputation for an intellectually rigorous, superior education. Here, again, printing was the inevitable prerequisite. Moreover, as Rome embarked upon a new missionary campaign using all available propagandist means, vast parts of Catholic Europe, especially in the more remote agricultural areas, were now properly Christianized for the first time. Once more, both abroad, in bringing European, Christian concepts to non-western peoples, and in Europe itself, where the mass of the faithful had to be mobilized to offer its prayers and its material support for the missionary effort, the new print culture provided an indispensable context. Obviously, the Church did not discard older methods, of proven worth, either. Thus, religious imagery, in painting and sculpture, was propagated on a scale larger, perhaps, than ever before in the history of Christianity and, again using print, was also distributed in mass form.

What with all these new or revitalized policies, and the impact of print that now helped to spread them, it is perhaps permissible to say that for the first time in 1,000 years Christianity actually became a vital force, even though, at the same time, its institutional unity was disrupted. Surprisingly, where there had been many local varieties of Catholicism during the first millennium of European Christianity, the religious culture of Catholic Europe and, with it, the code of norms and conventions, now became much more uniform.[49] It has also been said that it soon became modern, too. Of course, ever since the German sociologist Max Weber entered the sociocultural debate in the early twentieth century, the spirit of capitalism, which was to produce so much of Europe's subsequent modernity, has been closely associated with the 'Protestant' work ethic of sober, responsible, active, productive living. Recently, people have argued that the 'Counter-Reformation' ethic worked in the same way and, indeed, produced some of the same results in Roman Catholic societies.[50]

In their own ways, the Reformed Churches, too, succeeded in creating greater uniformity. Of course, the stress on the importance of reading and following Scripture seemed to lay primary responsibility with the individual believer. However, the locally organized churches, with their ministers and, in Calvinist countries, their elders elected from the local community, did not fail to influence the behaviour of the faithful through a regimen of religious and social control. They, too, used the printed word, in the form of moral and pious tracts, to drive home their notions of proper conduct.

Thus, the art of printing, used as a new and powerful instrument of government in both Church and State, greatly contributed to the standardization and uniformity of culture and thought. Moreover, this occurred not only in language and religion but also in many other areas of life where earlier there had been considerable variety. Thus, in 1520, the first 'Manual for Tailors' appeared in Seville, establishing, as it were, the prevailing Spanish dress habits. Through the distribution of this text via the press, people in other parts of Europe could now acquaint themselves with Spanish clothing conventions. Because Spain was looked upon as a culturally pre-eminent country, as a result of the wealth it had acquired from its colonies and its consequent European power policy, many Europeans felt they should even emulate Spanish fashion. Without books like the Seville guide, tailors could never have stimulated and satisfied their clients' demands.

Printing, therefore, contributed to something as essentially cultural as clothing being spread internationally. Inevitably, however, this led to a growing uniformity, with regional traditions often coming off worst, as had been the case with language. Publicizing prevalent dress conventions through printing also led to more rapid changes in what now became 'fashion' in the present sense of the word; indeed, it is a phenomenon that we can observe from the beginning of the sixteenth century. It is clear that this greatly altered man's consumption patterns and also, as a result, the economy. The same happened when the first cookery books were published: in food culture, too, habits from a particular region or social group now spread more quickly and became 'fashionable', which also meant changing and changeable, prone to manipulation by those who produced whatever was needed.

Thus, people increasingly discovered the possibilities of the printed word. Those with ideas about better methods of education, better codes of behaviour for young men and women who were courting, or better ways to build houses could now all try to impress their ideas and views on as many readers as possible.

Treatises on horsemanship and fencing,[51] on the theory and practice of dancing and music, on painting and the theatre appeared in bewildering numbers. Architecture is a good case in point. Both in building and in urban construction and layout, the virtues of 'classical' forms, that is the forms thought to be advocated by the great architect of ancient Rome, Vitruvius, were extolled in texts by such Italian Renaissance architects, either practising ones or only theorists, as Andrea Palladio and Sebastiano Serlio. Soon, this changed the way public buildings and towns in Europe looked for the following four centuries, and still influences modern or rather 'postmodern' architecture, which, from the 1980s onwards, has been eclectically referring to it.

Also, many of Europe's less obvious 'cultural' forms, which are, however, often deeply engrained as codes of behaviour, originate in the first period of the influence of printing. Don't eat with your mouth open; don't grab food with your hands, use a knife and fork; don't blow your nose with your fingers and then flick off the snot, use a handkerchief; don't start fighting another person after the first insult he offers you – these are all practices that were first adopted by specific, often powerful individuals or groups for no other reason than to create social distinction. Often, if new ideas received the support of government or of one of the sociocultural elites, the concepts propagated therein were spread in print, adopted in education, and thus helped to establish norms, as well as the material manifestations thereof, if only because, soon, others would want to ape those who acted out this behaviour because it indicated high sociocultural standing.

In short, a variety of manners and ideas acquired wide and sometimes even general application, both through the printed word and through the education made possible by it. Thus was inaugurated a development towards collective and indeed individual behavioural self-restraint that continues until the present day, despite the stress on 'individual expression' prevalent in contemporary culture. All over Europe, uniformity – although perhaps in manners more than in ideas – increased, while at the same time printing contributed to changes in what was 'in' and 'out', 'cool' or not 'cool', which were occurring faster and on a wider scale than ever before. However, this process, which has somewhat misleadingly been called the 'civilizing process',[52] has not necessarily made Europeans 'civilized' if the latter term is used as the equivalent of intrinsically humane, as it often seems to imply.

In short, culture in Europe underwent a gradual but definite transformation. For many, a new perception of reality developed. The 'literal' truth, the truth of the written word, stood increasingly central, especially in the Protestant world, where since Luther Holy Scripture, as the word of God, was presented as the only source of authority, which then led many believers to actually accept all 'authoritative' words as 'true'. Furthermore, people everywhere started to 'live according to the book', their thoughts and actions now becoming more uniform. However, at the same time, the need to escape from this compulsion and the restrictions it brought increased as well, because the individual 'I', the concept whose development since the fifteenth century had been put forward as educated man's goal in life, wanted to manifest itself. Standardization provoked reaction.

Many elements inherent in the culture of print as a new medium of communication are illustrated by one of its fascinating and successful products. In 1605, the Spaniard Miguel de Cervantes Saavedra (1547–1616), published a book. He intended it to be a comic novel about a man called Don Quixote, a man who had read too much and, moreover, believed everything he read to be true. Don Quixote's passion was reading novels of courtly love, in which knights errant went out on a complicated quest of honourable fighting to gain the hand of their beloved. Such novels had proliferated in the early years of printing, bringing a genre already popular in the manuscript culture of the preceding centuries to a new, larger public. Cervantes himself had travelled to Italy, and had fought both at Lepanto and at Algiers, two of Christian Europe's bloody battles with Islam, before returning to an unprofitable career in Spain. He soon became bitterly disappointed at the discrepancy between the courtly ideal held up to so many readers in novels and other texts and the social reality of his own times. In his *El ingienioso hidalgo Don Quixote de la Mancha* (The ingenious nobleman Don Quixote from la Mancha), the protagonist, accompanied by his servant Sancho Panza, sets out on a long journey, prepared to wage chivalrous battle against injustice wherever he meets it. Increasingly dejected by his experiences, Don Quixote gradually loses his idealism. Sancho Panza, on the other hand, the embodiment of an agricultural, down-to-earth, no-nonsense society, though very sceptical when he set outs with his master, becomes increasingly convinced of the essential value of knightly ideals. Thus, in his *Don Quixote*, Cervantes created one of the first 'modern' literary texts, a text that explores the psychology of its characters and even shows their development.[53] Due to the very fact of printing, the novel was soon famous all over Spain although, it has to be confessed, many contemporary Spaniards did not greatly appreciate this quirky image of a Spanish hidalgo and his society. However, translations were made in English, French and German, and numerous seventeenth- and eighteenth-century writers all over Europe loved and were influenced by the book. It was illustrated by well-known artists, too, for example, in the nineteenth and twentieth centuries, by the engraver Gustave Doré and the painter Salvador Dalí. It even inspired such composers as Jules Massenet, Manuel de Falla and Richard Strauss.[54]

From the beginning of the sixteenth century onwards, more than ever before, daily life in Europe became embedded in a body of common rules; man created a collective morality, and then became subject to it himself. It was spread and propagated more easily and intensively through the printed word. Yet, one should, of course, ask what were the relations between the world of print culture outlined above and the far larger world of the oral culture that continued to characterize Europe.

All over Europe, the orally presented power of traditional, individually and often locally recognizable authorities, the 'interpreters of information' or cultural intermediaries, became more dependent on texts put together by mainly anonymous creators of norms. Power itself, both religious and secular, increased though it became more anonymous precisely because the printed word distanced it further from its subjects. Orders that for centuries had been given orally by authorities who, even if only for that reason, retained some form of closeness to the 'common people', were now imposed in writing by the mainly invisible 'powers that be'. This also explains why many of those who could not read often saw printing as a threat, the new secret instrument of the powerful. The 'culture brokers', both the 'official' ones, the members of the various elites like the clergy and the bureaucracy, and the unofficial ones, like quacks and colporteurs, in short all those who contributed to the formation of established, standardized codes of behaviour, of 'ritual repertories', were now living the tension which arose between, on the one hand, the ambiguous space which for so long they had been able to exploit to their own use and advantage and, on the other, an official, normative, increasingly enforceable and controllable printed culture.

The illiterate, besides experiencing the new administrative pressure, were influenced, too, by the encoding in writing and in print of standardized norms because the written message was frequently imposed on them through the filter of the more traditional, yet still very effective media of oral culture: both songs – sung in the marketplace and on the street, or, of course, in the pub[55] – and various kinds of drama. The latter was, and, until the nineteenth century, remained one of the most influential means of communication, with its combination of word, image and emotive act. Often, new notions of what was civilized and uncivilized were expounded in plays. For example, from the sixteenth century onwards peasants were frequently portrayed as rough and wild, as characters who defecated, gorged themselves and copulated in public, behaviour that was no longer deemed acceptable or civilized. Thus, those who held power, both the nobility and the influential urban middle class, tried to impose new standards for the simple reason that they thought that 'different' also meant 'uncontrollable'.

A striking example of the way the educated, written, printed culture penetrated the oral culture of enacted word and song is the play *Mariken van Nieumeghen*, which was also translated from the original Dutch into English and German. Written in *c*.1500, it was printed and, obviously, enjoyed some success with an international readership. However, its message was probably heard and experienced by many more.

When the illiterate country girl Mariken is considering relinquishing her fate to the Devil, she asks him:

> Eer ghi met mi sult versamen in ionsten,
> suldi mi leeren di seven vrije consten,
> Want in alle dingen te leeren verfray ick.
> Ghi sullet mi all leeren, suldi?[56]

> Before you will couple with me,
> you will teach me the seven liberal arts,

for I very much want to learn everything and become a more rounded
person.
You will teach me everything, won't you?

The Devil agrees: 'Noyt vrouwe en leefde op eerde so abel also ic u maken sal'
('Never, my lady, was there on earth one so learned as I will make thee'). Not
surprisingly, from the sixteenth century onwards, demands were made for
women to be given more equality, which often stressed the need for better
education, obviously influenced by the Renaissance concept of man,[57] and
the diffusion of this concept in print. However, a severely patriarchal culture
still had problems in accepting these demands. For though Mariken gets her
education, she also descends into a life of sin. Only by a hair's breadth does
she finally escape from temptation, and from the worst fate, her union with the
Devil, by once more seeking communion with the Church. An essential part
of the message was that knowledge was not for each and everyone. So, while
the story acknowledges that knowledge is power, its moral is that the learned
aspirations of a woman cannot go unpunished if society is to remain stable and
free from chaos. Indeed, what was probably the most important cultural factor
in the gendered division of Europe, the educational disadvantage of the 'second
sex', was deliberately upheld by a male-dominated society until late in the
nineteenth century.

More generally speaking, as printing began to revolutionize all aspects of
life and culture in Europe, affecting even those who remained illiterate, contemporaries, mostly intellectuals and politicians, voiced their concern: might not
the common people – women and men – given the chance to acquire new ideas
and test them against their own opinions of their present position, come to voice
their criticism?[58] Thus, Europe's literate classes long continued to argue that the
number of people who could read and write should not become too great. They
would undermine the monopoly of power implicit in the monopoly of knowledge. If only for this reason, the Catholic Church forbade the reading of the
Bible in the vernacular. Inevitably, however, the fear that the printed word
that interpreted the world would also mobilize it, and might even lead to revolutions in the centuries to come, was to become reality indeed. Yet, it was
precisely those revolutions that would contribute to the genesis of European
society and culture as we now know it.

Europe and its frontiers: nation-feeling and cultural self-definition

The same *studium humanitatis* which opened up a clearer view of the classical
and Christian roots of European culture by calling for a careful analysis of the
Greek and Latin texts on which the learned tradition rested also led, in the
sixteenth century, to research into and a greater appreciation of all that was
valuable and had been written in the vernacular. In this way, Europeans gained
a better understanding of the past of their own communities, which had been
formed by interaction with, but to a certain extent also in opposition to, the

unifying rhetoric of the Catholic Church. Indeed, it was Humanism that, despite its cosmopolitan nature, also promoted the genesis of a gradually more 'national' culture. Consequently, while a new notion of Europe was slowly growing, at the same time it was a Europe that encompassed a variety of self-conscious entities, the new states. Surviving and, if possible, expanding their own power gradually became the most important aim for the majority of these states.

Not surprisingly, the earliest 'national' poems had developed in the regions where the threat to people's own culture appeared greatest: the Iberian peninsula and the Balkans. There, a typical 'frontier' mentality of constant alertness underlined the importance of propaganda.[59] A wide variety of ideological material – topics for poems and songs, mostly – was mined for those elements that would most effectively strengthen and motivate the people involved in the constant fight to survive, to help them establish or maintain their own identity. The topics were usually taken both from the *Christianitas* concept and from an often idealized past of shared emotions and actions strengthened by a sense of linguistically proven community.

At an early stage, south of the Pyrenees, the confrontation between Christendom and Islam had led to self-reflection and, thus, to 'border poems' written to bolster up regional identities: in the eleventh and twelfth centuries, in the region separating the Christian and the Muslim world, the *Chanson de Roland* and the *Poema del mio Cid* were created, epic poems which expressed first the Frankish and later the Castilian 'frontier feeling' with regard to the Islamic enemy. In late fifteenth-century Portugal, a similar feeling combined with a new front of contact and confrontation between the Portuguese and the world of Asia they now started to discover, resulting in Luis de Camões's epic and magnificent poem *Os Lusiadas*, which articulated Lusitanian nationalism.[60]

On Europe's other frontier, in the Byzantine Empire, even before the fall of Constantinople the threat of Islam produced the 'Akritic Songs', a variety of frontier poetry wherein, often, a Greek-Christian girl marries a Saracen, Islamic man who then converts to Christianity.[61] Further north, in the old town of Split in the Balkans – formerly a Roman imperial palace – Marko Marulić wrote his epic *Judita* in *c.*1500,[62] and the Serb Ivan Gundulić published his *Osman*, two works created in the face of the advancing Turkish forces. However, the religious, and in a broader sense cultural, emotions revealed in these poems could not obviously prevent the region's capture by the sultan's janissaries.

All of these texts seem to point to a slowly emerging sense of national identity, especially in regions where this served an obvious need against an enemy. The process also shows in the increasing use of the 'vernacular' both in literature and in government administration, education and so on. Indeed, the purity of the 'national' language became a symbol for the purity and the unity of the nation. Thus, Juan de Valdes, writing about the history of the Spaniards in 1535, noted that:

> This conquest . . . lasted until 1492 when the Catholic Kings, of glorious memory, took the kingdom of Granada and expelled the tyrannical Moors from Spain. But

during this time, the Spaniards were unable to keep the purity of their language and stop it from mixing with the Arab one, for even though they recovered kingdoms and cities, towns and other places, as many Moors stayed living in them, their language also stayed; and things remained like this until a few years ago the Emperor [i.e. Charles V] ordered that they become Christians or leave Spain. But speaking with them, many of their words have stuck to us.[63]

In Spain, the demand for the purity of language was soon combined with demands for religious and even racial purity as well. Although not all European states were to adopt the extreme measures used in Spain – after the Moors had been forced to convert or accept expulsion, the Jews were treated in the same way – many were embarking upon some kind of policy to safeguard that purity.

Meanwhile, in comparing the more obvious 'nationalist' texts, it is clear that inevitably the virtues now vociferously attributed to a people's specific culture were often the same as those claimed by other nations, rooted as they ultimately were in the Christianity which was their common context, and in the contact with classical civilization that increasingly became the touchstone of 'civilization'. Thus, an increasingly diverse 'Europe' still defined itself in these dual, although by now somewhat hidden, component parts.

9 A new society

Europe and the wider world since the fifteenth century

The 'old' world and the 'older' world

Even before the birth of Christendom, some of the peoples living in 'Europe' had been aware of their debts to 'Asia'. The Greeks revered the wisdom of Egypt and Mesopotamia and, indeed, for a considerable part of their culture they were indebted to the civilizations of the Near East, of Persia and of India, although they might not always acknowledge this debt. From the age of Alexander the Great onwards, the links with central Asia, with China and the Indian sub-continent remained consistently strong, even though contacts were almost always indirect, by means of intermediaries, such as, for example, the merchants who travelled along the so-called 'Silk Road', the chain of trading routes connecting the Chinese and the Mediterranean economies through the plains and deserts of central Asia.[1] Rome, too, continued to be aware of the powers and the products of the east if only because of its very extensive trade links which, according to some Romans, sapped the Roman treasury. Admittedly, in the centuries following the decline of the Roman Empire, the ties grew weaker, and Asia became more of a fantasy land, for the role of its silver in the resurgence of the European economy under the Carolingians was understood only dimly, if at all, by even the most knowledgeable of politicians and traders in the eighth and ninth centuries.

The connotation of riches and wonder that came to be attached to Asia undoubtedly grew stronger because of Christianity's roots in the Near East, which brought many a pilgrim to the Holy Land, where they were told stories about the fabulous wealth of the world beyond the Arabian desert. The very fact that the Bible told the Christians that God had created the world in its original, sublime form in a garden 'in Eden', and that this garden still existed somewhere in the east, greatly contributed to the magic of Asia. Thus, the lands beyond the Levant continued to attract many Europeans, even though few ever reached them.[2] At one time, the popes even wondered whether they should not conclude an alliance with the Mongol emperors to combat Islam together, and monks were sent to the Great Khan's court at Karakoroum – an incredible journey, given the lack of proper roads and the many perils that threatened them on the way. Although nothing came of their efforts, they returned with wondrous tales that did not fail to fire the imagination. The travels undertaken by the members of the Venetian merchant family of Polo at the end of the thirteenth century were certainly inspired by them.

Although the fact of Marco Polo's presence in China has been doubted from the moment he returned to tell his story to an attentive but disbelieving audience – his tale became one of the greatest bestsellers both of the last century of manuscript books and of the first age of printing – it seems that he definitely was where he told his amazed and unbelieving friends he had been: in Cathay.[3] There, paper money was used, because one could trust the state that issued the bills. There, the streets of the big cities were paved and lit. There, people travelled in safety. There, an emperor ruled with a might as great as the Roman rulers of old. There, in short, a civilization existed that in all respects was equal to Europe, if not superior to it. For indeed, even without the benefit of Christianity, it was a humane society that held values which in Europe, too, were deemed sacred.

Soon, Asia, India, China or the east – Europeans used all these terms indiscriminately to denote the world beyond the world of Islam – was not only coveted for its wealth but also admired for a culture that, when it became better known, sometimes made even Europeans wonder about the superior value and, indeed, uniqueness of their own achievements. Inevitably, despite all developments in scientific and technical culture that characterized Europe from the sixteenth century onwards, it continued to learn from the East. However, while the process definitely became less one-sided in the field of technology, it was rather more marked in a general, perhaps even philosophical sense. Gradually, Europeans began to wonder whether, perhaps, Asia was the land of origins: the origins of knowledge – for, after all, man had had amazing knowledge in the 'garden of Eden' until, desiring to know 'all', he overstepped the restrictions set him by God – but also the origins of language; and, perhaps, even the origins of religion.

Of course, travel, the possibility of broadening one's horizons, always had been part of European culture in a variety of ways. Undeniably, however, from the fifteenth and sixteenth centuries onwards, an increasing amount of Europeans dared leave their own, trusted world, if only because Arab tracts about seamanship and cosmography and maps drawn by Jewish cartographers had shown them the way both in the Mediterranean and beyond. Partly through a growing self-awareness, partly through the promises of wealth and power the many new ideas suggested, Europeans became more independent-minded, confronting the challenge that the unknown always presents. Undeniably, the genesis of the 'modern' state is an additional explanation for the expansion that would bring Europe increased economic and political mastery over large parts of the world, from the late fifteenth to the early twentieth centuries. For it was these states that had to vie with each other for what was, after all, a limited territory, which, by the sixteenth century, could simply no longer sustain a growing population; using all their resources, both material and human, as inventively as possible, these states, or rather the people who served them, set out to explore new possibilities.

During the fourteenth and fifteenth centuries, traders, discoverers, adventurers and missionaries – two or even all of these roles sometimes combined in one and the same person – already increasingly crossed the Mediterranean to travel to the worlds beyond the Levant, the Middle and Far East, and to the coasts of North Africa. However, from the late fifteenth century onwards, the balance of power in the Mediterranean area, especially in the eastern part, started to change. The struggle between the two regional superpowers, the Ottoman Empire and the Persian kingdom, severely decreased the profitability of the caravan and shipping routes which, through the deserts of the Near East and across the Mediterranean, linked the European markets with the Indian Ocean and the production centres in Asia. Europeans now needed to find their own routes to the east. Thus, when the Portuguese started to sail the Atlantic Ocean, searching for gold and slaves in the interior of West Africa, they were also searching for a route to the wealth of Asia, and, at the same time, for allies in the fight against Islam and a strategic southern detour to the Holy Land. During the last decades of the fifteenth century, their small ships still somewhat anxiously hugging the African coastline, they discovered a new route to the fabulous Orient: via the Cape of Good Hope and the Indian Ocean.

Both the development of shipbuilding and of the entire array of nautical instruments, such as the magnetic compass, originated in the body of knowledge that had reached the Christian west in the previous centuries via the Islamic Mediterranean. Therefore, it is one of the ironies of history not only that some of the most important technical phenomena instrumental in Europe's 'take-off' in the fifteenth century had been part of the technology transfer from Asia to Europe via the Islamic world, but also that these phenomena enabled Europe eventually to bypass the Islamic world in its search for the riches of the east where much of this technology originated in the first place.

Specifically, the vicissitudes of the compass present us with a problematic case of technology transfer. We know that it originated in ancient Chinese religious divination techniques as a board with a magnetite pointer and the representations of earth and heaven. Well before the year AD 1000, it had spawned a variety of measuring instruments. Yet we do not know how it reached Europe, where it was first mentioned in 1198. It may have travelled over land, through central Asia and the Islamic world, where it was used as a surveying instrument but, even more important, as a 'Mecca-finding' instrument – highly useful to the hundreds of thousands who on their annual sacred journey to the holy city had to navigate the seas of the deserts to do so; a compass of sorts was, of course, of great help there. It may also have reached Europe via the Indian Ocean, through Chinese and Arab mariners who also already used it in its compass form.[4]

As for shipbuilding, it is obvious that during the fourteenth and fifteenth centuries construction techniques, for example on the Iberian peninsula, reached a level of sophistication that explains, at least partly, the success of Portugal's subsequent enterprises in the Indian Ocean. Yet the building of the light, three-masted Iberian ships may well have been influenced by illustrations of the huge multiple-masted Chinese junks that braved the Indian Ocean; they were depicted on late-fourteenth- and early fifteenth-century European world maps and described in the tales of Marco Polo. Once again, the process of transfer may have taken place at the meeting point of east and west in the eastern Mediterranean. As early as the 1420s, the Jewish and Arab sailors and savants at Sagres, the base of the group of scientists, mariners and technicians stimulated by Prince Henry the Navigator of Portugal, combined the Douro *caravela* with the Arab *caravo* to construct a ship that could confidently expect to return home even sailing against the wind, now it was rigged with its lateen sails common on the Egypt coast and in the Indian Ocean.

Once the first Europeans had arrived in Asian waters, new, direct technological transfer between Europe and Asia could develop. After rounding the Cape in the 1490s, Vasco da Gama had already learned new navigational techniques from his Arab pilot, the famous Ibn Majid, author of the monumental encyclopedia of navigation and nautical technology *Kitab al-Fawa'id* (1490).

After their arrival on the Indian coasts, the Portuguese and later the British soon learned how to use local shipbuilding techniques, employing local materials, a process that continued until the eighteenth century. At that time, for example, the English East India Company adopted the 'rabet' work of the shipbuilders of the great Indian port of Surat, who sealed the joints with cotton and tar, finding that it produced more durable ships and reduced construction costs by almost a half.

Another irony of history was that the use of guns and cannon helped to underpin the Europeans' bid for power in the east. Although in both India and China, to name but two of the regions targeted by the Europeans, the armaments industry had continued to flourish since the period when the earliest technology in this field had started on its slow road to Europe, by the late fifteenth century developments in Europe had taken on a momentum that was lacking in Asia. Consequently, in the sixteenth and early seventeenth centuries, the Portuguese, on arriving in China, could profit from their ability to help the warring factions in the Chinese empire with their by now superior technology. In Japan, the shogunal authorities who gained power after the great civil wars of the sixteenth century retained the knowledge of gunpowder and cannon. Yet, they relied on the weapons of the Dutch, who arrived in the early years of the seventeenth century, to help them suppress the revolt of the Christian-Japanese peasants of Shimabara in 1638. In subsequent years, Japanese governments enforced an almost complete return to sword and bow, hallowed by ancient samurai tradition. Only with the arrival of westerners in the nineteenth century did Japan once more return to a gunpowder concept of warfare which, as in sixteenth-century Europe, considerably altered Japanese culture and society in a variety of ways, if only because the 'way of the samurai' and all it entailed became increasingly obsolete.[5]

Meanwhile, one may wonder what happened to the world of Islam, which for centuries had been the essential intermediary between Asia and Europe. Admittedly, many scholars argue that culturally, and more specifically intellectually, the world of Islam belonged to the Mediterranean-European *oikoumene*

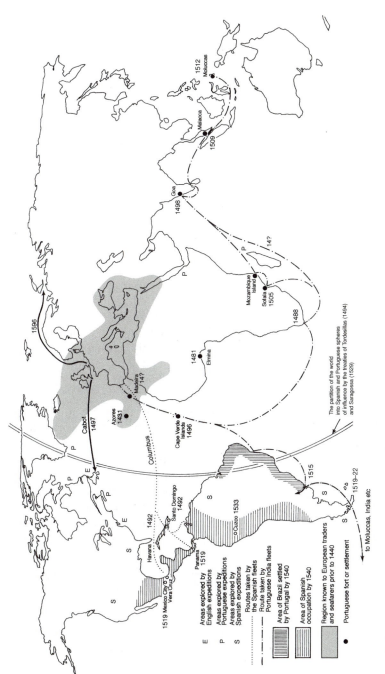

Map 5 European expansion at the end of the Middle Ages to *c.*1540

rather than to the civilizations of Asia, if only because of its great indebtedness to ancient Greek science and philosophy. Hence, it would seem that the Islamic cultural sphere could not but have participated in and made use of the numerous highly important inventions which it transferred to the Christian world and which enabled Europe to start upon its road to global economic, technological and political power.

However, by the late fifteenth century, the Islamic world had entered into a period of stagnation, especially in the field of technology, while Europe continued to develop. Here is not the place to explore in detail the reasons for this process – they are manifold, and the debate on their relative importance in this process is still ongoing. Most of the reasons belong to the same complex set of causes that also changed the technological, and consequently the economic, political and cultural balance between Europe and Asia, as outlined above. Some factors, however, can be singled out.

The challenging and, therefore, fruitful competition between states disappeared in the wake of the rise to hegemony of the Ottoman Empire, which tended to become ever more conservative. Also, one should stress the failure to develop in the world of Islam such a major technology as the art of printing. In Europe, it created a cultural revolution of enormous magnitude, contributing to the development of learning in general, and of education, scholarship and intellectual debate and exchange in particular, stimulating both further technological and material progress and, if slowly, altering civic society. Yet for various reasons, mainly of a religious and more broadly cultural nature, printing was not introduced in the Islamic world until the end of the eighteenth century, with lasting and, indeed, negative results if judged from an economic and social perspective.

Europe's discovery and subsequent domination of the ocean route to Asia, undeniably led to a decline in the importance of the Islamic world and the Mediterranean as the main route to the riches of Asia; and subsequently, its role as a receiver and transmitter of technology. Also, because of political strife in the Islamic Middle East, the costs of trans-Asian trade and hence of trade in Asian wares in the Levant rose considerably, which negatively influenced European willingness to go there. Therefore, it is difficult to determine whether the decline of the Mediterranean as a region of commercial and hence cultural exchange was a consequence of the general cultural, political and economic decline of the Islamic world, or one of its causes, robbing the Islamic world of its function as an intermediary and thereby reducing its vitality. Undeniably, however, as most cultures benefit from interaction rather than from seclusion, the long-term consequences were negative.

In the course of the fifteenth and sixteenth centuries, as commercial and industrial activity in Europe became concentrated in new centres – Seville and Lisbon, the French ports on the Atlantic coast, Antwerp, Amsterdam and London, mostly – the European trading economy shifted away from the Mediterranean to the Atlantic, increasingly so as other Europeans besides the Portuguese discovered their own routes to Asia. The cultural exchange that, from time immemorial, had developed along the maritime and overland routes through the Near East and central Asia now mainly, though not exclusively, took place on the ocean routes via the Cape. Inevitably, the organizations that dominated these routes became the main agents of cultural exchange, including the transfer of technologies from Asia to Europe. These, of course, were the great maritime-commercial companies of the northern European states, and the spiritual organizations of the Church of Rome, more specifically the Society of Jesus: merchants and missionaries became the main contacts between the old world and the older world. When a Swedish East India trader brought news of technical innovations in Chinese agriculture, his text was soon translated all over Europe;[6] and when a Jesuit priest first told Europe about the secret of porcelain manufacture, Europe was quick to take up the practice. But precisely because these organizations were forever looking for new and easier roads towards this older world, they also came to play an important role when Europe discovered an entirely new world.

For while the Portuguese were trying to find their way to India, succeeding when Vasco da Gama reached Calicut in 1498, the Spanish were navigating the dangerous western seas in Columbus's wake, sailing to the most distant corners of the earth. In doing so they discovered a new world. Subsequently, finding itself profitably placed between Asia and America, Europe definitely did well. International trade, which now became a permanent element of European commerce, acted as the pre-eminent booster for the European economy: commercial capitalism first really peaked in the late fifteenth and sixteenth centuries.

The 'old' world and the 'new'

It is important to stress that European culture is also, of course, very much about such deceptively simple things as the daily diet, which always express a culture's identity. Take, for example, the tomato, the potato, the coffee bean and tobacco that most Europeans take for granted. Tomatoes, of course, are supposed to be among the most essential elements of the daily diet. While more disputed in health terms, potato consumption and the daily cup of coffee are still essential elements of the overall European food-and-drink pattern. Tobacco, however, is easily the most controversial issue in food politics generally – since so many people still feel they cannot survive without it, while equally many argue that it is one of the major dangers threatening the health of the European population at large.

It is precisely these three items of Europe's daily diet that show that Europe's food culture was forever altered by what happened in 1492 and during the following century – the Spanish conquest of the Caribbean area, of Mexico and Peru, and the Portuguese colonization of Brazil during the sixteenth century. For these, of course, were the regions where these foodstuffs originated, just like the cocoa bean which produces the chocolate to which many people in the western world are as addicted as they are to alcohol. In short, the discovery of the 'new world' substantially changed some of the basics of European culture.[7]

Why did Europeans actually brave the westward ocean which most people felt held only the promise of death, since losing sight of the safe coast and sailing towards the horizon they would end up at the confines of the earth, where no man should dare go?[8] Did they long for adventure or hanker after fame, were they driven by religious fervour or fanaticism, or did they simply seek profit and the power it might bring? For some, it was a dream in which all these elements coincided, the dream of a paradise offering both the promise of innocence regained and the desire for material plenty fulfilled – for one should not forget that for Europeans in the fifteenth and sixteenth centuries, the prospect of starvation was terribly real and any notion of paradise had to be material as well, including an abundance of food.

The Genoese Cristóbal Colón or Christopher Columbus was one such European,[9] as is shown by the quite revealing log he kept on his first westward journey in 1492. While the original was lost in the sixteenth century, much of its substance was preserved in a transcription and re-arrangement of the original text by the monk Bartolomé de las Casas. Columbus regularly writes about gold and pearls and about the lucrative commercial contacts with China and Japan, the countries in the east he thinks he is going to reach by having chosen to sail west. Hopping from island to island in the Caribbean, he repeatedly notes that he will soon arrive in Cipangu or Cathay – Japan and China – and thus be able to hand to the Great Khan,[10] the fabled ruler of the Far East, his credential letters from the Spanish king Ferdinand of Aragon and his wife Isabella of Castille.

Europe only knew about the ruler of China from the garbled stories brought back by thirteenth-century monks and by Marco Polo. Columbus had read Marco Polo's travel story, using its first printed version – published in 1492 by a Dutchman, the Gouda printer Gerard Leeu. In his copy, the Genoese mariner had noted precisely the passages where the Venetian merchant wrote about a sea east of China that was said to beat the shore of mythical, hurricane-swept islands.

Yet the most striking observation in the many pages Columbus devoted to the Caribbean islands which he finally discovered is his continuous amazement at a country and people more beautiful than he has ever seen, at a climate so mild, a harvest so abundant, the likes of which cannot be found in Europe. Of course, these eulogies hid a propagandist purpose, as Columbus needed to stimulate the home front to further support for his enterprises. Yet, his rapturous descriptions sound genuine. In this world, peace reigns, while arms and laws are unknown; everyone understands each other, and belief in God, although not formalized in religion, prevails. Only at the end of his story does Columbus actually use the word 'paradise', yet his descriptions clearly show that he felt he had discovered a paradise. As Las Casas writes: 'He told that he felt like wanting to stay there forever'.[11] He had found a land that had retained the state of grace that had governed the earth before the Fall and the confusion of languages, with a landscape as glorious as that in the garden of Eden.

Others were moved by different emotions. Bernal Díaz del Castillo, companion of the Spaniard Hernán Cortés who, in 1519, was the first European to set foot in Aztec Mexico, voiced his feelings briefly but forcefully when, on dropping anchor at the place they christened 'Vera Cruz' (the True Cross), he noted that 'we came here to serve God and the King, and to become rich'.

The first generation of Europeans who crossed the Atlantic Ocean actually thought they had reached 'India', by which name they used to refer to Asia beyond the Indus river: a world where they expected to find the fabulous wealth that had fascinated them in the stories about the Orient they had read or been told for so many centuries. Convinced by Columbus, they thought that they had reached the coasts of Asia. They now hoped to obtain part of the mythical riches of an old continent: silk, spices, pearls and gems, the things that had for millennia reached them only via the complicated trade routes of the Mediterranean and the Near and Middle East.

However, it soon transpired that the supposed riches of 'India' were not to be found in these western lands. The explanation only dawned on them when they realized that the first Spaniards to cross the Atlantic had not landed in 'India', in Asia, at all, but in a new world that, as yet, had not figured on any of their maps – real or mental. Inevitably, the conquerors and the first colonists were disappointed, a feeling which remained until they discovered this new world offered its own, unexpected treasures: new stimulants and nourishing plants as well as gold and silver in seeming abundance.

The culture of the Americas that the Europeans now started exploring in the wake of Columbus was surprising indeed. Thus Hernán Colón, son of the discoverer, writes in his report about his father's arrival in Cuba:

> On the way they met many people who had a fire with them to light a certain herb of which they inhaled the smoke; they also used it to light the fire on which they roasted the roots, which they gave to the Christians to eat and which were their main nourishment.[12]

Men like Cortés and Pizarro, who conquered the empires of the Aztecs and the Incas were in for other surprises as well. Bernal Díaz, in his account of the first meeting between Cortés and the Aztec ruler Montezuma, relates what the Spaniards noticed when they were invited to attend the emperor while he ate: 'Sometimes they brought him, in cups of pure gold, a drink made of the cocoa plant which, according to them, he always drank before he went to visit his wives'.[13] He also noted that

> they (. . .) put three pipes on his table, painted and gilded, into which they poured fluid amber mixed with herbs called tobacco. After eating, Montezuma inhaled the smoke from the pipes. He only had a little, and then fell asleep.[14]

Soon, many items of native America's material culture were introduced in Europe. By about 1520, the first tobacco seeds had already arrived in Portugal from Brazil. The French ambassador in Lisbon then took them to France. As his name was Jean Nicot de Villemain,[15] 'Nicotine' began its conquest of the world. Some would argue that lung cancer was Montezuma's belated revenge of Europe's American imperialism.

In the 1550s, the potato was first introduced into Spain from Peru, which after Spain's defeat of the Incas, was now governed through a Madrid-appointed viceroy and a huge bureaucracy of Spanish officials.[16] The new potato plant was not a success, as the berries were poisonous as, at first, the tubers were thought to be, too. However, it went from Habsburg Spain to Habsburg Austria where, in Vienna, people learnt how to prepare the potato for human consumption. Gradually, it became popular, although not widely so until the seventeenth and eighteenth centuries. Only then did people grasp the value of the potato tuber as a cheap, stable and healthy staple food for the population of Europe, whose diet had been solely based on grain during the previous millennia. What with failed harvests a recurring problem of Europe-wide magnitude, it was always an endangered diet, and not a very healthy one at that. As the story goes, King Frederick the Great of Prussia desired that his army, on whose physical strength his power both at home and abroad was based, should adopt a diet of these nourishing and cheap potatoes. However, the soldiers, often farmers' sons, stubbornly refused. The king then decided to assemble his troops at Breslau, where he had a splendidly laid table placed on the balcony of the palace, with only one dish on it: a bowl of steaming potatoes. Making certain to visibly enjoy his meal, he set an example to his men.

In the course of the seventeenth and eighteenth centuries, the cultivation and consumption of the potato spread across Europe. Specifically in poorer regions, the tuber became the main part of the popular diet. As a result, some parts of Europe stopped farming grain altogether. This happened in, for example, seventeenth-century Ireland, where the potato first served as cheap rations for the British occupying army and where, subsequently, the local population became completely dependent on it.

Unfortunately, the contemporary state of botany was such that it could not prevent such devastating plant diseases as potato mould. Whenever these occurred, the harvest of one or even several successive years failed completely, as they did in Ireland. The failed harvests of 1847 and 1848 in particular are remembered there even today. A terrible famine followed in which hundreds of thousands of Irish died, and hundreds of thousands left hearth and home. Ironically, they turned towards America, from where the cause of their misery had arrived in Europe three centuries earlier. The Irish were followed by thousands of Dutch, and by much larger groups from the German states, from central Europe and from Scandinavia, when there, too, devastating potato epidemics occurred during the second half of the nineteenth century. Meanwhile, the massive depopulation that had taken place among the Indians in America in the first decades of the sixteenth century, though often blamed on the Europeans, unbeknownst to any of the parties involved was largely the result of such diseases as influenza, measles, mumps, smallpox and tuberculosis, carried by the Europeans. They wrought havoc among the Indians, since the native Americans, who for many thousands of years had lived in their own, insulated biological world, had no resistance to them. Unwittingly, the increasing number of emigrants who settled in the new world from the sixteenth century onwards – reaching many millions during the nineteenth and twentieth centuries – corrected the balance.

As indicated above, the importation of food from the new world was not limited to tobacco and potatoes.[17] Cocoa and coffee soon became popular as luxury drinks among more prosperous Europeans. Moreover, Europe's 'sweet tooth' was stimulated by the import of cane sugar from Brazil and the Caribbean area, replacing the honey used for so long.[18] Also, the first 'peppers' arrived from the Americas, greatly valued in the fairly uninteresting European cuisine because of their piquant, even sharp taste. Being first imported by Spain, they were called 'Spanish peppers'. However, Europeans, in their turn, transported these plants to Asia, where they had a very real influence on culinary habits in the East Indies and China. From there, they returned to the west in the twentieth century as part of a food culture wrongly seen as 'typically oriental'.

Another delicacy also caught the attention of Europeans. When the tomato was introduced in Italian cuisine, it was called *pomo d'oro* (golden apple). Long before the arrival of the Europeans, the Aztecs had discovered that the weed which grew between their corncobs and which was called *tomat* in Nahuatl, could be improved into a food crop. When the Spanish came, the Aztecs had already succeeded in creating many varieties, and had even written instructions on how to grow them. In Europe the tomato was first used as a 'love apple' or aphrodisiac. Only in recent years has it become a colourful part of Europe's vitamin-obsessed diet.

The 'Columbian exchange'

In the wake of Columbus, thousands and, later on, hundreds of thousands and even millions of Europeans migrated to America. First, Spaniards and Portuguese went there to escape poverty and hunger in their own countries, dreaming of the untold riches the new world seemed to hold in store for anyone willing to take the risk. Consequently, Central and South America were colonized by the Iberians.

Undeniably, the experience was a brutal one for the native Americans. Millions of them died. While a minority were killed in the bloody wars that were waged between the conquerors and the continent's original inhabitants, the great majority perished because of the above-mentioned diseases the Europeans, unwittingly, introduced. In the process, most native cultures were profoundly changed and some totally destroyed. Certainly, the process was influenced by the policy of the new, colonial authorities, both the secular and the religious ones; they wanted to create a political-administrative system and a society along European lines, with the true, Christian religion as the main instrument of cultural cohesion. In particular, the material remains of Indian culture disappeared: for example, most indigenous texts, seen as dangerous embodiments of a pagan culture and identity, were burnt, and precious

architecture and artifacts were destroyed, especially if they held religious meaning. Meanwhile, the slow imposition of new languages – both Latin and Spanish
– contributed to a gradual erosion and, sometimes, a total loss of collective
memory, and to the parallel genesis of a new, hybrid culture, a fusion of both
native American and European.[19]

To the Caribbean and to North America came a mixture of immigrants
– both Iberian and non-Iberian – whose decision to migrate was based on a
variety of motives. At the end of the sixteenth century, Jews settled there after
their forceful expulsion from the Iberian kingdom of Philip II of Spain. By the
beginning of the seventeenth century, Englishmen started crossing the sea to
the east coast of North America, in search of the gold and silver that reportedly
had brought fabulous wealth to Spain. They did not find these precious metals.
However, they found fertile soil, suitable for all kinds of highly profitable
agricultural ventures; soon, they had established plantations where black slaves,
bought in and brought from Africa, toiled to produce another kind of wealth,
based on tobacco, cotton and sugar. Other Englishmen – as well as Scotsmen
– fled their countries because they felt they could not freely express their
religious and political opinions. Along America's east coast, both 'puritan'
Protestants and Roman Catholics, repressed at home, founded colonies to create
their own 'promised land'. Meanwhile, Dutch and Swedes, as well as Germans
and French established settlements, too, sometimes to escape poverty or political
and religious persecution at home, sometimes because their governments
encouraged them to create overseas bases for profitable expansion.

To this 'new world' each group brought its own customs and ideas. Each
group also brought back or sent back some of the products of the new world,
thus establishing an exchange that, however unequal in many ways, has been of
prime importance to the cultural history of Europe and, indeed, of the world.
Yet it was not only precious metals and foodstuffs that the Spanish, the first to
return from America, imported into Europe. Without people knowing it, the
first phase of the 'Columbian exchange' also brought death. In 1493, the Indians
participating in the victory parade to welcome Columbus to Barcelona did
not carry gold and colourful parrots only. They also carried a latent disease they
themselves were immune to. Thus, after the first sexual contacts between
Indians and Europeans, syphilis was introduced into the old world.[20] For about
100 years, until late in the sixteenth century, it devastated Europe as it was spread,
mostly, by the armies which during the sixteenth century were continually on
the move. They brought syphilis to the remotest parts of the continent where,
soon, people blamed it on each other, with the French calling it the 'Italian
sickness' and the English defaming it as the 'French malady'. Worse still, in
their turn, European seamen, traders and soldiers brought this venereal disease
– after Venus, the goddess of love and sex – to Asia and Africa. In 1498, only
six years after the discovery of America, the first Portuguese to set foot in India
introduced syphilis there.

However, there are scholars, mainly biologists, who hold another theory. They
propose that forms of syphilis had always been present across the globe and that

Columbus therefore did not bring anything new and terrible back from America. There is little evidence to support that proposition. For the present, the Columbian theory seems the more convincing, if only because the first great syphilis epidemics in Europe did not break out until after 1492.

Meanwhile, whatever its origin, the cultural consequences of syphilis were widespread.[21] From the early sixteenth century onwards, prostitution, until then a more or less accepted practice, came to be severely frowned upon. Partly as a result, the habit of bathing in public bathhouses quickly disappeared from European culture. Authorities started to close the 'stews', as these places were called, rightly assuming that most of them were brothels. But the kiss, too, until then such a normal sign of friendship and emotion, suddenly became suspect. Shakespeare indicates as much in his play *Henry V* (1600), in which he describes a soldier's departure, implicitly warning those who want to say goodbye to him in this way.

Also all manner of medical treatments involving direct contrast with potentially contaminated persons were now eyed askance both by the common people and by the practitioners. Erasmus, always a reliable and astute chronicler of his times, sums up the dominant hysteria in one of the dialogues in his *Colloquia*: even the barber, wielding his knife as well as being in constant touch with the fumes coming from the open mouths and noses of his customers, is now advised to cover his face with a cloth and protect himself in other ways as well. The obvious parallel with the great fear that followed the first Aids epidemic in the 1980s and 1990s is both striking and disconcerting as public reaction in those decades seems to have been both as unpredictable and as cruel as it was five centuries earlier. Inevitably, some people pondered whether European civilization had progressed at all during those 500 years.

In addition to all sorts of fascinating foodstuffs, which lessened the initial disappointment about the absence of the highly prized spices, Central and South America provided the Spanish and later the Portuguese with an apparently inexhaustible supply of Europe's two precious metals: gold and silver. In retrospect, this discovery has been decisive not only for the further development of European culture, but also for its economic and political position in the world between the fifteenth and twentieth centuries.

As nature had not blessed Europe with sizeable deposits of precious metals of its own,[22] gold and silver, the basis of the economy, had always had to be imported from abroad, at, obviously, great cost. Especially since the recovery of trade in Carolingian Europe during the eighth century, bullion metals had become indispensable to pay for all sorts of interregional trade. When, in later centuries, trade with North Africa and the Near East was re-established, it soon appeared that only large amounts of gold and silver would support the slowly developing capitalist economy of the twelfth and thirteenth centuries. To enable Europe to engage in the kind of trade on which its growing prosperity and, of course, its cultural flowering, rested, access to 'cheap' precious metals was necessary. This became the more obvious as, in the fourteenth and fifteenth centuries, Europeans started travelling and trading beyond the Mediterranean

Sea themselves, rather than through intermediaries. The Middle East and East Asia, the main suppliers of highly lucrative luxury items such as spices, silk and porcelain, did not care to be paid in kind, if this meant being paid with the, to them, inferior European products. Rather than barter, they demanded cash: gold and silver.

During the fifteenth century, this caused serious financial and economic problems. European merchants were simply unable to acquire or buy enough bullion to pay for their imports and keep the economy growing. Therefore, the discovery of large quantities of gold and silver in the new world at the beginning of the sixteenth century was nothing short of a godsend. It saved the European economy from threatening stagnation and from a subsequent slow but certain decline. In retrospect, we can see that the discovery gave economic life in Europe a stimulus which allowed it to expand and, thus, to become the strongest in the world, for many centuries to come – indeed, until the middle of the twentieth century.[23]

The gold and silver mines in Mexico and Peru that were now opened by the Spanish, were worked very energetically from the 1520s and 1530s onwards, even though it was soon painfully obvious that the native Americans were physically unfit for this kind of hard labour. Therefore, black people from Africa were now imported, not as free labourers, as the Indian at least theoretically had been, but as slaves. Admittedly, the phenomenon of slavery had been endemic for, probably, more than 1,000 years already. Inter-tribal warfare was one of the main providers. Moreover, even after a major part of sub-Saharan Africa had converted to Islam in the ninth and tenth centuries, slave traders from the Maghrebine north used to come and capture their brethren in faith to sell them to the highest bidder. But now Christian Europeans became the main buyers on the African slave markets, trading their acquisitions to the markets across the ocean. Mostly, they used religious, even biblical arguments to justify their trade.

In short, to mine American ore, increasingly necessary to fuel Europe's trade with Asia, sub-Saharan Africa was now included in the ever more complex network of 'the European world economy'. Until the end of the sixteenth century, when the approaching exhaustion of the deposits first became manifest, an enormous quantity of bullion flowed from America to Europe. Until 1540, it was mainly gold. From then on, silver took over.

The annual bullion fleet, heavily protected by naval convoys, brought the precious metal into the Spanish economy by way of the Spanish monopoly port of Seville. However, the Iberian economy was no longer a specifically Spanish affair, since the kings of Spain, Charles V and Philip II, who were members of the Austrian Habsburg family, also ruled other vast parts of Europe, both in Italy and to the north of the Pyrenees and the Alps. Thus, gold and silver poured into Europe. It enabled Spanish nobles, prelates and private citizens to pay for the services of the hundreds of Dutch artists and artisans who flocked to Spain in the early decades of the sixteenth century, to build and decorate cathedrals, monasteries and palaces; they soon integrated into Spanish society. It also enabled the Spanish government to pay the soldiers who protected the Habsburgs' wide-ranging political interests. In the Dutch rebellion against Philip II, which became increasingly violent in the late 1560s, the thousands of mercenaries who fought for the Spanish against the rebels in the Netherlands were paid with American silver. Many of these soldiers stayed on, marrying local girls. Thus, the American bullion indirectly stimulated European migration.

In short, it is safe to say that the Spanish kings could not have engaged in international politics and in expensive wars if their American colonies had not contributed to the royal fisc in this way. Indeed, if a gold or silver fleet failed to arrive in Seville at the end of summer, because of head winds or because of piracy – the Dutch like to recall Piet Heyn, while the English think of Francis Drake and Walter Raleigh as national heroes who robbed the Spaniards of their ill-gotten wealth – the paymasters of the Spanish army faced empty coffers and the hirelings engaged to fight in Flanders' fields or in the German states stopped their fighting without further ado; often, they would take to plundering the countryside or rise in mutiny.

But bullion and the money coined from it did not only benefit Spain and Spanish power politics. Waiting for the annual fleet to arrive, the Spanish government had to negotiate gigantic loans to finance their current commitments. They did so with Portuguese, Italian and Flemish financiers and with the Fugger banking family of Augsburg; later, American gold would then pay off their debts. As a result, these financial companies invested their share of the new world's precious metal in their other ventures that, given their widespread economic interests, affected life in the whole of Europe. This influenced European society in three essential ways.

First, as American bullion and its economic consequences substantially contributed to the further extension of European trade with Asia – which started to grow from the second half of the sixteenth century – an old commercial and cultural link was now revived and strengthened. This proved fundamentally significant to Europe's budding self-image, as it now had to measure itself against the great civilizations of the east.

Second, it influenced government finance in the European states through its wide-ranging economic effects. Soon, the many new enterprises that were now founded started generating a larger tax volume, especially in Spain, France, England and the Netherlands. This tax income paid for the government bureaucracies that were expanding enormously in the sixteenth century. Thus, the basis was laid for the great power that, at least in Europe, the state came to hold over society – a power that has not decreased ever since.

A third result of the tidal wave of precious metal that flooded Europe for approximately 80 years was certainly negative for the average European. Galloping inflation affected all but the most wealthy[24] as the sudden and uncontrollable increase in the money supply was not immediately absorbed by a simultaneous growth in production. As a result, prices rose sharply everywhere. Those who had a fixed income experienced the greatest difficulties. Nor did this situation affect only the lower income groups. Big landowners, for instance, suffered as well. As many of them had let their lands on long-term leases, rising prices that

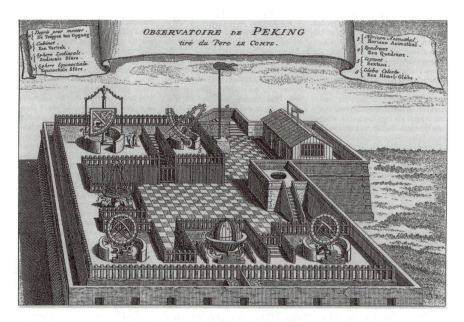

Plate 16 Across the world, Europeans tried to introduce Christianity. Travelling to Asia, they were especially fascinated by China. Though trading with the Celestial Empire was not made easy for European merchants, the Chinese authorities did allow the Jesuits to establish a mission in Peking, mainly, however, to allow them to teach China their technological skills, especially in the field of astronomical research, which they pursued in their observatory, here shown with all its measuring instruments in an eighteenth-century engraving.

Source: Centre for Art Historical Documentation, Nijmegen, the Netherlands

could not be translated in new contracts reduced their purchasing power. These nobles often became discontented and did not hesitate to show it, certainly when their power was threatened in other ways as well. This was the case in this very period. All over Europe princely governments had long been trying to reduce the competition from the old aristocracy and to strip it of its traditional military and administrative functions. Now, the changing economic climate, which slowly brought central governments more income from taxation, gave them the opportunity to free themselves of noble interference by replacing nobles with paid bureaucrats and mercenary soldiers. Most of the local and even national noble revolts which occurred in European countries during the second half of the sixteenth century and in the early seventeenth century, originated in this situation.

In France, during the co-called *frondes*, dissatisfied nobles, sometimes seeking an alliance with disgruntled urban elites, warred against an increasingly oppressive central authority that they blamed for everything. In sixteenth- and early seventeenth-century England, struggles continually flared up between sections of the aristocracy, many of whom felt restricted in their power and status by the changing economic and political situation. The protestant 'Beggars', the representatives of the minor nobility who, in 1566, presented the Spanish governor of the Netherlands with a petition in which they expressed their grievances and requested an adjustment of royal policy on, among other things, religious freedom, included many who had been adversely affected by the prevailing economic situation. It was one of the crises that led to the Dutch Revolt and the subsequent independence of the Netherlands.

In short, the influx of American precious metal was definitely no blessing for all Europeans. On the contrary, for many it felt more like a malediction, just as, in another context, syphilis and, later, the ill-fated dependence on the potato were seen as God's curse on his sinful people.

EUROPE, THE EARLY SIXTEENTH CENTURY: OPINIONS ON THE CONQUEST OF AMERICA AND ITS CONSEQUENCES

Contemporaries had a clear view of the consequences of America's inclusion in the European world. Spanish American bullion increased the credit of the House of Habsburg, enabling Charles V to purchase the imperial crown as, with the aid of loans provided by the Fugger banking firm, he managed to outbid his rival, King François I of France. In 1523, old Jacob Fugger did not hesitate to remind the new emperor of his obligations, with a frankness indicating the position of power men such as he now enjoyed:

> Your Imperial Majesty doubtless knows how I and my kinsmen have ever hitherto been disposed to serve the House of Austria in all loyalty to the furtherance of its well-being and prosperity; wherefore, in order to be pleasing to Your Majesty's Grandsire, the late Emperor Maximilian, and to gain for Your Majesty the Roman Crown, we have held ourselves bounded to engage ourselves towards divers princes who placed their trust and reliance upon myself and perchance on no man besides. We have, moreover, advanced to Your Majesty's agents for the same end a great sum of money, of which we ourselves had to raise a large part from our friends. It is well known that Your Imperial Majesty could not have gained the Roman Crown save with mine aid, and I can prove the same by the writings of Your Majesty's agents given by their own hands. In this matter I have not studied mine own profit. For had I left the House of Austria and had been minded to further France, I had obtained much money and property, such as was then offered to me.[25]

Old Jacob's words did not go unheeded. Among the ways Charles V chose to pay back his loans were lucrative mining concessions in Peru and a number of hugely profitable monopolies in the various states of the far-flung Habsburg Empire. The Fugger family prospered as never before. For a few decades, American precious metals flowed into Europe, until the first deposits had been exhausted. European politicians had been carefully watching the situation. In 1559, the Venetian envoy to the Spanish court, Michele Soriano, sent a cool and revealing assessment of the entire colonial situation to his masters, the aristocratic merchant rulers of the Republic of St Mark:

> From New Spain are obtained gold and silver, cochineal – little insects like flies from which crimson dye is made – leather, cotton, sugar and other things; but from Peru nothing is obtained except minerals. The fifth part of all that is produced goes to the king, but since the gold and silver is brought to Spain and he has a tenth part of that which goes to the mint and is refined and coined, he eventually gets one-fourth of the whole sum, which fourth does not exceed in all four or five hundred thousand ducats. . . . Nor is it likely that it will long remain at this figure, because great quantities of gold and silver are no longer found upon the surface of the earth, as they have been in past years; and to penetrate into the bowels of the earth requires greater effort, skill and outlay, and the Spaniards are not willing to do the work themselves, and the natives cannot be forced to do so, because the Emperor has freed them from all obligation of service as soon as they accept the Christian religion. Wherefore it is necessary to acquire negro slaves, who are brought from the coasts of Africa, both within and without the Straits, and these are selling dearer every day, because on account of their natural lack of strength and the change of climate, added to the lack of discretion upon the part of their masters in making them work too hard and giving them too little to eat, they fall sick and the greater part of them die.[26]

The Frenchman Jean Bodin (1530–96), one of the sharpest political analysts of his day, theorized about the consequences of the new situation, arguing from solid historical and statistical research, which, incidentally, shows the pervasiveness of the new scientific spirit. In 1568 he wrote:

> I find that the dearness we observe comes from four or five causes. The principal and almost the only one (to which no one has heretofore referred) is the abundance of gold and silver, which is much greater in this kingdom today than it was four hundred years ago. I do not go further back since the extracts of the registers of the court and of the chamber which I have do not go beyond four hundred years. The rest has to be drawn from old histories with little certainty.
>
>   The second cause of dearness comes in part from monopolies. The third is scarcity, which is caused as much by exports as by waste. The fourth is the pleasure of kings and great nobles, who raise the prices of the things they like. The fifth is the price of money, debased from its old valuation.[27]

Images of America and mirrors of Europe

Though my analysis of Europe's relationship with America may seem rather materialistic so far, it needs to be stressed that an empty stomach is but rarely conducive to great thoughts of a philosophical or religious nature. Moreover, without money no churches or palaces are built, no splendid paintings painted, no magnificent operas composed or produced. A healthy financial basis is necessary for every form of artistry or science.

Thus, almost inevitably, the discovery of America and the influx of bullion greatly strengthened the material basis of European culture. Indeed, from the sixteenth century onwards, European culture showed a new blossoming in many areas. Also, the very 'experience of America' became an intrinsic element in European culture, too, a source of continuous inspiration. To start with, both the prevailing world-view and Europe's concept of man had to be adjusted as existing geographical notions had to be adjusted almost daily and 'new' people integrated into the Christian view of creation.[28]

Until late in the sixteenth century, far and away the majority of Europeans still adhered to Kosmas's notion of the earth as flat, surrounded by a finite stretch of water that somehow ended in a bleak nothingness, where death awaited those who had dared so far. It had been that very image that made many simple sailors quail before the journeys their masters ordered them to undertake. Once on their way, these men had no idea of the actual vastness of the earth's seas and of the contours of its lands. Even after the discoveries were well under way, the great majority failed to be interested. Being land-bound, they could not care less about the wider world.

Only a tiny minority of Europeans, the ones influenced by the new knowledge gained by the contacts with Islam and, through these, ancient Greek science, had a completely different world-view; this was based on the spherical conception of the classical geographer Ptolemy. One of these was, of course, Columbus. But his dream of reaching 'India' – that is to say, East Asia – also indicates he was not completely aware of the actual dimensions of the globe.[29]

In 1492, the same year he set sail, one Martin Behaim of Nuremberg constructed a globe, according to many the first of its kind. Coincidence? Not really. Behaim came from the same Portuguese-Spanish maritime milieu as Columbus. He had lived in the Flemish merchant colony on the recently discovered archipelago of the Azores. This Bavarian scholar was therefore acquainted with the geographical data that the expeditions of the Portuguese along the west coast of Africa had produced. He also knew the Florentine scholar Paolo Toscanelli (1397–1492), whose world map and theories had indicated the possibility of reaching the east coast of 'India' by travelling westwards from Europe. In fact, Columbus had also corresponded with Toscanelli.

Behaim's globe does not show a 'new world'. He positioned an enormous ocean between Europe and Asia – containing only a small island, the mythical land of St Brendan, the Irish monk who was said to have ventured out long ago in search of a new world. But Behaim was the first to indicate the position of China and Japan. Yet almost everything else on his globe is as wrong as it could be from a present-day perspective. One must therefore conclude that, although for Europe the world now started opening up, most Europeans barely knew what it looked like. That the world was a globe, however, slowly became clear to more people, if only because of the material globes now being manufactured in increasing numbers, although they were very expensive. But maps, too, could convey this new notion and even though their reliability was as yet poor, they were now produced on a far larger scale through the new medium of printing, allowing an increased readership to acquaint themselves with the wonder that was the world.

Meanwhile, ever more energy was expended on improving cartographic reliability. The European economy, boosted by the discoveries, demanded scientifically based knowledge that could also be applied to its everyday needs. Map making soon became a valued craft and something of an industry, too; it was less fuelled by the disinterested intellectual pursuit of scientific accuracy and objectivity than by the awareness that progress and the success of Europe's international trade and politics depended on it. Indeed, maps soon came to determine and to show the economic and political agenda both of European rulers and governments as well as of all those who now ventured on an as yet often perilous path to riches and dominion in the world at large.[30]

During the first decades of the sixteenth century, following Columbus's expeditions, new data came pouring in almost every day. In 1513, Spaniards crossing the Isthmus of Panama in Central America, discovered that on the other side another great ocean stretched out: astonished at first, they soon realized what some had argued already, namely that Columbus had been mistaken in his conviction that he had reached the east coast of Asia. Incidentally, the situation created a new challenge: in the years 1519–21, the Portuguese Ferdinand Magellan (*c*.1480–1521), rounding the stormy capes of South America, was the first ever to circumnavigate the world, at least as far as can be established from research. Once more, one should again realize what such journeys meant to the people who undertook them. If not Magellan himself, at least his men, like the men sailing with Columbus before him, must have thought that they were going to and indeed 'over the edge of the world'.[31]

Inevitably, when the significance of the new discoveries of 1513 and 1519 dawned on Europe, a 'new world' was born, for no longer could the 'West Indies' be considered part of India, Asia, as the original name indicated. This new world had to be given its geographical place. To accommodate 'America', the image on European globes had to be reconsidered as well. In 1507, Martin Waldseemüller had already provisionally charted the east coast of the new continent, naming it after the Florentine navigator Amerigo Vespucci (1451–1512), accepting his claim to have been the first to reach the American mainland, on his voyage of 1497 or 1499. Whether Vespucci was indeed the first is not certain even now; and, of course, we do know whether Norsemen from Iceland had reached Newfoundland, by way of Greenland, five centuries earlier. Meanwhile, the American west coast was to remain a sketchy line for many years to come.

Summing up Europe's increased understanding and knowledge of the world, 1,000 years after Kosmas's *Kosmographia*, Waldseemüller could write:

> It is clear from astronomical demonstrations that the whole earth is a point in comparison with the entire extent of the heavens. . . . There is about a fourth part of . . . the world . . . inhabited by living beings like ourselves. Hitherto it has been divided into three parts, Europe, Africa and Asia.
>
> Europe is bounded on the west by the Atlantic Ocean, on the north by the British Ocean, on the east by the River Tanais [i.e. the Don], Lake Maeotis [i.e.

the Sea of Azov], and the Black Sea, and on the south by the Mediterranean Sea. Europe is so called after Europa, the daughter of King Agenor [i.e. the king of Phoenicia, in the Near East]. While with a girl's enthusiasm she was playing on the sea-shore accompanied by her Tyrian maidens and was gathering flowers in baskets, she is believed to have been carried off by Jupiter, who assumed the form of a snow-white bull, and after being brought over the seas to Crete seated upon his back to have given her name to the land lying opposite. . . .

Africa is bounded on the west by the Atlantic Ocean, on the south by the Ethiopian Ocean, on the north by the Mediterranean Sea, and on the east by the River Nile. . . . It is called Africa because it is free from the severity of the cold. . . .

Asia . . . far surpasses the other divisions in size and in resources. . . . Asia is so called after a queen of that name. . . .

Now . . . a fourth part has been discovered by Amerigo Vespucci. Inasmuch as both Europe and Asia received their names from women, I see no reason why any one should justly object to calling this part Amerige, i.e. the land of Amerigo, or America, after Amerigo, its discoverer, a man of great ability.[32]

The honour of giving America its proper place on the map should, according to many, be given to Gerard Mercator (1512–94). Having studied the humanities at Louvain, he continued his education there with the famous mathematician Gemma Frisius, to prepare for a career as a constructor of mathematical instruments. In 1536, with his master, he made the first celestial globe and, with a Louvain goldsmith, the second ever terrestrial globe. In the following years, Mercator, using all available data, drew and published maps of the Holy Land – a cultural 'must' in a Christian society and, moreover, of commercial interest for the pilgrim industry. He quickly gained a wide reputation. Even Charles V ordered him to manufacture astronomical instruments.

In 1579, roughly three-quarters of a century after Behaim, Mercator published a world map *ad usum navigatorum* (for the use of navigators). With it, he established his interpretation of the earth's outlines, having used a cylinder projection based upon straight lines of longitude and latitude intersecting at right angles. For the map's details, he combined Ptolemy's data and ideas with those of more recent vintage – Marco Polo's, regardless of their continued controversiality – and with the newest discoveries of Portuguese and Spanish navigators. The map also incorporated America. However, Mercator's image of South America was overlarge while North America, of which so little was yet known, appears far too small. Moreover, reflecting ancient beliefs, he also added two large polar continents. Still, even now the so-called 'Mercator Projection' is the one most humans envisage when they think of a map of the globe.[33]

The large number of maps produced by Mercator after he had published his map of the world show that cartography had become a field of evident scientific and economic importance. Indeed, however magnificent and costly the Mercator editions, they were all commercially successful.

Interestingly, Mercator still saw the world from one, in a sense metaphysical, point of view. He applied both his theoretical notions and his practical research to an integral, essentially Christian cosmological view that encompassed the earth and the heavens. This became more apparent after his death when, in 1596, the first part was published of what he himself considered the synthesis of his work, his own *Cosmographia*. Edited by his son, it consisted of five parts. The first part was called *Atlas*. In his 'Foreword to the Atlas', Mercator clearly suggests that the really wise person attempts to harmonize his knowledge of heaven and earth. The engraved print on the title page shows the mythical Atlas with the celestial globe on his knee and, at his feet, the terrestrial globe, now including the Americas. In this first so-called 'atlas', Mercator also discusses creation. He analyses the book of Genesis and the four Gospels. This section is followed by a new edition in four parts of map collections of various parts of Europe and the other known continents that he had published before.

The complete 'Cosmography' was published in Amsterdam. As the centre of the European economy had shifted from the Mediterranean to the coasts of the Atlantic in the early decades of the sixteenth century, by the end of the century it moved from the main commercial metropolis, Antwerp, to the harbours of Holland, partly because the Dutch, in their revolt against Spain, had chosen to permanently blockade the River Scheldt. Map and instrument makers now established themselves in the Dutch port towns, applying the results of empirical research to produce new technology and thus contributing greatly to the success and growth of international trade. Holland was also the place where Europe's most important printers and publishers settled, trying to market their knowledge of new worlds. Pouring out travel stories and novels, encyclopedias and atlases, they acquainted their readers with the rediscovered older world of Asia and the new world of America. For a long time, a disbelieving astonishment and an insatiable curiosity continued to ensure a lively demand for new texts and pictures.

Money is power. As Europe became richer, the size of armies which rulers sent into battle and the fleets that sailed the seas increased as well. Ever more parts of the non-European world submitted to the economic and, increasingly, political and cultural power of European states. Power induces a sense of superiority. Travelling the world, Europeans observed that, often, they were stronger than others, soon feeling 'better' than Asians, Africans and native Americans. First and foremost, they often proved themselves superior militarily, with their use of gunpowder. Inevitably, they wondered why this would be so. Their answer was, in fact, the simple answer of those who have an inscrutable faith: they were victorious, superior because, being Europeans, they were Christians, always supported by the one God who was true to his biblical promise. Admittedly, the more educated often followed a rather more complex argument. To Jean Bodin, it was clear that Europe dominated the world precisely because European culture, after first having based itself on the great achievements of Greek civilization, had now managed to surpass even many of these.[34]

This growing self-awareness was reflected in geographical representations as well. Maps now showed Europe as a region that dominated the world rather than as the remote corner of the great Eurasian land mass. Sometimes, Europe's geographical contours were so transformed that it represented a triumphant queen, as on the famous map in Sebastian Münster's *Cosmographia universalis*, published in Basle in 1588. Soon, this sense of superiority turned actual expansion into a 'mission', which, in creating its own legitimacy, then provided the arguments for further expansion, for new conquests.

A world-view, however, is not restricted only to a globe or map – indeed, one might argue these are rather translations of a pre-existing vision. Certainly, a world-view is a way of thinking, as can be shown in the complex process whereby the new world was fitted into the European mind. As America was, according to the stories, a world inhabited by people with totally different physical features and habits, a world where animals and plants existed that were not described in the traditional textbooks, Europeans experienced the discovery of America as a grave culture shock.[35]

Especially during the first decades after Columbus's voyages, many were so astonished by the reports about the new world that they thought that, after centuries of searching, the 'garden of Eden', the 'earthly paradise' had at last been discovered: surely, the Americas were the place where people still lived as God had created them, not corrupted by the Fall.[36] This belief was strong among the Franciscans – twelve of them, to symbolically represent the first Apostles, were the first missionaries to depart for Mexico in 1524. In trying to convert the Mexican Indians, they felt they had to protect them from the evil influences of godless Spanish colonists. Besides thus keeping power over the new Christians to themselves, in pursuing this policy they also hoped to realize God's kingdom on earth with these Indians, his as yet innocent children.

The same belief in the continued existence of a terrestrial paradise or, conversely, in the possibility of its recreation somewhere on earth can be found in many literary texts inspired by the Americas. The well-known English poet Andrew Marvell (1621–78), in a poem called *Bermudas*, praised God who had brought the English to:

> . . . an isle so long unknown,
> And yet far kinder than our own.
> He lands us on a grassy stage,
> Safe from the storms, and prelate's rage
> He gave us this eternal spring
> Which here enamels everything.[37]

He represents an island, therefore, where the English could live as they no longer could at home: in a world of freedom – freedom of religion, among other things – in a paradisical context. A few decades later, George Berkeley (1685–1753) wrote his *Verses on the Prospect of Planting Arts and Learning in America*:

> The Muse, disgusted at an age and clime,
> Barren of every glorious theme,
> In distant lands now waits a better time,

Producing subjects worthy of fame . . .
There shall be sung another golden age,
The rise of empire and of arts . . .
Not such as Europe breeds in her decay:
Such as she bred when fresh and young.[38]

The poem voices another theme that would recur for several centuries: the old world, Europe, is decaying. In the new world, Europeans can realize what is no longer nourished in the old. Indeed, Berkeley actually wanted to transplant what most eighteenth-century Europeans considered the essence of Europe: its arts and learning, thus showing that, essentially, Europe's self-definition had not changed since the same notions had been expressed in the fourteenth and fifteenth centuries, or even earlier.

A comparable, in some ways even more idyllic vision of the new world as the garden of Eden, and of the Indian as the 'Noble Savage', a man living, uncorrupted, in the natural state given him by God and in a nature still as pristine as created by God, can be found in many sixteenth- and seventeenth-century prints and paintings – by Albrecht Dürer and Jan Mostaert to name only two examples.[39] However, many other Europeans were convinced that Indian societies were not civilized societies at all. Judged by humanist norms of civilization, wherein communication developed along the lines of public oratory and eloquence, denoting an ordered, regulated polity, or by Christian norms of civilization, wherein the belief in the one, true, unseen God denoted the same, the Indians had to be educated, to be raised to the level of Europe. Nor was actual contact with the Indians as peaceful as the more idealistic images would have us believe. On the contrary, European connections with America were, if anything, often calculating and equally often cruel, even by contemporary standards.

The traces of this contact turned conflict can be found in one of Shakespeare's plays, *The Tempest* (1611), that tells of a group of Europeans who, lured there by the exiled Prospero, find themselves stranded on a strange island. The playwright is known to have been inspired by the sizeable number of stories of Europeans who were shipwrecked in foreign parts. Yet his play is more than a poetic fabrication of such travel stories. It is an allegory of the way Europeans behaved towards their new fellow men. *The Tempest* can therefore be read as follows. At first, the natives, represented by the wild man Caliban, are friendly and share their treasures and secrets with the foreigners if only because in return they are taught some of Europe's arts:

When thou camest first,
Thou strokedst me and made much of me; wouldst give me
Water with berries in't; and teach me how
To name the bigger light, and how the less,
That burn by day, and night; and then I loved thee
And showed thee all the qualities o' the isle,
The fresh springs, brine-pits, barren place and fertile.[40]

Then the foreigners, obviously Europeans, turn their back on the natives because they find them uncivilized. The Indians react in kind. Now, the Europeans, to enslave the natives and make them work for them, begin to use their superior technology, symbolized in the play by Prospero's magic. The natives try to defend themselves by combining forces with newly arrived foreigners. Caliban calls out:

> I'll show thee the best springs; I'll pluck thee berries . . .
> A plague upon the tyrant that I serve!
> I'll bear him no more sticks but follow thee,
> Thou wondrous man.[41]

But their fate is sealed: they become only more dependent. Moreover, they are now branded as bloodthirsty monsters.[42]

In the first decades of the seventeenth century, when in North America, too, Europeans and Indians entered into more frequent contact, the fight for land began. Many colonists, born and raised in the strict traditions of Protestantism, strengthened their moral position and defended their land-taking actions by using biblical arguments. Dozens of sermons and tracts use the image of an elite corps of believers whom God has placed in this 'wildernesse' as a test, just as He had once done with the people of Israel, leading them into the desert. But as in the past, the promised land is around the corner, 'a garden enclosed, a fountain sealed', and with God's help 'Jerusalem shall be inhabitable without walls', just as the Bible says.[43]

Yet this could not be attained without a struggle. Outright strife between the European settlers and the natives soon followed. In 1637, the first large-scale war was declared by a group of English colonists, and the tribe of the Pequot was exterminated completely. Admittedly, some colonists questioned whether all this bloodshed could be justified. An anonymous minister had no such qualms, answering 'I would refer you to David's war. When a People is grown to such a height of blood and sin against God and man . . . sometimes the Scripture declareth women and children must perish with their parents'.[44] Among the many texts that tell their readers to conquer the new world as the Jews had once conquered their promised land, that is with Old Testament violence, one is relieved to find sometimes a somewhat more nuanced judgement, like that of Robert Beverly, who concluded his 1703 outline of Indian society with the words:

> Thus I think I have given a succinct account of the Indians; happy, I think, in their simple State of Nature, and in their enjoyment of Plenty without the Curse of Labour. They have on several counts reasons to lament the arrival of the Europeans, by whose means they seem to have lost their Felicity, as well as their Innocence.[45]

Another colonist went one step further when, in 1708, he admitted that:

> We neither give Allowance for their Natural Disposition, nor the Sylvan Education and strange Customs (uncouth to us) they lie under and have ever been trained up

to; these are false Measures for Christians to take, and indeed no man can be reckoned a Moralist only, who will not make choice and use better Rules to walk and act by.[46]

Until well into the eighteenth century, some European Americans and many more Europeans indulged in an uncritical idealization of the 'Noble Savage'. Yet careful analysis of most of their writings shows that they are always addressing the European who must improve himself, if necessary by recognizing his own failings, by judging his actions against the original, still uncorrupted worlds and beings. Only rarely does one find a plea for accepting 'the Other' as intrinsically different, and thus as his own self. Indeed, as far as the problem of the relationship is addressed at all, the predominating view presents non-European man as dependent on European man. In the early eighteenth century it was codified in Daniel Defoe's famous story *Robinson Crusoe* (1719) which created a stereotype of the relation between the European and 'the Other' – in this case black rather than red. It shows that the discovery of America or, in general, of new worlds, and the meeting with 'the Other' substantially influenced the way Europeans viewed themselves: as superior, as natural-born leaders.

Further cultural consequences of European expansion

Undeniably, the process of contact and conquest by which Europe came to dominate a large part of the world, has caused great suffering all over the globe.[47] Obviously, history writing is not the forum to make moral judgements on those periods and people of the past who held values so different from our own. Yet one may conclude that colonialism and imperialism, though practised by many civilizations all over the world during known history, in their European form and by Europe's very technological possibilities, often transgressed even the norms of the time itself.

However, in surveying European history, one cannot fail to note also that the rediscovery of Asia and the discovery of America have been decisive factors in the creation of numerous and lasting forms of culture: of artistic masterpieces still to be seen all over Europe and now eagerly visited by many non-Europeans as well; of lifestyles and luxuries that, while a European prerogative for a long time, are now emulated and often enjoyed by non-European peoples, too; and, perhaps more important, of ideas and attitudes which shaped the European mind for centuries to come and, in their turn, have influenced the hopes and aspirations of the wider world, as is shown in the process of globalization.

To give but a few examples, one may think of the Florentine banking family of Medici, in whose coffers large amounts of Asian and American gold and silver ended up: they were Michelangelo's first patrons.[48] The new St Peter's which rose in Rome in the course of the sixteenth century – it took more than 100 years to build – was constructed in part from the ecclesiastical taxes which flowed in from Spain and Portugal and, hence, from the gold and silver mines in Iberian colonial America. In the seventeenth century, in that same Rome, on the Piazza

Navona, Gianlorenzo Bernini created the dream-like 'Fountain of the Four Rivers', one of which symbolized the Rio de la Plata, the 'River of Silver', while all four rivers supported an obelisk, seen as the representation of the oldest culture of the world, Egypt, but that one, in its turn, is topped by the Christian cross.

On the Iberian peninsula itself, the bullion that came from the Americas not only helped to create sumptuous buildings, among them Philip II's church-monastery-palace of the Escorial, in the mountains above Madrid, but also resulted in commissions for music to be played and sung in churches, monasteries and palaces alike, and in a wide demand for emotionally evocative baroque paintings and sculpture to adorn these buildings.

In the far north, in Amsterdam, Jacob van Campen's palatial town hall with its statues by Flemish sculptors, the proud symbol of the foremost mercantile city of the seventeenth century glorified the Dutch trading metropolis as 'mistress of the world'. Significantly, the façade of the building was crowned with a gigantic Atlas figure shouldering the globe. For good reason, two enormous world maps were represented in the multi-coloured marble pavement of the great hall. That globe and those maps certainly served to remind visitors and passers-by of the colonies the Dutch had conquered from the Portuguese in Brazil, as well as of the 'New Amsterdam' which Dutch traders and settlers had founded on Manhattan island in the Hudson river, later to become New York, and of the even vaster colonial empire they had built in the east.

The same satisfaction surfaced in a poem in which the Dutch poet Joost van den Vondel referred to Amsterdam's position of power in the old and in the new world. In more than 1,000 lines he gave the inauguration of the new town hall an allegorical–ideological context. It argues that Amsterdam, which knows all 'shores', including gold-filled America's, is, by right, the ruler of the earth. By Vondel's time, the Dutch East India Company, founded in 1602 to become the world's first multinational, had firmly established its hold over South Africa, over parts of the coasts of India, Ceylon and present-day Indonesia, while they were the only Europeans allowed to enter the magic island empire of Japan.

In France, at the end of the seventeenth century, sumptuous tapestries were woven to adorn the pompous palace of Versailles. Some show scenes derived from paintings made by Dutch artists in Dutch Brazil.[49] Other paintings were used as the basis for the engraved illustrations of several successful travel stories published in the Netherlands in the seventeenth century: Caspar Barlaeus's 1647 history of the Dutch conquest of Brazil, and the still more famous *Brasiliaensche Land-en Seereise* (Brazilian Land and Sea Journey), written in 1672 by Johan Nieuhof, servant of the Dutch West Indies Company, the global trade organization which focused, in particular, on the Americas.[50] But France, of course, longed to dominate the world all by itself. In 1662, young Louis XIV, for whom his first minister had even sought the imperial crown, entered the Place du Carroussel in a festive procession to mark the birth of the Dauphin. While he himself dressed as a Roman emperor, his brother and his first nobles had dressed as Persians, Turks, and men from India and the Americas; they all made their obeisance to the 'ruler of the world'. During the reign of the man who, if not actually gaining the dominion he sought, yet managed to have himself styled the 'Sun King' as another indication of his ambition, such acts of political propaganda were to recur regularly, always showing not only his own pretensions but also those of his state, of the French nation.[51]

All over Europe, comparable references to Europe's position in the world show the prevalence of such notions of superiority. In the first decades of the eighteenth century, Giovanni Battista Tiepolo painted the magnificent ceiling frescos for the immense vaulted staircase of the prince-bishop's baroque residence in Würzburg and at the prince-bishop's new summer palace Weissenstein, in nearby Pommersfelden. Representing the different parts of the world in colourful allegories, they depict Europe as 'queen of the continents', implying that she ruled the earth.[52] The palaces of the Habsburg emperors and their noble courtiers, as well as of other German courts in the eighteenth century, were adorned with pictures of America, too.[53] At those courts, one might also hear an opera by the composer Karl-Heinrich Graun whose theme was the tragic fate suffered by the Aztec Emperor Montezuma at the hands of the Spanish conquerors. The same story was also set to music by the Venetian composer Antonio Vivaldi, and a host of others. Indeed, these were only a few of the many operas and ballets in which the Indies, America, formed the location of the action, and the Indians were the characters. By this time, in a more 'enlightened' Europe the 'wild' Indian had become 'noble' again and it was possible to take a more nuanced view of his destiny at the hands of rapacious Europeans.

In England, the nobility's craze for gardening, or rather for having others lay out their gardens for them, received a new impulse when, at the beginning of the eighteenth century, engravings depicting the huge gardens at Jehol, the Chinese emperor's summer palace, were published by a Jesuit returning from the Far East. He had been part of a group of Christian missionaries staying at the imperial court, the fourth generation to do so since the beginning of Europe's new contacts with China in the sixteenth century. Now, in the early eighteenth century, Chinese pagodas began to appear in English gardens while Chinese-style furniture started to fill the country houses. Indeed, a wave of 'chinoiserie' swept over Europe, not only to satisfy the need for a new fashion, but also because the Jesuits in their travel tales had succeeded in portraying China as a powerful state with a civilization that did actually match that of Europe.

In short, many of Europe's works of art would not have been created without the material contribution that the peoples of Asia and America were forced to give, nor, for that matter, without the inspiration which the wonders of this new, foreign and to many dreamlike world had given to the European mind.

At an early stage, Europe had first become an independent world when the Greeks defined it as their world, in opposition to Asia. The concept of Europe had been further articulated when the peoples of Europe had felt the need to form a common front against Islam, to actually cooperate in the Crusades. Now, in the fifteenth, sixteenth and seventeenth centuries, the idea of Europe was elaborated once more in the often hostile contact with other cultures, not only those of Asia, the older world, but also those of America, the new world.

For Vondel's poem cited above was a glorification not only of Amsterdam. It also described Europe as the world where the 'burgher', the citizen, was the centre of society: he was the politically free individual, who continues the tradition of the ancient Greek city-states. Yet, these burghers now drank coffee and tea imported from Asia, and sat down to dinner at tables laden with porcelain, china-ware, sometimes decorated in patterns specifically requested by them, and ended a pleasant evening smoking a cigar made of American tobacco – undoubtedly unaware of or comfortably ignoring the fact that the tobacco was grown on plantations worked by black slaves from Africa, that the china was produced in ever more complex factories on the Chinese mainland, that the cultivation of tea and coffee was slowly disrupting traditional Asian economies and that many of their luxuries were bought with the profits they themselves made from the opium trade in India.

In their gardens they often grew plants from seedlings brought all the way from India or Indonesia by the ships of the Dutch East India Company. Some of the wealthiest Amsterdam burghers owned private zoos, where privileged visitors were allowed to gape at exotic animals collected from all over the globe. Such visitors were also invited to enter the luxurious townhouses that lined the Amsterdam canals, in order to view, or even to study the inanimate collections, the curio-cupboards stacked with strange objects brought from overseas: minerals and manuscripts, but also dodo eggs and unicorn horns. Indeed, all over Europe such collections were being formed by the curious and wealthy, to indicate culture and status, or for reasons of genuine learning and scholarship. In England, the German-born court physician Sir Hans Sloane bequeathed his own extensive collection of artefacts, books and manuscripts to the nation of his adoptive country on condition that it be publicly displayed, thus laying the foundation for the British Museum and its library.

These objects, as well as the animals and the plants, documented a world that, though new discoveries continued to fill in the blanks on its map, yet grew ever more complex, and hence asked to be interpreted, to be understood. The new and the strange could either be explained as being superficially different, but essentially the same as European things, and thus they were controllable, not dangerous; or they were seen as radically different and consequently dangerous, a challenge to be met, a world to be conquered in order to remove the threat of its uncontrolled otherness.

The fact that some of these cultures, like the Chinese and the Japanese, appeared to be highly developed themselves, even according to the criteria posed by Europe, only increased the necessity to underline Europe's own identity as a Christian and hence superior civilization. How else could one justify the use of guns and cannon in the many attempts to conquer other cultures for the purpose of expanding Europe's economic and military power?

Only by maintaining that in their very essence every other civilization lagged behind that of Europe, which rejoiced in its superiority founded on Christianity and the classical world, only by believing and proclaiming that for that very reason every other culture contentedly had to accept European supremacy and its resulting economic and political dominance, could Europeans legitimize their efforts to establish the overseas colonies and empires that now became the first manifestations of the globalization process. Economically, politically, religiously and culturally, large parts of the non-European world were gradually incorporated into what slowly became a 'European world system'.

From this time on those Europeans who consciously thought about their own world, about Europe, would always be influenced by dreams of other worlds. For the first time, leaving the security of home in large numbers, Europeans were also forced to account for their deepest fears and desires, emotions which could not so easily be given free rein at home, if only because they had to preserve the relative stability of their own environment. What forms of culture did Europe want to preserve, defend and even disseminate, and at what cost? What new, 'foreign' things should Europeans try to understand and accept?

Those who had made the journey to the distant worlds, which now began to form Europe's horizon, developed an altered understanding of what was 'own' and what was 'other' and thus contributed to the development of European self-awareness. For example, in 1544, the cartographer Sebastian Münster proclaimed that Europe, although the smallest of the known continents – a fact which now could and had to be recognized – was yet the most fertile, the most densely populated and consequently the strongest.[54] The English divine Samuel Purchas, who took great pleasure in listening to the tales that seamen told on returning from their trips, was rather more articulate in the collection of travel stories he published in 1625. He wrote that 'The Qualitie of Europe exceeds her Quantitie, in this the least, in that the Best of the world'. After all:

> If I speake of Arts and Inventions (which are Man's properest goods, immortall Inheritance to our mortalitie) what have the rest of the world comparable? First the Liberall Arts are most liberall to us, having long since forsaken their Seminaries in Asia and Afrike, and here erected Colleges and Universities. And if one Athens in the east (the antient Europaean glory) now by Turkish Barbarisme be infected, how many Christian Athenses have wee in the west for it. As for Mechanicall Sciences, I could reckon . . . the many artificiall Mazes and Labyrinths in our watches, the great heavenly Orbes and motions installed in so small a model. What eares but European have heard so many Musicall Inventions for the Chamber, the Field, the Church?

This very revealing panegyric, which enumerates many phenomena even now considered by many to constitute Europe's unique cultural heritage, continues for several paragraphs, until Purchas poses the question:

> And is this all? Is Europe onely a fruitfull Field, a well watered garden, a pleasant Paradise in Nature? A continued Citie for habitation? Queene of the World for power? A Schoole of Arts Liberall, Shop of Mechanicall, Tents of Military, Arsenal of Weapons and Shipping?

Garden, paradise, city, the very locations of civilization, archetypal images that had been grafted onto Christian thought by the tales in the first books of the

Old Testament. What kind of culture blossomed there? Besides music and instrument making there were art, technology and commerce, all of them empowering elements in the widest sense. It is fascinating to see Purchas creating an almost essentialistic relationship between them. For him not only the arts and sciences, but also the nascent commercial–industrial society of Europe itself is a cultural phenomenon. It was a notion that slowly gained wider acceptance until, in the nineteenth century, it had become the very basis of Europe's self-esteem, in all cultural and scholarly circles.[55]

Purchas's question naturally required an answer, and he himself provided it, in equally enthusiastic prose:

> Nay, these are the least of Her praises, or His rather, who hath given Europe more than Eagle's wings, and lifted her up above the Starres . . . Europe is taught the way to scale Heaven, not by Mathematicall principles, but by Divine veritie. Jesus Christ is their way, their truth, their life; who hath long since given a Bill of Divorce to ingrateful Asia where hee was borne, and Africa the place of his flight and refuge, and is become almost wholly and onely Europaean.[56]

Once more, the Bible provided the historical arguments that served to belittle the significance of the other old continents. However, Purchas also explicitly noted that Europe had discovered and conquered the world: its cultural qualities are not restricted to its religion, political structures and military might, to its arts and sciences, but include its capacity for expansion. After all:

> Who ever tooke possession of the huge Ocean, and made procession round about the vast Earth? Who ever discovered new Constellations, saluted the Frozen Poles, subjected the Burning Zones?[57]

Here, indeed, Purchas touches upon an important point. For it has to be admitted that no civilization but that of Europe had ever undertaken such large-scale travel. The spirit of adventure and discovery and, consequently, the will to expand one's horizons and one's power, if not specifically European, yet seem to be characteristics that Europe, more than any other culture, could claim to have translated into real, and indeed, world-wide action. Or should one term them Christian characteristics? After all, Christianity was a religion that, as Purchas himself indicated, was conscious of the fact that its roots lay outside the region where it had gained dominion. Consequently, this religion almost forced its believers to travel, the more so as the Christian belief in a paradise on earth as well as in a promised land proved an additional, perhaps even more powerful stimulus to engage in travel, however perilous.

Not only did Europe's often discordant contacts with other parts of the world, and the resulting reflection, result in a broadening of the definition of that which was considered to constitute its essence. Also, many Europeans now began to contemplate Europe's failings and to consider how to remedy these. Significantly, from the late fifteenth century onwards, time and again plans were devised for the establishment of a better society. These plans offered an intriguing insight both into the reality and into the ideals of the period in which they were formulated. Mostly, they stressed four topics.

A happy society was nearly always presented as a city, an idea for which the Europeans certainly were indebted to the Greeks. It also implied the notion that nature, essentially uncontrollable, had to be tamed. In this city, healthcare was optimal: obviously, the fear of death played a crucial role in the European, Christian view of man. Also, education – of the middle class, the ruler, and the learned – is given high priority. Last but not least, prosperity is divided according to principles of justice. The fact that the opportunity to publish and distribute one's collected works is sometimes named as the fifth characteristic of these ideal societies betrays their origin in the minds of intellectuals and scholars who were concerned about their future reputation.[58]

Even though, of course, none of these ideal societies were ever realized, they did influence the European self-image. In consequence, reality, both in Europe but more often abroad, in regions that could still be dreamt of as unspoiled by the negative characteristics of society at home, was frequently envisaged and depicted as if it were already the ideal situation. Also, such ideals often influenced the political and social demands that individuals or groups made of reality, showing their dissatisfaction with it. Inevitably, these demands, if reiterated and forcefully voiced, did help to slowly change that reality.

The above process can be traced from the visions of man and society in Thomas More's *Utopia* (London 1516) and Tommaso Campanella's (1568–1639) *Città del Sole*, 'Sun City' (1603), via Johann Valentin Andreae and his 'Description of a Christian Republic' (Nuremberg 1619), to the German philosophers Leibniz and Herder in the eighteenth century, and to the 'utopian' socialists of England and France in the nineteenth century. One aspect is particularly striking. A utopia really needs a virgin land. Many of the early utopian thinkers did not locate the world of their dreams in their own world, or in the older world of fabulous Asia but in the newly discovered America, as yet untainted by civilization.

In retrospect, one can see the fifteenth and sixteenth centuries as a period of change. In many fields of culture, old values and systems slowly disappeared while, mainly because of the communications revolution in Europe itself, new norms and institutions were born. At the same time, improved education and the increasing dissemination of texts ensured that the notion of a wider world – Europe itself, but also the worlds beyond, both of them expressed both in the mind and on the map – filtered down to an ever larger readership. Through their contacts with these worlds, a more complete, and also more secular vision of the European self took shape.

The poet Philip Freneau, fed on the often superficial, for largely uninformed, cultural relativism that took root in intellectual circles in the Atlantic world in the latter decades of the eighteenth century, in his poem *The American Village* of 1772, described the world of North America as the place where:

Renowned sachems once their empire rais'd
On wholesome laws; and sacrifices blaz'd.
The gen'rous soul inspir'd the honest breast
And to be free, was doubly to be blest.

Obviously, this was too idealistic a representation of Indian society as a community of noble, free, self-governing men, reflecting a yearning for a life no longer possible in the civilized colonies of the east coast. However, in another poem called *The Rising Glory of America*, Freneau observed:

How much obscur'd is human nature here!
Shut from the light of science and of truth.[59]

Unavoidably, and despite his dream of a romantically simple society, he shows himself to be rooted in European values that, precisely in the eighteenth century, increasingly considered science to be the basic norm of truth and progress.

10 A new society

Migration, travel and the
diffusion and integration
of culture in Europe

Migration, travel and culture

People sometimes wonder whether travel and the ensuing encounter with
other cultures is, indeed, a factor of cultural integration. It is true that someone
who travels does move to locations where people live and behave according to
different norms, creating a different culture. But do not most travellers carry
only themselves, namely their own identity and their own prejudices which are,
consequently and sometimes even agreeably, confirmed by confrontation with
'the Other'? Often, travel does not seem to lead to positive interaction at all, let
alone integration.

Yet this chapter will try to establish that travelling outside Europe but,
increasingly and perhaps more importantly, also within Europe itself, did in fact
lead to cultural change. Not considering long periods of actual domination of
one language over another, it was precisely travel, especially commercial travel,
that continued to result in linguistic interchange, contributing words and ideas
to Europe's various languages. Spain, of course, had its hundreds of Arabic words
after 700 years of Islamic domination, and likewise England, through its far
shorter contacts with France. Italy absorbed a fair amount of Turkish words
through trade and, in the golden age of Dutch commercial and technical superiority, Dutch shipping terms entered many languages, including Russian.

Travel also resulted in greater knowledge about such fields as the geography,
economics, politics and the morals and customs of other regions, both for the
individual traveller but also, as a result of a cumulative process, within the groups
who were the main culture makers in the regional cultures of which Europe
was, in fact, comprised. Finally, travel was an important element in the formation
of a cosmopolitan culture which increasingly tied together the elites of the
various countries at a European level.

This process was, of course, not exclusively determined by the phenomenon
of travel. Other factors were the invention of printing and subsequent developments in education, which resulted in a slow but nevertheless important
diffusion of culture during the sixteenth century, as well as the new phenomenon
of correspondence networks and cultural periodicals that further promoted this
movement. After all, only knowledge and information enabled people to write
the books that, from the sixteenth century onwards, brought new ideas to an

expanding readership. But without travel and epistolary contacts, that knowledge and information would certainly not have been amassed on such a scale that would allow us to characterize the period from the early sixteenth century onwards as one of growing cultural complexity. Precisely through the interaction of partly traditional, partly new elements that now started functioning together, did cultural life in the centuries between *c.*1500 and 1800 acquire a peculiarly 'European' character.

Non-voluntary travel: the cultural significance of migrations

In view of the land-bound lives of the majority of Europeans, until the early nineteenth century most people travelled rarely, if at all. The few who did, certainly did not do so for motives of cultural communication. While considerable numbers of people from all kinds of social groups have always been forced to travel either professionally or, even, to migrate because of life-threatening circumstances, these two types of travel, though of unmistakable cultural significance for Europe, did not lead to conscious communication, to a growing feeling of solidarity, to a concept of 'Europe'. Moreover, we know little about the collective or individual experiences of the vast majority of the people who travelled, especially those who did so involuntarily, mainly because they rarely recorded their experiences. Thus, the lack of important sources for the study of past travel experiences and of the ensuing reflections – letters and travel reports[1] – inevitably impairs the picture.

Only one of the numerically large groups who travelled was not forced to do so: the groups of pilgrims, who seasonally or annually visited the innumerable locally venerated shrines and the few universally revered holy sites of the Christian world, among which Rome and Santiago de Compostela were the two outstanding destinations – Jerusalem being too far and too expensive for most. Mostly on foot, and recognizable by staff and scarf, the pilgrims travelled to the holy places. Both the pilgrims' manuals and such literary texts as Chaucer's *Canterbury Tales*, which was successful precisely because of its recognizable stories, give an often vivid picture of what pilgrim life was like.[2] People did not just go on pilgrimage whenever they felt the urge to do so, not least because the major pilgrimages were bound to the seasons, undertaken only after the cold of winter had disappeared and before the new snow made the passes in the Alps and the Pyrenees impassable again. But even within England, the weather determined pilgrimage. Famously, Chaucer begins his story with the words:

> Whan that Aprille with his shoures soote
> The droghte of March hat perced to the roote
> . . . Thanne longen folke to goon on pilgrimages
> And palmeres for to seken straunge strondes.[3]

The number of people who went on pilgrimage was huge. The figures for the period before the sixteenth century are frequently unreliable but, fortunately, in Rome, careful counting took place. Thus, in the Holy Year 1600, according to estimates, at least half a million pilgrims from all over Europe invaded a city that at that time had only 100,000 inhabitants itself. The atmosphere on these trips was less pious than one might perhaps expect: it was the atmosphere of an outing. For most pilgrims – except penitents sent on a punitive pilgrimage by secular or religious judges – experienced it as a unique moment in their life, the only sanctioned, long-lasting interruption of a routine which was, for the most part, determined by work and sleep.

We know little about the individual experiences of pilgrims. Most of them were illiterate, unable to put their impressions and emotions on paper. Thus, we do not know how they reacted to the people they met on the road, or to the villages and cities they walked through, to the different languages, eating habits and other forms of behaviour they experienced on the way. Yet, returning home, they must have been full of stories, some obviously even wild ones, for such is the traveller's condition. Quite likely these stories did influence those who had stayed home and, consequently, unconsciously altered their view of the world beyond the horizon. Quite likely they also confirmed existing prejudices.

It is difficult to determine what was the impact of the phenomenon of involuntary travel, of the wanderings of the many poor wretches who, compelled by all manner of economic and social misery, left hearth and home often for long periods of time, signing up as mercenaries in the new states' armies or swelling the crews of the big trading fleets.

From the sixteenth century onwards, in most European states both the military themselves and their lifestyle became distinctly international. Between the late sixteenth and the early nineteenth centuries, Spanish soldiers' letters from the period of the Eighty Years' War[4] and Dutch soldiers' letters written at the time of the Napoleonic campaigns[5] tell us a little about the harsh life of the army experienced by those who had been forced to leave their native soil, often never to return. Huge numbers were killed in battlefields where, as a result of their actions, the map of Europe was continually redrawn. Yet their records support the idea that while all this 'travelling' may have led to a growth of knowledge, it certainly did not result in large-scale mutual understanding, in any form of 'European thinking' *avant la lettre*.

It is equally difficult really to gauge the effects on the dissemination and integration of culture of the economically and socially vital group of itinerant workers, the fascinating phenomenon of the *fahrende Leute* (the travelling people), often large groups of tramps who frequently crossed state borders.[6] Also, although they did not travel in the strict sense of the word, it is certainly worth noting the large group of migrants who left their homes and moved around until, sometimes after long periods, they settled down again, either at home or, frequently, elsewhere. First and foremost among these were, of course, religious refugees, who were exiled or, for fear of persecution, 'voluntarily' abandoned their native soil to settle in more liberal climes. They brought their own culture, their own world of ideas and lifestyles. Often adapting themselves with difficulty, they still had to find a place in the new world of the receiving culture.

Of this kind of life, of course, the Jews have both the longest and easily the most painful story to tell. After the Romans had conquered Israel at the beginning of the Christian era, they had subdued various Jewish rebellions. In AD 69, during one such revolt, they destroyed Jerusalem. Many Jews then fled and settled around the Mediterranean as well as in central Europe. For centuries, they were forced to live marginal lives on the border of an increasingly Christian and, to them, increasingly hostile world. Whenever local or regional problems occurred, they were often treated as scapegoats, branded as magicians, murderers of Christ, and so on. Obviously, one of the underlying reasons for this attitude was jealousy of the prosperity of many Jews: Jewish bankers and merchants were often very visible in European economic life, to which they contributed greatly. Additional reasons were, precisely, their otherness in such forms of culture as religion and language.

For a long time, in the Islamic world of the Iberian peninsula their lot had been relatively easy. However, after the Christians reconquered Spain, and the Spanish kings started to create a unified, homogeneous state, also in the religious-cultural sense, hundreds of thousands of Jews were expelled in the late sixteenth century.[7] Later, large groups felt forced to migrate from the states of eastern Europe to safer areas because of the bloody persecutions or pogroms that they faced there – a phenomenon that went on for several centuries until well into the nineteenth century. Moving, and moving again, or being moved, in their new worlds the Jews often lived in more or less official ghettos, which, if anything, limited their cultural influence. Yet there was a certain dialogue with the mainstream Christian culture, especially in the scholarly world.[8] The mysticism of the Jewish Kabbala as well as Jewish theological speculation within the rabbinical tradition inspired many Christian scientists and scholars until the nineteenth century. Moreover, discussing Hebrew and the other languages relating to the Bible contributed to the revival of European interest in the cultures of the Near East since the sixteenth century.

Another example of religious refugees are the Protestant Waldensians and Huguenots, who, as a result of the centralizing religious policy of Louis XIV as well as of their obvious economic power, were forced to flee France and north-west Italy in the last decades of the seventeenth century and to settle elsewhere. The French Protestants mainly sought refuge in the German states, the Dutch Republic and in England.[9] They gave an economic and technological boost to the budding manufacturing industry in all these countries, as had the Jews;[10] specifically the Huguenot intellectuals contributed to the growing influence of 'French' culture in many European cities, despite the fact that the horrific stories about the tragic lot of the Huguenots and Waldensians frequently fed the hostile vision of France that already existed all over western Europe because of Louis XIV's aggressive foreign policy.

Three types of cultural travel

Though the majority of Europeans who moved around, who travelled, even, did not do so from any conscious wish to broaden their cultural horizon, there were groups who did have this aim. Mostly, they came from Europe's literate population, who were in a position to actually communicate with their foreign surroundings. The question is, which group's cultures thus gained a more international character and gave Europe a more marked cultural unity?

Given the need for a certain economic background and the social and cultural preconditions of education, such travel by and large was limited to the land-owning aristocracy, the urban patriciate and the affluent upper-middle class. Consequently, travel in these centuries was principally, although not exclusively, an elite phenomenon which, if only for that reason, cannot be compared with the mass tourism that only started with the creation of mass transport in the late nineteenth century. Because of the elite background of most travellers, their experience initially contributed to the formation, consolidation and change of culture only within the elite.

The business trip: merchants and bankers

From days of old, business trips by merchants who operated on a European scale had been important. Even before Roman times, there had been trans-European trade contacts. In the period from the fourth to the seventh centuries of the Christian era – tumultuous centuries which saw mass migration, population decline, economic malaise and political crisis – commercial travel decreased considerably. However, as a result of the economic policies of the Carolingian rulers, from the eighth century onwards a revival set in which, with interruptions, lasted until the demographic-economic crisis of the fourteenth century.

In the fifteenth century, Europe's economic activity substantially intensified. Until then, leaving aside exceptions such as the Hanseatic network and transalpine and Mediterranean commerce, trade and industry had often been orientated locally. Now national and even international trade began to develop, soon stimulated by increased contacts with Asia, America and, finally, Africa. However, as had been the case for thousands of years, even now such contacts were often maintained not by a single person travelling over long distances but through a chain of merchants, each of whom travelled only regionally.

Yet the extent to which merchants contributed to a change in European culture is shown by the large number of travel guides published specifically to cater for the new needs of this group by printers keen to serve this market; one study counted almost 1,000 different titles for the period between 1500 and 1600.[11] These guides were mainly of a very practical nature. They outlined the most accessible and safest travel routes, but also gave information about local and regional currencies, which, because of their huge variety, necessitated conversion tables. Useful advice concerning market times and reasonable hotels was given as well. Some guides even contained short vocabularies to help people

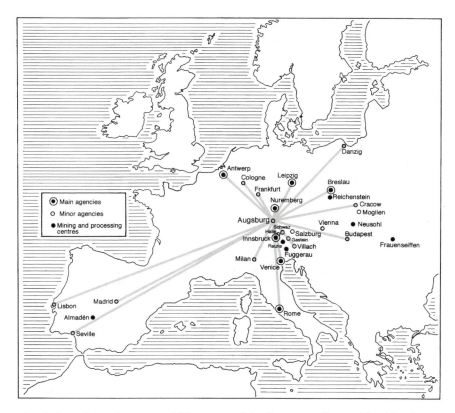

Map 6 Agencies and commercial interests of the Fugger trading and banking house, *c.*1500

make themselves understood in the various European languages.[12] Yet even though these guides greatly facilitated travel and communication, they also emphasized that elsewhere everything was different.

In this commercial world, so much larger than the agrarian world of the farming population, one meets the agents of the international trade and banking house of the Fugger family, the backers of the Emperor Charles V (1500–57), the first ruler since Charlemagne to operate on a really supranational scale. In their turn, the Fuggers and their clerks operated supra-nationally as well, using a network of offices that stretched from Warsaw to Lisbon, from Rome to Antwerp. Their outlook too became international. In their letters, national borders seem to fade and an awareness emerges of, at least, common economic problems, of factors that determined the growing global trade.[13] The big entrepreneurs and their travelling staff certainly operated and, hence, thought in 'European' terms.

Yet the question remains to what extent this sense of growing economic interdependence and unity also influenced other aspects of their world-view?

Plate 17 Trade and travel: Jacob Fugger, the Augsburg banker, and his chief accountant, Matthäus Schwarz, depicted in the Fuggers' headquarters with the filing cupboard labelled with the various branch offices that formed the Fugger empire, and between which the Fugger 'factors' journeyed to conduct their variegated business. From a coloured drawing dated 1516.

Source: Centre for Art Historical Documentation, Nijmegen, the Netherlands

Once more, their letters give us a clue. Besides the 'German' Fuggers and Welsers, there were other merchants and financiers working on a European scale, such as the Portinari and Della Faille, who hailed from Italy but soon established themselves in the new economic centre of Europe, the southern Netherlands, as well as the Burlamacchi, who came from Lucca to Amsterdam, but also Portuguese Jews like the Suassos. In their correspondence, these entrepreneurs show that they were thoroughly abreast of the cultural peculiarities of Europe's different trading regions. This certainly helped them to put the interests of states and their small political problems in their proper perspective.

Obviously, the growth of a more cosmopolitan, 'European' vision in these circles also depended on their level of education. Also, it was certainly stimulated by the frequent practice of sending abroad the younger members of the family firm – for this remained the basic organizational unit. By staying with foreign business relations, they not only learnt the basics of their trade, they also acquired a sense of what was different in the international economy. In his youth, Heinrich Floris Schopenhauer (1747–1805), father of the famous philosopher Arthur Schopenhauer and himself descended from a dynasty of Danzig wholesalers as well as the son of a Dutch merchant's daughter, spent several years in France and England. On his return, he accustomed himself to reading *The Times* every day. His library contained the works of French writers like Rousseau and Voltaire. Schopenhauer's wife, Johanna Trosiener – whom, nineteen years his junior, he had married in 1758 – had grown up in the same culture and spoke both English and French. Her most trusted friend was a Scottish doctor practising in Danzig.[14] In such cosmopolitan mercantile circles, which existed from Gothenburg to Seville, from Amsterdam to Narva, some sort of 'European' thinking was indeed normal.

The diplomatic trip: ambassadors and politicians

Of course, another group who travelled extensively were diplomats. They were a fairly new group, for ambassadorial diplomacy was developed as a system in the fifteenth and sixteenth centuries, in consequence of the rise of national states which, to retain their independence, had to constantly negotiate with one another. Diplomats were also a much larger group than nowadays, mainly because to uphold the honour of their nation, the ambassadors in the various European capitals usually kept a retinue of dozens, and on special occasions even hundreds of people, ranging from a suite of noblemen to a host of servants. Consequently, their significance for the 'Europeanization' of Europe certainly was as great as that of the merchants.

Moreover, the European royal courts, where these diplomats were accredited, were by their very nature the pre-eminent locations where culture was expressed in many ways. As a result of alliances between the various royal houses, courts were, by definition, the milieu where at least two, and often more, 'national' cultures continually mixed; perhaps it would be more appropriate to speak of 'regional' cultures in this period, during which nations were only slowly starting to take shape.

At first, contacts between 'Italy' – or rather, the Italian states – and France became frequent. Partly as a result of the struggle for power over the Italian peninsula between the French kings and the Habsburg rulers of Spain and Austria, in the sixteenth century people from France often travelled there. In the process, the diplomatic relations with the Italian courts became cultural relations, too, and resulted in a perceptible change of, specifically, French court culture. In the wake of, among others, Maria de Medici, daughter of the Florentine banking family turned dukes who, decked with gold, was married to the heir of France, Italian customs reached the French court at the end of the century. Many Frenchmen quickly found fault with this preposterous foreign culture, if only because it presented itself as superior. At the same time, however, they adjusted to it, in the visual arts, in science, in music, in food, in table manners; in short, in all expressions of elite culture.

Several decades later, in the retinue of Henrietta Maria of Bourbon, 'daughter of France', who had been given in marriage to Charles I of England, French culture travelled to the capital of the island kingdom. The famous diarist and chronicler of London life, Samuel Pepys (1633–1703), noted both its pleasant and to some, though not to him, its less attractive aspects: French influences on drama and music and even on food, but also on sexual mores.[15]

The presence of large contingents of diplomatic actors and spectators on these royal stages further increased the international and cosmopolitan character of these courts. In most European countries, the elite began to feel their education was not complete unless they had travelled on a diplomatic mission at least once in their life, preferably at an early age. The instructions set up for the education of royal children and young members of the aristocracy soon described such journeys as a necessity.[16]

Through this type of travel, a relatively large part of each nation's future leadership came into contact with various aspects of a number of foreign court cultures. Norms, ways of behaving and other cultural expressions were observed abroad and subsequently, consciously or unconsciously, adopted, if, that is, they were sufficiently attractive and dominant. In the late sixteenth and early seventeenth centuries this meant a growing ascendancy of what one might term the 'soft power' of, first, Italian and, later, Spanish culture in Europe's higher circles. In 1637, the imperial ambassador Johann Fürst Eggenbergh, who travelled from Vienna to Rome to offer Pope Urban VIII the obedience of his master, the newly elected 'King of the Romans' Ferdinand III, was received in regal fashion. The city and the papal court still considered themselves the trend-setters and arbiters of culture which, it went without saying – and thus usually remained unsaid – was to be understood as both Christian and European.

We do not know which of his Roman experiences impressed Eggenbergh most. However, undeniably the banquets that Francesco Cardinal Barberini, secretary of state and cardinal-nephew to the reigning pope, and many other high-placed inhabitants of Rome offered their guest were in the most luxurious and fashionable taste. Table culture at Italian courts was an important cultural element *tout court*. The 'ingredients' of this culinary culture – presentation, table etiquette and the food itself – were both native, Spanish and international.[17]

Soon, north of the Alps, civilized people felt that they had not yet reached the same degree of refinement. In a process comparable with what had happened through the Italo-French connection, in the wake of ambassadors like Eggenbergh the Italian norm, naturally experienced as Roman by the Romans, was slowly imposed on northern Europe. Continuing the influence of the Renaissance, dance and diet, fashion and music, literary and artistic conventions, all these cultural forms 'travelled' in the wake of diplomats. Consequently, during the sixteenth century the Italian example remained the European norm in many areas of culture.

However, in the second half of the seventeenth century, French court culture became the dominant one in Europe, and remained so until the end of the eighteenth century, for the simple reason that France had developed into Europe's most powerful state, both economically and politically. The French king was the embodiment of this power. In particular, Louis XIV, who ruled during the greater part of the century's second half, tried to emphasize and enhance his prestige through a sophisticated propaganda policy. Its central instrument was his court, which became a 'theatre of power', where everything was 'conspicuous consumption' in the prince's service.[18]

To realize his goal, Louis willed the palace of Versailles, a new creation, far from Paris, the cramped and politically troublesome capital.[19] The finished building was a veritable little town, containing hundreds of rooms and galleries and vestibules, where some 5–6,000 persons lived, from servants to France's most exalted nobles. In the state rooms, the curtains and the tapestries covering walls and furniture were changed twice a year: in winter, green and red velvet were used; in summer, silk embroidered with gold and silver.

The palace had two nuclei. First, the great *Gallerie des Glaces*, where seventeen huge mirrors covered the walls, each of them worked on by several artisans for many years. On the ceiling, the frescos represented Louis's military triumphs and the glory of France: it was the room where the king received the representatives of his foreign rivals, and where he fêted his court. The second centre was the royal bedroom. There, on a dais, stood the splendidly canopied royal bed where each royal day began and ended with the elaborate ritual of the *lever* and the *coucher du roi*. Each morning, France's most illustrious nobles assembled around Louis's bed to watch His Majesty rise. A happy few of the princes and dukes were chosen to help the king take off his night shirt and then some hundred people were allowed in to watch while another select group assisted the royal dressing. One by one they reverently handed the king his clothes: shirt, breeches, socks, shoes, rapier, mantle, feathered hat and so on. These ceremonies were called the 'little' and the 'grand' *lever*. People fought for the honour to be present. Huge bribes were given to be included in the group who handled the royal garments. At night, the entire ritual was repeated in reverse order. Between these two moments, the king's day ran according to an iron routine, described by the Duke of St Simon, one of the inner circle of court nobles, as 'the machine of Versailles', referring to the world of the theatre where increasingly clever stage machinery produced the effects desired by contemporary playwrights to bring the wonders of the world to the stage![20]

At each and every daily act of the king, tens or even hundreds of nobles and commoners were present: as he went to chapel, walked in the gardens that extended the architecture of the palace into the countryside, took his dinner, played at cards, or, to round of evening entertainments, danced – Louis was often the centre of great ballets and operas set to stately music by such composers as Jean-Baptiste Lully, which celebrated him as the 'Sun King'.[21] On the splendid stage of his palace, the king acted as a demi-god, whose most simple action was presented as of extraordinary significance. That, of course, was the very aim of this 'theatre of the state': the noble courtiers, the humble servants, the haughty foreign diplomats, all of them had to be impressed, to be persuaded that this king's power was absolute, that everything depended on him. To the untrained eye this was, indeed, the case: the king dispensed the most influential functions in government, the top military posts, the most lucrative bishoprics. Through royal favour, a person could reach the peaks of power. Incurring royal disgrace meant, to many, that life became lacklustre, not to say useless.

The French example was followed all over Europe. Every prince wanted a palace as splendid as Versailles, a court as magnificent as the one that displayed itself there; the cities and countryside of Germany which, at that time, was still divided into tens of dozens of small states, even now afford many examples of the beautiful but, of course, costly results of this desire for emulation. Indeed, below the level of European royals, in one way or another, all European nobles strove to emulate this French culture, too: in England and Poland, in Sweden and Spain they started building country palaces and town mansions after the French manner, filled them with treasures after the French example, dressed according to the fashions dictated by France, ate what and as was prescribed in the manuals produced by the French cuisiniers.[22] They even behaved as the French nobles did, aping the intricate court manners of Versailles, in the way they walked, waved their hands, bowed their heads, and so on. French was the fashion in everything, even in pornography and whoring.

Consequently, whether people visited the palaces of the rulers in the German states or the luxurious residences of the nobility in Swedish Skåne or in Austrian Styria, the signs of French culture were everywhere, partly as a result of the owners' experience while on diplomatic missions. However, even in an essentially non-noble, middle-class society like that of The Hague in the seventeenth century, Dutch culture was also heavily influenced by French examples, if only because of the influence of the diplomatic, largely aristocratic milieu on the local bourgeois elite.[23]

In short, during these centuries, elite culture slowly changed. First, interaction between the Christian values which the Church had proclaimed as universal since the eighth century, and the even older regional or popular cultures of Europe had resulted in the birth of 'national' elite cultures from the ninth and tenth centuries onwards. Since the fifteenth century, as a result of contacts with the courts in Italy and with French culture – that is, the culture of the French kings – these national cultures, while retaining their own character, yet acquired a more 'European' aspect as well. Reading the travel notes of that fascinating eighteenth-century Englishwoman, Lady Mary Wortley Montagu, it is obvious how easily this diplomat's wife moved among her class and kind when travelling around Italy and France.[24] In short, travellers, though always belonging to a specific national elite, quickly felt at home in their own circle elsewhere in Europe.

Yet another factor played an important role in the development of this cosmopolitan court culture. Due to the invention of printing, those who travelled only through the pages of their books could read all manner of reports about court life, first oriented mainly towards Italy and Spain and subsequently towards France. Particularly influential was the idealized picture of court culture given in novels such as Honoré d'Urfé's *L'Astrée* (1627) or Madame de la Fayette's *La Princesse de Clèves* (1678), the latter a moving and, to many aristocrats – especially aristocratic women – a recognizable psychological sketch of a woman's struggle between passion and reason that resulted from the stifling norms imposed by court society on its members. Indeed, in the seventeenth century, a flourishing and intriguing genre of what can be called 'court novels' developed, often of as little literary value as the sentimental novelettes of our own time yet certainly of great significance for the development of new norms, behaviour and expectations among their aristocratic and other readers.

The educational trip: students, scholars and artists

Undoubtedly, the contribution by the third group of cultural travellers, consisting of students, scholars and artists was the most important to the formation and transmission of a culture that, in the process, transcended its regional or national origins and became European. In so far as this group embodied culture in the written and printed word or in visual representation, their work had an important communicative function, far more penetrating than can be imagined now that electronic mass communication creates so many images that their impact is sometimes negligible.

Obviously, it would be a mistake to think the travels of this group had a less directly professional character than those of merchants and diplomats – that their travel was anchored in the ideal world of 'culture'. For many – a considerable number of the students and besides them the scholars and the artists – the world of high culture was also or would be their professional world. Theirs was the world of printed texts that would bring them jobs in education, in bookselling or with publishing firms, or in the world of art, in which the printed word, the 'theory' and the 'explanation' of the artistic product, played an increasingly important role in the reception and understanding of its visual message.

More than any of the above-mentioned groups, this group was the product of systems of education, as well as of a scholarship and a science whose basic characteristics were 'European'. These systems had their centres of excellence: certain universities, for example, Bologna, Heidelberg, Leiden, Orleans, Oxford, Paris and Salamanca enjoyed European fame, while others had a more limited but still respectable supraregional attraction.

Depending on their place of origin and their financial possibilities, students for whom a good education was a career necessity or a sociocultural requirement, travelled to the nearest or to the most famous academies. Thus, Swedes went to Heidelberg, Leiden or Utrecht if they were not happy with Abo, Lund or Uppsala. The Dutch, depending on their religious background, travelled either to the Catholic universities of Louvain or Orleans, or to Protestant Heidelberg, Geneva or Saumur.[25] The French travelled to Pisa or Bologna. Young Greeks from the Orthodox east flocked to the famous academy at Padua, the university of Venice, before taking up positions in the formerly Christian parts of the Ottoman Empire, or even in the Ottoman imperial bureaucracy. Thus, Padua, from the sixteenth to the eighteenth centuries, became the gateway to western learning for the south-eastern periphery of Europe. Bohemian students, 90 per cent of whom came from the urban middle class, sought places at academies all over the German 'Reich' as well as in Switzerland. Of the latter, we also know how old they were the moment they set off on their international journeys: usually 12 or 13 years of age.[26] This serves to remind us that the notions of 'child' and 'adolescent', in so far as they existed at the time, were interpreted quite differently and, inevitably, were experienced differently as well, both emotionally and even physically and biologically. Not until the eighteenth century did the age at which most people in Europe started their university study reach the present-day 'norm' of 18.[27]

Established scholars travelled the same roads as their students. Then, as now, state borders were of less importance to them, although religious differences sometimes imposed limits on their choice of destination. Basically, they would follow the call of lucrative salaries, accept prestigious professorships at famous universities or take up promises of challenging research possibilities.

In this way, the so-called *peregrinatio academica* (academic pilgrimage) became a permanent part of university education, at least for those students who could afford it. Many Dutch students – future government servants, doctors, lawyers, church ministers and university professors – followed a 'German route' or a 'French route', respectively, to study abroad for a shorter or longer period, while, conversely, between 1575 and 1814 some 5,000 foreigners from all over Europe flocked to the Dutch Republic, usually opting to study medicine or law.[28]

The value of studying abroad was impressed on everyone as early as the first decades of the sixteenth century, when Erasmus wrote about it. However, the most influential text in this field was a much-read and translated one by the Flemish humanist Justus Lipsius (1547–1606). In his *Epistolarum . . . centurio prima*, a 'collection of hundred letters' published in Antwerp in 1586, he made an impassioned as well as a practical plea for the academic journey. Lipsius's text, which went through many editions until well into the eighteenth century, greatly influenced educated Europeans through the way it stressed travel as one of the most important elements in the development of human knowledge and understanding, the way to a truly civilized life and behaviour – incidentally, this was the very reason why Lipsius's contemporary, King Philip II of Spain, fearing his subjects might get the wrong ideas, forbade Spanish students to travel abroad at all. It also emphasized the significance of Italy as the cradle of civilization. Lipsius did, of course, refer only to men. Girls, if they travelled at all, did so only to accompany their husband or father as his wife or daughter.

Besides Lipsius's treatise, other manuals soon appeared which gave more detailed information about academic travel for specific career preparations. Thus, there were travel guides specifically for lawyers and doctors, both for those who were still studying and for who were already established.[29]

Artists had comparable reasons for travelling though: for the completion of their training, they did not attend university but rather sought out the studios of famous colleagues or enrolled in professional academies. Mostly, they combined this with a visit to old and new monuments, sketchbook in hand. Just like the students, their travels almost always brought them to Italy, which, until late in the eighteenth century, was seen as Europe's most authoritative artistic centre. After they had finally succeeded in making a name for themselves, many artists would have acquired the same attitude as many scholars: they did not necessarily feel deeply about their 'national' culture anymore. They took up home where their clients lived, at the royal courts in the capital cities of the various European states or at the mansions of the great aristocrats who wanted to express their power and status through artistic patronage.

Thus, from the early sixteenth century onwards, painters travelled from Antwerp and Bruges, from Haarlem and Utrecht, to Italy, to Rome, where they sold their work to cardinals and curia officials – incidentally introducing perspective into the budding realism of Renaissance Italian landscape painting. On the other hand, they learned from Italy as well, especially from its by now long tradition of anatomically correct representations of the human body: in this respect, the quality of Albrecht Dürer's painting differed considerably before and after his stay in Italy. For some artists, travelling became a cultural must, for others a professional necessity. In 1521, the famous Dutch master Jan van Scorel even travelled to Jerusalem, afterwards representing his idealized impressions of the Holy Land in his paintings. In the same century, choristers and other musicians travelled from Burgundy and Flanders to the courts in Munich and Burgos, in Venice and Krakow, in Mantua, Florence and Rome, to sing in royal or papal chapels for which they composed their masses and madrigals. Some would stay for only a year, others for the rest of their lives, as can be shown from the example of Roland de Lattre (1532–94).

As a 12-year-old chorister, the young Roland, born in Bergen, or Mons in the Low Countries, accompanied the newly appointed viceroy of Spanish Sicily to his court at Naples and Palermo. Soon, he was known as Orlando di Lasso. At the age of 20, he became the choirmaster of the cathedral of St John Lateran in Rome. Subsequently, he worked in Antwerp where the publisher Tilman Susato saw that money could be made from his music. Its publication made Lasso famous all over Europe. In 1556, he left for the ducal court of Bavaria at Munich, where he first became a singer and, after eight years, Master of the Duke's Music. To hire other singers he travelled to the Netherlands again, and also visited Italy once more. The pope knighted him and the Bavarian duke raised him to the nobility.

In their turn, painters and other artists from Italy travelled northwards. In the sixteenth century, the Florentines Leonardo da Vinci and Benvenuto Cellini went to the court of François I of France at Fontainebleau, the one to paint, the other to make his astonishing pieces of silverwork. In the seventeenth century, the Roman architect-sculptor Gianlorenzo Bernini temporarily established himself in Paris in order to design palaces and statues that tickled the vanity of Louis XIV. In the eighteenth century, the Venetian Giovanni Battista Tiepolo worked for the prince-bishop of Würzburg's 'Residenz'. Many of his compatriots found employment in the creation and decoration of the sumptuous churches and monasteries which, to spread the message of counter-reformation Catholicism, began to adorn the towns and the countryside of southern Germany. However, they were soon supplanted by immensely talented – but often Italian-trained – native artists, such as the painter-sculptor Assam brothers and the five architects from the Dientzenhofer family, who built cathedrals, abbeys and palaces all over Franconia and Moravia.[30]

In the same period, generations of Italian architects erected the golden towers that rose against the steely blue sky of the new tsarist capital, St Petersburg. Meanwhile, in the London opera houses Italian sopranos, tenors and castratos sang the virtuoso arias of Georg Friedrich Handel (1685–1759), English court composer of German origin. They were arias written in a style Handel had made his own during his stay in Italy where, for several years, he had been employed by Italian aristocrats. In the same years, two of Handel's colleagues and contemporaries, the Italian composers Domenico and Giovanni Locatelli (who were unrelated) crisscrossed central Europe, seeking and finding employment at various German courts, both Catholic and Protestant, and even in Russia. The former ended his career in Kassel, the latter in Moscow. The great Johann Sebastian Bach (1685–1750) moved around, too, composing his cantatas for the services in Leipzig's St Thomas Church, but producing his six 'Brandenburg Concertos' for the electoral court at Ansbach. His numerous musical sons and other relatives found employment all over Germany.

And, finally, Mozart (1756–91) – as a boy, Wolfgang Amadeus was toured all around Europe by a proud but also money-conscious father, performing in Paris, London and The Hague. And while he began his career as court composer to the prince-archbishop of Salzburg, he went on to Vienna to make a name for himself in the imperial service as well as providing compositions to the great aristocrats of the Habsburg states. For the coronation of Leopold II in 1791, he travelled to Prague, where his beautiful opera *La Clemenza di Tito*, praising the new emperor's forgiveness of his enemies, paid witness to the influence not only of Italian musical style but also to the impact of classical themes on contemporary political propaganda-through-music.

A particularly good example of the phenomenon of the growing exchange of cultural forms and ideas is seventeenth-century Sweden. In the 1640s, Magnus Gabriel de la Gardie, favourite of Queen Christina and later chancellor of the realm, undertook several ambassadorial trips to the Dutch Republic and France. He subsequently arranged for Swedish nobles and artists to study there. Thus, David Klocker Ehrenstrahl, after having studied in the Netherlands and having married a Dutch woman, became the foremost painter of the Swedish baroque, decorating, for example, the ceiling of the new-built, classically styled Riddarhus in Stockholm with a painting of Svea, the goddess allegorically representing this proud nation. Foreign artists and scholars, too, were offered attractive conditions by De la Gardie to establish themselves in Sweden, at court or at the universities of Uppsala and Lund, which he patronized generously, also enriching their libraries with foreign acquisitions.

His colleague and competitor in the kingdom's government, Carl-Gustav Wrangel, a war commander who had become immensely wealthy as a result of the Swedish conquests on the eastern shores of the Baltic, tried to outdo him in building sumptuous dwellings, which he then filled with works of art confiscated on his military campaigns in imperial Germany – or buying them from all over Europe through a network of specialized agents. His Renaissance dream palace of Skokloster, a classically symmetrical structure in glistening white stone, was the jewel box for his magnificent collection. He also formed a splendid library there. In consequence of the patronage of such magnates, in a few decades Swedish culture began to show a humanist Renaissance face, with obvious Dutch and French features especially in architecture and interior decoration.[31]

Business trips, diplomatic trips, educational trips – were three types of travel which not infrequently occurred in complicated combinations.[32] Businessmen were often asked to carry out diplomatic missions as did, occasionally, artists like the famous Flemish painter Peter-Paul Rubens who was sent to England by his Spanish masters. Young members of the nobility or the sons of wealthy middle-class citizens regularly combined a trip as a member of an ambassador's retinue with a period of study at one or more universities and a visit to the most important sights.[33]

During the seventeenth and eighteenth centuries, the combination of the diplomatic and educational trip developed into a phenomenon that from then on became something of a European cultural constant: the so-called 'Grand Tour'.[34] This was understood as a grand trip if only because it was meant to influence the education of the European elite in a cosmopolitan-cultural sense. But it was also a trip that, certainly when seen from a north-west European perspective, was grand because it had to include Italy and in the seventeenth and eighteenth centuries often France as well. Indeed, for most Europeans, the 'Grand Tour' was characterized by a clear southerly gravitation. It was based on an 'Italy feeling'[35] that, until the eighteenth century, seems to have existed among most cultured Europeans, including the French, despite their growing cultural chauvinism.[36] This emotion, a *Drang nach dem Süden*, and soon a 'Mediterranean passion',[37] has in different guises continued to direct European travel until our own times.

Significantly, travel in the northern direction was far less frequent. Admittedly, the Italians and French journeyed to those bleak regions when the occasion arose, with the Dutch Republic being among their principal destinations.[38] In the seventeenth century, its policy of tolerance, driven by financial pragmatism and fundamental principle, had made the country a European centre of education, science and publishing. For the same reasons the northern Netherlands held an irresistible attraction for people in central and eastern Europe. After the Dutch Republic, England and the German states were good second choices for those who came from the south and east. And yet, though sufficient quantitative data are lacking, the impression remains that, generally, the south–north movement was far less important than the north–south movement.

Of course, this is not really surprising. After all, the roots of both classical civilization and Christianity, the two components of the cultural tradition that Europe's elite cherished most, were found in Italy. Moreover, while the material manifestations of that glorious past could be admired in Rome's ruins, the more recent cultural products inspired by it could be seen in the contemporary city. Soon, both the classical and the modern monuments and Rome's, or Italy's, other artistic expressions were considered a collective heritage that people, after

having partaken of it, wanted to recreate at home in order to continue that
tradition.

ROME, WINTER 1644–5: JOHN EVELYN VISITS THE ETERNAL
CITY

In May 1641, John Evelyn (1620–1706), a young Englishman from a comfortable background and with a somewhat lazy, pleasure-loving and yet inquisitive
disposition, set out on a journey through Europe that was to last for nearly nine
years, bringing him to the Netherlands, Germany, Italy, Spain and France, before
he returned to England and settled down to a long life mainly devoted to leisure
and amateur scholarship as well as to gardening. He has left an extensive and
delightful diary covering the larger part of his life and affording precious insights
both into his way of thinking and into the culture of his time.

The following selections tell of his visit to Rome and illustrate some of the
characteristics of travel, of daily life in an urban context, of the position of Jews,
besides the extent of a cultured visitor's interest in what to most Europeans
was still the 'Eternal City'.

I came to Rome on the fourth of November 1644, about five at night . . .
November 6, I began to be very pragmatic. In the first place, our sights-man (for
so they name certain persons here who get their living by leading strangers around
to see the city) went to the Palace Farnese, a magnificent square structure, built by
Michel Angelo, of the three orders of columns after the ancient manner, and when
architecture was but newly recovered from the Gothic barbarity.

[. . . eighth November] We visited the Jesuits' church, the front whereof
is esteemed a noble piece of architecture, the design of Jacomo della Porta and
the famous Vignola. In this church lies the body of their renowned Ignatius
Loyola, an arm of Xaverius, their other Apostle; and, at the right end of their high
altar, their champion, Cardinal Bellarmine. Here Father Kircher (professor of
Mathematics and the oriental tongues) showed us many singular courtesies, leading us into their refectory, dispensatory, laboratory, gardens, and, finally (through
a hall hung round with pictures of such of their order as had been executed
for their pragmatical and busy adventures) into his own study, where, with Dutch
patience [to Englishmen, Dutch and German were and often still are the same],
he showed us his perpetual motions, catoptrics, magnetical experiments, models,
and a thousand other crotchets and devices, most of them since published by
himself.

[. . . nineteenth November] I visited St. Peter's, that most stupendous and
incomparable Basilica, far surpassing anything now extant in the world, and perhaps,
Solomon's Temple excepted, any that was ever built.

[. . . 21st November] I was carried to see a great virtuoso, Cavaliere Pozzo, who
showed us a rare collection of all kind of antiquities, and a choice library, over
which are the effigies of most of our late men of polite literature. He had a great
collection of the antique basso-relievos about Rome, which this curious man had
caused to be designed in several folios.

[. . .fifteenth January] The *zitelle*, or young wenches, which are to have portions given to them by the Pope, being poor, and to marry them, walked in procession to St. Peter's, where the Veronica [i.e. the cloth with the imprint of Christ's face] was showed.

I went to the Ghetto, where the Jews dwell as in a suburb by themselves; being invited by a Jew of my acquaintance to see a circumcision. I passed by the Piazza Judea, where their seraglio begins; for, being environed with walls, they are locked up every night.

[. . . eighteenth January] From thence, through a very long gallery (longer, I think, than the French Kings' at the Louvre), but only of bare walls, we were brought into the Vatican Library. This passage now was full of poor people, to each of whom, in his passage to St. Peter's, the Pope gave a mezzo grosso. I believe they were in number near 1500 or 2000 persons. This library is the most nobly built, furnished, and beautified of any in the world; ample, stately, light and cheerful, looking into a most pleasant garden. . . . The largest room is 100 paces long; at the end is the gallery of printed books; then the gallery of the Duke of Urbino's library, in which MSS. of remarkable miniature, and divers China, Mexican, Samaritan, Abyssinian, and other oriental books.

[. . . After a trip to Naples] Thus, about the seventh of February, we set out on our return to Rome by the same way we came, not daring to adventure by sea, as some of our company were inclined to do, for fear of Turkish pirates hovering on that coast.

[. . .] On the thirteenth of February, we were again invited to Signor Angeloni's study, where with greater leisure we surveyed the rarities, as his cabinet and medals especially, esteemed one of the best collections of them in Europe. He showed us two antique lamps, one of them dedicated to Pallas, the other Laribus Sacrum, as appeared by their inscriptions; some old Roman rings and keys; the Egyptian Isis, cast in iron; sundry rare basso-relievos; good pieces of painting, principally the Christ of Correggio, with the painter's own face admirably done by himself, divers of both the Bassanos; a great number of pieces by Titian.

[. . .] The next day, we went to the once famous Circus Caracalla, in the midst of which there now lay prostrate one of the most stately and ancient obelisks, full of Egyptian hieroglyphics. It was broken into four pieces, when overthrown by the Barbarians, and would have been purchased and transported into England by the magnificent Thomas Earl of Arundel, could it have been well removed to the sea. This is since set together and placed on the stupendous artificial rock made by Innocent X, and serving for a fountain in Piazza Navona, the work of Bernini, the Pope's architect . . . Hence, to a small oratory, named *Domine, quo vadis?*, where the tradition is, that our Blessed Saviour met St. Peter as he fled, and turned him back again.[39]

All over Europe, the impressions gained on the Grand Tour led to a creative interaction between well-travelled clients and well-travelled or travelling artists, so that churches, palaces, country and town houses were built and paintings and sculptures were created according to aesthetic principles accepted in the whole of Europe. All this culture – paintings and buildings, but also literary and scientific works and music – referred to the 'universal', classical and Christian values, yet they increasingly contained a double reference: they also sang the praises of the excellence of their own state and nation, of the men who commissioned and the men who executed them. Consequently, while a general 'style' now developed that was immediately recognizable everywhere in Europe, it also showed national varieties.

In addition to business trips, diplomatic trips and educational trips, was there also a fourth type that we could simply call 'tourism', travel for the sake of travelling and sightseeing, for the sake of experiences without an ulterior, 'higher' motive? There certainly was. Beginning in the seventeenth century but especially during the eighteenth century, people influenced by a new, more positive, perhaps even 'romantic' perception of nature, started going on pleasure trips. However, as opposed to the trips mentioned earlier, these rarely went far; they were usually short and, finally, contributed little to the cultural integration of Europe.

The practice of travel

For present-day travellers, accustomed to the comfort of travel agencies and fast transport, it is difficult to imagine how laborious travel was until the beginning of the nineteenth century. How did European travellers tackle the limitations associated with it and the difficulties that accompanied it?[40] First, of course, they thoroughly prepared themselves for their trips, certainly when these were to last many months or even several years, as was often the case with the 'Grand Tour'. Their expectations were shaped by their upbringing and education; for many, intensive reading formed a basis on which their actual experiences would grow. Published travel stories and travel guides were important not only because they would briefly inform their readers about what should be seen but also because they contained many useful tips about, for instance, where to eat and, naturally, what.

Many people embarking on travel were instructed by family, friends, acquaintances, teachers or colleagues, telling them, first of all, who was to be to visited: local dignitaries, famous scholars or collectors with interesting collections of antiquities or curios, artists whose ateliers were open to visitors, and so on.

In his youth, the famous French bibliophile, researcher and collector Nicholas Fabri de Peiresc (1580–1637) travelled and studied in Italy for more than a year. He also crossed the Channel to England in the retinue of a French ambassador and, subsequently, went to the Netherlands on his own in order to talk to the leading scholars there. At the beginning of the seventeenth century, he enjoyed an international reputation because of his extensive correspondence with men of letters all over Europe. He regularly sent his younger friends and acquaintances memoranda indicating how they could make the most of a trip to England or Italy.[41] What to see, to whom to talk, which things to buy, Peiresc was able to indicate all this on the basis of his own rich, much-travelled experience.

People did well to arm themselves with letters of recommendation to this and that person, so as not to turn up unintroduced and thus unexpected and, perhaps, unwelcome. Passports and escorts were also very important in view of the fact that there was always a war going on somewhere in Europe. And people's financial affairs naturally had to be settled as well. Carrying cash was, of course, dangerous. Bills of exchange – the new medium of European finance, popular since the fourteenth century – could be cashed with bankers or merchants en route.

Many travellers embarked on long journeys, but only for the very rich can the experience have been a really comfortable one, although even they probably suffered from the jolting of carriages which, without adequate suspension, had to negotiate Europe's mostly unpaved roads. However, many had to make do without their own carriage and travelled by stage coach,[42] by horse or, if the opportunity arose, by barge or sailing boat. For poor students or artists, as well as for pilgrims, walking was normal, as appears from the useful guide that G. Grutarolus had published in Basle as early as 1561, called *De Regimine iter agentium vel equitum, vel peditum, vel navi, vel carru, seu rheda . . . utilissimi libri duo* (Two very useful books including a guideline for those who travel by horse, by foot, by ship, or with a two- or four-wheeled carriage). Many simply had to use whatever means of transport were available and affordable at a given place and time.

As streets were not normally lit and sailing vessels and carriages often did not carry lanterns, as well as for reasons of safety, it was wise to travel only during daytime. Hence one had to get up very early and end the day's travel in time to start searching for a place to stay the night. Travellers were, therefore, waylaid by cheeky youths who, representing rival innkeepers, loudly praised the qualities of their accommodation, qualities which not infrequently turned out to be complete fantasies. Inns where a night's rest was not spoilt by lice in a bed that, moreover, had to be shared with two or three other guests, were expensive and thus, for many, such as travelling students and artists, an unaffordable luxury. In short, the hostelry offered most travellers little rest. In his *Colloquia*, Erasmus, an experienced traveller, too – he had lived in Basle, Rome and England, among other places – fulminated against the poor quality of inns, mainly German ones.[43] Yet, frequent stops were unavoidable, for the tempo of travel was slow. Travelling by coach, it might be possible to cover 50 kilometres a day, but on foot this was obviously unthinkable.

Travellers looked around. The obvious and important question is what directed their gaze and what did they actually see? Admittedly, we know little about the process. As already indicated, to a certain extent people were prepared for their 'Grand Tour' or for other types of travel not only by the expectations created by their Christian-Humanist education but also by reading works of a general historical and cultural nature as well as special travel guides. However, once having reached their destination, most travellers frequently showed themselves very dependent on and mostly following, unquestioningly, the directions of professional guides who were either employed for the occasion or travelled as permanent escorts – by the seventeenth century, there were people who made a career of accompanying young members of the aristocracy on their tours.[44] Others decided on a route and a sightseeing schedule themselves but in doing so often used a printed guide as well.

Much of what we know about travel experiences in this period stems from the diaries people kept, mindful of the adage of, among others, Francis Bacon, one of England's leading scholars and intellectuals. In his essay 'On Travel', he wrote: 'Let diaries therefore be brought into use',[45] since any experience gained and any knowledge acquired had to be set down systematically in order to be profitable. A comparative study of the printed guides with the experiences that travellers chronicled in their letters and diaries results in striking although perhaps not unexpected conclusions. Many travellers only 'saw' what their travel guides told them to see. Indeed, describing their impressions, whether on the spot or later, as they sat down to recall their memories, they frequently recorded not so much their own views as the ones the book, which they often had at hand, had taught them to see. And as far as their emotions were concerned, a sometimes suspicious similarity is evident between the admiring commentaries, programmed, as it were, by the printed travel guides, and the feelings expressed by travellers in their own writings with, often, an ostensible air of originality.

Travellers met people. Or at least, they should have done so if they remembered another piece of advice in Bacon's essay: 'Let him [i.e. the traveller] sequester himself from the company of his countrymen and diet in such places where there is good company of the nation where he travelleth'.[46] Of course one may ask whether most travellers really were inquisitive and, if so, what were their opportunities to make actual contact with other people? Francis Bacon also wrote: 'He that travelleth into a country before he hath some entrance into the language, goeth to school and not to travel'.[47] Indeed, language was an essential means of communication, but in those days it was often an insurmountable barrier as well. Those who, numerically, were the most important group of travellers, the pilgrims, often spoke only their own language, relying on a small group of leaders to arrange everything for them. They travelled in and with their own world, outside of which another world was visible but basically incomprehensible – not unlike the majority of modern tourists who travel within the semi-closed context of their operated tour.

However, for the elite, language was far less of a problem. They had been taught Latin at an early age. Moreover, in the sixteenth and early seventeenth centuries, Italian had become a 'European' language, a function that French then took over in the seventeenth and eighteenth centuries. Thus, it was possible to communicate in one of these three languages with those who moved in the same privileged circle, who shared the same social and educational background. Reading contemporary travel letters and diaries, German and English aristocrats seem to have felt rather more at ease with Frenchmen or Italians of their own social class than with the labourers in their native country. They simply 'understood' each other better, culturally, down to the basic level of language.

To travel or not to travel?

Clearly, travel in Europe acquired a wider scope and frequency from the sixteenth century onwards. That much is obvious from the enormous increase in publications which were aimed specifically at the travel market and which, either by presenting practical information or by emphasizing the moral and educational aspects, intended to serve an apparently growing public. The boom in this sector occurred in the last decades of the sixteenth and in the early years of the seventeenth century and, again, in the last years of the seventeenth and the first decades of the eighteenth century.[48]

Many apparently shared the opinion articulated by the Englishman William Bourne. In his *A Booke called the Treasure for Travailers . . . contaynyng very necessary matters, for all sortes of Travailers, eyther by Sea or by Lande*, published in London in 1578, he writes: 'it is a playne case, that Travailers into other Countreies doo much profyte the common weale'. He underlines the need for contact with other countries, and, although he does not say this explicitly, with other cultures, arguing that if people do not travel, 'in process of time wee should become barbarous and savage'. As seen above, it was precisely for fear of such outside influences that Spaniards in the sixteenth and seventeenth centuries were forbidden to embark on educational travel. However, elsewhere, too, there were those who were less than certain that travelling was indeed a worthwhile experience. On the contrary, early in the seventeenth century one already finds commentators who judged the phenomenon negatively. By no means all parents and educators were convinced of the value of a southward trip, heading for Italy. All too often, young travellers passed the time eating and drinking, playing cards and roulette and, not infrequently, indulging in sex which, if things went wrong, affected one's purse as well as one's health.

Other objections were raised as well. In his tract *Quo Vadis? A just Censure of Travell*, published in London in 1671, the Englishman John Hall wondered whether all those young members of the English nobility who said they simply 'had' to travel to the continent and, especially, to France and Italy, would not get bad ideas, whether, in short, travel would not lead to 'private and publicke mischiefe'? And the German Johannes Thomasius, in his tract called *Programma XLII de peregrinationis usu et abusu*, 'a programme of 42 points on the sense and nonsense of travelling', published in Halle in 1693, argued that travel had actually become unnecessary now that books could be obtained so easily. He added that one of the dangers lurked in people's uncritical acceptance of what they encountered abroad, pointing out, particularly, the risk that travelling might 'dilute' the purity of proper Protestantism – Thomasius, being a Protestant pietist, clearly referred to the dangers of popery.

Such statements give cause for reflection. Other morals and customs, even if people encountered them within Europe, within the Christian world, apparently did not by definition evoke feelings of cultural solidarity. If anything, such men as Thomasius and Hall feared the propagandistic, even corrupting power of Catholicism which, after all, was now showing all its post-Tridentine, baroque splendour to the many travellers who visited southern Germany, France and especially Italy. It is a fear that for centuries continued to characterize European anti-popery, stemming from the opposition between Catholicism and Protestantism that had created such a fundamental schism in Christian unity.

For different reasons, the English philosopher and pedagogue John Locke (1632–1704) was not completely convinced of the usefulness of the 'Grand Tour' either. He wondered whether a person would not benefit more from a foreign trip when he had grown to manhood as he would, then, be less easily influenced.[49] The famous Swedish biologist Carl Linnaeus (1707–78)[50] used another argument when, in 1741, he gave his inaugural address as professor at the university of Uppsala. He regretted the 'wanderlust' of many young Swedes who travelled to distant lands yet hardly knew their own country at all. With some pride he pointed to his own past. After all, as a young man he had joined one of the first scientific expeditions to Swedish Lapland. He now felt that some experience of the unknown regions and cultures of a person's own country could be far more salutary.[51] However, in later years this opinion did not prevent Linnaeus from sending his students on overseas expeditions which explored even the remotest corners of the earth.

Those who did not heed such warnings, but yet were seldom, if ever, able to actually travel themselves, could, of course, indulge in 'armchair tourism'. Sitting by the hearth or at their desk, they enjoyed the products of what was quickly becoming one of the more successful genres in European book production, travel literature. Special books were even written for them. In 1600, the Englishman Samuel Lewkenor published a work in London with the telling title, *A Discourse not altogether unprofitable, nor unpleasant for such as are desirous to know the situation and customs of forraine cities without travelling to see them.*

Clearly, the craving for the exotic, the need to escape from everyday routine, greatly popularized precisely those travel stories in which a completely different and, therefore, preferably non-European world was described, a world where Europeans could still project their dreams of an earthly paradise or a promised land. Yet travel stories of journeys in Europe also enjoyed considerable success. After having completed his studies, the Guelders country squire Thomas Walraven van Arkel, who in the seventeenth century led a quiet life at his castle of Ammerzoden in the Betuwe area, rarely travelled. However, the inventory of his rich library – he owned approximately 2,000 titles – seems to prove that he read a great deal, especially travel stories, as well as, not surprisingly in view of his origins and status, many court novels of the genre described above. In this way, he and, as is shown by numerous other inventories, many members of his class in the rural backwaters of Europe kept up with the latest developments in a lifestyle which they considered theirs; which, perhaps in their youth, they had 'sniffed' during a diplomatic or educational trip, and which they still experienced as normative, even if they could only partly live it out in their own lives.[52]

Travel as an element in growing cosmopolitanism and cultural integration

Travel letters, travel diaries, published travel reports – do they allow us to conclude that besides growing cosmopolitanism, travel in the period from the late fifteenth century onwards caused or promoted some form of supraregional or even supranational solidarity, a concept of 'Europe'? The answer is twofold.

Admittedly, many travellers certainly gained some knowledge about other countries and peoples; yet, most of them but little understood or valued the different, national or regional cultures they met elsewhere in Europe. Reading their recorded experiences reveals the existence of prejudices that were hardly, if at all, removed by travelling. On the contrary, they frequently appear to have been confirmed by it. Maybe this was only to be expected. After all, the manuals that prepared the traveller for his new experience abounded with warnings regarding certain habits, certain patterns of behaviour that were deemed characteristic of specific European nations. Even the largely impartial Lipsius could not help enumerating them: French vanity, Italian degeneracy, German gluttony and, *nota bene*, Spanish 'Africanness' – for, indeed, many Europeans saw Spain as non-European, for the very reasons that made it so recognizable to the Moroccan ambassadors who, when visiting Madrid, travelled through Andalusia and were proud to note that in this otherwise dismal country Arab culture had survived, to become one of its few redeeming points.[53]

Thus, there were definite limits to the acceptance of the otherness of the various parts of Europe travellers got to know. Particularly in their appreciation of the various aspects of daily life – the 'low' culture of the 'small' tradition – travellers frequently showed their irritation. Without batting an eyelid, a mainly tolerant, relatively cosmopolitan traveller like John Evelyn still describes an incident as being 'after a true *trecherous* Italian guise'.[54]

Indeed, for many, the contemporary society of the countries they travelled in held little or no fascination. On the contrary, most travellers seem annoyed by foreign customs, by codes of behaviour they often considered bizarre and sometimes ill-mannered. Remarkably, central and north Europeans expressed this negative appreciation precisely about the countries of the south: for them, the vision of a glorious, all too idealized past, hoped for but certainly not always found, that was the basis of 'high' culture, of the 'great' tradition, inevitably clashed with the realities of daily life, of contemporary culture in that very region, a reality which, especially for many Protestants, was so evidently Catholic, and, or so they felt, superstitious. Also, growing differences between a northern Protestant culture and a southern Catholic civilization seem to emerge in the often disparaging descriptions of the perceived seediness of southern street life. Does this constitute proof of actual differences? Perhaps not – for if anything, street life in London was as dirty as it was in Rome. But it does constitute proof of a change in, especially, elite values and views of what proper culture, in a civilized world, should be.

Nevertheless, certain forms of culture were profoundly influenced by the phenomenon of travel, becoming characteristic of a larger Europe as a result. Returning home, travellers could not only look back upon their stay abroad as an enjoyable conclusion to their relatively carefree 'youth', a chapter they now closed before embarking on a responsible career. For many, the memory also remained a life-enhancing experience that somehow determined their future thoughts and actions. The elite vision of European culture was definitely altered by this increasingly close interaction between travel and other forms of educated communication.

11 A new society

The 'Republic of Letters' as a virtual and virtuous world against a divided world

The Republic of Letters: a quest for harmony

The political and religious divisions of Europe, which reinforced each other from the sixteenth century onwards because disputes on the one front were often fought out with arguments from the other domain, resulted in almost uninterrupted discord, in a general feeling of insecurity. Not only did all states actually fight each other, they also felt that their own identity, judged increasingly important, would be lost if a single state were to achieve hegemony.

In the sixteenth century, this fear centred around the imperial aspirations of the House of Habsburg, reflected in an ideology and a propaganda policy which linked this family, who had borne the imperial crown for several centuries, to Charlemagne, to the early German and Roman Empires, and even further to Japhet and Adam, while its acquisition, through marriage, of the Spanish crowns of Aragon and Castile and, consequently, of dominion over parts of the Mediterranean, and of America, Africa and Asia was seen as proof positive of their right to rule the entire world. In the seventeenth century, Europe feared the equally megalomaniac concepts of Louis XIV of France which continually threatened the quest for peace and quiet that now determined the foreign policies particularly of smaller states, admittedly rather more from pure necessity than from any idealism. Reactions to this situation, which regularly led to devastating wars, were twofold. Both can be interpreted as attempts to reach a more precise definition of 'Europe' and thus limit the results of war and dissension as much as possible.

First of all, one senses that, at least among the European elite, thinking and acting were to a large extent intensified by experiences gained during diplomatic and educational travel. A cosmopolitan culture recognizable all over Europe now developed; though limited to the upper classes, in the long run it did not fail to have a more widespread influence on very diverse areas of European life. Obviously, many lived this culture only as a superficial lifestyle, but specifically the intellectual elite began to embrace the values which appeared to guarantee the more fundamental ideals of unity, civilization and, it was hoped, the resulting peace: the values of Christianity in its original, universal form and classical culture. These values became internalized through common educational norms and practices and therefore were considered Europe's collective inheritance even if, depending upon the specific philosophy and the world-view of those involved, this was now felt to be Christian-European, European-Christian or perhaps just European, without any clear religious connotation.

Because unity, civilization and peace offered the possibility of escaping from the political and religious differences which so cruelly influenced or even disrupted the everyday lives of many, people made attempts to contact and stay in contact with each other across the very borders of the states that increasingly thought in 'national' terms, thus fuelling that very discord. The frequent travels undertaken by the elite to complete their cultural formation by a period of university study elsewhere, by visits to art collections and classical ruins and by contacts with scholars and other famous figures obviously did not create a fundamental sense of solidarity all by themselves. Other means of communication, too, contributed to the genesis of a culture and, finally, a mentality, a way of thinking in which it was possible to believe that the consequences of political and religious conflicts could, as it were, be transcended by emphasizing what was of essential importance, what should bind everyone: the belief in individual freedom and the chances for creative development, the improvement of the human mind – all this, at least for the majority of intellectuals, in relation to the challenges presented by the great miracle of God's creation. These ideals, which transcended and partly even had to deny the borders of one's own region and state, were given shape in what was very significantly called the *Respublica Literaria* – a concept frequently, but as time went by decreasingly, defined by the addition *Christiana*.[1] From the late fifteenth century onwards, the Republic of Letters was felt to be a non-institutionalized community based on commonly experienced norms such as brotherhood and tolerance and on a common aim such as the advancement of knowledge, of learning, in order to become more human. This ideal and its background are strikingly articulated in a poem by the sixteenth-century Englishman Samuel Daniel, who writes:

> It be'ing the proportion of a happie Pen,
> Not to b'invassal'd to one Monarchie,
> But dwell with all the better world of men,
> Whose spirits are of one communitie;
> Whom neither ocean, Desarts, Rockes nor Sands
> Can keepe from th' Intertraffique of the minde,
> But that it vents her treasure in all lands,
> And doth a most secure commencement finde.[2]

The Republic of Letters and the ideal of tolerance: theory and practice

However, this ideal, which implied a view of man and the world, of a tolerant fraternity, remained a dream only, voiced in the conscious and unconscious propaganda of its bearers. Indeed, later historiography that, after all, has often been the product of people who had their roots in this tradition, tended to depict

Plate 18 Religion and the practice of intolerance: people watching heretics and witches being burnt in a straw hut, depicted in a text on criminal law and procedure, the *Cautio Criminalis* of 1632.

Source: Centre for Art Historical Documentation, Nijmegen, the Netherlands

the *Respublica Literaria* as an achieved European cultural unity rather more than contemporary reality warranted. The expectations people cherished of the humanizing, civilizing influence of a brotherhood of all those who wanted to advance the *bonae litterae* contributed to this vision.

CHATEAU MONTAIGNE, NEAR BORDEAUX, AD 1580: MICHEL DE
MONTAIGNE ON EUROPE AND 'THE OTHER'

In 1580, Michel de Montaigne (1533–92), a French intellectual and one of the sharpest minds of his age, published a number of highly perspicacious essays, covering a great many aspects of contemporary culture in a spirit of criticism, not to say scepticism. In these *Essais*, he showed himself to be an example *par excellence* of undogmatic, cosmopolitan thinking, of the Humanism that had grown in the previous centuries. Later thinkers, from the seventeenth, eighteenth and nineteenth centuries, such as Pierre Bayle and John Locke, Jean-Jacques Rousseau and Friedrich Nietzsche, were influenced by him. With his essay 'On the cannibals', Montaigne joined one of the most fundamental debates of the Republic of Letters, indeed of Europe: the debate on tolerance. Reflecting on the 'otherness' of the newly discovered American Indians, he actually voiced a critique of the situation in contemporary Europe. On the basis of the travel tales he had read he sketches an idealized version of Indian culture and society: not hierarchical, not determined by birth and wealth. In this society, man lives 'in the wild', in a state of nature and, therefore, nobly, for as intended by creation:

> The discovery of an enormous continent deserves consideration. I do not know that I can be sure that some other may not hereafter be added, seeing that so many great men have been deceived in this. . . .
>
> I find . . . that there is nothing barbarous or savage about that people, as far as I have been able to learn, except that everybody will call anything barbarous that does not agree with what he is used to. Admittedly, we have no other test of truth and reason except the example and model of the notions and customs of our own country: the perfect religion, the perfect society, the perfect and complete employment of all things are natural here. Those others are savages, just as we call those fruits wild which nature produces unassisted and by its ordinary processes; whereas by rights we ought to apply the term to those which we by our science have changed and perverted from their proper state. . . .
>
> Those people, therefore, seem barbarous to me because they have received very little conditioning by the human mind and are still close to their original simplicity. The laws of nature, but little bastardized by ours, still govern them, and in such pure form that I am sometimes distressed by the thought that the knowledge of all this did not come sooner, at a time when there were men who could have brought greater insight to the matter than we can. I am sorry Lycurgus and Plato knew nothing of this; for it seems to me that what we have learned about those people there exceeds not only all images with which poetry has embellished the golden age and all the fanciful inventions about a happy state for man, but also the arguments and even desires of philosophers. These could not imagine so pure and simple a lack of artificiality as we now see before our eyes; they could not believe that our society could maintain itself with so little contrivance and human sweat.
>
> Those peoples, I would tell Plato, have no knowledge of trade or letters, no science of numbers, not the name even of a magistrate, no superiors to rule them; no use of services, of wealth or poverty; no contracts, no inheritance, no property rights, no occupations except those of leisure; no respect for ancestry except that which they all share, no clothes, no agriculture, no metal, no use of wine or wheat. The very words signifying lies, treason, deceit, avarice, envy, slander, pardon – all unheard of! How far would he find that his imaginary republic differs from such perfection? . . .
>
> [But they are] ignorant how dear their acquaintance with our corruption will one day cost their peace and happiness, and how this intercourse will bring about their ruin.[3]

May one interpret Montaigne's sketch as a form of European self-criticism, as a 'dream of Europe'? One certainly may. Does it imply a plea for tolerance of 'the other'? It obviously does. But yet, the Indians whom Montaigne glorifies lived far way. Had he chosen to portray the 'Moors', the Muslims, who lived nearby, in the Balkans, and who for many Europeans constituted the real danger, the message would have been rather more poignant, or more difficult to swallow – as is shown by the reality of Europe's reactions to those neighbours. Thus, Osmin, one of the main characters in Mozart's opera *Die Enführung aus dem Serail* (The Escape from the Seraglio) (1782), was ridiculed by the Austrian composer's librettist. In doing so, he provided his audience with one of the proven possibilities to ward off the danger of the nearby 'other', the foreigner who is seen as a threat. Monostatos, too, the 'Moor' in *Die Zauberflöte* (The Magic Flute) (1791), the Mozart opera in which white and black, light and darkness, good and evil are so child-like and yet so profoundly contrasted with each other, is clearly 'the enemy'. Both operas, based on texts in the vernacular, were very popular: real crowd-pullers, rather than purely elite events. They undoubtedly had the effect of confirming prejudices.

Still, one may maintain that Montaigne had tried to counter precisely such feelings. Nevertheless, his text shows that even he could not avoid explicitly taking the norms and even the terms he used to describe and analyse 'the Indians' from Europe's ideal-type civilization, that of classical Greece. Nevertheless, one cannot simply interpret Montaigne's argument as 'cultural imperialism'. Maybe, people can accept 'the foreigner' only if they are able to see and experience the potential 'enemy' as an ideal self.

For centuries, Europe, like most other cultures on earth, had wrestled with the problem of insiders and outsiders, the problem of tolerance. From the sixteenth century onwards, with religious unity finally broken, it became a central problem in understanding itself as a culture undivided, the more so as, generally speaking, the normative function of Christianity began to lose its force. Tolerance, between religions and, increasingly, different religious cultures, was now a major problem, as was tolerance between the peoples of the various states with their increasingly national, sometimes even nationalistic cultures. Consequently, tolerance remained a problem of European culture both in theory and in practice.

John Locke and Pierre Bayle (1647–1706), two of the many intellectuals who participated in the tolerance debate in the last decades of the seventeenth century, brought about a gradual change in the description of the concept through their writings, moving from a tolerance that resignedly accepted what could not be changed to the peaceful acceptance of other opinions – and behaviour? – that one did not necessarily approve of oneself.

Yet, their grand theories still left the practical problems all but unresolved. Indeed, it was an intellectual debate, mostly, in a context, moreover, in which at least for most participants the actual issues of toleration were not really problematic. Yet the growing conceptual consensus within the intellectual elite in no way guaranteed that people – those who lived in less comfortable positions but also intellectuals themselves, men of letters – now accepted, in everyday practice, those fellow men who were clearly different culturally. It was the more difficult if that acceptance had to be proven in an economic situation that did not favour tolerance.

The situation in seventeenth-century France provides a telling example. In 1589, King Henry IV had proclaimed the Edict of Nantes, according a measure of safety and even liberty to the French Protestants, a religious minority living in an overwhelmingly Catholic world. For a century, they had been able to enjoy this tolerance which, though it did not extend throughout the realm, had resulted in the powerful economic and cultural presence of these so-called Huguenots in French society. This irked Henry's most famous, or infamous successor, Louis XIV. In 1685, in the same period that the debate on tolerance was waged, the Protestants were given the choice either to convert or to leave their possessions and their native France. As victims of the religious intolerance of the Sun King, in their hundreds of thousands they went into exile, giving up their country and, of course, their culture.

Many European states gave them refuge, either moved by sincere sympathy, or because the host countries saw them as potentially profitable immigrant workers. Yet not all exiles proved easily employable. Many were and remained poor. Appealing to social funds, they were soon seen as a threat to local social stability. Obviously, it was only then that tolerance was – and still is – really tested. Many Huguenots realized that far-reaching assimilation, renouncing their own dreams, was the best, indeed the only protection against the resentment and spite with which many now treated them.

This in no way detracts from the fact that many Europeans genuinely tried to put their high-minded thoughts into actual practice. From the end of the sixteenth century onwards, in learned circles the most grandiose projects for 'eternal peace' were devised with increasing regularity. Mostly, they pleaded for some sort of federal political organization which would guarantee that violence and the other miserable consequences of the perverted use of power and intolerance be banished from Europe. Besides the creation of the *Respublica Literaria*, these projects constituted Europe's second attempt to realize some unity in a situation that so often threatened to slide into crisis.[4] However, even more than the Republic of Letters, these plans remained only paper ideals, though they contained many elements which, from the late nineteenth century onwards, were proposed for the unification of Europe and, indeed, have been realized in more recent years.

In 1693, the Englishman William Penn, leader of a Protestant sect known as the Quakers because its members were encouraged to publicly and sometimes vehemently – quakingly – voice their beliefs, published his *Essay towards the present and future Peace of Europe*. It is a powerful text in that it successfully avoids the usual long-winded references to the Bible or the classics, and hardly uses baroque or classical figures of speech. It is also a short text. It proposes a 'European parliament' in which all participating states are represented by a number of delegates – that number to be determined on the basis of their economic strength! The German Empire holds pride of place, with twelve seats; France and Spain are next, with ten votes each, etc. – one is forcefully reminded of the debate over the seats to be given to the various states under the proposed European constitution of 2004. Given his cultural or rather religious background of pacifism and tolerance, Penn argues: 'And if the Turks and Muscovites are also admitted, which is only just and right, then two times ten representatives will also be added [. . .]' – incidentally another, even more telling position in view of the decision yet to be taken by the present-day European Union in the coming decades. Thus, according to Penn, a political constellation is created that, admittedly, covers only 'a quarter, but still the best and richest, part of the known world, where religion and education, civilization and art have their place'.[5] Thus, while Penn's definition of the elements that constitute European civilization unmistakably refers to a long tradition, he also includes the two cultures which, precisely because they were not part of that tradition, most of his contemporaries would have excluded, even emphatically so. Fascinating also, from a present-day perspective, is Penn's awareness of the tensions that will inevitably develop between sovereign states and a 'parliament' of representatives.

However, one of the most significant aspects of Penn's plan is that while he does not attempt to achieve a traditional Christian world order, his inspiration was in its deepest essence biblical. However, economic and utilitarian considerations play a clear role, too, undoubtedly because the formation of his theory was partly based on the works of such 'common sense' thinkers as his contemporary John Locke.

In Penn's outline of a civilized society, the concept of 'freedom' stands explicit and central: not a single person must live in fear. As a result, 'justice', or controlled 'violence', is the basis of a state, and freedom of conscience is the logical consequence. Penn implicitly proposes that true Christianity lies in the acceptance of others, if only they, too, accept justice and freedom – thus, in a sense, entrusting the State with the protection of these basically religious values. Finally, he stresses the absolute necessity of education to realize these ideals.

Yet, it is characteristic of the problematic nature of Penn's idealistic vision that ten years earlier he had sought to realize his plans in the new world, on the other side of the ocean, where a century earlier many readers had situated Thomas More's *Utopia* (1516) and where, during the following years, so many people had actually attempted to make their dreams come true. 'Pennsylvania' and 'Philadelphia' – respectively 'Penn's colony in the Woods', in an Eden-like garden, and the 'City of Brotherly Love' – were the outcome of William's ideas on the ideal state and the ideal city. Yet, whereas he advocated equality of Indians and Europeans, on the condition that the latter would do some civilizing work – to be understood as Christian mission – among the former, his followers quickly proved unable to reconcile the requirements of practice with the ideals of theory.[6] Penn's utopian society soon became a 'normal' European colony using and even exploiting both Indian territory and the Indians themselves.

The Republic of Letters and its enemies: national cultural policies, or the political uses of culture

Plans like Penn's not only reveal the vision that many intellectuals held of Europe's ideal self, but also show that people were fully aware of the reality that had emerged from the sixteenth century onwards, the reality of increasingly powerful national states. They now formed the framework in which Europe's cultural self-awareness was articulated and shaped. The new awareness is fully outlined in a text by the French publicist Louis le Roy. Viewing the past in his *De la vicissitude ou variété des choses de l'univers* (Paris 1575), he writes:

> We in the west have, during the past 200 years, regained the value of knowledge and learning and have restored to honour the different branches of science which for so long appeared to be extinct. The constant dedication of many scholars led to so many successes that today our time can measure itself with the best that ever was. . . . The rulers who have done the most for the recovery of culture are Pope Nicholas V and King Alfonso of Naples, who welcomed those who offered them the Latin translations of Greek books with tributes and royal support. The King of France, François I, paid the salaries of professors in Paris and had a splendid library assembled at Fontainebleau. Without the support and generosity of the kings of Castile and Portugal the discovery of new countries and the journey to the Indies would never have taken place. The Medici lords of Florence, Cosimo and Lorenzo, also gained many merits because they received scholars from all over the world and supported their work.

In short, at the end of the sixteenth century and in the early seventeenth century, Europe's cultural elites were obviously well aware that society and culture had undergone great changes in the preceding 200 years.

While at the beginning of the period Le Roy described the aim of many Europeans had been to revive and relive the culture of the ancient Greeks and Romans, according to him, two centuries later, people no longer considered this the only worthwhile goal. Indeed, the development of knowledge and of the arts in Europe had been such that classical civilization had been superseded already.

Obviously, the state, in the person of the ruler, was now felt to play an important role in the advancement of the arts and sciences, not, of course, because of any innate civilization but rather because they valued the cultural prestige and the propagandist effects of this patronage. Equally important was that many of the products of culture and, especially, science, could be of eminent practical use, for example in the development of education and, thus, in the training of a well-informed bureaucracy, but also for all kinds of technological improvements, not least in military matters.

However, because state governments, growing powerful, began to use all sorts of cultural forms to increase their power further, the freedom to form and exchange ideas slowly became limited precisely because culture was now embedded in official structures. During the seventeenth century, royal academies of science and fine arts had been founded and educational institutions, especially at university level, had been used increasingly to support royal prestige which, of course, was now felt to be the prestige of the State, the nation.[7] This is most clearly shown in the writing of history, whether it be in the royal biographies commissioned from well-known authors via the system of 'gratifications' in France, or in the so-called *Pragmatische Geschichte* produced in the German states from the late sixteenth century onwards, or in the descriptions glorifying the past and present cultural and political achievements of a people, for example the *Italia Illustrata*.[8] In Spain, Juan de Mariana, linking his nation's fame to its military and colonial expansion, wrote:

> The name and valor of Spain, known to few and confined within the narrow limits of Spain, was in a short time, and with great glory, spread abroad, not only through Italy and through France and Barbary, but to the very ends of the earth.[9]

Indeed, until late in the eighteenth century, those expressions of culture principally produced for and dominated by the elite – the visual arts, literature, music – could exist only within the often limiting framework of patron–client relationships. Thereby, the leaders of State or Church, princes, nobles and prelates acted as patrons. For the artists involved, this was not always a pleasant situation. As early as 1508, in a letter to a friend, the painter Raphaello Santo lamented: 'You yourself have several times experienced what it means to be robbed of one's freedom and to live under the yoke of a patron'.[10]

By the seventeenth century, it was only the Catholic Church that still maintained its manifestations of grand culture which actually stemmed from and contributed to a universal cause. Most states had developed distinctly 'national' varieties of culture. In France, three powerful ministers – Richelieu, Mazarin and finally Colbert – used culture to enhance the glory of the monarch, the embodiment of the state, harnessing prose writers, playwrights and historians, but also architects, musicians and painters into a 'bureaucracy of the arts' hitherto unknown in European history. The creation of scientific academies (the *Academie Française* was founded in 1635), libraries and museums further strengthened government control over a culture that had to be 'national'. In the German principalities, too, culture increasingly became a concern of the State, a matter of national prestige. In 1700, the Prussian Academy of Sciences was founded in Berlin, directed by the famous philosopher Gottfried Wilhelm Leibniz (1646–1716).

Cultural nationalism manifested itself in a variety of forms and situations. As all over Europe, in England, too, classical architecture was highly valued. Yet the designs attributed to the famous Roman master builder Vitruvius – actually they were based on sixteenth- and seventeenth-century interpretations of him – were published in London under the telling title *Vitruvius Britannicus*, adapted to English needs and the English climate. And while Italian and French music may have delighted English ears, yet new melodies were presented in a guise both classical and national, as in *Orpheus Britannicus*, two volumes of songs published by the widow of the great composer Henry Purcell in 1698 and 1707, and in *Amphion Anglus*, in which John Blow collected his music in 1700. Indeed, the music itself was by now often unabashedly national(-istic), as demonstrated by Purcell's delightful tune to the very chauvinistic text 'Fairest Isle, all isles excelling', part of the equally chauvinistic masque 'King Arthur', written by the poet John Dryden in praise of England as the ideal island, a society where, as worries no longer exist, man only has to indulge in his sensual pleasures.

In Russia – first, the grand-duchy of Muscovy, later, the empire of the tsars – which attempted to come out of its economic, political and cultural isolation in these centuries, the process of interaction between cosmopolitan and national culture was even more complex. The full panoply of Byzantine coronation rituals, which, in a way, had survived in the west through the complex ceremonial of the papal court, was introduced in Russia in the late sixteenth century. Meanwhile, Italian Renaissance forms began to structure the great cathedrals built inside the Moscow Kremlin, the churches of St Michael the Archangel and of the Dormition of the Virgin. Yet the famous cathedral of St Basil, dominating the great square outside the palace, with its multicoloured façade and its bulbous domes, was built to show a visibly different style, that was considered less European, more 'Russian'.[11] From the end of the seventeenth century onwards, Tsar Peter not only ordered a great literacy campaign but also decreed the setting up of an imperial academy and a university – all following the European example but decidedly intended to serve Russia's national fame and prosperity.[12] And while Peter's new capital, St Petersburg – incidentally not named after the emperor but after the Apostle Peter, to stress Russia's ambitions to be the successor of imperial Rome – might function as a 'window on the west', the large-scale scientific expeditions to central and east Asia organized by the Imperial Academy from the 1720s, aimed to help Russia to map, literally, its growing empire in the east. Peter's successors continued his policy of western-style education and the advancement of modern, i.e. European, learning, but arguably this was successful only among the nobility and the bourgeois elites of a few towns. When, in 1767, Tsarina Catharine declared in one of her famous decrees, 'Russia is a European state',[13] she showed she was by birth a German princess and, moreover, a woman whose will, though it often became law, nevertheless revealed more about her wishes than about Russia's cultural reality.

The development of national cultures all over Europe is, perhaps, best represented in one characteristic moment. In 1700, at the book fair in Frankfurt, which had become Europe's largest in the late fifteenth century and has remained so ever since despite a decline in the eighteenth century,[14] only 4 per cent of the titles available were still in Latin, that once cosmopolitan language. European books were now published largely in the various national languages, as is eloquently shown in the fair's catalogues.[15]

The Republic of Letters, or how to communicate in an invisible institution

The community that transcended the State, which is what the *Respublica Litteraria* intended to be, was constantly being formed by travel and the resulting personal contacts, but in everyday practice it mainly continued through the writing and, thus, reading of letters. On this point, too, Bacon had clearly expressed himself in his essay on travel: 'When a traveller returneth home, let him . . . maintain a correspondence by letters with those of his acquaintance which are of most worth'.[16]

Unlike in today's e-mail society, the hand-written letter was the privileged means not only of personal but also of professional communication. Naturally, the printed word was influential, too. Its role in European culture gained considerable importance during the sixteenth and seventeenth centuries because the need for information in all areas of life and culture grew continually. Yet for daily communication the hand-written letter remained a primary carrier of information until the invention and introduction of the typewriter in the twentieth century.

All over Europe, literate people, while working in their often relatively closed milieus, were inspired by the vision of a larger world, held together by a network of correspondents to which they, along with thousands of others, belonged. Many who regularly corresponded with each other also knew each other, even if only through a few meetings during the academic peregrination or the Grand Tour they had made to round off their education. Yet some who wrote to each other for dozens of years never actually met. In short, for all of them, correspondence was one of the most important methods of keeping up with the latest news, whether personal or political, religious or scientific. The world of learning in particular was largely dependent on contact by letter. Thus, a man like Erasmus relied on more than 100 more or less regular correspondents, mostly in the Netherlands, England, France, Italy and the German countries, while a century later the French *érudit* Peiresc exchanged letters with more than 200 friends, living in an even wider world that included North Africa and the Levant.[17] Of course, their letters were not 'private' ones. The addressee would frequently share its scholarly contents with a wide circle of like-minded people who gathered at his house to hear the latest news. Despite the postal delays caused by climatic or political problems, one could circumvent such uncertainties by sending several copies. However, it was less feasible, and far more expensive, to send heavy loads of printed texts, whose postal distribution beyond one's own region was equally difficult as a result of commercial, financial and political limitations.

Yet printing indisputably caused a momentous increase in the diffusion of knowledge, both in a quantitative and a qualitative sense. After its invention, which in Europe coincided with the beginning of a century of unprecedented economic expansion and increased purchasing power, only some small technical and, in the case of very ambitious publishing enterprises, somewhat bigger financial problems still limited the distribution of the book and, thus, the further expansion of communication and the spread of knowledge. While there had been people trading in manuscript copies of mostly learned and devotional texts in the fourteenth and fifteenth centuries, as well as marketing such bestsellers as Marco Polo's tale, or the famous knightly romances, the sixteenth and seventeenth centuries really saw the beginning of the mass distribution of texts. The age of the printers and publishers had arrived, of people who saw a market for their products.

Some publishers were actually interested in the promotion of culture, but mostly they were in it only for profit. Besides the few famous 'scholar-publishers' – men such as Aldus Manutius in Italy,[18] Johann Amerbach and Johann Frobenius, the printer-publishers and friends of Erasmus in Basle, and Christoffel Plantijn and his descendants in Antwerp – there was a host of less scholarly and idealistic entrepreneurs who simply smelled money in the nascent information culture. Counting on improving education, on the growing group of readers and, of course, eagerly exploiting the change from one, universal language, Latin, to the many national languages, they adapted to the market or even took the lead. They introduced cheaper books that were also less awkward to handle than the heavy folio and quarto volumes that had dominated in the sixteenth century. Not only did the supply of titles in the various national languages grow expansively, so did the texts providing general information or entertainment. Gradually, literary prose and poetry, historiography and, especially, travel stories[19] became more popular than theological or scientific treatises.

In the first years of printing, book production had concentrated mainly in Italy, the land of many courts, the land of Rome and the papacy, the cradle of Humanism and of the Renaissance. Venice was a major centre, where publishers could use a long-established trade network and where the demand for Greek classical texts could be most easily met. As an important cultural consequence, the Orthodox Christians of the Balkans, who were deprived of the benefits of printing by Ottoman rule, were now educated mainly through the products of Venetian presses, which provided not only classical learning, but also started publishing a religious and popular literature in Greek, later enriched with works of modern science. This contributed considerably to the reintegration into Europe of the Orthodox Christian intelligentsia.

As the focus of trade in general moved north, by the beginning of the sixteenth century book production also moved to the north. There, first Antwerp and subsequently, in the seventeenth century, the cities of the Dutch province of Holland, with Amsterdam and Leiden in the lead, dominated the international book trade.[20] The arrival of the Huguenots, mentioned above, certainly contributed to Holland's increasingly important function as an intellectual trading centre. The Huguenots hoped to make money with books, not least because they rightly reasoned that the country from which they had been banished represented an enormous market which, as a result of French royal censorship, could be served more profitably from abroad. As some of their fellow believers had ended up in the German states and in England, it was easy to establish international contacts as well.[21] Thus, the eighteenth-century Leiden printer, publisher and publicist Elie Luzac, a Huguenot, cooperated with the secretary of the Prussian Academy of Sciences in Berlin, Samuel Formey, another Huguenot, on the publication of a periodical whose title, *Bibliothèque Impartiale*, clearly indicated the contemporary ideal of tolerant yet critical knowledge.[22]

While travel cost time and money, so did buying books. In the seventeenth and eighteenth centuries it had already become too expensive for many. Nevertheless, information was important to those wanting to keep up professionally or simply interested in new developments in all fields of culture. At the same time, the flow of information had already become uncontrollable. European publishers quickly devised a solution for people who, for whatever reason, could or would not buy new titles by the dozen. Thus, in the 1660s, a new phenomenon appeared on the European cultural scene: the periodical. Within a few years' time, specialized political, literary and scientific journals gained a central role in the spreading of knowledge and new ideas among people who travelled seldom, if ever, and had little money to buy expensive books. While serious scientific studies continued to be published, their contents were often disseminated in these periodicals which reached an increasingly large readership in the Republic of Letters. They were not primarily directed at specialist scholars who lived with their books and letters, but rather at a broader readership of educated people who wanted to keep up with the latest in a variety of fields: theology, philosophy, political theory and literature.[23]

Inevitably, those periodicals 'specializing' in general information or commenting on recent events satisfied an increasing demand. Still more popular were the periodicals filled with abstracts of new titles, preferably providing extensive, critical excerpts and reviews. Until the late eighteenth century, the market for these journals was mainly supplied by Dutch publishers. They were often written in French, whose role as a *lingua franca* had already been confirmed by diplomacy and was now reinforced by Europe's language of culture as well.

Yet, to many, even the regular perusal of periodicals was too much trouble. An even more concise, preferably critically acceptable form of collected knowledge was thought to offer a solution. Publishers soon realized there was a market to be explored and succeeded there as well. The encyclopedia, in itself a very old phenomenon, now appeared on the European market. It is difficult to judge whether stories about the printing of gigantic compendia of knowledge by the Chinese emperors, which became known in seventeenth-century Europe through the reports of the Jesuits and other travellers, contributed to its introduction. The fact is that in the second half of the seventeenth century, the first 'libraries without walls' were published: Louis Moreri's *Dictionnaire* was brought out in 1674, followed in 1697 by Pierre Bayle's *Dictionnaire Historique et Critique* which was talked about and read for decades.[24] The latter was an excellent example of the 'literature of recollection', a text which was, as it were, to be the memory of that European culture Bayle had become acquainted

with in his reading, and which he wanted to understand and interpret as a corpus
that had grown historically but which needed to be read and used critically.

The Republic of Letters and the 'intertraffic of the mind': three examples

At the end of the seventeenth century, the Dutch envoy in Stockholm, Christian
Constantijn Rumph (1633–1706), befriended most of the representatives
of Sweden's political and cultural elite. Also, for twenty-five years he exchanged
letters virtually every month with Gisbert Cuper (1644–1716), a Deventer
professor of classical languages but also mayor of his native city and member of
the Dutch States-General.[25] His contacts with the learned Cuper made Rumph
a godsend for his Swedish friends and acquaintances who frequently gathered
at his house, among whom were many professors from Uppsala who had studied
in the Dutch Republic in their youth and who retained the best memories
of those years. With Rumph's help, these Swedes could obtain the books and
periodicals discussed in the Republic of Letters but that could not be easily
bought, if at all, in their own country. Between them, Cuper, the insider, living
in the Dutch Republic, and Rumph, the outsider, living on the periphery of
European culture, were able to supply Sweden with the latest political and
cultural news.

Cuper's, or rather Rumph's, Swedish contacts also used their friends' epistolary
network to prepare the publication of their scientific work in the Dutch Republic
since there were as yet no up-to-date printing facilities in Sweden. Only for the
finishing touches did they have to undertake the difficult journey to Amsterdam
– difficult because, as a result of the many destructive wars in these decades, the
Baltic and North Seas were anything but peaceful waters. When their books were
finally published, Swedish knowledge of the geography of northern Europe
and central Asia, of the origins of the Goths and so on could be discussed in
learned Europe.

In his turn, Cuper corresponded regularly with dozens of men from all parts
of Europe, ranging from Cardinal Noris, a powerful member of the Roman curia,
and the Florentine librarian and erudite Magliabecchi to the English, Anglican
theologian and historian Burnet, and the German, Lutheran philosopher Leibniz.
News of all sorts from Italy thus ended up in Amsterdam and the Netherlands
and, subsequently, in Berlin and in Prussia, as well as in Sweden.

One of Cuper's best friends was the Amsterdam merchant and politician
Nicolaas Witsen (1641–1717), one of the richest and most powerful men in the
Dutch Republic and director of the Dutch East India Company. Both in his
palatial canal house and in his country house he kept an enormous library
and filled the rooms with collections of the most valuable and exotic rarities. In
his gardens grew choice shrubs from the east – he had introduced the coffee
plant to the city's botanic gardens – and his zoo was famous, too. Travellers from
all over Europe who visited Amsterdam asked permission to visit him.

Almost every month, Cuper sent Witsen a six- or seven-page letter and duly received a reply.[26] A considerable part of the Cuper–Witsen letters concerned questions which they, both fanatical readers of travel stories, asked in the margins of the multifarious information which their reading matter offered. What was the origin of language and was there, still, an 'original' language, from which all the others stemmed? Had Asia and America once been linked? Was Chinese Confucianism a pre-Christian form of Christianity? And so on. Witsen supplied Cuper with data from China, Japan and India, but also from Brazil and Canada. Cuper again informed his German and Swedish acquaintances, introducing Witsen to Leibniz, who asked him for material on the globe's innumerable tongues. Eventually, much of the information spread in this manner found its way into the scientific and other publications or periodicals that were published for the people involved in this learned exchange.

Unlike his correspondent, Witsen had travelled a great deal, even, quite exceptionally – for it was on his own account – as far as Russia. He regularly exchanged letters with a number of distinguished Russians as well as with French Jesuits and with members of the Royal Society in England. Frequently, his letters contained requests for more detailed information concerning the data he obtained from his scientific reading and from the travel stories he devoured. In the discussions which then followed, carried on by letter again, one can see Witsen's world-view, his concept of culture, gradually change, as he came to view the world as fundamentally one, a single creation under a veneer of cultural diversity which, on closer inspection, revealed surprising similarities.

Such correspondence networks spanning Europe enabled people to exchange ideas. This encouraged intellectual curiosity and resulted in a dynamic cosmopolitanism, especially in educated circles. In the 1720s, following the years in which Rumph, Cuper and Witsen had established their complex but rewarding epistolary north–south axis, the Phanariot Greek Nicholas Mavrocordatos kept up an exchange of letters with the Amsterdam Huguenot scholar and magazine director Jean Le Clerc. Mavrocordatos, scion of an intellectual Greek family, whose father had studied medicine at Padua and had published several books, was appointed by the Ottoman sultan prince of Moldavia and Wallachia, two of the Balkan border regions separating the Christian and the Islamic worlds. Not only did Le Clerc supply his friend with recent maps of central Europe and the eastern Mediterranean; also, answering Mavrocordatos's incessant requests for information about new developments in the world of arts and letters, he sent him the books of recent western learning which Nicholas asked for. Thus, Mavrocordatos enriched his library with the works of Newton and other scientists, and with John Locke's *Two Treatises of Civil Government* (1690), a highly influential tract about a more balanced political system in which royal absolutism was mitigated by representative institutions. Mavrocordatos's intellectual interests fully appear in his novel *Les Loisirs de Philothé*, which was the first text to introduce the names of Bacon and Hobbes into Greek culture and to declare that if Aristotle were alive he would gladly become a pupil of 'the Moderns'[27] – those who held that contemporary culture had, indeed, surpassed classical civilization.

At the end of the eighteenth century, the wealthy bibliophile Gerard Meerman (1722–71), former Pensionary of Rotterdam and former Dutch ambassador to England, lived in The Hague. He had travelled extensively, starting with a Grand Tour that lasted for three years and brought him to Germany, France, Switzerland and Italy. His luxurious house was crammed with books, manuscripts, coins and antiquities, all of which he generously showed to people provided with a proper introduction. By letter, Meerman remained in contact with all of Europe, including the erudite Spaniard Gregorio Mayans y Siscar (1691–1781).[28]

Although Meerman and Mayans never met, their letters, over a period of more than twenty years, totalled several hundred, each often three or four pages long. They helped the two men share a treasure of information in many fields. Mayans, one of the most critical and, hence, important figures in Spanish culture in the eighteenth century, benefited from the situation because it enabled him to write a number of works wherein he pleaded for a more modern view of science and society – less dominated by Church traditions – to achieve the cultural regeneration of Spain. Mayans's books were partly published abroad, including in the Dutch Republic, where Meerman, following his friend's instructions, provided essential assistance. In his turn, Mayans acted as intermediary in Meerman's purchase of Spanish books and manuscripts and supplied him with the details for a number of his own publications, especially concerning the history of the invention of printing, which Meerman considered one of Europe's central cultural feats and which he desperately wanted to ascribe to a Dutchman, Laurens Janszn Coster. Of course, the Dutch were not immune to cultural nationalism, either.

The Meerman–Mayans letters also reveal how the two friends tried to practise what they felt was their duty as 'men of letters': to gather and critically test knowledge. However, equally important, their epistolary exchange shows how much the correspondents – one a Protestant, the other a Catholic – were aware of the political and religious structures and traditions that separated their countries. Consequently, they expressed the need for tolerance and mutual understanding to demolish these barriers and to serve the interests of an ideal they never specifically named but clearly did feel: Europe's 'common culture' and, through it, their own humanity.

Contacts with like-minded people from other nations provided the basis for the very exclusiveness of the members of the Republic of Letters, of Europe's cosmopolitan elite. During these centuries, these men – the Republic being a predominantly male affair – were not yet heavily pressured to make their country's rather than their own intellectual and cultural choices. Undeniably, however, many of these people, too, were profoundly prejudiced against representatives of other nations, especially if the latter remained anonymous and did not belong to the same sociocultural group; yet, as soon as people got to know each other personally, or through letters, prejudices would often disappear.

Of course one should ask if the ideal of the Republic of Letters was a limited and elitist one? I feel it was. Undeniably, it was easier to pay lip-service to an abstract concept, in letters, books and periodicals, and to propose tolerance and even understanding on paper, than to be confronted – in one's daily life or on trips abroad – with other people's regional or national cultural peculiarities. Yet the indisputable limitations both of the ideal and of the various elite groups who were its bearer did not make the idea behind it less functional or valuable. Despite a growing nationalization of culture, in the Republic of Letters Europe enjoyed a form of communication, a form of culture that, de facto, created a certain unity that was almost completely lacking in other fields. This situation lasted for almost three centuries. Only at the beginning of the nineteenth century did it start to alter.

12 A new society

From Humanism to the Enlightenment

Humanism and empiricism between 'ratio' and 'revelatio'

Many Europeans shared the critical attitude towards all kinds of scriptural knowledge shown by such men as Abelard and Erasmus. This became increasingly obvious from the late fifteenth century onwards, as printing and epistolary networks intensified the dissemination of knowledge and the ensuing debate. It has been frequently suggested that the emphasis on texts, originating from or based on the classical tradition, combined with the great influence of the Church(es) on education hindered the development of the modern, more experimental sciences. However, this is certainly not the case. It was precisely the interaction between the empirical research methods of philology as used in the study of religious and literary texts and the fundamental problems which philosophy continued to formulate with regard to the nature of man and the cosmos that actually stimulated experimental scrutiny in other areas, for instance, in the natural sciences.[1] Thus, the Venetian Daniele Barbaro translated the work of Dioskurides which codified Greek botanical thought, yet to this text, which was not based much on empiricism, he added many an empirical observation of his own. Indeed, in the centuries of Humanism, a way of thinking developed which more than ever before raised profound questions concerning reality as it could be observed; inevitably, in the long run, the answers to these questions created a growing gulf between the real, that is to say physical world, which people now thought could be understood and explained rationally, and the world of the invisible, whose existence was acceptable only on the basis of arguments of authority and belief. The lives and works of the Polish astronomer Nicolaus Copernicus (1473–1543) and the Italian astronomer and physicist Galileo Galilei (1564–1642) are a good case in point.

Niklas Koppernigk, born in the Polish city of Torun, studied at the great university of Krakow, specializing in both philosophy and medicine, and in astronomy and mathematics. In the tradition of the academic peregrination, he then travelled to the Italian universities of Bologna, Ferrara and Padua, to continue his studies there, finally returning to his homeland to take up the practice of medicine. Afterwards, he became the administrator of the bishopric of Frauenburg. However, always continuing his studies, in 1543, shortly before his death, Copernicus – his Latinized name – dared publish his principal work, *De Revolutione Orbium Caelestium* (On the revolution of the heavenly spheres).[2]

The text bears witness to great intellectual courage because it went against everything that the sixteenth-century Church and State saw as the established order of man and God, of earth and heaven. Thus, it laid the foundation for the modern, western world-view. A few notions exemplify how revolutionary Copernicus's concepts were. In the foreword, addressed to Pope Paul III, it said:

> After long research I am finally convinced:
> That the sun is a fixed star, surrounded by planets which turn around it and of which it is the centre and the torch.
> That besides the major planets there are planets of the second order which circle around these major ones like satelites, and, all of them together, around the sun.
> That the sun is a major planet, subject to threefold movement.
> That all the phenomena of these daily and annual movements, such as the periodic return of the seasons, all the vicissitudes of light and the temperature of the atmosphere which accompany these movements, are the result of the rotation of the earth and its periodic revolution around the sun.
> That the seeming orbit of the stars is nothing but an optical illusion, the product of the actual movement of the earth and the oscillations of its axis.
> I do not doubt that the mathematicians will agree with me, if they will take the trouble to study, not superficially, but in a sound manner, the proofs I will give in this work.
> If some people, of a superficial and ignorant mind, want to use some passages of Holy Scripture against me, distorting their sense, I reject their attacks: mathematical truths can only be judged by mathematicians.[3]

The text clearly shows that the author was prepared for criticism from those who, adhering to a literal interpretation of the Bible, would always reject empirical considerations as irrelevant or even godless. Actually, Copernicus called into question the Bible's authority only as a book from which scientific knowledge can be deduced. Moreover, he maintained that there are certain forms of science the uninitiated cannot judge: the ability to do so rests with those who have mastered mathematics. Thus, his book marks the growing division between an old and a new world-view, stressing the importance of mathematics as a 'new language', as a medium of communication that turned the technical sciences into a territory unintelligible to the ordinary literate person. In the long run, this division – basically between 'the Humanities' and 'the Sciences' – came to characterize the culture of Europe.

In 1623, a century later, this was echoed by the Italian astronomer Galileo Galilei, who wrote:

> Philosophy is written in the big book, the universe. But one cannot understand the book unless one first learns the language and the signs in which it is written. It is written in the language of mathematics, and the signs in which it is written are:

triangles, circles and other geometric figures; without knowledge of these, a person cannot understand anything about the universe; without knowledge of these, one wanders lost, as in a dark maze.

Consciously or unconsciously citing the words of the great, twelfth-century Islamic scholar Ibn Rushd, whose work had done so much to re-introduce Greek science to Europe, Galilei, too, felt he needed to stress that the Bible, however sacred a book, was an allegory only, and, moreover, one specifically meant for those who could not read that other book, the book of nature, the book that, if read with an empirical eye, would disclose reality.[4]

Meanwhile, rather than concentrating on the discovery of the mysteries of the heavens, other scientists literally dug into the earth in order to discover the chemical basis of life. The sixteenth century saw the rise of mineralogy, of research into the secrets hidden in caves and held by fossils, but also an increased interest in alchemy, the quest for the elixir of life, and for the Stone of Wisdom that was thought to disclose all knowledge. Moreover, well into the seventeenth century, the belief in sorcery and witchcraft, in black magic and the stars, which, to the present-day mind, smacks of pseudo-science or sheer deception, was strongly present in literate, even scholarly environments and, indeed, among the very people who showed the greatest interest in the new, empirical sciences. Thus, life at the courts of Emperor Rudolph II, of Pope Urban VIII and of King Louis XIV was profoundly influenced by people claiming insight and power from these sources.

Inevitably, the contradiction hidden in the fusion which men like Augustine and Thomas had hoped to create between the rational views of the world and man as developed in antiquity, and Christian revelation and cosmology became ever more apparent. In the long run, the new view of nature as a complex but understandable machine of which man was only a small part led to conflicts with institutionalized religion. Until the 1630s, the papal court in Rome was a centre of the new sciences, where research in every field was welcomed. It was only when the Catholic authorities realized the doubts that would result from Galilei's speculations on the nature of matter – which touched upon the central doctrine of transubstantiation, rather than on his ideas about the universe – that he was silenced – and perhaps only then because the reigning pope himself, Urban VIII, who had protected the Florentine scientist, no longer felt able to manoeuvre between the Church's major religious orders, which were warring about power issues rather than scientific theories.[5]

Meanwhile, Galilei's predecessor Nicolaus Copernicus and his follower Johannes Kepler (1571–1630) – who had given a mathematical-mechanical explanation of the working of the universe and the movements of the planets in it – had been squarely condemned already by protestant leaders. Martin Luther, confronted with Copernicus's heliocentric views, had called the Polish scholar 'an ass who wants to pervert the whole art of astronomy and deny what is said in the book of Joshua [i.e. one of the books of the Old Testament], only to make a show of ingenuity and attract attention'. With his theologian friend,

Philip Melanchton, he vehemently defended the geocentric model as the only one that conformed to the Bible, whose literal truth could not be questioned.[6]

For even though men like Copernicus, Galilei and Kepler and a host of other scholars advocated the study of the 'book of nature' as being just as pleasing to God as the reading of the Bible, arguing that it was nature which revealed God's greatness, the new science and the new reasoned and reasonable language of 'numbers and figures', incomprehensible to ever larger groups within the intellectual elite, endangered the Christian tradition. Many felt that if nature were a power in itself and if, moreover, man could by his own capacity understand it, God and his saving grace would have completely lost their power and significance. The contradiction between 'reason' and 'belief' – to many a seeming one only, to others a very fundamental one indeed – continues to haunt many scientists as well as the ordinary literate public up to the present day.

Not surprisingly, besides the mainstream science that now started increasingly to influence people's lives in all its aspects, there were those who wanted to re-establish a central role for man in God's creation. In this period, Giordano Bruno (1548–1600) and Jacob Boehme (1575–1624) represented positions which returned to earlier attempts to narrow the abyss between belief and reason.

Bruno replaced the Platonic and Christian view of a transcendent God who, while having created the universe, no longer influenced it, with the idea that the universe itself is a living being, the soul of which is God; to him, God and nature are almost inseparable. It took the gentlemen of the Inquisition of the Catholic Church, which, because of its dogmas, could never accept such pantheistic proposals, eight years of deliberations before they condemned Bruno to death at the stake, an indication that these judges were not without intellectual scruples. Bruno was burnt in Rome, on Campo dei Fiori, in 1600. In the nineteenth century, he was adopted as the 'martyr' of science.

Meanwhile, the south German cobbler Jacob Boehme argued that there was no opposition between God and nature; to him, heaven and hell, good and evil, light and darkness were the essential characteristics of nature, and thus of God, and, of course, of man who, after all, is the manifestation of God. It had all started in a 'Nothingness' where space and, thus, time were absent. Substance, nature was formed in this:

> We understand that without nature there is only an eternal immobility and stillness, that is to say, Nothingness; and then we understand that in the Nothingness an eternal Will exists, which wants to form the Nothingness into Something, because the Will can know, feel and behold itself.[7]

Thus, God, man, the other organic creatures and the inorganic things had come into existence. Good and evil are the two options open to man because they represent a 'Will to Something' and a 'Will to Nothing'.[8]

Although the thoughts of these men for whom the *virtù* of man, his creative capacity, became united with nature, with God, certainly did not gain as wide an influence as the ideas of their empiricist contemporaries if only because, soon, these enjoyed the added prestige of technological success, they have yet helped people who otherwise would have been shattered by the choice between their faith and their reason. Indeed, not surprisingly, a considerable part of philosophical debate in Europe up until today has been concentrated on precisely these issues and the various positions taken by the men introduced above.

From – scientific – empiricism to new visions of man and society

Although most people tend to identify empiricism with the sciences, it has to be understood that as an attitude to and a vision of reality it existed outside and indeed before 'science' as we now understand it became a feature of European culture.

Thus, in the sixteenth century, both Martin Luther and Ignatius of Loyola (1491–1556), one the symbol of Protestantism, the other of Catholic reform, had induced man to look at himself and his place in the world in an empirical way, albeit with the ulterior motive that, in doing so, he would best understand his position in relation to God. For example, the so-called 'spiritual exercises' (1548) of Loyola, designed specifically for the members of the Society of Jesus, forced them to daily, methodically deconstruct themselves – on paper, of course – into the tiniest details of their emotions, thoughts and actions; in thus examining and analysing themselves, they actually reached a state of self-awareness that truly constituted them as individuals.[9] Protestants, too, were supposed to account daily for their sins, which entailed a similar process of individuation. Thus, the 'idea of the self', now one of western man's constituent characteristics, was already introduced in Europe in the sixteenth century.[10] Slowly, the concept of an 'inner self' with its own self-consciousness was now twinned with – at least in Christian, European culture – a new preoccupation with the physical body, with one's own flesh.[11] While many saw the body – especially the female body – as the prime vehicle of sin, in the eighteenth century people increasingly engaged in multifarious sexual experiments, doing so, moreover, in all sorts of places.[12] Indeed, the more comprehensive attitude towards sex that is common today originated in this period, including, perhaps, the notion of a homosexual identity – a notion, of course, that was totally different from homosexual activity as such.

Most scholars tried to carry out their scientific research without openly wondering whether they were acting in conformity with the basic values propagated by the Churches, without, that is, asking whether their ideas somehow impaired the traditional views of God, man and the world and the relationship between them. Inevitably, however, many who read their texts did ask these questions, because they touched upon the foundations of their culture.

Two men, specifically, influenced the attitude towards science in the early seventeenth century, precisely because, unlike Copernicus, Kepler and Galilei, they addressed the problems involved in 'natural' language rather than in mathematical equations. They were, of course, the Englishman Francis Bacon (1561–1626) and the Frenchman René Descartes (1596–1650).

Plates 19 and 20 Europe enters an era of expanding technology, between dream and reality. The spirit of the age is well illustrated by the enormous number of mechanical gadgets one encounters in contemporary publications. Some of them were actually realized, such as the water-driven organ-cum-automata devised by the learned Jesuit Athanasius Kircher (1602–80), from A. Kircher, *Iconismus*, Rome, vol. II, f. 343. To many, the new ideas seemed far-fetched and impractical, as is shown in an eighteenth-century print making fun of science, in a vision of an air-borne world.

EUROPE, THE EARLY SEVENTEENTH CENTURY: VIEWS ON THE
SCIENTIFIC METHOD OF FRANCIS BACON AND RENÉ DESCARTES

Sir Francis Bacon, scholar and statesman, contributed to the development of modern scientific thought with a number of wide-ranging discussions clearly aimed at a general, literate audience rather than at specialist scientists. In particular, he propagated the essential value of the inductive method:

> XIV   A syllogism consists of propositions, propositions consist of words, words are tokens for ideas. If therefore the ideas themselves (the foundation of the matter) are confused and rashly deduced from things, there is no sort of firmness in the superstructure. Therefore, the only true hope lies in *induction*.
>
> XVIII   All that has so far been discovered in the sciences pretty well remains subject to vulgar notions; if we are to penetrate to the heart and limits of nature, we shall have to find a more certain and better fortified way of inferring both ideas and axioms from things. Altogether, a better and more certain method of reasoning will have to be brought into use.
>
> XIX   There are, and can only be, two methods of enquiry and the discovery of truth. One flies upward from the sense-data and particulars to extremely general axioms and causes, and discovers from these principles and their unchanging truth the intermediate axioms; this is the method now in use. The other deduces axioms from sense-data and particulars by steadily and gradually climbing higher, coming at last to the most universal generalisations; this is the true method, but one not yet tried.
>
> XXI   The intellect, left to itself, in a sober, patient and serious condition (especially if not impeded by received teaching), tends markedly towards the second and right way, but at a very slow rate of progress; since the intellect, unless directed and assisted, is an inadequate weapon and altogether unable to overcome the obscurity of things.
>
> XXII   Both methods begin with sense-data and particulars, and culminate in generalisations of a universal order, but they nevertheless differ enormously. For the one only just touches on experiment and the particular, while the other employs these properly and by rote; the one from the first posits certain abstract and useless generalisations, while the other by stages arrives at the truly knowable aspects of nature.
>
> XXVIII   Anticipation [Bacon's word for hypothesis] is not the least more useful for the establishment of agreed facts than is interpretation [of phenomena]. Gathered from a few facts – and those as a rule the ones that occur familiarly – it only dazzles the intellect and stimulates the fancy. Interpretation, on the other hand, gathered all over the place from very varied and far separated data, cannot strike the mind with such sudden force; the facts must be treated, like opinions, as hard and discordant, not unlike the mysteries of the faith.
>
> XCV   All practitioners of science have been either empiricists or dogmatists. Empiricists, like ants, only collect and put to use; dogmatic reasoners, like spiders, spin webs from within themselves. The bee's is the middle way: it extracts matter from the flowers of garden and field, but, using its own faculties, converts and digests it. The true operation of philosophy is not unlike this. It neither relies

exclusively on the powers of the mind, nor simply deposits untouched in the memory the material provided by natural history and physical experiment. Rather it transforms and works on this material intellectually. Therefore we may have hopes of great results from an alliance so far unconcluded, between the experimental and rational methods.[13]

Against Bacon's proposition that only the experimental, inductive method can lead to valid knowledge, the Frenchman René Descartes proposed a mathematical and, moreover, deductive style of argumentation as the basis of all science. The resulting 'Cartesianism' subsequently influenced the western way of thinking for centuries, even if the actual results of Descartes's own scientific thought, for example in physics, were quickly overshadowed by empirical research and other theories. Descartes tells about his quest for the perfect method in an autobiographical way:

> When I was younger, I had devoted a little study to logic, among philosophical matters, and to geometric analysis and to algebra, among mathematical matters three arts or sciences which, it seemed, ought to be able to contribute something to my design.
>
> But on examining them I noticed that the syllogisms of logic and the greater part of the rest of its teachings serve rather for explaining to other people the things we already know, or even . . . for speaking without judgement of things we know not, than for instructing us of them . . . as to the analysis of the ancients and the algebra of the moderns, besides that they extend only to extremely abstract matters and appear to have no other use, the first is always so restricted to the consideration of figures that it cannot exercise the understanding without greatly fatiguing the imagination, and in the other one is so bound down to certain rules and ciphers that it has been made a confused and obscure art which embarrasses the mind, instead of a science which cultivates it.
>
> This made me think that some other method must be sought, which, while combining the advantages of these three, should be free from their defects . . . I believed that I should find the following four [precepts] sufficient, provided that I made a firm and constant resolve not once to omit to observe them.
>
> The first was, never to accept anything as true when I did not recognize it clearly to be so, that is to say, to carefully avoid precipitation and prejudice, and to include in my opinions nothing beyond that which should present itself so clearly and so distinctly to my mind that I might have no occasion to doubt it.
>
> The second was, to divide each of the difficulties which I should examine into as many portions as were possible, and as should be required for its better solution.
>
> The third was, to conduct my thoughts in order, by beginning with the simplest objects, and those most easy to know, so as to mount little by little, as if by steps to the most complex knowledge, and even assuming an order among those which do not naturally precede one another.
>
> And the last was, to make everywhere enumerations so complete, and surveys so wide, that I should be sure of omitting nothing.
>
> The long chains of perfectly simple and easy reasons which geometers are accustomed to employ in order to arrive at their most difficult demonstrations had given me reason to believe that all things which can fall under the knowledge of

man succeed each other in the same way, and that provided we only abstain from receiving as true any opinions which are not true, and always observe the necessary order in deducing one from the other, there can be none so remote that they may not be reached, or so hidden that they may not be discovered. . . . What satisfied me most with this method, was that by it I was assured of always using my reason, if not perfectly, at least to the best of my power.[14]

In fact, in his *Discours sur la Méthode* (1637), Descartes studied his own thought processes; he concluded that man frequently starts from the wrong suppositions because he fails to systematically take into account all the factors which influence a thought, perception or action. Descartes therefore introduced the concept of fundamental doubt: before one departs from a particular position, which one wants to assume as a relative certainty, one must examine one's own thoughts about it as thoroughly and impartially as possible. However, Descartes still left open the possibility that it is God who instils these particular references in man, his creature. So, while he had to erode the function of all authority that could not be made acceptable on the basis of reasonable arguments, the concept of God remained as unquestionable for him as it had been for St Augustine and St Thomas Aquinas. The debate over the Cartesian position was waged all over Europe. By the end of the seventeenth century, it was incorporated into mainstream scholarship and science by the 'journalist' and cultural commentator Pierre Bayle. In his widely read and highly influential compendium of European knowledge, the *Dictionnaire Historique et Critique* (1697), he adopted the Cartesian attitude of radical doubt which, in his view, would inevitably lead to both reliable knowledge and to tolerance.

In the same years, John Locke proceeded one step beyond Descartes, without acknowledging or denying God. In his *Essay concerning Human Understanding* (1690) he argues that, for example, observing children teaches us that man has no inborn ideas or principles. Everything he thinks and does during his life results from or builds on ideas and principles he has learnt or which are otherwise 'taught' him within his cultural context. Thus, man is not ruled by 'universal ideas' – from which the reader might infer that, if God, or another, perhaps platonic, agency existed, it did not determine man.

Meanwhile, the 'new science', now often characterized, in the Baconian way, as experimental physics, produced new findings almost every day. The invention of the microscope in the 1620s had opened up an 'invisible world' that showed the gradual development of many life forms from eggs or semen. Some argued that putting a slice of nature under the microscope would hardly contribute to a greater understanding of such a complex whole – and in a way they were right. Others, however, rejoiced in the idea that the realities of nature could now be seen beneath the surface of nature, which gave them a powerful weapon against the occultists who, for so many centuries, had used the book of nature only as a text full of secret signs.[15]

By the later decades of the seventeenth century, the concepts of the empiricists, whose thought was guided by the study of the cosmos and of the visible world, had become a new philosophy.[16] This was most clearly demonstrated in the writings of the physicist Isaac Newton (1642–1727), whose life shows a phenomenon that characterized European culture until the end of the eighteenth century, i.e. that science was not a 'professional career' but rather something people did while taking on other tasks as well. Newton himself was first a professor at Cambridge and later master of the Royal Mint of England.[17]

In 1704, Newton published his great work *Opticks*, or the 'Optica'. In this he explains the true method for attaining knowledge and insight, the right way to look at man and the world:

> analysis consists in making experiments and observations, and admitting of no objections against the conclusions but such as are taken from experiments or other certain truths. For hypotheses are not to be regarded in experimental philosophy, and although the arguing from experiments and observations by induction be no demonstration of general conclusion, yet it is the best way of arguing which the nature of things admits of, and may be looked upon as so much the stronger by how much the induction is more general. And if no exception occurs from phenomena, the conclusion may be pronounced generally.

The way of thinking adopted by Newton and his generation shows both a Baconian trust in the value of empirical research and in the use of the Cartesian method of 'fundamental doubt', resulting, for many, in a clear optimism with regard to the human capacity to know the world and even the universe. People now felt the cosmos was governed by general laws that one could uncover and understand through careful observation. This new epistemology was codified, so to speak, in Newton's *Philosophiae naturalis Principia mathematica*, published in 1687 with the support of the Royal Society. The book unleashed a revolution precisely because, as the title indicates, it was more than a treatise on physics. Let Newton speak for himself:

> I offer this work as the mathematical principles of philosophy, because the whole content of philosophy seems to exist in this – from the phenomenon of movement to the study of natural forces, and from these forces to the demonstration of other phenomena . . . I am induced by many reasons to suspect that (the phenomena of nature may) all depend upon certain forces by which the particles of bodies, by some causes hitherto unknown, are either mutually impelled towards each other and cohere in regular figures, or are repelled and recede from each other; which forces being unknown, philosophers have hitherto attempted the search of nature in vain. But I hope the principles here laid down will afford some light either to that or some truer method of philosophy.[18]

Elaborating on the speculations of Copernicus, Kepler and others concerning the movement of the planets, Newton wanted to present a sound system based on quantitative, physical arguments. To this end he used integral and differential calculus through which it was possible to establish the position of a body at a particular moment if the relation between the position and the speed of the body or the change in speed at another time were known. When Newton subsequently reflected on the existing concepts concerning gravitation in his general study of gravitation, he was able to describe the cosmos mathematically as a system in which the celestial bodies moved eternally in set positions determined by the relative gravitational force of sun, earth and planets.

The consequences were profound, for there now occurred a definite break with the Aristotelian cosmology of the Christian world, in which the Creator always had to be present because movement supposed the constant exercise of force. According to Newton, creation, made up of atoms, was, once God had brought it into existence, a dynamic mechanism that worked in accordance with a simple law of nature. Newton confirmed what many had already suspected, or feared: God does not continuously interfere in man's life. Yet, Newton was also continually searching for more intangible knowledge, through all kinds of chemical, some would say alchemical experiments, hoping even to find the 'philosopher's stone'.[19] It is an important reminder of the fact that what has been termed the 'Age of Reason' was, in fact, a time in which people, as always, were torn between the conviction that rational thought would uncover all the world's secrets and the conviction that there might yet be a truth behind the one thus revealed.

By the end of the seventeenth century, many Europeans who followed the developments in the world of learning may well have felt they were now thrown back on themselves. The Frenchman Blaise Pascal (1623–62), who formulated striking thoughts on many questions in his famed *Pensées*, had already voiced the 'angst' evoked by a new insecurity, writing:

> When I consider the brief span of my life absorbed into the eternity which comes before and after – as the remembrance of a guest that tarrieth but a day – the small space I occupy and which I see swallowed up in the immensity of spaces of which I know nothing and which know nothing of me, I take fright and am amazed to see myself here rather than there: there is no reason for me to be here rather than there, now rather than then. Who put me here? By whose command and act were this time and place allotted to me? . . . the eternal silence of these infinite spaces fills me with dread.[20]

Many still share this fear. Nevertheless, many others, especially those who experienced the power and authority of the Churches as a hindrance to a more rational world-view, rejoiced. To them, through Newton, Europe seemed at last to have seen the light: the universal explanation of the universe had been found. Of course, the fact that science, or rather the sciences, now became a power system, too, demonstrating its use through the public presentation of all kinds of experiments with, preferably, spectacular instruments, gave it increased standing in society.

However, empirical, rational observation not only began to dominate research in the natural or physical sciences, whose importance to the European economy and society increased especially though the stream of technological innovations it produced. The new attitude now began to affect and even direct the way people thought about themselves and about their position in the cosmos as well. Thus, the political philosopher Thomas Hobbes (1588–1679) analysed and described society as if it were a physical phenomenon. In his famous work *Leviathan, or the Matter, Form and Power of a Commonwealth, Ecclesiastical and Civil* (1651), he established that all citizens are separate bodies, individual entities, only; if they continue to act like swirling particles, they will be unable to avoid collision. Therefore, man has created the State, as an instrument to avoid calamity and to realize the highest attainable good for the greatest number of people, for 'we make the common wealth ourselves'.[21]

By the beginning of the eighteenth century, Newtonian physics and other scientific concepts had gained considerable influence over various non-physical domains of human thought, varying from practical aspects such as time and distance measurements on land and at sea to economic and political philosophies about man as an individual citizen, as an individual entrepreneur. Indeed, the new sciences began to change the way people observed their environment and interpreted the nature, the organization and functioning of society and politics.[22]

From Humanism to Enlightenment: a long dawn

A growing confidence in the results of man's capacity to know himself and his world, which was widely felt throughout the Republic of Letters, came to characterize European learned culture in the late seventeenth and early eighteenth centuries. Many people considered themselves and their time as 'enlightened', namely by the light of 'Reason', of solid common sense, which led them to collect data, analyse them and only then conclude their meaning and significance. Many educated Europeans felt less and less inclined to accept as truths ideas that could not be reduced to empirical observations. Consequently, they also began to doubt all claims to authority and power that were not founded on logically reasoned and thus acceptable principles. In short, people threw off the shackles of tradition.

Increasingly, people now argued that man should free himself of the paralysis of the past, of the authoritarian, unreasoned imposition of tradition used as an argument for the ideas and structures that, specifically, Church and State had created to hold their power over society and, even, man's soul. Inevitably, faith, by its very nature un-reasonable, was thought to deny the very qualities in man that must be the basis of his thinking and acting, namely, reason and tolerance. In short, people became critical, sceptical even, and judged the world around them accordingly. A more empirical, individual and secular way of thinking, which had begun during the Renaissance, now achieved its provisional completion in a vision of man and the world that has been called 'the Enlightenment', because its main champions were convinced that the world finally was ready to be illuminated by the light of reason.

This enlightened culture was increasingly governed by concepts that, though sometimes centuries old, were once more instrumental in distancing man from the traditional vision of God and his presence in creation, in the universe. For some, as for the French author La Mettrie, who voiced his widely discussed but, to many, abhorrent thoughts in a tract called *L'Homme machine* (The Machine-Man) (1747), the universe contained no God, but physical, moving bodies only. The most complex body ever evolved was man, a self-regulating machine that, in order to function, depended upon its fuel, food – if this man-machine lacked fuel, it would not function or, in human parlance, it would become 'ill'.[23] Such thoughts were naturally influenced by technological inventions and the consequent view of man, of the world, as mechanical instruments.

Yet, though a strongly materialist philosophy did now develop – continuing to the present day – in the long run most people adopted a mainly Christian 'enlightened' view, which allowed them to somehow reconcile the opposing ideas of religion and science. This 'moderate', religion-tinged enlightenment came to affect the minds of most educated Europeans well into the twentieth century, the more so as it became prevalent in Europe's major cultural institutions – for instance, in education and science. Obviously, this occurred because both the various Christian churches and the governments of the European states – for reasons of principle and of pragmatism – tried to hold on to their traditional power, eschewing revolutionary notions that would only cause upheaval.

The Enlightenment – whether radical or Christian – was to a large extent an urban phenomenon, as can be shown from the example of late-eighteenth-century Edinburgh. This was the town where, in the late seventeenth century, Presbyterian ministers had roamed the streets on Sundays to ensure that everyone attended divine service, using force if necessary, and, of course, they would sit in church both in the morning and the afternoon. It was the town where, at that time, witches were still being burnt, as, indeed, they were all over Europe.[24] Yet, a century later, all that was changing, and not only in Edinburgh but also in eighteenth-century Amsterdam and Middelburg, in 'enlightened' circles in Madrid and Valencia under the reign of Charles III, and in the bourgeois milieus of north Italian cities like Milan. In Great Britain, this 'Enlightenment' was embodied in scholars like George Berkeley (1684–1753) and David Hume (1711–76). In the German states, it found expression in the works of Gotthold Ephraim Lessing (1729–81) and, perhaps most of all, in Gottfried Wilhelm Leibniz.

He has rightly been called the last 'universal scholar'. Admittedly, he never developed the all-embracing scientific system he longed for, with a language to match it, based on the irrevocable logic of mathematics – though with Newton he shares the honour of having developed differential calculus. Yet he contributed seminal ideas to a wide variety of fields, ranging from linguistics to philosophy, from library science to political theory. His cosmology has influenced people up to the present day. It was built on the notion of the 'monad' as the essential, basic, conscious element of the universe, matter and spirit in one, on which all more complex structures are built including, somewhere in the range of complexity, man himself, but culminating in the all-encompassing structure that is God.[25]

Indeed, the problem of God weighed heavily on the enlightened mind. To a greater or lesser degree, most Enlightenment thinkers wrestled with the relation between physics, between the world of matter, a natural world, that could be known, and meta-physics, a world that one could speculate about but not know in the same way as the physical world. Obviously, the debate centred around the relation between matter and spirit. In the seventeenth century, the Jewish-Dutch philosopher Baruch de Spinoza had already decided that man, in an age of scepticism and doubt, needed scientific proof of God's existence, and he duly proceeded to give it.[26] In his highly complex but still very readable *Tractatus Theologico-Politicus* (Amsterdam 1670), he created an image of God very unlike the personal God who had been essential to Jews and Christians for thousands of years. Spinoza's God was a primeval force, of which all men, indeed all creatures were, in a way, part. In this concept of God, the opposition of matter and spirit dissolved. But to be able to conceive of such a God, Spinoza stipulated freedom. To him, liberty was the essential precondition both for public peace and for private piety, and both were the basic preconditions of a humane society.[27]

Ultimately, the major minds of the eighteenth century, too, were unable to really distance themselves from some sort of vision of God as an uncreated substance, as creator outside and above the world. Even the German philosopher Immanuel Kant (1724–1804) had to address the question. Admittedly, in his *Kritik der reinen Vernunft* (Critique of Pure Reason) (1781), he reasoned that all experience was realized only in rational categories and that ideas such as the soul, the world and God could certainly be thought but were not provable through reason, nor, however, were they refutable; in short, the world of belief, of faith, begins beyond the borders of theoretical reason. Yet in his *Kritik der praktischen Vernunft* (Critique of Practical Reason) (1788), he strongly argued for an acceptance of religion on ethical grounds, as a human and social necessity that, of course, implied some notion of belief as well.

In the 1760s, Kant had a fascinating discussion with the Swedish mining engineer and philosopher Emmanuel Swedenborg (1688–1772), which clearly articulates the eternal tension in European-Christian thought. In a series of works, of which the *Arcana Caelestia* (The Celestial Secrets) of 1749–56, and *De Caelo et Inferno* (On Heaven and Hell), were the most important, Swedenborg had developed a vision of man and the universe which made Kant his opponent but won him many adherents even in our own age. For the Swede, attempting to prove God's existence, the mind, the spirit is a substantial, organic whole in which man and God coincide in its successive stages of awakening. To him, churches and religions are irrelevant, and he unhesitatingly rejects the universal claims of Christianity: 'Everyone whose heart is enlightened can see that not a single person was born for hell' and 'the Church of the Lord is spread over the whole world and is therefore universal: all are members of it who live a life of brotherly love, in accordance with their own religion'.[28]

For others, the world and everything in it – including the most sold material objects – were merely projections of the human mind. So it was for Arthur Schopenhauer (1788–1860). In his *Die Welt als Wille und Vorstellung* (The World as Will and Idea) (1819) he accepted that man can acquire knowledge through experience but he questioned what man can reliably say and know about the nature of things. His answer was: not much, for each man is an object, a body, 'an idea', and at the same time, a subject, a self-awareness, a 'will'. To survive in this world, each man assumes that the same counts for all other humans:

> Wenn also die Körperwelt noch etwas mehr seyn soil, als bloss unsere Vorstellung, so müssen wir sagen, dass sie äusser der Vorstellung, also an sich und ihrem innersten Wesen nach, Das sei, was wir in uns selbst unmittelbar als Willen finden.

> Therefore, if we want to maintain that the material world is more than merely our idea of it, we must conclude that beyond idea it is, in its essence and according to its own innermost self, that which we, in ourselves, immediately will it to be.

Schopenhauer concludes that a world of sorts does exist but that, actually, though we have the illusion of its manifoldness, it is nothing but the projection of one essence: 'Jeder erkennt nur *ein* Wesen ganz unmittelbar: semen eigenen Willen, im Selbstbewustseyn' ('Everybody is able to know only one essence immediately: his own will, in his own consciousness of it').[29]

Among the countries of continental Europe, eighteenth-century France was, perhaps, most open to 'enlightenment'.[30] French society was characterized by innovation and diffusion, by production and distribution, by circulation and mobility. Books and ideas acted on social mores, practices and artefacts, and together they were interwoven in an ever tighter network of communication and, indeed, of change.[31] Enlightened thinkers such as Voltaire (1694–1778) reasoned that if their principles were widely disseminated – by making knowledge accessible in dictionaries and encyclopedias, through education and reading, by displaying nature and culture in museums and visualizing it in experiments – they could actively propel society along the road to progress.

Consequently, many ideas considered characteristic of the Enlightenment evolved mainly in France. Though some of them might have been very old already, they were now described and advocated more convincingly than ever before. In his *Du Contrat Social* (On the Social Contract) (1762), Jean-Jacques Rousseau (1712–78) reasoned his way towards revolutionary ideas about freedom, equality and fraternity. However much his notion of popular sovereignty was based on his rather limited experiences of a small city-state – his native city of Geneva – and was therefore difficult to apply to larger societies, Rousseau's ideals of political and social change impassioned many, in part because the rhetoric he used was appealing in its emotional variety. Indeed, it was precisely the inconsistency of his views that allowed everyone to interpret them as they pleased. However, few French *philosophes* were as radical as he was: many sought a middle course between existing economic and social structures and the necessity to effect change gradually, especially through politics.[32]

All over educated Europe, French writers were read and commented on,[33] even if their more extreme concepts were more admired than applied. In many countries, people soon felt a moderate version of enlightened thought might go a long way to effect change. Consequently, the notions that were most success-ful were those that, having been developed in earlier Humanist and cosmopolitan thinking, now accentuated growing tolerance, especially regarding freedom of expression, and showed an increasing confidence in the civilizing value of reason.[34]

Although the non- or even anti-religious aspect of 'enlightened' thinking was not shared by the majority of educated Europeans, both the Enlightenment itself and the many debates that were essential to it inevitably contributed to a quickening erosion of Christianity as the all-powerful normative framework of European culture. Following the division between the Churches in the sixteenth century, it was now the Enlightenment that reinforced the process which went on to deconstruct a way of thinking, a world-view that, regardless of one's judgement of its morals and practices, had formed Europe's most fundamental claim to unity.

Meanwhile, cosmopolitan thinking not only became less Christian, but also claimed to comprehend and understand the entire world rather than just Europe. The new belief, the new 'faith' now vested in the power of reason increasingly proclaimed ideas about man and society that heavily emphasized a universal morality; indeed, humankind, or so people now believed, was intrinsically imbued with a morality that, if applied in its pure form, would of itself result in such values as a sense of public responsibility and the search for beauty.[35] Obviously, the body of knowledge about the non-European world which had grown tempestuously in the two preceding centuries was at the basis of these new ideas. On the one hand, ethnology had engendered cultural relativism, affecting European thought about man and the world, about Europeans and others, and had often resulted in finding 'proof' of Europe's cultural superi-ority.[36] On the other hand, the universal values now envisaged were equally the result of a European vision of humankind, and indeed, imposed upon it a set of values specifically European, specifically enlightened.

In the development of this vision, one single text – pretending to encompass all knowledge – played a central role. Preceded, in 1728, by the English *Cyclopaedia* by Chambers, it was, of course, the French *Encyclopédie*, which was published in twenty-eight volumes between 1751 and 1772,[37] and was soon seen as the fundamental repository of Enlightenment culture. In thousands of articles it described, and often also judged 'the world': its geography, its history, its religions, its philosophies, its languages, its inventions – indeed, its all and everything. But though it was a monumental, radical and hugely influential text, that did much to spread enlightened views, it is perhaps characteristic of the new divisions in Europe that the Parisian scholars who produced it were unaware of the German enterprise of J.M. Zedler, who had been publishing his *Grosses Vollständiges Universal-Lexicon aller Wissenschaften und Künste* (Great and Complete Universal Dictionary of all Sciences and Arts) from 1732 onwards; it may not have been as critical, as enlightened as its French competitor, yet it was influential in the world of German culture. The situation indicates the limits of communication between the regional languages now that Latin had lost its position as Europe's lingua franca.

Enlightenment and Romanticism: poles apart?

Paradoxically, the process by which a mainly moderate, Christian version of the Enlightenment filtered down to wider circles of the educated population of Europe at the end of the eighteenth and in the first decades of the nineteenth century was reinforced by considerable criticism of some of the more far-reaching 'enlightened' concepts, the more so when these became connected to political and social revolution. This happened when, all over Europe, people outside the circle of those who called themselves progressive – first and foremost French-orientated intellectuals – reacted negatively to the 'spirit' of the political and social revolution that shook France from 1789 onwards, resulting in the fall of the monarchy and the institution of a dictatorship. According to them, the blatant secularism and the bloody chaos that characterized French politics in this period had been the inevitable outcome of those aspects of the Enlightenment which, to them, embodied materialism, lack of belief and inhumanity. At the same time they saw the revolutionary developments as proof positive that they were right in rejecting the Enlightenment altogether. They were strengthened in their conviction by the actions of General Bonaparte, later the Emperor Napoleon; specifically by his large-scale attempt to unite the whole of Europe politically, at first with the help of the youthful zest of the French revolutionaries but soon by means of destructive wars. To better understand what was happening around the turn of the eighteenth to the nineteenth century, it is necessary once more to look back.

Actually, something of a 'counter-Enlightenment' – others would prefer to call it a Christian Enlightenment – had been developing long before the revolutionary horrors of the 1790s dawned upon Europe. During the eighteenth century, in the complicated process of cultural transmission and borrowing between different social groups, a symbiosis had been growing in which the culture of Humanism, having gained a new stimulus in the (pre-)enlightened institutions of the Republic of Letters – a cosmopolitan culture though elitist both in its origins and essence – acquired a far broader social base. One of the explanations for this process can be found in the fact that learned, scientific culture in general had slowly been adopted by the various European states and, consequently, had been presented as the result of a national effort,[38] the more so since governments had decided that the new scientific, technological achievements should be harnessed to their own goals. Increasingly, the middle classes, who basically carried this culture, were imbued with an ethic that told them that serving the State was to be their prime objective. Significantly, while all over Europe people continued to admire classical civilization, Europe's common heritage, in the reading societies and debating clubs which now became the hotbeds of bourgeois cultural life[39] – the counterpart of the aristocratic salons – thought and action now focused on the cult of one's nation's own past.

This tendency, which grew during the eighteenth century, became much stronger in the aftermath of the French Revolution. For, now, a widespread aversion developed to all those ideas and other forms of culture that, in the wake of the Enlightenment, had been presented as generally valid. People only continued to accept enlightened, universal ideas if these could be fitted into more traditional, controllable frameworks. Instead of relying on the general, the universal, which was threatening in its vagueness and offered little security, people fell back on the particular, the local, regional or national that gave structure to their own country – its religion, its language, its customs and morals, which, unlike the high-flung, so-called universal philosophical principles, could function as the recognizable, comforting anchors of identity in an ever wider, threatening world.

Specifically in those countries where French culture in its eighteenth-century, strongly secular form had been less influential – parts of the German Empire, the Netherlands and Scotland but also Spain and Italy – traditional, and also religious, concepts fused with new scientific ideas influenced by although not always acknowledged as part of the Enlightenment. In a sense, the Enlightenment and the 'counter-Enlightenment' merged in these places. A strongly personal faith, frequently of a devout, pietistic nature, and a moderate form of progressive thinking interacted fruitfully with growing pride in the achievements of one's own state. Although all over Europe, on the local-regional level, certain forms of communal thinking had a long tradition, the search for common roots now became more crystallized; soon, the governing elites of the European states took care that this evolved into a well-defined national feeling.

What remained was admiration for the great achievements of Europe's classical civilization, which were experienced, at least by the more educated, as part of their identity, and indeed, as their own roots. It was an emotion greatly reinforced by the spectacular discovery and subsequent excavation (1738–48) from the ash and lava of Mount Vesuvius of the splendours of the Roman cities of Herculaneum and Pompeii. At the same time, and perhaps understandably in view of the growing tendency to idealize only Europe, or, indeed, only one's own nation, the undeniable Afro-Asian components of that classical civilization were gradually written out of ancient Greek and indeed European history by the guardians of tradition, the scholars, precisely to ensure that this tradition could be presented as uniquely 'European'.[40] Also, in response to the French Revolution and, even more so, the imperialistic politics of Napoleon, many European states expressed their disapproval of imperial aspirations; consequently, the 'popularity' of ancient Rome decreased, while that of classical Greece grew. Greece, where no one ruler had ever subdued the towns; Greece, where democracy had been born; Greece, where the intellectual had been able to claim a far more powerful position than in imperial Rome, became very popular indeed until the end of the nineteenth century, both in the German states and in England,[41] both of which claimed to be the true heirs not only of Greek culture but of the Greek ideal.

Meanwhile, in Greece itself, for several hundred years a backward province of the Ottoman Empire, as was the greater part of the Balkans, the ideas of the Enlightenment had taken hold as well, if only among a small urban elite. One such intellectual, Iosipos Moisiodax (*c.*1725–1800), boldly came forward to claim that the peoples of the Balkans should remodel their societies on European 'enlightened' lines. One of the main instruments should be a re-organization of education, wherein vernacular Greek, the 'national' language, should be the medium.[42] Soon, all over Europe, people enthusiastically flocked to Greece to help it gain independence from its non-European, Islamic, and therefore backward and tyrannical, rulers in Istanbul.

Inevitably, as European culture was slowly being nationalized, appreciation grew of that part of the past that could convincingly be argued as explaining the nature and uniqueness of one's own state and society. By this process, trends that had set in during the late seventeenth century now became more pronounced.

In England, in the 1750s, the composer Thomas Arne had produced a masque to be acted before the crown prince's court called *King Alfred* – along with the rather more mythical Arthur, Alfred was considered to be the founder of England's independence; it contained the rousing nationalistic song 'Rule Britannia'. In his *Ossian Poems* of 1761, James Macpherson harked back to an even more distant past, singing the praises of Celtic culture as a basic element in the formation of Britain. In the German states, Johan Wolfgang von Goethe (1749–1832) and Friedrich Schiller (1759–1805), while still inspired by classical Greece, also delved deeply into their 'own' Germanic past. Remarkably, in Spain, for the first time in its history, intellectuals, and, moreover, monks like Benito Feijóo and Martin Sarmiento pointed to the influence of Islamic civilization on Spanish culture, although, of course, they tended to concentrate on Spain's glorious *Siglo de Oro*, the 'golden' sixteenth century.

And yet, as if to prove that such appreciation of the past need not result in stultifying conservatism but could be a creative influence, many of these men also strongly voiced the need for change, to recapture the erstwhile grandeur of the nation. Even in Spain, considered by most northern, Protestant Europeans to be almost as backward as the Balkans if only because it was judged to be 'priest-ridden', enlightened monks and other thinkers, often from the provincial bourgeoisie, contributed to a climate wherein, for the first time in more than 100 years, part of the ruling elite did indeed consider and even implement new policies; in the economic and educational sectors, ideas from England and France were discussed and adopted.[43] The same occurred in Italy, especially in Milan and the other economically prosperous towns of Lombardy, where the rule of the Church was less oppressive than in the papal states. Intellectuals from the clergy as well as from the secular bourgeoisie and innovative entrepreneurs discussed both the past and the future, proposing reforms to restore Italy's ancient cultural and economic pre-eminence. In doing so, they created a situation wherein, by the end of the eighteenth century, northern Italy was on its way to becoming one of Europe's most enlightened and, also, most prosperous areas.

All the while, indeed, from the mid-seventeenth century onwards, another phenomenon had become increasingly manifest in European culture and now began to interact with the growing tendency to reduce the space of meaningful experience to one's own nation, and to glorify it, partly through its past greatness. This was the glorification of spontaneous, 'natural' feeling and, inextricably mixed with it, the cult of nature, of harmonious growth – though in the new fashion of natural garden architecture it had to be artfully arranged to achieve the desired effect. Feeling and growth, both seen as characteristics of nature, became elements of a new awareness, a new sense of life. Instead of the mathematically cold lines of classicist architecture, of a totally controlled society and environment as epitomized in the denatured court and also gardens of Versailles, people stressed the value of organic growth, both in art and architecture and in society and nature. Significantly, the woods, once the abode of the uncivilized, the wild, and of the old, pagan gods, now became the natural habitat of a man at ease, a man communicating with his roots and with the cosmos; indeed, while many still felt this cosmos was ruled by a personal, omnipotent God, others now, again, stressed that the cosmos, nature, was the ultimate force of life itself. This cultivation both of nature and of the past coincided in a vision of society as an organism that had grown 'naturally' through the ages, with time nurturing it and hallowing its results. The sum total of these complex sentiments has been termed Romantic. The term itself had already been in use for a long time; indeed, the famous English diarist Samuel Pepys had applied it in the 1660s to characterize an extra-ordinary contemporary of his, Margaret Lucas, duchess of Newcastle, precisely because she, in her dress, lifestyle and even emotions, indicated a tendency to reject fashion, to follow no rules, to be her own self.

The new, romantic views had a wide resonance. In the imperial capital, Vienna, Franz Joseph Haydn (1732–1809) was avidly reading the works of contemporary philosophers and other scholars.[44] He also travelled, to England among other places, in 1791 and again in 1794, because his music was greatly appreciated there. While in London, he acquainted himself with Handel's great choral works which inspired in him the wish to create something comparable. Back home, the baron Gottfried van Swieten, one of the Empress Maria Theresa's courtiers and her librarian, presented Haydn with the text of the Englishman John Milton's poem *Paradise Lost* (1658–67), depicting man's creation and life in paradise, which he had translated and adapted. Haydn set it to music in 1798. But paradise was not lost to these eighteenth-century musicians and thinkers. From an intriguing nexus of cultural lines reaching through time and space, the oratorio *The Creation* became a paean of praise to God's work, a joyous song about the sheer variety and life of nature. It is a vocal résumé both of Europe's continued Christian vision of its origins and development, and of its optimism for God's future achievements as ruler of the earth.

Yet, even in a vision like Haydn's, in which the overture depicting the seven days of creation should definitely be labelled Romantic, the idea of Europe's shared ideals inevitably receded into the background. Perhaps this is one of the most important elements distinguishing the Enlightenment from Romanticism.

Even while enlightened thinking had been gaining a firm foothold all over Europe by the end of the eighteenth century, reactions against it already started appearing, denouncing its so-called dehumanizing tendencies. Indeed, from the late eighteenth century onwards, many have found problems choosing between what by then were significantly termed the poles of positivism and poetry. In these years, Goethe conceived his greatest play, *Faust*, a 'scholar's tragedy' in which he, through Faust, empirical thinker and doubter, articulated weighty questions about the limits of knowledge and thus about the position and purpose of man in the world. Not surprisingly, both in Germany and, for example, in the Netherlands, Baruch de Spinoza, was rediscovered, by some as the anti-Christian, atheistic philosopher of a scientific, secular culture, but by others as the prophet of a convincing pantheism.

Indeed, it was in Germany, in the milieu of Jena University, that a new or rather an old philosophy using new terms and ideas was now preached. This 'Naturphilosophie', embodied in Friedrich-Wilhelm Schelling (1775–1854) but strongly present in the scientific and the poetic writings of men like Goethe and other Romantic authors as well, sought to reunite nature and culture, in the sense, too, that to them nature implied feeling, faith even, and culture stood for man's rational capacities and technological achievements. To reunite the two worlds, the new philosophy developed dynamic and even organic explanations for natural phenomena using both chemistry and mathematics and applying such concepts as polarity and complementarity, metamorphosis and identity. Although this philosophy did not go in for experiment, it did, in fact, generate important scientific results, precisely because such concepts as unity and polarity led to discoveries in the fields of contact-electricity and electro-magnetism. However, in the end, the largely deductive character of this approach was felt to be technically, materially unproductive; hence, in the 1830s, people once more embraced a very positivistic, inductive view of science which, for the time being, eschewed philosophical reflection. Yet the idea of a more holistic interpretation of nature lingered on, resurfacing every now and then, as, for example, in Germany itself, where, at the end of the nineteenth century, a new call was heard: 'zurück zu Goethe', meaning back to a humanizing science. It was a call that can be heard even now, reflecting both scientists' and the general public's feelings that the modern world should address 'the unfinished business of our times';[45] it is, in fact, a call heard by all those who, whether scientists or ordinary educated people, argue that a purely positivistic and moreover technological bias would be damaging to human culture.

It is necessary to consider these developments precisely because criticism of the Enlightenment and its consequences has echoed up to the present day, being voiced, specifically, by those who feel that the culture of 'modernity', of progress promised by the enlightened thinkers – a culture that, indeed, materialized in the highly technological, consumption-driven world of nineteenth- and twentieth-century Europe – has not become the humane world it also promised to be, a world of reason and tolerance. Consequently, depending on the extent to which one experiences the effects of that which initially developed in the Enlightenment as positive or negative, one will consider this period as a blessed or a cursed phase in European history.

In retrospect, many have judged the period between *c.*1650 and 1820, in which the Enlightenment slowly became manifest and, subsequently, triumphant, as a period that showed a growing awareness of the position of man as a free agent, an individual who should be the central point of reference in society, as well as a period of increasing rationalism. Undoubtedly, between them, these phenomena signalled a definite break with the 'harmonious universe' that most intellectuals had tried to maintain one way or the other since the union of the classical and Christian world-views sought and achieved in the Middle Ages. Together, humanism – by which I do not mean the scholarly Humanism of the fifteenth and sixteenth centuries – and rationalism greatly contributed to the decline of a European culture that had been determined by institutional religion and marked the transition to a more secular view of man and the world. To many, both then and now, the situation was aggravated precisely because the prevailing organic world-view had been supplanted by a mechanistic vision that was to hold an almost absolute sway over Europe until the middle of the twentieth century.

Undoubtedly, though Enlightenment ideas at first only affected a small group of intellectuals and the better educated, they were soon taken up by the middle class, during the nineteenth century, and then became the basis of European thought about man and the world in the twentieth century.

However, this happened only because the Enlightenment was certainly not as diametrically opposed to Romanticism as is often argued. The Enlightenment glorified empiricism, but it was an empiricism not only of reason but also of the senses! Thus it bore the fruit of the seeds that had already been sown in early Humanism and the subsequent Renaissance. The difference became manifest mainly in the more secular character of the Enlightenment. Yet, recent research has abundantly shown that in this very period innumerable creative combinations of reason and religion remained or even came into existence: from the esotericism of such secretive and indeed secret societies as the Rosecrucians and the Freemasons, to the Catholic 'Aufklärung'.[46] In particular, the moderate, bourgeois version of Romanticism continued to pose many of the questions which people in the Christian Enlightenment had asked too, even though these questions were now clothed in other words. Maybe one must conclude that it was only the extent to which the answers to a number of fundamental questions betrayed a clear return to a more religious, metaphysical view of the world that really differentiated Romanticism from the Enlightenment. Indeed, the two often seem to have fused, especially in the first decades of the nineteenth century.

Part IV

Continuity and change

New forms of consumption
and communication

13 Europe's revolutions

Freedom and consumption for all?

Material culture and conspicuous consumption: Europe's process of consumer change until the end of the eighteenth century

Until well into the eighteenth century and, in some areas of Europe, up until the end of the nineteenth century, most families, especially in the countryside, possessed little more than a dozen household goods – those that were absolutely necessary: some simple stools, a plank table, some cooking utensils, perhaps two or three beds and mattresses, and a few blankets. The fact is borne out by an investigation organized in the German countryside at the end of the nineteenth century. According to the survey:

> The bed was a wooden plank with a straw mattress; there was a cupboard, a rough-hewn wooden table, a few stools, all of which a carpenter could make in a few hours. In my youth the first stoves were introduced; before, we only had an open fire with a kettle hanging above it. Around 1860/1870 my father bought such a stove. . . . In the old house . . . we had an oven, which my parents had purchased when they married, a pump, and a sofa. We ate and lived in the kitchen, with its wooden floors, its scrubbed table, its settee and cupboard, all made by Father . . . The few clothes we had were hung on pegs, maybe behind a curtain. Mostly, two children shared a bed.[1]

In order to know whether this situation prevailed all over Europe and, moreover, whether it applied to the non-agrarian population as well, a cultural historian must delve into the archives. For the answers are, at least partly, given by the inventories enumerating the possessions of citizens and farmers in towns and villages. Research into the material culture of Europe is a fairly recent branch of scholarship. Formerly, most historians were more interested in the traces left by the great thinkers and artists, the ramifications of political intrigues and dynastic affairs, the mechanisms of social processes. But these certainly do not suffice in writing cultural history. We also want to know how ordinary people lived, what their houses looked like, what they ate and how they dressed in their daily lives; the culture of Europeans was shaped fundamentally by its basic material conditions.

One of the first results of this new type of research has been that we now know that all over western Europe the average number of household items gradually increased between the late fifteenth and the late eighteenth centuries. In the same period, material possessions were perceptibly, if slowly, more evenly spread across the social classes. Both developments were undoubtedly caused by the economic changes produced, in particular, by the growth of trade and industry.

Yet, up until the end of the eighteenth century, only a single social group lived a life resembling our modern consumer society. Only a single social group was always well fed, always able to buy luxury foods it did not need and, more-over, able to buy any amount of material objects which, judged from a survival perspective, were unnecessary as well. This group, of course, was Europe's elite, comprised both of the old nobility, its wealth largely based on landed income, and of a small number of top bureaucrats grown rich in the service of the State as well as of plutocrats who had amassed their fortunes in trade and banking. What did their material culture look like?

Their houses were big, even very big, boasting an amount of space far and above what was needed to give simple shelter: it showed society that its owners had the money to buy 'superfluous' space, space that was luxury and thus gave status to its proprietor; in short, it showed wealth and the social position usually associated with power. The rooms in these houses were filled with objects that were useless, too: sculpted wooden chests, huge armoires, Persian or other oriental carpets, richly embroidered tapestries, pictures large and small. The chests and cupboards stored rich clothes, and caskets full of jewellery, as well as china and plate. All these objects shared the function of the space they occupied, displaying wealth, distinguishing their possessor, referred to his power.

But the ideology behind it went deeper: the wealth of the elite, the money that did not have to be spent on life's bare necessities, was still put to good use. Building or buying the splendid mansions, castles and palaces, commissioning the beautiful and costly objects that filled them meant that the elite cared for culture and showed that the society of which they were the leaders was a truly civilized society. This argument was prevalent already in the sixteenth and seventeenth centuries. The mentality it expressed has been described as society's need for 'conspicuous consumption'. The function of spending money on luxury was to underline the privileged position of the possessors. Of course, the phenomenon also included not only luxury goods, but leisure too, as it indicated that those who were thus able to do nothing had, indeed, no need to work to stay alive – obviously because there were others who worked for them, others over whom they held power. Hence, leisure was a luxury as well, and one that gave status. But for leisure to have this function, it had to be as publicly displayed as the elite's material possessions.

Hence, the nobles and high officials of France, England and Sweden, of the Burgundian and the Spanish-Habsburg courts frequently organized hunt parties and tournaments that lasted for days. Dressed in their splendid clothes and decked with jewellery, they attended princely or aristocratic weddings that were often celebrated with week-long festivities. They were the guests at banquets that might last an entire day, if only because more than a hundred different dishes were served. It was 'conspicuous consumption', both of money and of time, that achieved its very function because it was played out before an audience; if maximum visibility was ensured – often, the common people were invited to watch their 'betters' eat and feast – power was not only represented but, in that very moment, created.

One can still see them, these aristocrats, in their costly garments of velvet and silk, threaded with gold and silver and stitched with pearls and gems, for they had themselves depicted in all their finery by such painters as François Clouet, Hans Holbein and Titian (Tiziano Vecelli), who portrayed the princes and nobles of fifteenth- and sixteenth-century Europe. And we know what they ate, too, because the banquets were often recorded for posterity, in written or even printed descriptions that tell us they ate dishes composed of the most exotic and therefore the most expensive ingredients like peacock tongues and salmon cheeks. The food was served on tables groaning under the weight of richly worked gold and silver vessels, crystal goblets and plate cutlery. While fountains spouted wine, musicians and dancers entertained the guests.

Both the events themselves, and their painted or printed records meant to display money and power, power and money. And, indeed, these events, and the visual and written records thereof, reproduced power: through these manifestations of power, the public was strengthened in its belief that the existing order was, indeed, the natural one. No more so, of course, than in the royal processions, when splendidly decorated floats passed under triumphal arches richly painted with all kinds of classical or mythological scenes, usually presenting a political and dynastic message. At such a moment, even such a cynical and critical observer as the Scotsman James Boswell, keeping a diary of his 1763 London sojourn, felt he had to note:

> This day being the Queen's birthday, I was amused by seeing multitudes of rich-dressed people driving in their splendid equipages to Court. Really, it must be confessed that a court is a fine thing. It is the cause of so much show and splendour that people are kept gay and spirited.[2]

Indeed, for a long time, the courts of the European princes were the very centres and even the motors of this 'system' that effectively taught people to equate consumption with power.

At the French court at Versailles, not only the power of France was concentrated, it was also a theatre where immense wealth and opulence were displayed. There, the French aristocracy were positively worn out by a continuous orgy of feasts that left some of them physically exhausted every day.[3] Some 3,000 to 4,000 nobles attended the court. Together, they made up approximately 1 per cent of the *c.*400,000 people who constituted the nobility of France. In their turn, this entire group constituted only 2 per cent of the country's population of some 20 million people. Surrounding this court elite were, of course, armies of servants, but also the French state's top bureaucrats, for the palace was the seat of government as well.

The court nobles lived a life of fierce competition. They all wanted to gain the king's favour, for the power and the riches it could bring. Flatteringly emulating the king's example, everybody wanted to show himself in as advantageous a light as possible. Man and wife dressed luxuriously, following the fashions set by the king and the queen, or rather, in this case, the king's official mistress. People felt forced to spend fortunes on festivities, hoping the king might deign to attend. They decorated their own house as a little Versailles. Indeed, they went out of their way to show they understood what it meant to be a courtier, to impress the world with the fact that they belonged to the centre of power. No wonder the Duke of Saint-Simon, who in his diaries left a surprisingly cynical description of life at court and of the 'Sun' who reigned over Versailles, writes that Louis deliberately urged his nobles to spend their fortunes, by making luxury a matter of honour, crippling them with debts and, thus, increasing their dependence on him.[4]

To judge by the many descriptions of foreign visitors, in the last quarter of the seventeenth century, Versailles did indeed become the stage where Europe's culture of 'conspicuous consumption' was daily enacted, precisely by the costly and time-consuming ceremonies and rituals that served to display and cement the power of royalty and aristocracy. The message was that people who could afford to live this kind of life, to spend so much money on such futile things and futile pastimes, were placed far and above the solid burgher, the industrious artisan and the hard-working farmer. Those who lived in this way belonged to the political, social and cultural elite.

Because the court aristocracy were the leaders of society in most of the states of Europe, other people seeking status, wanting to climb the ladder of social and political success, tried to live as the aristocrats did. Indeed, Saint-Simon indicated as much, concluding that the 'vice' of overspending spread from Versailles to Paris, and finally infected the general public. More specifically, the rich members of the bourgeoisie, who, though not born to this culture, yet had reached positions of considerable economic power by virtue of their own work, began to imitate the court nobility. Their number increased in the course of the seventeenth and eighteenth centuries. By 1800 the bourgeoisie made up some 10 per cent of the European population. Admittedly, most of them could not afford to spend their lives in a continuous *dolce far niente*, as did the leading nobles. However, they endeavoured to emulate the aristocratic lifestyle by publicly demonstrating as much leisure as they could afford to and, moreover, by surrounding themselves with all the trappings of riches and power, with as many luxury goods as possible. Thus, the upper echelons of the bourgeoisie aped the lifestyle of the aristocracy precisely through 'conspicuous consumption'.[5]

Inevitably, there were those who condemned these developments. Many even voiced moral objections to increasing consumption as *luxuria*, a sin destroying public harmony because it made people want to break the restrictions imposed upon them by the divine, by nature and by society. These critics maintained that all this luxury was but waste, turning people away from the real values of life and, hence, inducing moral decadence. At least from the fifteenth century onwards, governments, often using such moral arguments but also because they wanted to preserve class boundaries and, thus, the traditional order of society, repeatedly proclaimed so-called 'sumptuary laws', forbidding those of the middle and lower classes who were so inclined to indulge in various forms of luxury. Bourgeois women were not to dress in costly velvets or furs, and the ever-longer tips of shoes, which sometimes had to be tied to the knee to prevent a person from tripping over them, were denied to non-noble people. Also, the number of attendants at funeral processions was regulated in accordance with one's position in society, and so was the number of chimneys and, for that matter, street-facing windows one's house might boast. Still, such laws were hardly ever successful, if only because at the same time governments found it highly expedient to incite their subjects to spend as much as possible, precisely to profit from the taxes on production and consumption they imposed.[6]

No wonder, perhaps, that a clear-minded, non-moralizing philosopher like the Frenchman Voltaire, and a clear-minded, non-moralizing economic theorist like the Anglo-Dutchman Bernard Mandeville tried to counter the moral arguments. They argued that 'conspicuous consumption', though perhaps decadent from a moral point of view nevertheless did contribute to economic and social progress. Without this powerful stimulus, the European economy would have no motor, and Europe's progress would come to a standstill. Mandeville's was the most incisive comment. In his *Fable of the Bees: Private Vices and Public Benefits* (London 1714), which, essentially, is a debate on the morality of capitalism and consumerism, he showed that both the European economy and, in a specific sense at least, European society thrived on the unbridled spending of certain groups, even though that same society continued to condemn a spendthrift way of life as utterly sinful.[7]

Production and reproduction: a process of economic and demographic change until the end of the eighteenth century

Until the seventeenth century, in western Europe the 'normal' structure of the basic unit of social organization, the family, was not that of the so-called 'extended family' or clan, of several generations living together under the authority of a patriarch or matriarch. Indeed, in this part of Europe such clans probably never were the common type of family at all, unlike in other regions of the world. Instead, the conjugal family was well established: when children married, they went to live by themselves, creating their own household. They might take in one or more of their parents or elderly relatives when advanced age made them unfit to provide and care for themselves, and in this way the image of a three-generation household became common, but its nucleus was still the couple with its children.[8]

Outside of the aristocracy – the group most likely to forge marriage ties at an early age to secure the preservation of power and wealth for the next generation – people married rather late: well into adulthood, i.e. in their late twenties. Also, many never married at all, for marriage depended heavily on a future couple's potential to support themselves financially. In Europe's largely agricultural society this meant that, if they did not inherit a plot of land, both had to work before they could acquire a farm of their own. In trade and industry, too, people had to work for a long time before they were able to start their own business. As most boys and young men went out to work if they were not employed in the family business, so did the girls, even though their opportunities were fewer. By far the most common job for a girl was to serve in another household, whether in the country or in town. There, however, their plight often was not easy, what with being beaten by their mistresses and sexually harrassed by their masters. Normally, if they got pregnant, they had to leave the house. This often meant they had no alternative but to become a prostitute. In addition to those who freely entered the profession or, more likely, were forced to do so by sheer destitution, these girls account for the enormous number of prostitutes who populated European cities in the seventeenth and eighteenth centuries, amounting to many thousands in such capitals as London, Paris and Vienna.

Meanwhile, all kinds of sexual relations were practised both before and outside the marriage, as is shown by the many rules devised to regulate mating behaviour, and reflected in all kinds of popular customs connected with courtship. They all indicate a rather daunting measure of social control, especially in this area of life. Although lawful wedlock was propagated by both the Churches and the State, one should certainly not view European society at that time as even remotely as sexually restricted and, indeed, priggish as the picture conjured up by ideals developed and enforced in the nineteenth century. Thus, for example, the sexual allusions used in the very popular catches of seventeenth- and eighteenth-century England were broad indeed. Samuel Ives made his public sing along lustily to such texts as the following:

> Come pretty wenches more nimble than eels,
> and buy my fine boxes, my stones and my steels;
> let me touch but your tinder and you would admire
> how quickly my steel and my stones will give fire . . .
> take my steel in your hand, wench, and try but a blow:
> i'faith I dare warrant 'tis true touch and go.[9]

The sexual fulfilment of women, as well as of men, was openly discussed – a situation that would begin to change only by the end of the eighteenth century when, once more, the Churches embarked on a campaign to make marriage the only venue for sex, and procreation its sole justification.

Once married, birth control was, if not uncommon, not very effective, due to the lack of foolproof contraceptive devices. Though all kinds of ingenious devices did exist, still the most common and obviously not very reliable practice was *coitus interruptus*, the withdrawal of the penis before ejaculation. Hence, abortion flourished, though the methods used were highly primitive and, consequently, the death rate among the women appallingly high. It was, however, illegal and, moreover, condemned as a mortal sin, especially by the Churches.

While both Church and State tried to control marriage as the tie that secured the position of family as society's basic moral and legal unit, they tried to prevent some people from marrying at all: if allowed to procreate freely, the poor especially would only produce more children who were then abandoned, to die or to be brought up in an orphanage, to finally become paupers themselves who would roam and ravage the countryside, or make life in the towns unsafe and procreate again. Also, though quite extensive programmes of poor relief did exist, the authorities disliked spending too much money that way.

It is not unlikely that the pattern of marriage and family that characterized Europe during these centuries contributed to a mentality that differed considerably from that found in other cultures. At least in western Europe, couples of mature men and women formed the essential basis of society, people with a spirit of self-reliance and self-responsibility, which may have translated itself into forms of creativity both in the individual and in the community.

By the middle of the eighteenth century, a number of factors combined to effect profound demographic and consequently cultural changes. A 'rural revolution' took place when the three-course system was abandoned and farmers started working their entire property, expanding the yield through new systems of crop rotation and the use of new fertilizers. In the same period, the economy altered because people began using the opportunities increasingly offered by the cottage industry and, later, by more complex forms of industrialization. Especially in the more industrialized regions, marriages were now concluded earlier and, what is more, they were no longer dictated only by economic motives, but, as a romantic culture slowly spread even among the middle and the lower classes, also by sentiment. However, the number of illegitimate children rose sharply as well, especially in urban areas. This indicates a sexual, indeed, a cultural transformation, which ties in with the greater mobility of life in Europe in general and with the declining social control of closed communities in particular. It can also be explained by a general dissatisfaction with prevailing living conditions, with people turning against economic restrictions, against a society wherein legal separations divided the classes, against laws that forbade the poor to marry at all.

These changes coincided with an exceptionally long period of peace between 1763 and the end of the century, as well as with improving hygiene conditions: for example, as the paving of streets and the collection of refuse were introduced in the main towns of western Europe, and cures for some of the more devastating illnesses were finally found – for example, a smallpox vaccination was introduced in 1796. With the death rate considerably reduced, these changes resulted in what has been labelled 'the demographic transition'.

Yet, the life expectancy of newborn children remained dismal. Infant mortality was still very high: one in five children died before their first birthday, mostly from infectious diseases. The practice of breastfeeding – by the natural mother in the lower classes, by a wet nurse among the bourgeoisie and the aristocracy – did at least provide babies with a good diet. It also helped to reduce the birth rate, as it interfered with ovulation. Nevertheless, the practice of wet-nursing was, necessarily, a bad one. Not because of the commonly held belief, spread in many folk tales, that a woman employed to suckle a baby might change its character for the worse or even be inclined to kill the newborn left to her care in order to then take on the care and the money for another one, but because it was a business, after all, and most children tended to receive less care than they needed.

While the Christian Church at a very early stage of its existence had declared criminal one of the common practices of antiquity, infanticide, which was made punishable by death, Europeans, mostly for economic reasons, continued to kill their offspring – especially in the countryside. In towns, leaving children on the doorstep of one of the numerous churches was a less cruel solution for many parents. The number of foundlings in a major city ran into many thousands a year. Mostly, either church authorities or, increasingly, private charities or the State began to take care of these children as well the many orphans, who were the result of the high death rate among the adult population. Life inside these foundling hospitals and orphanages was less than healthy, for all their, sometimes palatial, external splendour, still visible in the huge buildings erected in London, Paris, Venice or Rome. Malnutrition, disease and only the most basic medical care led to an appallingly high mortality rate in these institutions, especially in times of economic or political crisis in the outside world.

Those children who survived faced a hard world. As to parental attitudes towards their children before the cult of the family became established in the bourgeois world of the nineteenth century, historians differ greatly in their judgement.[10] True, some of the visual evidence – especially the more intimate conversation pieces produced by Jan Steen and other Dutch painters of the seventeenth century, the 'Golden Age' of Dutch painting, or by that accomplished Frenchman Jean-Baptiste Chardin in the eighteenth century – seems to suggest harmonious family lives in which well-fed infants played contentedly with their toys or pet animals. Yet mostly, life for children in all socio-economic groups was emotionally harsh from a present-day point of view, even though their material circumstances might differ considerably.

A process of social and cultural change: the convergence of elites until the end of the eighteenth century

The growing influence of and interaction between the various means of communication, especially the printing press and travel, reinforced the cosmopolitan culture that, from the late fifteenth century onwards, came to characterize European court culture and, soon, also influenced the life of the educated in general, since their background in humanist education was now strengthened by a wide variety of mediated cultural stimuli. In a 'civilization process' that, in chronological order, was marked by influences from Italian, Spanish and finally French court culture and by the humanist culture which developed partly within and partly outside these circles, a distinct European elite culture was evolving.[11]

Yet, well into the sixteenth century, the Europeans who participated in this culture – the 'great tradition' – still belonged to two socially separate elite groups. On the one hand there was the intellectual, scholarly elite, recruited increasingly from the middle class, from people who, partly because they chose learning as a career, or profession, sought to improve their position. On the other there was the elite made up both of the land-owning nobility, whose power base was the European countryside, and of the non-noble, 'bourgeois' urban patriciate; together these latter two constituted a political and socio-economic upper class whose members definitely did not look upon culture – artistic and learned culture – as a career opportunity but nevertheless fostered culture in the widest sense, either from genuine interest in the arts and sciences or because it gave them distinction and status.

Now, from the sixteenth century onwards, the highest reaches of the well-to-do middle class – both the established 'notables' or 'patricians', who had been slowly gaining influence and wealth both in the service of the State – more specifically in state bureaucracy and the military – and people working in the professions, as well as in trade and industry, increasingly came to form a distinct, largely urban elite.[12] Indeed, in the whole of western Europe this group began to play a more important role in society, both economically and politically. Yet socially and culturally it continued to orientate itself on the norms and values of the traditional upper class culture of courts and nobles.

However, in the course of the sixteenth and seventeenth centuries, the old aristocracy lost its role as the principal carrier of the 'new', bureaucratic, centralized states, which needed new instruments of power for the effective exercise of that power. The connection between growing state power and an economy, a fiscal system increasingly directed by and tied to the State, was reflected in the fact that both successful entrepreneurs and powerful government officials now came mainly from the middle class. Since people now realized that 'knowledge' actually meant 'power', it was mainly the prosperous bourgeoisie who underpinned and consolidated its economic and political power and the social advancement associated with it through increased emphasis on education and knowledge. These were considered useful as well as 'dignified' because they were effective in helping to achieve position and wealth.

Thus, inevitably, members of the old aristocracy, too, realized that service to the state with its 'modern', bureaucratic-technical government was the means to maintain their economic, political and social position. For them, too, education, specialization even, became necessary. Thus, culture, especially in its form of useful knowledge, of science, of technology, was increasingly respected and fostered.

One of the places where the sociocultural process outlined above became visible were the 'salons' of seventeenth- and eighteenth-century Paris. There, daughters of the rich middle class, who had been able to marry into the nobility on the strength of their dowries, now received artists and scientists from the middle class in their aristocratic mansions, mixing them with the lords from the court nobility of Versailles.[13] At the innumerable courts in the German states the process was visible, too. In a cosmopolitan milieu like eighteenth-century Weimar, on winter evenings the reigning duchess and her noble courtiers might be observed sitting around the table with their learned advisers, among whom was Johan Wolfgang von Goethe – a commoner raised to the nobility, since the aristocracy remained, socially, the most desirable order – and with educated citizens from the town's leading circles.

Slowly but inevitably, middle-class norms and values started filtering through to the aristocracy who, in order to maintain their position economically and politically, no longer shunned people from other social groups. As a result, this group's composition, character and culture started to change. Even though the two groups never merged completely, they did come to share a common lifestyle and a cosmopolitan attitude, on the basis of which the English politician and thinker Edmund Burke could observe at the end of the eighteenth century that 'No European can feel completely like an exile anywhere in Europe'.[14] But of course he was still describing an elite, people who had been well educated and could afford to travel.

Perhaps the collision as well as the fusion of aristocratic and bourgeois elite cultures can best be observed in the learned periodicals that constituted the Republic of Letters. At first, in the seventeenth century, these principally aimed to further the 'correspondence' between scholars[15] or to help the economic-political elite to gain an informed opinion of the issues of the day. However, by the end of the seventeenth century, a different type of periodical was being published, which intended to popularize all manner of information and knowledge; significantly, instead of using the languages of the scholars and the court elite, i.e. Latin and French, they were now published in the vernacular: German, English, Dutch. A new reading public devoured such new periodicals as the 'European Library' or *Boekzaal van Europe*, which first appeared in the Dutch Republic in 1692.[16] *The Spectator* was very influential both in and outside England from 1712, and the fascinating *Biedermann* was widely read in the German-speaking region. In the eighteenth century, the number of such journals increased spectacularly: by 1780, in the German states alone approximately 1,000 different periodicals were being read. Many show signs indicating that the authors – and, thus, one may surmise, at least part of their readership – wanted to change or even abolish a culture, a set of traditional norms and values too distinctly associated with, and propagated by, the old aristocracy. *The Spectator* fulminated against the waste of money and time displayed by the nobility, and *Biedermann*, scathingly referring to the absentee parenthood practised in many an aristocratic household, asking its readers whether children raised by servants instead of by their own mothers would ever become worthy citizens. Indeed, the concept of responsible citizenship was central to this new culture.

Rather than listen to the elevated but, to many, unrealistic and outdated aristocratic conflicts between honour, love and duty articulated in the tragedies of seventeenth-century French playwrights like Pierre Corneille and Jean Racine and given musical expression in the allegorical and mythological operas of such eighteenth-century composers as André Campra and Jean-Philippe Rameau, people now read novels that dealt with the vicissitudes of 'real' men and women – that is to say, the inhabitants of comfortable bourgeois households, but not, of course, the labouring classes. It would take another century before they entered the mainstream of European cultural consciousness. By disseminating the principles of the happy family, of a sober, virtuous life – expressed in and achieved by proper education and the reading of elevating books, by applying utilitarian science, by a stable relationship between man and wife, parents and children – these often weekly papers aimed to civilize society on the basis of middle-class rather than aristocratic values.[17] Soon, this 'civilizing offensive' proved quite successful.

All over Europe, members of the bourgeoisie now felt the wish to search for knowledge, for truth; also, they knew they wished to do so in a sociable way, that is, in the context of a group of like-minded, well-educated, 'reasonable' people. Indeed, this sociability was now experienced as a road to virtue not only by members of the affluent middle class but also of the aristocracy.[18] Consequently, this sociability, expressed in gatherings that might choose salon, café, or reading circle as their venue – the latter because it helped shoulder the costs of reading material, still an obstacle to many – became a characteristic of the cosmopolitan culture of the eighteenth-century European elites. And yet, in many other ways, the lives of the people sharing in this culture might be very different, for while one member might return home to his town house in a private carriage, another was, perhaps, forced to walk.

Parallel to and soon in combination with this culture of sociability another development occurred, soon to become the single most important factor in the process that now shaped the increasingly dominant 'middle class' self-consciousness. It was the rise of voluntary associations, in which well-to-do burghers organized for all kinds of civic-social and sociocultural purposes and where, increasingly, a culture of free speech was fostered, irrespective of rank, wealth or even their legally circumscribed position in society. These associations became a kind of 'subscriber democracy'.[19] The many thousands of clubs that, by the end of the eighteenth century, dominated life in the towns of western Europe soon developed into miniature civil societies, characterized by self-government through their constitutions, elections and representatives. Constituting part of the growing power of bourgeois culture, they also became a hotbed of new ideas about social and political organization, and became the training ground for practices which people now thought they might also want to introduce into society at large.[20]

Two 'revolutions': one political, one economic, both cultural

All over Europe, control over political power had always been an issue that threatened the stability cherished by the rulers and the ruling elites alike.

In many states during the seventeenth and eighteenth centuries, the inevitable reaction to the growing power of the princes and their top bureaucrats tended to marginalize the consultative role which had been claimed by the 'estates' since the twelfth century; that reaction now took the form of constitutionalism. This was certainly not democracy in the present-day sense of representational government based on universal suffrage, in which the franchise, or right to vote, is given to all adults. Yet it was one step in this direction. Many people felt a growing revulsion at princely claims to 'absolute' power – a power that, theoretically at least, was not restricted by any other laws than those made by the sovereigns themselves, and by the general, 'natural' laws which God had instilled in his creation. People now argued there should be some balance of power, between government on the one hand, embodied in the sovereign, and the rights of subjects on the other, especially of those subjects who visibly contributed to the continued prosperity of the State, as did, in their own view, the cities and, of course, the nobles.

Since the fourteenth century, political groups all over Europe, exploring the limits of the balance between king and country, had tried to force their rulers to accept some kind of constitution that would bind them to laws made, preferably, by the traditional representative assemblies rather than by the prince only.

However, in their turn these assemblies had become instruments of power coteries. Inevitably, 'new men', especially those who had acquired power in new sectors of the economy from the sixteenth and seventeenth century onwards and now felt their stake in the State's economy warranted greater participation in its government as well, made themselves heard. Since elites were never unified groups, the wealthy representatives of the business and entrepreneurial classes in the European towns soon succeeded in manoeuvring themselves into positions that allowed them either to establish their own power – as, for example, they had done in the seven rebellious Dutch provinces in the 1570s and 1580s – or, if the political force field made this more viable, they sought alliances with, or were invited to ally themselves with, sections of the ruling elite dissatisfied with the current distribution of power, and of the populace, who expected, of course, to hold the balance themselves. Thus, in many states a more broadly based political system was achieved. But changes came only slowly. Much depended on the willingness or necessity experienced by princes and ruling elites to alter the existing political and social system. Not everyone agreed that traditional society – still largely organized along the lines of the 'three estates' – was obsolete. Indeed, for the time being, most monarchs only sought to increase their power.

Yet, in England, the Stuart monarchs' bid for 'absolute' power in the seventeenth century was checked by an uneasy alliance between part of the nobility, who largely dominated the country's constituencies and, thus, the majority of the seats in the House of Lords and in the House of Commons, and part of the non-noble elite, both land-based and town-based, the latter being the representatives of the influential banking and mercantile interests of the City of London and other commercial towns. In 1688, a *coup d'état* was staged, soon named the 'Glorious Revolution' by its winners. Its major importance lay in the fact that a new monarch was put on the throne – the Dutch stadholder William III of Orange – who, ruling with his wife Mary, the daughter of the deposed king, accepted a number of restrictions on royal authority; on the other hand, the successful alliance accepted its share in the responsibility for the State: now allowing government to systematically tax their wealth, they began to bear a considerable part of the increasingly burdensome state expenditure. Soon, the novelty and the advantages of this system were discussed all over Europe. One should realize, however, that post-1688 England was far from democratic. Indeed, the new political system was decidedly oligarchic. However, the fusion of old and new elites did help to prevent serious social and political unrest for more than a century to come. It also assured considerable though not total tolerance, especially of those who held alternative religious opinions.

One man who was deeply influenced by the apparent advantages of the new English system and now became an advocate of redressing the balance between state and citizen was the French nobleman Charles de Montesquieu (1689–1759). After travelling extensively in various European countries, he published his *De l'esprit des lois* (1748). In it, he proposed that at least the powers of the judiciary should be separated from those of the legislature and the executive, to prevent the concentration of power in a few hands, as this would lead only to corruption and abuse. His book was avidly read and commented upon in political circles all over Europe as well as in more liberal circles in the English and even the Iberian colonies on the other side of the Atlantic.

A prince who did think that change was necessary and might even be possible without, perhaps, conceding too many of his own rights, was King Frederick II of Brandenburg-Prussia, who ruled from 1740 to 1786. He wanted to create a more modern, efficient state which could rely on the support of all its citizens, instead of precariously navigating between hostile socio-economic groups. He greatly favoured agricultural innovations and experiments, as witnessed by the introduction of the potato,[21] but also furthered the various branches of industry. As a fervent friend of Voltaire – whom he admired as one of the most outspoken advocates of a more 'enlightened' society which would create equality of all before the law, a more rational and humane system of criminal justice, etc. – the king decided to act accordingly. In 1740, he decreed:

> His Royal Majesty in Prussia has, for weighty reasons, decided that in His States torture will be totally abolished in the Inquisition, except in cases of Crimen Laesae Majestatis and high treason, as well as in murder cases which involve the death of many people, and when it is deemed necessary to determine the accomplices of serious delinquents. In all other cases, criminals will be punished according to

the law, after hearing the strongest possible evidence of reliable witnesses, even if they do not confess of their own free will.[22]

Frederick II also made clear that he would heavily punish those landowners and government officials who ill-treated the taxpayers – the farming population, mostly. In 1750 he declared:

> As up until now various officials have ill-treated the farmers by having them beaten with sticks, and We cannot possibly tolerate such tyranny against Our subjects, We declare it to be Our will that when it can be proven that someone has beaten a farmer with a stick, he will immediately, and without any possibility of reprieve be imprisoned for six years, even if such an official were well in advance with paying the farm of his taxes.[23]

Noblemen and noblewomen who maltreated their servants were to be thus punished as well. But while things changed in England and Prussia, albeit in very different settings and with different intentions, it has to be admitted that few princes in western Europe entered into politics as enlightened and as forcefully as Frederick did.

In monarchic states like France, Spain and Sweden, but also in the Dutch Republic, to name but a few, traditional views lingered on considerably longer. This may have been one of the reasons why tensions built up there, eventually exploding in revolutions of varying degrees of violence which created great upheaval in European society in the decades from 1770 onward.

The case of France must be cited specifically, not only because it represented to the full the economic, social and political problems that characterized most European states, but also because the revolution that was the people's answer to these problems greatly influenced developments elsewhere in Europe. In France, the clergy and the nobility, the first two of the three traditional estates, were 'privileged' in, among other things, that from the sixteenth century onwards they had been allowed to pay little or no taxes. Thus, though economically they represented the better part of the country's tax capacity, they refused to bear the financial burden of the State which, consequently, was devolved to the mass of the urban and the rural population. The price that these two groups paid for their exemption was that, though individually they might rise to positions of great power, especially if they loyally served the king at Versailles, as a class they could not determine the course of government. Actually, the French kings retained the almost absolute authority they had won during the sixteenth and seventeenth centuries in their continuous struggles with the nobility, the Church and the towns. In the end, however, this situation proved the undoing of the *ancien régime*.

In the later decades of eighteenth century, it became obvious that France lacked a sound financial base, provided by a fiscal system that could tap the entire nation's wealth instead of mainly taxing the peasantry and the towns. In the 1780s, a grave financial crisis induced the advisers of King Louis XVI to suggest fundamental fiscal changes. The king let himself be persuaded but the nobility fiercely resisted. To be able to introduce reforms after all, Louis then felt forced to convene the States-General, the representative body of the three 'estates' which had not met since 1614. Not surprisingly, both the country and the townspeople now rose to make themselves heard. Their political leaders, who mainly hailed from the educated rural and urban middle classes, had been profoundly influenced by the often critical texts about the position of man in political society published by such men as Thomas Hobbes, John Locke and the baron De Montesquieu, and by the advocates of a reasonable, enlightened society; conversely, their willingness to uncritically accept the words of authority as spoken by the State and, even more so, the Church had greatly diminished.[24] Now they demanded that the representative system be changed drastically. Instead of convening and voting in the three estates which actually left out the great majority of the French people, they demanded that general elections should be held, to create a convention of true representatives, each to be given one vote, each to voice his own opinions according to his own responsibility to those who had elected him. These demands resulted, in 1789, in a veritable revolution which, during the following years, took on increasing momentum, resulting in fundamental political but soon also socio-economic changes.

The French Revolution articulated a number of principles in the form of a 'credo' which, with adaptations suiting other situations, was used to gradually restructure society in many European states in the period between 1790 and 1850. In these decades, all over western Europe, slowly but inexorably the power of the old elites, the first and second 'estates', was broken, in the sense that they lost their legally privileged position. Gradually, in most countries, every citizen – that is to say the educated, taxpaying, male citizen – was given the vote and legal barriers between social classes were demolished. Thus, the process of individualization that had become increasingly manifest in European thinking about man from the Renaissance onwards was now translated into the political, social and economic sphere, at least for the well-to-do male part of the population. As yet, women, of whatever social class, were given no such rights – it would take another 100 years before the first European states were willing to introduce female suffrage. Nor, it has to be added, did the revolutions help women acquire full legal rights in other fields. In most countries, their fathers and, if they married, their husbands continued to administer whatever property they might possess until well into the nineteenth century.

PARIS, 27 AUGUST 1789: THE CULTURAL IMPORTANCE OF THE 'DÉCLARATION DES DROITS DE L'HOMME ET DU CITOYEN'

On 27 August 1789, the members of the newly elected French *Assemblé Nationale* voted to adopt the so-called '*Declaration of the Rights of Man and Citizen*'. Not only did they hope to end centuries of what they felt had been the oppression of the French people at the hands of the country's aristocrats,

Plate 21 The first German railway, between Nuremberg and Fürth, was inaugurated in 1835.

Source: Centre for Art Historical Documentation, Nijmegen, the Netherlands

they also hoped to rally all well-intended Frenchmen behind a new vision of society. The text of the declaration, though originating in a European and, moreover, very specific sociopolitical situation, yet had universal pretensions, presenting man as being born with inalienable rights. These, of course, for the past two centuries have continued to resound in every discussion about the democratic relationship between state and individual. For this reason alone, the '*Déclaration*' is a major monument of European culture which, through European imperialism, has found wider application as well, now even determining the global political debate. It reads as follows:

> The representatives of the French people, organized in National Assembly, considering that ignorance, forgetfulness, or contempt of the rights of man are the sole causes of public misfortunes and of the corruption of governments, have resolved to set forth in a solemn declaration the natural, inalienable, and sacred rights of man, in order that such declaration, continually before all members of the social body, may be a perpetual reminder of their rights and duties; in order that the acts of the legislative power and those of the executive power may be constantly compared with the aim of every political institution and may accordingly be more respected; in order that the demands of the citizens, founded henceforth upon simple and incontestable principles, may always be directed towards the maintenance of the Constitution and the welfare of all.

Accordingly, the National Assembly recognizes and proclaims, in the presence and under the auspices of the Supreme Being, the following rights of man and citizen:

1 Men are born and remain free and equal in rights; social distinctions may be based only upon general usefulness.
2 The aim of every political association is the preservation of the natural and inalienable rights of man; these rights are liberty, property, security, and resistance to oppression.
3 The source of all sovereignty resides essentially in the nation; no group, no individual may exercise authority not emanating expressly therefrom.
4 Liberty consists of the power to do whatever is not injurious to others; thus the enjoyment of the natural rights of every man has for its limits only those that assure other members of society the enjoyment of those same rights; such limits may be determined only by law.
5 The law has the right to forbid only actions which are injurious to society. Whatever is not forbidden by law may not be prevented, and no one may be constrained to do what it does not prescribe.
6 Law is the expression of the general will; all citizens have the right to concur personally, or through their representatives, in its formation; it must be the same for all, whether it protects or punishes. All citizens, being equal before it, are equally admissible to all public offices, positions, and employments, according to their capacity, and without other distinction than that of virtue and talents.
7 No man may be accused, arrested, or detained except in the cases determined by law, and according to the forms prescribed thereby. Whoever solicit, expedite, or execute arbitrary orders, or have them executed, must be punished; but every citizen summoned or apprehended in pursuance of the law must obey immediately; he renders himself culpable by resistance.
8 The law is to establish only penalties that are absolutely and obviously necessary; and no one may be punished except by virtue of a law established and promulgated prior to the offence and legally applied.
9 Since every man is presumed innocent until declared guilty, if arrest be deemed indispensable, all unnecessary severity for securing the person of the accused must be severely repressed by law.
10 No one is to be disquieted because of his opinions, even religious, provided their manifestation does not disturb the public order established by law.
11 Free communication of ideas and opinions is one of the most precious of the rights of man. Consequently, every citizen may speak, write, and print freely, subject to responsibility for the abuse of such liberty in the cases determined by law.
12 The guarantee of the rights of man and citizen necessitates a public force; such a force, therefore, is instituted for the advantage of all and not for the particular benefit of those to whom it is entrusted.
13 For the maintenance of the public force and for the expenses of administration, a common tax is indispensable; it must be assessed equally on all citizens in proportion to their means.
14 Citizens have the right to ascertain, by themselves or through their representatives, the necessity of the public tax, to consent to it freely, to supervise its use, and to determine its quota, assessment, payment, and duration.

15 Society has the right to require of every public agent an accounting of his administration.

16 Every society in which the guarantee of rights is not assured or the separation of powers not determined has no constitution at all.

17 Since property is a sacred and inviolable right, no one may be deprived thereof unless a legally established public necessity obviously requires it, and upon condition of a just and previous indemnity.

In the course of the late eighteenth century, and with increasing speed during the early years of the nineteenth century, European society changed rapidly and drastically. Many of the traditional political, economic and social structures that had conditioned life in Europe for centuries now swiftly disappeared. For the political changes that culminated in the French Revolution and its successor movements had been embedded in and influenced by an equally fundamental Industrial Revolution which had slowly altered life in Europe between *c.*1750 and *c.*1850. Together, these two revolutions resulted in a veritable and almost complete transformation of European culture, making it, basically, into the culture we now know.

Of course, one should not think of the Industrial Revolution as one in which, over night, a dramatic reversal occurred in the European economy. It was actually a very slow process in which – in some regions of Europe – the existing, mainly agricultural communities turned into a mainly industrial society.[25]

The process had its roots in the beginnings of commercial capitalism and, therefore, was fundamentally related to Europe's ever-more important economic relations with Asia, the Americas and Africa. However, it was accelerated when agricultural prices started falling in the seventeenth century as related to industrial prices. Especially from the 1650s onwards, the demand for industrial goods increased and the cottage industries together with domestic commerce, rather than foreign trade, sustained an expansion of manufacturing in those regions where people had easy access to markets: England, the Dutch Republic, northern France, parts of Germany and so on. It was a complex interaction between a supply creating its own demand and a demand-initiated growth process. Essentially, in these regions households changed their attitude to labour and started to specialize: men, but increasingly also women and children filled a growing number of hours per day, and days per year with work instead of leisure; significantly, this was the period when the traditionally large number of Christian holidays was progressively reduced to raise the number of working days.

Self-exploitation as well as a marked rise in output per worker increased the household income and altered the demand pattern in the direction of manufacturing. The growing income was spent on consumption, on a market supplying both goods and services. This resulted in an 'industrial revolution' *avant la lettre*. It also resulted in a gradual and complex sociocultural change: more and more, women obtained a strategic position in the household economy, taking on the role of consumers, spending money on clothing and the home, in short on consumer goods.

The first country to properly industrialize was England. There, the surplus wealth created in agriculture, the cottage industries and trade during the early eighteenth century sought an outlet in new investments. Also, the surplus labour that resulted from increased agricultural productivity because a smaller percentage of farm labourers now sufficed to realize a greater yield, freed up men and women for other kinds of work. If only because there were often no longer sufficient jobs in agriculture and the closely related industries, people became more mobile, moving to places where they could more easily earn their wage, even if this meant they were forced to work and live in miserable conditions.

Spinning and weaving, which had been part of (western) Europe's small-scale, agriculture-related industry for a very long time, now became increasingly profitable alternatives, especially so when various technical improvements were introduced, such as the flying shuttle which facilitated the operation of a loom, and the spinning jenny, a kind of mechanized spinning wheel. The technological preconditions for a major economic revolution were created when, in the 1780s, Richard Arkwright started using the steam engine to drive his wheels. Soon, the new technology was applied in manufacturing everywhere where fuel – especially coal – and infrastructure – especially waterways – encouraged people to invest their money in factories – in the southern Netherlands and northern France, in the Rhineland area of Germany and northern Italy.

These developments occurred over several decades and resulted in the Industrial Revolution proper, a mainly organizational and technological restructuring of production in the factory system. Its effects were to be deeply felt first in the period *c.*1780–1830 – while, in subsequent decades, the new system spread to wider parts of Europe as well. Of course, to answer a growing demand, coal and iron mining now expanded into large, mechanized industries as well, providing employment for many.

At the beginning of the nineteenth century, the cultural consequences of both revolutions, the political-legal and the industrial, began to really show, first of all in their material aspects. A letter written in the 1830s by the German aristocrat Prince von Pückler-Muskau to his wife, narrating his observations during his trip through England, is quite revealing:

> Birmingham is one of the most prominent and at the same time most ugly towns of England. It numbers 120,000 inhabitants, two-thirds of whom must be factory workers; indeed, it looks like one huge workshop.
>
> Immediately after breakfast I went to the factory of Mr. Thomasson, our consul, the second largest as to size and extent; for the biggest, where 1,000 labourers are at work each day and where a steam engine with a strength of eighty horses produces an infinite amount of products, including buttons and needles, has been hermetically closed to all foreigners since the visit of the Austrian prince (some of whose suite are told to have stolen some important secrets). Here, I spent a number of hours, albeit in horrible, filthy and smelling holes serving as work rooms, and was mighty interested; I even made a button. . . . On the ground floor, in the better

rooms, all products made by the factory are exhibited: things made of gold, silver, bronze, sheffield plate, lacquer (which even surpasses the Chinese originals), steel of every sort, et cetera, to a number, and of an elegance which really astonish. ... Here, I got to know a great number of new and pleasant luxuries, both small and big.[26]

In a nutshell, this letter summarizes many of the characteristics of the new industrial society and its culture. The increase in population that cities like Birmingham experienced was the result both of greatly improved hygiene and the discovery of simple but effective remedies for some of the most destructive diseases. In turn, the population increase resulted in a rapid growth of the old towns, and in the foundation, in the industrially profitable areas, of new ones that fast became populous and wealthy as well. In these industrial centres, the factory owners settled their labourers, initially recruited from the mass of the agricultural poor but soon from the expanding urban proletariat itself. Soon, the very different circumstances of town life and factory labour as opposed to agriculture and rural life influenced the reproductive patterns of the industrial parts of European society. Sexual mores became less strict and marriages were now concluded earlier. This, in its turn, not only led to further population growth but also to different attitudes in the area of family relationships. The economic and social ties that had given cohesion to a peasant society became loosened or were severed altogether.

During the course of the nineteenth century, many Europeans became the dependants of the machine that enslaved them within the horrible working conditions of the industrial centres, where new forms of solidarity were called for. Factory workers started organizing themselves in fraternities to plead their rights with the owners – if necessary enforcing these pleas with strikes, although the political elite, by now partly consisting of wealthy industrialists, tried to make this action illegal. Both in England, which had the advantage of a quick start and, initially, flooded the European continent with its industrial products, and in other parts of industrialized Europe, people criticized the economic and social consequences of the new developments, using both economic and socio-ethical arguments. The *Kölnische Zeitung* of 1818 published an article that argued along the following lines:

> A steam engine often renders a thousand people jobless, and brings the profit which otherwise would be divided between all labourers into the hands of one person. Each new perfection introduced into a machine robs new families of their daily bread; each new-built steam engine increases the number of beggars, and one may expect that soon all money will be in the hands of a few thousand families, and that the rest of the population will be begging to serve them.

Indeed, many people rose in protest against what they saw as a huge plot to rob them of their labour, blaming the new machines for all the evil in European society. Soon, too, new ideologies were being formulated, voicing the demands of those who now depended on the jobs provided by factories, precisely because working conditions were often dismal. Meanwhile, the market economy came to rely increasingly on technological progress. Industrial espionage developed as factories realized the importance of new inventions. Technical colleges were founded and laboratories established, funds were given and prizes offered. Indeed, the technical sciences gained an ever more central position in society and culture. People wondered whether Europe's universities were not backward in adhering to a curriculum that mainly stressed the humanities. Others even wondered whether the success of science did not prove that the very methodology of the humanities was faulty because, unless it were based on empirical evidence, it would never be able to produce factual, 'positive', objective data. Knowledge that was not 'positive' would never benefit the new economy, the new society. Soon, the various branches of the humanities, primarily history, were trying to redefine both their objectives and their methods.

For the first time in human history, culture – in this case Europe's new, post-revolutionary, industrial culture – was a culture that, at least in its material aspects and, consequently, in its social outlook, began to level the differences between the various social groups without, however, necessarily altering the real power balance between these groups. One of the most influential long-term consequences of industrialization was the production of ever more consumer goods, rightly described by Pückler-Muskau as 'luxury'. The first to profit were the bourgeoisie: the industrial economy gave them not only increased wealth and power, but also numerous products that enhanced and facilitated their life. All kinds of household goods and knick-knacks, patent medicines and preserved foodstuffs that contributed to their comfort became available. Agricultural machinery also helped to supply provisions for their towns and trains brought them from their quiet, as yet unpolluted residential neighbourhoods to their shops and offices, or to their holiday destinations. And, of course, weapons that helped them win the wars that ensured their colonial possessions, from which they extracted the raw materials for their factories and to which they exported many of their products. In one 'symbolic year', the year 1851, all this materialized when, preceded and indeed inspired by a number of comparable, very successful French ventures, the British government organized London's 'Great Exhibition', staged in the so-called Crystal Palace, a mainly factory-built structure consisting entirely of iron and glass. It was a celebration of the new age, the machine age. Thousands of exhibitors from all over Europe, and also the USA, showed tens of thousands of products to a public that, within a few months' time, amounted to millions – with many travelling to London by train or steam ship for the first time in their lives. Indeed, many who went there had never left their village or town before. By now, Europe had entered its 'age of movement', with all the increased communication it entailed, and the cultural changes that would, inevitably, result from it.

The steam-driven machine that caused both a significant reduction in production time, and thus in wages, and an enormous increase in production volume, soon resulted in a markedly wider distribution of consumer goods across the various income groups. Just as, from the sixteenth century onwards, the invention of printing had resulted, through cheap, mass produced texts, in the spread of knowledge within groups previously denied access to it, now the mechanization that allowed for mass production in all kinds of fields made a wide range of cheap consumer goods available to an ever wider public.[27] Indeed, even printing itself was industrialized, with the introduction of the rotation press – that supplanted the hand press – and, soon, of colour printing. As in the sixteenth century, this again revolutionized education, allowing for cheap manuals and textbooks to be printed.

It was not long before 'the machine' was able to execute a number of techniques that gave its products a highly refined appearance. Machines made wooden furniture adorned with sculpted scrolls and flourishes closely resembling pieces made at far greater cost by the slow and judicious use of a hand-operated lathe. Mass-produced pottery was artistically decorated with intricate patterns that were stencilled instead of painstakingly painted by hand. New chemical processes enabled the factories at Sheffield and Solingen to turn out cutlery and other luxury metalwork that resembled hand-made silverware in everything but its price. In short, many products had an aristocratic air, exuding status, but nevertheless were within the reach of many. In short, luxury was democratized.

Developments in other fields contributed to the process as well. Precisely because the political upheaval in France, followed by comparable changes elsewhere, was closely linked to, not to say caused by, the Industrial Revolution – historians do not agree on this – the old society, which was now denounced as feudal, began to crumble. Most visibly, the old aristocracy had lost its constitutionally or otherwise legally guaranteed power. Although the right to vote was still restricted, being tied to a person's ability to pay taxes, with the advance of democracy, the way to the top, to power, was now open to practically all. Not surprisingly, the great entrepreneurs, who dominated the mercantile and now also the industrial economy, hastened to ensure that they would also dominate politics. Thus, once more, a new elite came into being. The older elites, desperately trying to hold on to their position, were now joined by a new upper class formed by these entrepreneurs: bankers, factory-, ship- and railway-owners, mining tycoons, men engaged in international trade.

As before, this new elite, too, tried to show off and enhance their new-found status, following the example set by the older elites: to demonstrate their wealth and power and to acquire the social and cultural position that were considered its logical corollary, they surrounded themselves with its outward symbols, with luxury consumer goods. The more luxury objects, manifestly useless, one could show, the more people would think, or know that one 'belonged' – as a character in Oscar Wilde's novel *The Picture of Dorian Gray* (1891) says: 'We live in an age when unnecessary things are our only necessities'. But in other ways, too, this new, industrial elite aped the lifestyle of the older aristocracy, for, as the same Oscar Wilde told his readers: 'the middle classes are not modern'.[28]

For example, as one of the consequences of the sociopolitical revolutions, the master chefs, the 'cuisiniers', and the couturiers who had worked for princely courts and aristocratic households had lost their patrons, and, if not exactly out of work, did feel the financial impact of the new situation. They now entered the market and thus one sees, at the beginning of the nineteenth century, the genesis of the fashionable restaurant and the great fashion shop; competing with one another for the favour of a new clientele, they offered the trappings of a luxurious lifestyle to a public that was quite willing to pay handsomely, but perhaps not as extravagantly as the old nobles had been. The food, the clothes, the furniture, the jewels, in short the luxury once reserved for the happy few could now be enjoyed by the new rich as well.

The revolutions also resulted in the abolition of the guilds that were felt to have imposed unacceptable restrictions on the free play of economic forces, limiting progress and continuing inequality. People were now free to set up shop and establish their business wherever they wanted, and to engage in competition as best they could. Now, well-trained artisans vied with one another for customers, creating a new, free market, less expensive than before. Indeed, many products whose prices had once been kept artificially high now came within the reach of a far greater group of customers and consumers.

During the course of the nineteenth century, both through continuing industrialization and through the enormous growth of state bureaucracy, another considerable group of well-to-do people emerged. Lacking inherited wealth, they could not aspire to the upper-class status of the old aristocracy, nor were they as wealthy as the new, industrial elite. Nevertheless, through solid education and solid, well-salaried jobs, they came to form a distinct addition to the middle class.

Soon, this group, too, adopted elements of the lifestyles of those they considered their social superiors. Hence, the culture of the aristocracy that had been democratized by wealthy traders and entrepreneurs in the seventeenth and eighteenth centuries, and by the new industrialists in the early nineteenth century, now found an even broader diffusion among a growing middle class.

Urban, industrial culture: the regulation and consumption of time

Increasingly, the Industrial Revolution visibly changed the aspect of Europe. Most visible were, perhaps, the consequences of the massive migration of people from the countryside to the towns, where a growing number of Europeans now came to live and work: Paris, for example, which had some 600,000 inhabitants at the turn of the eighteenth century, grew to a population of 1 million by 1851, and of 2.7 million by 1900.

The French painter Eugene Delacroix (1798–1863) was witness to the process. He saw numerous Frenchmen leaving their fields and villages to work in the factories and live in the towns. In his diary, he painted a very gloomy, sometimes one-sided picture of the changes resulting from this mass migration. His well-meant concern was shared by many all over Europe. However, they too easily forgot that agrarian life was far from a rustic idyll and that many farmers followed the call to a new life simply because it held a promise that their present conditions would never fulfil. Indeed, most of these cultural commentators were intellectuals, who had never handled a spade. In 1853, Delacroix noted in his diary:

> Will steam stop before churches and cemeteries? And will the Frenchman, returning to his fatherland after some years, be reduced to asking where it was that his village stood, and where the grave of his forebears was? For villages will be useless as the rest: villagers are those who cultivate the soil, for they have to stay in the place where their care is required at every moment. It will be necessary to build cities big enough to harbour this workless and disinherited mass of people, who will no longer find anything to do in the fields; it will be necessary to construct for them immense barracks where they will lodge pell-mell. And when they are there, the Fleming beside the man from Marseilles, the man from Normandy besides the man from the Alsace, what will they have to do but read the quotations in the newspaper, not to see if, in their region, on their beloved fields, the harvest has been good, whether they can advantageously sell their wheat, their hay, or their grapes, but to see whether their stocks in the unanimous universal property are going up or down? They will have paper instead of land! They will go to the billiard-rooms to gamble with this paper against their unknown neighbours, different in customs and in speech.
>
> O unworthy philanthropists! O philosophers without heart and without imagination. You think that man is a machine, like your other machines. You degrade him from his most sacred rights. . . . Instead of transforming the human race into a vile herd, let it retain its true heritage – its attachment, its devotion even to the soil. . . . And then, when new invasions of barbarians threaten what they still call their fatherland, they will rise with joy to defend it. They will not fight to defend the property of the machines. . . .
>
> Alas, poor peasants, poor villagers. . . . They are already abandoning the work of the field in haphazard fashion and with the most ill-founded hopes; they are rushing headlong into the cities, where nothing but disappointment awaits them . . . there, they complete the perversion of those feelings of dignity offered by the labour of love, and the more your machines feed them, the more they will become degraded! What a noble spectacle in this best of centuries – human cattle fattened by the philosophers.[29]

Quite obviously, Delacroix's fears concern the decline of the old, regional cultures with their agrarian economy, their distinct customs and their linguistic identity. He and his urban contemporaries witnessed two worlds, the rural and the urban which, for millennia, had been separate worlds, finally merging through the joint influence of continuing industrialization and the cultural integration brought about by the nation-state, which, in its turn, would not have succeeded without the wealth created by that very industrialization.[30]

In the process, both European material culture and, more specifically, the ways in which Europeans thought were deeply changed. Many now traded a life in the country, conditioned by the static work in the fields, by the rhythm of day and night and the inexorable change of the seasons, for a job in town. It would be a job in a factory, or in one of the growing number of shops and other businesses that catered for new consumer demands. Provided one had received some education, it might even be an office job, in the ever-growing bureaucracy that was needed to help the State control this increasingly complex society. It might also be a job in one of the numerous affluent bourgeois households, for the middle classes, aping the aristocracy, hired more and more servants. A well-to-do family of five or six easily employed an equal number of staff, and the really wealthy would be surrounded by dozens of servants. In *c.*1800, some 30 per cent of London's population was made up of those who served in the houses of the richest citizens, who comprised less than 20 per cent. A very considerable proportion of these domestic servants would be unmarried young females, coming in from the rural areas.

As did all people coming in from the countryside, they would soon notice that townspeople no longer reckoned their days from sunrise to sunset. The houses, the factories, the shops and the offices were artificially lit. Moreover, to remind people that time was money, clocks were introduced everywhere. In the towns, the bio-rhythms of Europeans started changing as the traditional sense of time slowly disappeared.[31] Soon, the clock reigned supreme, regulating work both in factories and offices, dictating the long hours – ten, eleven, twelve daily, far more than were ever worked on a farm – now put in by men, women and children alike, under conditions that were, often, horrific. Women especially now constituted a huge, flexible workforce: underpaid, liable to be fired without any warning, they often had to leave their children, their ageing or sick parents and other relatives unattended to go out to work. For to survive in the city, in the new economy, with its allure of cheap luxury, everybody had to work. However, besides being performed inside, town labour was both far harder and far more monotonous than in the countryside. Everything became routine, conditioned by the motions and the speed demanded by the clock-watching machines.

By 1838, the firm of Krupp, already one of the oldest and biggest industrial groups in Germany, set its workers the following rules:

> Each workman has to be faithful and unquestioningly loyal, behave himself decently both within and outside the factory, keep, exactly, the hours set for his task, and show by his diligence that he intends to work for the common good of the factory. In so acting, he may expect to be paid according to the value of his labour. Whosoever unintentionally or consciously forgets his duties, will be punished. Drinking spirits on the premises is not tolerated. Who spoils a piece of goods, or an instrument, will have to pay for it. Who arrives at the job 5 minutes after the bell has sounded, will lose ¼ day; who of his own desire stays away for ¼ day, will lose ½ day; for ½ day, ¾ will be subtracted from his wages, et cetera.[32]

Slowly, the outlook of the European towns changed as well. The division between rich and poor neighbourhoods became more visible than ever. The outskirts of most towns, such as the northern fringe of Paris, became the areas of poverty, immorality and vice where the police often did not dare enter when

Plate 22 A view of the Krupp firm's factories at Essen, Germany, in a (coloured) engraving of *c.*1860. Living conditions in the industrial centres were often appalling.

Source: Centre for Art Historical Documentation, Nijmegen, the Netherlands

riots broke out. People living in these quarters were termed the 'dangerous classes'. For the well-to-do, propertied classes, a visit to these parts of town was like going into another world. Or, as a French politician claimed:

> Workers are outside political life, outside the city. They are the barbarians of modern society. They should enter this society, but be admitted to it only after passing through the novitiate of owning property.[33]

Property, of course, was the very thing most people did not have. And it was precisely the reason why that other world encroached upon the more affluent neighbourhoods as well, as witnessed by the huge numbers of beggars, and the many unlicensed prostitutes roaming the streets day and night. For prostitution greatly increased with the massive influx of labour from the provinces, with the poverty that prevented men and women from marrying, and with the need for women to make ends meet, or even to survive.[34] As in the eighteenth century, when a child was born, infanticide was still an option. Of course, many women could not persuade themselves to do this. One of them said, presenting her baby to an orphanage:

> Why do I send this little child to the [foundling] hospital? Because I am without any resources. . . . But I don't want him to be lost for good. . . . I beg you to have the kindness to keep him there, so I can see him again when I can, because I am not married.[35]

In most towns, for those who had little money for food, the diet was considerably less varied than in the country. Despite the hygienic and sanitary improvements of the late eighteenth century, diseases now increased again, not only because of insufficient or bad nutrition, but also because of the poor living conditions. During the nineteenth century, towns, especially the regional and national capitals and industrial centres, evolved into huge clusters of mostly filthy tenements where five, six or seven people were often packed into one small room totally lacking in sanitary conveniences. Both outside and inside, everything was coated in the soot produced by the coals that were the fuel of progress. The English novelist Charles Dickens famously evoked the misery of the poor who lived in his country. While England was the first nation to fully show the effects of industrialization, all over Europe its consequences were felt, providing inspiration to artists and writers, philosophers and politicians to reflect on both the positive and the negative aspects of this new world.

14 Progress and its discontents

Nationalism, economic growth
and the question of cultural
certainties

The revolutions and their aftermath

As shown in Chapter 13, the industrial and the political revolutions had complex consequences, principally in western Europe, although changes made themselves felt in central and eastern Europe as well. Ideologically, conservatives and liberals in particular became the main opposition groups within the newly created constitutional, partly democratic political systems. The former, those who basically rejected the consequences of the revolutions, preferred to see the old power structures maintained or restored as much as possible. They also advocated vigorous government. The latter argued that social progress was best served by as free a play of social forces as could be realized without society degenerating into chaos; in their opinion, liberalism also implied the limited interference of government in economic, social and certainly cultural affairs.

Meanwhile, a third ideology, opposed to both conservatism and liberalism, gained increasing support. It was, of course, socialism, the most visible socio-political child born of the great European revolutions, principally the industrial one. But although its birth as a political force would not have occurred without the changes of the late eighteenth and early nineteenth centuries, its roots were much older, composed as they were of such diverse strands as guild solidarity in Europe's cities of the twelfth and thirteenth centuries, the growing individual-ism of Renaissance and (Counter-)Reformation culture, the organizational structures of the Enlightenment clubs and Romantic notions of the value of labour and the artisan as representative of traditional culture.[1]

Most socialists did not want to reverse the recent political-economic changes; mainly, they felt that their negative consequences should be remedied. The evident problems facing large parts of the working population required, accord-ing to socialist ideology, a steering of society – by the State, through a government that truly cared for all its people – in such a way that economic prosperity and, in a wider sense, sociocultural welfare would be adequately guaranteed to each and everybody.[2]

In the 1820s, the French author and social critic Henri, count of Saint-Simon, presented an interesting mix of the three political stances when he argued that:

At the outset, I wish to state that the only way to bring sustenance to people is through employment. The government has to be controlled by the heads of industrial enterprises. These men are the true leaders of the people, whom they direct in their daily labour. Therefore, directly and in their own interests, the heads of industrial enterprises will use their authority to expand business as much as possible. From this will result the greatest increase in economic activity, leading to larger employment.

Yet, while one may detect a strongly paternalistic tendency in Saint-Simon's society, he apparently held high hopes for the mitigating – or rather disciplining? – influence of education, writing:

I now come to another question. What is the best education for people, and in what ways should it be given? The education that people need most, and that will enable them to work best, should be based on the subjects of geometry, physics, chemistry, and hygiene. . . . incontestably the most useful as a preparation for life work. The scholars in the physical and mathematical sciences are the only ones fit to establish a good system of education.[3]

Of all the ideologies that were, more or less, the consequence of the new, industrial society, Saint-Simon's has perhaps been the most prophetic as to the direction actually taken by western capitalism, especially in the late twentieth century.

In the decades during which Saint-Simon contemplated his world, society and culture were already greatly influenced by the success of the 'modern' sciences – especially technology which, incorporated into the industrializing process, for the first time in history proved able to offer many people a modicum of prosperity. Due to the need to mechanize industry, the nineteenth century saw an increasingly far-reaching division of labour. This contributed to the genesis of many parallel, but by and large separate sociocultural networks and thus ultimately furthered the process of individualization. At the same time, standardization allowed production both to expand and to become more international. The consumer culture that now developed increasingly crossed the borders of states, nations and their traditions. These decades witnessed the first phase of material 'globalization'.

However contradictory, the national state yet proved itself the most adequate framework for all these developments, even increasingly so. Nationalism was – and perhaps is – both a component of and a reaction to the 'processes of modernization' which the economic and political revolutions expressed, processes which should more appropriately be called 'processes of change', since both 'modernization' and 'progress' are to a large extent immeasurable phenomena, mainly moral and, thus, subjective categories.

On the one hand, old cultural, social and political certainties were now lost. On the other, a strong state was clearly an effective vehicle for safeguarding a country's economic interests in view of growing international competition. Hence, from the late eighteenth century onwards, cultural notions were increasingly linked with state politics in an attempt to achieve a sense of national identity and thus of unity, which soon acquired rather extreme dimensions. Political and cultural elites, using such emotionally effective elements as a common name, the reference to a shared language and, where possible, a shared religion, the invocation of a common, though often mythical ancestry and of collective historical memories and traditions – though often invented – now succeeded in achieving nationhood for many European states.[4] Nationalism now became an ideological instrument used not only to reconcile the disparate and often conflicting sociocultural elements and regional identities that made up each and every one of the European states but also to buttress the expansionist politics of these states.

The development of nationalism in late eighteenth- and early nineteenth-century Europe was greatly strengthened by Europe's recent experience of a supranational dictatorship. In the wake of the French Revolution of 1789, Napoleon Bonaparte had tried and for a short time succeeded in uniting the whole of Europe, as far as the borders of the tsarist empire, excepting, of course, the British Isles. In order to do so, he had employed not only military means but also the same appeals to hegemony which in earlier centuries so many others had invoked: unity, even if achieved only by force of arms, would prevent division and its destructive consequences. Arguably, Napoleon's policies introduced or helped speed up a number of reforms that were of vital importance to the creation of a structured, economically free and legally more egalitarian society: legislative unification culminating in the famous Napoleonic Code (1804), the slow admittance, in large parts of continental Europe, of a metric system, of standard weights, of a standard coinage, in short, a number of structures which greatly facilitated the further development of the European economy as well as of socio-political change.[5] Indeed, judging France's first emperor dispassionately – which is hard in view of the tens of thousands of lives that his campaigns cost – his grand design prefigured the policies adopted by the European Community and, later, the European Union in the last decades of the twentieth century.

However, Napoleon's pan-European vision brought about a heightened awareness of problems existing in and even more so between the various European states. Indeed, opposition to Napoleon's conquests soon emerged. Politically and propagandistically, that opposition left no room for Bonaparte's more idealistic arguments for European unity, for a culture presented as a European culture; after all, the dictator had used these very arguments. Consequently, Britain, Sweden and, at a later stage, the Netherlands and parts of southern Europe joined against Napoleon. And so did the many states that, since Charlemagne, had been united in the fragile 'Holy Roman Empire of the German Nation', an empire Napolean had speedily abolished.

In 1805, the emperor had defeated the Prussians and imposed severe conditions on their country. In 1813, the Prussian king, Friedrich Wilhelm decided to join the alliance against Bonaparte. In an impassioned pamphlet, he admonished his subjects to fight for their country's indpendence. His words perfectly illustrate the various cultural elements that make up nationalism, in particular their common history as well as the achievements the Prussians had fought for in the past. However, a closer look reveals that those civilized and civilizing elements on which Europe had prided itself for so long were adduced as well, but, significantly, were now presented as characteristics of a national culture: freedom of conscience, industry and science stand beside honour and independence.

To my people

There is as little need to explain to My loyal people as to the Germans the causes of the war which is now beginning. They are clear for undeluded Europe to see. We succumbed to the superior power of France . . . The lifeblood of the country was sucked away, the principal fortresses remained occupied by the enemy, agriculture was crippled, as were the once-prosperous industries of our cities. Freedom of commerce was impeded, thus choking off the sources of profit and prosperity . . . I hoped to make things easier for My people and finally convince the French emperor that it was to his own advantage to leave Prussia its independence. But my wholly innocent intentions were rendered useless by his arrogance and faithlessness . . . Brandenburgers, Prussians, Silesians, Pomeranians, Lithuanians! You know what you have endured for seven years, you know what tragic fate will be yours if we do not end with honour the fight which now begins. Remember the past, the Great Elector, the great Frederick. Keep in mind the benefits which our forefathers won under them in bloody battle: freedom of conscience, honour, independence, commerce, industry and science. Think of the great example of our mighty allies, the Russians; think of the Spaniards, the Portuguese. Even smaller nations have joined battle with mightier foes for such benefits and have triumphed. Remember the heroic Swiss and Dutch. . . . No matter what sacrifices may be demanded of individuals, they do not balance the holy boons for which we make them, for the sake of which we struggle and must triumph, if we do not wish to cease to be Prussians and Germans. . . . You will go forward boldly . . . because a Prussian and a German cannot live without honour. But we must have complete confidence: God and our firm will shall bring victory to our just cause, and with it a secure and glorious peace and the return of better times.

Friedrich Wilhelm, Breslau, 17 March, 1813

The arguments proffered by the Prussian king essentially repeat the rhetoric used in other states by politicians now posing as national leaders in their opposition to the French dictator. Sometimes, these men were the ideological and even physical heirs of the old rulers, sometimes they were new men trying to cement their newly found power with an appeal to old traditions which were increasingly presented as inalienable and, indeed, almost innate national values.

Elements of nationalism: the political culture
of the nineteenth century

Even if the images in which, at the end of the eighteenth century, a 'Europe of nations' was revealed represent only a limited selection from Europe's cultural heritage, as images of earlier, more universal dreams, they constituted an ideology that presented the nation as a unique and essential unity, a living body, which, of course, represented its citizens. This idea was consciously constructed by the State, propagated with all possible means by governments and ruling elites in order to advance solidarity. Indeed, more than ever before, state policy now became a deliberate cultural policy as well.

In all European states, traditions were 'invented' to give the citizen the feeling of a centennial solidarity.[6] History was rewritten or written anew from the point of view of the State as the natural structure in which the nation and the community expressed itself politically. This new past was glorified by emphasizing the importance and results of commonly fought battles, the role of great men – rarely women – and the glorious feats of history; it was a 'national' past, the reflection of the nation's shared, collective heroism.

Everywhere, the school curriculum was emphatically historicized to contribute to this end. The arts were harnessed to the same end. In all states, splendid monuments arose to celebrate a nation's greatness. In Rome, itself the outstanding monument to the past and present of a millennial Church with universal pretensions, the very nationalistic and anti-clerical Roman republic, the outcome of the Napoleonic conquest of Italy, decided that secular culture should be remembered as well. In the Pincio Gardens, on a terrace overlooking the old town, dozens and dozens of marble busts were placed, honouring Italy's great sons and, admittedly, a few of its daughters as well. This tradition was continued when, after a temporary return to political division, Italy was finally united in the 1860s. The guide book to this 'remembrance park' was used as a prize gift in nineteenth-century Italian schools.[7] Meanwhile, the Bavarian kings built a classical Greek temple on a ridge overlooking the Danube, calling it the Valhalla, after the heavenly house of the ancient gods of the Germans; thus indicating the dual inspiration of contemporary German culture, they filled it with monuments glorifying the great men of Germany, for good measure 'adopting' many a genius who was manifestly not German at all. Old buildings and other places of historic interest, too, were now restored, as 'sites of memory';[8] they were made the object of secular pilgrimages, where the nation's past could be experienced as a living influence.

Inevitably, as most educated Europeans were increasingly fascinated with their own nation's past, which was glorified in literature and the visual arts and all remains of which were cherished, the centuries that by and since the Renaissance had been dismissively described as the 'Middle Ages', the period between the end of the classical world in the fifth century and its 'rebirth' in the fifteenth, were now glorified as well. After all, it was precisely in those ages that most European nations had first set foot on the road towards the formation of the sovereign, territorial states that now, in this blessedly prosperous and progressive nineteenth century, gave them such power and glory. Consequently, all over Europe a 'medieval' revival took place, most visibly manifest in architecture that chose the 'gothic style' as its preferred vehicle. In Cologne and Milan, the unfinished medieval cathedrals were now completed, but, mainly, hundreds of neo-gothic buildings were erected – churches, but also, as in, for example, such capitals as London and Budapest, the houses of parliament, for what better way to express a nation's confidence in the historic roots of its newly found democracy than to assemble its representatives in an architectural context harking back to those now hallowed ages.

All over Europe, literature served the national ideal as well: in poetry which evoked a past either distant or recent, but always decidedly romanticized, in plays which re-enacted the great moments of the nation's history, and in a genre that was relatively new but soon proved both hugely popular and politically particularly effective – the historical novel. Leo Tolstoy's monumental epic *War and Peace* (1863–9), referring to Russia's heroic battle against Napoleon, greatly helped to create a sense of the Russian nation's greatness through establishing its identity and destiny. In the person of the simple farmer-soldier Platon Karatayev, Tolstoy created the embodiment of the uncontaminated pure soul of the Russian people, whose example imbued the novel's noble protagonist, the aristocrat Pierre Bezuhov, with a sense of individual and collective suffering that helped him gain spiritual freedom.

Of course, people did create literary 'sites of memory' as well, if only by cultivating the places where the literary giants who were identified with national culture had lived. The English had been doing so in the Shakespeare cult staged at Stratford-upon-Avon since the middle of the eighteenth century; and in Germany, Goethe's city of Weimar became a place of pilgrimage, too. Due to improved and, more importantly, cheaper print technology, the nation's literary heritage could be brought to people's own homes, as it was when, for example, the publishing house of Macmillan decided to create its very successful *English Men of Letters* series in the 1870s; it was a veritable exercise in popular, national education,[9] as was, in a slightly more elitist way, the creation of the *Pleiade* series, the printed pantheon of the authors who were deemed to form the literary canon of France.

Last, but not least, all over Europe music was instrumental in inciting feelings of national pride, especially in the form of grand opera, both romantic and patriotic. In Brussels, in 1830, such an opera, *La Muette de Portici*, fuelled the already heated feelings of the 'Belgians' who were dissatisfied with Dutch rule. In due course, Belgium gained its independence as a nation from the Netherlands. During the political fragmentation of the Italian peninsula, the very name of the composer Giuseppe Verdi (1813–1901) came to be a rallying cry for those seeking to finally abolish both feudal and clerical authority and create a unified, national state under a new king. For the composer's name could be read as an acronym of the king of Sardinia's new title: 'Vittorio Emmanuele Re d'Italia'. In Germany, still divided into many states, the musical dramas of

Richard Wagner, such as the famous *Nibelungen* cycle, evoked the image of a common, though entirely mythical, Germanic past which soon served as a stimulus for action in the present, too. Wagner hoped that the German people would flock to his new opera house on the green hill at Bayreuth and, like the Greeks of ancient Athens in their theatres, be incited by the message encoded and enacted in the 'total art' he had devised and thus become better citizens of the German nation which, emerging out of its political division, soon would be a single state as well.

For in this climate of nationalism, new states were born to give political expression to the expectations and hopes of peoples who, instigated by the rhetoric of political and cultural leaders alike, felt that a state that was a veritable unity, encapsulating all who spoke the same language and shared the same traditions, would be a guarantee for a better life. During the course of the nineteenth century, the numerous German principalities were united under the Hohenzollern kings – soon to be emperors – of Brandenburg-Prussia, as was Italy under the kings of Sardinia of the House of Savoy-Piemonte. On the other hand, existing multicultural states, such as the old, far-flung Habsburg Empire, increasingly felt the centrifugal power of nationalist movements which, in the early twentieth century, led to its final dismemberment.

Frequently, in the process of nationalistic state formation, older, regional cultures were subordinated to and sometimes even violently forced to conform to the new ideal. All over Europe, language became an instrument of power that was used to help create the unity of the state. Consequently, all over Europe, national governments attempted to make the populations within their country's borders speak the same language, a policy that often evoked outbursts of regional particularism. Regional cultures now became nationalized. For the time being, such peoples as the Irish, the Balts and the Finns lost their cultural autonomy. Cruel campaigns of Anglification, Russification and Swedification superimposed the languages and frequently also the religions of the ruling elites on, or forcefully put them in the place of those who had not succeeded in retaining their power. Indeed, the terrible policy which came to be called 'ethnic cleansing' at the end of the twentieth century, had really started with such campaigns as the ones waged by the English against the Roman Catholics in Ireland from the times of Elizabeth I onwards until the nineteenth century. In consequence, all over Europe groups who were now put in the position of 'minorities' tended increasingly to cherish their own traditions. Secretly or openly they tried to defend their identity, defining it in cultural, including religious, terms, as well as on ethnic and political grounds, but always with linguistic arguments, too.

The ultimate reason for these nationalizing campaigns was that unity was required to secure internal cohesion and peace, necessary to pursue well-founded foreign policies and to maintain a leading position in the increasingly expanding world market. What a state needed was a general feeling of community among the people who would support the ruler's claims to sovereignty and the pretensions to power of those who led 'the nation'. Governability requires controllability. It was assumed that controllability was most easily achieved if a single system of norms and values were imposed on society. It was thought to be even more effective if it caused people in such a community to feel that those norms and values really formed their own specific identity, bound them together, making them strong against everyone who presented himself as an enemy – or who was presented to them as such. In the nineteenth century, to a greater or lesser extent, virtually all European states were each other's enemies, fighting for limited natural resources in order to make their economies as strong as possible and thus buttress their positions of power.

This is one of the reasons why science, especially in its applied, technological forms, interacting with increasing industrialization, was now seen as a pre-eminent manifestation of national culture, proudly presented as an expression of the national 'genius'. Thus, the great 'world exhibitions' such as that in London in 1851, despite their stress on the 'universality' of industrial and technological progress, were mainly windows for the display of national entries.[10]

New elites, new mechanisms of cultural diffusion, new manifestations of culture

The group who mainly articulated the national ideology was described succinctly by the nineteenth-century Hamburg publicist Johann Curio when he wrote:

> Wir haben keinen Adel, keine Patrizier, keine Sklaven, ja selbst nicht einmal Untertanen. Alle wirklichen Hamburger kennen und haben nur einen einzigen Stand, den Stand eines Burgers. Burger sind wir alle, nicht mehr und nicht weniger.[11]

> We have no nobility, no patricians, no slaves, no, not even subjects. All real Hamburgers know and have only one class, the class of burghers. Citizens we are, nothing more and nothing less.

As a result of economic and political change, by the 1840s it was mainly people from the affluent industrial and professional classes, partly new, 'self-made' men, partly descendants from the old urban notables, who dominated life and culture in Europe. Everywhere, their power grew, not only in the financial-economic world but also in politics, if only because officials who kept the wheels of state running were increasingly recruited from their ranks. Consequently, they began to control cultural life as well. This new elite was formed, intellectually and, in a broader sense, culturally, within and through a complex set of mechanisms of cultural diffusion.

States striving to achieve a heightened sense of national identity were helped in their endeavour by better communication. The construction of roads and railways facilitated the mobility of people who for ages had been tied to their villages. Increased migration as part and consequence of the industrialization process was another factor, and so was the recruitment of soldiers from the remotest corners of the country and from the entire population to serve in a 'national' army.[12] For to be able to obey orders, they now had to learn the 'national' language, rather than their own, local dialect. They also had to learn to read, if only because the new, technologically advanced arms often required a basic ability to understand written instructions.

Yet it was principally the enormous growth of education that contributed to the spreading of all sorts of ideas and traditions. To supply the needs of a growing technical-industrial economy, primary schools were founded on a grand scale and basic education was often made compulsory. Consequently, the literacy rate in Europe quickly rose, although this varied greatly from country to country.[13] Between 1870 and 1900, in the industrialized parts of Germany the number of illiterate people – measured among recruits for the army and among people who had to sign a marriage certificate – dropped from the remaining 2 per cent to nil. In a still largely rural Italy, the percentage dropped from a high 59 to 33 per cent, and among women, from 78 to 48 per cent.[14]

Also, education, especially at the secondary and tertiary levels, was now no longer limited to the old and new elites, but became open to large sections of the moderately well-to-do middle classes as well. Yet, it remained an education whose structure and content were based largely on the practices and concepts developed in the late fifteenth and early sixteenth centuries.

An authoritative 'educational philosopher' like the Englishman Matthew Arnold (1822–88) succinctly articulated the problem in his essay *Culture and Anarchy* (1869).[15] Arnold argued that good education is the basis of any society which claims the epithets 'civilized' and 'humane'. He wanted, first of all, to reform the 'public' schools – actually, the private boarding schools – where boys from the British aristocracy and the prosperous middle class were mostly educated. However, in his plans he referred explicitly to the situation in the German states.[16] There, Wilhelm von Humboldt (1776–1835) had voiced new ideas for reform of secondary and tertiary education as well; however, Humboldt felt such reforms should be realized through deliberate, government-controlled policies, instead of, as was normal in England and nearly the whole of Europe, being left to the Church and other private institutions.

For Arnold, 'Hebraism' and 'Hellenism' were the two pillars of European culture. The 'desire for reason' attributed to the latter combined with 'the will of God' inherent in the former produced those forms of culture which were worth propagating: 'the best that is known and thought in the world'.[17] There was every reason to propagate precisely this culture for, as Arnold significantly wrote in 1848: 'I see a wave of more than American vulgarity, moral, intellectual and social, preparing to break over us'.[18]

Like Von Humboldt, Arnold noted a growing and dangerous divergence between 'the strictness of conscience' that Christianity imposed on European man and 'the spontaneity of consciousness' that classical antiquity had fostered. He wrote: 'neither of them is the law of human development, as their admirers are prone to make them; they are, each of them, contributions to human development'.[19] Yet, reading between the lines, his deepest inclination was obviously to Hellenism, or rather to 'the habit of fixing our mind upon the intelligible law of things . . . [that] makes us see that the only absolute good . . . is the progress towards perfection, – our own progress towards it and the progress of humanity'.[20]

For some of Arnold's critics, this cultural ideal smacked of paganism. Moreover, many thought it was too elitist. Henry Sidgwick wrote that any culture worth propagating should:

> learn 'to call nothing common or unclean'. It can only propagate itself shedding the light of its sympathy liberally; by learning to love common people and common things, to feel common interests. Make people feel that their own poor life is ever so little beautiful and poetical; then they will begin to turn and seek after the treasures of beauty and poetry outside and above it.[21]

The influence of education was strongly reinforced by the culture of reading which was transformed by new techniques of printing and illustrating that made mass publishing far cheaper than before.[22] Since the end of the eighteenth century, all sizeable European cities boasted of reading rooms and lending libraries where newspapers, periodicals and books could be consulted.

Yet, if one were to ask what the visitors of these establishments actually read, the answer, as far as it is possible to give one, is disappointing. Analysis of inventories and loan records shows that in the eighteenth century relatively large numbers of informative, general publications were read but that, partly as a result of the censorship imposed all over Europe on these kinds of institutions in the years during and following the French Revolution, reading patterns changed in the early nineteenth century.[23] People still read daily papers and periodicals but their main fare consisted of novels.[24] The 'fiction industry', already in evidence at the end of the eighteenth century, now saw its first boom, precisely through an interaction between reading clubs and lending libraries.[25] When, in the course of the nineteenth century, general primary education became the norm in many European countries, this development continued to an even higher degree, especially when cheap magazines began to serialize the fiction both of hack writers and of more serious authors, influencing audiences hitherto untapped.

Novels, in so nationalistic a culture, were often constructed around a topic from the present or past of their own society. Yet few were the novelists who did not also articulate, albeit in a glorifying national context, the many Christian values that had characterized Europe for so long, though these values had been turned into middle-class shibboleths and, moreover, had often been secularized as well. Nor were novels entirely uncritical of contemporary society and culture. Indeed, they often vented opinions – popularized and 'filtered' precisely to suit a mainly middle-class readership – which had been expressed by elite cultural commentators but had not yet been divulged to the general public.

All the while, the continuing disadvantaged and indeed disenfranchised position of women, economically, socially as well as politically, robbed culture and society of many positive influences. That much was obvious even to Alfred,

Lord Tennyson (1809–92), Queen Victoria's 'best-selling' Poet Laureate. Admittedly, his very popular poetry, exalting the bourgeois family ideal, contributed to the consolidation of male–female relations in which the woman was denied virtually every right and even feeling. Not allowed to vote or to enrol at university and largely restricted to the roles of wife and mother, and, hence, confined to the house, middle-class women were increasingly dissatisfied. Yet society, and a cultural pattern that, having been shaped over many centuries, held both women and men prisoner, was not easily changed by the protests of a few courageous females, who were widely condemned as radical feminists and unwomanly women. Nevertheless, Tennyson at one time succumbed to the temptation to write a poem which not only made clear which spheres of cultural life women were excluded from but also – in its introduction – showed that he himself experienced the 'spirit' of his own time as restrictive and, hence, unproductive:

> At last
> She rose upon a wind of prophecy
> Dilating on the future: everywhere
> Two heads in council, two beside the hearth
> Two in the tangled business of the world,
> Two in the liberal offices of life,
> Two plummets dropt for one to sound the abyss
> Of science, and the secrets of the mind;
> Musician, painter, sculptor, critic, more;
> And everywhere the broad and bounteous Earth
> Should bear a double growth of those rare souls,
> Poets, whose thoughts enrich the blood of the world.[26]

Indeed, the early decades of the nineteenth century saw the coming of age of a new species, the female novelist. All over Europe, women took the opportunity that mass printing offered. Some of them did so to make a living, rightly assuming that the new market largely consisted of women as well. Others took to writing as an outlet for pent-up creative urges. Combining the two, some also used the novel to voice, either hesitantly or radically, their opinions about the position of women in an oppressively patriarchal society. Thus, the female readership of the majority of popular novels were slowly acquainted with new opinions on the relationship between men and women, which heralded the first step towards the movement that claimed liberty and equality for women. In England, Mary Ann Evans, writing as George Eliot, in her great novel *Middlemarch* (1872) explored the socio-economic and psychological boundaries that confined and restricted both men and women. Also, increasingly, specialized periodicals for both 'the family' and for 'women' were printed, which not only offered – mostly serialized – novels suitable for general reading but also acquainted this readership with developments in society and, interestingly, the sciences. If only to facilitate their educational role, women were enabled to take a stance in the often ferocious controversies between materialist scientists and those advocating a more conciliatory position aimed at retaining traditional theological views on the relationship between God and his creation.

Criticism of a society that was still essentially class-ridden also emerged. The German novelist and journalist Theodore Fontane, for example, in the exquisite novel *Effie Briest* (1895), set in late nineteenth-century Berlin and the surrounding Brandenburg countryside, painted a vivid portrait of the constraints which an aristocratic society imposed on its members, male and female alike. In France and Spain, Gustave Flaubert's *Madame Bovary* (1857) and Clarín's *La Regenta* (1884) depicted life in provincial towns, where the customary power of the Church and the local notables stifled any expression of individual emotion that threatened the limits of propriety set by tradition.[27] Meanwhile, it is worth noting that these three novels – among the most famous texts about the situation of nineteenth-century women – were still written by men.

Another point of sociocultural criticism effectively expressed in novels concerned the threats posed to the poor by increasing industrialization. It was most eloquently voiced in England by Charles Dickens (1812–70), the more effectively because his stories were usually serialized in periodicals first, thus reaching that part of the public which could not afford to buy his books. Such criticism as, for example, Dickens's on the appalling conditions of the urban labouring population did not fail to awaken the authorities to the need for actual social reforms.

Yet the danger of potentially more radical cultural changes, such as the growing significance of the machine for man, was taken less seriously. The unknown possibilities that, since the last decades of the eighteenth century, the sciences, especially mechanics and chemistry, had begun to offer had also revived fears about 'the mechanical human' in a number of books.[28] Mary Godwin Shelley's gripping novel *Frankenstein, or The Modern Prometheus* (1817) is one of the most important works in the genre precisely because she shows to what extent man, the maker of machines, can always choose to use them for his own purposes, good or evil. Towards the end of the first 'machine age', the English novelist Samuel Butler (1835–1902) published his satire *Erewhon* (1872), in which he contrasted the England of his time with a society which had consciously distanced itself from all sorts of 'modern' conveniences precisely out of fear of the machine, noting that:

> The largest machines will probably greatly diminish in size. . . . a day will come when . . . its language shall have developed from the cry of animals to a speech as intricate as our own . . . Man's very soul is due to the machines.[29]

The characters in Butler's novel articulate a perennial anxiety – the stronger because at the same time it voiced a desire? – that already had been expressed in the Roman version of the Greek Prometheus story, in which the hero, breathing life into a clay figure and, thus, god-like, creating life out of inane matter, subsequently loses control over it. The central question was, of course, the extent to which man could and should interfere in the process of creation.

Yet, the new 'bourgeois' elite, while educated within the culture outlined above, had often been raised in more limited financial circumstances than the aristocratic elite of earlier times. Moreover, they were firmly persuaded that their power and prosperity were principally bound to the destiny of their own national economy. Had they not been prepared to sacrifice money and life for their country, for example in the fight against Napoleon? Had they not subsequently forged a closer bond between nation and state because they had made a case for some form of popular representation? And was this process, which in many western European states had created at least the formal framework for democracy, not proof that they, these nations, Europe, essentially distinguished themselves from the greater part of the world, politically, institutionally, morally even? The German novelist Gustav Freytag depicted the new society, with its civic-national values and aspirations in his famous novel *Soll und Haben* (Assets and Liabilities) (1855), in which he pitted the bourgeoisie – educated, thrifty, idealistic, moralistic, concerned about both its own prosperity and the nation's progress – against a self-seeking, decadent aristocracy, and against the financial manipulations of Jewish bankers. For like so many other European novelists, he, too, openly voiced the growing, increasingly virulent anti-Semitism of the age, a sentiment that was certainly not tempered by growing nationalism and even expressed itself in the construction of theories of global Jewish conspiracies. While in Freytag's novel the latter groups lost out, the former, of course, triumphed.[30]

This atmosphere of triumphant middle-class nationalism almost seemed to suffocate the previous more cosmopolitan, Europe-centred spirit, precisely because nationalist thinking was so closely intertwined with the radical economic changes that had started to reshape large parts of Europe since the end of the eighteenth century. Now, even among the traditional elites, the old cultural ideal – the dream of Europe – largely disappeared. By now, these elites, too, felt they needed to identify with their own state and nation. Following the expansive growth of the European economy during the Industrial Revolution and in the subsequent phase of Europe's worldwide imperialism, following the political and social changes that the upheaval of the last decades of the eighteenth century had brought, these elites could no longer act and think as they had done in the past. Indeed, many historians argue that the beginnings of a cosmopolitan culture, felt and experienced all over Europe at royal courts and in the residences of the aristocracy, by the early nineteenth century had slowly disappeared. Or, one should rather say, the new power groups in European society had translated it into forms that could be more nationally experienced.

Of course, artists and scholars continued to read, write and travel, and many individual members of this principally intellectual part of the elite still cherished a sense of community that reached beyond their own country. Yet two phenomena began to undermine this cosmopolitanism. On the one hand, from the end of the eighteenth century, but certainly during the nineteenth century, the study and dissemination of classical culture increasingly became the domain of a professional class of 'career intellectuals' who gradually ensconced themselves in the ivory towers of universities and other academic institutions: the 'demolition' of the influence of the classical heritage in European society in a broad sense had begun.[31] On the other hand, most of those who were now, for the first time, able to look over their own fences and who did so by travelling and reading – the solid, proud bourgeois – were frequently informed by another mentality than the Grand Tour travellers of earlier times.

Admittedly, the new elite continued to look upon Mediterranean Europe as the cradle of classical culture. They travelled to Italy, which became a unified state in 1861. They also travelled to Greece, which in the 1820s had already fought itself free of Ottoman domination – helped by cultural enthusiasts from all over Europe as well as by European governments who wanted to increase their economic and political influence in the Ottoman provinces of the eastern Mediterranean. But Europe's well-heeled middle class no longer journeyed *en masse* to German universities or to the French court, with the aim of ending their trip and completing their education in Italy, and of turning themselves into members of a cosmopolitan elite whose representatives, recognizable across state borders by their common behaviour, shared certain norms and values. Increasingly, most of those who now went abroad did so only for pleasure, to enjoy themselves, preferably in an atmosphere in which an exotic landscape and a pleasant climate coincided with an interesting, status-enhancing cultural experience. The 'Grand Tour' was giving way to consumer tourism, for which the middle class's increased prosperity created the economic conditions. Improved means of transport – the steamship, the train – made it technically possible, while the cultural context made it into a mental, psychological imperative. Indeed, travelling or taking a holiday became fashionable and, as a result, a necessity as well, for a much bigger group than ever before – a group whose wishes and expectations also differed from the former Grand Tour-ists.

To reconstruct the new travel culture and the mentality behind it, one should turn to newspaper articles and to the brochures supplied by the first travel organizations – like Thomas Cook and Sons, who had made a fortune out of transporting people to the Great Exhibition of 1851 – as well as to travel guides like the German *Baedekers* and the English *Murray's*, which were written for the incipient mass tourism of the 1830s and 1840s. All these texts were clearly aimed at a group who, despite their classical education, still had a different attitude towards culture and towards Europe. Equally fascinating are the special magazines now created to publish only travel stories – indicative of a huge new market. A good example is the French magazine *Le Tour du Monde* (A trip around the Earth), which was translated into many languages and eagerly read by the bourgeoisie. Both the travel guides and these often illustrated periodicals not only described the exotic parts of the non-European world but also Europe itself which was now represented as a region made up of different, national cultures rather than as a single cultural world.

As most travellers came from western Europe, their views of central and eastern Europe are particularly revealing. There was a marked increase in people's interest in Russia. Yet, inasmuch as the world outside the imperial capital, St Petersburg, did not resemble the changed – meaning technologically and politically much improved – conditions 'at home', i.e. in western Europe, most travellers tended to comment negatively on and even judge the tsarist empire as part of 'barbaric' Asia rather than of 'civilized' Europe.

Searching such sources for the prevailing concepts of culture, national or European, one must conclude that the 'sense of Europe' was little developed. Indeed, they point to what was perhaps a growing gap between 'us' and 'them', the 'others', even within Europe itself; obviously, this was by and large caused by the nationalism that now constituted most people's political and cultural context, determining both their thoughts and their actions.

Yet, at the end of the eighteenth century, the German poet Friedrich von Hardenberg (1772–1801), better known as Novalis, had already proclaimed that the ghost of nationalism and the horror of revolution would disappear only if Europe once more drank from the source from which the inspiration for unity and civilization had once come, Christianity. However, though Novalis's mystic poetry was much admired, he did not find a large audience with his impressive and impassioned essay *Die Christenheit oder Europa* (Christendom or Europe) (1799). In it, he presented his vision of an all-encompassing humanity, based on democracy and the fruitful interaction between nature – mastered for man's progress by science and technology – and culture, as a system of values inspiring man's actions. Thus, he hoped to bridge the fundamentally threatening gap between an all too elitist humanistic vision of culture and an all too populist mechanistic, physical world-view. He also hoped to undo the results of a narrow-minded Eurocentrism. While Novalis certainly did not lapse into shallow cultural relativism and even less into reactionary traditionalism – he was far from preaching a romantic-medieval Christianity – his ideas were misunderstood, wilfully or not, by many,[32] and not surprisingly so. After all, the nations of Europe, instead of searching for unity, continued to struggle for hegemony.

BASLE, THE MIDDLE OF THE NINETEENTH CENTURY: JACOB BURCKHARDT (1818–97) CRITICIZES CONTEMPORARY CULTURE

Ever wider grew the gap between those who gloried in the measurability of nature and in the 'makeability' of everything that man could ever need, and those who maintained that this should not be the only, and certainly not the ultimate, concern of man. The Swiss historian Jakob Burckhardt gained European fame with his masterly analysis of the culture of the Renaissance. In his *Die Kultur der Renaissance in Italien* (1860), he virtually created the image of that period for many generations to come. However, his vision of the Renaissance was a highly positive one. Indeed, perhaps it was too positive, not least, one suspects, because in representing the past in a way suited to his feelings about the present this 'aristocrat of the mind' tried to find some sort of spiritual

Plate 23 While many Europeans eagerly entered the 'age of consumption', symbolized by the new phenomenon of the great department stores, such as the Parisian 'Au Bon Marché', here shown as it was in *c.*1870, others preferred to look back to times they thought more ennobling.

Source: Centre for Art Historical Documentation, Nijmegen, the Netherlands

refuge from the many unpleasant aspects he discovered in his own society and culture. Some fifty years later, the famous Dutch historian Johan Huizinga obviously succumbed to the same temptation with his powerful but equally one-sided recreation of the 'Waning of the Middle Ages'.

Burckhardt's private opinions – some of them clearly dated, some of them still relevant, most of them fascinating – can be gleaned from his correspondence. Some of them he expressed in his letters to his friend Hermaun Schauenburg, written in the fateful years 1848 and 1849, when revolutions occurred all over Europe because the new elites wanted more power and asked for more democratic rights – for themselves, only – while the common people simply hoped for improvement of their wretched living conditions in industrial society. These were also the years in which Karl Marx's *Communist Manifesto* (1848) was widely read and discussed. Burckhardt, betraying the continued fascination of Europe's intellectuals with the classical cultures of the Mediterranean, noted:

> I think I can detect a look of silent reproach in your eyes, because I am off so light-heartedly in search of southern debauchery, in the form of art and antiquity, while in Poland everything is going to pieces and the messengers of the Socialist Day of Judgement are at the gates. Good heavens, I can't after all alter things, and before universal barbarism breaks in (and for the moment I can foresee nothing else)

I want to debauch myself with a real eyeful of aristocratic culture, so that, when the social revolution has exhausted itself for the moment, I shall be able to take an active part in the inevitable restoration. . . . Just you wait and you will see the sort of spirits that are going to rise out of the ground during the next twenty years! Those that now hop about in front of the curtain, the communist poets and painters and their like, are mere *bajazzi* [clowns, PR], just preparing the public. You none of you know as yet what the people are, and how easily they turn into a barbarian horde . . . We may all perish; but at least I want to discover the interest for which I am to perish, namely, the old culture of Europe . . .

I hope for nothing from the future . . . for I am of the opinion that democrats and proletarians, even though they make most furious efforts, will have to yield to an increasingly violent despotism, for our charming century is made for anything rather than for real democracy.

Some twenty years later when, in the 1870s, Europe was, indeed, once more in turmoil as a result of the terrible war between France and Germany – the first 'industrial war', waged with weapons of mass destruction never before seen or used – Burckhardt wrote to his friend Friedrich von Preen:

The two great intellectual peoples of the continent are in the process of completely sloughing their culture, and a quite enormous amount of all that delighted and interested a man before 1870 will hardly touch the man of 1871. . . . The worst of all is not the present war, but the era of wars upon which we have entered, and to this the new mentality will have to adapt itself. O, how much the cultured will have to throw overboard as a spiritual luxury that they have come to love! And how very different from us the coming generation will be. . . . Anything that has to live on must contain a goodly portion of the eternal. And if anything lasting is to be created, it can only be through an overwhelmingly powerful effort of real poetry. To me, as a teacher of history, a very curious phenomenon has become clear: the sudden devaluation of all mere 'events' in the past. From now on in my lectures, I shall only emphasize cultural history . . .

Those who arranged those things [i.e. the Franco–German war] could all read, write and even compose newspaper articles and other literature. And the ones in Germany . . . are no less educated. But just look at England, bursting with wealth, and secretly kept in a state of siege by analogous elements! Up until now, for two hundred years, people in England have imagined that every problem could be solved through freedom, and that one could let opposites correct one another in the free interplay of argument. But what now? The great harm was begun in the last century, mainly through Rousseau, with his doctrine of the goodness of human nature. Out of this, plebs and educated alike distilled the doctrine of the golden age that was to come quite infallibly, provided people were left alone. The result, as every child knows, was the complete disintegration of the idea of authority in the heads of mortals, whereupon, of course, we periodically fall victim to sheer power. In the meanwhile, the idea of the natural goodness of man had turned, among the intelligent strata of Europe, into the idea of progress, i.e., undisturbed money-making and modern comforts, with philanthropy as a sop to conscience. . . . The only conceivable salvation would be for this insane optimism, in great and small, to disappear from people's brains. But then our present-day Christianity is not equal to the task; it has gone in for and it got mixed up with optimism for the last two hundred years. . . .

One of the principal phenomena which you emphasize reveals itself as clearly as can be in Switzerland: a flight from the risks of business into the arms of the salary-paying state is manifest in the fact that the moment farming is in a bad way the numbers who want to enter classes for teachers increases. But where on earth is it to end . . . Here in Basel we are now faced again with disbursements of two millions for new schools buildings! It's a single chain of related facts: free instruction, compulsory education, a maximum of thirty per class, a minimum of so and so many cubic metres per child, too many subjects taught, teachers obliged to have a superficial knowledge of too many subjects, etc. And, naturally, as a result: everyone dissatisfied with everything, a scramble for higher positions, which are of course very limited in number. Not to mention the absolutely insane insistence upon scholarship that goes on in girls' schools. . . . It may even be that the present educational system has reached its peak, and is approaching its decline.[33]

Inevitably, all over Europe urban life became more complex, representing an assault on man's senses: the crowdedness and filth of the smog-infested cities, where proper sewage systems were still often lacking, which meant that such epidemics as cholera claimed huge numbers of victims because human waste entered drinking water; the rampant prostitution and the consequent effects of venereal disease; the insecurity of the job market and the sense of a society constantly changing and on the move.

By the end of the nineteenth century, in the more industrialized regions of Europe, the elite's well-informed self-interest slowly, indeed, very slowly, resulted in improved working conditions in the factories as well as in better housing. Also, both the hospital and the medical service were now re-organized and extended. Large-scale vaccination campaigns were launched against such epidemic diseases as smallpox; initially, they aroused emotional, political and religious reactions revealing the widespread revulsion against the ways in which government and science increasingly invaded man's private life; indeed, it must be admitted that such policies did contribute to the growth of the power both of governments and of the medical profession, while, in retrospect, the health effects of the campaigns were debatable. Nevertheless, these developments have contributed to that aspect of European culture that has made medicine part and parcel of both the modern state and of modern society, with the latter, increasingly, relying on the former to deliver the 'health services' people now feel are their right.[34]

Also, some forms of insurance against illness, accident and old age were introduced – in Germany as early as the end of the nineteenth century. This and other, related, developments marked the final transformation of a society based on charity as a voluntary act to a 'social state', where the right to a minimal level of material comfort was guaranteed to every citizen. It was, perhaps, the major development that, besides increased overall prosperity and increasing political rights – and, of course, as a consequence thereof – came to distinguish European societies from those in the other worlds.[35] Admittedly, the industrial elite did not always adopt these changes of their own volition. Indeed, the ongoing social revolution was markedly influenced by the labour movement.[36]

One of the results of industrial action was that holidays were introduced for the labouring classes – albeit only a few days a year. Now, people started to save some of their hard-earned money to spend on an outing. They wanted to leave the overcrowded towns for the fresh air, deemed beneficial even if taken only for those few days. Actually, fresh air became they very symbol of escape from real and imagined illnesses, caused not only by the filth of factory towns and the terribly unhygienic living conditions, but also by 'stress', although the word had not yet been invented. Hence, people increasingly travelled to the mountains or the seaside.[37] Those who were better off could afford to be pampered by doctors and nurses in health resorts, mostly watering places that offered cures for each and every disease. Consequently, Europe is still dotted with spas, the monuments to a bourgeois society's growing concern with disease, real and imagined.

Within the context of both Romantic notions of nature and the need to escape from urban civilization, a new, far more positive attitude towards the natural environment developed, in which the erstwhile disdain for and fear of the countryside as something wild, untamed and uncontrollable was replaced by the feeling that only here the real life could still be lived, that only here man would find inspiration for really great visions and actions.[38] It was a notion visualized, especially, in landscape painting, which now tended to present man in the context of a 'sublime', awe-inspiring nature. Among the more daring and artistic, walking holidays, unheard of until that time and still looked upon with amazement by the working classes, became fashionable. Soon, the educated classes began to stress the view that if the labouring class could but experience nature, it would be a much-needed civilizing experience as well, that would keep them from their main, disturbing pastimes: drink and sex. In the process, Europeans also developed their passion for zoos and for pets. For of course, the animals that inhabited this sacred natural world should not be chased and killed, but lovingly protected. Taking a pet also meant bringing something of nature into one's own city-based existence. Soon, the animal world was highly senti-mentalized, especially in children's stories, where it was presented as a 'mode' for the values that should structure the human world.

Even though, for most Europeans, a real vacation was still limited to one or two day-trips a year, the more affluent citizens already took their holidays for two or three weeks. It was the wheel that turned this leisure revolution: both the wheels of the steam train, which permitted mass travel over long distances from the 1840s onwards and, by the end of the nineteenth century, the introduction of a safe and manageable bicycle which gave people greater mobility within their more immediate surroundings and revolutionized their thinking about space and time, immediacy and distance. Indeed, for many, bicycle tours became their first contact with a wider world.

All over the more prosperous parts of Europe, people came to think of leisure as both a symbol of status and a necessity of life: from the end of the eighteenth century onwards, consumer demands and consumption patterns increasingly revolved around free time, a commodity both scarce and expensive. The more leisure one was able to show, the more one moved away from the working poor, the lowest and largest group on the social scale.[39]

However, leisure time had to be filled and even regulated. If people became bored, they would only be tempted to start drinking or indulge in promiscuous sexuality or in wild games, all of which would lead to social unrest and chaos, specifically among the working classes: the culture of the people meant disorder. That, at least, was the argument of the mainly bourgeois political and social leaders who now controlled Europe's cities.[40] This resulted in a number of new cultural phenomena.

The well-to-do citizens – the men but also their wives, who were considered the natural keepers of civilized life – began to stage all kinds of activities to civilize and discipline the 'lower classes'. Temperance societies were formed to combat the demon of drink. Cookery classes taught women from these lower classes to be proper housewives according to the bourgeois model; it would help them to provide a welcoming home both for their husbands, who would be less inclined to go from the factory directly to the pub and spend their hard-earned wages on drink, and for their children, who would be reared in more congenial surroundings, and be taught to be proper citizens.

Obviously, all these activities were meant to help keep a tight rein on the large group of underpaid labourers who were suspected of the most shocking behaviour, which made them a potential threat both to the social and the political order. In 1825, the Prefect of the Rhône department in France wrote:

> I learned that men and women were sitting around a table in a separate upper room and . . . said indecent things and sang songs no less obscene. At dessert, everyone undressed completely. Paired off in couples, they proceeded to simulate the ceremony of marriage. One of them dressed in certain derisive garments . . . and married a couple in a parody of the religious ceremony of the Church. After . . . a sermon, the couple went into an adjacent room to consummate 'their marriage'. Afterwards they returned to wipe each other off. These ceremonies, as shocking as they are sacrilegious, continued as many times as there were couples to be joined in this scandalous manner.[41]

Concern for such and other forms of disorderly and indecent behaviour led civil and ecclesiastical authorities to collaborate in the transformation of all kinds of traditional popular pastimes. Thus, they tackled the phenomenon of the annual fairs and carnivals, which, according to bourgeois observers, always occasioned public drunkenness and, worse, the open manifestation of sexual acts. Precisely these two phenomena were felt to destabilize the family bond, the basic value of order that authorities held in high esteem. Therefore, such manifestations as fairs and 'kermisses' were sometimes banned completely, as was the case in many Dutch towns at the end of the nineteenth century. Often, however, the 'pillars of society', recognizing the need for popular relaxation, sought to give these festivities another, more controllable slant, focusing on religious processions and on such elevating activities as amateur theatricals, musical contests, flower shows and so on.[42]

Hence, in the same vein, importance was now attached to organized sports. They, too, could help to keep the 'mob' from the streets and out of the pubs where they would only create mischief. Moreover, participating in sports would imbue them with team spirit and, generally, incline them to a healthy way of living and thinking. The nineteenth century being the 'age of nationalism', celebrating the glory of 'King and Country', of *la Patrie* or of the *Vaterland*, in most countries the State, aided by the Churches, demanded the obedience of its subjects, if necessary to the point that they would be willing to give their lives for it. Social discipline was considered a basic civic virtue – and sport an excellent means to that end. Soccer especially soon became popular, not least among factory workers. Yet the game soon turned into an outlet for all kinds of suppressed aggression. Berlin's most authoritative newspaper around the turn of the century, the *Vossische Zeitung*, warning against the situation in Britain, reported on 23 April 1895:

> The losses of the football season 1894/5 during the past six months already amount to no less than 20 people killed, as well as several hundred badly wounded. However, it seems that only 10 per cent of the actual mishaps has been reported.
> . . .
> Quite deplorable is the custom, increasingly normal, to attack the umpire with bricks and iron bars when his decisions elicit the anger of the competing teams. Often, the public readily joins in, which means that the police, who are present at each match, cannot restore order. I know of English firms whose employees, on being hired, have to promise not to spend their leisure time playing football, as the number of accidents after the matches prevents the regular conduct of business.[43]

The well-to-do enjoyed sports as well, but not the same ones as those played by the labouring poor. Like all forms of culture, sports, too, have a specific status and a specific cultural value. In the eighteenth century, boxing was, to a certain extent, an elite sport, because aristocrats enjoyed watching it, often employing the contestants and at times even joining in themselves. In the nineteenth century, however, it became one of the 'common' sports. In the first decades of the nineteenth century, football was an elite sport, played mainly by the boys of English public, i.e. private, elite schools. At the end of the century, it became another 'common' sport. In the first decades of the twentieth century, hockey and tennis were elite sports, but after the Second World War 'everybody' entered the fields and the courts.

In short, all forms of culture that filled the free hours of the nineteenth century provided status and showed differences of status. But as the example of sports shows, in this fast-changing industrial society, the status of cultural forms changed equally fast, with the various social groups trying to find new ways of distinguishing themselves as older forms of culture were appropriated by other groups.

Factory and other blue-collar workers flocked to those theatres which, besides offering music hall and vaudeville shows, with bawdy songs and risqué scenes, also provided the highly popular genre of melodrama, packed with simple, recognizable emotional conflicts set in often improbable intrigues; the inevitable, though often equally improbable happy endings were judged sentimental and, worse, even morally corrupting by the bourgeoisie who were highly suspicious of these forms of 'low brow' culture.[44] They, in their turn, participated in those forms of public entertainment that provided status through their association with upper-class culture. Thus, 'high-brow' theatre continued to flourish, as did public reading rooms and the public lectures provided by scientific societies – a phenomenon that significantly contributed to the popularization of science, reinforcing the belief that this was, indeed, an era of progress. Indeed, it was this science that endorsed such physical notions as high brow and low brow in the first place and made them into stigmatizing characteristics – the high forehead being associated with intelligence or culture, because the upper classes were considered to have experienced a different development from the labouring poor with their low, almost animal-like foreheads.

Important developments took place in musical culture, too. Music had been part of European civilization for ages: the 'popular' music of the fairs and taverns, and the drawing-room music performed and enjoyed by the bourgeoisie and the aristocracy, besides, of course, the oldest music, that of the Church. The distinction between the three was far less than the present-day cult of classical, or serious, music might lead one to presume. Indeed, aristocratic opera and Church music were often constructed on the basis of popular, profane tunes, and court songs were whistled in the streets. However, although there were public concert halls in most European capitals – the seventeenth-century English diarist Samuel Pepys is forever telling us what he heard and saw in the London playhouses where music was played as well – their size was relatively small.

With the revolutions of the late eighteenth century, many court musicians, used to composing and performing for princes or wealthy private patrons – e.g. Joseph Haydn was employed by successive heads of the Eszterhazy family, one of the Habsburg Empire's most powerful dynasties – had to find new means of earning a living.[45] As the bourgeoisie, growing in number and with cultural aspirations of their own, were keen on good music, too, the step from the court theatre or court opera to the grand concert hall open to an increasingly numerous general public was not a big one. Thus, the first grand concert halls were built around the turn of the eighteenth to the nineteenth century. Not incidentally, they revolutionized European music: the size of the audiences necessitated composing on a grander scale, resulting in an increase both of the size of the orchestra and of the reach and pitch of the various instruments. Thus, Beethoven's symphonies were composed for and heard by a larger public than, for example, Mozart's.

It was a public who often enjoyed what it was offered but never forgot that attending these occasions gave status, too, showing that one was a culturally minded person. Audiences started to listen in silence. Having paid for the pleasure – or simply to be publicly seen imbibing 'culture' – they thought they should treat it as something special. And, in contrast to the aristocracy, who had considered musicians no better than servants, and music a *divertissement*, which should not interrupt polite conversation, the bourgeoisie, less secure, were afraid to speak. But the main change was that people increasingly looked upon music as an art, even as a religion, rather than an entertainment.[46] Indeed, some cultural historians feel that as the actual power of Christianity, of the Churches, fell, the power of music, romantically conceived as expressing all that was best in nature and man, rose, to become a 'substitute religion'.

Indeed, music, like reading, provides interesting clues to this development, especially within the context of the bourgeois cult of domesticity. For now the drawing room became the actual as well as the symbolic shrine of a culture whose specific task it was to instil the household and the family with the norms and values of this class. Reading, for example, the hundreds of 'romantic' poems set to music mostly for the drawing room by a composer like Franz Schubert (1797–1828), one of the most gifted musicians of the early nineteenth century, one detects the hopes and fears of this bourgeois society: a longing for love and a happy marriage; and a craving for solitude; the need to escape from the bustle of urban life into the fields and mountains, and the joy or melancholy born from a union with nature, with a God sometimes still manifestly present, but at other times unrecognizably hidden in the vastness of the cosmos.[47]

But besides this inward-looking romanticism, music, especially vocal music, was often the medium for expressing the values of a society not only bourgeois but also nationalistic: satisfied with its economic and political progress, in operas, cantatas and songs it often extolled the nation's glorious past in rousing melodies or obliquely commented upon Europe's superiority vis-à-vis the other worlds.[48]

One of the major questions raised by the changes of the nineteenth century is how the values of an urban middle class came to dominate the majority of the population. Between the early decades of the nineteenth and the early decades of the twentieth centuries, the transformation of parts of Europe from a rural into an industrial society and, moreover, into an urban or rather middle-class culture was inaugurated by the massive move of people from a slowly emptying countryside to fast-growing and even overflowing towns. Inevitably, for several generations, increasing numbers of Europeans were confronted with and bombarded by the norms and notions held by the bourgeoisie, whose affluence was a powerful stimulant for all those who sought to escape from poverty.

Great changes were brought about by the various civilizing, disciplining cultural policies successfully employed by the elite as described above, as well as by the increasing power the consumer economy of the towns came to hold over large sections of urban society. More important, however – for subconsciously, worlds were merging as well, they introduced the predominance of bourgeois morality in European society at large. Undoubtedly, the huge groups of male and, even more, female domestic servants were one of the main channels through which bourgeois family values slowly trickled down into the labouring classes, values epitomized in the ideal image of the non-working, mothering wife. Servants were also confronted with the growing taboo of sexuality in these middle-class households, where everything connected with intercourse and the childbearing process was becoming shrouded in secrecy. Besides the connotation of animal-like and thus non-human, i.e. non-civilized, behaviour, the bourgeoisie assumed that the seductions of sexuality pursued outside the restrictions of the marriage bond were a disruptive force, for men as well as, but perhaps even more so, for women. J.J. Virey, a widely read French medical publicist of the 1860s, revealingly wrote of the ideal coupling as one between:

> the most female woman and the most virile man, when a dark, hairy, dry, hot and impetuous male finds the other sex delicate, moist, smooth and white, timid and modest. The one must give in and the other is constituted to receive . . . to welcome, to absorb, out of a sort of need and feeling of deficit, the overflow of the other.[49]

Obviously, such representations of ideal sexuality, sanctioned by science – for by now medicine was definitely a science, and one increasingly demanded and, hence, respected as well – could not fail to influence people's expectations and behaviour. Men were allowed their evenings 'on the town', their drinking and smoking societies, and their liaisons, albeit reluctantly, for the notion of the 'double standard' was certainly not as universally accepted as has been suggested. Women, however, had no such distractions. The often intensely religious middle classes felt that the only outing becoming a respectable female was the daily walk to church or, perhaps, but then accompanied by a servant, a visit to dispense charity to the poor. Also, women were increasingly desexualized. As the guarantors of procreation and thus of the sacred family, they were idealized as innocent of the 'ways of the world' – always meaning the male world as self-effacing wives and mothers, as the natural keepers of the house. Slowly, such notions were introduced to and, moreover, interiorized by the working classes of Europe's urban, industrial regions.

Money and time, goods and leisure: towards a consumer culture

Besides the need for leisure – which increasingly became both a status symbol and a psychological craving – the 'culture of things', the acquisition of highly visible possessions remained a powerful expression of status. Never before had so many European houses been packed with so many useless objects.[50]

Not surprisingly, this was the century of the department store. These showcases of consumer culture proclaimed that, now, luxury goods were within everybody's reach, the material expression of the new democracy.[51] In 1883, the famous French author Emile Zola (1840–1902) published his *Au Bonheur des Dames*, one of a series of novels in which he aimed to provide a sociologically correct picture of the conditions of contemporary life. He had actually carried out research in and among the staff of one of Paris's grand new shops, the *Bon Marché*. Surprisingly, the technicalities of retailing he discovered and described seem as pertinent today as they were at the end of the nineteenth century. Probably because its subject matter struck a chord in the people inhabiting the changing townscape of England, too, it was the first of Zola's novels to be translated into English, as *The Ladies' Paradise* (1883). The novel opens with a scene showing a young girl and her two brothers who have left the country for the big city, Paris. Wandering around, overwhelmed by the bustle of the metropolis, they try to find their uncle's house. Suddenly, they come upon a palace-like building, all encased in glass, attracting the eye to all kinds of goods that seem to lure people inside. One of the windows shows, artistically presented, dozens of silk umbrellas, another item of luxurious ladies' wear. The youngsters gape at this unaccustomed spectacle of beautiful apparel. Showering the reader with an avalanche of consumer goods – as did and do, of course, department stores shower their customers – Zola makes plausible that, at this moment, the girl must have decided to try and 'make' it in Paris, to be able to enter this megastore as a customer herself. She had been sold to consumer culture, as her brothers had been:

> Denise had walked from the Saint-Lazare railway station, where a Cherbourg train had landed her and her two brothers . . . all three fatigued after the journey, frightened and lost in this vast Paris.
>
> But on arriving in the Place Gaillon, the young girl stopped short, astonished.
>
> – 'Oh! look there, Jean,' said she . . . 'that *is* a shop!'
>
> They were at the corner of the Rue de la Michodière and the Rue Neuve-Saint-Augustin, in front of a department store whose windows shone with bright colours, in the soft October light. . . .
>
> This, to her, enormous place, made her heart swell, and kept her excited, interested and oblivious of everything else. The high plate-glass door, facing the Place Gaillon, reached the first floor, amidst a complication of gilded ornaments. Two allegorical figures, representing two laughing, bare-breasted women, unrolled a scroll bearing the sign 'The Ladies' Paradise'. . . . The establishment comprised, beside the corner house, four others. . . . It seemed to her an endless extension, with its display on the ground floor, and the plate-glass windows, through which could be seen the whole length of the counters. . . .
>
> Denise was absorbed by the display at the principal entrance. There she saw, in the open street, on the very pavement, a mountain of cheap goods – bargains, placed there to tempt the passers-by, and attract attention . . . the establishment seemed bursting with goods, blocking up the pavement with the surplus.
>
> . . . following the shop windows and stopping at each fresh display . . . they were captivated by a complicated arrangement . . . an exhibition of silks, satins and velvets, arranged so as to produce, by a skilful artistic management of colours, the most delicious shades imaginable.

. . . just as she was entering the street, Denise was attracted by a window in which ladies' dresses were displayed . . . and the dresses were in this sort of chapel raised to the worship of woman's beauty and grace . . .

'How stunning they are,' murmured Jean, finding no other words to express his emotion. . . . All this female luxury turned him rosy with pleasure.

Essentially, since the beginning of industrialization proper at the end of the eighteenth century, cultural critics have discerned two situations, creating two basic problems for European civilization. After more than two centuries, these problems have lost nothing of their topicality.

On the one hand, some theorists reasoned that as the higher wages made possible by increasing employment and production would enable people to meet basic needs, the demand for leisure could increase and, moreover, be fulfilled. However, this posed the moral problem of the anarchy of undisciplined time. On the other hand, the emulative desire that many observers deemed structural in Europe and that was stirred by increasing luxury would spur additional effort. This, though, would lead only to a wholly work-driven society, based largely on false needs.[52]

At the end of the eighteenth century, Jean-Jacques Rousseau, as always reasoning within the, ultimately false, premises which he set by positing his small-scale *république* as man's normal political and social context, had prophesied that the problems would be solved by communal discipline.[53] The Scottish philosopher David Hume meanwhile had pleaded for individual self-control.[54] However, in the mid-nineteenth century, John Stuart Mill argued that the affluence brought by industrialization would lead to a democratic culture of leisure.[55] Many other thinkers, both liberal and socialist, followed him, differing only in their selection of the agency that would help achieve this goal: the State or the individual himself. The polarity between these two posed problems of balance that became manifest in other fields of culture as well. It has worried both politicians and social and cultural critics up to the present day.

15 Europe and the other worlds

Europe and its expanding world

Although the notion of 'the Columbian exchange' seems to suggest that in the wake of Columbus's 'discovery' momentous developments took place only on both sides of the Atlantic Ocean, because of the interaction between Europe and the new world of the Americas, yet the continued and, indeed, increasing interaction with Asia produced important changes in the old Eurasian world as well.[1]

From the sixteenth century onwards, the European maritime merchants who established trading posts all around the Indian and Chinese seas both satisfied and stimulated a European demand for Asian products such as chinaware, silk and spices. In the process, they slowly began to influence production and, consequently, the way of life of the producers in India, Indonesia and Ceylon. For in order to improve their control of supplies, they tried either to conquer or otherwise to dominate the production areas or, indeed, decided to transfer production to such regions as were under their power already. Thus, from the seventeenth century onwards, one finds the Dutch, English and French colonial companies shipping seeds all over Asia, planting them where they could be profitably grown. An unintentional but sometimes devastating process of ecological change set in; its long-term consequences for the world's biological and climate situation are even now difficult to determine.

It found its most poignant expression perhaps when, after their discovery in the 1770s, the islands of the Pacific Ocean were colonized. Whereas the first European visitors had described them as the 'last paradise', the true 'garden of Eden', the next generation turned these delicately balanced ecosystems into plantation societies with the sole function of producing fruit for the western market. Obviously, the introduction of these monocultures had serious social implications as well, changing power relations among the native population and all the values that went with them.

From the early seventeenth century onwards, something comparable happened in a region that had long remained at the margin of Europe's contacts with the wider world. The Russian tsars and their entrepreneurs, while turning to the west for its culture, started an eastward expansion to provide their realm with an economic base outside agriculture. The vast steppes stretching from the Ural Mountains to the Chinese Sea produced the furs that, as 'black gold', gave the rulers of Muscovy the wealth and, thus, power they sought. In a series of colonizing waves, sometimes prepared by the explorations of well-organized scientific expeditions, the Russians extended their power over this region, until in the 1720s they reached the Bering Straits, named after the Dane Vitus Bering, one of the explorers. They then crossed the Straits – as, some 30,000 years earlier, the Asian ancestors of the American Indians had first done – hoping to be able to colonize not only Alaska but also the entire coastal region of the North American Pacific. In this effort they were thwarted by the competition of the British and the Spaniards. Meanwhile, however, by toeing the line which separated their growing empire from the northern borders of China, and by playing off the scattered tribes who inhabited the sparsely populated region of Siberia against each other, using their gunpowder superiority, the Russians succeeded in subjugating the region, politically and economically. To help them do so they convinced themselves, as so many other European nations did, that they had a mission, that civilizing Siberia was their manifest destiny.[2] They turned it into a colony which, besides furs, now began to yield its enormous mineral riches as well. In the process, which was often as cruel as any of the European conquests in the south and north Americas, slowly but inexorably, traditional society disappeared.

Still, it would be unhistorical to blame European expansion for all the evil that befell the world, as many environmentalist campaigners would have it. Thus, for example, the great famines which devastated many of the world's tropical regions from the sixteenth to the end of the eighteenth centuries were caused by the occurrence of a so-called 'little draught age', in consequence of the oceanic movements that control fluctuations in the global climate.[3]

Europe and Latin America: a severed relationship?

For two centuries, the Spanish and Portuguese governments had succeeded in protecting their overseas territories against their European rivals in the colonial market, relatively easily at first, later only at great military expense which, towards the middle of the eighteenth century, no longer balanced the profits. The Iberian governments, moreover, were afraid that the indigenous population, especially in the peripheral areas of the empire, where Spanish and Portuguese power was barely effective, would unite with their European competitors, especially England and France: such crucial areas as Florida and, indeed, the entire Pacific coast could not really be defended without depleting the treasury. Therefore, by the mid-1750s, Spain in particular embarked upon a new phase of expansion.

This time, however, policy-makers in Madrid decided that costly military campaigns and the ensuing need to maintain expensive garrisons would not realize its aims. Looking at the colonial policies of the other European nations, which accomplished great results through commerce rather than conquest, men like the powerful minister Campomanes and the Viceroy Galves hoped for a peaceful incorporation of these territories. Trade with the Indians, to accustom them to all kinds of goods, among which especially alcohol, would soon bring them within the colonial consumer market and ensure their cooperation. Also, in the spirit of the Enlightenment which now pervaded part of Spain's governing elite, it was thought that it was more humane and, indeed, propagandistically opportune if the Indian nations should ally themselves freely to a civilized, enlightened empire which offered to protect them against possible enemies and which, now almost as an afterthought, would also bring them Christianity. In the ensuing process, many Indian tribes settled down to agriculture and trade, and their territories were eventually incorporated, while, of course, their culture was deeply affected.

All this meant a marked departure from Spain's earlier colonial policy, but as a new beginning it still came too late. It did not really solve Spain's grave financial and military problems. Nor did it lessen the pressure European commercial competition, now especially from England, put on the Iberian colonies. Finally, Spain and, though less so, Portugal, also had to counter the growing protests of the descendants of the original settlers of Central and Latin America, the erstwhile emigrants. The latter now considered the colonies their 'own' country, theirs to rule and enjoy. Indeed, they began to resent being administered and taxed by Madrid and Lisbon and, like the European-descended elites of Britain's former thirteen North American dependencies, began to voice definite ideas about self-government. In all American colonies, the educated classes had perhaps studied the political notions of the Enlightenment even more eagerly than the reformers in Madrid and Lisbon, or, for that matter, in London. This contributed to a climate in which the long-standing links between European centres and their colonial peripheries seemed decidedly less stable than they had been in the preceding centuries.

Consequently, the 'Atlantic revolutions' of the period between the 1770s and the 1830s which, among other things, resulted in the birth of the United States, were also felt in Central and South America. Virtually all former Spanish and Portuguese colonies fought for or were reluctantly given their freedom. During the seventeenth and eighteenth centuries, the protectionist–imperialist policy had considerably weakened the economic and cultural contacts between the Iberian part of the new world and the non-Iberian parts of Europe, with the consequence that Europe had largely lost its interest in the region. Now, the newly independent countries eagerly grasped their chance to open up to economic and cultural influences from non-Iberian Europe. Yet at first there was no marked increase in European emigration on a scale as great as that to North America. The main reason was that the new states soon proved to be no sensational economic success, while the new political structures did not inspire much confidence either.[4] The hot and humid climate also failed to attract the many potential emigrants who, after all, mainly came from the somewhat cooler north and west of Europe. Finally, they found the dominant role of the Catholic Church in these areas equally unattractive.

But even Roman Catholics, for instance from the Dutch and Belgian provinces of Brabant and Limburg that began to supply an amazing number of priests, monks and nuns to the worldwide missionary efforts of the Roman Church, felt less than stimulated by the often unexciting reports from the missionaries who had gone to Latin America in the 1820s and 1830s to strengthen the Christian belief among the Indians and black Africans in the Dutch territories, especially when the slave trade was finally abolished. As, in the same period, Dutch and Flemish priests did report with great enthusiasm about the freedom and hope held by the wide prairies of the American north, the choice for prospective missionaries was not a difficult one.[5]

During the course of the nineteenth century and in the first decades of the twentieth century, emigration to Central and South America did increase, especially from the poor regions of Europe's Catholic south, now hit by the effects of overpopulation and non-industrialization. Yet, for the time being this did not result in a renewed fascination with and a resulting cultural influence of that part of the new world on the elites of the old. Actually, it was only the new wave of artistic exoticism which swept Europe in the second half of the twentieth century that created a market for, mainly, the literary products of the intriguing cultural blend which had developed in Latin America from the fusion of European-Christian, Indian and African elements into a civilization of blacks, reds and whites; the novels of such authors as the Argentinian Jorge Luis Borges (1899–1986) and the Colombian Gabriel José García Márquez (1928–) became especially popular. The former often explored the intricate workings of a culture's memory; the latter, for example in his *Cien años de soledad* (One Hundred Years of Solitude) (1967, 1970), which became a worldwide bestseller, gave an almost mystical allure to this mixed culture. Thus, these writers, descended from European colonists but actually voicing a new, complex cultural tradition, were creating the new as well as undoing the old mythologies necessary to structure their, and indeed any society, as had their colleagues in the American north.

The 'old' world and the 'new': North America as a vision of freedom

In 1776, the revolt of Britain's North American colonies against the government in London and the independence that followed gave the former colonists a new self-awareness. Moreover, they were also liberated from the restrictions posed by a number of rules established by parliament, including those that had been devised to stop their westward expansion into protected Indian territory beyond the demarcation line established in 1763 in the Ohio valley. The endless, still largely unknown interior was now open to European settlers hungry for land, and the ideals which people like Benjamin Franklin had projected onto the pretended empty space now appeared realizable. Echoing the biblically motivated ideology of expansion voiced by the seventeenth-century immigrants, in 1792, General Benjamin Lincoln declared that:

> When I take a view of this extensive country . . . I cannot persuade myself that it
> will remain long in so uncultivated a state; especially, when I consider that to people
> fully this earth was in the original plan of the benevolent Deity . . . if the savages
> cannot be civilized . . . the whole race shall become extinct.[6]

The new nation's vision of itself became popular in Europe as well. Those who,
during the upheavals which drastically changed the political and economic
situation in large parts of western Europe between 1790 and 1830, sought an
ideology to legitimize the political revolutions, did so also by reflecting, often
in a sincere though highly uncritical way, on the admirable actions and ideas
that had shaped the foundation of the United States. For the sake of convenience,
these people forgot – just like the leading Americans themselves liked to do
– that the American form of government of the first decades after the declaration
of independence of 1776 was, in fact, aristocratic-oligarchic rather than democratic; some would argue it has continued to be just that, with more than a touch
of plutocracy mixed in.

Nevertheless, more and more Europeans were allured by visions of freedom
and space, of unlimited possibilities, of escape from the restrictions of the
old continent still associated with decadence and rigid structures. For though
the wealth of Europe greatly increased as a result of fast-paced industrialization,
the process frequently brought great misery to the lowest strata of its growing
population.

Many, if not all, of the above elements were described in the *Letters from an
American Farmer* which, first published in London in 1782, soon after its
translation into other European languages, became very influential in creating
an idealized image of North America. In his dedication, the author, Hector
St John, writes: 'You viewed these provinces of North America in their true
light, as the asylum of freedom; as the cradle of future nations, and the refuge
of distressed Europeans'.[7]

Besides containing very realistic analyses, St John's description of life in the
former colonies, which had recently begun their existence as an independent
nation, resounds with a clearly Arcadian undertone presenting the dream of
Eden, or its re-creation as a new, perfect world, to all those European readers
whose enthusiasm made the work into a 'bestseller'. A few quotations illustrate
his vision:

> we convert huge forests into pleasing fields, and exhibit through these thirteen
> provinces so singular a display of easy subsistence and political felicity. . . . Here
> nature opens her broad lap to receive the perpetual accession of new corners, and
> to supply them with food. . . . Here we have in some measure regained the ancient
> dignity of our species; our laws are simple and just, we are a race of cultivators, our
> cultivation is unrestrained, and therefore everything is prosperous and flourishing.[8]

Elsewhere, St John explains the reasons why most Europeans have made and
continue to make their momentous crossing:

The instant I enter on my own land, the bright idea of property, of exclusive right, of independence exalts my mind. . . . No wonder we should thus cherish its possession, no wonder that so many Europeans who have never been able to say that such portion of land was theirs, cross the Atlantic to realize that happiness.

However, with a prophetic glance, he indicates why the arguments for emigration could well change in the near future, as in the United States, too, the industrial economy will gradually eclipse the agrarian, rustic, noble way of life:

As it is from the surface of the ground which we till that we have gathered the wealth we possess, the surface of that ground is therefore the only thing that has hitherto been known. It will require the industry of subsequent ages, the energy of future generations, ere mankind will have leisure and abilities to penetrate deep, and, in the bowels of this continent, search for the subterranean riches it no doubt contains.

Equally prophetic is another pronouncement:

Many ages will not see the shores of our great lakes replenished with inland nations, nor the unknown bounds of North America entirely peopled. Who can tell how far it extends? Who can tell the millions of men it will feed and contain? For no European foot has as yet travelled half the extent of this mighty continent.

However, the inhabitants of the old continent will always be happier in the new:

In this great American asylum, the poor of Europe have by some means met together. . . . Everything has tended to regenerate them; new laws, a new mode of living, a new social system; here they are become men: in Europe they were as many useless plants . . . and were mowed down by want, hunger and war.

In short, America gives man, the European, the intensely longed-for perfection: 'Americans are the western pilgrims, who are carrying along with them that great mass of arts, sciences, vigour, and industry which began long since in the east; they will finish the great circle'.

In a simpler form, this eloquently articulated message, the verbal depiction of the American or, rather, the European dream of discovery, exploration and conquest occurs in the enthusiastic stories told by many other emigrants. From the late eighteenth century, the dream induced more and more inhabitants from the old world to try their luck in the new. 'There are always dreamers on the frontier', wrote the American novelist Willa Cather in *O Pioneers!* (1904),[9] her famous evocation of the life built up by Swedish migrants in the new world. It was these European emigrants who actually gave the United States its present contours. It was they who, in wave after wave, flooded across America, often in conjunction with economic calamities, political unrest or religious disputes in Europe. It was they who slowly shifted the frontier of the United States westwards, until in the 1860s even the Rocky Mountains were no longer a hindrance and the coast of the Pacific Ocean could now be conquered, too, from the Spanish, English and Russian merchants, soldiers and farmers who had settled there in the preceding century.[10]

In the latter decades of the nineteenth century, the flow of immigrants reached gigantic proportions. For many European countries, emigration to North America was a phenomenon of great economic and cultural significance although this was not appreciated for a long time.[11] It is splendidly articulated in Vilhelm Moberg's four-part epic *Romanen om Utvandrarna* (The novel about the migrants), in which he sketches, on the basis of extensive research of the sources, the historical and psychological circumstances behind this process as it took shape in late nineteenth-century Sweden. He probes into the tension between the lack of freedom in the old and the very real freedom in the new land – a freedom, however, which also poses existential choices: should one work for individual development or for the welfare of society?[12]

Capitalism and consumerism: freedom or slavery, progress or decadence?

By about 1870, the United States had reached its present extent and enormous parts of the country, certainly in the mid-west, had indeed been re-created as an agrarian 'paradise' that now seemed to reflect the vision of Hector St John and so many others. Some five decades later, however, the dream of Eden, at the hands of the new settlers themselves turned into the nightmare when the over-farmed plains changed into a barren dust bowl.

Meanwhile, on the east coast, industrialization had started at such a rate that the USA quickly became an economic giant on a scale hardly equalled by any European state or even by Europe. Yet, for the ever-increasing flow of emigrants, among whom were a growing number of farmers' sons from central and eastern Europe, American agriculture no longer had jobs to offer. They had to content themselves with low-paid industrial work: in the iron, steel and meat factories, in the coalmines and in the construction of railways. The same held for the numerous Jewish emigrants, who fled eastern Poland and the Ukraine, the region between Warsaw and Odessa, where they had been 'parked' by the Russian empress Catherine in the eighteenth century. Especially since the mid-nineteenth century, when they became the victims of new waves of the still widely pre-vailing anti-Semitism, in the form of gruesome pogroms, they left the bleakness of life in the old world hoping to find their promised country in the new world as well.

The same factors which contributed to the tempestuous expansion of American industry – a very liberal fiscal system and very liberal legislation – contributed to a situation wherein the labouring poor were hardly protected, if at all. For countless people who, often persuaded to do so under false pretences by unscrupulous 'dealers in human beings', boarded the badly equipped ships that would transport them across the ocean, the dream they had cherished quickly turned into a nightmare after their arrival in the 'Promised Land'.

The reports that the nineteenth-century immigrants sent home to the old world and which, often sentimentalized, began to fill popular magazines as well as the popular drama in which 'the rich uncle from America' or glowing stories about the new life of the emigrants quickly became favourite themes, certainly did not always reflect their true feelings about the situation they found themselves in. Indeed, many were ashamed to confess they had not been able to realize their dream, or still clung to the hope they might yet improve their situation.

Often, novelists succeed in vividly depicting the atmosphere of a certain period where other contemporaries fail to do so. The American author Upton Sinclair, after sound research and partly on the basis of interviews, wrote a fierce but to many of his readers entirely convincing indictment of the inhuman conditions in Chicago's meat-processing industry, where so many who had recently arrived from Europe had accepted a job in order not to die of starvation. In *The Jungle*, published in 1906, the hero, a farmer's son from Lithuania called Jurgis, considers 'that he would go to America and marry, and be a rich man in the bargain. In that country, rich or poor, a man was free, it was said'.[13] But the cruel fact soon appeared that:

> it was a land of high prices, and that in it the poor man was almost as poor as in any other corner of the earth; and so there vanished in a night all the wonderful dreams of wealth that had been haunting Jurgis.[14]

Chicago, 'Packingtown' in the novel, is a cold, damp and poisonous hell, where some 30,000 people, including children, toil in the meat factories, often for more than ten hours a day, for seven days a week, wading in the blood of the thousands of slaughtered, frequently diseased animals which, in the most horrifyingly unhygienic conditions, are processed into food that will subsequently endanger the health of countless consumers. Hundreds of thousands directly or indirectly depend on this kind of work for their livelihood. They are exploited, just like Jurgis and his family, by unscrupulous landlords, corrupt police officers and cunning tradesmen who tamper with the food they sell for high prices. If people become ill they are dismissed without mercy and, if things become worse, they die of hunger and cold. Consumption, as well as alcohol, claim their victims. When Jurgis, sick of it all, decides to improve his lot by joining a labour union he quickly notices that, rather than deciding his own fate, he has now become a mere tool in the hands of unscrupulous politicians. It is not long before he is among the many who hate the city 'with an all-inclusive hatred, bitter and fierce'. He also observes how one wave of emigrants after the other only results in mutual intolerance instead of creating solidarity. One evening, returning home after being forced to participate in a successful attempt to deceive a group of factory inspectors, he realizes 'how those might be right who had laughed at him for his faith in America'.

And yet, despite the often wretched circumstances which many immigrants had to live in, for countless people in Europe 'America' remained a magic word, the land *par excellence* where what definitely could not be reached at home could, apparently, be realized: prosperity and freedom. Thus, continued misery in the old world, as well as continued idealizing reports about the new world, combined with often consciously misleading propaganda on the part both of the American government and private entrepreneurs, went a long way to convince people to embark on the journey of their life.

NEW YORK, 1909: HERBERT CROLY (1869–1930) INTERPRETS 'THE PROMISE OF AMERICAN LIFE'

In 1909, Herbert Croly, an American journalist and the founder-editor of the influential periodical *The New Republic*, published a widely read pamphlet entitled 'The Promise of American Life'. In this tract, he voiced both his criticism of the state of contemporary culture and society in the United States and the hopes he yet held for the future if the dangers of excessive individualism, consumerism and, yes, even democracy were adequately met. Precisely because comparable developments took place in Europe, too, the text has a significance that transcends the American experience.

> All the conditions of American life have tended to encourage an easy, generous, and irresponsible optimism. As compared to Europeans, Americans have been very much favoured by circumstances. Had it not been for the Atlantic Ocean and the virgin wilderness, the United States would never have been the Land of Promise. The European Powers have been obliged from the very conditions of their existence to be more circumspect and less confident of the future. They are always by way of fighting for their national security and integrity. With possible or actual enemies on their several frontiers, and with their land fully occupied by their own population, they need above all to be strong, to be cautious, to be united, and to be opportune in their policy and behaviour.
>
> . . . We were for the most part freed from alien interference, and could, so far as we dared, experiment with political and social ideals. The land was unoccupied, and its settlement offered an unprecedented area and abundance of economic opportunity. . . .
>
> The moral and social aspiration proper to American life is, of course, the aspiration vaguely described by the word democratic; and the actual achievement of the American nation points towards an adequate and fruitful definition of the democratic ideal. Americans are usually satisfied by a most inadequate verbal description of democracy, but their national achievement implies one which is much more comprehensive and formative. In order to be true to their past, the increasing comfort and economic independence of an ever increasing proportion of the population must be secured, and it must be secured by a combination of individual effort and proper political organization. Above all, however, this economic and political system must be made to secure results of moral and social value. It is the seeking of such results which converts democracy from a political system into a constructive social ideal; and the more the ideal significance of the American national promise is asserted and emphasized, the greater will become the

importance of securing these moral and social benefits. The fault in the vision of our national future . . . consists in the expectation that the familiar benefits will continue to accumulate automatically. . . . But this is no longer the case. Economic conditions have been profoundly modified, and the American political and social problems have been modified with them. The promise of American life must depend less than it did upon the virgin wilderness and the Atlantic Ocean, for the virgin wilderness has disappeared, and the Atlantic Ocean has become merely a big channel. The same results can no longer be achieved by the same easy methods. . . .

If the fulfillment of our national promise can no longer be considered inevitable, if it must be considered as equivalent to a conscious national purpose instead of an inexorable national destiny, the implication necessarily is that the trust exposed in individual self-interest has been in some measure betrayed. No pre-established harmony can then exist between the free and abundant satisfaction of private needs and the accomplishment of a morally and socially desirable result. The promise of American life is to be fulfilled – not merely by a maximum amount of economic freedom, but by a certain measure of discipline; not merely by the abundant satisfaction of individual desires, but by a large measure of individual subordination and self-denial. . . . The traditional American confidence in individual freedom has resulted in a morally and socially undesirable distribution of wealth. . . . The existing concentration of wealth and financial power in the hands of a few irresponsible men is the inevitable outcome of the chaotic individualism of our political and economic organization, while at the same time it is inimical to democracy. . . . A more highly socialized democracy is the only practical substitute on the part of convinced democrats for an excessively individualized democracy. . . . Democracy may prove to be the most important moral and social enterprise as yet undertaken by mankind; but it is still a very young enterprise, whose meaning and promise is by no means clearly understood.[15]

Europe and 'America': a cultural symbiosis, or the growth of the 'western world'

Even during the colonial period, the more prosperous colonists and their descendants periodically returned to the old world, i.e. mainly to England, frequently to complete their schooling there. However, at the end of the eighteenth century, besides England – which, in the meantime, had become greatly mistrusted – France was the new place to go to: particularly Paris, the city of the 'enlightened' intellectuals, the centre of European civilization, a town not to be missed if one wanted to return to one's colonial world as a person of culture.

But whereas such trips were the perks of the colonial elite, during the course of the nineteenth century, in the United States, too, a prosperous middle class developed in this successfully industrializing economy. Now, this group also sought the benefit of a cultural formation in the same tradition that for centuries had formed the European elite; a journey to Europe, now including Italy as well, became a sort of 'Grand Tour' for many Americans, the rounding-off of their education. In the tale of his travels, the well-known writer Washington Irving (1783–1859) sighs:

> Europe held forth the charms of storied and poetical association. There were to be seen the masterpieces of art, the refinements of highly cultivated society, the quaint peculiarities of ancient and local custom. My native country was full of youthful promise: Europe was rich in the accumulated treasures of age. Her very ruins told the history of times gone by, and every mouldering stone was a chronicle.[16]

Irving was not the first and certainly not the last to enthuse thus over the old world. As emigration from Europe increased, more and more emigrants and especially their descendants thought about Europe as the land of the past; despite the often unhappy memories attached to it for the first generation, the second- and third-generation immigrants often wanted to visit the land where their roots lay. Moreover, American intellectuals in particular developed a vision of a Europe that was the embodiment of a millennial tradition of culture as a challenge to their creativity. Often feeling their own society to be constricted by Puritan norms, they also saw Europe as the land of freedom – a notion that is, of course, fascinatingly complementary to the reasoning that for centuries had caused so many European emigrants to make the crossing.

Many American artists and writers began to seek their inspiration in the old world. Henry James, for example, painstakingly chronicled in most of his novels the mutual fascination and antagonism of cultured Europeans and Americans. Still, both these intellectuals and the self-made billionaires who, like the Carnegies, the Morgans and the Rockefellers, spent fortunes buying European art and antiques, were criticized or even ridiculed by many on both sides of the ocean, albeit for different reasons: the majority of Americans rebuked their Europhile compatriots for failing to make an effort to create a true, indigenous culture rather than ape the old world, whereas Europeans mocked them for their manners and their crass belief in the power of money. And yet the phenomenon did contribute to a growing cultural *rapprochement* between the two worlds. The numerous affluent and educated Americans who, since the second half of the nineteenth century, made a long or short trip to Europe, did contribute to the formation of a positive image of the United States as well.

This context as well as the wealth shown by a number of sometimes only recently arrived immigrants and the position of power which the new state quickly achieved, by the end of the nineteenth century, explains both why and how the USA came to present a challenge to Europe more than ever before.

For those in the old world for whom progress in particular was measured in economic terms, America was the pre-eminent example of a 'modern', i.e. also a progressive, country; indeed, in European public opinion, especially in many (pseudo-)scientific and popular publications, the new nation was presented as a society both enviable and worthy of emulation. Thus, for many, America mirrored a very positive idea: it was the perfect state, pairing regulated spiritual freedom with high material development and thus also with civilization.

This admiration and the increasing economic interaction between North America and (western) Europe slowly led to a situation in which, in a number of fields, both cultures began to show marked similarities and looked upon each other as being closely related, democratic societies which, essentially, strove for the same values. To man in Europe, the coastal regions of the North Atlantic continued their own culture and economy: a new unity had been created which, in common parlance, soon became known as the 'western world'.

To the 'heart of darkness': Europe and Africa

Well into the seventeenth century, Europe's knowledge of sub-Saharan Africa had been restricted to the scant information it could obtain from the coastal forts built to enable slave-traders, merchants looking for gold and missionaries to do their work; indeed, few Europeans dared venture into the unknown, unhealthy interior. The slaves, mostly procured by indigenous rulers specializing in this 'commodity', and then sold to European companies, were sent to the Americas;[17] the gold went into financing Europe's increasing trade with Asia; and according to the missionaries, the souls of those who converted to Christianity went to heaven. Otherwise, European ships hopping from Portuguese fort to Dutch port on the so-called Gold and Slave coasts of Africa's western half, and then proceeding to the Dutch colony at the Cape of Good Hope and the Portuguese towns on the east coast of Mozambique, only saw Africa as an inhospitable continent they passed on their way to the riches of Asia.

By the end of the eighteenth century, this situation changed. On the one hand, the leaders of the European economy became aware of the possibilities of Africa both as a producer of raw material to be used by and as a market for the finished products of their industry. At the same time, the slave trade, which had uprooted many millions of black Africans, transporting them to the plantations of the Caribbean as well as of the American continent, came under increasing attack. Both 'enlightened' humanists and Church-related groups, especially in Protestant Europe, now started condemning a practice that caused such indescribable misery. Soon, campaigns were staged to provide public support for a Europe-wide effort to root out the problem. This, however, meant that the situation in Africa's interior would have to be explored, to provide the data which the so-called 'abolitionists' needed to convince their governments that action should be taken. Many governments eagerly assented to officially support fact-finding expeditions, partly for humanitarian reasons, partly however because they saw this as a marvellous opportunity to get to know the continent better and thus create possibilities for extending their economic power.

The slave trade and, later, slavery itself, were only abolished in the course of the nineteenth century. In the process, mission and trading posts had been established along Africa's rivers; the two were often complementary, for, as in South America two centuries earlier, many missionaries realized that the ways of Christ did not necessarily run parallel to the ways of the Mammon, and, therefore, started protecting 'their' negroes from the corruptive influences of soldiers and traders. It was not long before, in an outright 'scramble for Africa', fully fledged colonies were staked out by the major European powers. These now included imperial Germany which, after its political unification in 1870, decided it should be a colonial player as well; indeed, like the other industrializing nations, it increasingly needed the African markets as much as the German missionaries, both Protestant and Catholic, needed the African souls.[18]

Yet, it would be altogether too simple to present Africa as the silent victim of Europe's predatory politics. Much like in those regions of Asia and the Americas where Europeans had succeeded in establishing colonial rule in the seventeenth and eighteenth centuries, in Africa, too, they were successful only because local rulers often used the colonizing agencies as much as the latter used them, trying to implicate them and their superior weapons in their age-old power games. The small group of Europeans who for barely more than a century ruled large parts of Africa were able to survive only because local elites, for manifold reasons of their own, cooperated.

Nevertheless, the upheaval caused by European colonial rule – in Africa but, indeed, all over the world – was enormous. In economic terms, it sometimes created ecological change, which then led to famine and disease. In social life, it caused the disruption of traditional communities and societies. And, of course, there was upheaval in the cultural sphere. Thus, for example, European notions of clock-regulated time, of decent behaviour, beginning with decent clothes, and of work discipline were introduced to make Africans into willing workers and subjects, as well as Christians. However, one might also argue that the intrusion of Europe in Africa, and elsewhere, opened up roads for local elites to empower themselves, if only by appropriating the ideological and political tools of Europe. And, definitely, in many areas – though, perhaps, least so in Africa – larger groups now gained some prosperity, more than ever before.

Meanwhile, in Europe, many who would never visit Africa nor, perhaps, knew that many of the things they ate or wore were made of the materials produced by Africans, once more had to adapt their view of the world to include yet another world. They were informed, first, by the tales told by missionaries and widely published – again in the popular press – to serve as propaganda for the conversion policy of the Churches. Soon, scientific studies, especially in the newly defined branch of anthropology, were popularized, too, catering for Europe's desire for the exotic. They described a world full of creatures who might or might not be entirely human – were they not, perhaps, the embodiment of some stage between ape and man? As many missionaries, in their eagerness to get to know the region, acquired a vast amount of information, in a way that made them resemble an ethnographer or anthropologist, the resulting images were often mixed, creating a complex vision of the so-called Dark Continent and of its inhabitants.[19]

For a long time, many Europeans continued to hold extreme views. As early as 1864, the Anthropological Society of London debated the desirability of the extermination of the lower races, especially the African ones. When, in 1897, the German anthropologist Friedrich Ratzel published his *Politische Geographie*, it contained the same ideas, which were later eagerly adopted by the leaders of Nazi Germany.[20] Indeed, from the 1860s onwards, the advance of evolutionist theories in the wake of Darwin's epochal study inevitably helped to strengthen such views.

Finally, by the end of the nineteenth century, the notion that black Africans were some sort of wild animals was discarded by more enlightened Europeans. Nevertheless, native cultures were still depicted as 'primitive', sometimes with the same connotation of innocence that had once been applied to native America. During the late nineteenth and early twentieth centuries it was debated whether the process of evolution, instead of being interpreted negatively as if proving the backward species had no place in progressive society, should be positively advanced by education which, of course, meant Christianization. Others, for various reasons, did not want to embark upon such schemes, if only because educated Africans might come to resent European colonial rule as, of course, they eventually did. Often, those cultures of Africa that had been Islamicized were judged rather more harshly than the regions where animism reigned, the latter being seen as more receptive to the preaching of the Christian Gospel. Inevitably, in some regions the very introduction of that Gospel did increase the problems between native Islamic and native Christian groups.

Despite the many instances of individual Europeans working to their heart's content among their 'chosen' Africans, European public opinion often continued to stigmatize the people of Africa as stupid, lazy, addicted to alcohol and indulging in open sexuality. Perhaps even more than had been the case in Europe's perception of the other worlds it had encountered, the peoples of sub-Saharan Africa came to embody the emotions and actions which Europeans, precisely because they were now entering upon the 'bourgeois' phase of their culture, increasingly considered socially unacceptable and, therefore, morally evil. Consequently, they felt they had to combat these vices, if only to be able to continue believing that their own culture was, indeed, superior.

Meanwhile, the fact that, at the turn from the nineteenth to the twentieth century, many who belonged to Europe's artistic and musical 'avant garde' developed a decided penchant for the very 'primitivism' of African culture, for its emotionality which they saw as so much more in tune with the essence of being human than the over-refined, restrictive civilization of contemporary Europe, did little to alter the perception of the masses, who mostly thought these expressions of high culture an aberration or, even, a betrayal of European artistic values.

The 'old' world and the 'older' world

During the sixteenth and seventeenth centuries, the 'new' world, due mainly to the lack of effective resistance of indigenous societies and the demographic catastrophe that followed the first contacts, had been conquered and had become the embodiment of Europe's hope that paradise on earth might yet be found, or that at least the promised land could be built there. Africa was conquered too, in the nineteenth century, but was barely used for the large-scale resettlement of Europeans. Asia, however, sharing Europe's biological and bacteriological makeup and, moreover, ruled by powerful empires, for a long time resisted any easy conquest.

True, the Dutch had built their commercial rather than colonial empire in the East Indies, replacing the Portuguese, and the Spaniards retained their hold over the Philippines. Further expansion, however, did not prove easy. Japan, still traumatized by the Mongols' efforts at invasion in the twelfth century, had become afraid not only of firearms but also of Christianity as an ideological weapon which might be used by indigenous rebellious magnates – as had actually been the case after their introduction by the Portuguese in the latter half of the sixteenth century. Consequently, from the 1640s onwards, the shogunal government of the Tokugawa family closed its islands completely to all foreigners except the Chinese and the Dutch who were, however, allowed to live only in close confinement on two tiny artificial islands in Nagasaki Bay.[21] Nevertheless, the Dutch managed to see quite a bit of the country and, in a series of important books published in the seventeenth and eighteenth centuries, presented its history and culture to a highly appreciative European audience;[22] at the same time, the Japanese used the Dutch to become acquainted with those aspects of European culture they considered useful, such as medicine and some of the new sciences.[23]

China, too, successfully rebuffed any efforts made by European powers to enter the Middle Kingdom beyond the great port of Canton, where china, silk and tea were traded.[24] Only the Christian missionaries, and especially the Jesuits, were allowed to try and convert the Chinese. Their impact was minimal, but in order to gain material and moral support for their policies among the faithful in Europe, they spread highly one-sided, euphoric accounts of China as a society and a civilization uniquely worthy of Europe's attention; indeed, it lacked only Christianity to be truly admirable, but the conditions to impose the Gospel were favourable, for in the Confucian system of reverence for the gods – perhaps even the one God – and for the well-ordered family and the all-powerful state, China did have its share of proto-Christian ideas and values.[25]

If only for the relative mystery surrounding these two civilizations, Europeans, little aware of the actual state of affairs there, tended to idealize Chinese and, to a lesser extent, Japanese culture. Enlightenment intellectuals like Voltaire, highly critical of political and social conditions at home, and not hindered by profound knowledge of the realities of the Chinese political and social system, held it up as an example to the, in their opinion, backward monarchies of Europe.

The British, too, desiring to dominate the huge market of China from their Bengal commercial base, began to force their way into the heavenly empire by, among other means, the illegal import of huge quantities of debilitating opium. In the early decades of the nineteenth century, this resulted in violent controversy and in outright wars. Due to the military and technological superiority of the UK, the Chinese came out the losers, being forced to accept a series of highly humiliating treaties. From the 1840s onwards, not only did the British and, in their wake, other western powers begin their systematic economic exploitation of China, but also many in the western world lost their former admiration for Chinese civilization.

After being forcefully opened by and to the western world in 1854, Japan, in order to escape such a fate, embarked upon a remarkable policy of agricultural renewal as well as of industrial and technological 'westernization'. Y. Fukuzawa, one of the participants in the investigative missions sent out to explore and understand the factors that contributed to the success of the west, in his *Conditions in the West* (Tokyo 1866) concluded that the westerners were not intrinsically more clever than the peoples of the east but were definitely more rational and, because of that, valued 'clever people' more, who then tended to work for progress and power. Emulating what they saw and applying what they learned, the Japanese succeeded in keeping their economic and political independence as well as, in a way, earning the reluctant admiration of the western world, precisely because they so successfully aped its material achievements. Moreover, many artists of *fin-de-siècle* (turn-of-the-century) Europe, looking for new concepts and ever willing to be lured by the exotic, were inspired especially by Japan's woodblock art and its painting, as can be witnessed from the works of some of the impressionists and expressionists, such as Paul Gauguin and Vincent van Gogh;[26] more specifically it was the 'essentialist' tendency which came from the Zen form of Buddhist philosophy that now captured the western imagination. Soon, many Europeans who sought spiritual renewal in a world they felt increasingly devoid of any of the higher ideals turned to precisely these eastern philosophies, though they might only partly understand them.[27]

Perhaps the most amazing phenomenon in the continued interaction between Europe and Asia was the way Europe and, at a later date, the United States reacted to India. Until the eighteenth century, the vast subcontinent, too, remained largely outside European influence. By then, however, the French and, more successfully, the English had begun to encroach upon the crumbling Mogul Empire. Meanwhile, ever since the late sixteenth century, Roman Catholic missionaries had tried to convert the Hindus. Confronted with a stubbornly resistant culture, they had found out about the existence and power of India's sacred writings, the *Vedas*. As these were written in Sanskrit, a language kept secret by the caste of priests, the Brahmins, many missionaries tried to master it one way or another. Though they partly succeeded in doing so, their results were not widely publicized in northern Europe. At the end of the eighteenth century, the servants of the English and French colonial companies, also confronted with indigenous culture and society, experienced the same desire. Finally, a few managed to learn the language. From the 1780s onwards, the *Vedas*, the *Upanishads* and such ancient Indian epics as the *Mahabharata* were translated into French, English and German, and created a veritable craze.

Also at the end of the eighteenth century, Sir William Jones, himself a senior civil servant in the British colony of Bengal, though certainly not the first to formulate the idea, was the first to publicize the notion of Sanskrit being the

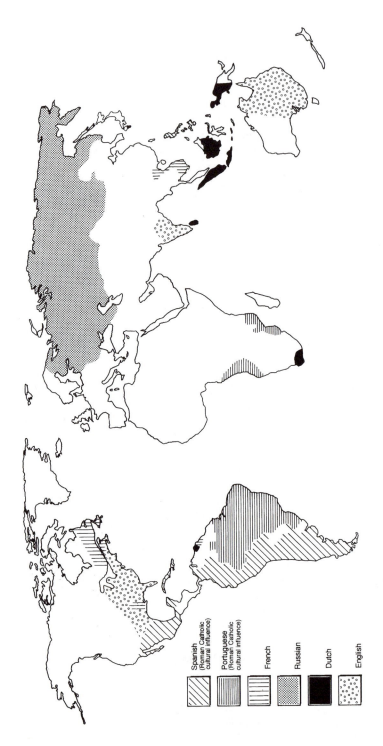

Map 7 Major spheres of European cultural influence, *c.*1800

Spanish
(Roman Catholic
cultural influence)

Portuguese
(Roman Catholic
cultural influence)

French

Russian

Dutch

English

oldest language on earth, the mother of all major languages of Eurasia, including Greek, Latin and all the Germanic ones. Written in the 'oldest' language, the Sanskrit texts were also considered to contain the oldest knowledge of things material and spiritual. Consequently, at many European universities professorships of Indology were established, studying the philology and the literature of India, as well as its religion and philosophy. Soon, the idea of a common linguistic origin was further elaborated in the scientific systematization of the now so-called Indo-European languages – including Persian and Sanskrit – which assumed them to be the offspring of one 'proto' Indo-European language. Therefore, Indian and European culture shared the same roots. As, however, Indian civilization had retained many of its pristine forms, indeed, had kept its childlike innocence – surely another sign of its great antiquity – many felt it to be a source to return to, to be drunk from in an effort to revivify European civilization as well.

Many of the theories supporting this view, from the late nineteenth century onwards were at least partly confirmed by archaeological research indicating the diffusion of culture into Europe and western Asia from a region covering parts of present-day Iran, Afghanistan, northern India and Asian Russia. It was not long before the notion of an ancient 'Aryan' people who had been the creators of all the major civilizations of the world – emphatically excluding the world of Islam – entered the European conscience. The idea was highly popular in England as well as in Germany, but also found adherents in other countries. In retrospect, one must conclude that the ensuing 'Indian Renaissance' was, in large part, an enchantment with origins, European society's romantic and revealing search for secure roots.

The second part of the nineteenth century shows elements of Indian culture being introduced into western literature and music, often shallowly but sometimes creatively. More important was the way in which Hinduist Indian philosophical notions – and in their wake also Buddhist ideas – about the essentials of man's self and his relation to the cosmos crept into European philosophy. Thus, for example, Arthur Schopenhauer, using Indian philosophical concepts, came to maintain that all human reality was *maya* (illusion) only, the projection of man's mind, the one reality, *brahman*; yet he also reasoned that this individual essence was part of the world-soul, *atman*.

To many, the culture of India, sometimes indiscriminately mixed with other oriental civilizations – Japan being perhaps the favourite one – was seen as less one-sidedly rationalistic than 'the European mind'. It fed their craving for a new spiritual dimension, which in their opinion Christianity could provide no longer. The foundation, in 1875, of the Theosophical Society, which tried to reconcile western scientific thought and eastern holistic visions is but one of its many manifestations. In their own way, the 'hippy movement' of the 1960s and the New Age ideas of the 1980s showed the continued attraction other cultures held for Europe. Interestingly, by now, the culture of the native Americans, too, was felt to have retained man's essential earth-bound force as well as being hailed as an example of an ecologically viable way of life.

Meanwhile, by the early nineteenth century, the Islamic Near East had become an area of actual European expansion as well, for the first time since the Crusades. Though 'God's Shadow on Earth', the sultan at Istanbul, who still claimed to rule it as the Prophet's heir, held only nominal authority, as his power had been steadily eroded by regional potentates since the seventeenth century. Internal weakness had come along with external pressure. For in the same period, the Ottoman Empire had grown important to European trade. Indeed, by the eighteenth century, its economy was partly run by Dutch, English and French firms, aided by Greek Christian middlemen. The reason the Ottoman world started acquiring even greater importance in the early nineteenth century was, of course, because through it ran a number of the vital overland routes linking Europe to its Asian colonies. Moreover, its Balkan provinces were becoming the battleground of two major expansionist European powers, the Austro-Hungarian monarchy and tsarist Russia; the latter was not only creating its eastern empire, but also strove for ice-free harbours in the Mediterranean. Consequently, all European powers which had a stake in south-eastern Europe, the Levant or central Asia were now interested in further weakening the sultan's power.

This economic and political interest ran parallel to and was often reinforced by a two-fold cultural factor. On the one hand, the Christian Churches from the early nineteenth century onwards experienced a revived interest in the Holy Land as the region where their religion had originated and, perhaps, would reach its fulfilment – might not Christ return there on Judgement Day? Partly connected with this movement, biblical scholarship, increasingly influenced by positivistic scientific thinking, sought to prove the holy book's literal truth by engaging in extensive archaeological research.[28] On the other hand, parallel to the discovery of India, the notion that perhaps Europe's culture was not based only on Graeco-Roman antecedents created a new fascination with the world of the ancient Near East. Its languages and its literature now became widely studied, often in combination with the newly discovered languages of central and eastern Asia. The first scholarly periodical devoted to oriental studies was founded in Vienna, in 1808, by the 'father' of Ottoman studies, Joseph von Hammer-Purgstall.

While, undeniably, many scholars were deeply fascinated by the new worlds that opened up for them, such learned journals as Hammer's *Fundgruben des Orients* as well as the slightly later French venture, *Journal Asiatique*, also show the growing interrelationship between oriental studies and the colonial policies of the European states: not surprisingly, Russia concentrated on the languages and cultures of central Asia, while England almost exclusively studied those of India. French scholars developed a specialism in Near Eastern and Indo-Chinese studies, still hoping to create an oriental empire there, after having lost their Indian possessions to Britain.

The knowledge about the cultures of Asia and the other continents was not gathered only by scientific explorers and other scholars. It was helped considerably by the greatly increased number of travellers who, sometimes with the aid of modern technology but often braving regions where conditions were still very primitive, reached the far corners of the earth. By the end of the nineteenth century and in the first decades of the twentieth century, for the first time in history Europeans could boast that they had 'discovered' the entire earth. From the impenetrable rain forests of the Amazon to the unscalable heights of the Himalayas, Europeans, whether economic adventurers, empire builders, expedition leaders, journalists or just more than normally enterprising tourists brought home their tales.

Also for the first time in history, a sizeable group of these travellers were women. Often they went to escape the restrictions of genteel life as an un-married 'maid' or, worse, a divorced wife in Europe, travelling either on the basis of some slender private means or even trying to finance their expeditions by writing up and publishing the stories of their experiences, catering to the ever-growing market for exotic tales. Whatever their background or motives, they, too, contributed to Europe's growing knowledge of the world while at the same time creating an alternative vision of European womanhood, suggesting that a woman could, after all, do the things only men were supposed to do.[29]

Thus, it was not only Henry Stanley who travelled to the heart of Africa, or the Swede Sven Hedin who crossed the Gobi Desert. The equally intrepid Scotswoman Isabella Bird journeyed along 'unbeaten tracks' to the northernmost parts of Japan and became one of the first Europeans ever to live among the Ainu tribes. The Dutch noblewoman Alexandrine Tinne first ventured into the Sudan and then moved among the Tuaregs. French-Danish Alexandra David-Nee claimed to be the first woman to have entered Lhasa, Tibet's forbidden city on the 'Roof of the World', where no Europeans had set foot after a handful of Jesuit and Capuchin missionaries who, without much success, had tried to bring Christianity there in the eighteenth century.

Irrespective of the gender of their authors, the majority of travel tales, both literary and scholarly, reflected European attitudes and values and stressed the superiority of European culture in all its respects, often sketching the world of the 'others' as timeless, or even stagnant and backward.[30] The 'sketching' should be taken literally as well, for the nineteenth century was the first period in European history in which considerable numbers of artists left their own world to travel. The few painters who had gone to Dutch Brazil in the seventeenth century, and who had accompanied Captain James Cook on his epochal voyages of discovery in the Pacific Ocean in the 1770s, had been the exception rather than the rule; moreover, in these early ventures artistic and scientific observations were clearly mixed.[31] Now, many artists left on extended trips, concentrating, however, on the Near and Far East. A wave of orientalist painting showed the new fascination for the brilliant light and, consequently, the equally brilliant colours created by the Orient's glaring sun. In the themes they chose, these painters also showed the dreams that they as well as their buyers had, and which Europe's increasingly industrialized, regulated society could no longer satisfy: dreams of a lost world, of a simpler life, of greater passions and of unrestricted sexuality.

Undeniably, such texts and, also, such paintings, idealizing and objectifying the Orient and all of Europe's 'other' worlds gave further argument to all those who were of the opinion that the east was neither modern nor progressive, and that Europe had a civilizing mission towards the rest of mankind. Yet a minority showed not only an increased interest in but also a growing awareness of the fact that these cultures, though they might be superficially different, were still somehow equal and even fundamentally the same. Friedrich Schlegel, for a few years the driving force behind a journal called *Europa*, in his *Ueber die Sprache und Weisheit der Indier* (On the Language and Wisdom of India) (1808), was one of the first scholars to alert Europe to the culture of India. He wrote:

> Now that in the history of peoples Europeans and Asians form one big family, Asia and Europe one inseparable area, we should try to see the literatures of all civilized peoples as a continuing cultural development, one tightly constructed building; this will allow us to view everything in its unity; many one-sided, restricted views will disappear, and, acknowledging the many interdependencies, we will come to understand things and see them in a new light.

And yet, Europe was forever creating new boundaries, in order to be able to define itself. One of the most fateful was also the nearest. For in the eighteenth century, notions about the 'difference' of the central and eastern part of Europe were ever more strongly voiced. True, as early as 1647, a book published by the German traveller Abraham Olearius on the culture of Muscovy had given Europe damning proof of its barbarism:

> If one were to judge the Russians by their character, customs and life-styles, it would be just to number them among the barbarians. . . . For the Russians do not love the arts and the sciences, nor have they any desire to get acquainted with them . . . Consequently, they remain unlearned and rude.[32]

Once more, Europe expressed itself as the embodiment of civilization, through its cultural accomplishments, especially in the arts and sciences. Translated into almost all western languages, Olearius's text was used by other travellers to Russia in the late seventeenth and early eighteenth centuries, who always wrote in confirmation of his views.[33] Since the mid-eighteenth century, these were being expressed rather more forcefully, and even began to include the whole of central and eastern Europe, from Russia to the Balkans.

Now, the entire region was described as 'oriental', being part of the strange world of Asia rather than of Europe. European public opinion began to deliberately cultivate the region's backwardness, if only to enable Enlightenment thinkers – Voltaire being one among many to air these views, despite his profitable relationship with the Russian empress Catherine – to more effectively present their own vision of Europe as the model of civilization. When Mozart, not normally given to reflection on such issues, went from Vienna to Prague, he felt that he entered another world, a Slav world, an oriental world.[34]

Of course, the fact that parts of central and eastern Europe were only marginally involved in the feverish economic development of the western European states, and that Russia was hardly involved in it at all, made the differences seem all the more glaring.[35] Even Poland, whose contribution to Humanism and the Renaissance had long been recognized, and which, being Roman Catholic rather than Orthodox, strongly felt part of the western, Christian world, now fell victim to the new view – not least, one suspects, because of the ease with which, at the end of the eighteenth century, the Polish kingdom was divided between contending neighbours. Thus, it lost a characteristic which 'Europe' had come to think of as vital to any civilization, namely its independence and its sovereignty.

Yet, the German philosopher Johann Gottfried Herder, reflecting on the course of world history in 1791, did ask himself whether eastern Europe and, more specifically, Russia, might not eventually emerge from this backwardness. Though according to him the Slav peoples might seem born to servitude, no doubt because they had been subjected to absolutist regimes for so many centuries, they did have the potential to imbibe the best elements of European culture. In doing so, might they not, at one time, follow the course of the United States, which had thrown off its colonial shackles to become a major power?[36]

16 The 'Decline of the Occident' – the loss of a dream?

From the nineteenth to the twentieth century

The sciences: positivism and increasing relativism

The tension between a humanistic view of man and society and a more materialist vision of the world which had been felt from the fifteenth century onwards heightened in the second half of the nineteenth and the early decades of the twentieth century. In particular, a way of thinking couched mainly in terms of the concept of progress, that in the eighteenth century had already started to reflect a rosy vision of the development of European culture and that was adopted by philosophers around the turn of the century, now seemed to acquire an empirical, scientific basis.

During each decade of the nineteenth century, the 'positive', 'exact' sciences and applied technology brought new discoveries, which sometimes could be put to immediate practical use, making life easier and more comfortable not only for the old elites but for the masses as well. The fact that not everyone could and did profit from them equally does not detract from their importance.

The list of new ideas and new techniques is long indeed, of which the following are but a few examples. In biology, Remak discovered cell division in 1852, and Mendel's theory of heredity appeared in 1865. In medicine, Morton developed ether anaesthesia in 1846, while in 1861 Semmelweiss showed how puerperal fever could be combated. Koch discovered the tuberculosis bacteria in 1882, and in 1883 Behring developed the diphtheria serum. In physics, Fresnel startled the world with the theory of light waves in 1815, while Faraday developed electric induction in 1831 and electrolysis in 1833. In 1888, Hertz wrote about electromagnetic waves and in 1895 Röntgen gave the world x-rays. Werner von Siemens (1816–92), a former army officer, had founded a telegraph company in 1849, and went on to introduce the dynamo in 1866–7 and the electric tram and train in 1879; in 1882, the Siemens firm electrified the Berlin street lighting system. Otto had developed the four-stroke engine in 1876, while, in 1884, Daimler patented the gasoline motor, and in 1885 produced the first car.

Many of these inventions contributed to the cultural unification of Europe and, indeed, of the world, if only because, by reducing the speed of communication, they intensified the process to an extent hitherto unknown. Thus, in

1855, Siemens Bros, which the founder envisaged as a worldwide enterprise that would surpass the sixteenth-century German venture of the Fugger family, was given the contract to put in a telegraph network across the Russian empire, connecting St Petersburg with the Pacific; in 1879, they linked Europe to India – a message from London to Calcutta now took 28 minutes, rather than two or three months; finally, they also linked Europe to the USA by putting cables under the Atlantic Ocean.[1]

Plate 24 This late nineteenth-century (coloured) lithograph of a Parisian telephone exchange shows not one but, actually, two 'revolutions'. The introduction, in the 1860s, of the telephone revolutionized communications in the western world. However, the manual operation of the exchange required a large staff. The new jobs involved were among the first considered 'suitable' for decent girls who were also nimble-fingered and thus able to handle the plugging system. Thus, besides being a factory worker, a household servant, and, more recently, a shop assistant, a new profession became available to women and, moreover, one that, for the first time, gave them some status.

Source: CKD RU Nijmegen.

BERLIN, 1877: HEINRICH STEPHAN REJOICES IN THE FIRST GERMAN TELEPHONE SERVICE

In November 1877, the German postmaster-general Heinrich Stephan wrote the following letter to Fürst Bismarck, chancellor of the newly formed German Empire, in which he outlined the general physical principles of the telephone, the history of its development and the possibilities of its use:

Your Grace knows that moving a piece of steel or iron within the reach of a magnet will induce an electric current that lasts while the movement of the iron or steel lasts. If one projects one's voice against a sheet of steel or iron so thin as to enable the human voice to make it tremble, and if a magnet, within a coil, is near, there will be electric vibrations in this coil which completely match the sound waves induced by the voice. The coil is connected to a normal telegraph cable, and through it the currents are transmitted to the receiving station. There, a similar instrument is connected to thin sheets of iron, through which the electric currents once more are transformed into air currents, and consequently into sound. . . .

On the above, the theory of the telephone is based. Only a century ago, people first conceived of the relationship between electricity and magnetism, when a stroke of lightning caused the magnetic pole of a compass to reverse. Fifty-eight years ago, Oerstedt established the principles of electromagnetism, and Ampere, only three years later, proved that magnetism was the consequence of electric vibrations. Nowadays, this research, combined with the principles of acoustics, which have been known for some time, has resulted in the invention of the telephone, which, I am convinced, will have a great future in the realm of human communication.

As far as is known today, in 1861, Philipp Reis, a Frankfurt school teacher, has been the first to have constructed a telephone capable of transmitting musical sound. Afterwards, the Americans have got hold of the idea, and Messers Bell, Edison and Gray have constructed various telephones to transmit human speech. As far as I can see, the most practical one is Bell's machine, which has served as the model for a number of telephones which I have ordered from the firm of Siemens and Halske. During the last weeks of October, we have first tried them out, to start with from my central office in the Leipziger Strasse to the General Telegraph Office in the Französischen Strasse. As these experiments were totally satisfactory . . . we started transmitting to Potsdam on the same day. With Potsdam, too, perfect communication has been established.[2]

Meanwhile, from the 1820s onwards, Nièpce, Talbot and Daguerre had developed photography. In 1839, a proud French government bought Daguerre's formula, presenting it as 'a gift to mankind'. But the breathtaking inventions of one generation were the old fashions of the next. The exact likenesses captured in the photograph soon seemed outmoded when film made images actually move. A new mass medium was born in 1897, which was to deeply influence European and indeed western society.[3]

In short, for many Europeans, life acquired a new speed, an almost breathless quality, not least because, for the first time in history, they could now look at themselves as they really were. Undeniably, these developments greatly helped to improve the material quality of life, facilitating not only transport and communication but also the movement of goods, thus, for example, contributing to a more varied and better diet. Moreover, through increased medical knowledge, the chemical industry, which developed in the wake of mechanical industrialization, through the mass production of patent medicine could help to increase life expectancy and reduce the death rate from all kinds of disease, though it also unscrupulously exploited people's fear of sickness and death for commercial purposes.

In a subtle and complex way, these new discoveries not only changed people's material lives but also their perception of themselves and of their relationship to nature. Understandably, most of these developments were hailed as triumphs of science and technology, of the genius that more and more seemed to characterize Europe, giving it its unique position in the world – to many, 'Europe' and 'progress' became almost synonymous. Yet the results of research in other fields, where the spiritual rather than the physical person and the material world was involved, were less unequivocally positive, not to say rather unsettling, especially to those who were convinced that the Christian Bible was the fount of all truth.

Around the turn of the eighteenth to the nineteenth century, French scientists like Buffon and Lamarck wrote about the variability of organic forms and their gradual evolution from monad to man, undermining the concept of the uniqueness of the human species. Meanwhile, geology showed the earth must have been shaped over the course of several million rather than several thousand years, considerably undermining the ideas proclaimed by the Churches about the age of the world and a creation process that was supposed to have been completed in a single week's time.

On the basis of these discoveries and speculations, biologists went on asking new questions about the development of life on earth. In the 1780s and 1790s, an English country doctor, Erasmus Darwin, had voiced his opinions about the creative force of natural or sexual selection in the origin of new species. Though he had carefully couched his ideas in such a way as not to irritate the religious establishment, he soon found that society was not yet ready to accept the notion that, perhaps, humans stemmed from apes. Some 60 years later, in 1844, the eccentric Scotsman Robert Chambers produced his *Vestiges of the Natural History of Creation*, presenting an evolutionist view of the genesis of life. He did so anonymously, undoubtedly afraid of adverse reactions within the conservative Christian community. Consequently, his work was not heeded.

Yet by that time, Charles Darwin (1809–82), building on the studies of all these predecessors, including his own grandfather,'[4] was thinking about biology in terms of evolution as well. Yet, he needed another decade to come to terms with his own discoveries. In 1859, his *On the Origin of Species by means of Natural Selection*, or the *Preservation of Favoured Races in the Struggle for Life* convincingly, and scientifically, 'proved' to many that new species developed in a constant process of evolution in which, in accordance with a fixed law of nature, stronger specimens of older species survived by adapting themselves, while the weaker ones disappeared.[5] When Darwin, although somewhat hesitantly, reached the logical conclusion of his own position and in 1871 published *The Descent of Man*, the human species lost its position at the apex of creation, the sole being created in the image of God. For many, Christianity in all its authoritarian institutional forms began to lose an essential part of its credibility.

Still, the success of Darwin's books, written in an almost novelistic style and, if only for that reason, appealing to a large audience,[6] shows the extent to which

the cultural climate had changed during the early decades of the nineteenth century. For though the Churches did react negatively to the notion of evolution and its theological implications, the scholarly community by and large did not, and nor did the general public: Europe had been ready for a 'change of paradigm', for a theory which answered the questions raised by a new society, a world of growing economic and social tensions and of global contrasts. Darwin's concepts were quickly popularized.[7] They flourished in a climate of continuing scepticism in the field of religion and to a large extent reinforced this, precisely because his and other new ideas bore the stamp of scientific method, of truth.

In these years, too, the human sciences, 'invented' in the late eighteenth century, began to dominate the scientific and cultural debate. Social theory – 'sociology', in the terms of the Frenchman Auguste Comte, who had been among the first to label it a positivist science – anthropology and, finally, psychology entered the world of scholarship and, far more important, the realm of popular culture that asked for scientific explanations of an increasingly complex society. Soon, they revolutionized the ways in which Europeans thought about themselves.[8] In 1859, which saw Darwin's biological theory unleashed upon the world, Europeans were shocked in their belief in the social make-up of the world as well. For in the same year Karl Marx (1818–83) published his *Zur Kritik der politischen Oekonomie*. Obviously influenced by the social misery and the political tensions caused by unbridled economic expansion in large parts of industrializing Europe, Marx proposed a scientific theory that showed society had developed as systematically as Darwin's nature: in a constant fight for the means of production, those who possessed the means of production had survived, had become stronger, while those who did not had weakened, and would for the foreseeable future continue to do so.

Soon science, rather than religion, became Europe's new faith.[9] For the first time in European history, an idea taken from the natural sciences had succeeded in influencing all fields of life, and in an unprecedentedly short period of time, too: the evolutionary perspective not only changed the other exact sciences but also politics and economics, as well as philosophy and literature, and, indeed, religion itself. A new view of man was born, strongly coloured by biological determinism. Free will as an essential human characteristic seemed to have disappeared. God, providence and deliverance had no place in the Darwinian world. Who could still believe in nature as a harmonious order? Was the entire physical world not a battlefield, in constant movement as a result of the struggle between

---

Plates 25 and 26 (opposite) An engraved representation of the 'Hall of the French Machines' at the 'Exposition Universelle' held at Paris in 1878. Machines, or mechanical and later electrical appliances, not only facilitated production in almost all sectors of the economy, they also entered the family home, being widely advertised as the means to finally free women of their heavy household chores.

Plate 25 Source: CKD RU Nijmegen.
Plate 26 Source: Centre for Art Historical Documentation, Nijmegen, the Netherlands

the representatives of the diverse species? In the face of a continuous struggle for survival, of the need to achieve progress, the notions of good and evil as advocated by, specifically, the Churches, seemed rather weak categorizations.

Notwithstanding such potentially dangerous developments as the monk Mendel's genetic experiments and, more generally, the boost to genetic research given by those who studied the implications of Darwin's ideas – indeed, all over Europe movements advocating eugenetic research and, sometimes, policies now cropped up – at the end of the technologically highly successful nineteenth century most Europeans were thrilled rather than worried by the prospects of science. Of course, the great majority did not understand the implications of the scientific debate. If anything, they would rather read the dozens of exciting and hugely popular adventure novels written by the Frenchman Jules Verne (1828–1905). He showed how machines and other technical devices – including a number of applications which, like Leonardo da Vinci before him, he 'invented' on paper only, though some of them were scientifically proven correct and then technologically realized in the later twentieth century[10] – would make life for people easier, more pleasant and more exciting.

The nineteenth century being the first 'century of children's books' on a scale to deserve this name, it is a highly significant aspect of European culture that Verne's massive output, translated into all European languages, aimed at an adolescent rather than an adult public. In such novels as *Voyage to the Moon* and *Robur the Conqueror*, the belief in the power of science was inculcated in the new generation from an early age. Nor was Verne the only one to incorporate new ideas. Those British children who read Charles Kingsley's highly popular *The Water Babies* (1863) were given a didactic fairy tale about a poor little chimney sweep who fled his persecutors by drowning himself and lived on in a new, clean, healthy world – a typical image of the age of pollution. Moreover, it was a watery world that confidently spelled out the benefits of progress through evolution and the survival of the fittest.

Yet one should note that in this age of triumphant positivism and materialism, the need to escape from reality seemed greater than ever, especially if judged by its manifestation in literature. The past, or at least a time when myth and a rural, village culture, rather than science and an urban, industrial civilization dominated man's life, became a powerful attraction. The first woman to win the Nobel Prize for literature, the Swedish author Selma Lagerlöf (1858–1941), wrote her *Gösta Berling's Saga* in 1891. This tale of the vicissitudes of a Lutheran minister who had fallen from grace was a powerful evocation of the landscape and the culture of her native Värmland, a mixture of realism and fantasy, of folklore and psychology, recreating a life that seemed both more simple and more passionate than the present. And in *Nils Holgersons underbara resa genom Sverige* (1907), fairy tale, travel book and *Bildungsroman*, which made her famous all over the world, she successfully tried to teach her youthful readership the history and beauty of the Swedish country. And yet, at the same time, both texts evince a kind of metaphysical Darwinism, showing man's evolution as a constant battle between his animal drives and his divine potential.[11]

This past-oriented tendency was dominant in many fields of elite culture. In 1859, 'Darwin's Year', Europe had first heard the long melodic lines of Richard Wagner's (1813–83) revolutionary opera *Tristan und Isolde*, in which physical love was openly shown as a passion that governs everything. It was now even coded in the notes themselves: Wagner's musical characteristics, the so-called 'leitmotiv', tried to express the compelling impulses that people experience and which determine their behaviour in the face of rationality and even all other emotions.[12] This and some of Wagner's other works were all set in a mythical, German past, though there were many among his audience who thought they could also detect messages for the present in his tales of superhuman heroes and heroines.

Rather than turning to an idealized or at least romanticized past, Friedrich Nietzsche, one of the many who were influenced by Darwin's thought, had proposed what he thought a more realistic analysis of the present, but did so in creating a heroic view of man that had not failed to influence Wagner: 'This world is the will to power – and nothing else! And you yourself are this will to power – and nothing else!'[13] Nietzsche called Christianity the symbol of the complete distortion of precisely all those natural values that help man to survive in this world, the only one he is given; to him, Europe's religion was the creed of 'the sick and dying who despised the body and the earth, and who invented heaven and the saving drops of blood, and they even deprive the body and the earth of that sweet, dark gift.'[14] 'Thus spoke Zarathustra', the ancient Persian philosopher whom Nietzsche used to voice his beliefs. Christianity had made the world into a vale of tears by damning all passions, instead of making optimal use of them as the positive forces that they were. Nietzsche wanted to undo this *Umwertung aller Werten* (The Revaluation of all Values) that had, in his view, negatively directed Europe for centuries.

In the same period, comparative ethnology flourished as never before, especially as a result of Europe's knowledge of the world's various peoples and cultures that arose from colonialism and imperialism. It was now slowly given form as a science of man in his cultural environment. One of its first influential practitioners, James Frazer (1854–1941), also developed comparative religious history. In his riveting twelve-part analysis of world religions and the myths associated with them, *The Golden Bough* (1890–1915), he set out to show that Christianity in its essence and functioning was definitely not unique, that both its beliefs and its characteristic rituals were to be found in many other religions as well. He convinced many readers. Yet many felt shocked when they realized that the distinction often made between magic and faith, between the many non-western 'superstitions' and the one, true western religion was built on sand, at least scientifically speaking.

Those who continued to cling to traditional beliefs and attitudes were certainly not well served by the practitioners of philology, of that textual science which already in the world of humanist learning had cleansed the Bible of all sorts of mistakes. For scholars now subjected the life of Jesus to historical analysis as well. They did so according to the rules developed by the nineteenth-century scientific, empiricist study of history. Among others, the highly controversial *Leben Jezu* (1839) by David Friedrich Strauss (1808–74) as well as Ernest Renan's (1823–92) *La Vie de Jesus* (1863) led to violent reactions all over the Christian world: many felt deeply pained when they were told the Son of God was an 'incomparable human being', an inspired revolutionary, only.[15]

Inevitably, in this cultural climate, secularization grew ever stronger. After Copernican physics had moved the earth from its place as the centre of God's universe in the sixteenth and seventeenth centuries, Darwinian biology now removed man from the pedestal on which he had placed himself as the culmination of God's creation and reduced him to an 'incidental' winner in the mechanistic process of evolution, while according to anthropology Christianity equally lacked any unique glory, being a culturally 'explainable' phenomenon among a multitude of other religions. In short, while many traditional values now became relative or even obsolete, only the belief in science seemed to reign supreme.

Europe in hiding, Europe surviving

While developments in the domain of high culture influenced Europe's intellectual upper crust, much larger groups were affected by the large-scale migration from the countryside to the towns that was connected with industrialization and urbanization, which in most countries became more marked from the 1860s and 1870s onwards.

People became detached from their traditional social and religious institutions, especially the rural community and its centre, the Church, where the clergy still held a powerful grip on the population. Removal to the ever more anonymous environment of the big city meant an erosion of the 'moral economy' of traditional societies. The bonds with the Church, but also with the old socio-emotional frameworks of family, village and neighbourhood were slowly weakened. When this became obvious to the spiritual authorities, the various Churches embarked upon a large-scale offensive. In doing so, they often allied themselves with secular governments who, for several decades already, had been equally alarmed at the disintegration of society and the political dangers inherent in increasing individualism.

A culturally fascinating situation now developed. From the 1840s onwards, the secular elites had used a variety of means to civilize the urban underclass, such as literacy campaigns, organized sports and large-scale community singing in amateur choirs that presented proper patriotic music, aided by the new mass education and the incipient mass media. Moreover, from the 1860s and 1870s onwards these same means were also employed by the colonial authorities to bring the increasing numbers of non-European subjects into the fold of European rule. The Churches, assisting the secular authorities through their global missionary activities, were particularly eager to employ these instruments of mass manipulation to convert the world to Christianity in its various forms. With renewed vigour, Rome staged extensive mission campaigns, partly out of fear of the equally energetic Protestant missionary movement which, from the early nineteenth century, had greatly affected the Catholic Church's near-monopoly on the proclamation of Christian, European values in large parts of the world. Significantly, however, by the late nineteenth century, the Churches felt that the industrialized cities and regions of Europe itself were the frontiers of a new paganism, of a world that had to be wrung from the new barbarism of individualism and of liberal or socialist doctrine. Europe itself now became a missionary field, to be worked with the same methods that were used in the non-European world.

The effectiveness of this religious-cultural offensive varied greatly from country to country, from social group to social group. Protestant communities, especially the less hierarchically organized ones, had problems binding their congregations to tradition, whether or not revamped and revitalized. After all, the role of the clergy in these Churches had traditionally not been very strong and individual believers had always played an important role in shaping religious policy; often, scepticism simply could not be checked by authority.

However, in some parts of the Catholic world, Rome's attempts to reinforce its hold over believers did result in the strong 'ultramontanism' which the papacy had hoped for: a renewed orientation towards the centre of the Catholic Church, 'beyond the mountains'. Consequently, in such countries as the Netherlands, Belgium and Austria, a growing 'sectarianism' developed that turned the Catholic communities into virtually self-contained worlds, wherein every aspect of life, of culture, was determined by religion and the clergy. Sometimes, however, the increasing demands of the Roman hierarchy had the opposite effect, resulting in a slowly more critical attitude and even in a political as well as cultural compromise with more recent movements like liberalism and socialism.[16]

In 1869, during the first Vatican Council, the Catholic Church, trying at least to keep its grip on the educated believers, supposed to be the leaders of these communities, decided to dogmatize some of Thomas Aquinas's thirteenth-century doctrines. In a large-scale campaign Rome once more tried to re-impose on the Catholic world its traditional views on the relation between man, the world and God. But this so-called neo-Thomism was only a reformulation of old positions, a fresh attempt to once again eliminate the tension the Christian faith itself had introduced into European culture almost 2,000 years earlier. Yet Rome hoped to rebuild the Catholic community as a power that could compete with the national states whose aims did not often run as perfectly parallel with the Church's ideas as had been hoped. It wanted to combat and finally destroy what it felt to be the destructive consequences of the Enlightenment and revolution, now summed up and condemned as 'Modernism' – i.e. materialism, individualism, the rejection of authority and secularization.

Nevertheless, even in such a religious society as existed in Spain, the combined forces of industrialization, the adoption of a constitution and the growing power of the bourgeoisie resulted in a new mood. Many were no longer willing to accept the Church's dominating position in cultural life. Liberal bourgeois leaders like Don Francisco Giner who, in 1875, founded his 'Institute of Free

Education', decided that Spain had to be educated anew, and, of course, preferably not by an undereducated priesthood. His educational reforms inspired a host of collaborators who crisscrossed the country, taking books, paintings and music to teach the new generation, and introducing them to sports and country walks. These efforts produced such painters as Pablo Picasso and Salvador Dalí, such musicians as Isaac Albeniz and Enrique Granados.[17] But as the Spanish government was unable to find the means for the large-scale adoption of this experiment, right-wing Catholicism continued its hold over the middle classes, who needed education as a means towards economic and social mobility.

Meanwhile, only a small group continued to feel that Europe was not only about material progress, but represented an ideal consisting of more profound norms and values that had to be cherished, if only to ward off the dangers of the increasing aggression between the European nations and of the growing gulf between the humanities and the natural sciences, two developments that would destroy Europe's cultural unity.

Just as in earlier centuries, concern about the outcome of these struggles caused intellectuals to devise all sorts of plans and strategies to maintain peace and bring about greater cohesion so that Europe might actually live up to its claim to be a humanistic civilization.[18] But even if people thought in terms of closer cooperation between states – one hears echoes of ideals like those which Dubois, Penn and Novalis had once articulated – the independence of Europe's sovereign nations was seldom discussed.

In this respect, the books written by the Danish state councillor Carl Friedrich von Schmidt-Phiseldek are intriguing. In 1820 he published his *Europa und Amerika oder die Künftigen Verhältnisse der civilisierten Welt* (Europe and America or the future situation of the civilized world) and in 1821 *Die Europäische Bund* (The European Union), to impress upon his readers the danger that the young United States posed to a divided Europe. In 1859, J. Fröbel was even more terse in his *Amerika, Europa und die politische Gesichtspunkte der Gegenwart* (America, Europe and the political aspects of the present), arguing that if Europe did not develop some form of unity it would very soon become a mere stage for the inevitable struggle between America and Russia. In 1867, the French writer Victor Hugo felt forced to point out that Europe was still at least the 'mother country of mother countries'. But three years later, such notions did not prevent a gruesomely bloody struggle between France and Germany. With the misery of this war still fresh in his memory, Friedrich Nietzsche tried yet to convince himself, in his 1886 essay *Jenseits von Gut und Bösen* (Beyond Good and Evil), that:

> nowadays the most obvious signs are not read, or even wilfully misinterpreted, which show that Europe will be one. In all people who, during this century, have looked beyond the surface, this has been the real direction their soul, in its mystical work, has been taking: to prepare the way towards that new *synthesis*.[19]

Yet, deep down he must have realized that this vision would remain a dream only, the dream of a handful of intellectuals. In a society dominated by political and cultural nationalism and socio-economic individualism, it seemed that the European ideal could no longer be a living force. Indeed, only a few Europeans still felt they could argue that their world was a world with unique, transnational values and norms shaping everybody's thoughts and actions regardless of their social or national background. Only a few felt that the nations of Europe collectively showed cultural characteristics which gave their part of the globe both unity and uniqueness, distinguishing it from the rest of the world. Only a few translated these notions into a concept of Europe that aimed to bridge differences or prevent disputes.

Nevertheless, such characteristics could be distinguished, even if only in the domain of elite culture, in which, because of its cosmopolitan character, they had been developed in the first place. A few should be named here.

Many Europeans did still admire the two great cultures of Greece and Rome which had so essentially influenced Europe's view of man and had contributed to the formation of Europe's notion of the State. For even though the practice of democracy in the ancient Greek city-states had not at all resembled what was now being created in the constitutional and representative democracies of nineteenth-century Europe, still the idealizing inspiration Europeans derived from ancient Greece and from the republican virtues of classical Rome had been a force in shaping political and social ideology from the sixteenth century onwards and, hence, in furthering the spirit of change that came to characterize the nineteenth century.[20] Another fundamental European characteristic was its empirical, later positivist, scientific thought; though not unique to Europe – if compared, for example, with developments in China until the seventeenth century[21] – yet nowhere was this way of thinking as all-pervasive as in Europe. In this field, moreover, the link with antiquity, though equally idealized, was actually far more real than in the domain of political thought. Besides the momentous consequences in the development of the sciences themselves, the ancient Greek notion of the free spirit that strives to know all greatly contributed to the climate of secularization and, hence, of cultural change that characterized nineteenth-century Europe as well.

Then, of course, there was the cultural unity brought about by certain motifs in the visual and literary arts, some of which seem to refer to an all-European emotion of contrasts and tension, such as, for example, the motif of the myth of Prometheus, the 'one who looks forward', one of the Titans, who, disobeying his father, Zeus, brought fire to the earth and thus embodied the spirit of creation and individualism with which Europe liked to identify its culture. It may be linked to the equally mythical figure of Faust,[22] who embodies the ancient tension between the powers of belief and reason: 'Zwar weiss ich viel, ich möchte aber alles wissen' (I do know much, but would like to understand all).

European music was by now quite unique among most other musical cultures in the world by its insistence on ever more complex harmonic polyphony, both instrumental and vocal, as well as in the quantity of the instruments and the performers used for large-scale religious and secular works. Indeed, no other culture created such a large and diverse corpus of religious music than the

Christian culture of Europe. True, the introduction, in the eleventh century, of a uniform, written musical notation, attributed to the monk Guido of Arezzo (*c*.990–*c*.1050), had led to the gradual loss of an important, orally transmitted musical culture – perhaps Portugal and Spain are among the few European countries that, with the flamenco and the 'fado', still have a significant tradition in this field. It had also resulted in a composers' rather than a performers' musical culture, which developed along lines that urged these composers to differ from their predecessors as much as possible; indeed, from the eighteenth century onwards, this urge for originality became imperative both in musical culture and, indeed, in most other creative arts, reflecting, of course, Europe's increased insistence on the uniqueness of the individual.

Yet despite its emphasis on individual expression, this musical culture, too, became a unifying force in European cosmopolitan culture. In the middle of the eighteenth century, composers like Christoph Willibald von Gluck (1714– 87), as well as Handel and Haydn, mentioned above, left their own country to work in Paris and London, adapting their compositions to French and English tastes. At the turn of the nineteenth to the twentieth century, the music of Pyotr Ilich Tchaikovsky (1840–93) and Modest Mussorgsky (1839–81) was brought from St Petersburg to the concert halls of Paris by such culture brokers as Sergei Diaghilev (1872–1929) – introducing a music that breathed a spirit of the exotic, of a Russia that, though trying to retain, or perhaps even regain its own character, was yet adopting western European culture in more than just music.

Though it seems paradoxical that during the very nationalistic nineteenth century all these forms of 'European' culture gained strength, it is perhaps precisely because, while less emphasis was placed on their common 'European' character, they were presented and experienced as 'genuinely German', 'specifically English/British' or 'typically French' achievements or expressions. Tennyson, while not creating great poetry when he wrote:

> Not in vain the distance beacons. Forward, forward let us range.
> Let the great world spin forever down the ringing groves of change.
> Thro' the shadow of the globe we sweep into the youngest day:
> Better fifty years of Europe than a cycle of Cathay[23]

did however clearly state Britain's pride in its conquests and progress. Yet in contrasting these achievements of British culture to China, he could not but present them as European as well.

In doing so, his poem – with its reference to the faraway Middle Kingdom which, in these very decades, was increasingly dominated by Britain and other European powers economically, politically and militarily – was an expression of what is yet another seeming paradox. Most European states, despite their constant and sometimes bloody competition in Europe itself, in the wider world took care to manifest themselves as the agents of a certain culture, a set of values they always presented as specifically European, and, as such, as the touchstones of civilization. Thus they justified their hold over the non-European world, which acquired its most trenchant expression in imperialism.

Consciously or unconsciously, many European civil servants, merchants, entrepreneurs and missionaries, in short, 'empire builders', experienced the need to emotionally and intellectually justify their participation in a policy of economic, political and cultural domination. Therefore, they created an ideology that would vindicate their actions. Sometimes, they would appeal to 'social Darwinism', a way of thinking in which the principles of Darwin's theory of biological evolution were misleadingly used to scientifically explain cultural, economic and political differences between peoples from racial distinctions. Far more often, the universal values of Christianity were adduced. And sometimes Europe's manifest power was felt simply to be its own justification. Always, Europeans were trying to excuse what they forcefully imposed on and asked of others: conversion to one of the forms of Christianity; acceptance of the capitalist system; the adoption of a lifestyle conforming to 'European' norms of civilized behaviour.

This imperial ideology, expressed in and imposed on Europe's growing colonial periphery, also helped to strengthen the cultural cohesion of the metropolis, Europe itself. All kinds of visual and printed propaganda, including a massive effort to educate Europeans, especially children, to an awareness of empire and its responsibilities, e.g. through highly romanticizing fiction, drove home the message that the nation and, on a deeper level, the concept of Europe, represented certain ideals, which had to be preserved and spread.[24] An author symbolic of this tendency was Karl May (1842–1912), who in terms of sales was easily the most successful German writer of all time. He influenced generations of boys and adults in works that were translated into dozens of languages. Though he never left his native country to engage in the adventures he so vividly described, he not only contributed outstandingly to the new genre of 'westerns', but also almost single-handedly created the genre of 'easterns', writing as convincingly about the noble Indian as about the noble Bedouin. Sincerely outlining the plight of the former at the hand of ruthless European/American land speculators and of the latter in a Near East beset by corrupt Turkish officials, he helped to cement the stereotypes Europe needed to rationalize its imperial policies. Despite May's open criticism of imperialism's rougher edges, in the end the indigenous protagonist – 'Winnetou, the red Gentleman' being the most famous one – was always saved by the humaneness and wisdom of the European hero, who epitomized a utopian vision of the power any individual could wield if only he let himself be directed by a benign, obviously Christian providence.[25]

A growing sense of *fin de siècle*: between pessimism and optimism

All over the world, both the Europeans who travelled and those who ruled presented a front of pleasant, uncritical and even uncompromising faith in the many positive characteristics and values they attributed to their civilization which, they maintained, differed immensely from the cultures they encountered and sought to dominate. Yet in Europe itself the continuous economic and political rivalry that was both the cause of and inherent in the phenomenon of nationalism resulted in increasingly bitter and bloody wars during the later nineteenth century: the machine had brought into use weapons which were vastly more effective and, thus, more destructive than anything ever seen before.

For those who seriously analysed contemporary life, the constant threat of war as well as the many changes wrought in society and culture by industrialization – the rise of new elites, of mass education, of mass consumption, the decline of 'old' values and traditions – created a sense of almost inevitable disaster. In 1907, John Little wrote about *The Doom of Western Civilization*. This feeling was enhanced by the relativism that became a dominant force in European elite culture from the end of the nineteenth century onwards. Despite all the changes, the ideas of a physical world built on the inalterable atom and the inalterable cosmos, and of man as a rational creature had remained unchallenged for most educated Europeans. But around the year 1900, even those certainties were threatened.

Many poets and philosophers – men such as Boehme and Bruno, Novalis and Goethe,[26] men such as Schopenhauer and Nietzsche – had cherished notions of the subconscious as the power which, unlike than the reason glorified by the Enlightenment thinkers, basically moved both man's thoughts and his actions. Now, the Viennese neuro-chemist turned 'psychologist' Sigmund Freud (1856–1939) took this idea a few steps further;[27] while obviously borrowing many of his ideas from Nietzsche and Schopenhauer, he denied having read their work at all. In his *Die Traumdeutung* (The Interpretation of Dreams) (1900) he showed how an 'archaeological' survey of the mind through research into man's dreams could reveal the – to many frightening – world of the subconscious. There, rational controls did not rule; on the contrary, deeply embedded anxieties and suppressed lusts seemed to steer man's life. Despite the abundant evidence that Freud doctored much of the data he used to support his theories about man, and despite the fact that his patients, rather than accepting his preferred role as an impersonal investigator, made him into a father-figure, an idealized lover, a saviour even, he nevertheless was a great clinical observer and a great writer. Perhaps more than any other author, he has altered the way people in the west have thought, talked and written about human nature since the early twentieth century.[28] Arguably, the Viennese psychoanalyst stood at the end of a long revolution. It had started when Newton, albeit implicitly, all but denied God's role as a continuous actor in the management of the macrocosm, of the universe. It had continued to the moment Darwin had robbed God of his role in the development of life on earth. It now found its climax in Freud, who seemed to suggest that even in man's soul God had no role.[29]

Yet, it soon appeared the revolution had not yet reached its final phase. For in physics, too, the turn of the century brought a revolutionary change. Traditional thinking on the structure of the microcosm was challenged and the idea of the unchanging atom was discarded: scientists began to accept that even atoms are unstable and produce energy when they disintegrate. Thus, it was increasingly evident that energy and matter were not separate worlds. Here, too, scientific proof was now presented for ideas that had been developed intuitively in earlier centuries, mostly by alchemists: matter can be altered, it can be changed into energy.

In the year 1900, the patrician American Henry Adams, thoroughly schooled in the humanist tradition of western culture, was in Paris. He wanted to visit the Universal Exposition, the umpteenth in a series that had started a century earlier, in 1798, also in Paris, with Europe's first ever industrial exhibition, a manifestation that had elevated the products of manufacture to the status formerly enjoyed only by the products of the 'arts'. Adams, who had been travelling and studying in Europe from the 1850s onwards, now wrote to his brother Brooke:

> As far as I have guessed the results of this Exposition, the Germans alone show very marked development of energy. But I see no one to give me a general idea of the whole field, and of course no single corner of it has value without the rest. The limit of the great economies may be near or far. Since 1889, the great economy has evidently been electricity. . . . Electricity must have altogether altered economical conditions. Looking forward fifty years more, I should say that the superiority in electric energy was going to decide the next development of competition. That superiority depends, in its turn, on geography, geology and race-energy. All these elements have somewhat exact numerical values, and the value of your theory depends on getting the values of these unknown quantities. We should both have gained by knowing a little mathematics. That deficiency, due to the shocking inefficiency of Harvard College, has destroyed half the working value of our minds as trustworthy machines.
>
> . . . I can see no reason for expecting any collapse at present, in Europe. . . . We ought to see a long period of rising prices and extensive economies. Apparently, Europe can go on indefinitely as she is, and the future type of England and France may be merely an extension of the Belgian and Dutch experience.[30]

Whereas Adams's political predictions proved false, his observations on economic development and the role of science and technology in it are quite interesting, as is his conclusion that to understand it all he lacks a basic precondition – some knowledge of mathematics, etc.

In the same year, Adams found a friend willing and able to explain to him the implications of the new sciences. From these lessons he proceeded to draw definite conclusions as to his own attitude towards culture, his need to understand and, perhaps, even somehow reconcile the old, Christian–humanist ideas and the new sciences. He tells about it in his autobiography, in a chapter he titled, significantly, 'The Dynamo and the Virgin':

> Until the Great Exposition of 1900 closed its doors in November, Adams haunted it, aching to absorb knowledge, and helpless to find it. . . . While he was thus meditating chaos, Langley came by, and showed it to him . . . Langley threw out

of the field every exhibit that did not reveal a new application of force, and naturally threw out, to begin with, almost the whole art exhibition. . . . He taught Adams the astonishing complexities of the new Daimler motor, and of the automobile. . . . Then he showed his scholar the great hail of dynamos, and explained how little he knew about electricity or force of any kind. . . . To Adams, the dynamo became a symbol of infinity. As he grew accustomed to the great gallery of machines, he began to feel the forty-foot dynamos as a moral force, much as the early Christians felt the Cross.

. . . The new forces were anarchical. . . . The force was wholly new. . . . In these seven years man had translated himself into a new universe which had no common scale of measurement with the old. He had entered a suprasensual world, in which he could measure nothing except by chance collisions of movements imperceptible to his senses, perhaps even imperceptible to his instruments, but perceptible to each other, and so to some known ray at the end of the scale. [. . . he] seemed prepared for anything, even for an indeterminable number of universes interfused – physics stark mad in metaphysics.

. . . the rays . . . were a revelation of mysterious energy like that of the Cross; they were what, in terms of mediaeval science, were called immediate modes of the divine substance. . . . Clearly, if he was bound to reduce all these forces to a common value, this common value could have no measure but that of their attraction to his own mind. He must treat them as they had been felt; as convertible, reversible, interchangeable attractions on thought. He made up his mind to venture it; he would risk translating rays into faith. . . . Here opened another totally new education, which promised to be by far the most hazardous of all . . . two kingdoms of force which had nothing in common but attraction.[31]

In view of his attitude towards the role of science in culture and society, Adams's experience may be deemed archetypal of one current of development of European, indeed of western man in the course of the twentieth century, the optimistic strand.

In 1900, the German physicist Max Planck (1858–1947) stipulated that subatomic radiation was not emitted in a steady stream, but rather in uneven little spurts, which he called 'quanta'. He also introduced a new constant in the field of physics, meant to determine the distribution of energy produced by a radiating body. This so-called 'Planck's constant', symbolized as h, soon proved fundamental in the development of a new mechanics of the atom, now named quantum mechanics. This spelled the end of the exclusive dominance of the classical, mechanistic interpretation of physics codified by Newton 200 years earlier.

Albert Einstein (1879–1955) synthesized many of the new developments in his 'General Theory of Relativity'. After his already revolutionary gravitational research that had upset traditional, Newtonian views, he now claimed, among other things, that time, space and movement should not be seen as absolute entities but, rather, be interpreted as relative in accordance with the position of the observer. Aristotelian logic, Euclidean mathematics and Newtonian physics – the three modes of thinking that, together, had structured the European vision of the universe – now seemed to collapse. And with it came the demise of a number of non-scientific certainties in the fields of ethics, philosophy and politics that had been loosely based on that structured universe with its fixed laws. Not surprisingly, Einstein's views led to a passionate debate in which theologians, philosophers and historians joined with their scientific colleagues.[32] Surprisingly, the Belgian-born priest-mathematician Georges Lemaitre (1894–1966), a member of the papal academy of science, took up Einstein's own mathematics and in 1927 came up with the idea of the primeval atom that was the beginning of life, when, some 15 billion years ago, the universe was born with a 'big bang' – the actual term was coined by the British astrophysicist Fred Hoyle in 1949. He also argued that this universe was anything but static. Einstein himself accepted Lemaitre's position only when, in 1931, the two of them got together with the American astronomer Edwin Hubble (1889–1953), who had presented the world with the proof of the existence of other galaxies besides the Milky Way. But despite the meeting of these three great minds, and their final consensus, the discussion about the precise nature of the universe as either contracting or expanding, or even static, continues.

Meanwhile, both Einstein and Planck tried to counter the indeterminist world-view that seemed to follow logically from their own arguments and which, moreover, was supported by their fellow physicists Nils Bohr and Werner Heisenberg. They held that a distinction should still be made between man the observer and the object of his observation, the physical universe.[33] But to many this distinction was no longer viable.

Since so many people perceived their own age as more revolutionary than any before it, a feeling of uncertainty pervaded the last decades of the nineteenth and the first years of the twentieth century. It was reflected in various forms of culture, as were the new ideas about man and the cosmos that were soon widely popularized. In a kind of wild abandon, a frenzy of creativity manifesting itself in painting and architecture as well as in literature and music, many artists now took up an 'avant garde' position. Re-examining the languages of the arts and using radically new techniques, they hoped to succeed in creating something that reflected the new age. Analysing, deconstructing and reconstructing reality as they saw or heard it, using such wide-ranging means as atonality and collage, cubism or expressionism, they did, indeed, succeed.[34] However, much of their creative production tended to present a pessimistic view of man and the world he had created.

In the visual arts, many artists felt that, despite all the efforts of the past century, indeed, despite the invention of photography, reality could not be represented. Paul Cézanne told his viewers that representation had to account for the effect of interaction between what one sees and the object one is looking at – one cannot paint reality, but only one's perception of it. Yet he also sought to find the basic structural forms of everything material – geometric solids. Thus, in 1907, Pablo Picasso (1881–1973) in his painting *Les Demoiselles d'Avignon*, represented his female figures as a 'cubist' composition. Though many were shocked by his choice of topic, prostitutes, far more were bewildered by his choice of form, by his proclamation of a new, anti-representational model of what one might call 'de-form-ation'. In his *Girl with a Mandolin* (1910), this idea of multiple, though simultaneous viewpoints is presented even more forcefully and logically. In a sense, the idea that when we look at an object, it never is fixed, but always shifting, that reality is a combination of variability and stability, was later demonstrated in physics as well.

In the 3,000-odd pages of the great cycle of novels *A la recherche du temps perdu* (Remembrance of Things Past) (1913–27), in which Marcel Proust (1871–22) tried to capture the mystery of time – and memory – and its relentless workings in man and society, he analysed, specifically, the ways and means of the new leaders, the bourgeoisie, who were trying to penetrate the bastions of the old aristocracy. In a series of merciless analyses of individual representatives of these various groups, Proust depicted the decline of the latter and the shallow, valueless drive for power and pleasure of the former, manifest in varieties of grotesque social opportunism and hypocrisy. The spirit of the time was also criticized, albeit rather more implicitly, in the works of the great Norwegian playwright Henrik Ibsen (1828–1906). He fathomed the growing conflict between an ever more restrictive society and the individual, between illusion and reality, in a series of haunting plays that, not incidentally, centre around powerful females in whose lives these conflicts are tragically shown. In *Samfundets Stotter, Et Dukkehjem* and *Gengangere – Pillars of Society, A Doll's House* and *Ghosts* – he described dilemmas that, as was shown by their success all over Europe, were felt increasingly by the bourgeois world of the west. Pablo Picasso, in the many still lifes he painted in the years between 1910 and 1914, often positioned his glasses and bottles against the background of a newspaper page: on each, something tragic is told – a chauffeur murders a woman, a soldier spits out a bullet, an actress poisons her lover; society is sick from moral decay and physical violence.[35]

Others, while convinced that western civilization was doomed and, worse, that it had brought down this doom on its own head, precisely by rejecting the old norms and values, were optimistic: out of the ashes of the past, if necessary the ashes left by another great war which seemed increasingly unavoidable, a new society would rise, not burdened by tradition but free. Thus, in Italy, the philosopher and cultural critic Benedetto Croce (1866–1952) tried to develop an open-ended historicism as an alternative to traditional religion and the culture of science. To him, reality was history: the human world forever grows as a result of the creative solutions individuals find to solve the problems that face them. He also argued that truth and morality do not dissolve if one denies transcendence and accepts historicity: men will always use these to order the world.[36]

A world between wars

Nevertheless, in 1914, a 'world war' was the almost inevitable outcome of the economic and political tensions that had built up during the preceding decades and which had been translated into military preparations by the three main imperialist nations of Europe – England, France and Germany – while they watched what was happening in the Balkans between the Habsburg Empire and Russia.

Admittedly, to term this conflict a 'world war' is, in a way, hypocritical, for it was, first and foremost, a war fought between the states and nations of Europe, for motives and interests entirely their own. The only reason why this struggle came to involve much of the non-European world was the very fact that Europe's economic and political interests had acquired global proportions, influencing even the farthest corners of the earth and the people living there, if only because so many men from French Africa and British India were now called upon to defend their 'mother country' in a world, Europe, they had never seen before.

Against the background of this 'world on fire', the dream of Europe turned into a nightmare. As before, part of the intellectual elite rejected their responsibility for the disasters befalling the old world. Yet they stated their claim to be seen once more as Europe's cultural conscience, demanding to be involved in the eventual building of a new one. With an acute insight into the social, mainly urban character of Europe's cultural elite, the Austrian literary critic and writer Hugo von Hofmansthal (1874–1929) wrote:

> We, we. I know very well that I cannot speak for the entire generation. I speak about several thousand people spread over Europe's big cities. Some of them are famous; some of them write . . . moving and gripping books; some . . . write only letters; . . . some of them leave no traces. . . . And yet these two or three thousand people have a certain significance; . . . they're not necessarily the leaders or the soul of their generation: but they are its conscience.[37]

Many intellectuals were convinced not only that a century had ended, but also that the end of civilization itself had come. This sense of doom was aptly coined in the phrase *Der Untergang des Abendlandes* (The Decline of the West), the title given by the German philosopher Oswald Spengler to the two-volume study he published between 1918 and 1922 – a book which was an instant bestseller and, as some of its analyses and criticism still stands, deserves to be read even now. Others, such as the Belgian historian Henri Pirenne in his *Mahomet et Charlemagne* (1937), created a vision of a European civilization that would have continued triumphantly from its ancient origins in the Mediterranean to its Christian fulfilment were it not for the coming of Islam, the power that had disrupted the cultural, religious unity still prevailing at the end of the sixth century – as if to alert Europe to the fact that, now, too, it could define itself only in contrast with other cultures, as if to remind Europe of the central, Christian roots and characteristics of its civilization.[38]

Meanwhile, many of the scientific ideas that evolved around the turn of the century, though often misunderstood or not understood at all, became highly influential in other fields of early twentieth-century culture, precisely because they seemed to support a view of man and his world as unstable and relative. They definitely contributed to the prevailing climate of disorientation and scepticism as is shown in the work of poets and other writers, such as the Czech author Franz Kafka (1883–1924).[39] On the other hand, these emotions, emphasized by the millions of deaths that had been the devastating inheritance of the First World War, confronted people with the question of the validity of these scientific ideas and their consequences, and, finally even with the question of the meaning of existence.

The sense of alienation that gripped many people was, perhaps, best voiced by the Austrian author Robert Musil (1880–1942), who, like Proust, used the novel to research the conditions of contemporary society. His gigantic, multi-volume *Der Mann ohne Eigenschaften* (The Man without Qualities) (1930–43) in its very construction of hundreds of short pieces showed the fragmentation of life and thought which, to many, seemed to characterize European culture in the first decades of the twentieth century.[40]

In this context, the relationship between Europe and America was reconsidered once more. Obviously, the appreciation of America fluctuated on the waves of Europe's self-image. In the early years of the twentieth century, Franz Kafka devoted the first of his great novels to America as the at-once alienating and yet challenging context in which his protagonist Karl Rossmann comes to know himself, through a series of situations that remind one forcibly of the bitter-sweet atmosphere that colours the movies of Charlie Chaplin, between naive innocence and world-wise cynicism. Landing in New York, Rossmann muses: 'Die ersten Tage eines Europäers in Amerika seien ja einer Geburt vergleichbar' ('the first days of a European in the United States after all resemble birth').[41]

However, most European cultural critics were less ambivalent. Indeed, those philosophers and social analysts who, at the turn of the century, had admonished Europe to copy the 'American model' now felt that contemporary American culture and society presented a mirror to be held up to Europe, to show it the dangers that would arise if the American example were indeed followed: here, too, human misery and cultural consumerism would be the result of the unbridled egoism and the rampant materialism that characterized the USA. They argued that the expectations voiced by Hector St John, that the best of the culture of the old world would find its fulfilment in the new, had been proven entirely wrong. On the contrary, America showed what would happen to man if he did not have the benefit of traditions to structure his thoughts and actions.

While they preached the American nightmare, millions continued to believe in the American dream. Either way, it was symbolized by the skyscrapers that seemed to touch the clouds: they were the embodiment of human pride, or of human tragedy, as those who knew their Bible were inclined to point out. All over Europe, the new media used the image to signify the United States. Indeed, photography, soon followed by the cinema, gave the skyscraper world-wide notoriety.[42] But the cinema often combined this skyscraper-world with another one, that of the all-powerful machine. Fritz Lang (1890–1976), whose fascinating film *Metropolis* was made in Germany in 1926, had had his first impression of New York's electrically lit skyline aboard ship, on his arrival from Europe. In the film, the machine inhabits the mile-high buildings and shows man his diminishing importance. In the end, it threatens to devour man, as a new Moloch.[43] This was the very fear that Europe had had for the past 100 years; the stormy developments of American technology only increased it.[44] A vision of technological science as a dehumanizing influence now combined with a pessimistic view of the equally dehumanizing effects of the metropolis, the machine-driven industrialized community, to create a deep-rooted anxiety about the approaching end of the individual, that proud, central figure in European culture. Hence, the heroic struggle of man against machine became a recurrent theme in western cinema. As if to show that after many decades the problems of western society had not been solved, as recently as 1988 the very images that made *Metropolis* unforgettable returned in the 'cult' film *Blade Runner*.[45]

The negative view taken of the United States by Europe's cultural elite from the end of the nineteenth century onwards had ended decades of positive propaganda. It was certainly the outcome of growing cultural pessimism, especially in intellectual circles which were profoundly influenced by the horrors of the First World War, when mass destruction ended the life not only of so many irreplaceable humans but also of so many irreplaceable monuments. In the Netherlands, the famous historian and cultural critic Johan Huizinga published his philosophically rather than historically founded opinions of the United States and their influence on the old world in his *Mensch en menigte in Amerika* (Man and multitude in America) (1918), followed in 1927 by *Amerika levend en denkend* (America as it lives and thinks). His views were shared by many all over Europe. On the one hand people felt there was no denying that America showed Europe the logical consequences of its own way of thinking and living that had originated in the optimistic, progressive attitudes of the eighteenth-century Enlightenment. Consequently, Huizinga, himself the heir of this intellectual tradition, decidedly admired the 'vitalistic attitude' inherent in the American way of life, an attitude of 'Dit, Hier en Straks' (of 'this, now and soon'). Yet, this admiration went hand in hand with an essentially pessimistic vision on the situation of contemporary European culture, that had lost its erstwhile vitality: the will to fight the inevitable decadence.[46] Moreover, his admiration was overshadowed by an equally clear aversion to the increasingly dehumanized mass culture created in and exported by the United States.

Meanwhile, the issue of European decadence was also addressed by one of Germany's, and indeed Europe's, most creative twentieth-century writers, Thomas Mann (1875–1955).[47] He analysed his world, the world of the first two decades of that century, in a monumental novel, *Der Zauberberg* (The Magic Mountain) (1924). Its hero, Hans Castorp, goes to visit a relative in a Swiss sanatorium. By the 'magic', the opaque language and actions of a staff of sinister, incomprehensible but apparently all-powerful doctors and psychologists, he is convinced that he, too, will succumb to the century's most dreaded illness, tuberculosis, if he does not follow their strange prescriptions. Hence, he decides to stay. Finally, he comes to know both himself and the maladies of his age: the conflict between freedom and responsibility, between art that can become anarchy, and civic values that can stultify the spirit if not inspired by art. The conflict, he fears, is between any form of tyranny, physical or spiritual, and chaos. In a gripping scene, set on the snow-capped mountain top, Castorp ponders the possibilities of a synthesis between the Apollonian and the Dionysian face of culture, of man: the harmony produced by a spirit of reason and the rapture produced by a spirit of emotion. When the novel ends, with Castorp leaving for the front, he dreams that, after death brought about by the war, Europe's fatal disease will be cured and there will be fraternity, a new humanity.

However, during the 1920s and 1930s the lessons of the terrible war of 1914–18 were not heeded at all, nor did the various forms in which Europe reconsidered the roles of man, of culture, produce the positive effects so many, including Mann, had hoped for. That much, at least, was clear when in 1939 a second all-European war seemed imminent. When it erupted it soon proved even more disastrous, and more far-reaching globally speaking, than its predecessor.

The rise of totalitarian modes of thinking, of totalitarian states, even, from the 1920s onwards, had been one of the most profound shocks ever felt by those who believed in Europe as a civil society based on certain norms and values, such as democracy, tolerance and responsibility vis-à-vis one's fellow human beings, precisely because most people deemed them almost intrinsically European and, therefore, invulnerable. Now, Europe itself produced a culture that almost denied the value of the individual. Worse, it resulted in the bloodiest war the world had ever seen.

And yet many have argued that the preconditions for this episode in European history lay in the very structure of its culture and society. The more or less liberal nationalism of the nineteenth century had helped the European states to further develop their power though their constitutional and parliamentary democracies; these resulted in and were the result of the gradual enlargement of the electorate until, finally, it encompassed all adult males and, by the 1920s, even females. Some have argued that despite the hopes raised by democratization, it was precisely the democratic system itself that facilitated the transformation into new totalitarian policies of the widespread feelings of resentment and vengeance felt by those states that had lost the First World War, or thought they had not gained enough. Both in Italy and, even more so, in Germany, these feelings galled from the moment the allied forces settled the terms of peace at the 1919 Paris Peace Conference. Now, the parliamentary democracy itself that, to many voters, seemed unable to prevent the degradation of their state and nation, gave easy access to power for those political leaders who exploited these feelings of hurt national pride and promised revenge and national glory if only they were given a free hand.

The capitalist economy and the society based on it had, from the late nineteenth century onwards, brought unprecedented wealth to Europe at large and raised the standard of living of the majority of its people to unknown levels. But allowed to develop unchecked, this socio-economic system had been unable to restrict the economic and social consequences resulting from the periodic crises inherent in it. Aggravated by irresponsible financial speculation, such a crisis occurred in the 1920s, resulting in mass poverty all over Europe, not least in defeated Germany. There, as elsewhere, the misery combined with a growing lack of faith in democratic institutions and solutions, and propaganda for totalitarian alternatives promising new national glory and new national wealth. Such a new medium as film was a perfect vehicle to drive the nationalistic message of salvation through strong, heroic leaders home to the masses.

In Germany, Fritz Lang – a trained architect and painter of large-scale canvasses – produced *Die Nibelungen* (1927), an impressive as well as oppressive film version of the ancient epic, dedicated 'to the German people'. It seemed to put the force of myth before the power of reason. Like its numerous historical counterparts elsewhere in Europe, it did not so much visualize the past as, more precisely, present the public with an idealized past of strong, even heroic men, and sometimes women, that might help it survive the unpleasant present. Other states, too, harked back to history to give new force to their nation. In France, which had a special bureau producing historical films, one of Europe's great cinematographers, Abel Gance (1889–1981), created his greatest work, *Napoléon* (1927), using the most daring of techniques – among other things projecting three different images simultaneously, on three screens, an innovation not taken up at the time but reinvented in the 1950s. In this epic, he illustrated the vital force of the French nation as embodied in the revolutionary hero. No wonder that in such a climate the warning message contained in the Dane Carl Dreyer's (1889–1968) moving masterpiece, *La Passion de Jeanne d'Arc* (1928), that the past had also been a time of fearful repression of the outspoken individual by powerful systems, Church and State, was definitely less welcome.

Indeed, without the technology that was greatly broadening Europe's perspective both of itself and of the world, the cultural and political consequences of social and economic change would not have been as serious as they were. Both the radio and the cinema, two of the most exciting technological manifestations of twentieth-century culture, provided the very means for the propaganda that helped Europe's would-be dictators on their way to power. Yet, undeniably, the technology that was used by nationalistic politicians also facilitated people's lives all over the western world, contributing greatly to their material well-being as well as to an easier and healthier life: the mechanical and chemical industries that provided food and medication, public transport and domestic appliances. To give but one example: the German state that, from the late 1930s onwards, ordered the mass murder of its Jewish population and of so many other citizens, also introduced mass transport – the much-vaunted 'Volkswagen' – and mass tourism, thus easing the tensions between collective goals and individual desires both in the working and the middle classes through a heightened consumerism.[48]

At the same time, the organizational skills and the technology involved were used to produce weapons that could bring death on a scale and with a thoroughness hitherto unknown. The very wings that in the early years of the century finally realized man's eternal dream of flying and that, through commercial machinations and a public demand for glamorized heroes, were almost immediately represented both in established and in popular culture through photography, the cinema, and songs[49] – soon brought bombs to the cities where other dreams of Europe had found their expression, both in magnificent works of 'high' art and in the by now highly improved 'popular' housing estates where many people lived in reasonable comfort. In the end, experimental physics, based on theories about the atom and the basic structure of matter going back to the ancient Greeks, created forces that could easily destroy the world that human culture had produced.

The social, or human sciences, by the end of the nineteenth century had begun to study politics and society and interpret it as a rational and therefore even makable organization. The work of the German scholar Max Weber (1864–1920), one of the most creative spirits in the field, still offers monumental insights into societal and cultural processes, even though he studied and implicitly judged other cultures such as the Chinese and the Indian by the standards of modernity and progress which Europe had set.[50] Empirically based on socio-historic data, and boasting some success in explaining the problems of contemporary society, these as yet mostly theoretical ideas about 'social engineering' seemed to offer the perfect proof to those who maintained they were able to liberate the world from its present predicaments and shortcomings: socialist politicians, social-democrat thinkers but equally more totalitarian-minded men. The modern state, with its efficient bureaucracy, had succeeded in almost eliminating private violence by concentrating the right to legal violence – jurisdiction and punishment, the use of the army – in its own hands. But that state could also be used as the highly accurate instrument that it was to enforce whatever policy carried the day in a democracy that lost its sense of human dignity. Indeed, in many respects these nationalist and nationalistic societies were conservative, not to say reactionary. Thus, for example, in Nazi Germany, notions of female emancipation were quickly suppressed, again by using the modern technology of film to create images of women contentedly staying at home, to take care of husband and family. In nationalistic France – the France of the Vichy regime – even the national heroine, Jeanne d'Arc – whose image has always been used by the various French governments to suit their own political and social ideals – was now presented to the French children as a thoroughly womanly woman who, when she was not leading the French army against the English, would do the sewing and the cooking and who, of course, had only denied herself motherhood in the cause of 'France'.[51]

In a Europe showing such great potential, the egotism of states – both the losers and the winners of the First World War – resulted in their failure to create an acceptable balance, an international order that did not breed dissatisfaction and war. In most states, the narrow-mindedness of various interest groups often resulted in a situation wherein the electorate failed to accept responsibility for society at large and for the weak in particular. Many felt they needed no excuse to break with traditional values now considered ineffective and to embrace other ideas, which were, after all, equally part of the European tradition and promised consolation for hurt national pride, solutions for deeply felt national problems: where democracy and tolerance disappeared, dictatorship and repression succeeded. Inevitably, this happened more easily in those states where industrialization, education and democracy were still comparatively recent developments, a thin veneer covering an older, rural, more traditionally hierarchical society.[52]

While Germany was, by the end of the nineteenth century, in many ways one of Europe's most civilized countries, producing musicians, painters, scientists and writers whose works still inspire European culture, yet it also was a country where almost all of the above mentioned preconditions were fulfilled at the same time. This helps us to understand the genesis there of a totalitarian system of unprecedented brutality and effectiveness, the 'Third Reich' and its 'final solution'.[53] The so-called Holocaust – a word meaning sacrifice to the gods and, hence, a totally inappropriate name for what was plain mass murder or genocide on the most gigantic scale known to history – saw the death of millions of people: not only the extermination of all but a few Jews from all over Europe, but also the slaughter of blacks, gypsies, homosexuals, mentally and physically disabled people and others,[54] because 'the system' – a government elected by the Germans themselves – had convinced society that it needed conformity and total obedience; to enforce this, it mobilized society against an enemy, against those who could be stigmatized as 'the other'. However, one should not forget that the leaders of Nazi Germany exploited a prejudice against 'strangers' that had been part of European culture for more than 1,000 years.[55] However, in the twentieth century not only were the Nazis able to give their racist ideology a pseudo-scientific gloss, more important they were able to use the instruments of modernity, like advanced technology and the bureaucratic apparatus of the modern state, to implement it.[56]

Meanwhile, comparable views were, indeed, being entertained elsewhere as well. In Italy, the birthplace of Humanism and the Renaissance, of new visions of man and society, a fascist dictatorship ruled from the early 1920s for more than twenty years; however, only at the end of the Mussolini era, did it also succumb to the attractions of racist policies. Moreover, France and Spain showed obvious totalitarian tendencies and parallel scapegoat ideologies; in France and in the countries of central Europe – Austria, Poland, Romania, etc. – the authorities were as explicit in their anti-Semitic form as in Nazi Germany. Also, there were small groups advocating strong leadership with little or no regard for democratic principles in Belgium, England and the Netherlands and, indeed, in almost all the countries of western Europe, as there were in other parts of central and eastern Europe, too.

In short, all over Europe a complex culture of 'modernity' had come into being, full of (technological) possibilities for good and evil, which goes a long way to explaining the origins of dictatorship in democracy, of war and mass murder in a society that, objectively judged, had never before been as educated and as prosperous. Most European societies manifested some form of what one might call hyper- or organic ultra-nationalism – 'nation-statism' – with para–militaristic tendencies. In most European societies, there were people who subscribed to utopian projects offering regeneration, promising a cleansing of the nation, as a remedy for prevailing problems. Arguably, the Nazi variety can only be understood if it is not seen as an anomaly, but as the outcome of obsessions that characterized Europe at large.[57]

17 Towards a new Europe?

Science, culture and society

By the first decades of the twentieth century, the dominant cultural forces in Europe were largely generated by an urban, industrial culture, in which the machine or rather technology had become an all-pervading presence, despite large regions remaining rural in their economic and cultural life. The new world was visualized in Walter Ruttmann's memorable movie *Berlin, Symphonic der Großstadt* (Berlin, the symphony of a metropolis) (1927). In the same years the concomitant features of this culture were voiced by the film actress Marlene Dietrich (1901–92), who sang:

> Es liegt in der Luft eine Sachlichkeit, es liegt in der Luft eine Stachlichkeit . . . Durch die Lüfte sausen schon Bilder, Radio, Telefon, durch die Luft geht alles drahtlos und die Luft wird schon ganz ratios, Flugzeug, Luftschiff.

> There's business–like rationality in the air, there's stimulation in the air . . . already, the air is filled with images, radio, telephone, all is going wireless and the air doesn't know how to handle it all: airplane, airship.

The song presents an image of a bewildering and bewildered world that finds itself completely dominated by the products of science and technology. Indeed, many wondered whether there were any limits to what science might produce. But equally many were afraid that, in the end, man might be the victim of the realization of his own dreams.

In 1929, the German composer Paul Hindemith (1895–1963) and his compatriot, the playwright Bertolt Brecht (1898–1956) collaborated in the creation of a fascinating theatre piece, combining an orchestra, a chorus, solo singers, a group of clowns and cinematic projection, to which they gave the title *Lehrstück* (Instruction piece), for in accordance with Brecht's idealist-socialist attitudes not only should it be staged and performed by and for the people,[1] it should also instruct them through its message. It tells of man's aspirations to dominate the world, nature, through technology, which has produced many marvellous machines and yet has not realized a society that prevents people from dying of starvation. In realizing his desire to fly like a bird, man has finally reached the limits of his ability. However, in the *Lehrstück*, a pilot, proud of his achievement, crashes. Asking for mercy as he lies dying, the multitude assembled around him yet denies him any help. On the contrary, they impress upon him the need for humility. Only when the pilot assents to his essential nothingness is he forgiven, and he can die in peace.

Seen against the background of the grave economic and social crises of the 1920s, Brecht's message projected a very negative vision of contemporary culture. One might ask whether it was not born from an increasing ignorance of modern science, from fear, even. I think it was, but the fear was understandable. In less than twenty years since the beginning of the century, science had come a long way since the British physicist Ernest Rutherford (1871–1937) had said that physics could be good, if only one could explain it to a barmaid. As one who had conducted basic research into the structure of the atom and received the 1908 Nobel Prize for chemistry, he may have slightly exaggerated.

For while the age-long gap between two of Europe's worlds, the rural and the urban, was being closed, a new one, in the making since Copernicus published his book on the cosmos in the fifteenth century, now opened up. For the time being, it was to create two worlds, one that could be understood, interpreted by all who had received a decent education, and another whose comprehension required a complex, non-verbal language understood by only a minority. Because the natural sciences speak a single, universal language, that of mathematics and, by and large, use a single methodology, since the early twentieth century the world of science has become, indeed, the World.

At the beginning of the twentieth century, the central field in the natural sciences was physics, and one of the central questions in it the nature of the atom. Further investigating its structure, so long seen as the stable building block of the physical universe, between 1911 and 1913 men like Rutherford and Bohr discovered its nucleus and the electrons circling around it. They also argued that a theory of causality relying either on waves or on particles would not suffice to explain its reality. Moreover, in 1927 Werner Heisenberg (1901–76) stated there is always uncertainty in the simultaneous measurements of the position of a particle, which would imply that the knowledge claimed of such an object is fundamentally limited as well – the idea has become known as Heisenberg's 'uncertainty principle'. He therefore claimed that we are unable to know the position and speed of the individual electrons. Hence, it is impossible to predict their behaviour. All these developments led to the further elaboration of Planckian quantum mechanics. It was now argued that a pattern of frequencies in the atom produced by successive quantum states manifest, putting matters simply, the complementarity of both waves and particles. To accept this, man, even scientific man, had to discard most theories held sacred in science for a long time, specifically determinist causality.

As in other fields of culture, the Second World War proved a catalyst in science, too. Concentrating on the powers of the atom, all contestants in the war had devoted enormous amounts of time and money to research in order to produce the technology to win the war. Indeed, 'pure' or theoretical science and 'applied' science, i.e. practical technology, though their union had first occurred in the nineteenth century, now effectively joined on a grand scale, never to separate again. Thus, the allied battle against Germany and Japan resulted, first, in the discovery of nuclear fission – the achievement of Otto Hahn (1879–1968), in 1939 – and, after the scientists told the politicians and the military of the possibilities, in nuclear warfare, when, in 1945, a team led by Robert Oppenheimer (1904–67) at Los Alamos, in the desert of New Mexico, managed to successfully test an atomic explosion. Tragically, the hydrogen bomb had to be actually used before many of the scientists involved started to have second thoughts, realizing its full and dreadful potential as well as the political use to which it had been put by the United States, ostensibly to end the war against Japanese, 'yellow imperialism' but, as some historians have argued, actually to deter Soviet Russia from advancing too far either into Asia or Europe.[2]

At the same time, the possibilities of the Englishman Alan Turing's (1912–54) speculations in mathematical logic, dating from the mid-1930s, had also become apparent. Soon, the machines that were constructed to help to decode enemy (i.e. German) messages evolved into the computers that now regulate many western people's most routine actions, from reading the bar codes on every piece of supermarket produce to giving access to worldwide telephone services or the information superhighway. Indeed, the moment these computerized systems fail, western society is increasingly faced with its daily and dangerous dependence on them.

By the end of the twentieth century, science had become the basis of society, of an economy and a culture that cannot exist without the technology it continues to produce, at ever greater speed, with such exciting developments as the reintegration of physics and chemistry.[3] Soon after research in solid-state physics showed the electromagnetic properties of crystals, the transistor revolutionized communication systems. However, a far more significant discovery followed a few years later. For only a short time after F. Crick and J.D. Watson discovered the structure of DNA in 1953 – the 'deoxyribo-nucleic acid' that was known to play a role in heredity but whose capacity for gene-copying and, thus, whose central function in the actual operation of heredity was as yet unclear – the so-called recombinant DNA techniques started to revolutionize biology and the life sciences in general.[4] By the 1980s, through combining the genes of one species with those of another, biotechnology altered such diverse fields as agriculture and medicine.

These developments, while obviously beneficial in a great number of ways, yet have negative effects as well. In agriculture, the concomitant pollution of the environment, and the many problems caused by foodstuffs containing heavy doses of growth-inducing chemicals and pesticides have become an object of political and, indeed, cultural debate, questioning the dependence of society on what many consider to be the unnecessary overproduction of irresponsibly doctored food that becomes a burden on the environment as well. In medical biology, the possibility of uncontrolled or uncontrollable genetic manipulation continues to pose worries, against a background of the increasingly consumerist attitude of many people, who may all too easily think that shopping for an altered or even a new body is as much everyone's individual right as is the acquisition of a newly enhanced personal computer.

Indeed, by the second half of the twentieth century Europe, and the wider world as well, was not yet completely at ease with the fundamental role of science. On the contrary, with its ascendancy, the cultural criticism of its power increased. There was widespread fear, mainly, one must conclude, because to most people science had become incomprehensible and, moreover, its practical and moral consequences unpredictable.

It is hardly accidental that, after the Second World War which had caused so many deaths through the means of 'improved' technology, which had created nuclear power, and which seemed to inaugurate an endless period of 'cold war' between the western and the communist world, two men engaged in a debate that raised the fundamental question of the role of science in a humane society.

C.P. Snow (1905–80) and F.R. Leavis (1895–1978) together created the famous image of a world of two cultures, defining the course of western civilization as running, continuously, through a field of tension between the 'natural sciences' and 'the humanities'. These two English intellectuals first crossed swords in 1959–61. Snow, a nuclear physicist and a senior science administrator, the embodiment of the fusion between the powerful exact sciences and the State that had gained much of its power controlling this field of knowledge, was yet a man from the humanities, the author of a series of novels called *Strangers and Brothers* which tried to depict the changes in English society between the 1930s and the 1960s. His opponent, Leavis, a famous as well as influential literary critic, taught at the old, traditional university at Cambridge, to many the embodiment of the 'ivory tower',[5] even though, of course, it was Cambridge itself that was increasingly known for its contributions to modern scientific research.

Snow publicly voiced his concern about the gap he saw growing between the two cultures. While acknowledging the traditional rivalry between the humanities and the natural sciences, his main concern was the increasing inability of the students and practitioners of the former to understand the basic assumptions and values governing the research and the motives of the latter. This, he argued, would be fatal to Europe, indeed to culture in general.

As Leavis did, many have accused Snow of surreptitiously playing on prevalent public fears, arguing that he was trying to establish the primacy of the sciences for economic development and, consequently, for prosperity, by implying that only a technologically educated and powerful and, hence, economically strong society would be able to compete with other ideologies, more specifically the communist one which was at that very moment felt to be threatening 'the west'. They also argued that Snow, in doing so, was willing to almost deny the contribution made by the humanities to the values many considered central to European civilization. Therefore, Leavis came to the defence of the humanities, of the arts, as an element in education, in society equally deserving of (economic) support.

Yet while Snow, as many politicians and cultural critics after him, certainly had his science-based agenda, his analysis did address a core issue of twentieth-century culture and society. Therefore, the Snow–Leavis debate has lost little of its actuality even now. Almost everything people have come to take for granted in the way of physical and material comfort has been the undeniable product of an increasingly complex and powerful science and technology, up to the medical and biological research that has not only prolonged the life of our bodies but now promises the perfection of our minds as well through genetic manipulation. Yet, while in Europe, nowadays, some one million people are actively engaged in scientific research and experimental development,[6] of a total population of some 700 million, few outside their circle understand even the most basic choices that govern this research. Averagely educated individuals, who are morally or otherwise concerned about the development of society, seem to have lost their grip on one of society's most creative cultural fields, as well as one of its most powerful tools. Partly, the lack of basic science education is to blame. Mostly, however, people consciously refuse to interest themselves, because science is perceived as difficult, impenetrable, even. Obviously, a large part of it is, but the basic principles determining its direction can be understood after all. In refusing to engage with the world of science, a responsible citizen can hardly expect to be able to confront the practitioners of the sciences with the validity of the values that the tradition of the humanities should continue to instill in that same society. Because western society at large seems unwilling and unable to discuss the responsibilities implied in the choices it makes, and the consequences of these choices, it seems content to leave things as they are, thus leaving science and technology, and the economic system on which they thrive, very much to make their own decisions, which means decisions that now implicate all of humankind and the entire planet. For example, the release of fluorocarbons – a substantial element in such comfort contrivances as refrigerators and aerosols – has greatly damaged the ozone layer that ensures our survival on this planet. And while the advances in molecular biology and the cracking of the genetic code will probably contribute to the elimination of much human suffering, they may also cause damage by allowing humans to go further along the path to, first, 'perfecting' themselves, at least physically, and then endlessly replicating these perfect beings, a possibility clearly proven by the animal cloning experiments of the 1990s. In both cases, only well-informed persons with at least some understanding of the issues involved may expect to participate in and exert some influence on the public debate which sustains a responsible society: a debate over the future of human culture and what we have come to see as its essential humanity, and a debate, moreover, not only with the scientists themselves but, equally important, with those who finance and hence at least partly control their work. For it is bureaucrats and politicians who, often equally ignorant of the basic issues, continue to fund and allocate the gigantic amounts of public money that keep science going.

In short, people should engage in a debate over the desired course of a civilization dominated by science instead of increasingly turning their back on its fundamental principles and only enjoying its fruits. They should accept science as an essential part of their cultural heritage but, with it, the responsibility to become acquainted with at least the fundamentals of its thinking. They should not become like the sorcerer's apprentice in the eponymous musical composition by Paul Dukas (1897), based on Goethe's *Der Zauberlehrling* (1797), who could not control the forces he unleashed because he refused to learn from his master and, hence, was confronted with chaos.

Admittedly, for the layman it is far from easy to enter the world of science as the questions that occupy scientists nowadays are extremely complicated. Take, for example, the continuing quest for the 'ultimate particle'. In the 1960s it resulted in a proliferation of 'quarks', and later of neutrinos – particles not yet 'seen', but proven, at least to many physicists, by their effects. Their very intangibility is, perhaps, reflected in the fact that the name for the 'quark' is taken from one of James Joyce's most enigmatic novels, *Finnegans Wake* (1939). Not surprisingly, twentieth-century scientists, themselves confronted with confusions and contradictions, have continuously tried to find new ways to describe the unity of nature in a single model that would reconcile or even efface all contradictions. Einstein worked on his 'unified field theory' to connect electromagnetism and gravitation. Bohr tried to do so with his idea of complementarity, arguing that the various modes of perceiving and understanding need not be mutually exclusive, indeed, will somehow probably contribute to a final comprehension, to a new unity of the sciences. It is a fascinating view, even more so if one realizes that he reached this conclusion partly on the basis of reading the American philosopher William James's *The Principles of Psychology* (1890), a work decidedly not part of the canon of the physical sciences. But then, Bohr was already trying to bridge the gap between the humanities and the sciences.[7]

Efforts by men like Bohr and Einstein, though not always understood, nor, for that matter, accepted by subsequent generations of scientists, seem to represent a basic yearning in western culture when faced with a nature that, however well explored, still remains a mystery. Indeed, they somehow mirror the emotional needs that had driven the physicists of the German *Naturphilosophie* of the early nineteenth century to try and reconcile the material and the spiritual universe and discover basic structures in each and every manifestation of life. This quest has continued, producing a series of 'solutions' that are still being debated. Meanwhile, discussions in the two scientific fields that cover the seeming opposites of the physical spectrum show how far removed man still is from final answers.

Brain research, though greatly advanced since the end of the twentieth century, still lacks consensus on what a human brain actually is, specifically in the dispute over the question of what, exactly, constitutes man as a free, creative agent.[8] Some have argued that the brain, being capable of non-computational intuition, can be understood only if a special type of physics, as yet unknown, is developed. Others have explained its functioning merely from the oscillation of our nerve cells. Yet others stress the necessity to understand the brain as an immensely complex (neuro-)chemical factory. Still, there have been many physicists, like the Nobel Prize winner John Eccles, who have said that understanding the brain will not make us comprehend man any better, because its study leaves out a spiritual soul – a point of view that certainly echoes the mind–body discussions of the ancient Greeks, of Descartes, of La Mettrie and so many others throughout the history of Europe.

Moving from the brain's tiny neurons to the origins of the universe, the most accepted cosmological solution, the so-called 'big bang' theory, which first emerged in the 1950s, maintains that it all began with a point, a mathematical singularity, some 15 billion years ago – a concept surprisingly made into something of a scientific hit by the British astrophysicist Stephen Hawking (b. 1942) in the 1980s. But for all its exciting vistas through space and time, these theories have not even started to answer the simple question that has perplexed man since he first formulated thoughts about the cosmos: what, then, is the origin of the cosmic seed from which the galaxies and, ultimately, life and mankind are said to stem?[9] Indeed, most modern cosmologists argue that the question of what came before the big bang is invalid, since besides matter and radiation, time and space also appeared – rather mysteriously – from the void at the moment of creation. Yet, that too leaves unanswered the questions that man has asked himself since time immemorial.[10]

Meanwhile, if anything, developments in the world of science and technology have shown that Europe is no longer the world's sole leader nor, one should admit, is it among the world's most creative and productive regions. True, some of the most influential and unsettling discoveries of the first half of the twentieth century were made in Europe, but since the Second World War the centre of 'big industry', the phenomenon of combining scientific research and technological developments, has moved to the United States. This happened partly because in the 1930s so many of Germany's most creative and productive minds were forced to move to the other side of the Atlantic – though others, after having worked for the Nazi regime, went on to do so for the victorious states of Europe. By the 1980s, however, another change became apparent. Both in Europe and in the USA, the creative input in, especially, the sciences came increasingly from students who had left their own, mainly east Asian countries to work in the west. Now, at the beginning of the twenty-first century, that situation has altered again, since many of those students now feel they would rather work in their own countries – where social, economic and political conditions have much improved. For the first time in the last 200 years of world history, this situation may well leave 'the west', i.e. both the USA and Europe, having to fight for its accustomed lead in scientific development.

Yet precisely because science and technology increasingly determine the course of mankind and the world, a Europe that tries to uphold certain values in the interplay between the sciences and that world, and to translate them into livable realities, can still be a force to the good. Conversely, without continued investment in research itself, Europe will not remain one of the world's 'big players'. This will both undermine the basis of its own prosperity and also weaken its credibility as a power that can actually presume to speak authoritatively on such issues.

Nowhere is the complexity of the issues involved demonstrated better than in the field of climate change. Some twenty years ago, British scientists first discovered the growth of holes in the earth's ozone layer. Yet, for two decades, most European societies have turned their back on the problems that this development is going to cause. Nevertheless, they were responsible for it in the first place, as, basically, the thinning and eventual disappearance of the ozone protection is caused by CFCs – the result of Europe's industrial, commercial, consumerist revolution of the past 200 years. The ways in which the world's climate is now ineluctably altering may, for one thing, cause many of Europe's low-lying regions to become inundated by the sea in the not-too-distant future. Now, many Europeans – including, admittedly, their politicians and governments, have simply denied the scientific evidence that should have alarmed them. Of course, they also fail to face the fact that the only way to counter the danger is by radically altering their consumer behaviour. While the USA clearly bears a large part of the responsibility, as do, by now, Russia, China and India, yet it may well be Europe that has to take the lead, politically and culturally-morally, in bringing about a long overdue change of mentality.

After the Second World War: deconstruction and reconstruction

Both the winners and the losers of the Second World War faced a number of grave problems. After mass destruction, economic reconstruction was, of course, imperative. But moral reconstruction was equally important. Germany had to come to terms with both losing another war and with the traumatizing stigma of having produced Nazism and the Holocaust. The allied states not only had to avoid a situation like Versailles and its aftermath recurring again, and therefore allow, even help Germany to recover its erstwhile position among Europe's civilized nations, they also had to ask themselves why a Europe of civilized nations had not prevented the war in the first place. A witch hunt for those who had collaborated with the German occupiers was the easiest way out – and besides punishing at least some of the worst war criminals, the Nuremberg Trials did in fact fulfil this function – but people soon realized that pointing an accusing finger at the guilt of others was too facile. It was certainly not going to answer the question of what structural conflicts within European culture and society, indeed within the people of Europe had resulted in the loss of precisely those values which many had thought to be fundamentally 'European'.

Another effect of the Second World War was the seemingly final division between east and west within geographical Europe. The power of Soviet Russia, which had been growing stronger since the Bolshevik Revolution of 1917, had brought about the downfall of the tsarist empire. It had been consolidated in the interwar period and had reached its apex in the Second World War. For during the war, the Soviet armies had spread over large parts of eastern and central Europe, overthrowing the existing regimes, some of which had collaborated with or had simply sold out to the Third Reich. By 1945, the Soviets were firmly entrenched there, establishing a series of satellite states to serve as a buffer zone between the Russian heartland and western Europe.

Last but not least, the Second World War accelerated the process of decolonization, forcing the leading nations of western Europe which had possessed colonial empires – some of them for more than 300 years – to face the fact that they no longer ruled the world. The process was enhanced by the obvious change in world politics brought about by the rise to global power status of the United States, which was accompanied by a growing American dominance in the economic, cultural and, specifically, scientific fields: Fröbel's predictions had come true after all.

Consequently, the traumas produced by the war and the grave prospect of a continuing conflict with the communist world, which might even result in the world's end now that nuclear arms had given man the power of total destruction, induced many western Europeans once again to examine fundamentally their hopes and policies for the future. Should the peoples of Europe accept that each nation continue to fight for its own ends, as had been the case for far too many years and with such obviously tragic results? Or was cooperation now called for, at least in the fields of economic and military policies? Would not this be a better answer to the challenges that a post-war world presented to a Europe that wanted to survive?

To avoid the ever-present danger of recurring chauvinism and nationalism and to foster a sense of European unity, as well as to create a bulwark against Bolshevism, a policy of formal economic and political-military cooperation between the states of non-communist Europe did indeed seem the best solution. Thus, western Europe went on its slow way to form a community,[11] slowly reformulating the ideas presented by so many Europeans during the previous centuries, to suit a now changed set of circumstances.

It was not, however, easy to eradicate the old, national ways of thinking which, after having gained their strongest expression in the nation-states of the nineteenth and early twentieth centuries, had become an almost innate set of oversimplified values inculcated in the minds of each citizen through education and constant propaganda. As the result of much soul-searching by intellectuals and politicians during the Second World War, in the years following it various bold and wide-ranging forms of economic cooperation were slowly realized – beginning, in 1952, with the 'Schuman Plan' that resulted in the European Coal and Steel Community, and ending with the 1957 'Treaty of Rome' which formed the European Economic Community. However, most politicians were aware that new, supranational institutions would not be enough. A new ideology was called for as well.

However prophetic their vision, in trying to present a concept of European culture, the 'European saints', the post-war founders of the European idea, those who 'rebuilt' the dream, were understandably still bound to their past, perhaps rather too much so. In this time of crisis, Konrad Adenauer, Alcide de Gasperi,

Jean Monnet, Robert Schuman and Paul-Henri Spaak – intellectuals or, at least, erudite politicians all of them – attempted, like so many of their predecessors, to formulate an ideal that could at least function as a political-rhetorical instrument. Perhaps not incidentally, most of them belonged to the Roman Catholic Church and pointed to (western) Europe as the geographical-cultural framework in which the classical tradition and Christian thought had provided the normative framework of European civilization. Indeed, Adenauer, Schuman and Spaak often conversed in German. Perhaps the spirit of Novalis was still present in them. However, even in their time the values and institutions that had once formed the core and expression of this European dream had already become less self-evident. The Churches especially have been losing influence since the 1950s.

Yet in the years since 1945 politicians and also historians have done their best to describe Europe's achievements as the result of a process that had evolved for more than 2,000 years; in doing so, they were certain to use a rhetoric that made people believe that their expectations for the present and the future were the logical outcome of this process. Admittedly, this was not an easy task. First of all because, as this book hopes to have shown, there is no such linear process linking our present to an inevitable evolution, to a European idea that has slowly grown and gained force over the ages. The task was difficult also because many, perhaps even the majority of Europeans, soon felt that the disadvantages of centralization under the aegis of 'Brussels', where for a number of reasons the new Europe had its administrative capital, seemed to outweigh the advantages which were all too quickly taken for granted. Indeed, even despite the as yet virtual absence of a clear-cut concept of European identity, over the past three decades a growing number of people have felt forced to take action against what they experience as 'the dangers of the European ideal'. To them, that ideal threatens to demolish the nation-state and, worse, its cultural identity. Obviously, we should ask whether that fear and the implied accusations are legitimate?

Analysing the actions of the founders of the 'European dream' after the Second World War, one cannot avoid feeling that their first intention was rebuilding their own states on the ruins of post-war Europe: cooperation, starting in the economically and strategically central sectors of coal and steel, was mainly deemed necessary to create the economic conditions for their own recovery.[12] This recovery had to prevent another devastating war which, like previous wars, would be waged for economic reasons, whatever the ideologies it might represent as well. While, admittedly, the power of 'the Community' has been growing, the Euro-pessimists who continue to defend the nation-state have been very successful in doing so, up to the point that, certainly at the moment, a 'United States of Europe' seems farther away than ever.

Meanwhile, one may well ask what, exactly, is this 'Community', this 'Union'? Is it, after decades of almost unchecked growth, any more than a hugely expensive, to some Kafkaesque, and ultimately self-serving bureaucracy with overpaid officials, a machine that regulates economic, social and political life for the sake of old and new capitalists – the image often presented in the media and adopted by many Europeans? Or should we accept this 'united Europe' and its admittedly sometimes absurd and often costly consequences as the price we should not be afraid to pay if only to prevent the inhumanity that characterized the two materially and morally devastating European wars of the twentieth century occurring again, at least not on the 'Union's' territory? Should we, also, acknowledge that precisely because of the economic policies pursued by 'Brussels', such European countries as Spain and Portugal, which had been virtual dictatorships for several decades during the mid-twentieth century, could become more democratic, open societies in the 1960s and 1970s? For one thing, the post-war, free-trade spirit that followed the protectionist policies of the 1930s did at least help to demolish the tariff walls that shielded these countries economically as well as culturally from the rest of Europe. With greater economic freedom, and, of course, with the massive influx of northern European tourists, came, slowly, an exchange of views, a greater spiritual freedom which woke up the Iberian peoples and considerably contributed to the final demise of these authoritarian regimes. Moreover, there are those who argue that it is precisely the success of western Europe which, in many ways, has been the success of Brussels, of Community politics, which has created a world that became both an economic and political power and, perhaps even more important, a persuasive role-model. As such, it could not but influence the millions who were ruled by the Soviet regime, contributing to its slow erosion. The very symbolic demolition of the wall that separated east and west Germany, and the far more important – and sometimes painful – demolition of the divisions between the two cultures that had been created in Europe from the 1940s onwards, would, I feel, not have happened if Europe's western half had not taken the path it actually did.

Since the early 1970s, another important question has been asked over and over again. Will the states and the peoples of Europe be willing to pay the costs of communal solidarity only if and as long as things are going relatively well, or will they retract the moment their own economy, as a result of this very solidarity, suffers from the lesser performance of other countries within – or aspiring to membership of – that 'Union'? This question obviously relates to another one, since most observers argue that for the time being the efforts at communality have resulted in a Europe of bureaucratic elites rather than a Europe of citizens who feel they are actually part of the project. Indeed, bureaucracy and democracy have not gone hand in hand in the development of European institutions, as shown by the even now restricted role of the (incidentally equally costly) European Parliament at Strasbourg. To counter, if only through a change of practice, the negative feelings this situation causes among many 'Europeans' – resulting in a continued lack of enthusiasm for the European elections – is one of the challenges of the future. All the time, almost inexorably, 'Europe' seems to be going its own way, economically, socially, politically and, in all this, culturally. In the long run, those who show their scepticism of more in-depth integration by defending the sovereignty of states may well be fighting a rearguard action.

Obviously, assuming that no one would argue that a state is an aim in itself, one must ask why people have created states in the first place. Well, during the past centuries its essential *raison d'être* seems to have been to serve the *res publica*, and promote the welfare of the state's subjects. Arguably, to a considerable extent as well as with considerable success, this task has been entrusted to 'the European Union', even if results do not always yet reflect its intentions and promises; and consequences are still difficult to gauge. Moreover, there are those who feel that, precisely by giving up some of their sovereign rights, the states of Europe over the past decades have been able to maintain a far greater measure of actual independence than otherwise would have been possible.[13]

Indeed, we should not construe the nation-state – which, after all, is not a centuries-old but on the contrary a fairly recent construction, a 'created tradition'[14] – as an untouchable ideal, under no condition to be destroyed by 'Brussels'. It is quite interesting to note that in many cases the nation-states of Europe are far less strong than people think; indeed, often a much older notion of a mainly regional cultural identity still seems to hide behind it. Here, too, one might argue that precisely the security the new Europe offers enables states to accept a growing measure of regional independence of a variety of cultures within their national structures. In Germany, the construction of the post-war state has from the beginning acknowledged the importance of regions in the field of culture. In Spain, Catalonia among others offers a fine case of the continuous strength of regional culture, as does Scotland in the UK. Indeed, the results of the 1997 vote demonstrated the latter region's wish to be formally identified as an independent culture and polity, to demolish, at least in part, a state structure erected nearly – or perhaps better: only – 200 years earlier. Often, a notion of a shared past, however revitalized beyond its erstwhile reality or, even, completely invented, appears to be the powerful basis for regional identity; often, too, it is associated with language and, sometimes, religion.[15] Perhaps these older roots have to be cherished, if only because nothing but healthy 'provincialism' can lead to any fruitful 'universalism', at least in a cultural sense.

Undeniably, the actions of those who press the ideal of European unity to its furthest limits appear to be stopped in many states by the as-yet solid walls of these more concrete structures which have, apparently, influenced and even formed man for longer and more radically than any concept of Europe which, despite all its undeniable practical and ideological purposes, is to many no lived reality as yet. Some would say this is so because a politically and culturally convincing definition of the essentials and characteristics of European culture has not been presented, even though the second millennium of what is, by the way, still called the 'Christian era' has now turned into the third.

Others would prefer it if a simple concept of European culture were never introduced at all. After all, such concepts can all too easily be manipulated by politicians who set out to rouse the masses, as, in the past, has been shown by the more extreme efforts to defend national or religious identity based on cultural criteria and characteristics.

From the 1950s onwards, within the context of Europe's search for its own identity, its relationship with America – or rather the United States – became an issue once more. However powerful the voice of the many critics cited above, these had reached intellectual circles only. However, certainly from the 1920s onwards, the popular press had continued to publicize the success story of the new world. The new medium of film, which, in its American form, dominated the European market in the years following the First World War because indigenous production had all but collapsed, only seemed to prove the truth of what the papers proclaimed: in images that 'could not lie', the Hollywood dream factory triumphantly showed a world of desires come true in every field from consumer culture to sexuality.

Subsequently, the undeniably crucial role of the United States in the liberation of the greater part of western Europe from fascist dictatorships had greatly strengthened its popularity with the peoples of Europe. But the ambivalence of the relationship remained.[16] A small group who felt and did not hesitate to proclaim themselves to be a cultural elite continued to warn the public against the danger of moral, cultural decadence in the old world precisely because of the soulless materialism that reached it from the new world, both in the form of consumer goods and in the messages contained in films and, later, television. Yet, for all the patronizing words of their self-appointed cultural leaders, the public at large continued to enjoy what the new world had to offer. Indeed, during the first post-war decade, their very power to consume at all had been made possible by the USA's 1947 'Marshall Plan', a gigantic financial injection with which the US government had helped to restore the European economy, out of a mixture of altruism and of understandable economic and political self-interest, for only a strong western Europe could be both a market for American consumer goods and a bulwark against communism.

In the 1960s and 1970s, as American culture in its commercial manifestations of film, fashion and music definitely conquered the European market, agitation ran high and many people asked for a concise, rhetorically effective concept of Europe to counter the assault of American mass culture and its values, or rather lack thereof. France, in particular, openly fought against these influences. Inevitably, the French, for all their pride in their own national culture, fought this battle under the banner of European values and traditions, claiming they needed everyone's support to uphold European civilization.[17] Yet the campaign was rather surprising. The market that these Euro-defenders wanted to protect, had to a large extent been revived and expanded by the Marshall Plan.

Whatever one's opinions on the merits or demerits of this mostly cultural anti-Americanism, the American influence, economically and, therefore, culturally, seems here to stay. Just as Columbus had portrayed the Indians as the ideal people and in doing so had given his European readers a vision of a physical perfection that resembled God's image of man, so American movies since the 1920s, American cars since the 1930s, American soldiers in the 1940s – captivating European women with their cigarettes and nylons – American advertising since the 1950s, American Barbie dolls since the 1960s, American music since the 1970s, American videos since the 1980s and, of course, American PCs since the 1990s have shown many Europeans a vision of man that is far more forceful than Columbus's description of a physically and morally ideal man and society: 'America' has become a compelling influence on the perception Europeans have both of themselves and of their society. It has resulted in an all-pervading obsession with the human physique which, in the 1980s and 1990s, led to, among other things, an increase in the incidence of anorexia. Since then, it has led to a massive interest in plastic surgery, in a 'total make-over'. Indeed, following the American example, many European TV shows dangerously suggest that such physical changes are not only easy but will totally improve one's life as well as one's position in society.

Beyond the culture of the body, Europe has adopted, and still adopts – though it sometimes also adapts – American food culture and other fashions, indeed everything money can buy. However, it also adopts and adapts American ideas through the visual arts, literature, music, the cinema and television. Thus, it seems that 500 years of communal history have only intensified the Euro-American relationship. Since Columbus, basic elements of culture such as the European diet as well as the rather more complex ways of looking at man and the world have altered. Europe has gone from the potato and cocoa to the hamburger and Coca-Cola; and it may have to rethink itself from being a free agent to, perhaps, one that has to work long hours during the better part of the year to pay for them. In short, ever since the discovery of America, the culture of Europe has shown its presence there. But conversely, what Europe is now, what Europeans are now is, to a large extent, incomprehensible if one does not take into account the economic, political and cultural influence of America, a process of interaction and integration that began in 1492.

A culture of time versus money

Nowadays, an analysis of the manifestations of European culture and its under-lying structures and assumptions no longer has to rely – at least not solely – on the often one-sided individual testimonies that have helped us to reconstruct the more remote past. Though historians will have to continue to painstakingly collect the data about pre-statistical times, advances in the social sciences and their research methods, combined with improved communications and data-collecting and processing systems, has created the possibility of large-scale investigation, producing extensive surveys that cover the practices and ideas of peoples across national or even continental borders. A decided but unavoidable disadvantage is that in the telling of the story that is history, the individual experience now tends to disappear behind anonymous categories, and is often even reduced to sheer numbers.

One of these surveys, the so-called 'European values research', carried out in the decade between 1980 and 1990 in Europe and North America, has parted from the assumption that this Atlantic region does indeed form a cultural continuum. It has contributed fascinating data for the analysis of late twentieth-century culture, even though one must be careful when dealing with the results and interpretations of such very global overviews based on random samples.[18] Some of the material has contributed to the following analysis.

With the advance of the mass market and the ensuing democratization of goods at the end of the nineteenth century, scepticism about the cultural consequences became more marked. Intellectuals noticed that capitalism and democracy together, resulted in both endemic overproduction and the multiplication of occasions for imitation, rather than creating a rational, cultured society based on clear and limited means. They saw the dangers of competition and conformism in the pursuit of luxury by a crowd whose taste was untrained and who would, in the end, swamp 'high' culture.

Yet the solutions that were proposed remained, by and large, the same as those formulated a century earlier, although they were worded differently.[19] In the 1880s, Paul Lafargue denounced the right to work as a false fixation causing a growing dependence on and increasing waste of material things. One of the founding fathers of sociology, Emile Durkheim, asked for some sort of social control of luxury, hoping to find exemplary asceticism in the individual and the genesis of 'social' religion among the population at large.[20]

Yet, by the beginning of the twentieth century, mass-production technology continued to promise and deliver an endless quantity of goods. Average purchasing power rose steeply, first in the United States and then in Europe as well. It was now assumed that economic growth and increased production would result in free time and in a 'mass leisure society'. Debates about the question of how to democratize leisure soon followed, but it was rather the liberal-leftist intellectual elite who worried over the issue than the majority of people themselves.[21] Many well-meant experiments were undertaken, especially in the 1920s and 1930s, by intellectuals, cultural educators and social workers to reintegrate those who were considered socially and culturally lost in urban, anonymous mass-production society; they mostly favoured the ordered free time of cultural and sports clubs. However, most capitalists argued strongly against increased leisure as it limited their access to flexible production, while many workers were more concerned about job and wage security.[22]

By and large, the optimists had the day, those economic and social theorists who peppered their works, however empirically based, with highly moralistic ideas. The French sociologist Eugène Tarde, who published his *The Laws of Imitation* in Paris in 1890, while admitting that mass-goods society arose from the imitation by the urbanized masses of the models of a creative class, yet voiced the hope that, in the end, the trend would reverse itself and a cultured democracy would emerge in which the masses – educated by now under the system of compulsory primary education which had been introduced by most European states – would operate discriminatingly between the poles of consumer goods and spiritual goods. Some decades later, the English economist John Maynard Keynes touchingly assumed that after the satisfaction of absolute needs people would devote their further energies to non-economic purposes and fill their leisure with the 'art of life itself'.[23]

However, the Depression of the 1930s and the Second World War only left most Americans and Europeans with an increased craving for material gratification.[24] When the war had ended, women returned to their homes from the factories and offices, by and large resuming their by now dual traditional role, of home-maker and of decision-maker in the spending of the family income. Ideas about the reduction of work time and leisure planning that were voiced in the immediate post-war period were soon deemed obsolete. Full employment and a vision of unlimited consumption were what most people, both politicians and workers, wished to realize. There was wide-ranging acceptance of the ideals of mass production and high wages.

A manipulated need creation on an unprecedented scale soon followed. Thus, after 1945, a 'consumerist consensus' seemed to be the prevalent attitude.[25] Indeed, consumerism was hailed everywhere. With a rise in the standard of living in accordance with – and matching, market-wise – an increase in production, everyone would be able to aspire to and eventually acquire the lifestyle of the well-to-do middle-income groups. Social classes would disappear as the United States and Europe reached the 'last stage of economic growth' prophesied by the popular economist W.W. Rostow.[26] In Europe, the adoption of what was called 'the American model' did not encounter great opposition. The French politician Jean-Jacques Servan-Schreiber, in his *Le Défi Americain* equated liberty with consumer choice and democracy with mass access to consumer goods.[27]

Intellectuals did ponder over the desirability of this situation, but, mostly, they failed to influence decision making.[28] An economist like J.K. Galbraith might point out the cultural, ecological and social consequences of unrestrained growth, in his famous book *The Affluent Society*,[29] and Raymond Aron voiced his fears in an equally famous study of *Les Desillusions du Progrès* but most westerners – both Americans and Europeans – were more optimistic.

Admittedly, by the late 1950s, first in the USA and later in Europe, people began to express some concern as television began to show its influence. The new medium was soon thoroughly commercialized when advertising began to direct programming. Ever more, leisure became consumption as many people began to spend their free time and their hard-won money in increasingly long hours of shopping, induced therein by merchandisers via television.[30] The half-joking, half-critical expression 'shop 'til you drop' became an adage. Even when not directly sending advertising messages, the home screen still projected lifestyles leading to consumerism through films and the family dramas sponsored by the household detergent industry, the so-called 'soap operas', a genre that continues the highly popular melodramatic theatre so beloved by both the lower-middle classes and the working population during the nineteenth century. In Britain, the percentage of homes provided with a television set rose from zero to 66 per cent between 1955 and 1959, and to 90 per cent by 1969. By that time, people spent about half of their leisure time in front of the screen and have continued to do so ever since.[31]

Though they professed to enable people to pursue their individual life-style, the merchandisers' efforts to manipulate the culture industry resulted in a conformist mass culture, mostly led by the needs they discerned among the middle classes, the 'status seekers' so aptly analysed in Vance Packard's eponymous sociological study of 1959.[32]

Tourism and its cultural connotations provide a fascinating case in point. Travel for pleasure, indicating almost unbounded leisure – albeit legitimized by the consumption of high culture – had been an elite phenomenon until the end of the eighteenth century, culminating in the southbound Grand Tour. In the nineteenth century, increased wealth and new modes of transport made such travel available to the well-to-do bourgeoisie. They were no longer satisfied with a week in the mountains or at the seaside, if only because by then the better-off members of the 'working classes' were going there too. Of course, the middle classes were also eager to ape an aristocratic culture that enhanced status as well as affording an escape from an industrialized, increasingly stress-ridden world. So, they now took a southerly trip as well. Innovative entrepreneurs like the firm of Thomas Cook and Sons or the Belgian *Compagnie Internationale des Wagons Lits* soon realized that there was a new market to open up and manipulate.

However, most people from north-western Europe continued to avoid the summer heat of the Mediterranean, travelling in the relatively mild autumn, winter and early spring periods. Once in southern France or in Italy, they used huge parasols to protect their faces from the sun. Not only did they originate in agricultural societies in which a fair complexion traditionally distinguished the rich landlords from the poor peasants and, consequently, had become a sign of beauty both in women and men, they also wanted to stress their difference from the darker-skinned 'locals' of southern Europe, whose ancient culture they admired but whose contemporary lifestyle they considered much less civilized and progressive than their own democratized, industrial society. However, in the course of the twentieth century, as transport – especially with the coming of the motor car and the aeroplane, as well as increased income – made long-distance travel available to the masses, a tanned face came to denote a holiday in the sun and, hence, became a status indicator. Soon, of course, marketing strategists were exploiting the argument that a suntan equated to health. Such is the strength of cultural stereotypes that even though in the 1980s medical research pointed to the increased danger of skin cancer, even nowadays the majority of European holidaymakers still flock to the world's sunny beaches.

As early as the 1950s, critics began to doubt the potential of such leisure as there was to be a really liberating force in society, fulfilling the individual. It seemed rather to be a simple release from the permanent tensions induced by long hours of wage-earning.

By the late 1960s and the early 1970s, a more decided reversal seemed to set in. Largely, the generation that had experienced the Depression of the 1930s and had lived to work for new prosperity was dead. By now, the greater part of the European population had been reared from childhood in a world of consumerism. Among them, a 'post-materialist' movement was born. Not only did merchandisers realize that not everybody might be willing to share their rose-coloured vision of unlimited consumer demands but the sacred tenet of the full-employment economy also came under attack, implying, at least in (western) Europe, a re-evaluation of the work ethic towards a more flexible use of work and leisure time.

This situation has had various, sometimes contradictory, cultural consequences.[33] The 'children of affluence' began to voice consumer demands, asking for participation. The market quickly realized the potential of the increasing number of young consumers who, structurally, rebelled against the more traditional values of their elders. Moreover, many of the current cultural educators were no longer classically trained humanists with ideas about a 'Hellenist', 'high' culture à la Matthew Arnold or Wilhelm von Humboldt. Rather, they were attuned to all kind of forms of popular, 'low' culture. The very fact that traditional culture had been unable to prevent the horrors of the 1940s had somewhat discredited it. Also, the increased post-war access to education and, consequently, to positions of relative power for large parts of the former 'lower middle' or even 'working' classes – groups not traditionally reared in this culture – altered society's perspective on what culture should prevail.

Meanwhile, intellectuals continued to voice hopes for a society with more free time that would liberate workers from routine and stress, as they had been doing ever since the early 1920s. But their analyses of the present and of the future were – and often are – contradictory and, anyhow, met with great opposition from the circles of economists and political decision-makers who, mostly, continued to advocate the ideal of growth.

Also, with real wages rising, the 'cost' of leisure time rose as well. Workers tended to intensify their consumption of leisure and aided it by time-saving pastimes like camping or gardening, which, however, involve consumer goods which have to be earned: paradoxically, people do long for community and self-expression but goods tend to get in the way of their enjoyment of time and of each other. When questioned, most workers, from the 1960s onwards, have preferred a 40-hour week and early retirement rather than shorter working days,[34] although among the economically more privileged groups the demand for free time is much higher.[35]

In the 1950s and 1960s, with more women entering the workforce, a more equal division of the public and the domestic work sphere between men and women and a redefinition of gender roles seemed possible. Job sharing was advocated as well. Still, it seems illusory to expect radical changes from the realignment of gender. Some theorists and sociopolitical activists have expressed hopes that women, choosing part-time jobs, may effectuate a new balance between work and leisure. However, with the increasing cost of housing, transport and recreation, in dual income families most women follow a largely male career-centred model. Deftly or desperately adjusting their wage and domestic work time, they try to minimize disruptions in the traditional family sphere. On another level, non-commercial leisure seemed to survive – in 1980, some 40 per cent of the British population joined in participatory sports. There was a sharp increase in do-it-yourself activities, while some 80 per cent of the men and 60 per cent of the women belonged to an endless variety of clubs.[36] In France, the same picture emerged, with a sharp increase in cultural activities more narrowly defined like visiting museums and art exhibitions.[37] In the Netherlands, the numbers attending the theatre, concerts of classical music and the opera were increasing as well.[38]

This trend seemed to hold even though economic growth slackened in the 1980s. As had happened in the 1920s and 1930s, the social consequences have been considerable. Once more, there was a confrontation between pressure for further reduction of the working week – which in most European countries had reached 40 hours by 1970 – to *c*.35 hours and prophecies of economic doom as a consequence of it. Indeed, by the 1990s, many employers were still fearing stagnation and increasing competition while a considerable group of economists favoured even raising the 40-hour standard and campaigned for an end to the policies aimed at lowering the compulsory retirement age. This trend seems to continue even today.

Meanwhile, the real danger may well lie elsewhere. From the 1950s onwards, something of a 'welfare state' was realized in many countries of western Europe. With its health benefit schemes and old age pensions, its paid holidays and its largely free education it was and is a monument both to economic prosperity and to the democratically expressed will of civic society not only to root out as much human suffering as possible but also to realize as much equality, at least of chances, as possible.

Yet even before it was fully realized in all the countries of western Europe, by the end of the 1980s this 'welfare state' seemed unable to sustain its high level of publicly fuelled social services. An increasingly consumerist society that sees its material prosperity threatened tries to reduce or even withdraw its support for the governments who have embraced this ideal. With growing unemployment, a possibly fatal gap opens between those who have a job and an income, as well as the position in society that both provide, and those who, though reasonably or even well educated, remain jobless, and whose children may well remain so, too. Research shows that precisely in these groups, where prospects for the future are bleak, educational performance decreases and criminality rises – in a sphere of forced, largely unstructured 'leisure'. This is certainly a major concern for the future, as is a continued, slavish adherence to a work-and-spend ethic which will certainly create even more tensions between the fully employed and the jobless.

So, on the whole, affluence, while greatly increasing the material well-being of the majority of Europeans, does not so far seem to have produced the structural social harmony envisaged by many idealists.

Perhaps the most profound cause of the many predicaments of present-day culture is the continued existence of hierarchy and emulation that makes people seek for 'signs' – whether in the time-leisure or in the money-consumption spheres – to bolster their individual or group confidence, the more so as the security offered by such traditional, primary groups as family and neighbourhood, is fast disappearing. As these signs tend to be the very consumer goods that can be bought only through the triumph of mass production, we now see that time does indeed collapse into money.[39] Economic growth does not liberate free time but rather creates affluence and the incentive to work more and harder. Insofar as it does produce leisure, it results more in private pleasure than in public commitment, especially among the young.

For the majority, free time and spending are happily reconciled both within domestic consumption, largely concentrated in the weekend, and in tourist consumption – the dream of the (summer) holiday. Liberty of choice and democracy of leisure seem intellectual, elitist concepts, only, which definitely do not figure on the agenda of the population at large. Also, non-profit cultural groups have little influence on the use of public space and time. Business and politics mostly control the finance of leisure services, and they tend to be somewhat conservative, channelling 'pleasure' into safe arenas, commodifying free time in such ways that, for many, it has become equivalent to passivity and emptiness.

Utopian schemes to stop what many critics consider cultural and social decline in individuals, groups or society have been presented, mostly calling for a break from unlimited, emulative and manipulated consumption and for the formation of non-political, non-market oriented values. However, even if they are humanist populists, these critical intellectuals have but little power to structurally redirect economic, social and cultural needs and to realize alternative forms of individuality and community both in work and in leisure. The dilemma of time versus money will be with Europe and the entire western world for some time to come.

From 'familyman' to 'salaryman' – from group identity to individual identity?

In Europe, the twentieth century has witnessed the completion of a socio-economic and sociocultural revolution that, especially since the 1950s, has changed its outlook fundamentally.

The first fascinating aspect in which change after the Second World War became manifest was that women 'became visible'.[40] The emancipation movement of the last decades of the nineteenth century, the first so-called 'feminist wave', had brought women the right to enter higher education and, after the First World War, the even more coveted right to vote, which finally made them into citizens. Yet their economic dependency remained appalling. Admittedly, some job sectors had become feminized from the beginning of the century onwards – for instance, secretarial and shop work, and soon such indispensable services as the manually operated telephone exchanges. However, most women who were forced to engage in paid work to enable their families to survive, taking the most menial of jobs, were in grossly underpaid positions. On the other hand, those women who wanted to work were often not allowed to, their sociocultural, bourgeois context practically forbidding them to enter the job market.

After 1945, not only did women from the working classes go out to work in far greater numbers than before, if only to enable their children to have a better education, but educated women from the middle class now entered the labour market too, often not because they wished to add to an already comfortable family budget, but from an urge for freedom and autonomy as well as, of course, equality. Such material changes as the introduction of all kinds of domestic appliances gave them the practical means to do so. Yet far more important was the control that women were gaining over their own lives, starting with the growing use of contraceptives in the face of enormous opposition from such traditional, family-centred cultural institutions as the Churches.

Slowly, women began to present themselves as a culturally and politically conscious group, in a striking revival of feminism. One of the most far-reaching consequences can be seen in the field of family law which, since time immemorial had been very paternalistic, in many European countries was now fundamentally changed for the first time to accommodate such notions as divorce and abortion. Though all over western Europe the Churches fought bitterly to counter this movement, women managed not only to claim but also to win the right to decide over their own lives, even in Italy, in the famous referendums of 1974 and 1981. Admittedly, the rates of divorce and subsequent remarriage are still definitely lower in those European countries that have a Roman Catholic background, and the more compelling moralities that still tend to go with it, than in the non-Catholic ones. Thus, whereas in Britain, almost one in three marriages ends in divorce, the percentage is lower in Belgium, France and the Netherlands, and even more so in Italy and Spain, but even there the rate is growing quickly, shifting towards a Europe-wide pattern. Incidentally, in large parts of the Soviet Union, the participation of women in the labour process since the Second World War had greatly exceeded the rate in the countries of western Europe; also, their independence in family matters had been far greater, with divorce rates consequently much higher.

Inevitably, as the public roles of women unalterably changed all over Europe, so did the 'western family'. Despite regional and temporal variations, over the ages the European family had retained its traditional characteristics of a formal, legal marriage, a distinct patriarchal mentality and a nuclear structure, i.e. that its core was a couple of parents and their children, even though there might be in-living relatives and even though it might function within a larger kin group.

But whereas, from a traditional point of view, the nuclear family may be said to have undergone a severe crisis since the 1950s, new forms of relationships have come to exist alongside it. With the relaxation of sexual rules in the sphere of the traditional, heterosexual family has come an acceptance of various other forms of sexuality hitherto considered deviant. Since the 1960s, both lesbianism and homosexuality have slowly been decriminalized. By the 1990s, same-sex unions have been legalized in a number of European countries, adding as yet non-traditional forms of family living to the spectrum of European society. As child adoption by same-sex couples may become an option in many countries as well, this will only further alter the aspect of 'the European family'. Culturally, this seems, by and large, a middle-class phenomenon, as well as an urban one. Apparently, the process of 'coming out', much discussed in the 1970s and 1980s – and, not incidentally, resulting in a massive, sometimes very creative, artistic output in film, theatre and literature – was easier in the milieu of the relatively free-thinking, higher educated groups who dominate the cities, and in the socially less restrictive atmosphere that characterizes city life. As always in European history, in this as in many other fields, urban milieus have remained the centres of cultural growth.[41]

Quite another development has surfaced in the post-war years as well, becoming more apparent by the 1980s and 1990s. By that time, in many west European countries the number of single-person households had risen to an average of some 20 per cent – with rates peaking in the urban centres. To many, the fact that the overwhelming proportion of these households are formed by single mothers in the lower income bracket is distressing indeed, if only because of the obvious emotional and socio-economic disadvantages this situation creates for future generations.

As many traditional forms of emotional and social allegiance have disappeared, so have, at least superficially, class structures and their distinctions, not only at the bottom of the so-called social pyramid but also at the top. Indeed, the three main, well-defined social classes which had emerged in the nineteenth century – working class, middle class and elite – have been eroded. The admittedly slow improvement in social mobility through improved education as well as the slow rise in average income and the advent of consumer culture with its egalitarian tendencies – the democratization of luxury – have largely demolished socio-cultural barriers and with them the traditional division between 'popular culture' and 'high culture'.[42]

The first major change saw the peasantry as a distinct socio-economic group all but disappear, at least in western Europe, and with it the way of life of the agricultural countryside. Whereas in the 1920s and 1930s farming and fishery still involved 25 per cent of the population in countries such as Britain and Belgium, rising to 50 per cent in, for example, Portugal and Spain, by the 1960s the percentage had fallen below 15 per cent in the latter, and even below 10 per cent in the former countries.[43] Consequently, most people born after the Second World War hardly know what a farm looks like. And yet these countries, which all belong to the group of developed industrial nations, are among the major producers of agricultural goods for the world market, both through an enormous increase in capital-intensive productivity per agriculturist and, in recent years, through the successes of agricultural chemistry, selective breeding and biotechnology, which shows the fundamental influence of science on even the most basic aspects of daily life.

A second major change was the disappearance, since the 1950s, of a distinct, single working class with an equally distinct consciousness and culture, which had been growing since the end of the nineteenth century.[44] Its way of life – the lack of mobility, the segregation in working-class neighbourhoods with little private space, resulting in a mainly public-centred, group-experienced culture of pubs and clubs and in strong organizations with a socialist or otherwise radical political orientation – has been utterly transformed by the social and economic developments that have taken place since the Second World War, specifically by two decades of almost full employment, the coming-of-age of consumer society and the democratization of education.

Yet it is precisely this group, not yet entirely liberated from its erstwhile restrictions, that has been hit hardest by the unemployment which, since the late 1970s, has been almost endemic in Europe, partly in consequence of the high cost of labour in the industrialized countries, and compounded by the exodus of many industries to low-wage countries in Asia and Africa. Indeed, this situation has resulted in a veritable erosion of the industrial workforce, both numerically and culturally.[45] Inevitably, among this group, the problems caused by the new phenomenon of mass immigration – unknown to western Europe for almost 1,500 years – became most painfully manifest. From the 1960s onwards, many indigenous Europeans felt threatened by the workers imported from Turkey and Maghrebine North Africa to enable the European economy to realize its dreams of consumption and social welfare. Soon, there was competion within the same labour market, especially since the immigrant workers started bringing their families, and inevitably there was a clash of cultures as well.

Whereas a small portion of the working class, the skilled, professional part, has entered the middle class, quite often altering its political allegiance accordingly and even assuming many of the bourgeoisie's largely conservative cultural and political values, the far larger part is increasingly condemned to a life on public welfare which many of their fellows, including those who used to belong to the same group, tend to think of as expensive and, perhaps, over-generous since the economy that once sustained it seems to be doing decidedly less well.

While the role of the peasantry and an unskilled urban working class has declined drastically, both the number and the importance of jobs demanding secondary or even higher education has increased, both in industry and in the tertiary sector. Especially after the Second World War, industrial and government planners realized that economic reconstruction and the creation of a modern society required a great number of skilled workers and administrators. Since then, helped by a state providing modest student aid, many families – of public officials, who had a long tradition in trying to take care of their offspring's future through good education, but now also of white-collar employees, small business people and even skilled workers – decided it was worth spending part of the slowly increasing family budget on a longer educational career and, hence, better job prospects for their children.

Consequently, in most European countries university students amount to between 1.5 and 2.5 per cent of the entire population. Secondary and even tertiary education is now deemed an inalienable right of youth. However, with on the one hand expenditure in this field growing, and on the other hand unemployment seemingly inescapable for a structural percentage of the population,[46] even among the better-educated groups, it is uncertain whether this right can be upheld to the level of the 1970s and 1980s. Perhaps the transformation of a 'providential state' to an 'insurance society' will increase the gap between rich and poor, and the increasing cost of education will only intensify the process.[47]

Some would say that all these developments and changes affect the visible, the external appearances of culture more than the remaining traces of, especially, elite power structures and the accompanying mentality, although this varies from country to country. Whereas, for example, Britain is still a distinctly class-structured society, where both differences in income and status are extremely visible, the Scandinavian countries and the Netherlands, to name but a few, are far less so. However, all over Europe, incomes still vary considerably and the various professions, obviously, carry quite different status connotations, partly depending on the amount of education needed to enter them. Also, the codes of behaviour associated with cultural sub-groups continue to create dividing lines and distinctions. If only, therefore, because patterns of spending are anything but uniform and, hence, material consumption both in terms of quantity and quality is still driven by emulation, difference is still used to shape identity, the meaning or symbolic value of things and action is still used to establish or underline power.[48]

Nevertheless, one may argue that, to a large extent, European society has become one big middle class, not only in its material manifestations but also in sharing the same values and expectations, which can be realized by all those who belong to the species of the 'salaryman'.[49]

Dimensions of identity – culture as communication: towards an 'anonymous mass culture'?

In 1951, the German-Italian scholar Romano Guardini published his *Das Ende der Neuzeit* (The End of the Modern Era), in which he tried to analyse Europe's history in order, also, to offer a prognosis of its future.[50]

One of his most interesting observations concerned the growing discrepancy between the cultural ideal of the free, autonomous person – an ideal dear to European intellectuals through the ages, but especially cherished since men like Von Humboldt and Arnold had incorporated it into their educational philosophies and systems – and a culture of the masses which, according to Guardini, now was both imminent and inevitable.

In a society characterized by organizational planning in the service of industry and technology, man is 'massified', not least because, through the mass media and mass consumption, norms and values are becoming massified as well. And yet this does not necessarily imply that man should become degraded to a mere 'homo sociologicus', a bearer of functions. The very possibilities of mass culture could and should be used to make man more free, to save the essence of European civilization. Yet, to judge the culture that has emerged since the 1950s dispassionately, one will have to accept that conformity is one of its main characteristics. Moreover, schools and the media are its centralizing agencies.[51] Even while admitting that, however, superficially, many group cultures and subcultures have displayed their 'individualistic' manifestations, while many cultural critics feel that anonymity and mass culture are the two basic characteristics of the present. Many, also, interpret these characteristics as negative and, hence, feel the present is a period of decline. Obviously, such a view will always prevail among those who fail to see that culture is, intrinsically, a system that changes, not only in its outward appearances but also, though more slowly, in the pattern of its norms and values. The sociological survey cited above outlines some of these changes.

In the second half of the twentieth century, individualization, in the sense of both enlarged 'freedom' of choice in all areas of life and of an appreciation which highlights the individual as the norm for all action, appears to be a characteristic of culture in all European countries.

Religiosity, certainly in the sense of Church-bound orthodoxy, is declining everywhere and secularization is advancing. With the loosening of group allegiances and the increased belief in the power of the sciences, both the intrinsic and the social construction of formal religiosity have been undermined. In the past, belonging to a church and adhering to religious traditions were often imposed within and through social groups and the pressure they exerted upon the individual. With the decline of these structures, institutionalized religion is no longer a central force in any of the countries researched, and is certainly no longer a national characteristic. Indeed, in the everyday life of many Europeans the moral guidance offered – imposed – by the Churches is only minimally accepted. Yet it has also been established that many Europeans, though they may not turn to any transcendental power in those situations in which the sciences provide many, if certainly not all, the solutions, still say they rely on 'God' or on a somewhat less defined 'higher power' to give them spiritual guidance.[52]

To cite but a few of the interesting phenomena of the past decades, one might refer to the growing number of people who once more travel along the pilgrim road to Santiago. They may not go as penitents, or to acquire as many indulgences as possible to secure a better place in heaven, but they still seem to be doing it both from a wish to communicate with Europe's past and its cultural remains as from the need to find themselves in the process. Also, the increasing interaction between the various world religions, more specifically between Christianity and Buddhism, is a very interesting development. Though one might point out that most of the insights people try to find in Vedic texts or in Zen could as easily be culled from the Christian mystical tradition – most texts written by such authors as Master Eckhart, St Teresa of Avila and St John of the Cross, to name but a few, offering insights specifically stressing the individual's relationship to the divine or the cosmos – the contacts between Europe and Asia cannot but help to create greater mutual understanding. Yet, to avoid presenting a distorted image, one must also admit that such phenomena are confined to the well educated. Moreover, this interest in non-European cultures is often highly superficial and self-indulgent: only seldom does the desire for 'enlightenment' from non-European sources go hand in hand with respect for the different dynamics of these cultures and their necessarily different sociopolitical value systems.

Whether or not one defines tolerance as an aspect of morality, one cannot argue that in this field Europe is showing a decline in its erstwhile pretensions and practice. Despite the problems surrounding the economic and cultural acceptance of post-war immigrants, in many respects greater tolerance, though interpreted by pessimists as mere social and moral indifference, is still growing. Indeed, widespread acceptance of the singularities of one's fellow countrymen is unmistakable, although it varies as to the issues at hand and in relation to the ethno-cultural background of those concerned and the socio-economic position of those whose tolerance is tested.

If, however, traditional religious and moral norms are no longer central to European identity,[53] have other forms assumed that function? When asked about their sense of national pride, more than three-quarters of the respondents declared they did indeed feel such a sentiment, although not a single European country equalled the high percentage of national pride found in the United States. The 'fear' of an increasingly united Europe varied from nation to nation, although the number rarely exceeded 30 per cent. However, it is perhaps more significant that the most important dimension of identity that was named was neither Europe nor the nation but rather a person's own city or region. Maybe the English writer G.K. Chesterton was right when he wrote: 'For anything to be real it must be local?'

Hence, one would assume that the prevailing outlook of most Europeans would be anything but global. Apparently, however, the two can exist together. Indeed, most manifestations of European culture in the twenty-first century are closely, if not intrinsically related to the growth and the growing power of the mass communications media that operate worldwide. These are definitely forces of cultural globalization, not perhaps idealistically so but certainly because their economic basis demands it.[54]

During the last decades of the twentieth century, there was a tendency to describe and interpret European culture from the 1970s onwards as 'post-modern'. Now, there is a definite lack of conceptual resources behind the term, which makes it unfit to serve as an instrument for historical analysis. However, one may define the prevailing outlook on the world as 'post-modern' if it means characterizing contemporary culture as essentially eclectic, in the sense that it does not seem to be ruled by one given set of values, by one tradition, whether it be that of Christianity, of secularized Humanism, of the Enlightenment or even of 'modernity'. It seems that the change in communications and information culture – the two, while not the same, do overlap to a considerable extent – may be at the root of this situation. Within the ever more complex communications landscape, several trends can be discerned, which are shaping culture in ways unknown in previous centuries.

With the coming, first, of cinema, then of television and video, and also of computerized services, more specifically the personal computer and the internet, with their 'virtual spaces, real histories and living bodies',[55] everyone who has access to these media can delve into the gigantic store of information and pleasure they provide. But control over this store reposes less and less with those groups in society who used to be the – partly self-appointed – guardians and distributors of culture: the State, the Church, the university, etc, and the elites who were the often self-serving inhabitants of these cultural strongholds until the end of the nineteenth century. More and more, control over information, knowledge, culture and the communications media which are instrumental in spreading it is a commercial affair, value-neutral in the sense that it is mainly or even only ruled by the laws of profit and loss, although these, of course, represent a system of values in themselves, reflecting a capitalist, consumerist society.

It is too early, yet, to predict whether a situation wherein these media are increasingly available to most Europeans, regardless of their economic and educational background, will result in a democratization of information in the same way that the Industrial Revolution resulted in a democratization of luxury. The same holds for the question of whether the quality, the content of communication itself is really being improved by this situation.

Thus, the linking of the internet to television will undoubtedly greatly alter, and perhaps even further democratize information.[56] However, some critics say that this will not only spell the end of the 'book' as we have known it since the beginning of scripture on clay tablets or palm leaves, but will also fragmentize knowledge. Others argue that the seemingly free, global exchange of information will only hide a continuing, age-old localism or regionalism. Yet others, while admitting that such a phenomenon as e-mail has greatly facilitated all worldwide contact – not only in commerce but also in entertainment and 'infotainment', by creating groups of people sharing the same interests – have noted that it reduces face-to-face communication. For example, even in the work-place, its too immediate and imperative *modus operandi* tends to increase unwanted individuality while decreasing much-needed cooperation.

Both in the communications media and increasingly in the information media as well, there are a number of big, semi-industrial, often multinational companies providing most of the popular fare, a development that really started in cinema after the Second World War. However, more than the cinema, television and, linked to it, the video screen, has come to dominate European daily life. Judging by the amount of hours a day people in all sociocultural classes and age groups spend watching television and the screen of their 'personal computer' – another indication of increasing individuality – it is now the major cultural factor. Also, television and, indeed, cinema in general show a clear shift from the written word to the visual image and this in turn tends to rely more and more on the message of sound, which sets the mood and marks emotions.

This development may well be one of the causes negatively affecting the literacy rate in Europe. Once the world's foremost literate culture, many European countries now face the fact that the amount of people who are functionally illiterate – as well as, often, innumerate – is increasing; they may well have been taught the three Rs at school, but their mostly 'visual' daily life does not force them to actually practise what they learned. While this is a culturally dramatic change for the worse, it also has consequences for the proper functioning of society and, specifically, the economy. For there, almost paradoxically, the importance of the written word is growing: even those with little formal schooling now need to be able to read and, even more important, to write correctly, precisely because our (economic) life increasingly demands the ability to concisely and unambiguously communicate through e-mail. Also, of course, more than ever before people's lives are being dictated by the paperwork produced and demanded by state and private bureaucracy. Already, all over the western world there are signs that this is going to be one of the future's graver problems.[57]

Since the Second World War, a kind of television largely if not only like that produced in the United States has come to dominate visual culture in Europe and, increasingly, in Africa and Asia as well. Both for financial reasons and because of the west's leadership in consumer and, hence, behavioural fashion, this will greatly reinforce a tendency towards global uniformity.

However, the multiplication of TV channels and the widespread use of home videos from the early 1980s onwards may have opened up the possibility for greater public choice, and for independent, small companies to survive on productions not aiming at the whole market, but at segments of it. This is of potentially great value to any society that wants to retain some pluriformity and, equally important, wants to nourish its multiculturalism. Most societies in western Europe will need to do this somehow.[58] Many cultural critics have feared that all programmes, whether in the audio-visual media or in the computer landscape, will increasingly tend towards a dulling sameness, robbing Europeans of their freedom to choose, of the possibility of retaining their own, regional culture. This does not seem to have happened yet, though, admittedly, mainstream visual culture does indeed tend towards the uniform, unavoidably so in view of the market position of television. This was accentuated as the home screen, even more than the cinema, entered the economically fruitful but for a diversified culture a less interesting relationship between the various agencies that determine the world distribution of images, such as the fashion industry and the pop music business. The latter, with the rise of the video clip, once more stresses the centrality of the eye in western culture.[59]

Connected with it, at least in mainstream television, is the importance of the instant recognizability factor. In a complex interplay between the desires of the audiences and the wishes of producers and their financial backers, many programmes have come to depend on the routines of meaning they conform to in the appreciation of the viewers. The latter want to be able to recognize types of programmes within seconds of selecting them, as they have developed a need to link broadcast TV to their fragmented daily routines. This has resulted in the phenomenon known as 'zapping' or 'channel hopping', practised by the majority of the audience, which is increasingly made up of young children and adolescents. Moreover, even though cinematographic or even television melodrama still tends to conform to older forms of representation, these genres, too, are being influenced by the fragmentized and stereotyped structure of most television.[60]

By reason of its near-universal availability, television has become a stubborn sociocultural medium. It mostly takes ideas that already have current value and thus more easily regulates the discourse of large groups or even of an entire national society. The images projected by one of the new media's most maligned but also most powerful expressions, i.e. the soap opera, provide the attentive observer with an interesting mirror of the values it presupposes in and projects on its public. Relationships are, indeed, central to the genre, but they are constantly changing relationships, reflecting the tension between the almost unlimited autonomy of individual desire and the need for some kind of emotional stability. On yet closer inspection, the genre shows itself to be morally ambiguous, with a subversive potential within the overall framework of middle-class cultural ideals that television in general mediates.[61] In representing general human problems as domestic, personal crises and, moreover, in showing the enigmas of life without offering permanent solutions, the soap has a certain ideological neutrality which allows a broad audience to participate and, consequently, view their own lives in such terms. Indeed, the very structure of the soap allows for an adaptability by which new ideologies and moral positions can constantly be woven into new episodes or characters. Far from being restricted to only an adult, female, home-bound, marginally educated audience – which has long been its negative image in intellectual circles – the genre's influence is increasing for it now attracts adolescents and adults of both sexes, across a broad socio-economic and cultural spectrum.

Though the visual mass media have become essential institutions in European culture, the question of whether their introduction can be regarded as another cultural revolution in the positive sense is hotly debated. Undeniably, however, they have contributed greatly to some of the major changes in twentieth-century European culture. Among the most important surely is the way they have accelerated and intensified the change from a culture dominated for thousands of years by the wishes of the adult, middle-aged group to a culture dominated by youth.[62]

In the twentieth century, in the countries of the west the average maximum human height, as well as the onset of puberty was reached at an earlier age than ever before.[63] The most obvious cause is, of course, increased prosperity and, with it – at least for some social groups – better diet. However, it has even been suggested that structural exposure to television radiation may also be responsible for a change in western hormones. At the same time, prolonged education has prolonged the period of puberty, resulting in a distinct new age-band which, with the baby boom of the post-war period, has become very large indeed. As adolescents have been inclined to do for as long as we know, so the post-war youth, too, defined themselves in opposition to their elders. With the increasing prosperity realized by their parents, as well as by those who entered the job market immediately after the age of compulsory education, 'the youth market' became an economic factor to be reckoned with, representing massive purchasing power. For example, in 1990, western Europe, with less than 5 per cent of the world population, accounted for *c*.35 per cent of the world market of personal products such as cosmetics.[64] Much of it was bought by young people.

As youth became such an important, even dominant, economic force, the images used to seduce it to buy and consume have become younger as well. Meanwhile, over the past two decades, the age of first sexual intercourse has dropped considerably. Obviously, this does not automatically result in marriage at a rather earlier age than was customary. Yet, it has contributed to a general tendency to view youth not as a transitional stage towards a much desired, independent adulthood, but rather as the most interesting phase of life *par excellence*. The adolescents of the 1960s, who have become the still youngish parents and, sometimes, even grandparents of the 1990s, are caught up in this trend, feeling they should live and look young as well.

As a result of these two trends, youth culture now tends to include both a group which, in former times, would have considered itself middle-aged, accepting the cultural expressions that went with it, and a group that, a generation ago, would have been defined as old. Now, many who are in their forties or even early fifties still call themselves young, and try to act accordingly, thus intensifying the hold of youth culture and the youth economy over culture in general while at the same time imbuing it with undeniable middle-class elements.

The most obvious characteristic of the youth culture that emerged in the second half of the twentieth century is its internationalism – at least in the field of material culture. It began with the enormous influence of the American film industry on European culture from the early decades of the century onwards. It was an influence that extended to such material aspects as hairstyles, clothes and interior decoration, but also, along with the growing force of advertising in the consumer society, to the physical appearance of men and, even more visibly, of women. The broad-shouldered, slim-hipped male and the round-hipped, full-bosomed or, in a later period, almost anorexic female became standard models both for American and European adolescents.

The record industry has become another vector of the cultural hegemony of the United States or, to be more precise, of the Anglo-Saxon world, for we should, of course, recall the great importance of The Beatles and other British rock bands or pop groups both in the development of new forms of music and for the music industry. Since the 1960s, its reliance on the purchasing power of youth has been almost all-inclusive – some 75 per cent of its output was and still is sold to adolescents.[65]

The world of popular music provides one more clue to contemporary youth culture. The disco dancing of the 1960s and 1970s, and the 'house music' of the 1980s and 1990s are the heirs of a long and exciting tradition of popular music, on which especially the Afro-American element introduced into Europe from the United States from the 1930s onwards has had an enormous impact. Indeed, both in the USA and in Europe, jazz and blues have very much become part of establishment popular music – to create what may sound like a contradiction.

The hours per week spent dancing by adolescents and adults up to the age of 40 represent various aspects of contemporary culture. Of course, certainly since the Renaissance, dancing had come to signify social order and patterned, ritualistic existence. But nowadays, increased leisure among a variety of social and age groups is at the basis of the contemporary nightclub existence. Watching and being watched, moving in – from the crowd onto the floor, individually, as a couple or in a small group – and moving out again, the dancers represent a microcosm of their society. There is participation and sharing, there is peer group cohesion, but there is also a strong sense of individual creativity. There is no greater contrast than with the ball scenes that so tellingly symbolized the social structure of the bourgeois world of the nineteenth and early twentieth century, where the elderly, sitting sedately along the walls, watched their off-spring amuse themselves, meanwhile closely controlling the proper behaviour of the couples or prospective couples who whirled around the room. Such a scene was nowhere better depicted than in the evocative pages devoted to an aristocratic ball in early nineteenth-century Palermo, in Giuseppe Tomasi di Lampedusa's *Il Gattopardo* (The Leopard) (1958), one of the most brilliant novels ever written in Italy, and filmed in 1963 by one of Italy's foremost cinematographers, Luchino Visconti (1906–76); he rightly extended the ball scene far beyond the scope of the book, to make it the symbol of a vanishing society.

The new fashion for dancing, which was visualized in such 1970s films as *Saturday Night Fever*, also provides western youth with a culturally acceptable form of more openly exhibiting erotic and sexual feelings, based on a strong rhythm that pervades body and mind. Indeed, it reminds one of Igor Stravinsky's (1882–1971) famous ballet of the early twentieth century, *Le Sacre du Printemps* (The Rite of Spring) (1913), in which he broke the code of polite culture with its harmless drawing room music, by evoking an image of a primitive Asian tribe sexually celebrating the rebirth of nature.[66] The ballet, choreographed by the famous dancer Vaslav Nijinsky (1890–1950), sent shock-waves throughout Europe, creating an uproar among an audience who were not yet accustomed to seeking this part of human culture openly exposed. The parents of the children of the post-war period were equally shocked when their offspring first started to exhibit themselves and their feelings this way.

From a wider perspective, the so-called popular music enjoyed, in all its variety, by millions all over Europe and, indeed, the world, presents an illumi-nating view of contemporary culture as well. Apart from its musically creative aspect, fed by an eclecticism that is both engaging and commercially profitable, the texts of pop songs show the great variety of feelings of adolescents and adults alike. They voice both the more negative, sometimes self-destructive emotions that people have – whether as a result of the problems peculiar to their age group or, more often, as an expression of the lack of ideals that structure their lives – and the more positive, that give a clue to the yearning for emotionally satisfactory relationships and for some spiritual values to give guidance in everyday life.

EUROPE SINCE THE 1960S: POPULAR MUSIC – HIGH CULTURE?

Seen in retrospect, the adverse reaction of many adults of the 1950s and 1960s to the popular music of such groups as The Beatles seems surprising. Judging by the texts of many of their songs, their message was anything but negative or even critical. They mainly mused on the age-old theme that has characterized European popular and, indeed, classical songs for centuries: love, mostly un-requited love. Therefore, it must have been the changed context that brought about the often condemnatory response: the growing self-awareness of the young, lounging on street corners, riding their motor bikes, dressing in a defiantly different way – yet adhering strongly to new group codes – and dancing, obscenely, as their elders lamented, to the aggressive rhythm of rock 'n' roll.

At the end of the 1960s, and in the course of the following decade, a rather more markedly critical attitude transpires in the lyrics of many popular songs, a certain disenchantment with the political tensions that threatened to disrupt the western world, as well as with the emptiness of consumer society. Punk music, developing in the 1970s, was clearly politically engaged, and critical of social and economic conditions as, for example, shown in the lyrics of the Sex Pistols.

For a group like Fischer Z, the world they explored in songs like *Multinationals Bite* and *Wristcutter's Lullaby* was grim indeed. They specifically targeted the inhumanity of the division between eastern and western Europe, and the threat it posed. On a record they made in 1980, they included the song *Cruise Missiles*:

> We share a common destination,
> Each person has their time to die.
> But men are speeding up our journey,
> By seeing what they can destroy with their
> Cruise missiles (We're near those)
> Cruise missiles (We're looking for those)
> Cruise missiles (They're not five years away)

and in *Berlin* they told their audience:

> Those sore red eyes explore the room again.
> The signed pictures of film stars who stayed here in eras that knew of no wall.
> Berlin . . . Berlin . . . Berlin . . . Berlin
> Part of the old world lives on this island in Germany
> And still out there through the window at six in the morning. The essence
>   survives.
> Berlin . . . Berlin . . . Berlin . . . Berlin

Incidentally, Berlin was, indeed, something of an icon in 1970s and 1980s European popular culture – as shown in the work of song writers and singers like Lou Reed and David Bowie[67] – if only because people romanticized the undeniable musical and sexual freedom of the Berlin of the 1920s and 1930s, which had become a cultural magnet to the young and daring – or desperate – from all over Europe.

In the 1980s, the musical landscape showed an ever greater variety, with 'punk' giving way to 'funk', 'new wave' and 'heavy metal', representing not only the eclecticism of the 'post-modern' day but also a growing wariness in matters political and social, as well as a growing explicitness in matters erotic and sexual, as represented in the high-selling hits of such megastars as Prince and Madonna, who reinforced their songs with elaborate videos feeding on a wide variety of images, some of them overtly harking back to the Christian tradition.

The group Iron Maiden sang a song called *Public Enema Number One* that told its audience about the normlessness of the streets, the corruption of politicians served by a press that looks only for the sensational, and all the while the earth is dying:

When it all comes down the line / And the lines they turn to greed
And you race off with you tyres screaming / Rolling Thunder
And the people choke with poison / Children cry in fear
But you've got your fast bullet / One way ticket outta here.

[*Chorus*: Fall on your knees today / And pray the world will mend its ways get to your feet again / refugees from the heartbreak and the pain]

In the cities in the streets / there's a tension you can feel / Breaking strain is fast approaching / Guns and Riots / Politicians gamble and lie to save their skins
And the Press get fed the scapegoats / Public Enema number one.

[*Chorus*]

A million network slaves / in an advertising new age
I don't need a crystal ball to sell ya / Your children have more brains
Than your drug infested remains / California dreaming as the Earth dies screaming.

Yet in the later 1980s, the singer Sting voiced both a complete distrust in the 'lessons of the past' and a hope for the ultimate victory of humane reason in a song titled *History will Teach us Nothing*:

If we seek solace in the prisons of the distant past
Security in human systems we're told will always last
Emotions are the sail and blind faith is the mast.
Without the breath of real freedom we're getting nowhere fast.
If God is death and the actor plans his part
His words of fear will find their way to a place in your heart.

Without the voice of reason every faith is its own curse. Without freedom from
   the past things will only get worse.
Sooner or later, just like the world's first day
Sooner or later, we learn to throw the past away
History will teach us nothing. Our written history is a catalogue of crime.
The sordid and the powerful, the architects of time,
The mother of invention, oppression of the mild,
The constant fear of scarcity, aggression as its child.
Sooner or later convince an enemy, convince him that he's wrong.
To win a bloodless battle where victory is long.
A simple act of faith in reason over might.
To blow up his children will only prove him right.
History will teach us nothing.
Sooner or later, just like the world's first day
Sooner or later, we learn to throw the past away
History will teach us nothing,
Know your human rights,
Be what you come here for.

In the 1990s, serious popular music – which, it should be stressed here, is not
at all the same as run-of-the-mill commercial music – seems to have experienced
so much fragmentation that it no longer presented the unified voice of
European, or western youth. There were no dominant themes though, perhaps,
some would argue that the disillusionment that, in the 1980s, was often
mitigated by a romantic vision of the world as it yet could be, now stood out
somewhat more starkly.

It has been argued that the cinema, television and popular music all highlight
another aspect of contemporary culture, its 'plebeian' characteristic, a not
altogether felicitous term. Admittedly, instead of projecting bourgeois or even
elitist, aristocratic lifestyles, norms and values, as had been the case in many
forms of popular culture during the preceding centuries, since the turn of the
nineteenth to the twentieth century, these forms of communication began to
show a tendency in which influences generated by and reflecting the lifestyles
of the former working class or even the proletariat moved systematically up the
social ladder, while, at the same time, many of the outward manifestations
formerly associated with upper-class lifestyles were accepted by ever greater
groups. It is this material eclecticism, in the body cult, dress habits, dietary habits,
interior decoration, music and entertainment, but also in other such areas
as sexual mores and language codes, and so on, that increasingly creates a mass
culture which is, perhaps, better termed a new 'middle-class' culture that actually
combines 'high' and 'low' in a way that Europe never has experienced before.
At the same time, acknowledging that there is no such thing as absolutely
individual choice, one may argue that all the ensuing manifestations of at least

apparent 'individual choice' are, of course, made possible by a spectacular rise in the average levels of prosperity experienced in most European countries from the 1960s onwards.

Despite the strict codes imposed upon it by a prudish, self-censuring and censured Hollywood from the 1930s to the 1960s and by only slightly less restrictive European censorship bureaus, the cinema and, to a lesser extent, television began to openly show various aspects of sexuality which, in earlier times, could only be seen on the stage in vaudeville theatres and cabarets – that is to say in the milieus shunned by the bourgeoisie as decadent or immoral, though, of course, the young, the consciously deviant and the outcasts always sought out this culture, helping to perpetuate it and introducing it, piecemeal, into the very society that rejected it.

One might even suggest that the visual media, precisely in exploring the limits of acceptability and showing the results of new customs and mores in the field of sexuality, have contributed to behavioural changes all over the world – as shown, for example, in the popularity of the so-called French kiss which, while still repellent to some other cultures of this world, has captivated the west.

Meanwhile, music not only introduced many elements from minority cultural traditions and from the social ghettos, it also used a verbal language that to older generations, with a background in bourgeois culture, was shocking if not obscene. Indeed, pessimists claim that the influence of the media both on language and, worse, on the behaviour and mentality especially of children, is pernicious, pleading for (self-)censorship, both of the unexpunged showing of increased violence and the commodification of sexuality, as well as what many parents still think of as 'strong' language. Yet, the resulting fierce debates have not noticeably altered the products of this commercial communication culture.

In the field of clothes fashion, one example exemplifies the 'plebeian' development in its entirety. It is, of course, the introduction of blue denim jeans in Europe and, indeed, all over the world, where they are now worn by the 'young' up until the age of 50, as well as, indicating the growing equality between the sexes, by girls and women. Moreover, despite the distinctly working-class origin of denim jeans, they have been adopted by the middle and what remains of the upper classes as well. Another development, perhaps even more interesting, has occurred in home furnishing. There, the IKEA brand, devised by the Swede Ingvar Kamprad in the 1950s to sell his flat-packed furniture through his mail-order firm, has conquered both Europe and the other worlds. His vision was to combine the minimalist aesthetic of modernist furniture – a 1930s concept of, mainly, intellectual designers who wanted to un-clutter the homes both of the middle and the working classes – with affordable prices. He turned his ideal into a philosophy which, he claims, will alter the life 'of The Many', as his slogan goes, since buying IKEA will positively affect people's well-being, create harmony in their house and in their soul. Yet, however laudable his ideas, one consequence is that, with the enormous success of the brand in the 1980s and 1990s and into the current century, all over Europe millions of interiors have become far more uniform than they ever were. A third, potentially far more dangerous, development is occurring in Europe's food culture. With, among other things, more women working and with television taking up an increasing amount of people's non-working time, the traditional family meal is slowly disappearing. In its place has come the culture of fast food – whether it is the hamburger-and-pizza variety introduced from the USA or the fish-and-chips tradition of Britain, both, incidentally, very much part of a plebeian culture. In consequence, all over Europe, meals tend to be less healthy – among other things fast food is cheaper as well as taking less time to prepare than a properly cooked dish. It now appears that this has enormous consequences for public health. Indeed, obesity is becoming one of the major health risks in European society in the twenty-first century. Inevitably, it also burdens the already overstretched budgets that most European countries have to set aside for medical care.

Another form of twenty-first-century culture that reveals many aspects of contemporary society is the role of sports and, more specifically, the function of football. Football, too, is an example of the demotic character of modern culture, having evolved from a decidedly lower-class status at the beginning of the century to the position of the number one popular sport which has also become a huge industry. For though it is not, perhaps, among the most popular active pastimes, television has brought it to every living room.[68] Part of this popularity can be explained from the fact that in most European countries it has become a symbol first of lower class, and also local group identity and then, through the internationalization of sports, of national identity. The victory of one national team over another is celebrated with an intensity generated by few other national events, what with the anonymity of elected heads of state and the increasingly limited emotional appeal of the hereditary dynasts. Indeed, both the former and the latter, like their predecessors in earlier times, realize the importance of being seen when their subjects, now no longer knights jousting, participate in what is still a mock battle, like the tournaments of old. Unhappily, football matches have tended to end in destruction and physical violence as well, even among those for whom the outcome is victorious. They seem to provide an outlet for emotions that state and society have suppressed for the sake of social order. It reminds us of the fact that celebrations and violence have always gone together, and that, according to some cultural theorists, this is the price we pay for no longer having blood feuds and wars.[69] However, the very case of football excesses confronts European society with an expression of individuality that it will probably not permit itself to tolerate.

The moral individualism that, within an at least materially uniform culture, permeates contemporary Europe and, indeed, the western and westernized world, can be interpreted either as the triumph of the individual over society's strictures or the uprooting of human beings from the cohesion provided by social structures. If one assumes that the seemingly unlimited right to choose is a basic constituent of human freedom as it has come to be understood in the west during the nineteenth and twentieth centuries, one cannot in earnest judge the 'new' culture as intrinsically reprehensible. One can only hope that each individual will make good use of this freedom. Europeans, who pride themselves on some of the most daring experiments in freedom, and have found mythical expressions for them in the figures of Prometheus, Icarus and Faust, should realize that real freedom will exist only in the acceptance of a system that will limit the individual's wish to express himself in order to guarantee the essence of that individualism.

Specifically, democracy should ultimately not be defined as unlimited individual rights, but rather reflexive rights, incorporating an element of responsibility. Indeed, the prevalent liberalism combined with socialism that seems to characterize most western societies is plagued by contradiction and paradox. For the liberal quest is an essentially unsolvable but entirely necessary and therefore continuous struggle to construct a rational political order under the rule of law, while respecting the ideal prospect of man's 'natural' individuality and equality, in face of the fact that nature continues to produce inequalities.[70] The major question that now has to be answered is, of course, what will be the results of man's efforts to reduce or even end these inequalities, in providing prosperity – a consumerist life? – for each individual through the continued exploitation of the earth and in making all individuals equal to the extent that even genetic differences are eliminated. Obviously, it is a question that cannot be answered in and by Europe alone.

Epilogue

Europe – a present with a future

Es irrt der Mensch, so lang er strebt.

Man errs as long as he strives.

God, in the Prologue to Goethe's Faust I[1]

In the prologue, I compared this book to an extended walking tour, through space and time – through the geographical part of Eurasia commonly called Europe and through the thousands of years during which it has gained recognizable traits. Obviously, I did not intend it to be an aimless walk; rather, I set out with a number of questions in mind that subsequently guided me as I went along. Having arrived at the end of my journey, I would like to think I have reached a new vantage point. Standing here, now, and looking back, it seems that this journey through the past has resulted in questions for the present, and thus for the future. The English historian Robin Collingwood, being asked what purpose was served by the study of history, replied: to bring man to knowledge of himself, and added, 'the only indication of what man can do, is what man has done; . . . the value of history lies in that it teaches what man has done and, thus, who he is'.[2] Indeed, in my view, in their exploration of the past, historians ultimately not only depart from questions which fascinate them in the present, but also want to return there; if they do their job properly, it is their journey which determines where, in the present, they finally find themselves. Since, in that sense, writing history is a scientific form of self-discovery, the resulting questions, though they may claim only a limited general validity, yet they will help an author and his readers to better understand their own world.

In the course of seventeen chapters and an interlude, I have attempted to show how, in the long period since Europe was first introduced as a geographical concept, people all over that part of the world have expressed themselves in a variety of cultural forms. Over the centuries, many of these coagulated into a set of norms and values which people began to ascribe to 'Europe', thus transforming it from, at best, a specious territorial designation, a geographical coincidence within the Eurasian landmass, into a cultural concept, a real world. Slowly, Europe has emerged as an increasingly complex and compelling definition people used to identify themselves with, usually in hours of need. However, any identification implies a distinction that, automatically, marks others as, indeed, 'other' – in this case as 'not European'.

Among these cultural forms, Christianity, absorbing a number of older beliefs and customs, slowly became the norm of all things, the challenging and at the same time restrictive context for Europe's ideas and actions. Undeniably, for a very long time Christian culture was the most influential denominator of the world that felt itself to be distinctly 'European'. Also, it decisively influenced the process in which, far more recently, a series of territorial political unities sought closer cooperation for reasons both eminently pragmatic and, many like to think, idealistic.

When the history of Europe had run its course to and through the Second World War, a climate of liberation and reconstruction, and the demand for peace and unity followed. Yet, a new divisive element quickly became manifest: the estrangement between, on the one hand, a group of basically democratic states in western Europe and, on the other hand, a number of countries in central and eastern Europe which had been brought under the totalitarian power of communist regimes, resulting, soon, in a new war, the 'Cold War'. In that situation, in 'the west' a 'dream of Europe' developed, perhaps even had to develop. But while most politicians viewed this new Europe primarily as a political and military necessity for which economic reconstruction was a prerequisite, many also felt that to win over the citizens of their states an appeal to old, partly forgotten, images and ideas might prove helpful.

Significantly, Jean Monnet, one of the architects of 'modern Europe', at the end of his life is said to have remarked that if he had to start building the 'European House' anew, he would first address culture rather than economic or political life. Similarly, another early 'European', Gonzague de Reynolds, wrote: 'Wenn ich noch einmal meine Europaische Arbeit beginnen konnte wurde ich mit den Kultur anfangen' (If I were to start again on my work for Europe, I would start with culture). Yet, as in the past, when perceived dangers had engendered a process of self-reflection and self-definition, those ideas again proved difficult to formulate, and still more difficult to establish as indisputably valid for everyone. Indeed, I do not know what these two eminent men meant, exactly, for they did not define their concept of European culture. In this epilogue, it might be useful to try and find out what one might like it to mean, especially since the economic and political Europe, in May 2004, expanded beyond the dreams of its erstwhile founders and since, in November of the same year, a European constitution was signed which, despite not having been ratified by the European Union's member states, will create a unity that definitely pretends to be cultural as well as economic and political. Indeed, the preamble to that constitution states that 'The people of Europe are determined to transcend their ancient divisions, and, united ever more closely, to forge a common destiny'. In doing so, they will create a Europe based on 'equality of persons, freedom, respect for reason', and will draw 'inspiration from the cultural, religious and humanist inheritance of Europe'. These seemingly simple words are the result of some extremely violent political and, therefore, cultural debates. Also, they show how even on this exalted level words can be used to confuse. For, of course, religion is part of culture. And while, also, of course, Humanism in the above sense is no longer defined and monopolized solely by the Churches, yet it is the outcome of a struggle to create a set of values that, at least in Europe, was first articulated by and, indeed, spread through institutionalized religion, i.e. Christianity. Symbolically, but also rather ironically, the twenty-five heads of government who lined up to sign the constitution did so in Rome, the city that considered itself for so long the 'capital of the (civilized) world'. To many, Rome, as the embodiment of the legal, secular values of the Roman Empire, is the preferred ancestor of present-day Europe.[3] Yet to subscribe to the European constitution, these leaders actually had to sit down at the feet of a huge bronze statue of Pope Innocent X in the act of blessing the world – significantly, he was the pope who had to watch as Europe's religious division was finally politically sanctioned at the Peace of Westphalia which, in 1648, ended perhaps the first all-European war. Arguably, the papacy represents that other strand of Europe's culture, Christianity, the religion that, after years of debate, was emphatically not identified in the constitution. Though one might feel that the constitution thus shows Europe turning its back on part of its past, one might also argue that it heralds a Europe turning its face towards the future. Some prefer it to be a future without religion. Others know it will be a future of many religions. Some feel that religion accounts for much that has been wrong in Europe, for much that Europe has done wrong. Others feel that without religion(s), Europe will fail to survive as a moral community and, therefore, a viable culture. Though one might argue that religion is not, perhaps, the sole fount of a consistent set of moral values, the fact that such values are needed to sustain a community seems indisputable. Problematically, the question is at the heart of Europe's present and future. What will be Europe's stance on religious fundamentalism – especially Islamic fundamentalism? What will be its stance on the admission of Turkey to the European Union? Some people now argue that, after all, Europe is what it is because it once was – and, basically, still is? – Christian. Including Turkey would be betraying Europe, because most Turks are supposed to be Islamic at heart. Others feel that, precisely because Europe is no longer Christian, but secular, the inclusion of a state which for many decades has proclaimed its secularity and, moreover, its adoption of European, secular values, is purely a logical step that will strengthen what Europe stands for.

All these problems notwithstanding, there are those who argue that Europe already has much to be proud of.[4] The euro zone has a trade surplus with most of the rest of the world though, of course, that creates problems of its own. By and large, the European economy is doing well. Also, Europeans have better public services than almost any other region of the world, and they are better educated than most other peoples, too. Moreover, they are healthier, and seem, increasingly, to choose quality of life over increased consumption and its implicit ties to the workplace. Europeans cherish the environment, though, admittedly, in face of the global dimensions of the climate change problems, their attitude can be little more than an example which, if not followed, will not help them very much. By creating a flexible system of sovereignty-sharing, Europe may well be able to better adapt to new threats and possibilities; but, then again, some might argue that this precisely precludes taking the stronger stance often necessary in today's increasingly complex global politics and the threat of terrorism that goes with it.

Yet, despite the grand claims of Europe's first constitution, pessimists hold that any appeal to define 'Europe' as more than a mere geographical entity and an economic association that is still debating whether it wants or needs to go towards political union, will sound hollow as long as the pan-European institutions that have been created to manage shared sovereignty manifestly fail to attract the loyalty of Europe's citizens. Indeed, one sometimes wonders whether over the past two decades many have not felt their allegiance should rather lie with the 'old', or at least tradition-hallowed national institutions which are, or seem to be, sustained by a familiar community narrative.

Others feel pessimistic about the future of a value-imbued Europe since fundamental intolerance has not disappeared and equal opportunities for all have not yet been realized there. Some argue that the so-called 'Age of Reason', 'the Enlightenment' that, to many, is one of Europe's distinctive and distinguishing cultural characteristics, while it did contribute to the growth of tolerance and equal opportunity, has also fostered a specific, potentially negative kind of rational, scientific thinking. Stressing analysis, classification, inclusion and exclusion, privileging modernity and individualism as specifically European, that culture threatens one of Europe's oldest – Judaeo-Christian and Roman – tenets, the fundamental equality of all humankind.[5]

Optimists, on the other hand, feel that one of the essential qualities of the European tradition is, precisely, that it has succeeded in creating unity out of diversity, while, at the same time, allowing diversity to continue to exist. They feel that though economic inequality has still not been eradicated, Europe, and more specifically the European welfare states, have realized a degree of prosperity and well-being for the majority of their population which has no precedent in the world's past and is, indeed, what distinguishes Europe from and makes it so attractive to most other societies in the present-day world. They hold that this is or should be one of Europe's contributions to humanity.

While the study of Europe's history provides both groups with some justification, it is the future that will prove either of them right. However, Europe's future will not be one in which it dominates the world as it has done over the past 200 years. Many predict that the third millennium of the Christian era will not be 'ours' anymore. With Europe having lost its global predominance – it symbolically ended in 1997, when Britain and Portugal handed over their former colonies of Hong Kong and Macao to China – it is predicted that the third millennium will be 'Asian' instead of 'European'.[6] Yet Europe will have a role to play. Having inherited a past that has helped to shape the world, it cannot but feel politically, economically and also morally obliged to contribute to its future. Precisely the interpretation and use of Europe's past will determine the course of its future.

Demonstrably, many cultural expressions that, over time, have given Europe a certain cohesion as well as distinction were produced and experienced only by an elite, by the educated and the powerful. For more than 1,000 years, this elite was a Christian elite, though from the sixteenth century onwards Christianity was fragmented into a multitude of denominations. Since the seventeenth century, part of that elite operated in increasing opposition to the Churches and, even, to Christianity itself; they reformulated old ideas and created new ones, willing them to be secular, free from the shackles of any religion, truly human and, indeed, universal. Nevertheless, much of this elite culture – religious and secular – was not articulated by the majority of Europeans and, indeed, had little meaning or relevance for them. The institutions that were the embodiment and the bearers of culture were mostly dominated by the elite, too, and often also reserved for them. Of these, 'Church' and 'Education' were perhaps the most important. Moreover, as this culture communicated, basically, through texts, both in the arts and the sciences, and through travel, it was biased towards the elite as well.

Yet, the majority of studies charting 'the' cultural history of Europe fail to state the crucial fact that most Europeans, being illiterate until the very recent past, hardly participated in that specific culture. During the past millennia, through lack of education and reading, as well as through lack of travel or other physical communication, most Europeans lived unaware of their common culture and its historical roots, nor did they share in the ideas and values which the elite called its most noble expression and frequently propagated as universally applicable. Consequently, what was a literate, educated and therefore elite culture only, is usually characterized as 'the' European tradition *par excellence*. Often, this reflects a political and propagandistic point of view. It is not a scholarly one.

Undeniably, all Europeans, through the religions of the many Christian Churches, did become acquainted with a few core concepts. Perhaps the most important of these was the equality of every person before God in heaven and the ensuing idea of the equality under law of all people – on earth. The Apostle Paul had argued: 'There are neither Jews nor Greeks, men nor women, masters nor slaves – for the Eternal One, all are equal'. Nor did some values vaguely derived from such tenets as 'social justice' fail to exercise great influence on the expectations of many people in Europe, though for a long time they existed as political rhetoric only. Only when the French and the Industrial Revolutions brought about a veritable, all-embracing cultural revolution as well, did Europe really begin to change, and a real European consciousness begin to take shape.

Basically, it was the expansion of education from the nineteenth century onwards that confronted the majority of Europeans with a set of values that were now considered essential by state governments. These values still derived from or were developed out of an originally Christian stock of ideas. Since the end of the nineteenth century, general education became available to the entire population. Yet, until the Second World War this was primary education only for most Europeans, and of very limited content and scope at that. Moreover, the quality of even this basic education differed greatly between north-west, central, eastern and southern Europe.

Since the last decades of the twentieth century, the influence of Christianity, both as a personal religion and as a general cultural tradition has declined. This has become manifest in people's actual experience of beliefs in their everyday life as well as in education. With knowledge of classical antiquity and its traditions declining as well, people's notions about life and the values that should guide their actions are no longer firmly rooted in a known past. Living their lives without a historical perspective, they also lack the foundation for self-criticism.

Meanwhile, since the late nineteenth century, mass communication has slowly become a major force in everyday life. However, its message was and is usually directed at reinforcing consumer culture – especially since it is dominated by largely anonymous, profit-oriented global corporations. Many feel that, as yet, the media have contributed little of significance to the (re-)creation of ideas and values, as opposed to lifestyles and a culture of everyday pleasures and emotions. Moreover, it is to be doubted whether mass tourism, though having evolved out of more elitist forms of 'cultural travel', will be a significant moral force, though, undeniably, it has increased a general awareness of cultural diversity and, at the same time, has fostered some cultural cohesion.

Yet, though in many European countries more or less similar ideas have been spread and are still being spread by similar cultural institutions, many of the so-called indisputable 'European values' have still materialized in widely different political-ideological systems. They were and are implemented in parliamentary-constitutional institutions, but within these have manifested themselves in a variety of liberal, social- or religious-democratic ways of thinking and acting. However, these values have also been appropriated by conservative-authoritarian ideologies, themselves the products of extreme or fundamentalist social or religious convictions. Frequently, during the recent past, in adopting these ideologies people have eliminated the possibility of thinking and acting within a parliamentary-constitutional context. Even in the new Europe, the danger of such a situation recurring still exists, if only because of the cultural contradictions recently resulting from the massive influx of people who have not been educated – and it is necessary to stress the concept of education here – to accept Europe's basic human values.

Moreover, though for the time being Europe itself seems unlikely to be devastated by the horrors of war, many feel its pretensions to a unique humaneness and an exemplary role have not been translated into a policy that prevents the systematic oppression and even extermination of fellow humans elsewhere. This situation posits a question fraught with practical-political and, indeed, moral problems. If Europe has the strength of its convictions, should it 'impose' its ideas on the rest of the world – as, in another sense, it did during its colonial-imperialist phase – and should it then create a military force of its own to be able to do so? Or would it, in doing so, risk following the course taken by the USA that is, precisely, a course many Europeans condemn?

Therefore, some may be inclined to ask whether the inhabitants of this Europe can rightfully maintain that the appellation 'European culture' designates more than a mere location. Others will argue that this culture has not formed every 'European' now included in the Union that claims it in the same way and to the same degree. Finally, there will be those who feel that, for many people living in Europe, this specific cultural Europe is a thing of the past.

While I do not presume to pronounce on the direction that Europe should follow culturally and politically, I do feel that it is precisely in these fields that the past has helped to shape the present. Therefore, the reader of this epilogue may benefit from a final, albeit short, in-depth look at the qualities people in the past have wanted to attribute to 'Europe'. For using the name consciously or unconsciously, but always with a certain intention, Europeans need to know what their 'being European' does, and perhaps should, mean. Indeed, as the preamble to the 2004 constitution seems to suggest, asking what 'Europe' means essentially is asking about the moral-ethical load necessarily implicit in every definition of group identity. As, moreover, 'European', used as an adjective, frequently seems to imply a criterion for quality – if not outright superiority – the following nuancing of the complex reality of present-day 'Europe' seems apposite.

During the last three or four decades, 'Europe' has presented itself as a relative unity. It partly legitimizes itself by pointing to a number of economic and political choices and achievements that are said to imply moral choices as well. More importantly, it tries to defend certain values, the results of a rich cultural tradition. Yet one sees how between Europeans themselves, on every level of political or sociocultural organization, the description 'we' and 'the others' results in narrow-mindedness and restrictive behaviour. Frequently, even the freedom and, hence, the tolerance often put central stage in many definitions of 'the European tradition' are lacking, let alone that others are actually accepted.

For centuries, Europeans have used disconcertingly simple but nevertheless deeply felt we–other, insider–outsider oppositions to define their world: such oppositions as civilized vs. barbarian, Christian vs. heathen, believer vs. heretic, town vs. country, 'high brow' vs. 'low brow' and, in a later period, white vs. black – or red, or yellow – and 'modern and progressive' vs. 'old-fashioned and static'. Moreover, there were the oppositions of north vs. south and west vs. east.[7] As for these latter two, they, too, implied differences of quality, strengthened by the influence of the Industrial and French Revolutions on the material and political-social conditions of parts of Europe. Since the early nineteenth century, the north-west has tended to present the prosperity realized within its own region and the genesis of certain political institutions there as absolute criteria for civilization and progress – as signs of a superior culture, even. These criteria have been applied to describe, measure and judge differences both outside and within Europe. Moreover, within Europe itself, the lack of understanding of other national or regional customs and traditions has created opinions of and attitudes towards others that, though mostly voiced only laughingly, are in times of conflicting interests caused by scarcity or other restrictions, articulated rather more fiercely and, also, reprehensibly.

The question of whether Europe's values of freedom, tolerance and equal opportunity were living realities within a democratic system surfaced once again when, in the 1980s, a new phenomenon appeared, which was quickly and propagandistically referred to by many as a new 'enemy'. It was the phenomenon of the culture of the hundreds of thousands of migrant workers whom, since the 1960s, north-west Europe had brought in especially from southern Europe, from Turkey and from the countries along the north coast of Africa – while, of course, Britain and the Netherlands also saw an influx of people from their former colonies. Indeed, by 2004, one in thirty British people descends from black or Asian settlers who have come to the United Kingdom during the past fifty years. Meanwhile, in the Netherlands nearly 10 per cent of the population consists of people who have newly arrived there from outside Europe, or their first- or second-generation descendants. Though some of the immigrant groups did assimilate surprisingly quickly, others manifestly did not. This has created a situation that, rather poignantly, has come to serve as a test of the strength and indeed the validity of European values.

For many 'Caucasian' Europeans surely the three most important questions, namely whether they feel European, whether they consider the non-Caucasian people inhabiting their world to be Europeans as well and, finally, which norms and values they share with each other, seem to be slowly receding before their need to define themselves against 'others'. These are not necessarily the people whose skin colour is different; far more important, they are the people whose cultural expressions, especially in religion and in the various customs and norms resulting from it, diverge from or are precisely more pronounced than what most Europeans now consider 'normal'; many 'old', 'real' Europeans' feel the presence of these 'new' Europeans will endanger both Europe as a social and cultural system and its prosperity. Now, of course, all over the world such opposition between 'us' and 'the others' always results from a need to ensure group safety, in which 'same' and 'different' serve as criteria on which distinction, self-assurance and power can be founded. Also, any social system – the tribe, the nation-state or Europe – will only be able to provide cohesion as long as it can remain true to its dream, and to the promises, material or immaterial, that its dream holds. Consequently, each and every system has its limits of capacity; it can only expand if, by some form of common consent, it alters its cultural premises, its self-image.

Undeniably, the second wave of immigrants, who originate from the various and diverse non-Christian cultures of the eastern and southern Mediterranean, have contributed to a very large extent to the unprecedented economic flowering which Europe experienced in the 1960s and 1970s and which has made Europe the affluent society it now is. Though tens of millions of Europeans now are Islamic,[8] it would be both dangerous and rather stupid to see or represent them as belonging to a 'monolithic' Islam, just as Christians themselves cannot be so represented. Knowing, as we do, that these 'new' Europeans often represent the second, third or even fourth generation to be born here, and yet doubting their right to live in Europe by (re-)drawing a dividing line between 'us' and 'them' is not only inhuman but also reveals the lack of historical perspective that so often seems to blight Europeans, politicians not least. For we should, of course, consider the very genesis of European culture itself, analysing it as the result of millennia-long, constantly recurring contacts with 'others' – often migrating into Europe from non-European regions. Moreover, it is increasingly evident that Europe – i.e. everyone living in it now – faces an enormous demographic problem, with its population falling and drastically ageing. Alongside the position of the USA and the inevitable rise of China and India, this will inevitably decrease Europe's share of world GDP and, at the very least, jeopardize its continued superstatehood. Nor, of course, will it guarantee the level of economic and social welfare to which Europeans have become accustomed. In short, immigration on a scale greatly exceeding the influx of the 1960s and 1970s seems the only way to prevent Europe from becoming a second-rate region in almost every conceivable respect. For this reason alone, addressing the question what Europe wants to be is more pressing than it ever has been. Obviously, the problems created by the continuing clash between national identities and a European multiculturalism are severely compounded by the hostility to integration provoked by, in particular, militant Islam.

Meanwhile, simply as a result of the demographic factor – for the time being the birth rate among the new Europeans is considerably higher than reproduction amongst the older groups – the descendants of the 1960s and 1970s immigrants will play an increasingly active role not only in every 'national' culture but also in 'European' culture. They are an undeniable factor in European society which is being changed by them as much as it changes them. For Europe, the confrontation with the dark-skinned African, a believer in Islam, was one of the oldest historical confrontations with 'the other'. In Shakespeare's *Othello* (1611) the eponymous 'Moor' is the protagonist. This tragic character, a Moorish admiral in Venetian service, was, one might say, Europe's first immigrant worker. Shakespeare sketched Othello 'objectively', that is to say, with his positive and negative sides, which are indicated as generally human. Moreover, Othello's opponent, the 'white' Iago, is the real scoundrel of the piece, as if the playwright wanted to indicate that stereotypes must be avoided. It has been suggested that, preferably, the 'Moor' be played by a white actor wearing a black mask, and Iago by a black actor with a white mask. Perhaps Europeans, of whatever background, should more frequently try such a form of 'role playing' in the drama of everyday life.

Shakespeare's plea for tolerance, however, seems to go still further. When Prospero in *The Tempest* eventually calls the 'wild' Indian Caliban his 'shadow', he recognizes the essential 'darkness' in himself, in every human being. Yet although tolerance can thus acquire a function as the self-criticism and, hence, the self-acceptance of any human amidst other humans, either permanent or not according to the extent to which a person enters into confrontation repeatedly with new 'others', this certainly does not explicitly guarantee complete acceptance of the fundamentally different. Even if only in order to remain himself or itself, every human, every culture will consider certain behaviour or situations to be unacceptable as long as the confrontation has not led to gradual adaptation, change or inculturation. Tolerance without norms and values ends in chaos, arbitrariness and, inevitably, repression.

Whether Europe's three-fold post-Second World War confrontation with 'the other' – the people from the former European colonies, the immigrant workers from, mostly, the Islamic Mediterranean, the political exiles from Africa and Asia – will be a process of acculturation or of inculturation cannot yet be ascertained. That Europe might perhaps return to its Mediterranean, partly Asian-African, origins is a fascinating thought. That the culture of any political unity in or of Europe during the third millennium of the 'Christian era' can be no longer specifically Christian seems to me indisputable.

Despite widespread nostalgia among the 'old' Europeans, Europe will be a world in which the church towers, the crosses and the ringing of bells will no longer almost instinctively evoke a multitude of emotions and images which, all-encompassing, describe culture and solidarity. But among the group of Islamic Europeans, too, secularization will become stronger and the power of the mosques, the minarets and the muezzin to retain or even recreate their group spirit will inevitably weaken as well. The same, perhaps, will happen to other religious cultures that have come to live in Europe. However, economic problems such as long-term unemployment coupled with inadequate education obviously create a climate of frustration that induces some to turn to fundamentalist interpretations of their own religious and cultural traditions, and, more dangerously still, to act accordingly. To provide the very different cultural traditions – Christian, Islamic, humanist, religious and secular, western and eastern European – that now are struggling to shape Europe with a set of common values, with shared ideals, is one of Europe's greatest challenges.

The challenge is all the greater because of another development. Since 1989, the communist regimes which had ruled the economy, politics and society of most states in central and eastern Europe for two or sometimes even three generations have collapsed, at least formally. The question as to whether these states and their inhabitants will take – or be given – the opportunity to adapt to the achievements of the western world cannot definitely be answered at present. Undeniably, the change from an until recently totalitarian political and economic system to one that sets a high store on a liberal or social democracy and a free market economy will be difficult despite, or perhaps even because of, the inclusion, in 2004, of so many formerly communist-dominated societies in the European Union – which, one needs to be reminded, does not equal Europe, for Finland, Iceland and Norway have not joined it.

Yet, the ten new states completely altered the cultural make-up of this 'united' Europe. No longer can we say, as H.A.L. Fisher did in his 1935 *History of Europe*: 'We Europeans are the children of Hellas'. If that ever was true, it is certainly no longer so. Of the new states, only two, namely Cyprus and Malta, have a Mediterranean culture with some obvious 'Hellenic' elements – although, of course, the Maltese language is a mixture of Italian and Berber-Arabic. Of the eight that have no such obvious 'classical' roots, six are, by and large, Slavonic, linguistically and culturally – Latvia, Lithuania, Poland, the Czech Republic, Slovakia and Slovenia – while Estonia and Hungary, at least linguistically, share Finnish-Ugric ties with Finland. Also, these eight states have all been subject to long-time imperialism: German, Austrian and, of course, Russian and the latter both tsarist and communist. Indeed, only three of them have existed as independent states since the early 1990s. While other European states have a long history of shared traditions that have coalesced in a definite 'national' culture, the Union's new members, with the exception, perhaps, of Poland, are still trying to find their own, national traditions, sometimes inventing them. Has their joining a Europe that, in its form as a union, is an economic institution, first and foremost, increased the chances of that Union ever becoming the embodiment of a cultural Europe? The problem is all the more complex because it is not clear whether new economic choices will result – automatically? – in new, i.e. western-European, cultural attitudes and manifestations. Does, for example, the consumer culture eagerly adopted by many in central and eastern Europe after decades of relative hardship necessarily entail the adoption of western forms of democracy and secularization as well? It remains to be seen. Also, of course, the inclusion of so many new countries in the European economic system has increased tensions between 'old' and 'new' Europeans. Those parts of the original Union that feel and indeed are demonstrably poor, for whatever reason – e.g. southern Italy, parts of Greece, eastern Germany, etc. vociferously claim that they should by right be given preferred treatment. Indeed, even such manifestly wealthy countries as Britain, France, Germany and the Netherlands are now staunchly defending their privileges to retain their own economic, and social, systems.

The process of adaptation certainly cannot be one-sided. For the present, the values that have come to characterize western Europe now seem to be triumphant all over the continent as well as, or so it seems, all over the world. But whereas the state-dominated socialism of the former eastern Europe definitely no longer seems to be a viable way, we should not forget that one of its most important, underlying values, the wish to create a system of social justice, of human dignity, was created in and by Europe, and, moreover, should remain one of its fundamental values. Perhaps it can be redefined as a capitalist society's form of radically reformist self-criticism – as it was conceived, originally, in the nineteenth century. Arguably, to continue or, where necessary, to introduce it is another of Europe's great challenges for the future.

The final question is, of course, which of Europe's many professed ideals will prove strong enough to give it cohesion in the years to come? It is a question which historians may ask, but which they cannot 'scientifically' answer.

It is quite difficult to prove that man has an innate morality that keeps him from doing wrong, if only because the notions of right and wrong seem, at least partly, culturally conditioned. The quest for a 'global' ethics, a quest that many Europeans are now pursuing in order to find spiritual coordinates in a secularizing and increasingly global society, is real if not yet very successful.

Nevertheless, we assume that all people have moral instincts, at least such as that make them want to protect those they know and feel close to. In this sense, morality almost precedes social reality. It is imperative to preserve this morality as a weapon against the possible dehumanizing aspects of social structures with a high degree of organizational rationalism – the 'modernity' that now characterizes European society. To be able to do so, pluralism, with its political concomitant, democracy, seems the essential prerequisite. However, we cannot assume that everybody shares these views. As recent discussions between Europe and Asia show – or, to avoid dangerous reification, between a number of western European states and a number of south-east Asian states – Europe's assertion that the rights of the individual should always rank highest and that democracy is their best guarantee are offset by Asian, more specifically Confucian ideas about the primacy of the community's stability, to which the individual should subordinate himself.

Nevertheless, many Europeans feel that this notion of pluralism – both within the existing nation-states and, *a fortiori*, in the European Union – is the best cultural guarantee for a society that wants to foster ideals, and be fostered by them. It seems the best way to create a civilization in which culture as a set of values keeps social structure and the economy in check. It helps to prevent society from being ruled by automatisms and single-issue movements. It checks the growth of authoritarian or even totalitarian attitudes and organizations. It forces people to take responsibility for themselves though, perhaps, at the risk of creating a situation in which no one person or group can claim the moral authority to provide the rules and regulations that help to give society the cohesion it needs.[9]

For the intellectual background of such ways of thinking one might refer to the analysis of present-day European culture offered by the Jewish-Lithuanian-French philosopher Emanuel Levinas (1905–93), who survived the Nazi efforts to destroy the Jews. In growing opposition to the great German philosopher Martin Heidegger (1889–1976), whose *Sein und Zeit* (Being and Time) (1927) had such enormous impact on European thinking between the two wars, Levinas held that 'to be' is not man's ultimate function, but 'being' is, because it means living with the constant reminder of 'the other' and his needs. This does not lead to alienation, non-comprehension. On the contrary, it results in a basic form of Humanism, an awareness of the other that generates an ethic with such basic moral precepts as 'thou shalt not kill' and 'thou shalt do unto others . . .'.[10]

Indeed, there seems to be a consensus in Europe that looks at man in society in a three-fold aspect: each man is unique, each person has to make his own choices for good and evil but, first and foremost, being human means taking responsibility for others, means protecting others to preserve the quality of society at large. Freedom, safety, prosperity for everybody seem to be the values European culture has come to cherish most; they transcend man's egocentric instinct for simple everyday survival. And yet, these values do not come naturally: they have to be constantly reaffirmed within the context of the culture that holds them.

Confronting an always uncertain future from the vantage point of the past, we might say that those Europeans who want the culture they have built and which they cherish to provide a continuing stimulus, in the context of the myth and reality which 'Europe' has now become,[11] will have to evaluate constantly and critically the actual meaning of the great values and traditions which have been articulated and codified in the past – first by intellectuals,[12] but from the late eighteenth century onwards increasingly by larger groups.

This participation is, of course, precisely the process we should continue to foster. After all, intellectuals on their own will never make Europe into an experienced reality of the pretensions that have grown in the past,[13] or, as the Oxford professor of ancient history, Rostovtzeff, who was of Russian origin, wrote: 'Our civilization will not survive unless it is a civilization not of one class, but of the masses'. However, consciously or unconsciously revealing his own position as an intellectual, he added two rather telling questions:

> Is it possible for the lower classes to participate in a higher civilization without lowering its level and diluting its quality to the stage where it disappears? Is not every civilization doomed to disappear as soon as it filters through to the masses?[14]

The above was written in 1926 and even then, raised unpopular questions with uncomfortable presuppositions. Nowadays, political correctness seems to forbid their being openly uttered at all. However, they are at the back of every debate about culture, whether in the media or in politics or in academia. Undoubtedly, Europe's greatest challenge is to make certain that the values which it deems important are constantly reaffirmed and, indeed, practised by as large a part of its people as is possible. If Europe wants to preserve its cultural heritage, it requires, to paraphrase the German poet Novalis, ordinary people who share the same ideals; for, as he said, with a few words betraying his hopes and beliefs: 'Mit den Menschen ändert die Welt sich' ('The world changes as man changes').

Consequently, the most apposite answer to Rostovtzeff's implied question, 'What to do?', would be to pay as much attention as possible to sound education. For the transmission of any ideology, of moral values which can create cultural cohesion, remains the most important task of education, increasingly so since it is one of the few 'socializing institutions' still functioning within the traditional state for the whole of society. Yet this poses the question as to who determines the values that education will teach? In the wake of the indisputable globalization of culture, will there still be values which circumscribe some sort of national identity, as well as a European culture which is experienced as the logical sum of a number of such identities, through a complex of common roots?

At least, to create a climate for the continuity of these values, we should be concerned with raising historical awareness among the many Europeans who are increasingly in danger of losing it. With the State and industry stressing the need for vocational or in-house training, and those who enter secondary and tertiary education increasingly involved in non-school activities, the lack of a common body of knowledge and values makes itself painfully felt.[15]

Does this result from the fact that pupils and students know less and less about the cultures from which these values supposedly stem? Should it be blamed on the fact that the ideals that have come to constitute the 'canon of European values' especially in the economically dominant north-west of Europe after the Enlightenment and the French Revolution, were for several decades during the past century certainly not structurally guaranteed in Greece and Italy, the so-called cradles of civilization, nor, indeed, in Spain, in Germany and in the better part of central and eastern Europe? Or should we raise an accusing finger at growing materialism, at the commercialization of life and culture that is, perhaps all too easily, blamed on the influence of the United States?

To provide Europeans with a critical perspective on the present and thus enable them to make balanced choices for the future, education should certainly ensure they know that the past matters: it is man's only more or less reliable experience, the horizon he needs to know if he wants to position himself in the present and plot his path into the future. A sound perspective, i.e. a vision that balances tradition and renewal, seems essential. Now, increased communication, especially through the cinema and even more so through television and computerized information services has created a visual 'knowledge' of almost every aspect of the present as well as of the past that somehow can be visualized. On the one hand this would seem to ensure the working of one of history's basic mechanisms, the increase of human interdependence, because people and groups, social configurations, will have to continue to learn from each other. But precisely because of the deliberate unreality of much that is shown by the new media, the resulting encyclopedic memory is in danger of being turned into an unreal, largely sentimental, less than human vision of the world. It is futile to refer to the classical roots of European civilization and the way it has creatively intertwined with the Christian tradition if these and other aspects of European culture are not outlined, interpreted and, in their consequences for our own age, criticized both in teaching situations and in the modern mass media, which hold an enormous responsibility in this respect.

Therefore, history education in its broadest sense will have to give an adequate survey of the genesis of the culture that has developed in most (west) European countries in the course of the past millennia stressing, more than has been the case, that, originally, there was little that can be named 'European' and, also, emphasizing the contingent character of the development towards what, by now, can be called European after all.

This education will need to explain how and why fewer and fewer recognizable sociocultural cores can be distinguished which, traditionally, have provided security: (extended) family, neighbourhood, religious community, and so on. It will ask whether, as some believe, life in the present lacks dimensions of identity. It will show that, perhaps, other forms are in the making.

Such education will also outline the consequences of the influence of Christian religion and Christian culture on Europe, showing that the Churches, both the united Roman Catholic Church as well as the Greek Orthodox and the many Reformed Churches, however controversial their policies, have for centuries been the bearers of civilization, profoundly influencing Europe's norms and values. It will also need to stress that, though unbeknownst to many, Islamic civilization has been a prime force in European culture for centuries as well, challenging it and infusing it with many of its profoundest ideas. It will analyse the process of disenchantment, in which a formalized belief in the supranatural power of the divine, especially in matters of this physical world, has slowly declined, at least in most societies of western and, increasingly, central and eastern Europe. It will explain why, after the Second World War, in the west the Churches lost their traditional authority to set strict norms for everyday behaviour while also, in a broader sense, losing their cultural authority. It will also draw attention to the genesis of other, more recent certainties, whether based on an intrinsic belief in the sciences or in forms of Humanism and, sometimes, spiritual forces; while less institutionally powerful than the traditional Churches, these new certainties seem yet to be emotionally satisfactory and, thus, culturally important to many.

History teaching will then analyse the growth of a more rationalist way of thinking and acting both in economic life and in culture at large, and explain the parallel ascendancy of the sciences. Both processes have become evident since the sixteenth century and have increasingly dominated European life since the eighteenth century. It will stress that these processes have created enormous prosperity and also show how this situation has resulted in all sorts of creative internationalization that now manifests itself in the 'globalization' not only of the economic but also of the cultural sphere. It will ask whether these developments threaten to accentuate and reinforce the declining value of group solidarity, traditions, and national identity or if, rather, cultural uniqueness and cohesion need no longer always be tied to a specific location: religion and science, music and film, for example, have increasingly transnational or even global dimensions easily accepted by many.

Yet precisely because the people born in the 1950s and 1960s will probably be the last 'Eurocentric generation',[16] the education of their children and grandchildren will have to show how, in the course of the past centuries, the appeal to the central values which had been, or were thought to have been articulated in the culture of classical Greece and Rome – freedom, individuality, creativity, democracy, in short pluralism – has been continuously adapted to suit changing needs. It will try to explain why this appeal had not yet sufficiently proven itself in the first half of the twentieth century. It will also show that, after the Second World War, it regained its impact, even if reformulated.

Exploring the past and, through it, understanding the present, is the main purpose of history. Society and politics should, therefore, give it pride of place both in education and in the media, in order to provide the contemporary world with a sound intellectual basis. But though history's purpose has always been and will be to give guidance, to provide hope, one has to admit that the validity of values does not result from historical example, only, but has to be proven from everyday practice. Therefore, I feel safe in saying that only by continuing to distinguish itself humanely, will 'Europe' continue to have a meaning that goes beyond the economical and the political. At the same time, taking pride in one's cultural inheritance should not imply uncritically or unthinkingly imposing it on others. In the recent past, many of the values and other cultural forms that have originated in or been elaborated by 'Europe' have all too easily been termed 'universal'. We would do well to discard this much-discussed notion as scholarly irrational and morally irrelevant. The only test of any culture – as a set of values and institutions and, through it, as a way of life – is whether it enhances human welfare. If Europe can convince the world that its most cherished traditions do so enhance this, Europe's past will, indeed, contribute to a better future, both for Europe and for humankind.

Notes

Prologue: Europe – a present with a past

1 G. Erler, ed., *Johann Wolfgang Goethe, Werke, VIII, Faust*, Berlin 1984, Faust I, 77.
2 For this and the following: Zigmantas Kiaupa, *et al.*, *Geschichte des Baltikums*, Tallinn 2002.
3 Cf. P. Sztompka, *From East Europeans to Europeans: Shifting Identities and Boundaries in the New Europe*, Wassenaar 2004.
4 M. Kunze, ed., *Winckelmann und Egypte*, Tubingen 2003; D. Wildung, *Preussen am Nil*, Berlin 2002.
5 S. Marchand, *Down from Olympus: Archaeology and Philhellenism in Germany, 1750–1970*, Princeton 1996.
6 M. Wellen, *Die Deutschen sind im Treppenhaus. Der Fries Otto Geyers in der Alte Nationalgalerie*, Cologne 2002.
7 Peter Rietbergen, 'Orientalisme: een theorie van ficties – de fictie van een theorie? Een poging to contextualisering en herinterpretatie', *Tijdschrift voor Geschiedenis* 111 (1998), 545–75, esp. 552–70.
8 Some surveys: C. Curcio, *Europa: Storia d'un Idea I–II*, Florence 1958; J.-B. Duroselle, *L'Idée d'Europe dans l'histoire*, Paris 1965; H. Foerster, *Europa: Geschichte einer politischen Idee*, Munich 1967.
9 G. Colli, M. Montinari, eds, *Fr. Nietzsche: Kritische Gesamtausgabe der Werke*, III/2, Berlin 1973 [=Fr. Nietzsche, *Nachgelassene Schriften, 1870–1873: Ueber Wahrheit und Lüge im aussermoralischen Sinne I*], 378.
10 For example, his *Capitalism and Material Life, 1400–1800*, London 1973, with his *Afterthoughts*, Baltimore 1977, and then elaborated as *Civilization and Capitalism*. Also, his *Grammaire des Civilisations*, Paris 1987. However, there is, I find, little of a really unifying concept behind Braudel's often rambling writings.
11 One may think of his *The Civilizing Process*, I–II, Oxford 1978, 1982, though these two volumes do seem to follow two different strands of thought.
12 Obviously, this is not to say that such theories cannot be fruitful. Yet I find, for example, G. Arrighi, *The Long Twentieth Century: Money, Power and the Origins of Our Times*, London 1994, not entirely convincing.
13 For a spirited defence of the historian's craft against some of the sillier post-modernist claims, see R. Evans, *In Defense of History*, London 1994.
14 The dangers of such an approach are evident in the recent and surely ridiculous effort by H. Bloom, *The Western Canon*, New York 1994; of the twenty-six authors included, about three-quarters are Anglo-Saxon.
15 B. Geremek, *The Common Roots of Europe*, London 1996, gives an interesting, short survey of the genesis of the concept of Europe; he also argues that, at the end of the twentieth century, the notion of European civilization is felt rather more strongly in central than in western Europe. Ph. Longworth, *The Making of Eastern Europe*,

London 1992, goes into the long history of the diverging paths of east and west. Ernest Gellner, *Conditions of Liberty*, London 1994, seems to view the ancient German lands as the frontier region between east and west.

16 See also P. Burke, 'Did Europe exist before 1700?', *History of European Ideas* 1 (1980), 21–9.
17 For example, A. Corbin, *Time, Desire and Horror*, Oxford 1995, viii–ix.

1 Before 'Europe': towards an agricultural and sedentary society

1 M.F. Ashley-Montagu, *Edward Tyson, 1650–1708, and the Rise of Human and Comparative Anatomy in England*, London 1943.
2 D.J. Boorstin, *The Discoverers*, II, New York 1991, 888–90.
3 For a stimulating, though debated view: D. and A. Premack, *Original Intelligence. Unlocking the Mystery of Who We Are*, New York 2004.
4 For this and the following paragraphs: G. Bosinski, *Homo Sapiens*, Paris 1990; P. Mellar, C. Stringer, eds, *The Human Revolution*, Edinburgh 1989; R. Klein, *The Human Career*, Chicago 1989; C. Gamble, *The Paleolithic Settlement of Europe*, Cambridge 1986.
5 P. Mellar, *The Neanderthal Legacy: An Archaeological Perspective from Western Europe*, Princeton 1996. See also R. Foley, *Humans before Humanity*, London 1995.
6 See S. Oppenheimer, *Out of Africa's Eden: The Peopling of the World*, Jeppestown 2003.
7 See P. Bahn, J. Vertut, *Images of the Ice Age*, London 1988. The sexual interpretations of A. Leroi-Gourhan, *The Art of Prehistoric Man in Western Europe*, London 1968, are now being widely debated.
8 See the interpretations of J. Clottes, D. Lewis-Williams, *Les Chamans de la préhistoire: transe et magie dans les grottes ornées*, Paris 1996.
9 For a survey: Ph. Lieberman, *Uniquely Human: The Evolution of Speech, Thought and Selfless Behaviour*, Cambridge, Mass., 1991; J. Wind *et al.* eds, *Language Origin: A Multidisciplinary Approach*, Dordrecht 1992.
10 T.D. Price, A.B. Gebauer, eds, *Last Hunter, First Farmer*, Santa Fé 1995.
11 A valuable survey: A. Sherratt, *Economy and Society in Prehistoric Europe*, Edinburgh 1997.
12 D.R. Harris, ed., *Origins and Spread of Agriculture and Pastoralism in Eurasia*, London 1996.
13 See for a survey A.B. Knapp, *The History and Culture of Western Asia and Egypt*, Chicago 1988; M. Silver, *Economic Structures of the Ancient Near East*, London 1986.
14 An impressive, comparative and long-term study of this region is J. Krejci, *The Civilizations of Asia and the Middle East*, London 1990.
15 See M. Beard, J. North, eds, *Pagan Priests: Religion and Power in the Ancient World*, New York 1990.
16 B.J. Kemp, *Ancient Egypt: Anatomy of a Civilization*, London 1991; J.N. Postgate, *Early Mesopotamia: Society and Economy at the Dawn of History*, London 1992.
17 J. Chadwick, *The Mycenaean World*, Cambridge 1976.
18 J.P. Mallory, *In Search of the Indo-Europeans: Language, Archaeology and Myth*, London 1989. The Kurgan thesis has been most vociferously voiced by Maria Gimbutas, especially in the culmination of her life's work: *The Civilization of the Goddess: The World of Old Europe*, San Francisco 1991.
19 C. Renfrew, *Archaeology and Language: The Puzzle of Indo-European Origins*, London 1987.
20 N. Klengel, *Hammurapi von Babylon und seine Zeit*, Berlin 1977.
21 J.B. Pritchard, ed., Th.J. Meek, trans., *The Ancient Near East: An Anthology of Texts*, Princeton 1958, 138–67, passim.

22   N.J.G. Pounds, *An Historical Geography of Europe, 450 BC–AD 1330*, Cambridge 1973, 1–16.
23   See C. Bailey, ed., *Hunter-Gatherer Economy in Prehistory: A European Perspective*, Cambridge 1983.
24   J. Hoddes, *The Domestication of Europe*, London 1990.
25   See J. Bintloff, ed., *Europe's Social Evolution: Archaeological Perspectives*, Bradford 1984.
26   M. Gimbutas, *The Civilization of the Goddess: The World of Old Europe*, San Francisco 1991.
27   S. Piggott, *The Earliest Wheeled Transport, from the Atlantic Coast to the Caspian Sea*, London 1984.
28   E.M. Brumfiel, T.K. Earle, eds, *Specialisation, Exchange and Complex Societies*, Cambridge 1987.
29   See N.K. Sandars, *The Sea Peoples*, London 1978; A. Harding, *The Myceneans and Europe*, London 1984; J. Bouzek, *The Aegean, Anatolia and Europe: Cultural Interrelations in the Second Millennium BC*, Lund 1985.
30   See V.R.d'A. Desborough, *The Last Mycenaeans and their Successors*, Oxford 1964.
31   See P. Johnson, *Civilization of the Holy Land*, London 1979; J. Maier, *Geschichte des Judentums im Altertum*, Darmstadt 1989.
32   J.H. Hayes, J.M. Miller, eds, *Israelite and Judaean History*, London 1977.
33   S. Moscati, *The World of the Phoenicians*, London 1973.
34   P. Mathiae, *Ebla: un impero ritrovato*, Milan 1977.
35   Cf. G. Nisbit, *Ancient Greece in Film and Popular Culture*, Bristol 2004.
36   O. Murray, *Early Greece*, London 1980; A. Snodgrass, *Archaic Greece: The Age of Experiment*, London 1980.
37   J. Latacz, *Troy and Homer*, Oxford 2004.
38   W. Burkert, *The Orientalizing Revolution: Near Eastern Influence in Greek Culture in the Early Archaic Age*, Cambridge 1992; orig. Munich 1984.
39   J. Bleicken, *Die Athenische Demokratie*, Paderborn 1986; C. Farrar, *The Origins of Democratic Thinking: The Invention of Politics in Classical Athens*, Cambridge 1988; J. Ober, *Mass and Elite in Democratic Athens*, Princeton 1989; D. Stockton, *The Classical Athenian Democracy*, Oxford 1990.
40   See the essay by Ch. Hedricks in R. Osborne, S. Hornblower, eds, *Ritual, Finance, Politics: Athenian Democratic Accounts Presented to D. Lewis*, Oxford 1993.
41   In a very interesting study, P. Vidal-Nacquet, *Politics Ancient and Modern*, London 1995, explores the ways in which widely diverse notions about Greek democracy have been formulated since the Renaissance, always to support contemporary ideas about politics.
42   From A. de Sélincourt, trans., *Herodotus, The Histories*, Harmondsworth 1972, III, 8–83, 238–40.
43   A fine survey: S. Blundell, *Women in Ancient Greece*, London 1995.
44   A.R. Hands, *Charities and Social Aid in Greece and Rome*, London 1968.
45   See A. Richlin, ed., *Pornography and Representation in Greece and Rome*, Oxford 1992.
46   W. Burkert, *Greek Religion*, Cambridge, Mass., 1985.
47   D. Cohen, Law, *Violence and Community in Classical Athens*, Cambridge 1995.
48   R. Buxton, *Imaginary Greece: The Contexts of Mythology*, Cambridge 1994.
49   S. Goldhill, *Love, Sex and Tragedy: How the Ancient World Shapes our Lives*, London 2004.
50   Chr. Meier, *The Political Art of Greek Tragedy*, London 1993, focusing on Aeschylus, provides a very interesting discussion.
51   R. Meiggs, *The Athenian Empire*, Oxford 1972.
52   T.B.L. Webster, *Athenian Culture and Society*, London 1973.
53   J. Boardman, *The Greeks Overseas*, Harmondsworth 1973.
54   For these questions see, e.g., G. Lloyd, *Magic, Reason and Experiment. Studies in the*

Origin and Development of Greek science, London 1999, and his *The Ambition of Curiosity. Understanding the World in Ancient Greece and China*, Cambridge 2002.

55 T. Champion, J.V. Megaw, eds, *Settlement and Society: Aspects of West European Prehistory in the First Millennium BC*, Leicester 1985.

56 B. Cunliffe, *The Celtic World*, London 1979.

57 N. Chadwick, *The Celts*, Harmondsworth 1984; N.N., *Au temps des Celtes, Ve–Ie siècle avant J-C*, Daoulas 1986.

58 J. Collis, *The European Iron Age*, London 1984.

59 See M.C. Fernandez Castro, *Iberia in Prehistory*, London 1995, which gives an excellent survey of the history of the peninsula in the first millennium BC.

60 J.-P. Mohen, A. Duval *et al.* eds, *Les Princes Celtes et la Méditerranée*, Paris 1988; B. Cunliffe, *Greeks, Romans and Barbarians: Spheres of Interaction*, London 1988.

61 A very readable survey: S. Moscati, ed., *I Celti: la prima Europa*, Venice 1991.

62 General surveys: W. Fritzemeyer, *Christenheit und Europa: zur Geschichte des europäischen Gemeinschaftsgefühls von Dante bis Leibniz*, Munich-Berlin 1931; P. Brezzi, *Realtà e mito dell'Europa dall'antichità ai giorni nostri*, Rome 1954.

63 The oldest known 'map of the world' shows the earth divided into two parts: *Lexicon der Alten Welt*, Zürich-Stuttgart, 1947.

64 De Sélincourt, *Herodotus*, IV, 37–45.

65 M. Führmann, *Europa: zur Geschichte einer kulturellen und politischen Idee*, Konstanz 1981, 7, n. 3.

66 F.M. Snowden, Jr, *Before Color Prejudice: The Ancient View of Blacks*, Cambridge, Mass., 1993.

67 J. Jüthner, *Hellenen und Barbaren*, Leipzig 1923; H. Diller, 'Die Hellenen-Barbaren Antithese im Zeitalter der Perserkriege', in *Grecs et Barbares: entretiens sur l'antiquité classique*, VIII, Geneva 1962, 37 sqq.

68 See D. Wood, *The Power of Maps*, London 1993.

69 P. Cartledge, *Alexander the Great. The Hunt for a New Past*, London 2004.

70 P. Green, *Alexander to Actium: The Historical Evolution of the Hellenistic Age*, Berkeley 1990. The term 'Hellenism' was coined by the nineteenth-century German historian J.C. Droysen, in his famous study *Hellenismus*, 1836–43.

71 See also A. Bullock *et al.* eds, *Images and Ideologies: Self-definition in the Hellenistic World*, Berkeley 1995.

72 See R.S. Agarwal, *Trade Centres and Routes in Northern India (c. 322 BC–AD 500)*, Delhi 1982.

73 E.S. Gruen, *The Hellenistic World and the Coming of Rome* I–II, Berkeley 1984.

2 Rome and its empire: the effects and limits of cultural integration

1 Cf, for example, M. Winkler, '*Gladiator': Film and History*, Oxford 2004.

2 E. MacNamara, *The Etruscans*, London 1990, but also, because of its use of recent archaeological material: G. Barker, Th. Rasmussen, *The Etruscans*, London 1996.

3 See, for example, J. Wernicke, *Die Kelten in Italien: Die Einwanderungen und die frühen Handelsbeziehungen zu den Etruskern*, Stuttgart 1989.

4 R.M. Ogilvie, *Early Rome and the Etruscans*, Glasgow 1979.

5 See R.P. Saller, *Patriarchy, Property and Death in the Roman Family*, Cambridge 1994.

6 A. Alföldy, *Early Rome and the Latins*, Ann Arbor 1965; A. Keaveney, *Rome and the Unification of Italy*, London 1987.

7 J. Bleicken, *Die Verfassung der Römischen Republik*, Paderborn 1978; L.R. Taylor, *Roman Voting Assemblies*, Ann Arbor 1990.

8 J. Heurgon, *Rome et la Méditerrannée occidentale jusq'aux guerres puniques*, Paris 1969.

9 Z. Yavetz, *Slaves and Slavery in Ancient Rome*, Oxford 1988.

10 G. Rickman, *The Corn-Supply of Ancient Rome*, Oxford 1980.

11 P. Veyne, *Le Pain et le Cirque*, Paris 1976.

12 K. Christ, *Krise und Untergang der Römischen Republik*, Darmstadt 1979.

13 A.H.M. Jones, *Augustus*, London 1977.

14 See F. Millar, *The Roman Empire and its Neighbours*, London 1967.

15 H.H. Scullard, *Roman Britain: Outpost of the Empire*, London 1979.

16 A survey: J.F. Drinkwater, *Roman Gaul: The Three Provinces, 58 BC–AD 260*, London 1983, 35–53, 143–60.

17 For a survey: R.M. Cimino, ed., *Ancient Rome and India: Commercial and Cultural Contacts between the Roman World and India*, New Delhi 1994.

18 See, for example, M. Benabou, *La Résistance africaine à la romanisation*, Paris 1975.

19 R. Chevallier, *Les Voies romaines*, Paris 1972.

20 For the following: F. Millar, *The Emperor in the Roman World*, London 1977.

21 S.R.F. Price, *Rituals and Power: The Roman Imperial Cult in Asia Minor*, Cambridge 1984.

22 C.G. Starr, *The Roman Empire, 27 BC–AD 476: A Study in Survival*, Oxford 1982.

23 An up-to-date and interesting survey: J.S. Richardson, *The Romans in Spain*, London 1996.

24 F. de Zuleta, ed., *The Institutes of Gaius*, Oxford 1946, I, i–xi, xlviii–xlix.

25 N. Lewis, M. Reinhold, eds, *Roman Civilization: Selected Readings. II: The Empire*, New York 1990, 500–5, 509.

26 J.F. Gardner, *Women in Roman Law and Society*, London 1986. See for a nuanced view of patriarchical authority Saller, *Patriarchy*.

27 See Suetonius, in his section on Augustus of *De Vita Caesarum*, 89; P. Harvey, *The Oxford Companion to Classical Literature*, Oxford 1937, 451.

28 Horace, *Odes*, III, 6.

29 B. Severy, *Augustus and the Family at the Birth of the Roman Empire*, London 2004; B. Rawson, *Children and Childhood in Roman Italy*, Oxford 2004.

30 B. Isaac, *The Invention of Racism in Classical Antiquity*, Princeton 2004. See also: F.M. Snowden, Jr, *Blacks in Antiquity: Ethiopians in the Greco-Roman Experience*, Cambridge, Mass., 1970.

31 S.F. Bonner, *Education in Ancient Rome*, London 1977; M. Beard *et al.* eds, *Literacy in the Roman World*, Ann Arbor 1991.

32 From J.A. Shelton, *As the Romans Do: A Sourcebook in Roman Social History*, New York 1988, 32–3, 106, 117.

33 J. Balsdon, *Romans and Aliens*, London 1979, still provides a very readable overview.

34 C.R. Whittaker, *Rome and its Frontiers. The Dynamics of Empire*, London 2004.

35 B. Cunliffe, *Greeks, Romans and Barbarians: Spheres of Interaction*, London 1988.

36 This and the following quotations from B. Cunliffe, 'Iron Age societies in Western Europe and beyond, 800–140 BC', in B. Cunliffe, ed., *The Oxford Illustrated Prehistory of Europe*, Oxford 1994, 361, 362, 363.

37 B. Kruger, ed., *Die Germanen*, I–II, Berlin 1976, 1986; R. Christlein, *Die Alamannen*, Stuttgart 1978; P. Perrin, L.-C. Feffer, *Les Francs*, I–II, Paris 1987; W. Menguin, *Die Longobarden*, Stuttgart 1986.

38 N. Downs, ed., *Basic Documents in Medieval History*, New York 1959, 9, 10.

39 A survey: M. Todd, *The Early Germans*, London 1992.

40 A discussion of the slow development of tribes into 'proto'-states: L. Hedeager, *Iron-Age Societies: From Tribe to State in Northern Europe, 500 BC to AD 700*, London 1992.

41 As examples: W.A. van Es, *Wijster: A Native Village beyond the Roman Frontier*, Groningen 1967; M. Stenberger, *Vallhagar*, Stockholm 1955.

42 N. Downs, *Basic Documents in Medieval History*, 11.

43 A.A. Lund, *Zum Germanenbild der Römer: Eine Einführung in die antike Ethnographie*, Heidelberg 1990.

44 F. Dvornik, *The Slavs: Their Early History and Civilisation*, London 1956.

45 Ammianus Marcellinus, *History* (Loeb Classical Library), XXXI, ii.
46 Ammianus Marcellinus, *History* (Loeb Classical Library), XVI, iv.

3 An empire lost – an empire won? Christianity and the Roman Empire

1 M. Hengel, *Juden, Griechen und Barbaren: Aspekte des Judentums in vorchristlicher Zeit*, Stuttgart 1976.
2 J. Collins and G. Sterling, eds, *Hellenism in the Land of Israel*, Notre Dame 2000; L. Levine, *Judaism and Hellenism in Antiquity: Conflict or Confluence?* Berkeley 1999.
3 Obviously, biographies of Jesus abound, despite the dearth of reliable sources. A stimulating account is J.D. Crossan, *The Historical Jesus. The Life of a Mediterranean Jewish Peasant*, New York 1991.
4 M. Jack Suggs *et al.* eds, *The Oxford Study Bible*, New York 1992, 1271 sqq.
5 See E.P. Sanders, *The Historical Figure of Jesus*, New York 1993.
6 R.E. Brown, *The Birth of the Messiah*, London 1994.
7 Recently, an effort has been made by G. Vermes, *The Authentic Gospel of Jesus*, Oxford 2003.
8 Many have speculated about early contacts between Israel and India: e.g. H. Goodman, ed., *Between Jerusalem and Benares*, Albany 1994. Obviously, trade continued to be a medium for cultural transfer. Cf. J. Innes Miller, *The Spice Trade of the Roman Empire*, Oxford 1969.
9 A competent survey of Christian Mariology is M. Warner, *Alone of All her Sex. The Myth and the Cult of the Virgin Mary*, New York 1985.
10 R. Turcan, *Mithra et le mithraicisme*, Paris 1993; D. Ulansay, *The Origins of the Mithraic Mysteries: Cosmology and Salvation in the Ancient World*, New York 1985; M.J. Vermaseren, *Die Orientalische Religionen im Römerreich*, Leiden 1981. M. Clauss, *Cultores Mithrai. Die Anhängerschaft des Mithras-Kultes*, Stuttgart 1992, gives the archaeological sites.
11 Cfr. W. Sommerfeld, *Der Aufstieg Marduks*, Kevelaer 1982.
12 Warner, op. cit., is rather vague about this.
13 Cfr. F. Dunand, *Isis: mère des dieux*, Paris 2000; T.T. Tinh, *Isis lactans*, Leiden 1973.
14 For a survey, see A. Böhlig, *Der Manichaeismus*, Zürich 1980, and M. Tardieu, *Le manichéisme*, Paris 1981. Cf. A. Böhlig, 'Der Synkretismus des Mani', in A. Dietrich, ed., *Synkretismus im Syrisch-Persischen Kulturgebiet*, Göttingen 1975, 144–69.
15 J. van Oort, *Jerusalem and Babylon: A Study into Augustine's 'City of God' and the Sources of his Doctrine of the Two Cities*, Leiden 1991.
16 R.M. Ogilvie, *The Romans and their Gods*, London 1979.
17 H.W. Obbink, *Cybele, Isis en Mithras*, Amsterdam 1965; M.J. Vermaseren, *Die orientalischen Religionen im Römerreich*, Leiden 1981.
18 For this and the following quotation: N. Lewis, M. Reinhold, eds, *Roman Civilization: Selected Readings. II: The Empire*, New York 1990, 542, 548–9.
19 R. MacMullen, *Christianizing the Roman Empire*, AD 100–400, New Haven 1984.
20 For a survey: W. den Boer, ed., *Romanitas et Christianitas*, Amsterdam 1973. Also R. Lane Fox, *Pagans and Christians in the Mediterranean World from the Second Century AD to the Conversion of Constantine*, Harmondsworth 1986.
21 See P. Brown, *The World of Late Antiquity*, London 1971, 53.
22 Lewis, Reinhold, *Roman Civilization*, 553–4.
23 B. Knopf, *Ausgewählte Märtyrerakten*, Tübingen 1929, third edition, no. 6.
24 Lewis, Reinhold, *Roman Civilization*, 556–7.
25 N. Downs, ed., *Basic Documents in Medieval History*, Princeton 1959, 17.
26 Cl. Pharr, trans., *The Theodosian Code*, Princeton 1952, XVI, x, 12.
27 Eusebius, *Historia ecclesiastica*, X, vii.
28 R. MacMullen, *Constantine*, London 1987.

29 See Lane Fox, *Pagans and Christians*, but also J. Blecken, *Constantin der Grosse und die Christen: Überlegungen zur konstantinischen Wende*, Munich 1992, 64 sqq.
30 See the analysis in E. Pagels, *The Gnostic Gospels*, London 1982.
31 R. Lim, *Public Disputation, Power and Social Order in Late Antiquity*, Berkeley 1996.
32 Pharr, *Theodosian Code*, XVI, i, 2.
33 Cf. M.R. Salzman, *The Making of a Christian Aristocracy*, New Haven 2004.
34 Pharr, *Theodosian Code*, IX, xvi, 4.
35 Pharr, *Theodosian Code*, II, viii, 18.
36 Pharr, *Theodosian Code*, XVI, x, 12 and 19.
37 Pharr, *Theodosian Code*, XVI, v, 62.
38 See P. Heather, *Goths and Romans, 332–489*, Oxford 1994, who argues that the Goths entering the Empire were not yet a settled group.
39 P. Scardigli, *Lingua e Storia dei Goti*, Florence 1964 [translated as *Die Goten: Sprache und Kultur*, Munich 1973].
40 Scardigli, *Lingua*, 95–132.
41 See E.A. Thompson, *Romans and Barbarians: The Decline of the Western Empire*, Madison 1982.
42 For a survey of these two centuries: A. Cameron, *The Mediterranean World in Late Antiquity: AD 395–600*, London 1993.
43 Cf. J. Liebeschuetz, *Decline and Fall of the Roman City*, Oxford 2001.
44 See R. van Dam, *Leadership and Community in Late Antique Gaul*, Berkeley 1985, esp. 141–52.
45 J. Lindsay, *Byzantium into Europe: The Story of Byzantium as the First Europe (AD 326–1204)*, London 1952; J. Décarreaux, *Byzance ou l'autre Rome*, Paris 1982; M. Whittow, *The Making of Orthodox Byzantium, 600–1025*, London 1993.
46 J. Vogt, *Kulturwelt und Barbaren: zum Menschheitsbild der spätantiken Gesellschaft*, Wiesbaden 1976, 21. See also M. Pavan, *La politica gotica di Teodosio nella publicistica del suo tempo*, Rome 1964.
47 Vogt, *Kulturwelt*, 24.
48 Lewis, Reinhold, *Roman Civilization*, 627.
49 G. Cardona *et al.*, *Indo-European and the Indo-Europeans*, Philadelphia 1970; W.B. Lockwood, *A Panorama of Indo-European Languages*, London 1972.
50 One among many vehement denials of any outside influence on India is P. Choudhury, *The Aryans: A Modern Myth*, New Delhi 1993.

4 Towards one religion for all

1 See J. Fischer, *Oriëns-Occidens-Europa: Begriff und Gedanke 'Europa' im späten Antike und im frühen Mittelalter*, Wiesbaden 1957.
2 G. Wijdeveld, trans., *Augustinus: De Stad van God*, Baarn–Amsterdam 1984, 760.
3 J.W. McCrindle, ed., *Cosmas: The Christian Topography*, London 1897.
4 See J.-G. Arentzen, *Imago Mundi Cartographica: Studien zur Bildlichkeit mittelaltlicher Welt- und Ökumenekarten unter besonderer Berücksichtigung des Zusammenhanges von Text und Bild*, Munich 1980, which, on plates 1 and 1a, has the Kosmas map.
5 R.L. Wilken, *The Christians as the Romans Saw Them*, New Haven 1982, 79 sqq.
6 Some testimonies in M. Führmann, *Europa: zur Geschichte einer kulturellen und politischen Idee*, Konstanz 1981, 23, n. 10.
7 See N. Cohn, *Noah's Flood: The Genesis Story in Western Thought*, Yale 1996.
8 Some testimonies in Führmann, *Europa*, 23, n. 10.
9 The text is in Th. Mommsen, ed., *Monumenta Germaniae Historica: Auctores antiquissimi*, XIII, Berlin 1898, 149 sqq.
10 J. Vogt, *Kulturwelt und Barbaren: zum Menschheitsbild der spätantiken*, Wiesbaden 1976, 39.

11 For the Merovingians see I. Wood, *The Merovingian Kingdoms, 450–751*, London 1993.

12 L. Duchesne, ed., *Liber pontificalis*, Paris 1886, 420.

13 B. Pullan, ed., *Sources for the History of Medieval Europe, from the Mid-eighth to the Mid-thirteenth Century*, Oxford 1966, 176–7.

14 P. de Letter, ed., *St. Prosper of Acquitaine, The Call of All Nations*, London 1950, 46.

15 See R. Fletcher, *The Conversion of Europe: From Paganism to Christianity, AD 371–138*, New York 1997.

16 P. Anderson, *Passages from Antiquity to Feudalism*, London 1974.

17 The text is in R. Rau, ed., *Briefe des Bonifatius: Willibalds Leben des Bonifatius*, Darmstadt 1968, 483, 30; 41–2; 493, 19–23.

18 J. Haldon, *The State and the Tributary Mode of Production*, London 1993, provides a stimulating reappraisal of developments in the west, compared with, especially, the Ottoman Empire.

19 See R. McKitterick, *The Frankish Kingdoms under the Carolingians, 751–987*, London 1983, but also the excellent survey by P. Riché, *Les Carolingiens: une famille qui fit l'Europe*, Paris 1983.

20 See R. Hodges, D. Whitehouse, *Muhammad, Charlemagne and the Origins of Europe: Archaeology and the Pirenne Thesis*, Ithaca 1983.

21 Bartholomew of Lucca, in the fourteenth century, quoted in J. van Laarhoven, *Europa in de Bijbel: kanttekeningen bij een middeleeuws concept*, Nijmegen 1991, 23.

22 J.W. Smit, 'Karel en zijn Kring', *Lampas* 18/2 (1985), 98–108.

23 See the discussion in *Nascità dell'Europa ed Europa Carolingia: un'equazione da verificare*, Spoleto 1981.

24 See a letter from Alcuin, AD 790, in E. Dümmler, ed., *Monumenta Germaniae Historica: Epistolae*, IV, Berlin 1895, 32.

25 See also A. Barbero, *Charlemagne. Father of a Continent*, Berkeley 2004.

26 W. Henze, ed., *Monumenta Germaniae Historica: Epistolae*, VII, Hanover 1928, 388, letter from Emperor Louis II to Emperor Basilius I.

27 Pullan, *Sources*, 27–8.

28 N. Downs, *Documents in Medieval History*, New York 1959, 33.

29 See B. Bischoff, *Manuscripts and Libraries in the Age of Charlemagne*, Cambridge 1994, 61.

30 See T. Stoianovich, ed., *Balkan Civilization: The First and Last Europe*, London 1992.

31 See R. Bartlett, *The Making of Europe: Conquest, Colonization and Cultural Change, 950–1350*, Princeton 1993.

32 A. Hofmeister, ed., *Ottonis Episcopi Frisingensis, Chronica*, V, prologue, in *Monumenta Germaniae Historica: Scriptores Rerum Germanicarum in usu Scholarum*, Hanover 1912, 227.

33 For the background the important synthesis by P. Riché, *Education et culture dans l'Occident barbare, VIe–VIIIe siècle*, Paris 1995.

34 For an example: V.I.J. Flint, *The Rise of Magic in Early Medieval Europe*, Oxford 1991.

35 J.C. Russell, *The Germanization of Early Medieval Christianity*, Oxford 1994.

36 See P. Biller, A. Hudson, eds, *Heresy and Literacy, 1000–1530*, Cambridge 1996; R. Copeland, ed., *Criticism and Dissent in the Middle Ages*, Cambridge 1996.

37 For a survey: C.H. Lawrence, *Medieval Monasticism: Forms of Religious Life in Western Europe in the Middle Ages*, London 1984. A useful reconsideration: L. Milis, *Angelic Monks and Earthly Men*, Woodbridge 1992.

38 For an example: N. Metzer, *Cultural Interplay in the Eighth Century: The Trier Gospels and the Making of a Scriptorium at Echternach*, Cambridge 1994.

39 See P. Dronke, *Intellectuals and Poets in Medieval Europe*, Rome 1992.

40 See Bischoff, *Manuscripts*, 134 sqq. on the role of Benedictine monasteries.

41 E.M. Wischermann, *Grundlagen einer Cluniacensische Bibliotheksgeschichte*, Munich 1988, 8 sqq.

42 P. Dronke, *Women Writers of the Middle Ages: A Critical Study of Texts from Perpetua (d. 203) to Marguerite Parete (d. 1310)*, Cambridge 1984.

43 See J.L. David, R.K. Ehrmann, eds, *The Letters of Hildegard of Bingen*, London 1994; J. Buehler, ed., trans., *Schriften der Heiligen Hildegard von Bingen*, Frankfurt 1980; P. Dronke, *Poetic Individuality in the Middle Ages*, Oxford 1970, 150–79.

44 For a later example: C.B. Bouchard, *Holy Entrepreneurs: Cistercians, Knights and Economic Change in Twelfth-century Burgundy*, Ithaca 1991.

5 Three worlds around the Inner Sea: western Christendom, eastern Christendom and Islam

1 I have borrowed the idea from G. Fowder, *Empire to Commonwealth: Consequences of Monotheism in Late Antiquity*, Princeton 1992.

2 For a survey: A. Hourani, *A History of the Arab Peoples*, Cambridge, Mass., 1991, and P. Crone, *Meccan Trade and the Rise of Islam*, London 1988, who argues that the trade routes, although profitable, were not a source of great riches and of a specific culture based upon it which would account for the genesis of Islam.

3 For a vast survey of the relationship between the three monotheistic religions, see: F.J. Peters, *The Monotheists. Jews, Christians and Muslims in Conflict and Competition*, Princeton 2004.

4 A. Özek, ed., *The Holy Qur'an with English Translation*, Istanbul 1992.

5 See H. Kennedy, *The Prophet and the Age of the Caliphates*, New York 1986.

6 For a survey: A. Dhanun Taha, *The Muslim Conquest and Settlement of North Africa and Spain*, London 1989.

7 See also the interesting survey by: H. Kennedy, *The Court of the Caliphs*, London 2004.

8 For the following: A.Y. al-Hassan, a.o. eds, *Science and Technology in Islam*, Paris 2001.

9 See Ph.K. Hitti, *The Arabs: A Short History*, Chicago 1964, 120.

10 R. Morris, *Monks and Laymen in Byzantium, 843–1138*, Cambridge 1995.

11 D. Baker, ed., *Relations between East and West in the Middle Ages*, Edinburgh 1973.

12 R. Byron, D. Talbot Rice, *The Birth of Western Painting*, New York 1968; see also J. Beckwith, *Studies in Byzantine and Medieval Western Art*, London 1989.

13 D.J. Geanakoplos, *Interaction of the 'Sibling' Byzantine and Western Cultures in the Middle Ages and Italian Renaissance (330–1600)*, New Haven 1976, provides an extensive survey that yet shows the paucity of proof for really intense interaction.

14 A. Davids, ed., *The Empress Theophano: Byzantium and the west at the Turn of the First Millennium*, Cambridge 1996.

15 See R.P. Hughes, I. Piperno, eds, *Christianity and the eastern Slavs II: Russian Culture in Medieval Times*, Berkeley 1994.

16 For a survey: B. Gasparov, O. Raevsky-Hughes, eds, *Christianity and the eastern Slavs I: Slavic Culture in the Middle Ages*, Berkeley 1993; D. Obolensky, *Byzantium and the Slavs*, Crestwood 1994.

17 A. Papadakis, *The Christian East and the Rise of the Papacy*, Crestwood 1994.

18 For the background: W. Montgomery Watt, *Muslim–Christian Encounters: Perceptions and Misperceptions*, London 1992.

19 For a balanced survey: C. Cahen, *Orient et occident au temps des croisades*, Paris 1983.

20 H. Hagenmeyer, ed., *Fulcher von Chartres, Historia Hierosolymitana*, Heidelberg 1913, 130–8, passim.

21 N. Downs, ed., *Basic Documents in Medieval History*, New York 1959, 75–6.

22 F. Gabrieli, trans., ed., *Arab Historians of the Crusades*, 1957; London 1964, 1984, 10–11, 79–80, 83–4, 82.

23 See S. Schein, *Fideles Crucis: The Papacy, the West and the Recovery of the Holy Land,*

1274–1314, Oxford 1991; N. Hously, *The Later Crusades, 1274–1580: From Lyons to Alcazar*, Oxford 1992.
24 W. Stubbs, ed., *Willelmi Malmesburiensis, De Gestis Regum Anglorum*, London 1887, 394–8, passim.

6 One world, many traditions. Elite culture and popular cultures: cosmopolitan norms and regional variations

1 For the following: P. Anderson, *Passages from Antiquity to Feudalism*, London 1978; G. Duby, *The Early Growth of the European Economy: Warriors and Peasants from the Seventh to the Twelfth Century*, London 1978.
2 See H. Clarke, B. Ambrosiani, *Towns in the Viking Age*, London 1995.
3 B. Pullan, ed., *Sources for the History of Medieval Europe, from the Mid-eighth to the Mid-thirteenth Century*, Oxford 1966, 237–8.
4 'Formulae Turonenses', edited by K. Zeumer, *Monumenta Germaniae historica: Formulae Merowingici et Karolingi Aevi*, Hanover 1886, 158.
5 L. Vanderkindere, *Ghislebert de Mons, Chronicon Hanoniense*, Brussels 1904, 13–14.
6 Vanderkindere, *Ghislebert*, 119–20.
7 See the 'iconoclastic' vision proposed by Susan Reynolds in her magnificent study: *Fiefs and Vassals: The Medieval Evidence Reinterpreted*, Oxford 1994.
8 J. Strayer, *On the Medieval Origins of the Modern State*, Princeton 1970.
9 J.A. Hall, *Powers and Liberties: The Causes and Consequences of the Rise of the West*, Oxford 1985, 125 sqq., is highly illuminating on this and related issues.
10 The case defended by J. Boswell, *Christianity, Social Tolerance and Homosexuality: Gay People in Western Europe from the Beginning of the Christian Era to the Fourteenth Century*, Chicago 1980, is definitely strong. It seems, however, that his argument for widespread acceptance of same-sex unions – in *A Marriage of Likeness: Same-sex Unions in Pre-modern Europe*, London 1995 – is less convincing.
11 J.B. Holloway *et al.* eds, *Equally in God's Image: Women in the Middle Ages*, New York 1990; M. Williams, A. Echols, eds, *Between Pit and Pedestal: Women in the Middle Ages*, Princeton 1993.
12 See R.I. Moore, *The Origins of European Dissent*, Oxford 1985, 58.
13 For an example, see A. Classen, ed., *Women as Protagonists and Poets in the German Middle Ages*, Göttingen 1991; H. Solterer, *The Master and Minerva: Disputing Women in French Medieval Culture*, Berkeley 1995.
14 For a survey of the many aspects of the cult of Mary through the ages: N. Perry, L. Echevarria, *Under the Heel of Mary*, London 1989.
15 M. Halissy, *Clean Maids, True Wives, Steadfast Widows: Chaucer's Women and Medieval Codes of Conduct*, Westport 1993.
16 Hall, *Powers*, 130–2.
17 For a survey: D. Sweeney, ed., *Agriculture in the Middle Ages: Technology, Practice and Representation*, Philadelphia 1996.
18 On indigenous developments in Europe: A. Pacey, *The Maze of Ingenuity: Ideas and Idealism in the Development of Technology*, Cambridge, Mass., 1976.
19 On the evolution of the water-mill since its early origins in the eastern parts of the Mediterranean: T.S. Reynolds, *Stronger than a Hundred Men*, Baltimore 1983.
20 J. Gimpel, *The Medieval Machine: The Industrial Revolution of the Middle Ages*, London 1977.
21 J. Landes, *The Field and the Forge. Population, production and power in the pre-industrial west*, Oxford 2004.
22 G. Duby, *The Early Growth of the European Economy*, Ithaca 1977.
23 A.Y. al-Hassan, D.R. Hill, *Islamic Technology: An Illustrated History*, Cambridge 1986.
24 For the following: J. Needham, *Science and Civilization in China*, 7, Cambridge 1986, passim.

25 A.P. Smyth, *King Alfred the Great*, Oxford 1995.

26 J. Krynen, *L'Empire du roi: idées et croyances politiques en France, XIIIe–XVe siècle*, Paris 1993.

27 Cf. B. Reynolds, *Kings and Communities in Western Europe, 900–1300*, Oxford 1997, 34–5, 118–19.

28 Hall, *Powers*, 141 sqq.

29 For example, Krynen, *L'Empire*, for developments in France.

30 Ch. Tilly *et al.* eds, *Cities and the Rise of States in Europe, AD 1000 to 1800*, Oxford 1994, provides a sweeping interpretation. See also E. Pitz, *Europaeisches Staedtewesen und Buergertum: von der Spaetantike bis zum hohen Mittelalter*, Darmstadt 1991.

31 An interesting study is D. Harrison, *The Early State and the Towns: Forms of Integration in Lombard Italy, AD 568–774*, Lund 1993.

32 See the essays in R. Holt, ed., *Houses and Households in Towns, 1000–1600*, London 1998.

33 For a survey: D.C. North, *The Rise of the Western World: A New Economic History*, Cambridge 1976.

34 Pullan, *Sources*, 265–6.

35 For the importance of the towns for the growth of the European concept of freedom, see R.W. Davies, ed., *The Origins of Modern Freedom in the West*, Stanford 1995.

36 Ph. Dollinger, *La Hanse*, Paris 1962.

37 R.S. Lopez, I.W. Raymond, eds, *Medieval Trade in the Mediterranean World*, New York 1955, 416–18, passim.

38 See Davies, *The Origin of Modern Freedom*, as well as G. Dilcher, ed., *Respublica: Burgerschaft in Stadt und Staat*, Berlin 1988.

39 W.-D. Heim, *Romanen und Germanen in Charlemagnes Reich: Untersuchung zur Benennung Romanischer und Germanischer Völker, Sprachen und Länder in Französischen Dichtungen des Mittelalters*, Munich 1984.

40 M.R. James, C.N.L. Brooke, R.A.B. Meyers, eds, *Walter Map De Nugis Curialium: Courtiers' Trifles*, Oxford 1983, 73, 173, 169, 183.

41 L. Wieland, ed., *Deutsche Chroniken. Monumenta Germaniae Historica: Scriptorum qui vernacula lingua usi sunt*, II, Hanover 1876; Zürich 1971, 115, 10; 116, 45; 133, 13–14; 139, 28–30; 150, 28–36.

42 See H.J. Graff, ed., *Literacy and Social Development in the West*, Cambridge 1982.

43 P. Strauch, ed., *Jansen Enikels Werke. Monumenta Germaniae Historica: Scriptorum qui vernacula lingua susi sunt III*, Hanover 1900. For the passages quoted in this chapter: 55, 2,847–53; 382, 20,021; 484–5, 24,837, 24,843; 498, 25,524 sqq.; 499, 25,576; 536, 27,393; 549, 27,661.

44 Strauch, *Jansen Enikel*, 535, 27,509–11; 535, 27,501–4; 536, 27,523–5.

45 His 'Noticia seculi' have been published by H. Grundmann, H. Heimpel, eds, *Monumenta Germaniae Historica: Staatsschriften des späten Mittelalters I*, 1, Stuttgart 1958; for this quote: 155–6.

46 See C. Beaune, *Naissance de la nation française*, Paris 1985, or its enlarged 2nd edition: *The Birth of an Ideology: Myths and Symbols of Nation in Late Medieval France*, Berkeley 1991.

47 F. Kempf, 'Das Problem der Christianitas im 12. und 13. Jahrhundert', *Historisches Jahrbuch* 79 (1960), 104 sqq.; P.E. Schramm, *Kaiser, Rom und Renovatio*, I, Darmstadt 1962, 3rd edition, 74 sqq.

48 R.F.M. Brouwer, trans., ed., *Dante Alighieri, De Monarchia en andere politieke teksten*, Baarn 1993, I, ch. 5; III, chs 13–15.

49 Ch.-V. Langlois, ed., P. Dubois, *De Recuperatione Terrae Sanctae*, Paris 1891, 1 sqq.

50 A. Gewirth, ed., trans., *Marsiglio of Padua: The Defender of Peace*, New York 1956.

51 See A. Erlande-Brandenburg, *The Cathedral: The Social and Architectural Dynamics of Construction*, Cambridge 1994.

52 L.J. Lekai, *The Cistercians: Ideals and Reality*, London 1977.
53 C. Stephen Jaeger, *The Origins of Courtliness: Civilizing Trends and the Formation of Courtly Ideals, 939–1310*, Philadelphia 1985.
54 A survey: A.S. Bernardi, S. Levin, eds, *The Classics in the Middle Ages*, Binghampton 1990.
55 An impressive case study: M.T. Clanchy, *From Memory to Written Record: England, 1066–1307*, Oxford 1992.
56 See I.D. Reynolds, N.G. Wilson, *Scribes and Scholars: A Guide to the Transmission of Greek and Latin Literature*, Oxford 1991.
57 For Notker Balbulus: G.H. Pertz, ed., *Monumenta Germaniae Historica: Scriptores, II*, Hanover 1829, 330; his *Gesta Karoli*, in R. Rau, ed., *Quellen zur Karolingischen Reichsgeschichte*, III, Darmstadt 1964, 344, 366; for Nithard: Rau, I, Darmstadt 1962, 386, 448.
58 For the background of the concepts 'little' and 'great' tradition: P. Burke, *Popular Culture in Europe*, London 1978, 28.
59 For a still masterful survey: M. Bloch, *La Société féodale*, Paris 1968; orig. 1939–40.
60 B. Reynolds, trans., *Dante Alighieri, la Vita Nuova*, Harmondsworth 1980, 97.
61 Good reading is provided by J. Sumption, *Pilgrimage: An Image of Medieval Religion*, London 1975; R. Stoppani, *Le grandi vie di pellegrinaggio del medioevo: le Strade per Roma*, Florence 1986.
62 A survey with many illustrations: N.N., *Santiago. Camino de Europa: Culto y Cultura en la Peregrinación a Compostela*, Santiago 1993.
63 D.G. Rossetti, trans., *The New Life by Dante Alighieri*, London 1904, sonnet 40.
64 N. Coghill, ed., trans., *Geoffrey Chaucer, The Canterbury Tales*, Harmondsworth 1960, 20–1.
65 R. Lafont, *La Geste de Roland*, I–II, Paris 1991; W. van Emden, *La Chanson de Roland*, London 1995, gives the text of one of the many versions.
66 A good survey of the many elements that made up the 'world of the knight' is R. Barber, *The Knight and Chivalry*, London 1996.
67 M.E. Lacarra, *El Poema de Mio Cid: realidad historica e ideologia*, Madrid 1980. The text has been translated by P. Such, J. Hodgkinson, *The Poem of my Cid*, Warminster 1987.
68 S. Reynolds, *Fiefs and Vassals: The Medieval Evidence Reinterpreted*, Oxford 1995.
69 G. Duby, *Les Trois ordres ou l'imaginaire du féodalisme*, Paris 1978.
70 Ch. Potoin, ed., *Oeuvres de Ghillebert de Lannoy, voyageur, diplomate et moraliste*, Leuven 1878.
71 See Th. Bender, ed., *The University and the City: From Medieval Origins to the Present*, New York 1988.
72 A survey that is also a plea for the notion that this specific culture dominated Europe until the end of the eighteenth century is R.W. Southern, *Scholastic Humanism and the Unification of Europe. I: Foundations*, London 1995.
73 Pullan, *Sources*, 104.
74 Migne, *Patrologia Latina*, 178, cols 1339–49.
75 G. Makdisi, *The Rise of Humanism in Classical Islam and the Christian West: With Special Reference to Scholasticism*, Edinburgh 1990.
76 A. Lewis, *The Islamic World and the West*, AD 622–1492, New York 1970.
77 B. Reilly, *The Contest of Christian and Muslim Spain, 1031–1157*, London 1992.
78 A synthesis: S.K. Jayyusi, ed., *The Legacy of Muslim Spain*, Leiden 1992.
79 Cf. G. Andress, a.o. eds, *Averroes and the Aristotelian Tradition*, Leiden 1999.
80 Quoted in H.-J. Störig, *Geschiedenis van de Filosofie*, I, Utrecht 1972, 246–7.
81 N. Downs, ed., *Documents in Medieval History*, New York 1959, 134–5.
82 Pullan, *Sources*, 105–8.
83 For a history of the phenomenon of language as a constructor of identity: P. Burke, R. Porter, eds, *Language, Self and Society*, London 1991.

84 F.P. van Oostrom, *Het Woord van Eer: Literatuur aan het Hollandse hof omstreeks 1400*, Amsterdam 1987, 18–22.
85 S. Bertino, *Le Strade della Civiltà: I grandi itinerari della Storia di ieri e di oggi*, Milan 1984.

Interlude: the worlds of Europe, *c*.1400–1800

1 For a general survey of this 'world', which many would think of as the world of the Middle Ages, see A. Gurevich, *Historical Anthropology of the Middle Ages*, Cambridge 1992. W. Rosener, *The Peasantry of Europe*, London 1994, provides a survey from the early Middle Ages to the present.
2 A. Cowan, *Urban Europe, 1500–1700*, London 1997, provides a very competent overview of life in Europe's cities.
3 B. Lepetit, J. Hoock, eds, *La Ville et l'innovation: relais et reseaux de diffusion en Europe, 14e–19e siècles*, Paris 1987.
4 See P. Hohenberg, *The Making of Urban Europe, 1000–1994*, Cambridge, Mass., 1995; G. Huppert, *After the Black Death: A Social History of Early Modern Europe*, Bloomington 1986, esp. ch. 1, 'The eternal village'.
5 The near all-importance of food has been sketched, albeit impressionistically, in two studies by P. Camporesi, *Bread of Dreams: Food and Fantasy in Early Modern Europe*, London 1989, and *The Magic Harvest: Food, Folklore and Society*, London 1993, as well as in his *The Land of Hunger*, London 1995.
6 W.H. McNeill, *Plagues and Peoples*, Oxford 1977.
7 Cf. R. Chartier, 'De praktijk van het geschreven woord', in Chartier, ed., *Geschiedenis van het Persoonlijk Leven 3: Van de Renaissance tot de Verlichting*, Amsterdam 1989, 95–139.
8 This, at least, is the outcome of the research by H. Roosenboom, *De Dorpsschool in de Meijerij van 's-Hertogenbosch van 1648 tot 1795*, Tilburg 1997.
9 See V. Fumagalli, *Landscapes of Fear: Perceptions of Nature and the City in the Middle Ages*, Cambridge 1993.
10 J. Riess, *Luca Signorelli's Orvieto Frescoes*, Princeton 1995.
11 See: P. Stanford, *Heaven: A Traveller's Guide to the Undiscovered Country*, London 2003.
12 See P. Burke, 'The invention of leisure in Early Modern Europe', *Past and Present* 146 (1995), 136–50.
13 See C. Ginzburg, *The Cheese and the Worms: The Cosmos of a Sixteenth-century Miller*, London 1980, who deals with the methodological problems involved.
14 The best survey to date of this complex way of writing cultural history is P. Burke, *Popular Culture in Early Modern Europe*, London 1978.
15 For a survey of this field, on which opinions between scholars continue to clash: G. Duby, ed., *Amour et sexualité en Occident*, Paris 1991.
16 J. Delumeau, *Une histoire du paradis*, Paris, 1992.
17 G. Klaniczay, *The Uses of Supranatural Power: The Transformation of Popular Religion in Medieval and Early Modern Europe*, Cambridge 1990.
18 See the position taken in L. Milis, ed., *De heidense Middeleeuwen*, Brussels 1991.
19 A. Murray, *Reason and Society in the Middle Ages*, Oxford 1978, provides a fine introduction to the phenomenon of the mathematization of European culture. It does so rather more satisfactorily than A. Crosby, *The Measure of Reality: Quantification and Western Society, 1250–1600*, Cambridge 1996.
20 For a survey: M.L. Bush, ed., *Social Orders and Social Classes in Europe since 1500*, Harlow 1992.
21 For example, J. Kaplow, *The Names of Kings: The Parisian Labouring Poor in the Eighteenth Century*, New York 1972.

22 A survey of the attitudes involved: M. Sommerville, *Sex and Subjugation: Attitudes to Women in Early Modern Society*, London 1995.
23 N. Davis, ed., *Paston Letters and Papers of the Fifteenth Century*, I–II, Oxford 1971, 1976.
24 See N. Armstrong, L. Tennenhouse, eds, *The Ideology of Conduct*, New York 1987.
25 An interesting case: A. Pardailhé-Galabrun, *The Birth of Intimacy: Privacy and Domestic Life in Early Modern Paris*, London 1991.
26 The problem of childhood is one of the most discussed topics in recent cultural history. It seems that the original thesis about the 'invention' of childhood in the seventeenth century, voiced by Ph. Ariès, *L'Enfant et la vie familiale sous l'ancien régime*, Paris 1960, should definitely be revised; see e.g. S. Shahar, *Childhood in the Middle Ages*, London 1990; B.A. Hanawalt, *Growing Up in Medieval London: The Experience of Childhood in History*, New York 1993.
27 From the vast literature: S. Brauner, *Fearless Wives and Frightened Shrews: The Construction of the Witch in Early Modern Germany*, Amherst 1996, as well as R. Briggs, *Witches and Neighbours*, London 1997.
28 For a survey that compares the European experience to that of other cultures: A. Burgière *et al.* eds, *A History of the Family*, II, London 1996.
29 L. Bogaers, 'Geleund over de onderdeur: Doorkijkjes in het Utrechtse buurtleven van de vroege Middeleeuwen tot in de zeventiende eeuw', *Bijdragen en Mededelingen betreffende de Geschiedenis der Nederlanden* 112 (1997), 336–64.
30 Instances are given in P. Burke, *The Historical Anthropology of Early Modern Italy: Essays in Perception and Communication*, Cambridge 1987.
31 For example, E.M. Benabou, *La Prostitution et la police des moeurs au XVIIIe siècle*, Paris 1981.
32 Instances in M. Barberito, ed., *Giacinto Gigli, Diario di Roma, 1608–1670*, I–II, Rome 1994.
33 See R. van Dülmen, 'Das Schauspiel des Todes', in R. van Dülmen, N. Schindler, eds, *Volkskultur: zur Wiederentdeckung des vergessenen Alltags*, Frankfurt 1984, 203–45.
34 See A. Demandt, ed., *Mit Fremden leben: eine Kulturgeschichte von der Antike bis zur Gegenwart*, Munich 1995.
35 See: R. Briggs, *Witches and Neighbours. The social and cultural context of European witchcraft*, Oxford 2002, maps 1 and 2.
36 See: L. Roper, *Witch Craze*, New Haven 2004.
37 Cf. P. Burke, *Languages and Communities in Early Modern Europe*, Cambridge 2004.
38 R.A. Houston, *Literacy in Early Modern Europe: Culture and Education, 1500–1800*, London 1988, 207.
39 See L. Trenard, 'L'enseignemant de la langue nationale', in D.N. Burke, ed., *The Making of Frenchmen: Current Directions in the History of Education in France, 1679–1979*, Waterloo 1980, 95–114; R.A. Houston, *Literacy in Early Modern Europe: Culture and Education, 1500–1800*, London 1988, 40 sqq.
40 E. Weber, *Peasants into Frenchmen*, London 1976.
41 P.J.A.N. Rietbergen, 'Beeld en zelfbeeld: "Nederlandse identiteit" in politieke structuur en politieke cultuur tijdens de Republiek', *Bijdragen en Mededelingen betreffende de Geschiedenis der Nederlanden* 107 (1992), 635–56.

7 A new society: Europe's changing views of man

1 See R. Jacoff, ed., *The Cambridge Companion to Dante*, Cambridge 1993.
2 A very perceptive study of the thinkers of the Renaissance is L.M. Baktin, *Gli Umanisti Italiani: Stile di Vita e di Pensiero*, Rome 1990. E. Garin, ed., *L'Uomo del Rinascimento*, Rome 1988, provides an attractive series of portraits of various Renaissance 'types'.

3 A masterly succinct survey is given by G. Nauert, *Humanism and the Culture of Renaissance Europe*, Cambridge 1995.
4 An exhaustive survey: A. Rabil, ed., *Renaissance Humanism: Foundations, Forms and Legacy*, I–III, Philadelphia 1988.
5 Piccolomini's treatise on Europe is in A.S. Piccolomini (Pius II), *Opera*, Basle 1551, 387 sqq.
6 W. Fritzemeyer, *Christenheit und Europa*, Munich-Berlin 1931, 18.
7 Fritzemeyer, *Christenheit*.
8 See Piccolomini's *Oratio de Constantinopolitana clade*, in his *Opera*, 682.
9 See Piccolomini's *Bulla de profectione in Turcos*, in his *Opera*, 923.
10 P.O. Kristeller, *Il pensiero filosofico di Marsilio Ficino*, Florence 1953; a German edition was published in 1972. Further: E. Garin, *La cultura filosofica del Rinascimento italiano*, Florence 1961; P.O. Kristeller, *Marsilio Ficino and his work after five hundred years*, Florence 1987.
11 D.J. Geanakoplos, *Constantinople and the West*, Madison 1989; J.J. Yiannias, ed., *The Byzantine Tradition after the Fall of Constantinople*, London 1991; D.M. Nicol, *Byzantium and Venice: A Study in Diplomatic and Cultural Relations*, Cambridge 1992.
12 R. Sabbadini, *Storia del Ciceronianismo*, Turin 1885, 82.
13 G. Christianson, Th. Izbicki, eds, *Nicholas of Cusa in Search of God and Wisdom*, London 1991.
14 A.G. Weiler, *Desiderius Erasmus: De spiritualiteit van een christen-humanist*, Nijmegen 1997, provides an up-to-date evaluation of Erasmus' spiritual significance. For a biography see L. Halkin, *Erasme parmi nous*, Paris 1987; trans. as *Erasmus: A Critical Biography*, Oxford 1993.
15 P.S. Allen, ed., *Opus Epistolarum Des: Erasmi Roterodami*, Oxford 1913, III, 587 sq., Erasmus to Cardinal Wolsey, 18 May 1519.
16 C. Nicholl, *Leonardo da Vinci: Flights of the Mind*, New York 2004.
17 G.L. Hersey, *The Evolution of Allure: Sexual Selection from the Medici Venus to the Incredible Hulk*, Cambridge, Mass., 1996.
18 R.J. Clements, ed., *Michelangelo: A Self Portrait*, Englewood Cliffs, NJ, 1963, 37, 44.
19 G. Bull, ed., trans., *The Autobiography of Benvenuto Cellini*, Harmondsworth 1956, 15, 28, 29, 31, 37–8.
20 E. Garin, ed., *La Disputa delle Arti nel Quattrocento*, Florence 1947, 5–6.
21 Cf. P. Rietbergen, *De Retoriek van de Eeuwige Stad: Rome gelezen*, Nijmegen 2003.
22 The preceding is surveyed succinctly in G. Quazza, *La Decadenza Italiana nella Storia Europea*, Turin 1971.
23 P. Bange, ed., *De doorwerking van de Moderne Devotie*, Hilversum 1988; R.R. Post, *The Modern Devotion: Confrontation with Reformation and Humanism*, Leiden 1968.
24 M.M. Phillips, *Erasmus and the Northern Renaissance*, Woodbridge 1981.

8 A new society: Europe as a wider world

1 W.Ch. Jordan, *The Great Famine: Northern Europe in the Early Fourteenth Century*, Princeton 1996, is a good survey.
2 F. Chabod, 'L'Idea di Europa', *Rassegna d'Italia* II (1947), 7.
3 F.-M Arouet, Voltaire, *Le Siècle de Louis XIV*, Paris 1752.
4 E.J. Jones, *The European Miracle: Environment, Economies and Geopolitics in the History of Europe and Asia*, Cambridge 1987.
5 Francis Bacon, *Novum Organum*, London 1620 or later editions, aphorism 129.
6 M. Devèze, R. Marx, trans., eds, *Textes et documents d'histoire moderne*, Paris 1967, 77–8.
7 An excellent introduction is provided by L. Avrin, *Scribes, Script and Books: The Book Arts from Antiquity to the Renaissance*, Chicago 1991; a beautifully illustrated survey

of all aspects of medieval manuscript production is J. Glenisson, ed., *Le Livre au moyen âge*, Paris 1988.

8 See P. Gumbert, *The Dutch and their Books in the Manuscript Age*, London 1989.

9 C. Bozzolo, E. Ornato, *Pour une histoire du livre manuscrit au moyen âge*, Paris 1983, especially part I: 'La production du livre manuscrit en France du Nord', 15–121.

10 H. Bresc, *Livre et société en Sicile (1299–1499)*, Palermo 1971, 187, table 2.

11 For the general background: Tsien Tsuen-Hsuin, *Paper and Printing*, Cambridge 1985 [= J. Needham, ed., *Science and Civilisation in China*, 1].

12 J. Moran, *Printing Presses: History and Development from the Fifteenth Century to Modern Times*, Berkeley 1973.

13 For the following: E.L. Eisenstein, *The Printing Press as an Agent of Change: Communication and Cultural Transformation in Early Modern Europe*, I–II, Cambridge 1979.

14 The problem of economic and technological stagnation in the east in general, and in the Chinese Empire in particular has been much discussed, lately, with very interesting but largely non-conclusive and always contradictory interpretations being brought forward by various authors. See M. Elvin, *The Pattern of the Chinese Past*, London 1973; C.A. Alvares, *Homo Faber: Technology and Culture in India, China and the West from 1500 to the Present Day*, The Hague 1980.

15 D.S. Landes, *Revolution in Time: Clocks and the Making of the Modern World*, Cambridge, Mass., 1983.

16 W. Schivelbusch, *The Railway Journey: The Industrialization of Space and Time*, New York 1986.

17 G.R. Elton, *Renaissance and Reformation, 1300–1648*, London 1963, 135–40.

18 For a splendid overview, see D. MacCulloch, *Reformation. Europe's House Divided, 1490–1700*, London 2003.

19 A.R. Wentz, ed., *Luther's Works*, Philadelphia 1959, XXXVI, 66–7.

20 J.I. Packer, O.R. Johnston, trans., eds, *Martin Luther: On the Bondage of the Will*, London 1957, 80–1, 313–14.

21 Cf. B. Erne, ed., *De Gentse Spelen van 1539*, The Hague 1982.

22 J. Black, *Kings, Nobles and Commoners: States and Societies in Early Modern Europe*, London 2004.

23 The problematic nature of the term 'intellectual' as used in European cultural history is best illustrated by the following three studies, each a valuable contribution in its own right: J. le Goff, *Intellectuals in the Middle Ages*, Oxford 1993, originally Paris 1957; D. Masseau, *L'Invention de l'intellectuel dans l'Europe du XVIIIe siècle*, Paris 1994; C. Charle, *Naissance des intellectuels 1880–1900*, Paris 1990. I take an intellectual to be a person who, from a certain background of erudition or perhaps even specialized scholarship, participates in the wider debate regarding the functioning and direction of his culture and society.

24 See among others: E. Kaeber, *Die Idee des Europäischen Gleichgewichts in der publizistischen Literatur vom 16. bis zur Mitte des 18. Jahrhunderts*, Berlin 1907.

25 W. Schmale in his introduction to W. Schmale, N.L. Dodd, eds, *Revolution des Wissens? Europa und seine Schulen im Zeitalter der Aufklärung*, Bochum 1991.

26 R. O'Day, *Education and Society, 1500–1800: The Social Foundations of Education in Early Modern Britain*, London 1982, 13, 42.

27 D. Cressy, *Literacy and the Social Order: Reading and Writing in Tudor and Stuart England*, Cambridge 1980, 175–89.

28 F. Furet, J. Ozouf, *Lire et ecrire: l'alphabétisation des français de Calvin à Jules Ferry*, Paris 1977, 59–68.

29 K.P. Luria, *Territories of Grace: Cultural Change in the Seventeenth-Century Diocese of Grenoble*, Berkeley 1991.

30 J.M. Lloyd Thomas, ed., *The Autobiography of Richard Baxter*, London 1931, 3–4.

31 See R. Gawthrop, G. Strauss, 'Protestantism and literacy in early modern Germany', *Past and Present* 104 (1984), 31–55; G. Strauss, 'Lutheranism and literacy: a reassessment', in K. von Greyerz, ed., *Religion and Society in Early Modern Europe, 1500–1800*, London 1984, 109–23; R.A. Crofts, 'Printing, reform and the Catholic Reformation in Germany', *The Sixteenth Century Journal* 16 (1985), 369–81; R.B. Bottigheimer, 'Bible reading, "Bibles" and the Bible for children in early modern Germany', *Past and Present* 139 (1993), 66–89.

32 For example, T. Watt, *Cheap Print and Popular Piety, 1550–1640*, Cambridge 1991.

33 See also P.E. Grendler, *Schooling in Renaissance Italy: Literacy and Learning, 1300–1600*, Baltimore 1989, 111 sqq.

34 H. Chisich, *The Limits of Reform in the Enlightenment: Attitudes toward the Education of the Lower Classes in Eighteenth-century France*, Princeton 1981.

35 This argument has been raised by A. Grafton, L. Jardine, *From Humanism to the Humanities: Education and the Liberal Arts in Fifteenth- and Sixteenth-Century Europe*, Cambridge, Mass., 1986, 17; see also G. Strauss, 'Liberal or illiberal arts?', *Journal of Social History* (1981), 361–7.

36 N. Kolowski, J.B. Lasek, eds, *Internationales Comenius-Kolloquium*, Bayreuth 1991; G. Michel, *Die Welt als Schule*, Hanover 1978.

37 R.A. Houston, *Literacy in Early Modern Euope: Culture and Education, 1500–1800*, London 1988, 83 sqq.

38 See, for example, R. Kagan, *Students and Society in Early Modern Spain*, London 1974; L. Brockliss, *French Higher Education in the Seventeenth and Eighteenth Centuries*, Oxford 1987.

39 See also: W. Frijhoff, 'Grandeur des nombres et misères des réalités: la courbe de Franz Eulenburg et le débat sur le nombre des intellectuels en Allemagne, 1576–1815', in D. Julia *et al.* eds, *Histoire sociale des populations étudiantes I*, Paris 1986, 23–64.

40 See also: H. Blumenberg, 'Der Prozess der theoretischen Neugierde', in his *Die Legitimität der Neuzeit*, Frankfurt 1966, 201–433.

41 N.G. Wilson, *From Byzantium to Italy: Greek Studies in the Italian Renaissance*, London 1992.

42 D. Baggioni, *Langues et Nations en Europe*, Paris 1997.

43 R. Myers, M. Harris, *Censorship and the Control of Printing in England and France, 1600–1910*, Winchester 1992.

44 For the following: M.U. Edwards, *Printing, Propaganda and Martin Luther*, Berkeley 1994.

45 R.W. Scribner, *For the Sake of Simple Folk: Popular Propaganda for the German Reformation*, Oxford 1994.

46 J.L. Koerner, *The Reformation of the Image*, Chicago 2004.

47 See T. Watt, *Cheap Print and Popular Piety, 1550–1640*, Cambridge 1991.

48 For an overview of, often conflicting, interpretations, see M. Luebke, ed., *The Counter-Reformation*, London 1990.

49 See also: L. Chatellier, *The Europe of the Devout. The Catholic Reformation and the Formation of a New Society*, Cambridge 1989.

50 M. Novak, *The Catholic Ethics and the Spirit of Capitalism*, New York 1993.

51 See for an illuminating example S. Anglo, ed., *Chivalry in the Renaissance*, Woodbridge 1990, 1–12, for Anglo's essay 'How to kill a man at your ease: fencing books and the duelling ethic'.

52 Especially by the great historian of the process, Norbert Elias, in his *The Civilizing Process. I: The History of Manners*, New York 1978.

53 E.C. Riley, *Don Quijote*, Winchester, Mass., 1986.

54 See A. Flores, M.J. Bernadete, *Cervantes across the Centuries*, New York 1947.

55 R. Palmer, *The Sound of History*, Oxford 1988, 1–29.

56 C. Kruyskamp, ed., *Mariken van Nieumeghen*, Antwerp 1982, vs. 227–30.

57 See L. Smith, *Reason's Disciples: Seventeenth-Century English Feminists*, Urbana 1982.

58 E.L. Eisenstein, 'Revolution and the printed word', in R. Porter, M. Teich, eds, *Revolution in History*, Cambridge 1986, 190–2.

59 On the problem of the frontiers of Europe: R. Bartlett, A. Mackay, eds, *Medieval Frontier Societies*, Oxford 1994.

60 See J.-Cl. Margolin, ed., *L'Humanisme portugais et l'Europe*, Paris 1984; M. Simões, 'Camões e a Identidade Nacional', *Peregrinação* 5 (1984), 3–8; J. Kaye, 'Islamic imperialism and the creation of some ideas of Europe', in F. Barker, *et al.* eds, *Europe and its Others*, Colchester 1985, 59–71.

61 R. Beaton, *Folk Poetry of Modern Greece*, Cambridge 1980; R. Beaton, D. Ricks, eds, *'Digenes Akrites': New Approaches to Byzantine Heroic Poetry*, Aldershot 1995.

62 H.R. Cooper, *Judith*, Boulder 1991.

63 C. Barbolani, ed., *Juan de Valdes, Diálogo de la Lengua*, Madrid 1992, 132.

9 A new society: Europe and the wider world since the fifteenth century

1 I.M. Franck, D.M. Brownstone, *The Silk Road: A History*, New York 1986.

2 For a brilliant survey of this world: K.N. Chaudhuri, *Asia before Europe: The Economy and Civilization of the Indian Ocean from the Rise of Islam to 1750*, Cambridge 1990.

3 The most recent in a long line of authors who have doubted Polo's presence in China, F. Wood, *Did Marco Polo Go to China?*, London 1995, cannot really substantiate her claim.

4 J. Needham, *Clerks and Craftsmen in China and the West: Lectures and Addresses on the History of Science and Technology*, Cambridge 1970, 239 sqq.

5 N. Perrin, *Giving Up the Gun: Japan's Reversion to the Sword, 1543–1879*, Boston 1979.

6 C.G. Ekeborg, *Kort Berättelser om den chineska Landthusholdningen*, Stockholm 1757. A German translation followed in 1765; English and French ones in 1771.

7 A fundamental study is J.H. Elliott, *The Old World and the New, 1492–1650*, Cambridge 1992.

8 The most recent documentation can be found in *Amerika 1492–1992. Neue Welten, Neue Wirklichkeiten. Eine Dokumentation*, Berlin 1992, and *Amerika 1492–1992. Neue Welten, Neue Wirklichkeiten. Geschichte – Gegenwart – Perspektive*, Berlin 1992. Besides these, H.J. König, *Die Entdeckung und Eroberung Amerikas*, Berlin 1992, is fascinating as well for the visual material of the time presented in it.

9 The already substantial amount of literature on the 'discoverer' greatly swelled in 1992. One of the useful titles is W.D. Phillips, C.R. Phillips, *The Worlds of Christopher Columbus*, Cambridge 1992.

10 W. Uitterhoeve, H. Werner, eds, *Christoffel Columbus: De Ontdekking van Amerika. Scheepsjournaal 1492–1493*, Nijmegen 1992, 48, 55, 65, 79, 80, 81, 84, 88, 114, etc., for mentions concerning Cipangu and Cathay.

11 Uitterhoeve, Werner, *Columbus*, e.g. 66, 71, 73, 78, 83 etc., on the beauty of the islands; 90, 100, on the beauty of language; 96, 97 on the absence of evil; 65, 97–8 on the natural belief in God; 93 on the absence of weapons and laws. For the quote: 116.

12 Quoted in D. Divine, *Ontdekkers van een Nieuwe Wereld*, Bussum 1973, 249.

13 Quoted in Divine, *Ontdekkers*, 245.

14 Quoted in Divine, *Ontdekkers*, 246.

15 For an overview of the influence of tobacco on different cultures of the world see J. Goodman, *Tobacco in History: The Cultures of Dependence*, London 1993.

16 R.N. Salaman, *The History and Social Influence of the Potato*, Cambridge 1949.

17 E. Forster and R. Forster, eds, *European Diet from Preindustrial to Modern Times*, New York 1975; R. Forster, O. Ranum, eds, *Food and Drink in History*, Baltimore 1979.

18 S.W. Mintz, *Sweetness and Power*, New York 1985.

19 A very informed case study: S. Gruzinski, *The Conquest of Mexico: The Incorporation of Indian Societies into the western World, sixteenth–eighteenth Centuries*, London 1993.

20 A. Crosby, Jr, *The Columbian Exchange: Biological and Cultural Consequences of 1492*, Westport 1972.

21 Crosby, *The Columbian Exchange*, 158–60.

22 For the following: H. Kellenbenz, ed., *Precious Metals in the Age of Expansion*, Stuttgart 1981; J.F. Richards, ed., *Precious Metals in the Later Medieval and Early Modern Worlds*, Durham 1983, especially 397–496.

23 H. Pohl, ed., *The European Discovery of the New World and its Economic Effects on Pre-Industrial Society, 1500–1800*, Stuttgart 1990.

24 See R. Pieper, *Die Preisrevolution in Spanien (1500–1640)*, Stuttgart 1985.

25 R. Ehrenberg, *Capital and Finance in the Age of the Renaissance: A Study of the Fuggers and their Connections*, New York 1963, 80.

26 H. Rowen, C.I. Ekberg, eds, *Early Modern Europe: A Book of Source Readings*, Ithaca 1973, 74–5.

27 Rowen, Ekberg, *Early Modern Europe*, 77.

28 On the problem: E. Zerubavel, *Terra Cognita: The Mental Discovery of America*, New Brunswick 1992.

29 See also J.B. Russel, *Inventing the Flat Earth: Columbus and Modern Historians*, New York 1910.

30 Two recent surveys: J. Brotton, *Trading Territories: Mapping the Early Modern World*, London 1997; J. Black, *Maps and Politics*, London 1997.

31 L. Bergreen, *Over the Edge of the World: Magellan's Terrifying Circumnavigation of the Globe*, London 2004.

32 J. Fischer, F. von Wieser, eds, trans., *Martin Waldseemüller: Cosmographiae Introductio*, Ann Arbor 1966, 68–70.

33 A. Taylor, *The World of Gerard Mercator*, London 2004.

34 See Bodin's *Methodus ad facilem historiarum cognitionem*, in P. Mesnard, ed., *Jean Bodin, Oeuvres Philosophiques*, Paris 1951, 223 sqq.

35 The following studies deal with this problem: S. Greenblatt, *Marvellous Possessions: The Wonders of the New World*, Oxford 1991; A. Grafton, A. Shelford, N. Siraisi, *New Worlds, Old Texts: The Power of Tradition and the Shock of Discovery*, Cambridge, Mass., 1992.

36 L.E. Huddleston, *Origins of the American Indians: European Concepts, 1492–1729*, Austin 1967.

37 K. Crossley-Holland, ed., *The Oxford Book of Travel Verse*, Oxford 1986, 364–5.

38 Crossley-Holland, *Travel Verse*, 365–6.

39 J.A. Levenson, ed., *Circa 1492: Art in the Age of Exploration*, Washington, DC, 1991.

40 Shakespeare, *The Tempest*, Act I, Scene II, 407–14.

41 Shakespeare, *The Tempest*, Act II, Scene II, 163–4, 166–8.

42 For the psychological background: O. Manoni, *Prospéro et Caliban: psychologie de la colonisation*, Paris 1984.

43 P.N. Carroll, *Puritanism and the Wilderness: The Intellectual Significance of the New England Frontier, 1629–1700*, New York 1969, 72, 112, 134.

44 R.H. Pearce, *Savagism and Civilization: A Study of the Indian and the American Mind*, Berkeley 1988, 23.

45 L.B. Wright, ed., *Robert Beverly: History of the Present State of Virginia*, Chapel Hill, NC, 1947, 235.

46 Lawson's *History of North Carolina*, Richmond 1937, 251–2.

47 A short but excellent survey of the process is U. Bitterli, *Cultures in Conflict: Encounters between European and Non-European Cultures, 1492–1800*, London 1993.
48 D. Heikamp, *Mexico and the Medici*, Florence 1972.
49 G.Th.M. Lemmens, 'Die Schenkung an Ludwig XIV. und die Auflösung der brasilianischen Sammlung des Johann Moritz 1652–1679', in G. de Werd, ed., *Soweit der Erdkreis reicht: Johann Moritz von Nassau-Siegen, 1604–1679*, Cleves 1979, 265–93.
50 P.J.A.N. Rietbergen, 'Zover de aarde rijkt. De werken van Johan Nieuhof (1618–1672) als illustratie van het probleem der cultuur- en mentaliteits geschiedenis tussen specialisatie en integratie', *De Zeventiende Eeuw* 2–1 (1986), 17–40.
51 J.-M. Apostolides, *Le Roi-machine: spectacle et politique au temps de Louis XIV*, Paris 1981.
52 Th. Hetzer, *Die Fresken Tiepolos in der Würzburger Residenz*, Frankfurt 1943; see also C. le Corbeiller, 'Miss America and her sisters: personifications of the four parts of the world', *The Metropolitan Museum of Art Bulletin*, April 1961.
53 *Federschmuck und Kaiserkrone: Das barocke Amerikabild in den Habsburgischen Ländern*, Schlosshof im Marchfeld 1992.
54 S. Münster, *Cosmographia Universalis*, Basle 1559, 40–1.
55 See also U. Nef, *Cultural Foundations of Industrial Civilization*, Cambridge 1958.
56 S. Purchas, *Hakluytus Posthumus or Purchas His Pilgrimes*, New York 1965 [originally *Works of the Hakluyt Society*, Extra Series I, London 1905], 248, 249, 250, 251.
57 Purchas, *Pilgrimes*, 251.
58 M. Eliav-Feldon, *Realistic Utopias: The Ideal Imaginary Societies of the Renaissance, 1516–1630*, Oxford 1982; J.C. Davis, *Utopia and the Ideal Society: A Study of English Utopian Writing, 1516–1700*, Cambridge 1981, 299.
59 Pearce, *Savagism*, 86.

10 A new society: migration, travel and the diffusion and integration of culture in Europe

1 Much has been written on the development of the travel story, which became a literary genre in the course of time, and on the use of such stories as historical sources. I mention only B.I. Krasnobaev *et al.* eds, *Reisen und Reisebeschreibungen im 18. und 19. Jahrhundert als Quellen der Kulturbeziehungsforschung*, Berlin 1980, and A. Maczak, H.J. Teuteberg, eds, *Reiseberichte als Quellen Europäischer Kulturgeschichte. Aufgaben und Möglichkeiten der historischen Reiseforschung*, Wolfenbüttel 1982.
2 D. Brewer, *Chaucer and his World*, London 1978.
3 A.W. Pollard *et al.* eds, *The Works of Geoffrey Chaucer*, London 1923, 1.
4 J. Brouwer, ed., *Spaansche reis- en krijgsjournalen uit de Gouden Eeuw*, Groningen 1932; Brouwer, *Kronieken van Spaansche soldaten uit het begin van de tachtigjarige oorlog*, Zutphen 1933.
5 J. van Bakel, P. Rolf, eds, *Vlaamse soldatenbrieven uit de Napoleontische tijd*, Bruges 1977.
6 For an impression, see A. Kopecny, *Fahrenden und Vagabunden: Ihre Geschichte, Ueberlebenskunste, Zeichen und Strassen*, Berlin 1980, and C. Kother, *Menschen auf der Strasse: Vagierende Unterschichten in Bayern, Franken und Schwaben in der zweiten Hälfte des 18. Jahrhunderts*, Göttingen 1983.
7 J. Edwards, *The Jews in Christian Europe, 1400–1700*, London 1988; J.I. Israel, *European Jewry in the Age of Mercantilism, 1550–1750*, Oxford 1985.
8 See M.A. Shulvass, *The Jews in the World of the Renaissance*, Leiden 1973; B.D. Cooperman, ed., *Jewish Thought in the Sixteenth Century*, Cambridge, Mass., 1983; D.B. Ruderman, *Jewish Thought and Scientific Discovery in Early Modern Europe*, New York 1995.

9   For an overview see M. Yardeni, *Le Refuge protestant*, Paris 1985, especially 129–54, 179 sqq. and 201 sqq.

10   For example S. Jersch-Wendel, *Juden und 'Franzosen' in der Wirtschaft des Raumes Berlin/Brandenburg zur Zeit des Merkantilismus*, Berlin 1978, especially 182 sqq.

11   P. Jeannin, 'Guides de voyage et manuels pour marchands', in J. Céard, J.-Cl. Margolin, eds, *Voyager à la Renaissance*, Paris 1987, 160.

12   See, for example, G. Miselli, *Il Burattino veridico . . . per chi viaggia*, Rome 1682.

13   V. von Klarwill, *Fugger-Zeitungen: Ungedruckte Briefe an das Haus Fugger aus die Jahre 1568–1605*, Vienna 1933.

14   K. Pisa, *Schopenhauer: Kronzeuge einer unheilen Welt*, Vienna 1977.

15   R.L. Latham, *The Illustrated Pepys*, London 1983, passim; in this splendidly illustrated work, in which Latham summarizes his monumental eleven-volume edition of the diary, there are many passages which illuminate this statement in more detail.

16   Julius Bellus, *Justinopolitani Hermes Politicus sive de Peregrinatoria Prudentia Libri tres*, Frankfurt 1608; S. Von Birker, *HochFürstlicher Brandenburgischer Ulysses*, Bayreuth 1669.

17   P.J.A.N. Rietbergen, 'Prince Eckembergh comes to dinner: food and political propaganda in the seventeenth century', *Petit Propos Culinaires: A Journal of Culinary History* VI (1983), 45–54. See also S. Bertelli *et al.* eds, *Rituale. Cerimoniale. Etichetta*, Milan 1985; M. Jeanneret, *A Feast of Words: Banquets and Table Talk in the Renaissance*, Oxford 1991 (originally Paris 1987).

18   See for the following paragraphs: N. Elias, *Die höfische Gesellschaft*, Darmstadt 1969; translated as *The Court Society*, Oxford 1983; R. von Krüdener, *Die Rolle des Hofes im Absolutismus*, Stuttgart 1973.

19   For a survey: G. Walton, *Louis XIV's Versailles*, Harmondsworth 1986.

20   See L. Norton, *Saint-Simon at Versailles*, Hamilton 1985.

21   See Ph. Beaussait, *Lully, ou le musicien du soleil*, Paris 1992.

22   An entertaining and informative study is B. Ketcham Wheaton, *Savouring the Past*, Baltimore 1983, esp. ch. 7 and following.

23   P.J.A.N. Rietbergen, 'Den Haag, 20 april 1660: de bruiloft van Susanna Huygens', *De Zeventiende Eeuw* III–2 (1987), 181–9.

24   E.B. Johnson, ed., *The Letters of the Right Honourable Lady Mary Wortley Montagu, 1709–1762*, London 1906, passim.

25   For example, H. Bots *et al.* eds, *Noordbrabantse Studenten, 1550–1750*, Tilburg 1979, passim.

26   J. Pesek, D. Sanan, 'Les étudiants de Bohême dans les universités et les académies d'Europe centrale et occidentale entre 1596 et 1620', in D. Julia *et al.* eds, *Histoire sociale des populations étudiantes*, I, Paris 1986, 89–112.

27   R.A. Houston, *Literacy in Early Modern Europe: Culture and Education, 1500–1800*, London 1988, 85.

28   W.Th.M. Frijhoff, *La Société neerlandaise et ses graduées, 1575–1814: une recherche sérielle sur le statut des intellectuels*, Amsterdam 1981, 83 sqq., 102, 106.

29   For example, J.G. Klinger, *Commentario de promotionibus studiosorum iuris ad iter iuridicum pertinentibus*, Leipzig 1744; Th. Bartholinus, *De peregrinatio medica*, Copenhagen 1674.

30   See H. Zimmer, *Die Dientzenhofer: Ein bayerisches Baumeistergeschlecht in der Zeit des Barock*, Munich 1976.

31   P.J.A.N. Rietbergen, 'Magnaten en Maecenassen in Zwedens Stormakstid: Magnus Gabriel de la Gardie (1622–1686) and Carl-Gustaf Wrangel (1613–1676)', *Artilleri* III–3 (1986), 67–80; IV–1 (1986), 35–50.

32   We are well informed about the experiences of all these sorts of trips by the travellers from at least one country, England, during the seventeenth century: J.W. Stoye, *English Travellers Abroad, 1604–1667: Their Influence in English Society and Politics*,

London 1993; J. Lough, *France Observed in the Seventeenth Century by British Travellers*, Stocksfield 1984.

33 One example among many is P.J.A.N. Rietbergen, 'Papal policy and mediation at the Peace of Nijmegen', *Acta. International Congress of the Tercentenary of the Peace of Nijmegen, 1678–1978*, Amsterdam 1980, 29–96.

34 A. Frank-Van Westrienen, *De Groote Tour: Tekening van de educatiereis der Nederlanders in de 17e eeuw*, Amsterdam 1983; J. Black, *The British and the Grand Tour*, London 1985.

35 N.N., *Het Italië-gevoel: Nederlandse schrijvers over Italië*, Amsterdam 1989.

36 H. Harder, *Le Président de Brosses et le voyage en Italie au dix-huitième siècle*, Geneva 1981.

37 The expression is derived from a fascinating study by J. Pemble, *The Mediterranean Passion: Victorians and Edwardians in the South*, London 1988. He mainly describes the motives for and experiences of nineteenth-century English travellers, yet also exposes structures which already determined the southerly tendencies of northerners during the ancien régime.

38 As an example: G.J. Hoogerwerff, ed., *De twee reizen van Cosimo de Medici, prins van Toscane, door de Nederlanden (1667–1669)*, Amsterdam 1919.

39 W. Bray, ed., *The Diary of John Evelyn*, I–II, London 1950, I, 101, 102, 107–8, 128, 136, 139, 140, 161–2.

40 An excellent survey: A. Maczak, *Travel in Early Modern Europe*, London 1995.

41 Such lists can be found in: *Carpentras, Bibliothèque Ingouimbertine*, Mss. 1821, folios 494, 496 and 497.

42 P. Charbon, *Au temps des malles-postes et des diligences: histoire des transports publics et de poste du XVIIe au XIXe siècle*, Strasbourg 1979.

43 L.E. Halkin, ed., *Desiderius Erasmus, Colloquia*, Louvain 1972, 333–8.

44 One such professional guide was the seventeenth-century Englishman Richard Lassels, who recorded his experiences: R. Lassels, *Description of Italy, With Instructions for Travellers*, London 1660.

45 Pitcher, *Bacon, Essays*, 113.

46 Pitcher, *Bacon, Essays*, 114.

47 Pitcher, *Bacon, Essays*, 113.

48 M. Rassem, J. Steigl, *Apodemiken: eine räsonnierte Bibliographie der reisetheoretische Literatur des 16., 17. und 18. Jahrhunderts*, Paderborn 1983.

49 J. Locke, *Some Thoughts Concerning Education*, London 1693, 189–201.

50 W. Blunt, *Linnaeus: the Complete Naturalist*, London 2004.

51 Carl von Linné, *Oratio, qua peregrinationum intra patriam asseritur necessitas*, Uppsala 1741.

52 P.J.A.N. Rietbergen, 'The Library of a Guelders country squire: Thomas Walraven van Arkel van Ammerzoden (1630–1684): a contribution to the history of Dutch aristocratic culture in the seventeenth century', *LIAS* IX-2 (1983), 271–84.

53 See H. Peres, *L'Espagne vue par les voyageurs musulmans de 1610 à 1930*, Paris 1937.

54 W. Bray, ed., *The Diary of John Evelyn I–II*, London 1907; for this passage, see I, 118.

11 A new society: the 'Republic of Letters' as a virtual and virtuous world against a divided world

1 For a short introduction: F. Wacquet, H. Bots, *La République des Lettres*, s.l. 1997.

2 A.B. Grosart, ed., *The Complete Works in Verse and Prose of S. Daniel*, I, London 1885, 106.

3 Michel de Montaigne, *Essais*, Paris 1580.

4 Most of these plans were published and commented on in German translation by K. von Raumer, *Ewiger Friede: Friedensrufe und Friedenspläne seit der Renaissance*, Munich 1953.

5 Von Raumer, *Ewiger Friede*, 321.

6 Von Raumer, *Ewiger Friede*, 89 sqq.

7 See: G. Kanthak, *Der Akademiegedanke zwischen utopischem Entwurf und barocker Projektmacherei*, Berlin 1987, especially 64 sqq. An example is R. Hahn, *The Anatomy of a Scientific Institution: The Paris Academy of Sciences, 1666–1803*, Berkeley 1971.

8 O. Ranum, ed., *National Consciousness, History and Political Culture in Early Modern Europe*, Baltimore 1975, 54 sqq., 73 sqq.

9 Juan de Mariana, *Historia de España*, Book 26, ch. 1.

10 M. Warnke, *Hofkünstler: zur Vorgeschichte des modernen Künstlers*, Cologne 1985, 314.

11 M. Cherniavsky, 'Russia', in Ranum, *National Consciousness*, 118–43.

12 P.J.A.N. Rietbergen, 'Onderwijs en Wetenschap als instrumenten van cultuurpolitiek: Rusland in de tweede helft van de zeventiende en in de achttiende eeuw', *Ex Tempore* 11 (1992), 147–59.

13 See W.F. Reddaway, ed., *Documents of Catharina the Great*, Cambridge 1931, the nakaz of 1767, ch. 1, sec. 6.

14 See A. Dietz, *Zur Geschichte der Frankfurter Büchermesse, 1462–1792*, Frankfurt 1921.

15 See H. Kiesel, P. Münch, *Gesellschaft und Literatur im 18. Jahrhundert*, Munich 1977.

16 Pitcher, *Bacon, Essays*, 114.

17 See the map in R. Mandrou, *Des humanistes aux hommes de science*, Paris 1973.

18 M. Lowry, *The World of Aldus Manutius: Business and Scholarship in Renaissance Venice*, Oxford 1979.

19 For a case see H.-J. Martin, *Livre, pouvoirs et société à Paris au XVIIe siècle (1598–1701)*, I–II, Geneva 1969, 1064, 1073.

20 See C. Berkvens-Stevelinck *et al.* eds, *Le Magasin de l'Univers. The Dutch Republic as the Centre of the European Book Trade*, Leiden 1992.

21 G.C. Gibbs, 'The role of the Dutch Republic as the intellectual entrepot of Europe', *Bijdragen en Mededelingen betreffende de Geschiedenis der Nederlanden* 86 (1971), 323–49; Gibbs, 'Some intellectual and political influences of the Huguenot émigrés', *Bijdragen en Mededelingen betreffende de Geschiedenis der Nederlanden* 90 (1975), 255–87.

22 J. Marx, 'La Bibliothèque impartiale', in M. Couperus, ed., *L'Etude des periodiques anciens*, Paris 1972, 89–108.

23 See, too, for background information: E.L. Eisenstein, 'The cosmopolitan enlightenment', in her *Grub Street Abroad*, Oxford 1992, 101–30.

24 H.H.M. van Lieshout, *Van Boek tot Bibliotheek: de Wordinggeschiedenis van de 'Dictionnaire Historique et Critique' van Pierre Bayle (1689–1706)*, Grave 1992.

25 P.J.A.N. Rietbergen, 'Light from the North: Christian Constantijn Rumph, Gisbert Cuper and cultural relations between Sweden and the Dutch Republic during the last quarter of the seventeenth century', in J.A. van Koningsbrugge *et al.* eds, *The Netherlands and the Balticum, 1524–1814*, Nijmegen 1991, 315–42.

26 For the following, see P.J.A.N. Rietbergen, 'Witsen's world: Nicolaas Witsen (1642–1717) between the Dutch East India Company and the Republic of Letters', *Itinerario* IX–2 (1985), 121–34.

27 J. Bouchard, 'Les relations épistolaires de Nicolas Mavrocordatos avec Jean Le Clerc et William Wake', *O Eranistis* 1 (1974), 67–92; Bouchard, ed., *N. Mavrocordatos, les loisirs de philothée*, Athens 1989.

28 For the following, see P.J.A.N. Rietbergen, 'Dutch and Spanish "Enlightenments"? The case of Gerard Meerman (1722–1777) and Gregorio Mayans y Siscar (1691–1781)', in Rietbergen, ed., *Tussen Twee Culturen: Nederland en de Iberische wereld, 1500–1800*, Nijmegen 1988, 105–34.

12 A new society: from Humanism to the Enlightenment

1 See on this subject A. Grafton, *Defenders of the Text: The Traditions of Scholarship in an Age of Science, 1450–1800*, Cambridge, Mass., 1993.

2   A French translation was made in 1934 by A. Koyré, a German one in 1939 by Cl. Menzer.
3   M. Devèze, R. Marx, eds, *Textes et documents d'histoire moderne*, Paris 1967, 119–20.
4   On Galilei: P. Redondi, *Galilei eretico*, Turin 1983, which, although not accepted by all scholars in the field, is a stimulating study.
5   See Redondi, *Galilei*.
6   Cited from G. de Santillana, ed., *The Age of Adventure: The Renaissance Philosophers*, New York 1956, 159.
7   See Bax, ed., trans., *The Signature of All Things, with Other Writings by Jacob Boehme*, London 1926, 14, II, no. 8.
8   Bax, *Boehme*, 268.
9   For an interesting analysis: R. Barthes, *Sade, Fourier, Loyola*, Paris 1971.
10 Though I date the phenomenon a century earlier, one should also consult: J. Seigel, *The Idea of Self. Thought and Experience in Western Europe since the seventeenth Century*, Cambridge 2004.
11 R. Porter, *Flesh in the Age of Reason*, London 2004.
12 J. Peakman, *Lascivious Bodies. A Sexual history of the Eighteenth Century*, London 2004.
13 Francis Bacon, *Novum Organum*, London 1620.
14 R. Descartes, *Discours sur la méthode*, Paris 1637.
15 C. Wilson, *The Invisible World*, Oxford 1995.
16 A good background study: M.F. Cohen, *The Scientific Revolution: A Historiographical Enquiry*, Chicago 1995.
17 R.S. Westfall, *Never at Rest: A Biography of Isaac Newton*, London 1981.
18 I. Newton, *Foreword to Philosophiae naturalis principia mathematica*, London 1687.
19 Cf. e.g. M. White, *Isaac Newton: the Last Sorcerer*, Addison 1997.
20 A.J. Krailsheimer, trans., *Blaise Pascal, Pensées*, Baltimore 1966, 48, 95.
21 Cf. B. Gert, ed., *Thomas Hobbes, 'de Homine' and 'de Cive' – Man and the Citizen*, Boston 1972, 110–11; J. Watkins, *Hobbes' System of Ideas*, London 1973, 23–4, 89 sq., and 47 for the quote.
22 For a survey of developments in science: R. Olson, *Science Deified and Science Defied: The Historical Significance of Science in Western Culture. II: From the Early Modern Age Through the Early Romantic Era, ca. 1640 to ca. 1820*, Berkeley 1990.
23 A. Thomson, ed., *La Mettrie: Machine Man and Other Writings*, Cambridge 1996.
24 Cf. L. Roper, *Witch Craze. Terror and Fantasy in Baroque Germany*, New York 2004.
25 R.M. Adams, *Leibniz: Determinist, Theist, Idealist*, Oxford 1994.
26 For a short introduction to this highly complex thinker: R. Popkin, *Spinoza*, Oxford 2004.
27 For an introduction, see H.E. Allison, *Benedict de Spinoza*, London 1987.
28 J.H. Spalding, F. Bayley, eds, trans., *Heaven and its Wonders, and Hell: From Things Heard and Seen: by Emmanuel Swedenborg*, London 1920, nos 318, 328.
29 See: A. Schopenhauer, *Die Welt als Wille und Vorstellung*, I, 125 ff, and II, 366, in A. Hübscher, ed., A. Schopenhauer, *Sämtliche Werke I–VII*, Wiesbaden 1972.
30 For a survey: D. Goodman, *The Republic of Letters: A Cultural History of the French Enlightenment*, Ithaca 1994.
31 A very inspiring analysis is D. Roche, *La France des lumières*, Paris 1994.
32 H.C. Payne, *The Philosophes and the People*, New Haven 1976.
33 R. Porter, M. Teich, eds, *The Enlightenment in National Context*, Cambridge 1981.
34 For example, R.B. Sher, *Church and University in the Scottish Enlightenment: The Moderate Literati of Edinburgh*, Princeton 1985.
35 Th.J. Schlereth, *The Cosmopolitan Ideal in Enlightenment Thought*, Notre Dame 1977.
36 H. Vyverberg, *Human Nature, Cultural Diversity and the French Enlightenment*, New York 1987.

37 For a brief overview: Ph.N. Furbank, *The Encyclopédie*, Milton Keynes 1980; P. Swiggers, 'Pre-histoire et histoire de l'encyclopédie', *Revue Historique* 549 (1984), 83–93; J. Lough, *The Encylopédie*, London 1971, Geneva 1989.

38 U. im Hof, *Das gesellige Jahrhundert: Gesellschaft und Gesellschaften im Zeitalter der Aufklärung*, Munich 1982; R. von Dülmen, *The Society of the Enlightenment: The Rise of the Middle Class and Enlightenment Culture in Germany*, Cambridge 1992 (originally Frankfurt 1986).

39 O. Dann, ed., *Lesegesellschaften und bürgerliche Emanzipation: ein europäischer Vergleich*, Munich 1981.

40 See J. Bernal, *Black Athena: The Afroasiatic Roots of Classical Civilization*, London 1987.

41 F.M. Turner, 'Why the Greeks and not the Romans in Victorian Britain', in G.W. Clarke, ed., *Rediscovering Hellenism: The Hellenic Inheritance and the English Imagination*, Cambridge 1989, 61–81. For Germany, see B. Näf, *Von Perikles zu Hitler? Die athenische Demokratie und die deutsche Althistorie bis 1945*, Berne 1986.

42 See P. Kitromilides, *The Enlightenment as Social Criticism: Iosipos Moisiodax and Greek Culture in the Eighteenth Century*, Princeton 1992.

43 See D. Ringrose, *Spain, Europe and the 'Spanish Miracle', 1700–1900*, Cambridge 1996.

44 E. Sisman, ed., *Haydn and his World*, Princeton 1997.

45 A. Harrington, *Reenchanted Science: Holism in German Culture from Wilhelm II to Hitler*, Princeton 1996.

46 A. Faivre, *Mystiques, theosophes et illuminés au siècle des lumières*, Hildesheim 1976.

13   Europe's revolutions: freedom and consumption for all?

1 Quoted in G. Wurzbacher, R. Pflaum, *Das Dorf im Spannungsfelde industrieller Entwicklung*, Stuttgart 1961, 13.

2 F.A. Pottle, ed., *Boswell's London Journal, 1762–1763*, London 1982, 159.

3 See M.C. Moine, *Les Fêtes à la cour du Roi Soleil, 1665–1715*, Paris 1984.

4 A. Chéruel, ed., *Mémoires de Saint-Simon, XII*, Paris 1857, 461 sqq.

5 For a case study: J.H. Plumb *et al.* eds, *The Birth of Consumer Society: The Commercialization of Eighteenth-Century England*, Bloomington 1982.

6 See D. Roche, *The Culture of Clothing: Dress and Fashion in the Ancien Régime*, Cambridge 1995.

7 See F.B. Kaye, ed., *Bernard Mandeville: The Fable of the Bees*, Oxford 1924.

8 For a survey: B. Gottlieb, *The Family in the Western World from the Black Death to the Industrial Age*, Oxford 1987.

9 See B.W. Robinson, R.F. Hall, *The Aldrich Book of Catches*, London 1989, 79, no. 56.

10 A survey: H. Cunningham, *Children and Childhood in Western Society since 1500*, London 1995.

11 N. Elias, *The Civilizing Process. I: The History of Manners. II: State Formation and Civilization*, Oxford 1982.

12 See J. Barry, C. Brooks, eds, *The Middling Sort of People: Culture, Society and Politics in England, 1550–1800*, Basingstoke 1994, esp. 1–27; D. Blackbourn, R.J. Evans, eds, *The German Bourgeoisie*, London 1991; P.M. Pilbeam, *The Middle Classes in Europe, 1789–1914: France, Germany, Italy and Russia*, Basingstoke 1990.

13 See D. Roche, *Les Republicains des lettres: gens de culture et lumières au XVIIIe siècle*, Paris 1988. An important case: C. Lougee, *Le Paradis des Femmes: Women, Salons and Social Stratification in Seventeenth-Century France*, Princeton 1976.

14 F. Chabod, 'L'Idea di Europa', *Rassegna d'Italia* II (1947), 3.

15 See H. Bots, ed., *Henri Basnage de Beauval en de histoire des ouvrages des savans, 1687–1709*, I–II, Amsterdam 1976.

16 P.J.A.N. Rietbergen, 'Pieter Rabus en de "Boekzaal van Europe", 1692–1702', in H. Bots, ed., *Pieter Rabus en de Boekzaal van Europe*, Amsterdam 1974, 1–102.
17 See on the moralizing nature of many weeklies: W. Martens, *Die Botschaft der Tugend*, Stuttgart 1968.
18 P.J. Buijnsters, 'Sociologie van de Spectator', *Spiegel der Letteren* 15/1 (1973), 1–17.
19 P. Clark, *Sociability and Urbanity: Clubs and Societies in the Eighteenth-Century City*, Leicester 1986.
20 M.C. Jacob, *Living the Enlightenment: Freemasonry and Politics in Eighteenth-Century Europe*, Oxford 1992.
21 R. Stadelman, *Preussens Könige in ihrer Tätigkeit für die Landeskultur. II: Friedrich der Grosse*, Leipzig 1882, 333.
22 G. Schmoller, ed., *Acta Borussica*, I/2, Berlin 1892, 8.
23 Stadelman, *Preussens Könige*, 287.
24 R. Chartier, *Les Origines culturelles de la revolution française*, Paris 1991.
25 Among the numerous introductions, for background information one might read Ph. Deane, *The First Industrial Revolution*, Cambridge 1979, and J. Goodman, K. Honeyman, *Gainful Pursuits: The Making of Industrial Europe, 1600–1914*, London 1988. An illuminating case study is D. Sabean, *Property, Production and Family in Neckarshausen, 1700–1870*, Cambridge 1990.
26 H. Ch. Mettin, ed., *Fürst Pückler reist nach England: aus den Briefen eines Verstorbenen*, Stuttgart 1958, 107 sqq.
27 For a non-English case study: R. Sandgruber, *Die Anfänge der Konsumgesellschaft*, Vienna 1982, which deals with Austria in the eighteenth and nineteenth centuries.
28 O. Wilde, *The Picture of Dorian Gray*, London 1891, chs 8 and 6.
29 A. Joubin, ed., *Eugène Delacroix, Journal. 1822–1863*, Paris 1981, 346–7.
30 See R. von Dülmen *et al.* eds, *Volkskultur: zur Wiederentdeckung des vergessenen Alltags, 16.–20. Jahrhundert*, Frankfurt 1984.
31 For a survey: R. Wendorff, *Zeit und Kultur: Geschichte des Zeitbewusstseins in Europa*, Opladen 1980.
32 K. Jantke, D. Hiler, eds, *Die Eigentumslosen*, Freiburg-Munich 1965, 178.
33 *Journal des Débats*, 18 April 1832.
34 See the fine study by J.M. Meriman, *The Margins of City Life: Explorations on the French Urban Frontier, 1815–1851*, New York 1991.
35 Quoted in P. McPhee, *A Social History of France, 1780–1880*, London 1993, 203.

14 Progress and its discontents: nationalism, economic growth and the question of cultural certainties

1 For a very perceptive study of similarities and continuities in this field, see R. Wuthenow, *Communities of Discourse: Ideology and Social Structure in the Reformation, the Enlightenment and European Socialism*, Cambridge, Mass., 1989.
2 A comparative survey of the sociopolitical consequences: G.A. Ritter, *Der Sozialstaat: Entstehung und Entwicklung im internationalen Vergleich*, Munich 1989; as well as S. Padgett, W.E. Patterson, *A History of Social Democracy in Europe*, London 1991.
3 Henri de Saint-Simon, *Le Système industriel*, Paris 1821, 19.
4 For further arguments: S. Woolf, *Napoleon's Integration of Europe*, London 1991.
5 B. Anderson, *Imagined Communities: Reflections on the Origin and Spread of Nationalism*, London 1983.
6 For a general survey: B. Tobia, *Una patria per gli Italiani: spazi, itinerari, monumenti nell'Italia unita (1870–1900)*, Rome 1991.
7 For the concept: P. Nora, ed., *Realms of Memory: Rethinking the French Past*, I, New York 1996.

8 See S. Collini, *Public Moralists: Political Thought and Intellectual Life in Britain, 1850–1930*, Oxford 1991.

9 For the background see P. Greenhalgh, *Ephemeral Vistas: The Expositions Universelles, Great Exhibitions and World Fairs, 1851–1939*, Manchester 1988.

10 P.E. Schramm, *Neun Generationen: Dreihundert Jahre deutscher 'Kulturgeschichte' im Lichte des Schicksals einer Hamburger Bürgerfamilie, 1648–1948*, Göttingen 1963, I, 295.

11 For example, D. Blackburn, R.J. Evans, eds, *The German Bourgeoisie: Essays on the Social History of the German Middle Class from the Late Eighteenth to the Early Twentieth Century*, London 1991; see also the essays in J. Kocka, A. Mitchell, eds, *Bourgeois Society in Nineteenth-Century Europe*, Oxford 1993 (originally Munich 1988). Pamela Pilbeam, in her wide-ranging *The Middle Classes in Europe, 1789–1914*, Basingstoke 1990, has raised the question of the continuity of the pre-revolutionary urban patriciate and the new industrial elite.

12 For example, E. Weber, *Peasants into Frenchmen*, London 1976.

13 See, too, H.J. Graff, *The Legacies of Literacy: Continuities and Contradictions in Western Culture and Society*, Bloomington 1987.

14 Kocka, Mitchell, *Bourgeois Society*, 430, table 16.3.

15 See S. Collini, *Matthew Arnold: A Critical Portrait*, Oxford 1994.

16 M. Arnold, *Popular Education and the State*, London 1861; *Arnold, Schools and Universities on the Continent*, London 1868.

17 J. Dover Wilson, ed., *M. Arnold, Culture and Anarchy*, Cambridge 1971, 129 sq.; M. Arnold, *Essays in Criticism I*, London 1865, 18.

18 G.W.E. Russell, ed., *M. Arnold, Letters I*, London 1895, 4.

19 *Culture and Anarchy*, 138.

20 *Culture and Anarchy*, 195.

21 quoted by J. Dover Wilson in his introduction to *Culture and Anarchy*, XXXV.

22 P. Anderson, *The Printed Image and the Transformation of Popular Culture, 1790–1860*, Oxford 1994.

23 See O. Dann, ed., *Lesegesellschaften und bürgerliche Emanzipation: ein europäischer Vergleich*, Munich 1981, 22, 159 sqq.

24 See the details in F. Parent-Lardeur, *Lire à Paris au temps de Balzac: les cabinets de lecture à Paris, 1815–1830*, Paris 1981, 171, 172, 178.

25 G. Jäger, J. Schönert, eds, *Die Leihbibliothek als Institution des literarischen Lebens im 18. und 19. Jahrhundert. Organisation, Bestände, Publikum*, Hamburg 1980, 11 sqq.

26 Quoted in H. Nicolson, *Tennyson: Aspects of his Life, Character and Poetry*, London 1923, 1960, 235.

27 *La Regenta*, written by L. Alas (1852–1901), whose pen-name was Clarín, was translated into English in 1984.

28 See L. Sauer, 'Romantic automata', in: G. Hoffmeister, ed., *European Romanticism: Literary Cross-Currents, Modes and Models*, Detroit 1990, 287–306.

29 S. Butler, *Erewhon*, London (Everyman's Library) 1951, 144, 145, 147.

30 See M. Schneider, *Geschichte als Gestalt: Gustav Freytag's Roman 'Soll und Haben'*, Stuttgart 1980.

31 This is the drift of most of the essays in M.I. Finley, ed., *The Legacy of Greece: A New Appraisal*, Oxford 1981, and R. Jenkyns, ed., *The Legacy of Rome: A New Appraisal*, Oxford 1992, even if the limitation of culture to art and literature in the latter volume is debatable.

32 See P.J.A.N. Rietbergen, 'Een Europeaan droomt: Novalis tussen Europa, Christendom en Wereld', in his *Dromen van Europa: een cultuurgeschiedenis*, Amersfoort 1993, 255–81.

33 From Alexander Dru, ed., *The Letters of Jakob Burckhardt*, London 1955, 97; 107–8, 145–8, 150–1, 219–20.

34 A. Corbin, *Time, Desire and Horror: Towards a History of the Senses*, Oxford 1995.

35 H. Kaeble, *Auf dem Weg zu einer europäischen Gesellschaft: eine Sozialgeschichte Westeuropas, 1880–1980*, Munich 1987.

36 See K. Tenfelde, ed., *Arbeiter und Arbeiterbewegung im Vergleich*, Munich 1986, which compares developments in Britain and Germany.

37 For the background: A. Corbin, *Le Territoire du vide*, Paris 1988; translated as *The Lure of the Sea: The Discovery of the Seaside in the Western World, 1750–1840*, Oxford 1994.

38 For the complexity of Europe's attitude towards nature: K. Thomas, *Man and the Natural World: Changing Attitudes in England, 1500–1800*, Harmondsworth 1982.

39 For a survey: A. Daumard, *Oisiveté et loisirs dans les sociétés occidentales au XIX siècle*, Amiens 1983.

40 See S. Easton *et al.*, *Disorder and Discipline: Popular Culture from 1550 to the Present*, Aldershot 1988.

41 Quoted in J.M. Merriman, *The Margins of City Life: Explorations on the French Urban Frontier, 1815–1851*, New York 1991, 67.

42 An important introduction to the problems involved is W. Kaschuba, *Volkskultur zwischen feudaler und bürgerlicher Gesellschaft: zur Geschichte eines Begriffes und seinen gesellschaftlichen Wirklichkeit*, Frankfurt 1988, as well as Van Dülmen, Schindler, eds, *Volkskultur*, passim.

43 Quoted in G. Schönbrunn, ed., *Das bürgerliche Zeitalter, 1815–1914*, Munich 1980, 826.

44 See V. Lidtke, 'Recent literature on workers' culture in Germany and England', in Tenfelde, *Arbeiter und Arbeiterbewegung*, 337–62.

45 A good biography: M. Marnot, *Joseph Haydn: la mesure de son siècle*, Paris 1996.

46 See W. Weber, *The Rise of Musical Classics in Eighteenth-Century Orchestral Concerts: A Study in Canon, Ritual and Ideology*, London 1992; J.H. Johnson, *Listening in Paris: A Cultural History*, Berkeley 1995.

47 One of the best analyses of, especially, Schubert's solo songs still remains the one written by the singer who was probably their most convincing performer in the twentieth century: D. Fischer-Dieskau, *Auf den Spuren der Schubertlieder*, Munich 1976. A good biography: P. Guelke, *Franz Schubert und seine Zeit*, Laaber 1991.

48 See S. Finkelstein, *Composer and Nation: The Folk Heritage in Music*, New York 1960.

49 Quoted in P. McPhee, *A Social History of France, 1780–1880*, London 1993, 125.

50 See A. Briggs, *Victorian Things*, London 1988.

51 M. Miller, *The 'Bon Marché': Bourgeois Culture and the Department Store, 1869–1920*, Princeton 1981.

52 See G. Vickert, 'The theory of conspicuous consumption in the eighteenth century', in P. Hughes, D. Williams, eds, *The Varied Pattern: Studies in the Eighteenth Century*, Toronto 1971, 253–67.

53 See the English translation: *Jean-Jacques Rousseau, The First and Second Discourses*, New York 1986, 4–5, 175, 180–1.

54 D. Hume, *Treatise on Human Nature*, Oxford 1978.

55 J.S. Mill, *Principles of Political Economy*, originally London 1848; Toronto 1965, 753–96.

15 Europe and the other worlds

1 For a survey, albeit a not always balanced one: A. Crosby, *Ecological Imperialism: The Biological Expansion of Europe, 900–1900*, Cambridge 1986.

2 G. Lantzeff, R. Pierce, *Eastward to Empire: Exploration and Conquest on the Russian Open Frontier to 1750*, Montreal 1973; M. Rywkin, *Russian Colonial Expansion to 1917*, London 1987; G. Diment, Y. Slezkine, eds, *Between Heaven and Hell: The Myth of Siberia in Russian Culture*, New York 1993.

3 D. Arnold, *Environment, Culture and European Expansion*, Oxford 1997.

4 See D. Gregory, *Brute New World: The Rediscovery of Latin America in the Early Nineteenth Century*, London 1992.

5 See P.J.A.N. Rietbergen, 'Aan de vooravond van "het Groote Missie-uur": een onderzoek naar de Nederlandse missiebeweging gedurende de eerste helft van de negentiende eeuw en de rol van "missietijdschriften" daarin', *Nederlands Archief voor Kerkgeschiedenis* 70 (1990), 75–108.

6 R.H. Pearce, *Savagism and Civilization: A Study of the Indian and the American Mind*, Berkeley 1988, 69.

7 J. Hector St John de Crevecoeur, *Letters from an American Farmer*, London 1782. Here quoted from the Everyman's Library, London, edition, 5.

8 The following quotations are from *Letters*, 11, 24–5, 13, 41, 41–2, 43–4.

9 W. Cather, *O Pioneers!*, New York 1913; Harmondsworth 1989, 301.

10 See W.C. Davis, *The American Frontier: Pioneers, Settlers and Cowboys, 1800–1890*, New York 1992; J.D. Unruh, *The Plains Across: Emigrants, Wagon Trains and the American West*, New York 1992; and the illustrative volume of eyewitness accounts in *Westward Expansion*, New York 1992.

11 For a general overview see D. Baines, *Emigration from Europe, 1815–1930*, London 1991.

12 The novels appeared between 1949 and 1959; G. Eidevall, *Vilhelm Mobergs emigrantepos: studien i verkets tillkomsthistoria, dokumentära bakgrund och konstnärliga gestaltning*, Stockholm 1974.

13 Upton Sinclair, *The Jungle*, New York 1965, 29.

14 The following quotations are from *The Jungle*, 32, 59, 64.

15 H. Croly, *The Promise of American Life*, New York 1909, 17–25, passim; 452.

16 W. Irving, *The Sketch Book*, London, 2.

17 P.E. Lovejoy, *Transformations in Slavery: A History of Slavery in Africa*, Cambridge 1983.

18 For a case study: H. Gruender, *Christliche Mission und deutscher Imperialismus*, Paderborn 1982.

19 For a survey of British attitudes: R. Robinson, J. Gallagher, *Africa and the Victorians: The Official Mind of Imperialism*, London 1981.

20 F.J. McLynn, *Hearts of Darkness*, London 1992; S. Lindquist, *Exterminate All the Brutes*, London 1997.

21 D. Massarela, *A World Elsewhere: European Encounters with Japan in the Sixteenth and Seventeenth Centuries*, New Haven 1990.

22 P. Rietbergen, *Nihon door Nederlandse Ogen: the VOC en Japan, c. 1600 – c. 1800*, Amsterdam 2003.

23 G.K. Goodman, *Japan: The Dutch Experience*, London 1986.

24 For a survey: N. Cameron, *Barbarians and Mandarins: Thirteen Centuries of Western Travellers in China*, Oxford 1989.

25 See D.E. Mungella, *Curious Land: Jesuit Accommodation and the Origins of Sinology*, Honolulu 1985.

26 See E. Evett, *The Critical Reception of Japanese Art in Late Nineteenth-Century Europe*, Ann Arbor 1982.

27 S. Wichmann, *Japonismus: Ostasien-Europa. Begegnungen in der Kunst des 19. und 20. Jahrhunderts*, Herrsching 1980.

28 See N.A. Silberman, *Digging for God and Country: Exploration, Archaeology and the Secret Struggle for the Holy Land, 1799–1917*, New York 1982.

29 S. Mills, *Discourses of Difference: An Analysis of Women's Travel Writing and Colonialism*, London 1991.

30 This, of course, has been the central, though debatable, argument of E. Said, *Orientalism*, London 1978, which he repeated in his *Culture and Imperialism*, London 1993.

31 A survey: M. Jacobs, *The Painted Voyage: Art, Travel and Exploration, 1564–1875*,

London 1995. See also D. Mackay, *In the Wake of Cook: Exploration, Science and Empire, 1780–1801*, London 1985.

32 A. Olearius, *Neue Beschreibung der Moskovitischen und Persischen Reiche*, Leipzig 1656, 184.

33 See W. Leitsch, 'Westeuropäische Reiseberichte über den Moskauer Staat', in A. Maczak, H.J. Teuteberg, eds, *Reiseberichte als Quellen Europäischer Kulturgeschichte*, Wolfenbüttel 1988, 153–76.

34 Basic reading is the fine study by L. Wolf, *Inventing Eastern Europe*, Stanford 1994; for this: 7–8.

35 See D. Chirot, ed., *The Origins of Backwardness in Eastern Europe: Economics and Politics from the Middle Ages until the Early Twentieth Century*, Berkeley 1989.

36 D. Groh, *Rusland und das Selbstverständnis Europas*, Neuwied 1961, 65 sqq.

16 The 'Decline of the Occident' – the loss of a dream? From the nineteenth to the twentieth century

1 J. Scott, *Siemens Brothers, 1858–1958*, London 1958.

2 W. Lautemann, M. Schlenke, gen. eds, *Geschichte in Quellen*, Munich 1980, 825.

3 C. Harding, S. Popple, *In the Kingdom of Shadows: A Companion to Early Cinema*, London 1997.

4 A good introduction to the period is J. Barzun, Darwin, Marx, *Wagner: Critique of a Heritage*, New York 1958, esp. 38–55: 'The evolution of evolution'. See also R. Olson, *Evolution: The History of an Idea*, Berkeley 1989.

5 The study of Darwin has become a veritable industry. There is an avalanche of recent biographies. Instructive is L.S. Bergmann, 'Reshaping the roles of Man, God and Nature: Darwin's rhetoric in On the Origin of Species', in J.W. Lee, J. Yaross, eds, *Beyond the Two Cultures: Essays on Science, Technology and Literature*, Ames 1990. *Proteus: A Journal of Ideas* VI/2 (1989) is entirely devoted to the various aspects of Darwin's life and works.

6 See the very perceptive study by S.E. Hyman, *The Tangled Bank: Darwin, Marx, Frazer and Freud as Imaginative Writers*, New York 1962, which has not received the attention it deserves.

7 For example: G. Levine, *Darwin and the Novelists: Patterns of Science in Victorian Fiction*, London 1988.

8 Ch. Fox *et al.*, eds, *Inventing Human Science*, Berkeley 1995.

9 D. Knight, *The Age of Science: The Scientific World View in the Nineteenth Century*, Oxford 1986, provides an excellent introduction.

10 P. Costello, *Jules Verne, Inventor of Science Fiction*, London 1978; G. Proteau, *Le Grand Roman de Jules Verne: sa vie*, Paris 1979.

11 B. Holm, *Selma Lagerlöfs litterära profil*, Stockholm 1986.

12 See Barzun, *Darwin*, passim.

13 E. Förster-Nietzsche, ed., *Nietzsche's Werke XVI*, Leipzig 1912, 402. It has to be said that a text titled *Der Wille zur Macht: Versuch einer Umwerthung aller Werthe*, as presented by Elisabeth Nietzsche as Nietzsche's chief work, does not exist. What exists is a collection of 'aphorisms', very difficult to interpret. See M. Montinari, 'Vorwort', in G. Colli, M. Montinari, eds, *Friedrich Nietzsche: Sämtliche Werke. Kritische Studienausgabe*, 14, Berlin 1980, 1–12.

14 See Colli, Montinari, eds, *Fr. Nietzsche: Kritische Gesamtausgabe der Werke*, VI/2, Berlin 1968) [= Fr. Nietzsche, *Also sprach Zarathustra: ein Buch für Alle und Keine*], 33, 8–1.

15 See B. Reardon, 'Ernest Renan and the religion of science', in D. Jasper, T. Wright, eds, *Critical Spirit and the Will to Believe*, New York 1989, 199–205.

16 For example, W. Loth, ed., *Deutscher Katholizismus im Umbruch zur Moderne*, Stuttgart 1991.

17   M. Artola, *Antiguo Régimen y revolucíon liberal*, Barcelona 1978; L.G. San Miguel, *De la Sociedad Aristocrática a la Sociedad Industrial en la España del siglo XIX*, Madrid 1973.

18   See the texts in Foerster, *Die Idee*, as well as H. Wehberg, *Ideen und Projekte betreffende die Vereinigten Staaten von Europa in den letzten 100 Jahren*, Bremen 1984.

19   See G. Colli, M. Montinari, eds, *Fr. Nietzsche: Kritische Gesamtausgabe der Werke*, VI/2, Berlin 1968 [= Fr. Nietzsche, *Jenseits von Gut und Böse*], 209, no. 256.

20   See J.G.A. Pocock, *The Machiavellian Moment: Florentine Political Thought and the Atlantic Republican Tradition*, Princeton 1975.

21   See M. Elvin, *The Pattern of the Chinese Past*, London 1973.

22   W. Lautemann, M. Schlenke, gen. eds, *Geschichte in Quellen*, Munich 1980, 825.

23   A. Tennyson, 'Locksley Hall', in *Poetical Works of Alfred Lord Tennyson*, London 1917, 103.

24   For the case of Britain, which is the best researched: J.M. Mackenzie, ed., *Imperialism and Popular Culture*, Manchester 1896.

25   M. Lowsky, *Karl May*, Stuttgart 1987.

26   R.D. Gray, *Goethe the Alchemist*, Cambridge 1952.

27   A very readable biography has been written by P. Gay, *Freud: A Life for our Time*, New York 1988.

28   A balanced, up-to-date analysis is given by F. Forrester, *Dispatches from the Freud Wars*, Cambridge, Mass., 1997.

29   See L.B. Litvo, *Darwin's Influence on Freud*, New Haven 1991.

30   H.D. Cater, ed., *Henry Adams and his Friends: A Collection of Unpublished Letters*, New York 1970, 499–500.

31   H. Adams, *The Education of Henry Adams: An Autobiography*, Boston 1918, 379, 380, 381–2, 383.

32   See the study by H.A. Klomp, *De relativiteitstheorie in Nederland*, Groningen 1997.

33   See H. Hartmann, *Max Planck als Mensch und Denker*, Frankfurt 1953.

34   Chr. Butler, *Early Modernism: Literature, Music and Painting in Europe, 1900–1916*, Oxford 1994.

35   A. Stassinopoulos Huffington, *Picasso, Creator and Destroyer*, New York 1988, ch. 4.

36   See D. Roberts, *Benedetto Croce and the Uses of Historicity*, Berkeley 1987.

37   Quoted in R. Wohl, *The Generation of 1914*, London 1980, 240, n. 1.

38   H. Pirenne, *Mahomet et Charlemagne*, Paris 1937.

39   For example, P. Barker *et al.*, eds, *After Einstein*, Memphis 1981; D.P. Ryan *et al.*, eds, *Einstein and the Humanities*, Westport 1987.

40   G. Blasberg, *Krise und Utopie der Intellektuellen: kulturkritische Aspekte in Robert Musils Roman 'Der Man ohne Eigenschaften'*, Stuttgart 1984; G.M. Moore, *Proust and Musil: The Novel as Research Instrument*, New York 1985.

41   M. Brod, ed., *Franz Kafka, Amerika*, Frankfurt 1953, 38.

42   For the background: E. Timms, ed., *Unreal City: Urban Experience in Modern European Literature and Art*, New York 1985.

43   The very negative interpretation of Lang's film by Siegfried Kracauer in his *Von Caligari zu Hitler: eine psychologische Geschichte des deutschen Films*, Frankfurt 1979, originally 1949, seems unfounded, induced by Kracauer's wish to detect a growing glorification of totalitarianism in every movie made in these years. Rather, I think Lang's vision to be a generally pessimistic one.

44   For the background *Revue du Dix-Neuvième Siècle* 13, 1983, and *Cahiers Victoriens et Edwardiens* 31, 1990. Also Th.P. Dunn *et al.*, eds, *The Mechanical God: Machines in Science Fiction*, Westport 1982.

45   J.B. Kerman, ed., *Retrofitting Blade Runner*, Bowling Green 1991, especially in 110–23, as well as the illuminating analyses by J. Douchet, 'La Ville Tentaculaire', N.N., *Cités-Cinés*, La Villette 1987, 61–71; F. Chaslin, 'Dans les villes crépusculaires', ibid., 103–9. See also: Y. Birle *Profane Mythology: The Savage Mind of the Cinema*, Bloomington 1982, 57–62.

46 For Huizinga's reactions: W.E. Krul, 'Moderne beschavingsgeschiedenis: Johan Huizinga over de Verenigde Staten', in K. van Berkel, ed., *Amerika in Europese ogen: Facetten van de Europese beeldvorming van het moderne Amerika*, 's-Gravenhage 1990, 86–108.

47 K. Harpprecht, *Thomas Mann: Eine Biographie*, Reinbek 1995.

48 Cf. S. Baranowski, *Strength Through Joy: Consumerism and Mass Tourism in the Third Reich*, Cambridge 2004.

49 See R. Wohl, *A Passion for Wings: Aviation and the western Imagination, 1908–1918*, New Haven 1995.

50 H.J. Fügen, *Max Weber*, Hamburg 1991; D. Käsler, *Max Weber: An Introduction to his Life and Work*, Munich 1988.

51 E. Jennings, 'Re-inventing Jeanne. The iconology of Joan of Arc in Vichy schoolbooks, 1940–1944', *Journal of Contemporary History*, 29/4, 1994, 711–34.

52 For the above, mostly B. Moore, *Social Origins of Dictatorship and Democracy: Lord and Peasant in the Making of the Modern World*, New York 1966.

53 For a survey of the historiography of this very complex problem see P. Lambert, *The Weimar Republic and the Rise of Hitler*, London 1997.

54 Cf. S. Evans, *Forgotten Crimes: the Holocaust and People with Disabilities*, London 2004; also D. Bloxham, T. Kushner, *The Holocaust: Critical Approaches*, Manchester 2004.

55 See R.I. Moore, *The Formation of a Persecuting Society*, Oxford 1987.

56 Z. Baumann, *Modernity and the Holocaust*, London 1989.

57 S. Payne, *A History of Fascism, 1914–1945*, London 1995, and M. Mann, *Fascism*, Cambridge 2004, put the phenomenon in a comparative perspective.

17 Towards a new Europe?

1 In Brecht's final version of 1930, the title was changed into *Das Badener Lehrstück vom Einverständnis*, which better indicated the central theme: man's basic need to accept death.

2 G. Alperovitz, *The Decision to Use the Atomic Bomb*, New York 1995.

3 See M.J. Nye, *From Chemical Philosophy to Theoretical Chemistry: Dynamics of Matter and Dynamics of Disciplines*, Berkeley 1993.

4 Watson himself wrote a highly readable first-hand account: J. Watson, *The Double Helix*, London 1968.

5 See C.P. Snow, *The Two Cultures* and *A Second Look: An Expanded Version of The Two Cultures and the Scientific Revolution*, Cambridge 1964, as well as J.S. de la Mothe, *C.P. Snow and the Struggle for Modernity*, Austin 1992. Significantly, Snow's text was translated into German as: *Die Zwei Kulturen: literarische und naturwissenschaftliche Intelligenz*, Stuttgart 1967. Also F. Leavis, *Cultures: The Significance of C.P. Snow*, Cambridge 1964, as well as D. Thompson, ed., *The Leavises*, Cambridge 1984.

6 See *Unesco Statistical Yearbook*, 1991.

7 See A.P. French, P.J. Kennedy, eds, *Nils Bohr: A Centenary Volume*, Cambridge, Mass., 1985; G. Holton, *Thematic Origins of Scientific Thought*, Cambridge, Mass., 1988.

8 For a very lucid survey: S. Greenfield, *The Human Brain*, London 1997.

9 See A.H. Guth, *The Inflationary Universe*, London 1997.

10 A layman's – *c.*500 pages long – guide through the complexities of the issue is provided by S. Singh, *Big Bang: The Most Important Scientific Discovery of All Time and Why You Need to Know about It*, London 2004.

11 A survey: D.W. Urwin, *The Community of Europe: A History of European Integration since 1945*, London 1995.

12 See the important, 'demythologizing' study by A.S. Milward (with G. Brenner, F. Romero), *The European Rescue of the Nation-State*, London 1993, as well as A.S. Milward, *The Reconstruction of Western Europe, 1945–1951*, London 1984.

13 See A. Milward, V. Sorensen, 'Interdependence or integration? A national choice', in A.S. Milward *et al.*, eds, *The Frontier of National Sovereignty: History and Theory, 1945–1992*, London 1993, 1–32.

14 E.J. Hobsbawm, T. Ranger, eds, *The Invention of Tradition*, Cambridge 1983; E.J. Hobsbawm, *Nations and Nationalism since 1780: Programme, Myth, Reality*, Cambridge 1990.

15 This has already been argued by L. Kohr, *The Breakdown of Nations*, London 1957; more recently: Chr. Harvie, *The Rise of European Regionalism*, London 1993.

16 For the following see R. Kroes, *De Leegte van Amerika*, Amsterdam 1992.

17 For example, R.F. Kuisel, *Seducing the French: The Dilemma of Americanization*, New York 1993. For a parallel study: R. Willett, *The Americanization of Germany: Post-War Culture, 1945–1949*, London 1989.

18 S. Harding, D. Phillips, *Contrasting Values in Western Europe: Unity, Diversity and Change*, Basingstoke 1986; S. Ashford, N. Timms, *What Europe Thinks: A Study of Western European Values*, Aldershot 1992; and the reports of the *European Values Studies Project*, published in Tilburg, the Netherlands, from 1993 onwards.

19 For a survey: R. Williams, *Dream Worlds*, Berkeley 1982, 298–384, passim.

20 E. Durkheim, *Formes élémentaires de la vie religieuse*, Paris 1912.

21 See M. Birman, *All that is Solid Melts into Air*, London 1982; A. Ross, *No Respect: Intellectuals and Popular Culture*, London 1989.

22 See M.A. Bienefeld, *Working Hours in British Industry: An Economic History*, London 1972.

23 J.M. Keynes, *Essays in the Art of Persuasion*, London 1931, 365 sqq.

24 For a general survey: R. Williams, *Culture and Society, 1780–1950*, London 1961.

25 G. Poujol, R. Labourie, *Les Cultures populaires*, Toulouse 1979.

26 W.W. Rostow, *The Stages of Economic Growth*, Cambridge 1961.

27 See P. Yonnet, *Modes et masses: la société française et le moderne, 1945–1985*, Paris 1985.

28 See P. Brantlinger, *Bread and Circuses: Theories of Mass Culture as Social Decay*, New York 1983.

29 J.K. Galbraith, *The Affluent Society*, New York 1958, 139 sqq.

30 See R. Butsch, ed., *For Time and Profit: The Transformation of Leisure into Consumption*, Philadelphia 1990.

31 From G. Cross, *Time and Money: The Making of a Consumer Culture*, London 1993, 193 sqq. This perceptive study has been of great value in the writing of this section.

32 V. Packard, *The Status Seekers*, New York 1959; W. Whyte, *The Organization Man*, New York 1956.

33 See R. Inglehart, *Cultural Shift*, Princeton 1990.

34 See P. Blyton, *Changes in Working Time: An International Review*, New York 1985.

35 W. Gossin, *Le Temps de la vie quotidienne*, Paris 1974.

36 A. Veal, *Sport and Recreation in England and Wales*, London 1979; J. Bishop, P. Higgett, eds, *Organizing around Enthusiasm: Mutual Aid in Leisure*, London 1986.

37 J. Dumazedien, *La Révolution culturelle du temps libre, 1968–1988*, Paris 1988.

38 Report of the Dutch Bureau for Social and Cultural Planning (The Hague), May 1995.

39 This is the argument persuasively sustained by Cross, *Time and Money*, passim.

40 For the background: L. Tilly, J.W. Scott, *Women, Work and Family*, London 1987.

41 U. Hannerz, *Cultural Complexity: Studies in the Social Organization of Meaning, States, Markets, Movements*, New York 1992.

42 A penetrating survey: H.J. Gans, *Popular Culture and High Culture: An Analysis and Evaluation of Taste*, New York 1974.

43 See ILO *Yearbook of Labour Statistics: Retrospective Edition on Population Censuses 1945–1989*, Geneva 1990.

44 E.J. Hobsbawm, *The Age of Empire, 1870–1914*, London 1987, esp. ch. 5.

45 P. Bairoch, *Two Major Shifts in Western European Labour Force: The Decline of the Manufacturing Industries and of the Working Class*, Geneva 1988.

46 See J. Rifkin, *The End of Work: The Decline of the Global Labor Force and the Dawn of the Post-market Era*, New York 1995.

47 F. Ewald, *L'Etat-providence*, Paris 1986.

48 A. Gray, J. McGuigan, eds, *Studying Culture: An Introductory Reader*, London 1993.

49 The point is much discussed; see, e.g. F. Zweig, , London 1961, as opposed to J. Goldthorpe *et al.*, *The Affluent Worker in the Class Structure*, London 1971, although both rely heavily on the somewhat atypical case of Britain.

50 On Guardini: H. Kuhn, *R. Guardini, der Mensch und das Werk*, Darmstadt 1961. In 1962, Guardini was awarded the Erasmus Prize.

51 See Hannerz, *Cultural Complexity*, passim. *The Polity Reader in Cultural Theory*, Cambridge 1994, significantly starts with mass communication.

52 Cf. J. Carrette, R. King, *The Selling of Spirituality*, London 2004.

53 See P. Berger, 'Social sources of secularization', in J.C. Alexander, S. Seidman, eds, *Culture and Society: Contemporary Debates*, Cambridge 1992, 239–49.

54 R. Wilson, W. Dissanayake, eds, *Global/Local: Cultural Production and the Transnational Imaginary*, London 1996.

55 R. Shields, ed., *Cultures of Internet*, London 1996.

56 For a survey of various opinions: F. Webster, *Theories of the Information Society*, London 1996.

57 S. Dillon, 'Office workers fall short when building a sentence', *International Herald Tribune*, December, 8, 2004, 1, 10.

58 J. Ellis, *Visible Fictions: Cinema, Television, Video*, London 1992, esp. 109 sqq., 270 sqq.

59 Chr. Jenks, ed., *Visual Culture*, London 1995.

60 Ph. Drummond, R. Patterson, eds, *Television and its Audience: International Research Perspectives*, London 1988.

61 R.C. Allen, *Speaking of Soap Opera*, Chapel Hill, NC, 1985.

62 For a survey: M. Mitterauer, *Sozialgeschichte der Jugend*, Frankfurt 1986.

63 R. Floud *et al.*, *Height, Health and History*, Cambridge 1990.

64 From the Financial Times, 11 April 1991, quoted in Hobsbawm, *Age of Extremes*, 326.

65 E.J. Hobsbawm, *The Jazz Scene*, New York 1993.

66 Stravinsky, though presenting himself as a 'cosmopolitan', was far more influenced by Russia's musical past than he cared to admit: R. Taruskin, *Stravinsky and the Russian Tradition*, Oxford 1996.

67 With thanks to my colleague, Dr Remco Ensel.

68 For the role of television in the public domain: M. Price, *Television, the Public Sphere and National Identity*, Oxford 1996.

69 O. Marquard, 'Moratorium des Alltags: Eine Kleine Philosophie des Festes', in W. Haug, H. Warnung, eds, *Das Fest*, Munich 1989, 684–91.

70 See P. Manent, *An Intellectual History of Liberalism*, London 1994.

Epilogue: Europe – a present with a future

1 G. Erler, ed., *J.W. Goethe, Werke*, VIII, Berlin 1984, 77.

2 Quoted in W.C. Bark, *Origins of the Medieval World*, Stanford 1958, VII.

3 P. Rietbergen. *De Retoriek van de Eeuwige Stad. Rome gelezen*, Nijmegen 2003.

4 Most articulate, recently is J. Rifkin, *The European Dream. How Europe's vision of the future is quietly eclipsing the American dream*, Cambridge 2004.

5 This vision was defended by A. Finkielkraut, *L'Humanité perdue*, Paris 1997.

6 F. Fernandez-Armesto, *Millennium*, London 1995.

7 An elegant though limited survey written by Josep Fontana, *Europa ante el espejo*,

Barcelona 1994, has been translated in several European languages; however, he omits the important north–south and east–west oppositions.

8 G. Nonneman *et al.*, eds, *Muslim Communities in the New Europe*, Reading 1996.

9 Z. Bauman, *Modernity and Ambivalence*, London 1990.

10 E. Levinas, *Totalité et infini*, The Hague 1961.

11 P. Brezzi, *Realtà e mito nell'Europa dall' antichità ai giorni nostri*, Rome 1954, 22.

12 M. Beloff, *Europe and the Europeans: An International Discussion*, London 1957.

13 A. Lemaire, *Twijfel aan Europa: Zijn de intellectuelen de vijanden van de Europese cultuur?*, Baarn 1990. The contribution by C. Nooteboom, *De ontvoering van Europa*, Amsterdam 1993, as the reflection of someone who calls himself a 'European' traveller and thinker, is a disappointment.

14 M. Rostovtzeff, *The Social and Economic History of the Roman Empire*, Oxford 1926, 486–7.

15 R. Barnett *et al.*, eds, *The End of Knowledge in Higher Education*, London 1997.

16 See C.W. Bynum, 'The last Eurocentric generation', *Perspectives* 34/2 (1996), 3 sqq.

Index

À la recherche du temps perdu, cycle of novels by Proust, 432

Abelard, Peter, monk and scholar, 160

Academy at Padua, 283

Académy of Plato, 196

Academy of Sciences at Berlin, 305, 306

Academy of Sciences at St Petersburg, 306

Accademia Platonica, at Florence, 191

Adam, the father of Man, 296

Adams, Henry, American intellectual and author, 429–30

Adenauer, Konrad, German politician and statesman, 450

The Affluent Society, by Galbraith, 456

Aeneas, main character in the eponymous poem by Virgil, 55

Aeschylus, Greek playwright, 36

Akademie der Wissenschaften, or Prussian Academy of Sciences, 292, 296

'Akritic songs': Byzantine poetic genre, 237

al-Khwarizmi, Islamic mathematician, 113

al-Ma'mun, caliph, 113–14

al-Rashid, caliph, 114

Alanus, descendant of Japhet, 94

Alaric, leader and king of the Goths, 81

Albeniz, Isaac, Spanish composer, 424

Alexander the Great, king of Macedonia, 34, 35, 43, 44, 59

Alfonso, the Learned, king of Castile, 162

Alfred, the Great, king of Wessex, 138, 146, 322

Alkuin, monk, one of Charlemagne's advisers, 100–1

Alskog Tjangvide, with limestone tomb showing the Germanic cosmology, 88

Also sprach Zarathustra, by Nietzsche, 421

Altamira cave paintings, 6

Amerbach, Johann, publisher at Basle, 308

The American Village, poem by Freneau, 270

Amerika, Europa..., by Fröbel, 424

Amerika levend en denkend, or 'America living and thinking', by Huizinga, 435

Ammianus Marcellinus, Roman writer, 56, 57, 60, 61

Amphion Anglus, collection of songs by Blow, 306

Amsterdam Town Hall, 265

Andreae, Johann Valentin, German author, 270

Anti-Barbari, text by Erasmus, 193

Antiquités celtiques et antediluviennes, by Boucher, 4

Apologeticum, Tertullian's text in favour of the Christians, 72

L'Apprenti Sorcier, musical piece by Dukas, 446

Aquinas, Thomas, Christian theologian and philosopher, 118, 163, 192, 322, 423

Arcadius, Roman emperor, 81

Arcana Coelestia, by Swedenborg, 327

Archimedes, Greek scientist, 40

Ardèche cave paintings, 6

Aristotle, Greek philosopher, 26, 27, 32, 37, 52, 88, 92, 113, 149, 163, 191, 201, 207, 227, 311

Arkwright, Richard, English factory owner and inventor, 357

Arminius, or Hermann, German war leader against the Romans, 58

Arne, Thomas, English composer, 322

Arnold, Matthew, English author, 374–5, 458, 464

Aron, Raymond, French sociologist, 456

Assam family, dynsaty of painters and sculptors, 285

Asser, bishop of Winchester, biographer of Alfred the Great, 138

L'Astrée, novel by D'Urfée, 282

Atlas, the first part of Mercator's *Cosmographia*, 259

Au Bon Marché, one of the first, French, department stores, 381, 390

Au Bonheur des Dames, or *The Ladies' Paradise*, novel by Zola, 390

Augustine, Christian saint and author, 66, 88, 91–2, 163, 316, 322

Augustine, monk and Christian saint, buried in Canterbury cathedral, 96, 153

Augustus, Gaius Octavius, the first Roman emperor, 41, 42, 43, 44, 48

Averroës, or Ibn Rushd, Islamic scholar, 163, 303

Avicenna, or Ibn Sinna, Islamic scholar, 163

Bach, Johann Sebastian, German composer, 286

Bacon, Francis, English statesman and philosopher, 207–8, 212–13, 292, 307, 311, 319–23

Bacon, Roger, English monk and scholar, 137

Baedeker, the first German travel guide, 379

Barbaro, Daniele, Venetian scholar, 313

Barberini, Francesco, cardinal, 280

Barbie dolls, 453

Barlaeus, Caspar, Dutch writer, 265

Barnabas, writer of a very early 'Life of Jesus', 64

Basil I, Byzantine emperor, 100

Baugulf, abbot of Fulda, 101

Baxter, Richard, English theologian, 223

Bayle, Pierre, French publicist and philosopher, 299, 301, 309, 322

Bayreuth, shrine to Wagner and his music, 372

Beatles, The, English pop group, 470, 472

Beethoven, Ludwig van, German composer, 387

Behaim, Martin, German globe maker, 257, 259

Benedict of Nursia, Christian saint, founder of the Benedictine Order, 106

Bering, Vitus, Danish-Russian explorer, 393

Berkeley, George, English philosopher, 326

Berkeley, George, English poet, 261–2

Berlin, song by Fischer Z, 472

Berlin, Symphonie der Grossstadt, film by Walter Ruttmann, 440

Bermudas, poem by Marvell, 261

Bernard, monk and Christian saint, founder of the Cistercian Order, 150

Bernini, Gianlorezno, Roman architect and sculptor, 265

Bessarion, Johannes, Byzantine scholar and book collector, 208–9, 227

Beverly, Robert, American poet, 263

Bezuhov, Pierre, character in Tolstoy's *War and Peace*, 371

Bibliothèque Impartiale, scholarly periodical, 309

Biedermann, German periodical, 348

Bird, Isabella, Scottish explorer, 411

Blade Runner, film, 435

Blow, John, English composer, 306

Boccaccio, Giovanni, Florentine writer, 158

Bodin, Jean, French political theorist, 256, 260

Boehme, Jakob, German philosopher, 317, 428

Boekzaal van Europe, Dutch learned periodical, 348

Bohr, Nils, Danish physicist, 431, 424

Boniface, Irish monk and saint, 97

A Booke called the Treasure of Travailers, by Bourne, 293

Borges, Jorge Luis, Argentinian writer, 395

Bosch, Hieronymus, Netherlandish painter, 204

Boswell, James, English diarist, 341

Boucher de Perthes, J., French scholar, 4

Bourbon, Henrietta Maria of, French princess, 279

Bourne, William, English author, 293

Brançion: fresco cycle at church of, 121

Brandenburg Concertos, by Bach, 286

Brasiliaensche Land-en Seereise, by Barlaeus, 265

Braudel, Fernand, French historian, xxvii

Brecht, Bertolt, German playwright, 441–2

British Museum, 267

Brown, Ford Maddox, English painter, 382

Bruni, Leonardo, Italian humanist writer, 200

Bruno, Giordano, Italian philosopher, 317, 428

Burckhardt, Jacob, Swiss historian, 380

Burke, Edmund, English political thinker, 348

Burlamacchi family, 278

Burnet, Gilbert, English theologian and historian, 310

Butler, Samuel, English novelist, 377

Caesar, Gaius Julius, Roman general and dictator, 9, 44, 56, 71

Caliban, character in Shakespeare's *The Tempest*, 262–3, 486

Calvin, John, Swiss Church reformer, 218

Campanella, Tommaso, Italian freethinker and author, 270

Campra, André, French composer, 349

Canterbury Tales, a cycle of stories by Chaucer, 154–8, 178, 273

Casimir III, king of Poland, 201

Cather, Willa, American novelist, 397

Catherine, the Great, tsarina of Russia, 398, 412

Cato, the Elder, Roman politician, 43

Cautio criminalis, a text on legal procedure in criminal affairs, 299

Cavallini, Pietro, Italian painter, 150

Cecilius Metellus, Roman politician, 52

Cellini, Benvenuto, Italian artist, 199, 285

Cervantes, de Saavedra, Miguel, Spanish author, 234

Chambers, E., English encyclopedist, 329

Chambers, Robert, Scottish scholar, 418

Chanson de Roland, epic tale, 155–6, 237

Chansons de Geste, genre of epic tales, 157

Chaplin, Charles, American actor, 434

Chardin, J.-B., French painter, 346

Charlemagne, or Charles, the Great, king of the Franks, first Holy Roman Emperor, 98–102, 104, 112, 114, 116, 118–20, 127, 138, 145, 150, 155–6, 221, 277, 297, 368

Charles I, king of England, 267

Charles III, king of Spain, 312

Charles IV, emperor, king of Bohemia, 184

Charles Martel, king of the Franks, 89, 111, 112

Charles V, emperor, king of Spain, 239, 242, 243, 246, 266

Chartres Cathedral, 149

Chaucer, Geoffrey, English civil servant and writer, 154–8, 178, 273

Chesterton, G.K., English author, 466

Chlodwig, leader and king of the Franks, 82, 95

Die Christenheit oder Europa, essay by Novalis, 380

Christina, queen of Sweden, 286

Chrysoleras, Manuel, Byzantine neo-platonist scholar, 191

Cicero, Roman orator and author, 55, 143, 189

Citeaux, main monastery of the Cistercian Order, 150

Città del Sole, Campanella's major work, 270

Clarin, or L. Alas, Spanish novelist, 377

La Clemenza di Tito, opera by Mozart, 286

Clouet, François, French painter, 341

Cluny, main monastery of the Cistercian Order, 116

cocoa, 245, 247, 249

Codex, collection of imperial Roman decrees, 51

Codex Argenteus, manuscript copy of Wulfila's Bible in Gothic, 72

coffee, 245, 249, 267, 310

Colbert, J., French statesman, 305

Collingwood, R., English historian, 478

Colloquia, text by Erasmus, 251, 291

Cólon, Hernan, son of Columbus, 246

Columbus, Christopher, Genovese mariner and explorer, 215, 245–7, 249–51, 257–8, 261, 392, 453–4

Comenius, or Komensky, Johann Amos, Czech scholar and author, 224

Comte, Auguste, French sociologist, 419

Confessiones, one of St. Augustine's main works, 91

Confucius, Chinese scholar and political theorist, 218

Constantine, first Christian Roman emperor, 67, 68, 69, 71, 83, 87, 138, 192

Constantius Augustus, Roman emperor, 76

Contra Christianos, a work by Porphyry, 92

Cook, James, English explorer, 411

Cook, Thomas, first English travel agent, or tour operator, 379, 457

Copernicus, or Kopernigk, Nicholas/Niklas, Polish scholar, 314–18, 323, 442

Corneille, Pierre, French dramatist, 157, 349

Corpus Iuris Civilis, main Roman law code, 51

Cortés, Hernan, Spanish conquistador of Mexico, 246–7

Cosmographia, Mercator's major collection of maps, 260

Cosmographia universalis, 261

Coster, Laurens Janszn, Dutch printer, 312

Council of Trent, 220

Cracow University, 201

The Creation, or *Die Schöpfung*, oratorio by Haydn, 433

Crick, F.H.C., English molecular biologist, 443

Croce, Benedetto, Italian philosopher, 432

Croly, Herbert, American journalist, 400

Cruise Missiles, song by Fischer Z, 472

Culture and Anarchy, by Arnold, 374

Cuper, Gisbert, Dutch politician and scholar, 310–11

Curio, Johann, Hamburg publicist, 373

Cusanus, or Chrypffs, Nicholas, scholar and scientist, 192

Cyclopedia, 329

Cyrillic writing, 117

Cyrillus, Greek Orthodox monk, and saint, 117

D'Urfé, Honoré, French author, 282

Da Gama, Vasco, Portuguese mariner and explorer, 215, 242, 245

Da Palestrina, Giovanni Pierluigi, Italian composer, 203

Da Vinci, Leonardo, Italian scholar and artist, 285

Daguerre, L.J., French inventor, 416

Daimler, G., German engineer, 414, 430

Dali, Salvador, Spanish painter, 234, 424

Daniel, Samuel, English poet, 298

Dante Alighieri, Florentine poet, 148, 152, 153, 187, 188

Darwin, Charles, English biologist, 405, 418–22, 427–8

Darwin, Erasmus, physician and scholar, 418

Das Ende der Neuzeit, by Guardini, 464

Das Leben Jesu, by Strauss, 422

David, king of the Jews, 22

De Bello Gallico, Caesar's story of the war in Gaul, 56

De Buffon, G.L.E., French biologist, 419

De Camoes, Luis, Portuguese poet, 237

De Civitate Dei, one of St Augustine's major works, 91

De Coelo et Inferno, by Swedenborg, 327

De Falla, Manuel, Spanish composer, 234

De Gasperi, Alcide, Italian statesman, 450

De Iure Belli ac Pacis, or 'On the Right of War and Peace', by Hugo Grotius, 215

De l'esprit des lois, by Montesquieu, 351

De la vicissitude…des choses de l'Univers, by Le Roy, 304

De la Fayette, Mme, French authoress, 282

De la Gardie, Magnus, Swedish statesman and patron of the arts, 286

De Lamarck, J.B., French biologist, 417

De la Mettrie, J.O., French scholar, 326, 447

De Lannoy, Guillebert, Burgundian nobleman and traveller, 159, 165

De las Casas, Bartolomé, Spanish monk, missionary and historian, 246

De Mariana, Juan, Spanish historian, 305

De Monarchia, political treatise by Dante, 148

De Nugis Curialium, or 'On Courtiers' Trifles', by Map, 146

De Peiresc, Nicholas Fabri, French scholar, 290, 307

De regimine iter agentium, by Grutarolus, 291

De Revolutione Orbium Coelestium, by Copernicus, 315

De servo Arbitrio, or 'On the bondage of the will', by Luther, 218

De Valdes, Juan, Spanish historian, 237

Dead Sea Scrolls, 62

Decameron, collection of stories by Boccaccio, 158

Déclaration des Droits de l'Homme et du Citoyen, 353–5

Decree of Milan, 71

Defensor Pacis, political treatise by Marsiglio of Padua, 149

Le Défi americain, by Servan-Schreiber, 453

Defoe, Daniel, English author, 264

Delacroix, Eugène, French painter, 362–3

Della Faille family, 278

Der Mann ohne Eigenschaften, novel cycle by Musil, 434

Der Untergang des Abendlandes, by Spengler, 433

Der Zauberberg, novel by Mann, 435

Der Zauberlehrling, by Goethe, 446

Descartes, René, French mathematician and philosopher, 319–22, 447

The Descent of Man, by Darwin, 418

Description of a Christian Republic, treatise by Andreae, 270

Di Lasso, or De Lattre, Orlando/Roland, Netherlandish composer, 285

Diaghilev, Sergei, Russian impressario, 426

Diaz de Vivar, Rodrigo, Spanish warrior, hero of the *Poema de mio Cid*, 155

Diaz del Castillo, Bernal, companion of Cortés, 246–7

Dickens, Charles, English novelist, 364, 377

Dictionnaire, by Moreri, 309

Dictionnaire Historique et Critique, by Bayle, 309, 322

Didactica magna, by Comenius, 224

Dientzenhofer family of architects, 285

Dietrich, Marlene, German actress and singer, 441

Digests, collection of Roman private law texts, 51

Diocletian, Roman emperor, 68

Dionysios, Greek fertility god, 31, 75

Dioskurides, Greek scientist, 112

Discours sur la Méthode, by Descartes, 322

A Discourse, by Lewkenor, 294

Don Quixote, novel by Cervantes, 234

DNA, 443

Doré, Gustave, French artist, 347, 348

Dormition of the Virgin, church of, at Moscow, 306

Drake, Francis, English buccaneer and naval commander, 253

Dreyer, Carl, Danish film maker, 437

Dryden, John, English poet, 306

Du Contrat Social, by Rousseau, 328

Dubois, Pierre, French political theorist, 148, 434
Dukas, Paul, French composer, 446
Dürer, Albrecht, German painter, 198, 262, 285
Durkheim, Emile, French sociologist, 455

Eccles, John, English physicist, 447
Edict of Villiers-Cotterets, 227
Edict of Nantes, 302
Effi Briest, novel by Fontane, 377
Eggenbergh, Johann, prince of, Austrian diplomat, 280
Ehrenstrahl, D. Kl., Swedish painter, 286
Einhard, monk, Charlemagne's biographer, 100
Einstein, Albert, German physicist, 430–1, 446
Elementai, Euclid's mathematical treatise, 39, 430
El ingenioso hidalgo Don Quijote de la Mancha, novel by Cervantes, 234
Elias, N, German historian, xxvii
Eliot, George, or Evans, Mary Ann, English novelist, 376
Elizabeth I, queen of England, 222–223, 372
Encyclopédie, 329
English Men of Letters series, 371
Enikel, Jansen, Viennese chronicler, 146–7
Die Entführung aus dem Serail, opera by Mozart, 301
Epistola de litteris colendis, Charlemagne's memorandum on learning, 101
Epistolarum...centurio prima, treatise by Lipsius, 284
Erasmus, Desiderius, Dutch humanist scholar, 193–4, 204, 211, 218, 251, 284, 291, 307–8, 314, 418
Eratosthenes, Greek scientist, 39
Erewhon, novel by Samuel Butler, 377
Essay concerning Human Understanding, by Locke, 322
Essay towards the . . . Peace of Europe, by Penn, 302
Eszterhazy family, of Hungarian magnates, patrons of Haydn, 387

Et Dukkelhjem, or *The Doll's House*, by Ibsen, 432
Etymologiae, encyclopedia written by Isidore of Seville, 79
Euclid, Greek mathematician, 39, 430
Euripides, Greek playwright, 30, 31
Europa, mythological Phoenician maiden, abducted by Zeus, 35
Europa und Amerika, by Von Schmidt-Phiseldek, 424
Die Europäische Bund, by Von Schmidt-Phiseldek, 424
Eusebius, biographer of the Emperor Constantine, 74
Evelyn, John, English diarist, 288, 295
Ezekiel, Jewish prophet, 61

Fable of the Bees, treatise by Mandeville, 343
Fairest isle, all isles excelling, Air by Purcell, 306
Faraday, M., English chemist, 414
Faust, play by Goethe, xvii, 334, 425, 477–8
Feíjoo, Benito, Spanish monk and author, 322
Ferdinand III, 'King of the Romans', 280
Ferdinand, king of Aragon, 161, 246
Ficino, Marsilio, Floretine neo-platonist scholar, 191, 196
Finnegans Wake, novel by Joyce, 446
Fischer Z, German pop group, 472
Flaubert, Gustave, French novelist, 377
Fontainebleau Palace, 285
Fontane, Theodore, German novelist, 377
Formey, Samuel, German Huguenot scholar, 309
Formulae of Tours, a set of models for legal practise, 129
Fountain of the Four Rivers, by Bernini, 265
François I, king of France, 227–8, 254, 285
Frankenstein, novel by Mary Godwin Shelley, 377
Franklin, Benjamin, American politician and writer, 395

Frazer, James, English anthropologist, 421

Frederic I, emperor, 159

Frederick II, the Great, king of Prussia, 248, 351–2

Freneau, Philip, American poet, 270

Fresnel, A.-J., French physicist, 414

Freud, Sigmund, Austrian psychologist, 428

Freytag, Gustav, German novelist, 378

Friedrich Wilhelm, king of Prussia, xxii, 368–9

Fröbel, J., German author, 424

Frobenius, Johann, publisher at Basle, 308

Fugger, Jacob, of the German banking family, 253, 255, 277, 278

Fulbert, bishop of Chartres, 128

Fulcher of Chartres, historian, 122

Fundgruben des Orients, scholarly periodical, 410

Fust family, firm of Gutenberg's backers, 211

Gaius, Roman legal writer, 51

Galbraith, J.K., American economist, 456

Galen, Greek physician, 40, 112

Galilei, Galileo, Italian scientist, 314, 316–17

Gallerie des Glaces, at Versailles, 281

Gance, Abel, French film maker, 437

Il Gattopardo, by Lampedusa, 471

Gauguin, Paul, French painter, 408

Genesis, the first book of the Old Testament of the Bible, 25, 94, 260

Gengangere, or *Ghosts*, play by Ibsen, 432

Gerusalemme Liberata, poem by Tasso, 203

Ghosts, play by Ibsen, 432

Gibbon, Edward, author of the *Decline and Fall of the Roman Empire*, 41

Gigli, Giacinto, Roman diarist, 179

Gilgamesh, Summerian epic, 25

Giner, Francisco, Spanish intellectual and educational reformer, 423

Giotto, di Bodone, Italian painter, 150, 187

Godwin Shelley, Mary, English feminist and novelist, 377

Goethe, J.W., German author and philosopher, xvii, 317, 332, 334, 348, 371, 428, 446, 478

The Golden Bough, by Frazer, 421

Gösta Berling's Saga, novel by Lagerlöf, 420

Granados, Enrique, Spanish composer, 424

Graun, Karl-Heinrich, German composer, 224

Graves, Robert, English novelist and screenwriter, 41

Great Exhibition, at the Crystal Palace, London, 359

Gregorian chant, 116

Gregory I, the Great, pope, 96

Gregory III, pope, 95

Gregory IX, pope, 164

Grimm, Jacob and Wilhelm, German scholarly brothers, collectors of folk tales, 174

Grosses Vollständiges Universal-Lexicon, by Zedler, 329

Grotius, Hugo, Dutch legal scholar, 215

Grutarolus, G., German author, 291

Guardini, Romano, German-Italian scholar, 464

Guido of Arezzo, tenth-century musicologist, 426

Gundulic, Ivan, Serbic poet, 237

gunpowder, 137, 207, 212, 214, 243, 260, 393

Gutenberg Bible: the first printed book in the West, 210–11

Gutenberg, Johann, inventor, credited with the invention of printing in Europe, 210–11

Hahn, Otto, German physicist, 443

Hall, John, English author, 293

Ham, or Cham, patriarch of the H/Chamites, or Africans, 94. 146

Hammurápi, Babylonian king, 15–16

Handel, Georg Friedrich, German composer, 286, 333, 426

Hannibal, Carthaginian general, 43

Hawking, Stephen, English astronomer and physicist, 447

Haydn, Joseph, Austrian composer, 333, 387, 426

Hedin, Sven, Swedish explorer, 411

Heidegger, Martin, German philosopher, 431, 442

Heifetz, Jascha, Jewish musician, xix

Heisenberg, Werner, German physicist, 414, 423

Hekataios of Miletos, Greek writer, 35

Helen, princess of Troy, character in the *Odyssey*, 25, 30

Henry IV, king of France, 302

Henry VII, king of England, builder of King's College, 150

Henry, the Navigator, prince of Portugal, 242

Henry V, play by Shakespeare, 251

Herder, J.G., German philosopher, 174, 270, 413

Herodotus, Greek historian, 27, 33, 35–6

Hertz, H.R., German physicist, 414

Heyn, Piet, Dutch buccaneer and admiral, 253

Hildegard, abbess of Bingen, 107

Hindemith, Paul, German composer, 441

Hippocrates, Greek physician, 112

Historia Brittonum, a seventh-century Christian history, 94

Historiai, Herodotus' history of the Near East, 27

History of the Goths, by Isidore of Seville, 79

Historia Animalium, or the 'History of Animals', text by Aristotle, 52

History will Teach us Nothing, song by Sting, 473

Hobbes, Thomas, English philosopher, 311, 325

Holbein, Hans, German painter, 341

Holocaust, 439

Hollanda, Francesco de, Portuguese painter, 197

Hollywood movies, 453

Homer, Greek poet, 24, 25, 32, 39, 55, 191

L'Homme machine, by La Mettrie, 326

Horace, Roman poet, 52, 55

House of Wisdom, academy of sciences at Baghdad, 112

Hroswitha, abbess of Gandersheim, 107

Hubble, Edwin, American astronomer, 431

Hugo, Victor, French author, 424

Huizinga, Johan, Dutch historian, 381, 435

Hume, David, Scottish philosopher, 326, 391

Husayn ibn-Ishaq, Nestorian physician, 112

Hus, Jan, Czech Church reformer, 217

Husayn, Muhammad's grandson, leader of the Sh'ites, 110

Ibn Majid, African sailor and nautical scholar, 242

Ibn Rushd, also: Averroës, islamic scholar, 316

Ibsen, Henrik, Norwegian playwright, 432

Icarus, Greek mythological figure, 477

I, Claudius, British television series, 41

Iconismus, a work by Kircher, 319

IKEA, Swedish funrniture brand, 475

Iliad, 24, 25, 30, 191

Imitatio Christi, by Thomas à Kempis, 203

Institutio Oratoria, treatise by Quintilian, 53

Institutiones, treatise by Gaius, 50

Irving, Washington, American author, 402

Isabella, queen of Castile, 161

Isaiah, Jewish prophet, 61

Isidore, archbishop of Seville, Christian author, 79, 94

Isolde, Celtic legendary figure, 34, 421

Ives, Samuel, English composer, 344

Izz ad-Din ibn al-Athir, Islamic historian, 123

James, Henry, American author, 402

James, William, American psychologist, 446

Japhet, patriarch of the Japhites, or Europeans, 94, 146, 297
Jehol, Chinese imperial summer palace, 266
Jena University, 334
Jenseits von Gut und Bösen, by Nietzsche, 424
Jeremiah, Jewish prophet, 61
Jerome, Christian saint and author, 81
Jerusalem, site of the Jewish temple, 20, 262
Jesus of Nazareth, 62–6, 93, 109, 121, 421
John of the Cross, Christian saint and mystic, 446
John of Damascus, Christian scholar, 118
Jones, William, English Sanskrit scholar, 408
Journal Asiatique, scholarly periodical, 410
Joyce, James, Irish writer, 446
Judita, epic by Marulic, 237
The Jungle, novel by Sinclair, 399
Justinian, Byzantine emperor, 51, 115
Juvenal, Roman poet, 52

Ka'ba, the House of Worship at Mecca, 109
Kafka, Franz, Czech writer, 434
Kant, Immanuel, German philosopher, 327
Kamprad, I., Swedish furniture designer and producer of the IKEA-brand, 475
Karatayev, Platon, character in Tolstoy's *War and Peace*, 371
Kepler, Johannes, German scholar, 316–317, 319, 323
Keynes, John Maynard, English economist, 455
King Alfred, opera by Arne, 322
King Arthur, Celtic legendary figure, 34
King Arthur, opera by Purcell, 306
King James' Bible, 222
King's College Chapel, Cambridge, 150
Kingsley, Charles, English author, 420
Kircher, Athanasius, German Jesuit scholar, 288, 319
Kitab al-Fawa'id, nautical treatise by Ibn Majid, 242

Koch, Robert, German bacteriologist, 414
Kölnische Zeitung, German newspaper, 358
Komensky, Johann Amos *see* Comenius
Kopernigk, *see* Copernicus
Kosmas, monk, first Christian cosmographer, 89–90, 257, 258
Kremlin palaces, Moscow, 306
Kristianikè Topographia, Kosmas' cosmological treatise, 89–90
Kritik der reinen Vernunft, by Kant, 327
Kritik der praktischen Vernunft, by Kant, 327
Krupp, German industrial family, 363, 364
Die Kultur der Renaissance in Italien, by Burckhardt, 380

Lafargue, Paul, French sociologist, 455
Lagerlöf, Selma, Swedish author, 420
Lang, Fritz, German film maker, 79, 435, 437
La Passion de Jeanne d'Arc, film by Dreyer, 437
Lascaux cave paintings, 6
Laus Hispaniae, text by Isidore of Seville, 79
The Laws of Imitation, by Tarde, 455
Le Clerc, Jean, Dutch Huguenot publisher and scholar, 311
Le Roy, Louis, French publicist, 304
Leavis, F.R., English author and literary critic, 444
Leeu, Gherard, Netherlandish printer, 246
Lehrstück, play by Brecht, 441–2
Leibniz, G.W., German philosopher, 270, 305, 310, 311, 326
Lemaitre, Georges, Belgian mathematician, 431
Leopold II, emperor, 286
Les Desillusions du progrès, treatise by Aron, 456
Les Loisirs de Philothé, novel by Mavrocordatos, 311
Lessing, G.E., German author, 326
Letters from an American Farmer, by St John, 396

Leviathan, socio-political treatise by
Hobbes, 325
Levinas, Emanuel, Jewish-French-
Lithuanian philosopher, 489
Lewkenor, Samuel, English author, 294
L'Homme-machine, by La Mettrie, 326
Liber Sancti Jacobi, manual for pilgrims to
Santiago, 153
Lincoln, Benjamin, American general
and writer, 395
Linnaeus, Carl, Swedish biologist, 294
Lipsius, Justus, Netherlandish humanist
author, 284
Lipschitz, Itzak, Jewish sculptor, xix
Locatelli, Domenico, Italian composer,
286
Locatelli, Giovanni, Italian composer,
286
Locke, John, English philosopher, 294,
299, 301, 303, 311, 322
London, a Pilgrimage, picture book by
Doré, 347
looms, 136
Louis II, emperor, 100
Louis XIII, king of France, 228
Louis XIV, king of France, 228, 265,
275, 280, 297, 302, 316
Louis XVI, king of France, 352
Lucas, Margaret, English scholar. 333
Luke, one of the disciples of Jesus, and
writer of a gospel, 63, 64
Lully, Jean-Baptiste, French composer,
281
Luther, Martin, German monk and
reformer, 217–19, 316
Luzac, Elie, Dutch Huguenot publisher
and publicist, 308

McCartney, Paul, English singer and
composer, 451
Machiavelli, Niccolò, Italian political
scientist, 200, 206, 207
Macmillan, English publishing house,
371
Macpherson, James, English poet, 322
Madame Bovary, novel by Flaubert, 377
Madonna, pop singer and actress, 473
Magellan, Ferdinand, Portuguese
mariner and explorer, 258

Magliabecchi, Antonio, Florentine
librarian and scholar, 310
Magna Carta, English constitutional
document, 139
Mahomet et Charlemagne, by Pirenne,
433
Mandeville, Bernard, Dutch-English
publicist, 343
Mani, Persian prophet, 67
Mann, Thomas, German novelist, 435
Manual for Tailors, 232
Manutius, Aldus, Venetian scholar and
publisher-printer, 212, 308
Map, Walter, English-Welsh civil servant
and courtier, 145
Maria Theresia, empress, 333
Mariken van Nieumeghen, Dutch play,
171–3, 235–6
Mark, one of the disciples of Jesus, and
writer of a gospel, 64, 160
Márquez, Gabriel Garcia, Columbian
writer, 395
Marshall Plan, 453
Marsiglio of Padua, Italian scholar, 149
Marulic, Marco, poet from Split, 237
Marvell, Andrew, English poet, 261
Mark, Karl, German philosopher and
historian, 38, 419
Mary, princess of Orange, 351
Mary, mother of Jesus, cult of, 66, 88,
132, 157
Massenet, Jules, French composer, 234
Master Eckhart, Christian mystic, 465
Matthew, one of the disciples of Jesus,
and writer of a gospel, 63, 64, 93,
100, 160
Mavrocordatos, Nicholas, Greek ruler
and scholar, 311
May, Karl, German popular novelist, 427
Mayans y Siscar, Gregorio, Spanish
scholar, 312
Mazarin, Jules, Italian-French statesman
and cardinal, 305
Medea, play by Euripides, 30
Medinet Habu temple, 21
Medici, de' Cosimo, Florentine ruler and
patron of the arts, 191
Medici de' family, Florentine bankers
and dynasts, 264

Medici, de' Lorenzo, Florentine ruler and patron of the arts, 196

Medici, de' Maria, Florentine princess, 279

Meerman, Gerard, Dutch diplomat, bibliophile and scholar, 312

Melanchton, Philip, German theologian, 317

Mendel, Gregor, Austrian monk and geneticist, 414

Mensch en menigte in Amerika, or 'Man and Mass in America', by Huizinga, 435

Mercator, Gerard, Dutch cartographer, 259, 260

Methodius, Greek Orthodox monk, and saint, 117

Metropolis, film by Lang, 434

Michelangelo Buonarotti, Italian artist, 197, 199, 200, 202, 203, 264

Middlemarch, George Eliot's major novel, 376

Mill, John Stuart, English economist, 391

Milton, John, English poet, 433

Minucius Felix, Roman author, 67, 70

Mithras, Persian god, 67

Moberg, Vilhelm, Swedish author, 398

Moisiodax, Iosippos, Greek intellectual, 322

Monnet, Jean, French statesman, 450, 479

Monostatos, character in Mozart's opera *The Magic Flute*, 301

Montaigne, de Michel, French philosopher, 299–301

Montesquieu, de Charles, French political thinker, 207, 351

Monteverdi, Claudio, Italian composer, 203

Montezuma, last Aztec emperor, 247, 248, 266

More, Thomas, English statesman and author, 270, 303

Moreri, Louis, French scholar, 309

Morton, W.T.G., American anaesthesiologist, 414

Moses, Jewish leader and law giver, 61

Mostaert, Jan, Dutch painter, 262

Mozart, Wolfgang Amadeus, Austrian composer, 286, 301, 387, 412

La Muette de Portici, opera by Aubert, 371

Muhammad, founder of Islam, 64, 108–12, 118, 119, 146

Multinationals Bite, song by Fischer Z., 472

Münster, Sebastian, German cartographer, 261, 268

Museion, at Alexandria, 38

Musil, Robert, Austrian writer, 434

Mussolini, Benito, Italian dictator, 439

Mussorgsky, Modest, Russian composer, 426

Napoleon Bonaparte, French general, and emperor, 100, 330–1, 368, 370–1, 378

Napoleon, film by Gance, 437

Napoleonic Code, 368

Nassau, Maurice of, prince of Orange, Dutch statesman and military innovator, 214

The New Republic, American periodical, 400

Newton, Isaac, English mathematician and philosopher, 311, 323–4, 326, 428–9

Niaux cave paintings, 15

Die Nibelungen, film by Lang, 437

Nibelungenlied, early German epic, 79

Nicot de Villemain, Jean, French diplomat, 247

Nièpce, J.-N., French chemist, 416

Nietzsche, Fr., German philosopher, xxvi, 299, 421, 424, 428

Nieuhof, Johan, Dutch traveler and travel writer, 265

Nijinsky, Vaslav, Russian choreographer and dancer, 471

Nils Holgersons underbara resa, or 'Nils Holgerson's Strange Voyage', by Lagerlöf, 420

Nithard, monk and historian, 151

Noah, biblical figure, 25, 89, 94, 146

Noris, Enrico, cardinal and scholar, 310

Notker Balbulus, monk and historian, 151

Novalis, or Von Hardenberg, Friedrich, German poet, 380, 424, 428, 450, 490

Novum organum, by Francis Bacon, 207

O Pioneers, Willa Cather's major novel, 397

Octavius, dialogue by Minucius Felix, 67

Odin, Germanic god, 88

Odyssey, 25, 30, 55, 191, 227

Olearius, Abraham, German traveler and travel writer, 412

On the Origin of Species, by Darwin, 419

On Travel, essay by Bacon, 292

Oppenheimer, J. Robert, American physicist, 443

Opticks, or 'Optica', by Newton, 323

Orang-Outang, sive Homo Sylvestris, by Tyson, 3

Organon, work by Aristotle, 207

Orpheus Britannicus, collection of songs, 305

Os Lusiadas, Portuguese epic by Camoes, 237

Osman, Serbic epic by Gundulic, 237

Ossian, cycle of poems by Macpherson, 322

Osmin, a character in Mozart's *The Escape from the Seraglio*, 301

Othello, play by Shakespeare, 486

Otto I, emperor, 107, 116, 131

Otto II, emperor, 116

Otto, N., German engineer and inventor, 414

Pachomius, Christian saint, founder of the first monastery proper, 105

Packard, Vance, American sociologist, 457

Palladio, Andrea, Italian architect, 233

paper-making, 134, 135, 212

Paradise Lost, poem by Milton, 433

Pascal, Blaise, French philosopher, 324

La Passion de Jeanne d'Arc, film by Dreyer, 437

Paston, Margaret, English noblewoman and writer of letters, 177

Paul, apostle and Christian author, 69, 482

Paul III, pope, 315

Penelope, Odysseus' wife, character in the *Odyssey*, 30

Penn, William, English statesman and religious leader, 302–4, 424

Pensées, by Pascal, 324

Pentateuch, the first five books of the Old Testament of the Bible, 61

Pepys, Samuel, English diarist, 279, 333, 387

Periplous, mariner's manual from Marseilles, 34

Perrault, Charles, French writer and collector of folk tales, 174

The Persians, play by Aeschylos, 27, 36

Peter, apostle and first pope, 75, 76, 93, 95, 153, 202, 306

Peter, the Great, tsar of Russia, xviii, 306

Petronius, Roman author, 189

Philip Augustus, king of France, 142

Philip II, king of Spain, 250, 252, 253, 265, 284

Philip IV, king of France, 144

Philosophiae naturalis Principia mathematica, by Newton, 323

Picasso, Pablo, Spanish painter, 424, 431

The Picture of Dorian Grey, novel by Wilde, 343

Pieterpad, or St. Peter's Way, pilgrims' road to Rome, 153

Pincio Gardens, open-air gallery of national heroes in Rome, 370

Pillars of Society, play by Ibsen, 432

Pirenne, Henri, Belgian historian, 433

Pius II, or Aeneas Sylvius Piccolomini, pope and humanist author, 180, 181

Pius V, pope, 211

Pizarro, Francisco, Spanish conquistador of Peru, 247

Planck, Max, German physicist, 430, 431, 442

Plantijn, Christoffel, publisher at Antwerp, 308

Plato, Greek philosopher, 26, 30, 36, 88, 92, 113, 149, 191, 196, 237, 300

Pletho, Byzantine neo-platonist scholar, 191

Pliny, the Elder, Roman writer of a 'Natural History', 54

Pliny, the Younger, Roman author, 46
Plotinus, neo-platonist philosopher, 92
Poema de mio Cid, Spanish epic tale, 237
Politeia, Plato's treatise on politics, 26
Politika, Aristotle's treatise on politics, 27
Politische Geographie, by Ratzel, 404
Polo, Marco, Venetian traveller, 216,
    240, 242, 246, 259, 308
Polyglot Bibles, 193
Porphyry, neo-platonist philosopher, 92
Portinari family, 278
Poseidonios, Greek writer, 57
potato, 235, 242
La Princesse de Clèves, novel by Mme De
    la Fayette, 283
Il Principe, or 'The Prince', Machiavelli's
    major work, 200
Principles of Psychology, by James, 446
Prodigal Son, painting by Bosch, 204
Programma XLII de peregrinationis, by
    Thomasius, 293
Prometheus, Greek mythological figure,
    377, 425, 477
Prosper of Aquitaine, Christian saint, 96
Prospero, character in Shakespeare's *The
    Tempest*, 262, 263, 486
Proust, Marcel, French author, 432, 434
Prudentius, Christian scholar, 95
Ptolemy, Greek cosmographer, 40, 214,
    257, 259
Punch, English satirical journal, 386
Purcell, Henry, English composer, 306
Purchas, Samuel, English collector of
    travel tales, 306
Pythia, Greek oracle at Delphi, 35

Quintilian, Roman paedagogue and
    writer, 55, 189
Quo Vadis? A Just Censure of Travels, by
    Hall, 294

Racine, Jean, French playwright, 349
Raleigh, Walter, English buccaneer and
    naval commander, 253
Rameau, J.-Ph., French composer, 349
Rameses II, Egyptian pharaoh, 21
Raphael(lo) Santi, Italian painter, 197,
    205
Ratzel, Friedrich, German scholar, 404

La Reggenta, Clarin's major novel, 377
Renan, Ernest, French scholar, 422
Republic, one of Plato's texts, 113
Richelieu, J.-A. Duplessis, de French
    statesman and cardinal, 305
Riddarhus at Stockholm, frescoes at, 286
Ring des Nibelungen, cycle of operas by
    Wagner, 372
The Rising Glory of America, poem by
    Freneau, 270
Robert, monk and chronicler, 123
Robinson Crusoe, novel by Defoe, 264
Robur the Conqueror, novel by Jules
    Verne, 420
Romance of the Rose, tale of courtly love,
    157, 187
Romanen om Utvandrarna, novel by
    Moberg, 398
Romantic, new cultural term, 333
Röntgen, W.C., German chemist, 415
Rostovtzeff, M., English historian, 490
Rostow, W.W., American economist,
    456
Rousseau, Jean-Jacques, French
    philosopher, 279, 299, 328, 382, 391
Royal Society, 311
Rubens, P.P., Netherlandish painter, 287
Rublev, Andrej, Russian painter, 117
Rudolp II, emperor, 316
'Rule Britannia', song by Arne, 332
Rumph, Chr. C., Dutch envoy at
    Stockholm, 310–11
Rutherford, Ernest, English physicist,
    442
Ruttmann, Walter, German film maker,
    441

Sancho Panza, character in Cervantes's
    Don Quixote, 234
Le Sacre du Printemps, or The Rite of
    Spring, by Stravinsky, 471
Said al-Andalusi, Islamic legal scholar,
    161
St Petersburg, churches and palaces at,
    273
St Basil's cathedral, at Moscow, 306
St James' shrine at Compostela, 153
St John, Hector, French-American
    writer, 396, 398, 434

St Mark's basilica, at Venice, 116

St Michael the Archangel, church of, at Moscow, 306

St Peter's, the main church of Roman Catholic Christianity, xxviii, 93, 202, 288, 289

St Simon, Duke of, diarist at Versailles, 281, 342

Saint Simon, Henri, count of, French social theorist, 366–7

Samfundets Stotter, or *The Pillars of Society*, play by Ibsen, 432

San Clemente church, Rome: Mithraic frescoes, 69

San Vitale church, Ravenna: Byzantine mosaics, 45, 177

Sarmiento, Martin, Spanish monk and author, 332

Saturday Night Fever, film, 471

Savery, Roelant, Dutch painter, 158

Schelling, Fr.-W., German philosopher, 334

Scheherazade, one of the main characters in the *Thousand and One Nights*, 113

Schiller, Friedrich, German author, 332

Schinkel, Karl, German architect, xx

Schlegel, Friedrich, German linguist, 412

Schopenhauer, Arthur, German philosopher, 278, 328, 409

Schopenhauer, H. Fl., German merchant, 278

Schopenhauer, Johanna, née Trosiener, 229

Schubert, Franz, Austrian composer, 388

scriptoria, centres of manuscript book production, 106, 151, 209

Sein und Zeit, by Heidegger, 489

Semmelweis, I.P., Hungarian obstetrician, 414

Serlio, Sebastiano, Italian architect, 233

Servaas, or Gervase, bishop of Maastricht, saint, 153

Servan-Schreiber, J.-J., French politician, 456

Shakespeare, William, English playwright, xxxvi, 251, 262, 371, 486

Shamash, Summerian sun god, 15

Shem, or Sem, patriarch of the Semites, or Asians, 94

Sic et Non, treatise by Abelard, 160

Sidgwick, Henry, English politician and intellectual, 375

Le Siècle de Louis XIV, by Voltaire, 207

Simon, *see* Peter, apostle and first pope

Sinclair, Upton, American novelist, 399

Skokloster castle, 286

Sloane, Hans, German collector of books and curios, 267

Smith, Adam, English economic theorist, 207

Snow, C.P., English civil servant, scientist and author, 444

soap opera, 456

Society of Jesus, 231, 244

Socrates, Greek philosopher, 30, 31

Soll und Haben, novel by Freytag, 378

Solomon, king of the Jews, 22

Solon, Greek law-giver, 26

Sophocles, Greek playwright, 31

Sorbonne University at Paris, 149, 157, 163

Soriano, Michele, Venetian diplomat, 255

Soutine, Chaim, Jewish painter, xix

Spaak, Paul-Henri, Belgian statesman, 450

Spanish peppers, 249

The Spectator, English periodical, 348

Spengler, O., German scholar, 433

Spinoza, Baruch de, Spanish-Jewish-Dutch philosopher, 327, 334

Stanley, H.M., Welsh journalist, 411

Statenvertaling, or Dutch State Authorized Bible, 222

The Status Seekers, by Packard, 457

Steen, Jan, Dutch painter, 346

Stephan, Heinrich, German postmaster-general, 415

Stonehenge sanctuary/temple, 19

Stoss, Veit, Bohemian sculptor-painter, 150

Strabo, Greek geographer, 56, 214

Strangers and Brothers, cycle of novels by Snow, 444

Stratford-upon-Avon, Shakespeare's shrine, 371

Strauss, D. Fr., German theologian and scholar, 422

Strauss, Richard, Austrian composer, 234

Stravinsky, Igor, Russian composer, 471

Strettweg bronze chariot, 21

Sturm, Jacob, humanist scholar from Strasbourg, 226

Suasso family, 278

Summa Theologica, by St Thomas Aquinas, 118

Sunna, the corpus of texts explaining Muhammad's teaching of Islam, 109

Susato, Tilman, Antwerp music publisher, 285

Svea, allegory of Sweden, 286

Swedenborg, Emmanuel, Swedish philosopher, 327

Symposium, one of Plato's main works, 92

Synesius, Roman orator, 81

syphilis, 179, 250–1, 255

Tacitus, Roman historian, 52, 55, 57–9, 164

Talbot, W.H.F., English physicist, 416

Tarde, Eugène, French sociologist, 455

Tasso, Torquato, Italian poet, 203

Tchaikovsky, P.I., Russian composer, 426

The Tempest, play by Shakespeare, xxxvi, 262, 486

Tennyson, Alfred, English poet, 376, 486

Teresa of Avila, Christian saint and mystic, 465

Tertullian, Roman author, 72

The Modern Prometheus, by Mary Shelley, 377

The Times, English newspaper, 279

Themistius, Roman orator, 81

Theodora, Justinian's wife, empress of Byzantium, 49

Theodosius, Roman emperor, 75, 81

Theophano, Byzantine wife of emperor Otto II, 116

Thomas à Becket, English statesman, martyr and saint, 153, 154

Thomas à Kempis, or Thomas Haemerken, Netherlandish writer, 203

Thomasius, Johannes, German author, 293

Thomsen, Chr. J., Danish scholar, 3, 4

Thousand and One Nights, collection of (Arabic) tales, 113

Tiepolo, Giovanni Battista, Italian painter, 266, 285

Timaios, one of Plato's works, 92

Tinne, Alexandrine, Dutch traveler, 411

Tischbein, W., German painter, 363

Tizian, or Tiziano Vecelli – also: Titian –, Italian painter, 211, 341

tobacco, 245, 247, 249, 250, 267

Tokugawa family, rulers of Japan from the seventeenth to the nineteenth century, 406

Toledo School of Translators, 136, 161, 162

Tolstoy, Leo, Russian writer, 371

Tomasi di Lampedusa, Giuseppe, Italian writer, 471

tomato, 245, 249

Toscanelli, Paolo, Florentine geographer, 257

Le Tour du Monde, French periodical of travel stories, 379

Trajan, Roman emperor, 46

Die Traumdeutung, by Freud, 428

Tripitaka, the Buddhist canon, 210

Tristan, Celtic legendary figure, 34

Tristan und Isolde, opera by Wagner, 421

Turing, Alan, English mathematician, 443

Two Treatises of Civil Government, by Locke, 311

Tylor, Edward, English anthropologist, xxiv

Tyson, E., English physician, 3

Ueber die Sprache...der Indier, by Schlegel, 412

Upanishads, ancient Indian texts, 407

Urban II, pope, 122, 125

Urban VIII, pope, 280, 316

Usama ibn Munqidh, Islamic nobleman and diarist, 124

Utopia, Thomas More's major work, 270, 303

Valhalla, Bavarian monument, 370

Van Arkel, Thomas Walraven, Dutch country squire, 294

Van Campen, Jacob, Dutch architect, 265

Van den Vondel, Joost, Dutch poet, 265

Van Gogh, Vincent, Dutch painter, 408

Van Scorel, Jan, Netherlandish painter, 285

Van Swieten, Gerard, Dutch-Austrian courtier and writer, 333

Vedas, ancient Indian texts, 82, 408

Verdi, Giuseppe, Italian composer, 371

Verne, Jules, French author, 420

Versailles palace, xviii, 265, 281, 282, 333, 341, 342, 352

Verses on the Prospect of Planting Arts, by Berkeley, 261

Vespucci, Amerigo, Florentine navigator, 258

Vestiges of the Natural History of Creation, by Chambers, 418

Victoria, queen of England, 376

La Vie de Jesus, by Renan, 422

Virey, J.J., French medical publicist, 389

Virgil, Roman poet, 55

Virtù, the creative potential of man, 188, 189, 201, 206, 317

Visconti, Luchino, Italian film maker, 471

Visegrád palace, 201

Vita Constantini, Eusebius' 'Life of Constantine', 74

Vita Karoli, Charlemagne's biography by Einhard, 102

Vita Nuova, cycle of sonnets by Dante, 152

Vitry, Jacques de, French clergyman, 163

Vitruvius Britannicus, English architectural treatise, 305

Vitruvius, Roman architect, 233, 305

Vivaldi, Antonio, Italian composer, 266

Vladimir cathedral, 117

Voltaire, or François-Marie Arouet, French philosopher, 207, 279, 328, 343, 351, 406, 412

Von Behring, E.A., German pharmacologist, 414

Von Bismarck, Otto, chancellor of Germany, 415

Von Freising, Otto, German historian, 103

Von Gluck, Chr. W., German composer, 426

Von Hammer-Purgstall, Joseph, Austrian orientalist, 410

Von Hofmansthal, Hugo, Austrian author, 433

Von Humboldt, Wilhelm, German politician and intellectual, 374, 458, 464

Von Pückler-Muskau, Prince, German traveller and author, 357, 359

Von Roes, Alexander, German civil servant and writer, 147

Von Schmidt-Phiseldek, Fr., Danish politician and author, 424

Von Siemens, W., German industrialist and inventor, 414–16

Vossische Zeitung, Berlin newspaper, 386

Voyage to the Moon, novel by Jules Verne, 420

Wagner, Richard, German composer, 79, 372, 421

Waldseemüller, Martin, German cartographer, 258, 415–16

Walter of Henley, author of a famous agricultural treatise, 135

War and Peace, epic novel by Tolstoy, 371

Wasa, Gustavus, king of Sweden and military innovator, 214

The Water Babies, novel by Kingsley, 420

Watson, J.D., American biochemist, 443

Weber, Max, German intellectual and sociologist, xxxii, 232, 438

Weimar, Goethe's shrine, 371

Weissenstein palace near Pommersfelden, 266

Welser family, 278

Die Welt als Wille und Vorstellung, by Schopenhauer, 328

Wilde, Oscar, English author, 360

William, duke of Aquitaine, 128

William III, prince of Orange, king of England, et cetera, 351

William of Malmesbury, monk and chronicler, 125

William of Roebroeck, monk and missionary, 137

William, the Conqueror, duke of Normandy, king of England, 138

Willibald, monk, biographer of St Boniface, 97

windmills, 133, 134

Winnetou, the red Gentleman, character from novel by May, 427

Witsen, Nicholas, Dutch politician and scholar, 210–311

Wortley Montagu, Lady Mary, English traveler and writer of letters, 282

Wrangel, C.G., Swedish military leader and patron of the arts, 286

Wristcutter's Lullaby, song by Fischer Z, 472

Wulfila, or Ulfilas, bishop of the Goths, 78, 117

Würzburg episcopal palace, frescoes at, 266, 285

Wycliffe, John, English Church reformer, 217

Zagorsk monastery, frescoes at, 117

Die Zauberflöte, opera by Mozart, 301

Zedler, J.M., German author, 329

Zeus, Greek god, 35, 36, 425

Zola, Emile, French novelist, 390

Zoroastrianism, Persian cult, 66

Zur Kritik der politischen Oekonomie, by Marx, 419

Routledge History

British Culture
2nd Edition
David P. Christopher

In the new millennium Britain is changing rapidly. Global influences have created a more open but also more complex society, with a high degree of cultural diversity. At the same time, the arts have become more central to everyday life, with both specialists and the general public joining the debate over their meaning and merit.

Exploring a wide range of areas including literature, film, TV, magazines, sport and popular music, David P. Christopher observes and investigates key movements and issues, placing them in a clear, historical context. This creates a comprehensive introduction which allows students of British society to understand, study and enjoy a fascinating range of unique cultural material.

This second edition of David P. Christopher's book offers a wider range of topics, and gives special emphasis to outstanding artists and developments in the field. Also included are:

- fully revised and updated chapters
- new chapters on sport, newspapers and magazines
- authentic extracts from novels, plays and TV series
- discussion of recent developments such as the greater commercialisation of cultural life and wider public participation through increased exposure in the mass media
- follow-up activities and suggestions for further reading to strengthen study skills.

This book is an engaging study of contemporary life and arts, and is essential reading for every student of modern Britain.

Hb: 0-415-35396-3 Pb: 0-415-35397-1